"I love your book. As a UNIX geek with SS7 telco background, I have had a fledgling NT 4.0 system plopped in my lap. The fellow who built the two servers and Exchange has left and the Mucky Mucks have decided I will be the MS systems administrator. Humph, now I have to learn THIS?! I bought your book and it has warmed my heart to Microsoft NT 4.0 and Exchange Server. Thank you for a well thought out endeavor. I look forward to the Exchange Server 5 book you will write.

P.S. I bought your book because of the Mastering NT Server *and* Mastering NT Workstation *books by the same publisher."*

GEORGE F. MISHLER
SYSTEMS ADMINISTRATOR
TeleServ CORPORATION

"I would like to thank you for writing such an informative book. We have been able to utilize your material to set up our own Exchange organization."

IAN D. CARLSON
A.O. SMITH AUTOMOTIVE

"I referenced your book many, many times during our migration to Exchange Server. Keep up the good work."

DAVID MISTRETTA
NETWORK ENGINEER
HARBINGER CORPORATION

Mastering™ Microsoft® Exchange Server 5

Second Edition

Barry Gerber

SYBEX®

San Francisco • Paris • Düsseldorf • Soest

Associate Publisher: Gary Masters
Acquisitions Manager: Kristine Plachy
Acquisitions & Developmental Editor: Peter Kuhns
Editor: Ben Miller
Technical Editor: Ron Sanfilippo
Book Designer: Suzanne Albertson
Graphic Illustrator: Pat Dintino
Desktop Publisher: Franz Baumhackl
Production Coordinator: Alexa Riggs
Proofreaders: Jennifer Metzger, Theresa Gonzalez
Indexer: Matthew Spence
Cover Designer: Design Site
Cover Photographer: The Image Bank

Screen reproductions produced with Collage Plus and
Paint Shop Pro.
Collage Plus is a trademark of Inner Media Inc.

Library of Congress Card Number: 97-65362
ISBN: 0-7821-2053-9

Manufactured in the United States of America

10 9 8 7 6 5 4 3 2 1

To Jane, my wife and best friend,
for reminding me in so many ways
that technology should serve
and not control humanity

ACKNOWLEDGMENTS

Writing a book about a communications-support product such as Exchange Server is a lot like trying to catch a bunch of TCP/IP packets in a fishnet. Things changed so rapidly during the Exchange Server 5.0 development cycle that I often found myself rewriting the same paragraphs two or three times in the span of a week. Without the help and support of a number of fine people, this second edition of Mastering Microsoft Exchange Server would never have happened.

Deepest thanks to the marketing folks at Microsoft and Microsoft's public relations support firm, Waggner Edstrom, for their early encouragement and continuing assistance in opening doors I never even knew existed.

Words really cannot express both my indebtedness to and respect for the Exchange Server 4.0 and 5.0 development teams. I'll never forget the patience they showed with my seemingly endless and not always well-articulated questions, especially as product delivery deadlines approached. My *Exchange Book* e-mail folder overflows with helpful, timely, and just-in-time responses from them all: Behrooz Chitsaz, August Hahn, David Johnson, Bill Kilcullen, Eric Lockard, Mark Ledsome, Steve Masters, Tom McCann, Ramez Naam, Jim Reitz, Todd Roberts, Rob Sanfilippo, Elaine Sharp, Rob Shurtleff, Aaron Snow, Bill Sorinsin, Paul Waszkiewicz, Jeff Wilkes and Rusty Williams.

Finally, my heartfelt and everlasting thanks to the team of editors who kept me honest and articulate through both editions of the book. John Read at Sybex listened to my ideas for the first edition and helped shape them into a book. Peter Kuhns very ably picked up the ball for the second edition. Maureen Adams, with help from Lorraine Fry, shepherded my first edition draft manuscript through all the highs and lows of the production process. Ben Miller took over for the second edition and made me look like the most articulate technoid ever to come down the pike. I'd also like to thank everyone on the Sybex production team who helped to produce this book, including Pat Dintino, Franz Baumhackl, Alexa Riggs, Theresa Gonzalez, Jennifer Metzger, and Robin Kibby. And last, but far from least, Eric Lockard (first edition) and Rob Sanfilippo (second edition) were the very best technical editors I've ever been privileged to work with. They both read every word and looked at every diagram and screen capture in an effort to ensure that what you read here is both accurate and understandable.

Thanks to everyone for all your help. Whatever errors of fact or judgment remain are mine and mine alone.

Barry Gerber (gerber@deltanet.com)

Los Angeles, California

CONTENTS AT A GLANCE

Introduction   *xxv*

PART I **Exchange Concepts, Basics, and Design**   1

   1   Introducing Exchange   3

   2   The Exchange Hierarchy   31

   3   The Architecture of Exchange   47

   4   Exchange and Windows NT Server   69

   5   Designing an Exchange System   95

PART II **Installation**   145

   6   Installing Windows NT Server   147

   7   Installing an Exchange Server   193

PART III **Basic Exchange Server Administration and Management**   225

   8   The Administrator and Its Menus   228

   9   The Exchange Server Hierarchy and Core Components 291

   10   Backing Up an Exchange Server   333

PART IV **Exchange Clients for Windows**   **357**

11   Installing Exchange Clients for Windows   359

12   Exchange Clients for Windows 101   383

PART V **Expanding an Exchange Organization**   **421**

13   Administering and Managing Multiserver Exchange Sites   423

14   Administering and Managing Multisite Exchange
     Organizations   455

PART VI **Connecting to Other E-Messaging Systems**   **533**

15   External Links Using Exchange Connectors   535

16   Directory Synchronization with MS Mail PC Systems   589

PART VII **Advanced Topics**   **609**

17   Advanced Exchange Administration and Management   611

18   Advanced Exchange Server Internet Protocols   671

19   Application Development with Exchange Forms Designer   745

     Index   775

TABLE OF CONTENTS

Introduction   *xxv*

PART I   **Exchange Concepts, Basics, and Design**   **1**

1   Introducing Exchange   **3**

Exchange and the E-Messaging Decade   4
Exchange Applications   5
   E-Mail Is Only the Beginning   5
   Just a Step beyond Mail   9
   Off-the-Shelf Messaging-Enabled Applications   10
   OLE 2.0 Objects   12
   Electronic Forms   13
   Applications Built on APIs   14
   Applications Using Exchange Public Folders   15
Some Exchange Basics   16
   Exchange as a Client/Server System   17
   A Quick Take on the Exchange Client   20
   Exchange Server's Dependency on NT Server   23
   Exchange Server's Object Orientation   25
   Exchange Server Scalability   26
   Exchange Server Security   26
   Exchange Server and Other E-Messaging Systems   27
Conclusion   28

2   The Exchange Hierarchy   **31**

A Conceptual View of the Hierarchy   32
A More Practical View of the Hierarchy   33
   Organizations   34
   Sites   34

Servers 35
Recipients 36
Reasons to Be Careful about Exchange Hierarchy Design 43
The Exchange Hierarchy and Exchange Management 43
The Exchange Hierarchy and E-Messaging Address 43
Conclusion 45

3 The Architecture of Exchange **47**

Exchange Server's Core Components 49
The Directory 49
The Information Store 50
The Message Transfer Agent 52
The System Attendant 54
Optional Exchange Server Components 55
The Exchange Administrator Program 56
The Directory Synchronization Agent 57
The Key Management Component 57
Exchange Internet Protocol Access Components 57
Exchange Connectors 58
Exchange Gateways 63
Exchange Client Components 64
The Exchange Client 64
Schedule+ 65
The Outlook Client 65
The Microsoft Exchange Forms Designer 66
Microsoft Exchange Forms Designer Forms 66
Other Client-Based Applications 66
Conclusion 67

4 Exchange and Windows NT Server **69**

Why NT Server? 70
NT Server Can Handle Heavy Multiuser Loads 70
NT Server Supports RAID Levels 1 and 5 71
NT Server Is a Piece of Cake 73
NT Specifics for the Exchange Server Crowd 73
NT Services 75
NT Networking 76

Microsoft Network Domains 77
Cross-Domain Trusts 80
Domain Models 82
The NT User Manager for Domains 87
The NT Server Manager 89
NT and Multiprocessing 90
The NT Event Viewer 91
The NT Performance Monitor 92
Conclusion 93

5 Designing an Exchange System 95

Assess User Needs 97
Questions to Ask 99
An Example: Assessing GerCom's User Needs 100
Study Your Organization's Geographical Profile 105
An Example: GerCom's Geographical Profile 106
Assess Your Organization's Network 108
What's Connected to What, and How? 108
How Much Bandwidth Have We Got on Each Network? 108
How Reliable Are Our Networks? 109
An Example: GerCom's Networks 109
Establish Naming Conventions 111
Naming the Organization, Sites, and Servers 111
Naming Recipient Mailboxes 112
An Example: GerCom's Naming Conventions 115
Select a Microsoft Networking Domain Model 116
An Example: The GerCom Domain Model 116
Define Site Boundaries 118
Exchange Sites and Domains 118
Required Networking Capabilities 119
An Example: GerCom's Site Boundaries 120
Plan Intersite Links 121
Site Link Options 121
An Example: GerCom's Intersite Connections 125
Plan Servers and User Links to Them 125
Designing Your Exchange Servers 126
Backing Up Your Exchange Servers 129

Networking Your Exchange Users   130
An Example: GerCom's Servers and User Links   131
Plan Connections to Other Systems   133
Connection Options   133
An Example: GerCom's External Links   135
Validate and Optimize the Design   136
Guaranteed Delivery   137
Message Integrity   137
Message Security   137
System Versatility   138
Optimization   138
An Example: Validating GerCom's Design   138
Roll Out the Plan   139
An Example: The GerCom Rollout   140
Conclusion   143

PART II	Installation	**145**

6   Installing Windows NT Server   **147**

Installation: An Overview   148
Setting Up the Server Hardware   149
Getting Server Components in Order   150
Testing Key Components   153
Installing NT Server Software   155
Starting the Installation   156
Detecting Mass Storage Devices   156
Insert the NT Server CD-ROM Disk   157
Licenses   157
Checking for Software and Hardware   157
Preparing Disk Partitions   158
Copying Files from the NT Server CD-ROM Disk   158
Setup's Installation Wizard   159
Installing Internet Information Server   164
Finishing Up   164
Setting Up and Formatting Other Disk Partitions   166
Installing an Uninterruptible Power Supply   169
The UPS Itself   169

Configuring UPS Support 170
Testing the UPS 171
UPSs with Special Software 171
Setting Up NT Backup 172
Hardware 172
Installing Tape Device Drivers 172
Setting Up a Basic Backup 174
Giving Domain Access to Users and NT Systems 177
Creating Domain Accounts and Groups 177
Giving Domain Access to NT Servers and Workstations 180
Setting Up NT Server Clients 181
Windows 95 181
Windows NT Workstation 189
Windows for Workgroups 190
Novell NetWare and Other Clients 190
Conclusion 191

7 Installing an Exchange Server 193

Getting Ready 194
Verifying Server Hardware Setup 194
Gathering NT Server Information 194
Gathering Account Information 195
Gathering Exchange Server Information 196
Setting Up Security 197
Running the Exchange Server Setup Program 199
Selecting Installation Options 200
Selecting a Licensing Mode 204
Entering Organization and Site Names 205
Specifying a Site Services Account 205
File Installation and System Setup 206
Postinstallation Activities 210
Exchange Server's Windows Program Group 211
Verifying That Exchange Server Processes Are Running 213
Starting the Exchange Administrator 214
Setting Permissions for the Exchange Server
Administration Group 217
Conclusion 222

PART III	**Basic Exchange Server Administration and Management**	**225**

8	**The Administrator and Its Menus**	**228**

Administration and Management	229
Administrator Windows	229
Multiple Windows	230
Manipulating the Splitbar	233
Preliminary Settings	233
Setting Auto Naming Options	233
Setting Permissions Options	234
Setting the NT Account Deletion Option	236
Setting the Option to Find a Matching Windows NT Account	236
Changing Site Addresses	237
The File Menu	238
Connecting to a Server	239
Closing a Window	239
Creating a New Mailbox	239
Creating a New Distribution List	261
Creating Custom Recipients	266
New Other Options	268
Properties	279
Duplicating Objects	280
The Edit Menu	280
The View Menu	280
What to View	281
Recipient Attributes and Views	281
Sorting Lists	283
Fonts	284
Move Splitbar	284
The Toolbar	284
The Status Bar	285
The Tools Menu	285
Finding Recipients	286
Moving a Mailbox	287
Adding to an Address Book View	287
Cleaning Mailboxes	287
Starting a Monitor	288

Tracking a Message, Administering Forms, and Working with
   Newsgroup Hierarchies 288
Saving Connections 289
Customizing the Toolbar 289
Options 289
Conclusion 290

9   The Exchange Server Hierarchy and Core Components   291

The Exchange Server Hierarchy 292
The Organization 293
Sites 296
Servers 297
Specific Servers 298
Recipients: A General Overview 306
Administering and Managing Public Folders 308
Exchange Server Core Components 313
Administering and Managing the Directory Service 315
Administering and Managing the DS at the Site Level 315
Administering and Managing the DS at the Server Level 320
Administering and Managing the MTA 321
Administering and Managing the Information Store 321
Administering and Managing the Information Store at the
   Site Level 322
Administering and Managing the Private Information Store
   at the Server Level 325
Administering and Managing the Public Information Store
   at the Server Level 329
Administering and Managing the System Attendant 330
Conclusion 331

10   Backing Up an Exchange Server   333

Some Backup Basics 334
The Archive Bit 334
Backup Types 335
General Backup Strategies 335
Exchange Server Component Backup Strategies 336

Exchange Server Transaction Logs and Backup 337
Setting Up an Exchange Server Backup 338
  Selecting Exchange Servers and Components 338
  Backing Up NT Server Drives 339
  Selecting Backup Options 340
  Monitoring Backup Progress 343
Restoring from an Exchange Server Backup 345
  Specifying What to Restore 346
  Specifying How to Restore 347
Automating a Backup 349
  Creating a Batch File for Backup 350
  Using NT's Scheduler to Automate Backups 351
Conclusion 355

PART IV   **Exchange Clients for Windows**   **357**

11   **Installing Exchange Clients for Windows**   **359**

Installing Exchange Client Software on a Server 360
  Preparing Exchange Client Software for Installation 362
  Installing an Exchange Client on a Workstation 375
  Notes for NetWare Administrators 379
  Ensuring Proper Routing 380
  NetWare Clients and Exchange Server 380
Conclusion 381

12   **Exchange Clients for Windows 101**   **383**

Starting Up a Newly Installed Client 384
Sending and Receiving a Message with an Exchange Client 389
  Sending a Message 390
  Reading a Received Message 394
Creating a New Public Folder 395
Creating, Accessing, and Using a Shared Mailbox 400
  Creating a Shared Mailbox 401
  Accessing a Shared Mailbox 403
  Hiding a Shared Mailbox from the Address Book 406
  Sending a Message to a Shared Mailbox 406
A Quick Tour of the Exchange Client's Main Window Menus 407
  The File Menu 408

The Edit Menu   410
The View Menu   410
The Tools Menu   412
The Compose Menu   417
Conclusion   419

PART V   **Expanding an Exchange Organization**   **421**

13   **Administering and Managing Multiserver
Exchange Sites**   **423**

Installing an Additional Exchange Server in a Site   424
   Installing an Additional NT Server   424
   Installing an Additional Exchange Server   425
Using the Exchange Administrator in Multiserver Sites   428
   The Default Server   428
   Connecting to Multiple Exchange Servers   429
   Navigating the Site Configuration Hierarchy   432
Administering and Managing Multiserver Sites   433
Administrator Menu Items in Multiserver Sites   434
   Server Monitors   434
   Link Monitors   438
Exchange Core Components in Multiserver Sites   444
Administering and Managing the DS in Multiserver Sites   445
   Server-Level DS Administration and Management in
   Multiserver Sites   445
Administering and Managing the MTA in Multiserver Sites   447
   Site-Level MTA Administration and Management in
   Multiserver Sites   447
   Server-Level MTA Administration and Management in
   Multiserver Sites   450
Conclusion   453

14   **Administering and Managing Multisite Exchange
Organizations**   **455**

Installing an Exchange Server in a New Site   456
   Installing an NT Server in a New Domain   456
   Installing an Exchange Server in a New Site   463

Setting Up Required Cross-Site Permissions   464
Setting Up a Site-to-Site Link   470
   Setting Up the First Site   470
   Setting Up the Second Site   476
   Did It Work?   478
Setting Up Directory Replication between Sites   479
   Setting Up Directory Replication in the First Site   479
   Setting Up Directory Replication in the Second Site   481
   Did It Work?   482
Using the Exchange Administrator in a Multisite Organization   486
Setting Up Direct Site-to-Site Links Using Other Exchange
   Connectors   488
   Setting Up an MTA Transport Stack   489
Administering and Managing Multisite Exchange Organizations   494
   Setting Up a Site-to-Site Link Using the X.400 Connector 494
   Setting Up a Site-to-Site Link Using the Dynamic RAS Connector 503
Some Clarifying Comments on Site-to-Site Connections   507
Adding New Servers to Server and Link Monitors   508
Setting Up Cross-Site Public Folder Access   508
   Allowing Users in One Site to Connect to Folders in Another Site 510
   Cross-Site Public Folder Replication   513
Site-Level Addressing and Routing Administration and
   Management   528
   General Properties   528
   Routing Calculation Schedule   529
Conclusion   531

PART VI   Connecting to Other E-Messaging Systems   533

15   External Links Using Exchange Connectors   535

The X.400 Connector   536
   General Properties   537
   Advanced Properties   538
   Setting Up an Indirect Site Link   539
   Did It Work?   541
The Internet Mail Service   541
   The IMS and TCP/IP   542

Installing the IMS   544
Setting IMS Properties   553
Setting Up a Site Link Using the IMS   568
Did It Work?   569
The MS Mail Connector   569
Interchange   570
General Properties   571
Connections   571
Connector MTAs   576
Local Postoffice   581
Starting the MTA Service   581
MS Mail PC Post Office Setup   582
Did It Work?   584
The cc:Mail Connector   586
Exchange Gateways   586
Conclusion   587

16 Directory Synchronization with MS Mail PC Systems

589

Understanding Dirsync   590
Adding an Exchange System to Dirsync   592
General Properties   592
Import Container   594
Export Containers   596
Settings   597
Schedule   598
Dirsync Server Settings   598
Did It Work?   600
Building a New Dirsync System That Includes an Exchange
  Organization   601
Setting Up a Dirsync Server on an Exchange Server   601
Setting Up a Remote Dirsync Requestor   603
Administering and Managing the Exchange Directory
  Synchronization Service   604
Conclusion   606

PART VII Advanced Topics   609

17 Advanced Exchange Administration and Management   611

Creating New Information Stores   612
Moving Mailboxes   615
Tracking Messages   616
   Tracking User Messages   616
   Tracking System Messages   625
Setting Up Advanced Security   626
   Installing the Key Management Server   628
   Advanced Security Administration and Management in
     Other Sites   630
   Administering and Managing the Key Management Server   631
   Sending and Receiving Digitally Signed and Encrypted Messages 642
   Additional Advanced Security Administration and Management
     Options   642
Migrating Users from Other E-Messaging Systems   643
   Importing Information into the Exchange Directory   645
   Extracting Information from Other Sources for the Exchange
     Directory   649
   Exporting Directory Information from Exchange Server   651
   Exporting a Directory   653
Moving Mailboxes between Exchange Sites   655
Working with Address Book Views   655
   Adding an Address Book View   656
   Adding an Address Book View Container   661
   Adding to an Address Book View   662
Other Advanced Exchange Administrator Options   663
   Add-Ins   663
   Addressing   664
Remotely Administering Exchange and NT Servers   665
Supporting Remote Users   666
Supporting Roving Users   667
A Quick Look at Schedule+   668
Conclusion   669

18 Advanced Exchange Server Internet Protocols   671

The Post Office Protocol   672
   POP3 Set Up: The Exchange Server Side   673
   POP3 Set Up: The Client Side   681
Web Browser Access to Exchange Server   689
   Active Server Component (HTTP) Set Up: The Server Side   690
   Active Server Component (HTTP) Set Up: The Client Side   694
The Lightweight Directory Access Protocol   698
   LDAP Set Up: The Server Side   698
   LDAP Set Up: The Client Side   702
The Network News Transport Protocol   711
   NNTP Set Up: The Server Side   713
   Managing Newsgroups   735
   NNTP Set Up: The Client Side   736
   Becoming a USENET Newsfeed Provider   740
Configuring Protocols Containers   741
Conclusion   743

19 Application Development with Exchange Forms Designer   745

The Exchange Application Design Environment   747
Installation   748
Building an Exchange Electronic Form   748
   Getting Started with the Form Template Wizard 750
   Using EFD to Continue Building a Form   753
Installing a New Exchange Form   766
   Creating an Organization Forms Library   767
   Installing a Form   768
   Using a Form   770
   Don't Stop Here!   773
Conclusion   773

Index   775

INTRODUCTION

I wrote this book because I want to share the excitement I feel about the future of electronic messaging in general and about Exchange Server in particular. I also want to help you determine if there is a place for Exchange in your organization and, if so, to provide the information you'll need to set up an Exchange system of your own.

Your explorations of Exchange Server will open many new doors in the area of electronic communications. In addition, your work with this exciting product will afford you a peek at Microsoft's next iteration of NT Server. Exchange Server implements much of the object-oriented structure of Microsoft's NT Server 5, formerly known as Cairo. *Mastering Microsoft Exchange Server 5* will, at the very least, give you a leg up when you tackle NT Server 5.

What's So Exciting about Exchange Server 5?

While this book covers all aspects of Exchange Server 5, it is still pertinent to Exchange Server 4. Exchange Server 4 was one of the most powerful, extensible, scalable, easy-to-use, and manageable electronic messaging back ends on the market. Exchange Server 5 retains all of 4's features and adds extensive support for a range of advanced Internet communications protocols.

Version 3 of the Post Office Protocol (POP3) enables nonproprietary, lightweight client access to Exchange Server messages. Microsoft's Exchange clients for Windows and the Macintosh are full-featured and very easy to use, but they only run on those operating systems and they require large amounts of workstation disk and memory resources. Any POP3 client, whether running in MS Windows, Macintosh, any flavor of UNIX or another operating system, can access Exchange Server to send and receive messages. Furthermore, POP3 clients such as Qualcomm's Eudora, Microsoft's Internet Mail client, and Netscape's mail client demand fewer workstation resources. So, they can run on those lower-end workstations still in heavy use in corporate America.

The Hypertext Transport Protocol (HTTP) makes possible web browser access to Exchange Server mailboxes and public folders. Like POP3 clients, web browsers are both nonproprietary and lighter in weight than the standard Exchange clients. So users and their organizations realize the same benefits they get with POP3 clients, while using a client that is on virtually every desktop. HTTP support also enables controlled and selective access to Exchange Server environments by anonymous users.

The Lightweight Directory Access Protocol (LDAP) opens the Exchange Server directory of user e-mail addresses and other information to Internet users. Exchange Server users with LDAP-enabled POP3 clients can find e-mail addresses in the Exchange directory from anywhere in the world. This adds an unprecedented and a most welcome level of user friendliness to the POP3 world. The Exchange directory also can be made available to anonymous non-Exchange Server users armed with LDAP clients.

The Network News Transport Protocol (NNTP) brings those popular USENET newsgroups to Exchange Server public folders. An Exchange server can function as a full-fledged NNTP server. Users of Exchange clients, web browsers, or standard newsgroup reader software can participate in all or a select portion of the newsgroups hosted on an Exchange server.

With these and an impressive array of other features, Exchange Server 5 can help your organization move smoothly and productively into what I like to call "the e-messaging decade."

What You Need to Run Exchange Server

Exchange Server is a complex product with a remarkably easy-to-use interface for administration and management. All of this complexity and parallel ease of use requires an industrial strength computer. The minimum server computer suggested below is for testing, learning about, and evaluating the product. It's also enough for a small, noncritical installation. However, as I discuss in the book, when the server moves into critical production environments where it will be accessed by large numbers of users, you'll need to beef up its hardware and add a number of fault-tolerant capabilities. On the client side, with the broad range of clients available for Exchange, the lower-end machines now on desktops in most organizations should be more than adequate.

At a minimum, to test, learn about, and evaluate Exchange Server you'll need:

- Microsoft Exchange Server 4.0 or greater

- Exchange Server 4.0: Microsoft NT Server 3.51 or greater (upgraded to NT 3.51 Service Pack v4 or greater)

- Exchange Server 5.0: Microsoft Windows NT Server 3.51 w/SP5 or 4.0 (upgraded to NT 4.0 Service Pack v.2 or greater)

- A 166MHz Pentium-based PC with 64MB of RAM and one 1GB disk drive

- Tape backup hardware

- A local and/or wide area network

- At least one 486 66MHz or equivalent computer with 32MB of memory running Microsoft, Novell Netware, or Apple Macintosh networking and a Microsoft Exchange or Outlook client, or a POP3 client or web browser

How This Book Is Organized

I've divided this book into 7 parts and 19 chapters. As you proceed through the book you'll move from basic concepts to several increasingly more complex levels of hands-on implementation.

I'd prefer that you step through each chapter before going on to the next. Understanding the concepts and planning carefully are central to implementing a sophisticated electronic messaging system like Microsoft Exchange.

However, if you're in a hurry to get your hands dirty, start with Chapters 6, 7, 8, 9, 11, and 12. They'll help you get an NT server, an Exchange server, and some clients up and running quickly. As long as you're not planning to put your quickie server into production immediately, there should be no harm done.

Before going live, however, I do strongly suggest that you take a look at Part I; it will help you fix up any "little" problems that crop up and guard against a lot of future headaches.

Conventions Used in This Book

There are many notes in this book. Generally, they are positioned below the material to which they refer. There are three kinds of notes: Note, Tip, and Warning.

NOTE Notes give you information pertinent to the procedure or topic being discussed.

TIP Tips indicate practical hints that might make your work easier.

WARNING Warnings alert you to potential problems you might encounter while using the program.

Remember, Exchange is designed to help your organization do what it does better, more efficiently, and with greater productivity. Have fun, be productive and prosper!

PART I

Exchange Concepts, Basics, and Design

This section focuses on concepts and features of Microsoft's Exchange client/server electronic messaging system. It's designed to prepare you for installing, administering, and managing small and large Exchange Server systems.

Chapter 1 explores the role of Exchange in the "e-messaging decade" and looks at some of the things you can do with Exchange. Chapter 2 looks at the basic structure of Exchange Server and how it relates to real-world business and social structures. Chapter 3 focuses on the components of Exchange Server. Chapter 4 looks at Microsoft Windows NT Server—how it works and how it integrates with Exchange Server. Chapter 5 addresses the complex process of planning for the implementation of an Exchange system.

CHAPTER

ONE

Introducing Exchange

- Exchange and the "e-messaging decade"

- Exchange applications; e-mail and way beyond

- Exchange basics

Microsoft's Exchange client/server electronic messaging system is a major player in what I call the "e-messaging decade." It lets people work together in a variety of productivity-enhancing ways. The Exchange system is one of the most exciting, innovative, and promising software products I've ever seen. I can't wait to get started, so let's go to it.

Exchange and the E-Messaging Decade

Electronic messaging is more than e-mail. It is the use of an underlying messaging infrastructure (addresses, routing, and so on) to build applications that are based on cooperative tasking, whether by humans or computers. We can expect the years 1996 to 2005 to be the decade of electronic messaging (*e-messaging*), when store-and-forward-based messaging systems and real-time interactive technologies will complement each other to produce wildly imaginative business, entertainment, and educational applications with high pay-off potential.

Microsoft's Exchange Server will play a key role in e-messaging. Exchange Server is one of the most powerful, extensible, scalable, easy-to-use, and manageable e-messaging back ends currently on the market. Combined with Microsoft's excellent Exchange clients, Internet-based clients from other vendors, and third-party or home-grown applications, Exchange Server can help your organization move smoothly and productively into the e-messaging decade.

In writing this book, I was guided by three goals:

- To share the excitement I feel about both the promise of electronic messaging and the Exchange client/server system

- To help you decide if there's a place for Exchange in your organization

- To provide the information and teach you the skills you'll need to plan for and implement Exchange systems of any size and shape

The rest of this chapter introduces you to the Exchange client/server system. We start with a quick look at several of the neat ways you can use Exchange for e-mail and more, then focus on some of Exchange's key characteristics and capabilities.

This is just an introduction, so don't worry if you don't understand everything completely by the end of this chapter. All that we discuss here we will cover in more detail later in the book.

By the way, when I use the word *Exchange* or the words *Exchange system* from here on, I'm talking about the whole Exchange client/server system. *Exchange Server* means just the server product, and an *Exchange server* is any computer running the Exchange Server product. *Exchange client* refers to any client that lets you access all of the features of Exchange Server, for example, Microsoft's stable of Exchange clients. *Exchange client* does not refer to general purpose clients like POP3 clients or Internet browser–based clients that provide limited access to Exchange Server's features. When I talk about these, I'll use either their commercial or generic names or both, for example, *the Eudora POP3 client*. Got that? Okay, explain it to me.

Exchange Applications

I dare you not to get excited about electronic messaging and Exchange as you read this section. Just look at what's possible and imagine what you could do with all of this potential.

E-Mail Is Only the Beginning

Together, Exchange Server and its clients perform a variety of messaging-based functions. These include e-mail, message routing, scheduling, and supporting several types of custom applications. E-mail is certainly a key feature of any messaging system. And the Schedule+ 7.5 client that comes with Exchange Server is far and away better than previous versions of the appointment and meeting–scheduling software. (Figure 1.1 shows the Exchange and Schedule+ clients for Windows in action.) Take a look at Figures 1.2, 1.3, and 1.4 for a glimpse of the new Internet-based POP3, web browser, and fully Exchange client–compliant Microsoft Outlook e-mail clients you can use with Exchange 5.0. Finally, take a look at Figure 1.5 to see how the Outlook client handles your schedule.

FIGURE 1.1

The Exchange and
Schedule+ clients for
Windows

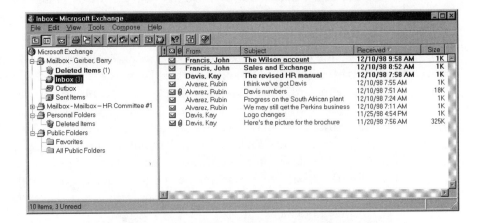

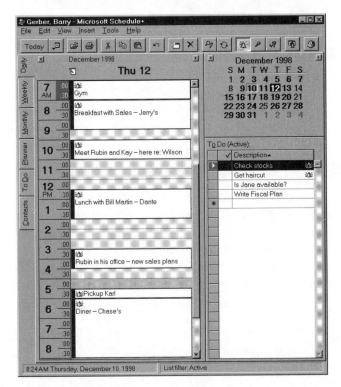

FIGURE 1.2

Qualcomm's Eudora Pro 3.0 POP3-compliant client accesses mail stored on an Exchange server.

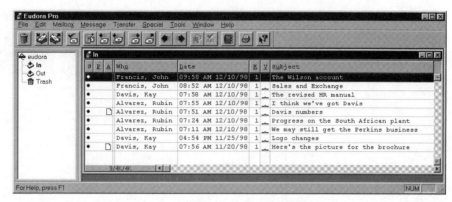

FIGURE 1.3

Microsoft's Internet Explorer 3.0 web browser accesses mail stored on an Exchange server.

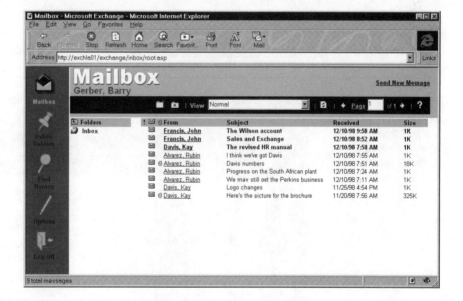

FIGURE 1.4

Microsoft's Outlook
client for Exchange
Server accesses mail
stored on an Exchange
server.

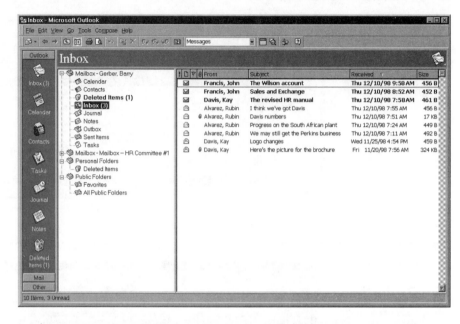

FIGURE 1.5

Microsoft's Outlook
client for Exchange
Server accesses a
schedule stored on an
Exchange server.

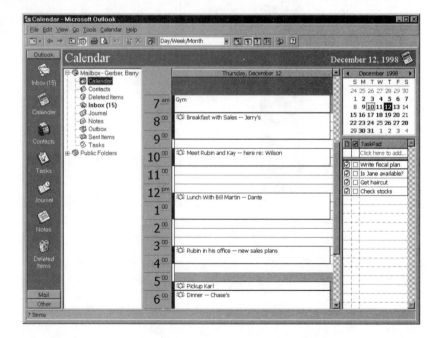

Change Is the Name of the Game

Some of the marvelous user interfaces you see in Figures 1 through 5 may look very different by the time you read this book. Software development and marketing, especially in the world of electronic communications, is running at hyperspeed. Updates and even major revisions hit the market at a breakneck pace. The Internet makes it even easier for vendors to market and deliver their wares. New pieces and parts of applications appear almost daily for manual or totally automatic download and installation.

The basic architecture of Exchange Server and its clients are unlikely to change much over the next couple of years. The outward appearance of user interfaces are likely to change dramatically. As far as Exchange goes, plan for change as a way of life. Keep an open mind and at least one eye on Microsoft's Internet pages.

In the long run all of this hyperactivity will prove a good thing. Our requirements will find their way into and bugs will find their way out of products faster. I will admit, however, that I sometimes long for the days of yearly or less-frequent updates on low density 5¼-inch floppies.

E-mail clients are exciting and sexy, but to get the most out of Exchange, you need to throw away any preconceptions you have that messaging packages are only for e-mail and scheduling. The really exciting applications are not those that use simple e-mail or scheduling, but those that are based on the routing capabilities of messaging systems. These applications bring people and computers together for cooperative work.

So what do these hot apps look like? Let's start with the simplest and move toward the more complex.

Just a Step beyond Mail

You're probably familiar with e-mail *attachments*—those word processing, spreadsheet, and other work files you can drop into messages. Attachments are a simple way to move work files to the people who need to see them.

Sure, you could send your files on floppy disk or tell people where on the network they can find and download the files. But e-mail attachments let you make the files available to others with a click of their mouse buttons: They just double-click on an icon, and the attachment opens in the original application that produced it (if your correspondent has access to the application, of course).

Using attachments has the added advantage of putting the files and accompanying messages right in the faces of those who need to see them. This leaves less room for excuses like "Oh, I forgot" or "The dog ate the floppy disk."

As great as attachments can be, they have one real weakness: The minute an attachment leaves your Outbox, it's out of date. If you do further work on the original file, that work is not reflected in the copy you sent to others. If someone then edits a copy of the attached file, it's totally out of sync with the original and all other copies. Getting everything synchronized again can involve tedious hours or days of manually comparing different versions and cutting and pasting them to create one master document.

Exchange offers several ways to avoid this problem. One of the simplest is the *attachment link:* Instead of putting the actual file into a message, you put in a link to the file (see Figure 1.6), which can be stored anywhere on the network. The real kicker is that the file can also be stored in Exchange public folders. (More about these later.) When someone double-clicks on an attachment link icon, the linked file opens. Everyone who receives the message works with the same linked attachment. Everyone reads and can modify the same file.

Off-the-Shelf Messaging-Enabled Applications

Here's another way to guard against dead work files: Microsoft Windows enables messaging in many word processing and spreadsheet applications. For example, when you install the Exchange client on your computer, Microsoft's Office products like Word and Excel are e-messaging enabled. You can select Send or Route options from the apps' File menu; this pops up a routing slip. You then add addresses to the slip from your Exchange client's address book, select the routing method you want to use, and assign a right-to-modify level for the route. Finally, you ship your work off to others with just a click of the Route button.

Figure 1.7 shows how all of this works. Though it's simple, application-based messaging can significantly improve user productivity and speed up a range of business processes.

FIGURE 1.6

Exchange links keep
attachments alive.

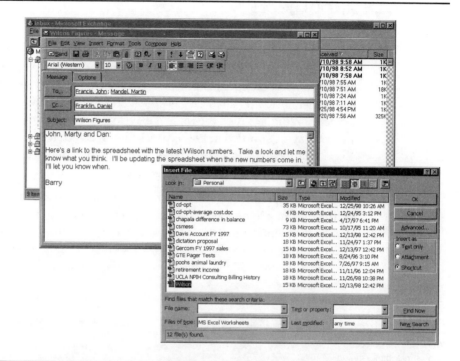

FIGURE 1.7

Microsoft Word 97
includes messaging-
enabled Send and Route
functions.

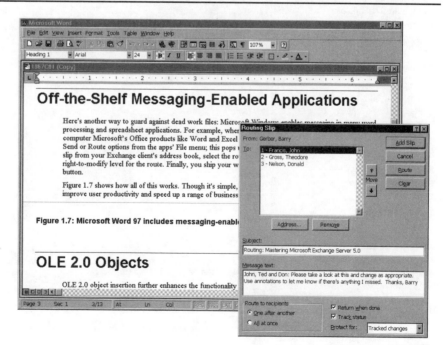

OLE 2.0 Objects

OLE 2.0 object insertion further enhances the functionality of the Exchange messaging system. Take a close look at Figure 1.8. Yes, the message includes an Excel spreadsheet and chart. The person who sent the message simply selected Object from the Insert menu that appears on every Exchange message. The Exchange client then inserted a blank Excel spreadsheet into the message as an OLE 2.0 object. Having received the message, we can see the spreadsheet as an item in the message, as shown in the figure. When we double-click on the spreadsheet, Excel is launched and Excel's menus and toolbars replace those of the message (Figure 1.9). In essence, the message becomes Excel.

The Excel spreadsheet is fully editable. Though Excel must be available to your recipients, they don't have to launch it to read and work on the spreadsheet. Even if your recipient doesn't have Excel, they can still view the contents of the spreadsheet, though they won't be able to work on it. (That is, even if they don't have the app, they can still view the object when they open the message.)

FIGURE 1.8

With OLE 2.0 objects, sophisticated messaging-enabled applications are easy to build.

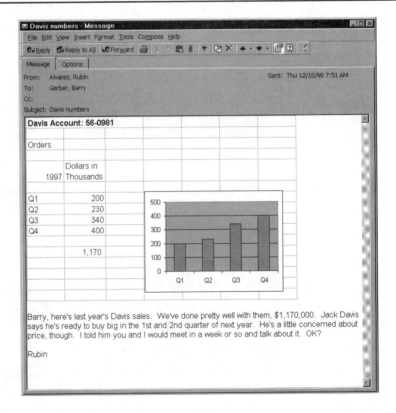

FIGURE 1.9

Double-clicking on an OLE 2.0-embedded Excel spreadsheet in a message enables Excel menus and toolbars.

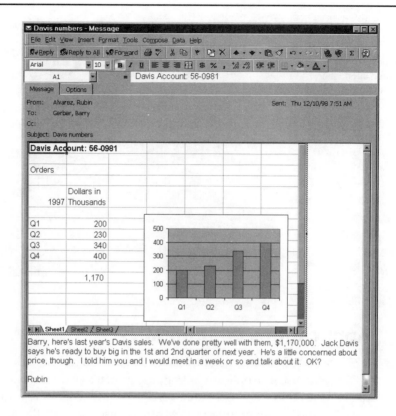

Electronic Forms

Exchange Server comes with the Exchange Forms Designer that is based on Microsoft Visual Basic. You can use the Forms Designer to build information-gathering forms containing a number of the bells and whistles you're used to in Windows applications. These include drop-down pick list boxes, check boxes, fill-in text forms, tab dialog controls, and radio buttons.

The forms manager, which is easy enough for nontechnical types to use, includes a variety of messaging-oriented fields and actions. For example, you can choose to include a preaddressed To field in a form, as shown in Figure 1.10, so users of the form can easily mail it off to the appropriate recipient. Once you've designed a form, it can be made available to all or select users, who can access the completed form by simply selecting it while in the Exchange client.

FIGURE 1.10

Electronic forms turn messages into structured information-gathering tools.

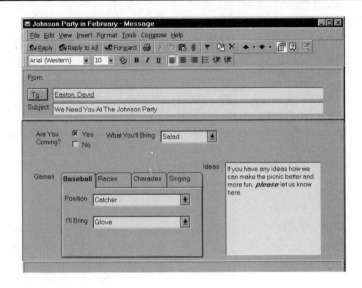

Applications Built on APIs

If all of this functionality isn't enough, you can go to the heart of Exchange Server and use its Application Program Interface (API). Exchange Server supports both the Simple and Extended versions of Microsoft's Windows-based Mail Application Program Interface (MAPI). It also supports the X.400-oriented, platform-independent Common Mail Call (CMC) APIs, which have functions similar to those of Simple MAPI. Using Simple MAPI or CMC, you can build applications that use e-messaging addresses behind the scenes to route data between users and programs. Extended MAPI lets you get more deeply into Exchange's storage and e-messaging address books to create virtually any messaging-enabled application you can imagine.

These custom-built applications may involve some level of automation, such as regular updates of your company's price lists for trading partners or sending a weekly multimedia message from the president to employees at your organization. Building apps based on MAPI or CMC requires someone with programming skills in languages like Visual Basic or C++.

Applications Using Exchange Public Folders

As you'll discover later in this chapter and chapters to come, Exchange Server supports both private and public folders. Both kinds of folders can hold messages and any kind of computer application or data file. Private folders are the place where Exchange users store and manage their messages and files. Public folders are for common access to messages and files. Files can be dragged from file access interfaces like the Explorer in Microsoft's Windows 95 and NT 4.0 and dropped into private or public folders. If you begin thinking of private and public folders as a messaging-enabled extension of Explorer, you'll have a fairly clear picture of Microsoft's vision of the future in regard to how an operating system organizes and displays stored information.

You can set up sorting rules for a private or public folder so that items in the folder are organized by a range of attributes, such as the name of the sender or creator of the item or the date the item arrived or was placed in the folder. Items in a private or public folder can be sorted by conversation threads. You can also put applications built on existing products like Word or Excel or with Exchange Forms Designer or the API set into private or public folders. In private folders these applications are fun for one, but in public folders, where they are accessed by many people, they can replace the tons of maddening paper-based processes that abound in every organization.

If all of this isn't already enough, Exchange is very much Internet aware. With Exchange 5.0, you can publish all or selected public folders on the Internet where they become accessible with a simple Internet browser. You can limit Internet access to public folders to only those who have access under Exchange's security system or you can open public folders to anyone on the Internet. At present you're pretty much limited to text-based information. But just think about it: Internet-enabled public folders let you put information on the Internet without the fuss and bother of web site design and development. Any item can be placed on the Internet by simply adding a message to a public folder. Figure 1.11 shows a public folder–enabled price list for the one product produced by my favorite fictitious company, GerCom, about which more later.

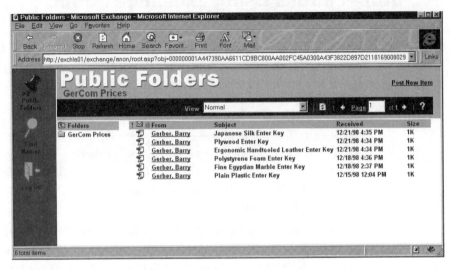

FIGURE 1.11

Using Exchange public folders to publish a price list on the Internet

Before we leave public folder applications, I want to mention one more option. Exchange Server 5.0 and greater lets you bring any or all of those devilishly delightful USENET Internet news groups to your public folder environment. With their Exchange clients, users then can read and reply to news group items just as though they were using a standard news group reader application. Exchange Server comes with all the tools you need to make it so. All you need is an Internet connection, access to a newsfeed provider, and a set of rules about which groups to exclude. Remember, this is where the infamous alt.sex news groups live.

Some Exchange Basics

It's important to get a handle on some of Exchange's key characteristics and capabilities. Once you do, you'll better appreciate the depth and breadth of Microsoft's efforts in developing Exchange, and you'll be better prepared for the rest of this book. In this section, we'll take a look at:

- Exchange as a client/server system

- The Exchange client

- Exchange Server's dependency on Microsoft's Windows NT Server

- Exchange Server's object orientation

- Exchange Server scalability

- Exchange Server security

- Exchange Server and other e-messaging systems

Exchange as a Client/Server System

The term *client/server* has been overused and overworked. To put it simply, there are two kinds of networked applications: shared-file and client/server.

Shared-File Applications

Early networked applications were all based on *shared-file* systems. The network shell that let you load your word processor from a network server also allowed you to read from and write to files stored on a server. At the time, it was the easiest and most natural way to grow networked applications.

Microsoft Mail for PC Networks is a shared-file application. You run Windows, OS/2, DOS, or Macintosh front ends, which send and receive messages by accessing files on a Microsoft Mail for PC Networks post office that resides on a network file server. The front end and your PC do all the work; the server is passive. Figure 1.12 shows a typical Microsoft Mail for PC Networks setup.

Easy as it was to develop, this architecture leads to some serious problems in today's networked computing world:

- Changing the underlying structure of the server file system is difficult, because you have to change both the server and the client.

- System security is always compromised, because users must have read and write permissions for the whole server file system, which includes all other users' message files. Things are so bad that a naive or malicious user can actually destroy shared-file system databases in some cases.

- Network traffic is high, because the front end must constantly access indexes and hunt around the server's file system for a user's message.

- Because the user workstation acts directly on shared files, these can be destroyed if workstation hardware or software stop functioning for some unexpected reason.

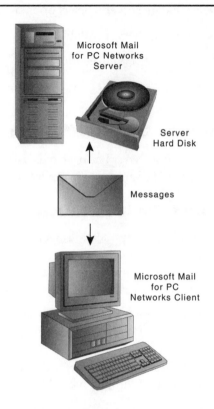

FIGURE 1.12

Microsoft Mail for PC
Networks is a typical
shared-file e-messaging
system.

Shared-file applications are in decline. Sure, plenty of "legacy" (that is, out-of-date) apps will probably live on for the data processing equivalent of eternity, but client/server systems have quickly supplanted the shared-file model. This is especially true in the world of electronic messaging.

Client/Server Applications

Today, more and more networked applications are based on the client/server model. The server is an active partner in client/server applications. Clients tell servers what they want done, and if security requirements are met, servers do what they are asked.

Processes running on a server find and ship data off to processes running on a client. When a client process sends data, a server receives it and writes it to server-based files. Server processes can do more than simply interact with client processes. For example, they can compact data files on the server or—as they do on Exchange Server—automatically reply to incoming messages to let people know, for instance, that you're going to be out of the office for a period of time. Figure 1.13 shows how Exchange implements the client/server model.

Client/server applications are strong in all of the areas in which shared-file apps are weak:

- Changing the underlying structure of the server file system is easier than with shared-file systems, because only the server processes access the file system.

- System security can be much tighter, again because only the server processes access the file system.

FIGURE 1.13

Microsoft Exchange is based on the client/server model.

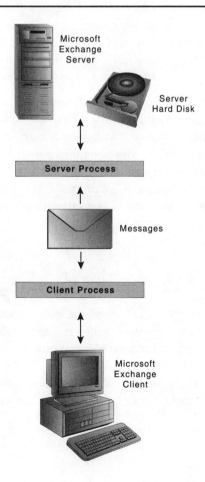

- Network traffic is lighter, because all the work of file access is done by the server, on the server.

- Because server processes are the only ones that access server data, breakdowns of user workstation hardware or software are less likely to spoil data. With appropriate transaction logging features, client/server systems can even protect against server hardware or software malfunctions.

As good as the client/server model is, it does have some general drawbacks. Client/server apps require more computing horsepower, especially on the server side. With Exchange, plan to start with very fast Pentium machines, lots of RAM, and plenty of hard disk capacity—and expect to grow from there.

Client/server applications are more complex than shared-file apps. This is partly due to the nature of the client/server model and partly due to the tendency of client/server apps to be newer and thus filled with all kinds of great capabilities you won't find in shared-file applications. Generally, you're safe in assuming that you'll need to devote more resources to managing a client/server application than to tending a similar one based on shared files.

The good news is that Microsoft has done a lot to reduce the management load and to make it easier for someone who isn't a computer scientist to administer an Exchange system. I've looked at many client/server messaging systems, and I can say without any doubt that Exchange Server is absolutely the easiest to administer. Exchange Server's administrative front end, called the *Exchange Administrator*, organizes the management processes very nicely and provides an excellent system based on a graphical user interface (GUI) for doing everything from adding users and network connections to assessing the health of your messaging system (see Figure 1.14).

A Quick Take on the Exchange Client

As should be clear from our look at some of its applications earlier in this chapter, the Exchange client is the sexy part of Exchange. It's where the action is—the view screen for the backroom bits and bytes of Exchange Server. While this book is mostly about Exchange Server, you can't implement an Exchange system without the clients. So we'll spend some time on the Exchange client in various places throughout this book. Meanwhile, let's discuss some client basics.

FIGURE 1.14

The Exchange Administrator makes management easier.

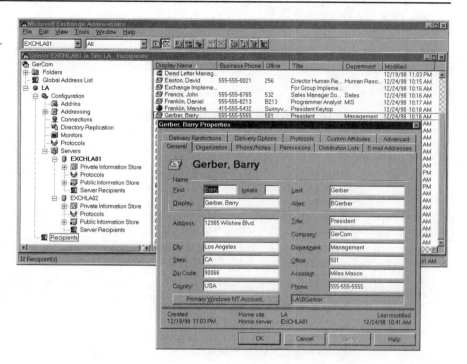

Information Storage

The client stores information in one of two places—private and public information stores. Each has a different purpose and function.

Private Information Stores   Though you can share them with others, private information stores generally hold items that you and you alone have access to. There are two basic kinds of private information stores: mailboxes and personal folders. You access mailboxes and personal folders using an Exchange client.

Mailboxes can send and receive messages. You can add folders to a mailbox to help you organize your messages. If you have the rights to other mailboxes, you can open them in your Exchange client as well.

Personal folders do not have the send and receive capabilities of mailboxes. You can create as many personal folders as you desire. Like the folders you add to mailboxes, personal folders help you organize information. You can drag and drop messages between folders. Using *rules* (discussed below) you can direct incoming mail into any of your personal folders.

The contents of mailboxes are stored inside the Exchange Server database. Personal folders are stored outside of Exchange Server on private or networked disk space.

Public Information Stores   Public information stores are often called *public folders*. Let's use that term here. Public folders hold items that you want others to see. Users whom you authorize can create public folders and drag and drop anything they wish into them. Public folders can also be nested and rules can be applied to them.

Public folders are stored inside the Exchange Server database. They are key to the organization-wide implementation of Exchange. Some, all, or none of an Exchange server's public folders can be automatically replicated to other Exchange servers. This lets you post items to public folders on one Exchange server and have them quickly and painlessly appear on any combination of the Exchange servers in your system. Even without replication, users all over your organization can access public folders.

Sharing Information

You can share information with others by sending it to them or placing it in public folders for them to retrieve on their own. You can drop messages, word processing documents, and other work files—even whole applications—into public folders. You can use public folders to implement many of the kinds of applications I talked about at the beginning of this chapter.

For example, instead of electronically routing a draft word processing document to a bunch of colleagues, you can just drop it into a public folder. Then you can send e-mail to your colleagues asking them to look at the document and even to edit it right there in the public folder.

Organizing Information

Creating a set of personal and public folders and dropping messages in them is a simple way to organize information. More sophisticated approaches include the use of rules, views, and the Exchange client's Finder.

Rules   As a user, you can set up a range of *rules* to move mail from your Inbox into personal or public folders. For example, you might want to move all the messages from your boss into a folder marked URGENT. Rules can be based on anything from the sender of a message to its contents. Because Exchange is a client/server system, rules run on the Exchange server, so the Exchange client doesn't have to be running for your rules to execute (unless the rules involve personal folders).

Views   Exchange messages can have numerous attributes. These include the obvious, such as sender, subject, and date received, as well as less common information, including sender's company, last author, and number of words. You can build views of messages using any combination of attributes and any sorting scheme. Then you can apply a particular view to a folder to specially organize the messages it contains.

The Finder   You can use the Exchange Finder to search all folders or a single folder for messages from or to specific correspondents, messages with specific information in the subject field or message body, and even messages received between specific dates or of a specific size.

Exchange Server's Dependency on NT Server

Exchange Server is a component of the Microsoft BackOffice suite. Like Microsoft's SQL Server and Systems Management Server, Exchange Server runs only with Windows NT Server. It won't run on top of NT Workstation or with Windows 95; even though both are 32-bit operating systems, they can't host Exchange Server.

Among operating systems, NT is the new kid on the block. As a longtime Novell NetWare user, I initially faced NT with not just a little fear and foreboding. That was then. Now I am a confirmed NT user and supporter. My personal workstation is an NT-based machine, and all of my servers but one run NT. (The one holdout is a NetWare server I use to ensure that NT- and Windows-based software works with Novell's IPX/SPX.)

It took me two weeks to get comfortable with NT, and a month to become totally productive with it. What sets NT off from all other operating systems for workstations and servers is Microsoft Windows. NT, whether the workstation or server version, *is* Microsoft Windows. If you can use Windows, you can use NT. Networking with NT is a breeze, and running apps on top of NT Server is a piece of cake. Figure 1.15 shows one of my NT/Exchange server desktops with some

NT and Exchange management applications running. This shouldn't be foreign territory for any Windows aficionado.

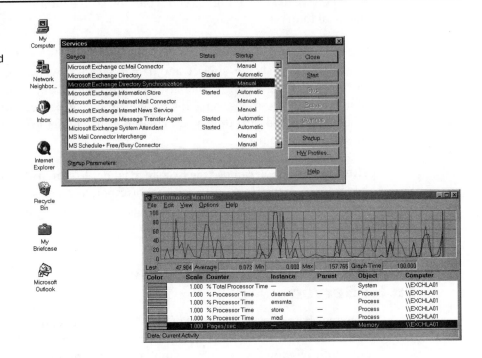

NT is chock-full of features that make it an especially attractive operating system. One of these is its very usable and functional implementation of Microsoft's domain-based security system. Domains have names—one of mine is called LA for my hometown, Los Angeles—and include NT servers, NT workstations, and all flavors of Windows- and DOS-based machines. Though there are a number of domain security models, the general rule is that the members of a domain can use any resource they have been given permission to use—disk files, printers, and so on—in the domain without having to enter a password for each. Exchange Server depends on NT domain security for a good deal of its security.

Later in the book you can read a whole chapter on NT and what you need to know about it to run Exchange Server. There's also a chapter on installing NT Server.

Exchange Server's Object Orientation

Exchange is a classic example of an *object-oriented* system. Take another look at Figure 1.14. See all those items on the tree on the left-hand side of the Exchange Administrator menu, such as GerCom, LA, EXCHLA01, EXCHLA02, and Recipients? Each of these is an *object*. Each object has attributes and can interact with other objects in specific ways. Exchange objects can hold other objects, serving as what Microsoft calls *containers.*

GerCom is the name of the fictitious organization I created for this book; it is the equivalent of a company name like IBM or TRW. (People often ask if I'm related to the baby-food Gerbers. I'm not, but GerCom at least lets me dream. Want to buy some stock?) Microsoft refers to this object as *the organization.* The GerCom organization contains all of the objects below it.

LA is the name of a physical site in the GerCom corporate hierarchy, Los Angeles. It is also a home for Exchange servers. The GerCom/LA hierarchy has two servers, named *EXCHLA01* and *EXCHLA02.*

The Recipients object way down at the bottom of the hierarchy is a container for Exchange Server recipients. *Recipients* are objects that can send or receive messages. Among other things, recipients include user mailboxes and distribution lists. Each recipient object can contain a large number of attributes. The tabbed Properties dialog box in Figure 1.14 should give you some idea of the breadth of attributes that can be assigned to a mailbox.

Notice that the Recipients container is a part of the LA site hierarchy. *Sites* are the most important containers in Exchange. They hold configuration information about recipients and how to reach them, as well as information about servers and other Exchange objects. This information is stored in what Microsoft calls the *Exchange Server directory.* Though specific instances of the directory are stored on the servers in a site, any instance of the directory actually contains information about all of the servers in an organization.

Object orientation makes it easy for Microsoft to distribute Exchange Server's functionality and management, and it makes it easy for you to administer an Exchange Server environment. For example, based on my security clearances I can manage any set of recipients—from those in only a single site to all of the recipients in my organization.

Exchange Server Scalability

Exchange Server scales very well both vertically and horizontally. NT runs on top of computers based on single and multiple Intel, DEC Alpha, and PowerPC processors, so it's very easy to scale an Exchange server upward to more powerful hardware when increased user loads make additional computing power necessary. Since you'll be taking both Exchange Server and NT with you, you really won't have to learn much more about your new machine than the location of its power switch.

If vertical scalability isn't what you need, horizontal scaling is also a breeze with Exchange Server. You can set up a new Exchange server and quickly get its directory and public folders in sync with all or some of your other servers. You can even move mailboxes between Exchange servers in a site with a few clicks of your left mouse button.

How do you know if it's time to scale up or out? Microsoft has an answer for this, too: You can use the LoadSim application included with Exchange Server to simulate a range of different user loads on your server hardware. By analyzing the results of your LoadSim tests, you'll get some idea of the messaging loads you can expect a server to handle in a production environment.

Exchange Server Security

Exchange Server security starts with NT's security system. Several different NT security models are available; the one that's right for you depends mostly on the size and structure of your organization and the department that supports Exchange Server. In all cases, the idea is to select a security model that puts the lightest burden on users and system administrators while still appropriately barring unauthorized users from messaging and other system resources. (More on this in Chapter 4.)

NT also audits security. It can let you know when a user tries to add, delete, or access system resources.

The security of Exchange Server is enhanced in several ways beyond the NT operating system's security. Access to Exchange Server objects such as public folders can be limited by the creator of the folder. Data encryption on the server and client protects messages and other Exchange resources from eavesdropping by those with server or workstation access. Digital signatures prove the authenticity of a message. Even traffic between servers can be encrypted.

Exchange Server and Other E-Messaging Systems

The world of electronic messaging is far from a single-standard nirvana. A good e-messaging system must connect to and communicate with a variety of other messaging systems. Microsoft has done a nice job of providing Exchange Server with key links, called *connectors,* to other systems. The company has also built some cross-system message-content translators into Exchange Server that work automatically and are very effective. With these translators, you're less likely to send a message containing, say, a beautiful embedded image that can't be viewed by some or all of the message's recipients.

In the case of Microsoft's legacy messaging systems—Microsoft Mail for PC Networks and Microsoft Mail for AppleTalk Networks—you have an option beyond connectivity. You can choose to migrate users to Exchange. Migration utilities for other messaging systems like Lotus' cc:Mail are also provided with Exchange.

X.400

A fully standards-compatible X.400 connector is built into Exchange Server and can be used to link Exchange sites. The 1984 and 1988 standards for X.400 are supported. The connector also supports attachment to foreign X.400 messaging systems.

SMTP

As with X.400, a Simple Message Transport Protocol (SMTP) connector is built into Exchange Server; unlike the old Microsoft Mail for PC Networks SMTP gateway, it is a full-fledged system capable of executing and responding to a range of Sendmail commands. UUencode/UUdecode and MIME (Multipurpose Internet Mail Extensions) message-content standards are also supported. So, once you've moved your users from MS Mail for PCs to Exchange, you won't hear any more of those vexing complaints about the meaningless MIME-source attachments that users get because the SMTP gateway was unable to convert them back to their original binary format.

Microsoft Mail for PC Networks

A built-in connector makes Microsoft Mail for PC Networks 3.*x* (MS Mail 3.*x*) post offices look like Exchange servers to Exchange clients and vice versa. If connectivity isn't enough, you can transfer MS Mail 3.*x* users to Exchange with a supplied migration tool. If all of this is too much, Exchange clients can directly access MS Mail 3.*x* post offices. So you can keep your MS Mail 3.*x* post offices, at least until you've got Exchange Server running the way you want and have moved everyone off of the legacy mail system.

Microsoft Mail for AppleTalk Networks

Connectivity for Microsoft Mail for AppleTalk Networks systems is also provided by a connector built into Exchange. When connectivity isn't enough, Mail for Apple-Talk users can be migrated to Exchange Server.

cc:Mail

If Lotus' cc:Mail is running in your shop, you'll be happy to hear that Exchange 5.0 comes with tools to connect and migrate users to Exchange. Never let it be said that Microsoft doesn't care about users of IBM/Lotus products. At least there's a way to pull them into the MS camp.

Other Messaging Systems

Gateways are or will be available for links to other messaging systems such as Notes, PROFS, SNADS, fax, and MCI Mail. Both Microsoft and third parties will build and support these networks. You can even extend the benefit of these gateways to your MS Mail users.

Conclusion

In this chapter you learned about some of the exciting things you can do with Exchange. You also had a first look at some key aspects and characteristics of the system. The rest of this book is devoted to helping you understand Exchange— how it works and how you can implement some of the nifty applications I've only hinted at in this chapter.

2

The Exchange Hierarchy

- A conceptual view of the Exchange hierarchy

- A practical view of the Exchange hierarchy

- Exchange organizations

- Exchange sites

- Exchange servers

- Exchange recipients

- How Exchange hierarchy design affects server administration and e-messaging addressing

Microsoft has built Exchange around a set of four key elements:

- Organizations
- Sites
- Servers
- Recipients

The relationship between these elements is hierarchical. The organization is at the top of the hierarchy, and recipients are at the bottom. The Exchange hierarchy imposes an organizational structure on both the real world and the Exchange world. The hierarchy also determines at least the defaults used to construct e-mail, or even better, e-messaging addresses for Exchange users.

A Conceptual View of the Hierarchy

The four key elements in the Exchange hierarchy stand for two conceptually different but related realities. First, the elements represent real people, places, and things. An *organization* is a collection of people who have some reason for associating with each other. An organization can be a business, an academic institution, a club, or some other entity. A *site* is a suborganizational unit like a geographical location or a department. *Servers* are computers running Exchange Server software. And *recipients* are the people and things that can send or receive mail. In the real world, each of these elements includes all of the elements below it: Organizations include sites, which include servers, which include recipients.

The four key Exchange elements represent a second set of realities: Exchange *objects*. Remember when I talked about Exchange's object orientation in Chapter 1? I noted that each of the four Exchange objects serves as a container for the objects below it. Organizational objects include site objects, which include server objects, which include recipient objects.

In this latter case, the language of object orientation replaces the language of social organization, but the effect is the same. The Exchange hierarchy orders the way we think about both the real world and Exchange itself. Take a look at Figure 2.1 to see how the Exchange Administrator brings these two conceptual views together in a single, easy-to-use interface.

FIGURE 2.1

The Exchange Administrator makes it easy to deal with Exchange's hierarchy.

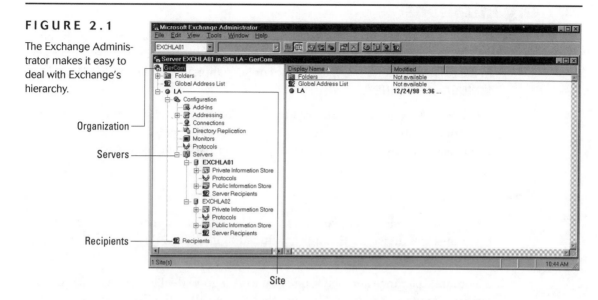

While there are four key elements in the Exchange hierarchy, other significant elements are contained within each of the four elements. We'll talk about these later in this chapter.

A More Practical View of the Hierarchy

Concepts are important, and I'll assume that you're comfortable with the ones presented above. However, we "systems" types can't live by concepts alone. We need to move quickly from concepts to designing, installing, and running systems.

So let's look at the four elements in the Exchange hierarchy from a more practical perspective. As you read on, you'll begin to see where you'll have to make some very specific design decisions related to the four elements before you can even think about installing an Exchange server. You'll also begin to see just how central the Exchange hierarchy is to setting up and managing an Exchange environment.

Organizations

By now it should be pretty clear to you that an Exchange organization can be all or part of a company, a school, a club, or another entity; it's the master container in the Exchange hierarchy. Examples of organizational names include IBM, IBMUSA, and IBMENG.

In Figure 2.1, GerCom is the organization. The name GerCom represents *all* of the fictitious little company I created for this book. That means I can include all the subdivisions of my empire within this particular Exchange hierarchy.

Sites

Sites are subdivisions of the organization. Generally, they encompass geographical or business divisions. Examples include Engineering, NY, and SFO. Currently, GerCom has only one site, LA (see Figure 2.1).

For fault tolerance and faster performance, a good deal of key information is replicated automatically and frequently between all of the Exchange servers in a site. That can make for some heavy-duty network traffic. Sites should be geographically contiguous enough that Exchange servers within them can be connected at reasonable cost by higher-bandwidth (128Kb/sec or greater) wide area networks (WANs).

Sites are usually connected by slower WANs, since replicating information between sites is usually done in a more selective way and at a more leisurely pace. Sites include a range of subelements or objects. For example, Exchange connectors let you link sites together and to the outside world. Exchange contains tools for setting up and administering these objects, including tools for administering and managing Exchange connectors. Figure 2.2, another view of the Exchange Administrator, shows the tool for the Internet Mail Service (IMS), which links my LA site to the Internet mail system and can even be used to link my LA site to other sites in my Exchange hierarchy through the Internet.

The IMS tool has a number of what Microsoft calls *property pages*—so called because this is where you set the attributes, or *properties*, of the service. Figure 2.2 shows the Internet Mail property page of the IMS tool, as you can see from the tab at the top of the page. The IMS tool has a total of 12 property pages, as indicated by the 12 tabs. Each tabbed page covers a different set of properties required to administer and manage an Internet mail link.

FIGURE 2.2

Working with the Internet
Mail Service in a site

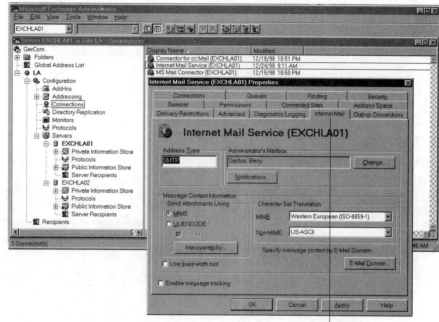

Internet Mail
Property Page Tab

Servers

Servers are the physical Exchange servers within a site. At the moment, there are
two Exchange servers in the LA site. They're called EXCHLA01 and EXCHLA02,
which stand for "Exchange [Server] in Los Angeles #1" and "Exchange [Server] in
Los Angeles #2." You'll find the servers toward the bottom of the Exchange hierarchy tree in Figure 2.1; notice that they are in the Servers container.

Some organizations like to base their Exchange server names on departments,
such as engineering or marketing, within a geographical site (for example, site =
LA; server = Marketing). Working with my imaginary MIS department, I've
decided to use a different naming scheme for GerCom. To start, I put all of my LA
employees on one server, EXCHLA01. As I ran out of capacity on EXCHLA01, I
added EXCHLA02. As GerCom grows—and I know it's going to grow—I'll add
more servers, called EXCHLA03, EXCHLA04, and so on. (There's nothing inher-
ently good or bad about my naming scheme; I just think it's better for GerCom
than a scheme based on department names. My company is relatively small right
now, so two servers are enough for all employees. I don't want to pop for servers

for each department, and I'm willing to tolerate Exchange servers with "meaningless" names. So there!)

As with sites, a number of tools are available for administering and managing server-based Exchange objects. Among other things, each server has tools for managing local message storage and for replicating public folders between servers. In Figure 2.3, the Exchange Administrator is used to set some default limits for EXCHLA01's private information storage area.

FIGURE 2.3

Exchange servers include tools for managing private information storage areas.

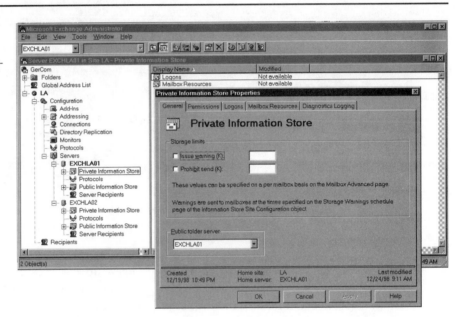

Recipients

Exchange has four major types of recipient objects: mailboxes (the most widely used of which is the primary mailbox), public folders, custom recipients (essentially aliases for addresses outside of an Exchange organization), and distribution lists. Each of these plays a different role and can be used to good advantage depending on the needs of your organization. As with other entities in the hierarchy, Exchange has tools for administering and managing recipient objects.

Mailbox Agents: Recipient Objects That Serve the System

There is a fifth kind of recipient object, though it's one you have little control over. It's called a *mailbox agent*. Mailbox agents are generally created by the system and used to support system-level information passing. I'll talk about one of these mailbox agents in a bit, the Schedule+ Free/Busy mailbox agent.

Recipients live in recipients containers. In Figure 2.4, which is a view from the Exchange Administrator, recipients containers show up five times in the GerCom tree. The Folders container near the top of the hierarchy holds, among other things, public folders. The Global Address List, down a bit from the Folders container, holds all recipients for an organization. Each of the two servers in the LA site has a recipients container named *Server Recipients*. And there is a site-level recipients container, named *Recipients*, at the bottom of the hierarchy.

FIGURE 2.4

A site-level recipients container includes all five recipient object types.

Recipient Container: Public Folder

Global Address List

Server Recipients

Recipients (Site)

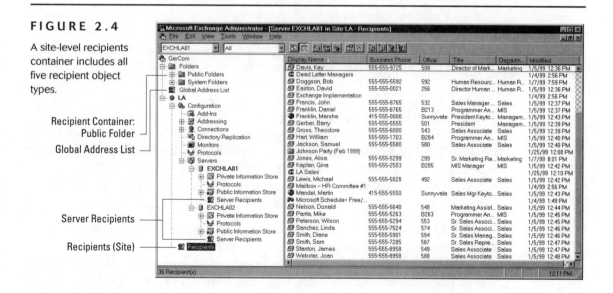

Each of the four types of recipients containers—Folders and the Global Address List at the organization level, Server Recipients at the server level, and Recipients at the site level—plays a special role in Exchange Server.

- The Global Address List holds all the recipients in an organization. It is used by Exchange clients to address messages and can be used by Exchange administrators to administer and manage recipients. For reasons of corporate policy or for the purpose for which they were created, some recipients may be hidden from the Global Address and other address books. Exchange administrators with the proper rights can readily access hidden recipients and even unhide them if necessary.

- The Public Folders container holds all the public folders in an organization. Even hidden public folders are visible in the Public Folders container, which is available only to Exchange administrators with the proper access rights.

- Unlike the other three types of recipients, which are or can be replicated to other servers, each Exchange mailbox physically resides on one and only one Exchange server. Server-level recipients containers hold these mailboxes and make it easy to find, administer, and manage the mailboxes on a server.

- Site-level recipients containers hold all mailboxes on all servers in a site, as well as the three other types of recipients for a site. A good deal of recipient administration and management is done in site-level recipients containers. For example, although a mailbox is stored on a specific Exchange server, you create the mailbox in the site, not on the server.

Figure 2.4 shows what's in the site-level recipients container for GerCom. As you can see, all five of the recipient object types are included in this container. Distribution lists, public folders, and custom recipients appear only at the site level. That little icon marked *Microsoft Schedule+ Free/ ...* is a mailbox agent. It represents the Microsoft Schedule+ Free/Busy Connector for the LA site. The connector lets users of Schedule+ for Exchange Server see the schedules of users of Schedule+ for Microsoft Mail for PCs, and vice versa.

Now just to verify that server-level recipients containers hold only mailboxes and, to be totally correct, mailbox agents, take a look at Figure 2.5. There's not a distribution list, custom recipient, or public folder to be seen—just a sea of mailboxes. Well, almost. Our old friend the Schedule+ Free/Busy Connector is there, too. It's there because, although it serves the whole LA site, it lives on my server EXCHLA01 or, in Microsoft-speak, it is *homed* on EXCHLA01. (That is, mailbox agent recipients appear in the Server Recipients container of the server they're homed on.)

FIGURE 2.5

A server-level recipients container includes only mailboxes and mailbox agents.

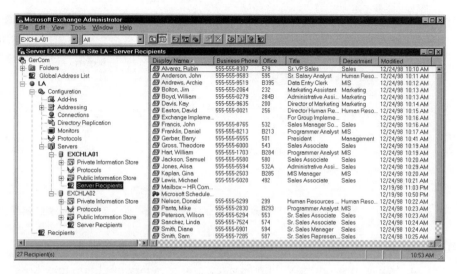

Let's take a closer look at each of the four major Exchange recipient objects.

Mailboxes

Mailboxes hold private messages and other objects such as word processing documents or spreadsheets, which belong to individual Exchange users. Any mailbox may contain folders created by the system or users. There are four system-created folders in Exchange: Inbox, Outbox, Deleted Items, and Sent Items. Generally, messages are received in the Inbox folder, sent from the Outbox folder, put into the Sent Items folder after transmission, and held in the Deleted Items folder after deletion. As you'll see below, not all mailboxes include all of these system-created folders.

Users can create as many folders in a mailbox as they wish and can give the folders any name they choose. Users can delete folders they create, but they cannot delete system-created folders. Any folder, whether system- or user-created, can have folders nested below it.

All mailboxes are stored on the user's Exchange server in an Exchange database called the *private information store.* You must be connected to your Exchange server to access your mailbox. Figure 2.6 shows my own Exchange client and its mailbox; my Inbox is open.

FIGURE 2.6

An Exchange client with
its mailbox

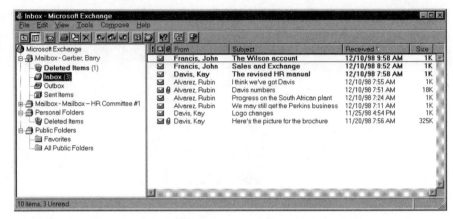

You can give others access to your mailbox. This lets them see and, if you wish, respond to your messages, as a secretary might do for a boss. You can also create mailboxes just to support specific activities or projects. By assigning certain people the rights to these kinds of mailboxes, groups can work cooperatively without turning to the public folders I'll discuss later. If you have rights to multiple mailboxes, they can all be made available simultaneously in your Exchange client. Figure 2.7 shows that my colleagues and I are using a shared mailbox to plan our Exchange system.

FIGURE 2.7

An Exchange client
with access to multiple
mailboxes

Shared Mailbox to plan
Exchange Server System

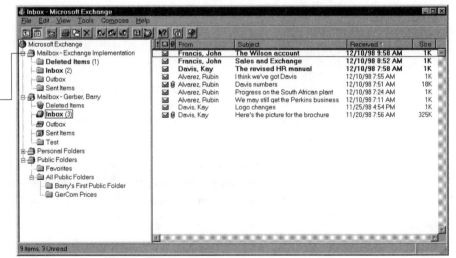

Personal Folders

To hold messages outside of the Exchange server environment, Exchange users can create personal folders. Unlike mailboxes, which are stored in a specific Exchange database called the *private information store*, personal folders are stored, at least initially, as standard files on a local or networked disk. When created, personal folders have only one system-created folder, Deleted Items. Personal folders can help you organize information in special ways. As Figure 2.8 shows, I'm using a personal folder named *Exchange Book* to isolate and manage messages and other information related to this book. In the folder named Chapter 1, I've dragged and dropped the items with .TIF and .DOC extensions into the folder using the Windows NT Explorer. The item from Rubin Alvarez, which is flagged with an envelope icon, is a message that I dragged and dropped into the folder from my mailbox's Inbox.

You can tell that my Exchange Book personal information store is stored on a local or network disk (and not inside the Exchange private information store database) because it's not in either of the two mailboxes in my Exchange client. To store the personal information store and all of its subfolders on my Exchange server, all I have to do is drag it into one of the two mailboxes.

FIGURE 2.8

An Exchange client with a personal information store for a special project

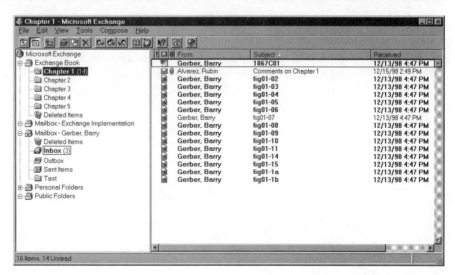

Public Folders

Though public folders can originate messages, most of the time you'll use them to receive messages. They're created by users and allow groups of users to share data. When you create a public folder, you can choose who has access to it—all users or only some. When you use a public folder, you can mail or directly post messages or files to it or simply drag and drop them into the folder. (Remember that messages can be anything from simple text to complex applications.)

Custom Recipients

When Exchange Server users need to communicate with people outside of your Exchange system, you can add these "foreigners" to your directory as custom recipients. Then Exchange users can pick them from directory lists just as they would select any internal Exchange recipient. You'd do this, for example, with someone who has an SMTP mail account on another system.

You don't have to create a custom recipient for every foreigner, however. If only a few Exchange users need to access a particular outsider, they can create an address for that person in their own address books or do "one-off" addressing on a per-message basis.

Distribution Lists

Distribution lists group together all other types of recipients, including other distribution lists. They make it easy to send a message to lots of people and places using a single address.

Hiding Recipients

You can hide any of the four recipient objects. Hidden recipients can send and/or receive mail, but they don't show up in address books. You can use them, for example, to protect the anonymity of specific recipients or to support applications.

Reasons to Be Careful about Exchange Hierarchy Design

The Exchange hierarchy does a nice job of imposing an organizational structure on both the real world and Exchange's own little world. If that were all it did, we could stop right here. But the hierarchy plays two more very significant roles: It shapes the way you manage your Exchange system, and it defines the default e-messaging addresses of everyone inside it.

The Exchange Hierarchy and Exchange Management

Look at Figure 2.1 once more. No matter how much GerCom grows as a real company, I'll always be able to easily think about and manage all of the sites, servers, and recipients inside it from the same Exchange Administrator session.

Furthermore, if I had more than one Exchange organization, I'd have to treat the organizations as foreign to each other when I linked them together. That could significantly increase the networking and administrative cost of operating my Exchange system. For example, I'd have to set up and manage separate Internet links for each organization.

It's not all that easy to fix problems like the one I'd create by dividing my company into a bunch of suborganizations. You'll welcome the ability to bring together Exchange organizations when your real-world organization changes— for example, when it merges with another organization. Still, it's better not to rely on futures. Define your organization as broadly as you can from the start, unless you've got some social, political, or economic reason for doing otherwise.

The Exchange Hierarchy and E-Messaging Address

In Figure 2.9, you can see how my default cc:Mail, Microsoft Mail for PC Networks, SMTP, and X.400 addresses are dependent on the way I've named the first two elements—organization and site—in my Exchange hierarchy. Server names are not included in addresses. Once a message gets to the organization, the sites are smart enough to guide the message to the appropriate server (to extend this, you might say that once a message gets to the organization, the sites in the organization are smart enough to get the message to the appropriate site as well).

FIGURE 2.9

The Exchange hierarchy defines everyone's default e-mail addresses.

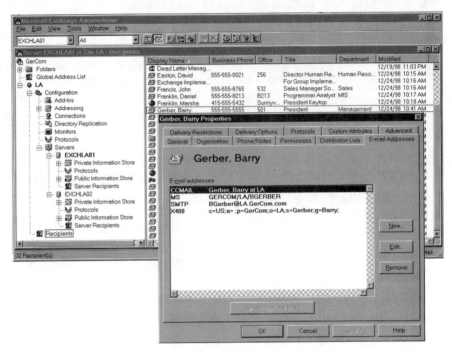

It's quite easy to change the default addresses that Exchange Server assigns to one or more recipients or even to add more addresses of a given type for any recipient. This way you're not trapped by your original Exchange hierarchy naming scheme. Still, it's best to get everything as right as possible from the get-go.

Although a variety of social and political barriers can get in the way of doing so, it's best to make your Exchange organization as all-inclusive as possible. Try to include the whole company, university, club, or whatever. If you don't, you may end up with a bunch of folks running around with addresses like jones@marketing.*acmela*.com and smith@marketing.*acmeny*.com.

One of the few times that centralized MIS or general management should rear its sometimes ugly head is in the early stages of Exchange hierarchy design. If yours is a decentralized organization, you can get back on your own horse as soon as this phase of the design process is finished.

Conclusion

In this chapter, you learned about the Exchange hierarchy. You saw how the objects in the hierarchy organize both the real world and Exchange itself. You learned key terms that you'll see again and again throughout this book. And you learned to be careful in designing the key elements of your Exchange hierarchy. How you define and name these elements will determine both how easy your Exchange system will be to manage and what your default Exchange e-messaging addresses will look like.

The Architecture of Exchange

- Exchange Server's four core components

- Optional Exchange Server components

- Exchange client components

Exchange is a client/server electronic messaging system. In this chapter, we'll take a close look at the architectures of both the Exchange server and client. We'll also see how the Exchange client and server interact from an architectural perspective, as illustrated in Figure 3.1.

This is an important chapter. It exposes you to a range of Exchange terminology that you'll find useful later on, and it gives you a sense of how the whole Exchange system hangs together and works. Remember that virtually all of the architectural components we discuss here are, in whole or in part, real program code running somewhere on an Exchange server or client machine. We'll revisit all of these components later in the book.

FIGURE 3.1

The architecture of Exchange.

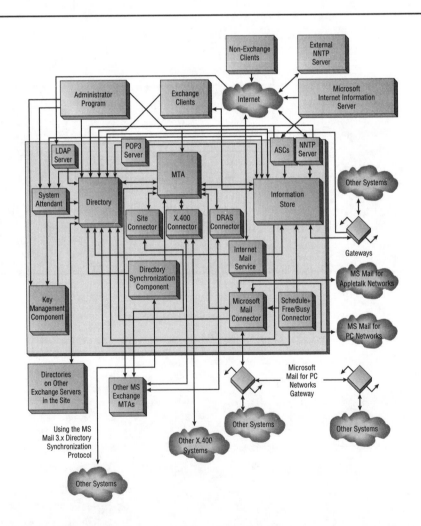

No, Figure 3.1 isn't a bird's-eye view of a spaghetti factory; rather, it's more or less a complete diagram of the Exchange hierarchy based on a diagram originally developed by Microsoft. It shows the components in the hierarchy and how they relate to each other. Everything inside the large, heavy-lined rectangle is part of a single Exchange server running all of the required and optional Exchange Server components. Everything outside the rectangle is external to the server itself. The lines indicate communications between components. All communications are two-way; where there is only one arrowhead, the arrowhead points away from the Exchange component that initiates communications. A line with an arrowhead at each end indicates that either of the two components can initiate communications at different times, depending on the function being carried out.

Don't get too hung up with the details of Figure 3.1. It's here partly to give you a sense of the complexity of Exchange, and partly to get you thinking about Exchange as a set of real processes that do real work. We won't go through every line and arrowhead of the figure in gory detail. However, when you come to the end of this chapter you should have a pretty good idea of how the various components in the Exchange hierarchy work, both alone and in league with their fellow components.

Exchange Server's Core Components

Exchange Server cannot provide messaging services to users unless all of its core components are up and running. Core components include:

- The Directory
- The Information Store
- The Message Transfer Agent
- The System Attendant

Let's take a closer look at each of the core components.

The Directory

The Exchange Server directory functions as both a database and a service. The directory is a container holding information about all of a site's objects that are required to send and receive messages within and to the site. These include recipients (as defined in the last chapter) as well as servers and all kinds of message-routing information. Copies of the directory for a site are stored on all Exchange servers in that site. If an organization includes multiple sites, information for all sites is included in every site directory.

The directory service (DS) is the access point for the directory database. Other processes on the Exchange server and on Exchange clients talk to the DS to provide and obtain information.

One of the key functions of the DS is to send and receive directory update information. Within an Exchange site, the DS sends this information directly to and receives it directly from the DSs on other Exchange servers. Across Exchange sites, the DSs send and receive directory update information as standard messages through the message transfer agent (MTA) on each Exchange server. The Exchange Server directory uses this update information for regular intrasite and intersite replication of directories across an Exchange organization. (More about all of this in later chapters.) The DS can also exchange directory update information with "foreign" e-messaging systems. The optional directory synchronization component does this.

Note that I use the term *replication* to describe the directory update process inside an Exchange organization, while I use *synchronization* to describe updates with foreign e-messaging systems. Though the processes are similar, Microsoft has chosen to use different terms to describe them. Remembering the differences in meaning between the two words will make your hands-on experience with Exchange Server much easier.

In addition to cross-server and cross-system updates, the DS is responsible for such things as managing and presenting system address books to Exchange users and enforcing security on all recipient objects. Figure 3.2 shows how the directory and the DS work together to present address information to users. Figure 3.3 shows some of the major functions of the directory in graphical form.

The Information Store

Like the directory service, the information store (IS) functions as both a database and a service. Each Exchange server contains one IS which can, at your pleasure, contain one or two databases. One database, the private information store, holds user mailboxes. The other, the public information store, holds public folders. Figure 3.4 shows the basic structure of the Exchange Server IS.

FIGURE 3.2

The active directory ser-
vice is the access point
for the passive directory
database.

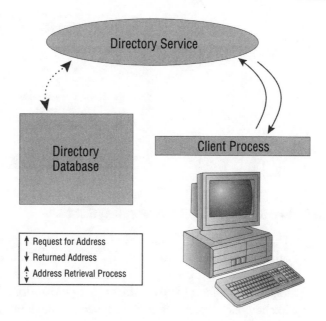

Incoming messages are placed in the Inbox, which, as I noted in Chapter 2, is a
special folder in a mailbox. Public folders are used to give all or some recipients
in an Exchange system access to specific messages.

To balance network loads and reduce access costs, public folders can be
replicated in whole or in part to other Exchange servers, either in the same site or
in remote sites. Additionally, to lighten the load on servers with mailboxes, you
can place public folders on separate Exchange servers and direct clients to those
servers when they need access to public folders.

The *IS service* is a buffer between the IS databases and other components of
Exchange Server. It performs a number of functions. Among other things, it
receives incoming mail from and delivers outgoing mail to the message transfer
agent, notifies clients of the arrival of new mail, looks up addresses in the
directory, and creates directory entries for public folders. Figure 3.5 shows some
of the major functions of the IS service.

FIGURE 3.3

Major functions of the
directory

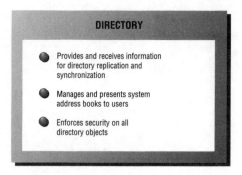

The Message Transfer Agent

The message transfer agent (MTA) routes messages between its server's IS and other Exchange systems. Within a site, the MTA routes messages directly to the MTAs on other Exchange servers. When it routes messages to Exchange servers located in different sites in the same organization, the MTA gets help from other Exchange components called *connectors*. Back in Figure 3.1, you can see three of these connectors—Site, X.400, and DRAS—directly below the MTA. I'll discuss these in more detail later in this chapter.

The MTA also routes messages to certain foreign e-messaging systems, including legacy Microsoft Mail 3.*x* systems, Internet systems, and those based on the X.400 standard. As with inter- and intra-site routing, when routing to these foreign systems the MTA gets help from special Exchange connectors, such as the Microsoft Mail, X.400 connectors, and the Internet Mail Service. For other systems such as CompuServe, gateways are used. (Refer back to Figure 3.1.)

FIGURE 3.4

The Exchange Server
information store

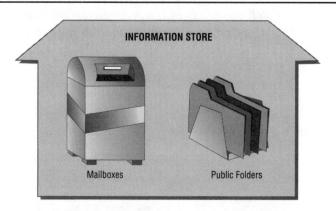

FIGURE 3.5

FIGURE 3.5

Major functions of the
IS service

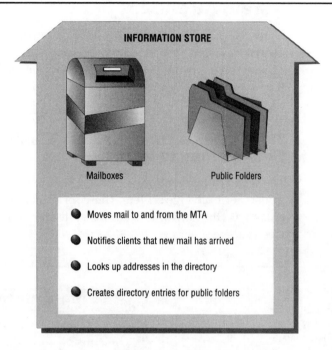

INFORMATION STORE

Mailboxes   Public Folders

- Moves mail to and from the MTA
- Notifies clients that new mail has arrived
- Looks up addresses in the directory
- Creates directory entries for public folders

The MTA has one other major function: When X.400 systems are involved, the MTA converts messages in Exchange's default Microsoft MAPI format to native X.400 format, and vice versa. This allows Exchange Server to readily trade messages with X.400 systems. Figure 3.6 presents the MTA's major functions graphically.

FIGURE 3.6

The MTA is a message
router and format
translator

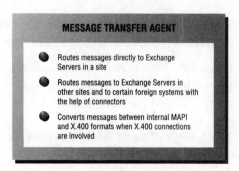

MESSAGE TRANSFER AGENT

- Routes messages directly to Exchange Servers in a site
- Routes messages to Exchange Servers in other sites and to certain foreign systems with the help of connectors
- Converts messages between internal MAPI and X.400 formats when X.400 connections are involved

The System Attendant

Other Exchange Server components cannot run without the system attendant (SA); it's the first Exchange component to activate on start-up and the last to stop on shutdown. The SA performs a range of functions, six of which are key to Exchange Server's operation. Let's take a closer look at each of these functions, as shown in Figure 3.7.

The SA Helps Other Servers Monitor Network Connections to Its Server

The system attendant receives and replies to network link integrity messages from other Exchange servers. These servers know that something is wrong— either with the network link or the system attendant's own server—if they fail to receive these replies.

FIGURE 3.7

The system attendant performs six key functions for Exchange Server.

The SA Monitors for and Corrects Directory Inconsistencies on Its Server

The SA automatically checks the consistency of its copy of the directory against those of other Exchange servers in its site. If it finds inconsistencies, the SA attempts to reconcile and fix them.

The SA Collects Message-Tracking Data for Its Server

The SA logs data about sent messages, which can be used for tracking a message's status and the route that it traveled once sent. This capability is especially useful when used in conjunction with similar data gathered by the SAs on other Exchange servers.

The SA Builds Site-Based Message Routing Tables for Its Server

Like any network, an Exchange Server network needs *routing tables,* which are used specifically for routing messages. The SA interacts with the directory to build tables that the MTA can use to route messages to servers in its site.

The SA Triggers and Retriggers the Generation and Regeneration of Foreign E-Messaging Addresses for Recipients on Its Server

The SA generates X.400, SMTP, Microsoft Mail, and cc:Mail addresses by default. When gateways are installed, the SA generates gateway-specific e-mail addresses for users. When creating addresses, the SA interacts with the directory.

The SA Participates in Certain Security Functions

Security in Exchange is very good. An Exchange mailbox can use both digital signatures and encryption. The SA is involved in enabling and disabling these two components of Exchange security. To do this, it interacts with the *Key Management Component,* which is discussed later in this chapter.

Optional Exchange Server Components

Exchange Server comes with all of the following optional components except gateways. These components are "optional" not because you always have to pay extra for them, but because Exchange Server can run without them. Optional components include:

- The Exchange Administrator program
- The Directory Synchronization Agent
- The Key Management Component

- Exchange Internet protocol servers

- Web Service

- Post Office Protocol 3

- Network News Transfer Protocol

- Lightweight Directory Access Protocol

- Exchange connectors:

  - Site Connector

  - X.400 Connector

  - Dynamic RAS Connector

  - Internet Mail Service

  - Microsoft Mail Connector

  - Schedule+ Free/Busy Connector

  - cc:Mail Connector

- Exchange gateways

You might find it helpful to refer back to Figure 3.1 as I discuss each component.

The Exchange Administrator Program

You've seen examples of the Exchange Administrator program in action in Chapters 1 and 2, and you'll get to know it very well as we move along. The main point I want to make here is that the Exchange Administrator is *home*. It's where you go whenever you need to do almost anything with Exchange Server—from creating and managing users to linking with other Exchange servers or foreign mail systems to monitoring the activities on your server. The Administrator is the single point from which you can manage anything, whether it's one Exchange server or your entire Exchange organization.

The Administrator is home in another way, too: It's easy. Soon after you start using the Administrator, you'll feel about it the way you feel about that comfortable old chair in the den. Really!

The Directory Synchronization Agent

The Directory Synchronization Agent (DXA) lets you create address books that include addresses from outside your Exchange system. It also allows you to send Exchange Server address information to other e-messaging systems. It sends directory update information to and receives it from Microsoft Mail for PC Networks 3.*x* and Microsoft Mail for AppleTalk Networks systems.

The DXA uses the Microsoft Mail 3.*x* Directory Synchronization Protocol, so any foreign, non-Microsoft e-messaging system that is compatible with this protocol is fair game for cross-system directory synchronization.

The Key Management Component

Exchange supports RSA public key encryption and digital signatures within an Exchange organization. These help ensure the authenticity of a message and the person sending it. Exchange Server's Key Management Component supports these services. With this component in place and running, Exchange client users can create very secure messages.

Exchange Internet Protocol Access Components

Exchange 5.0 comes with a set of four Internet protocol servers. These let you extend the reach of Exchange users beyond Microsoft's very good, but proprietary electronic messaging protocols. The four components are the Microsoft Active Server Components (ASCs), the Post Office Protocol (POP3) server, the Network News Transfer Protocol (NNTP) server, and the Lightweight Directory Access Protocol (LDAP) server. If you try really hard, you'll find all four of these in Figure 3.1's spaghetti factory.

Active Server Components

The Microsoft Active Server Components let users access everything in their Exchange mailboxes as well as items in public folders using a web browser like Microsoft's Internet Explorer or Netscape's Navigator. Active Server Components work in conjunction with the Active Server (AS) subsystem of Microsoft's Internet Information Server.

POP3 Server

Exchange Server's POP3 server gives users with standard POP3 e-mail clients, like Eudora or the mail clients in both Microsoft's Internet Explorer and Netscape's Navigator, limited access to their Exchange mailboxes. Users can download mail from their Exchange Inboxes, but that's all. Users have no direct access to other personal or public information stores or to their schedules. This is due to limitations in the POP3 protocol itself, and not in Microsoft's implementation of the protocol.

NNTP Server

The NNTP server lets you bring all of those exciting USENET news groups into your Exchange server's public folders where your users can read and respond to them with the same e-mail clients they use to read their regular messages.

LDAP Server

New to the 5.0 release of Exchange Server is support for the Lightweight Directory Access Protocol (LDAP), a protocol that works with X.500-compatible directories. Any client with LDAP capability can access information in the directory on an Exchange server via the Internet. Thus, users of non-Exchange e-mail clients can use the Exchange directory to find the addresses of people they wish to send mail to. LDAP also opens the Exchange directory to other exciting things like communications applications (e.g., Web browser–based paging or faxing apps) that use the directory to get the information they need to reach a particular Exchange user. LDAP is a really neat way to open the Exchange directory to the non-Exchange world.

Exchange Connectors

You use Exchange connectors to link Exchange sites to each other and to connect them to foreign e-messaging systems. You link Exchange sites to each other so that they can exchange user messages and can cross-replicate their directories and public folders. You link Exchange sites to foreign systems primarily so that Exchange users can trade messages with users of those systems and/or synchronize directories with them. As an added bonus, you can also use connections to foreign sites to link Exchange sites to each other; more on this in just a bit.

Exchange connectors run on—surprise—Exchange servers. You can run one or more instances of any Exchange connector within a site; one instance can service all of the Exchange servers in a site or even all of the sites in an organization.

Before we dive into the connectors themselves, we need to talk a bit about a really impressive feature of Exchange Server, *indirect site links.* When Exchange servers connect sites, they conduct their business using standard messages; that is, they move user-to-user communications as messages. And they replicate directories and public folders by means of system-generated messages. Users generate user messages, but directory and public folder replication messages are generated by the Exchange Server system itself. Directory and folder replication messages are marked as system messages to indicate their special content. Figure 3.8 shows how this works.

When an Exchange server sees a system message, it treats the message differently from a user message, using it to update directory or public folder information.

Because site links are message-based, you can connect Exchange sites *directly* (point-to-point) and/or *indirectly* (through foreign e-messaging systems). Direct site links are easy to understand: You just run a connector on an Exchange server in each of two sites and tell the connectors to link to each other. Direct site links are done in real time without any intervening systems between the Exchange servers. (Figure 3.8 shows a direct site link.)

FIGURE 3.8

Site links are based on the exchange of messages.

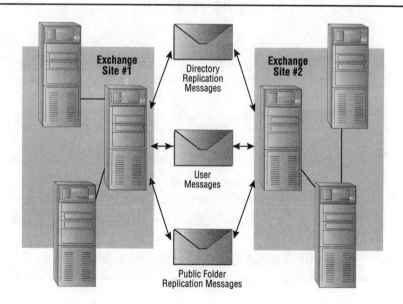

Indirect site links are a bit less self-evident. When two or more Exchange sites are connected to a foreign e-messaging system such as the Internet or a public X.400 system, not only can users trade messages, but the servers in the sites can also exchange system messages that let them cross-replicate directories and public folders. Indirect site links are not done in real time. An Exchange server in one site sends its user and system messages to an intervening e-messaging system such as the Internet. The intervening system then passes these messages on to the Exchange server in the other site. The effect is the same as a direct link, though the process is different.

That wasn't so bad, was it? Take a look at Figure 3.9, if you're still a bit in the dark.

Okay, now we can talk about the Exchange connectors. There are a number of different Exchange connectors including: Site, X.400, Dynamic RAS, Internet Mail Service, Microsoft Mail, Schedule+ Free/Busy, and cc:Mail. You'll find each in Figure 3.1. Now let's look at each of the connectors.

Intrasite Communications: Two Out of Three Ain't Bad

Exchange servers in the *same* Exchange site require no special connectors. They're linked to each other automatically as soon as they are up and running. Connections *between* sites require that you set up direct or indirect links through Exchange connectors. User communications and public folder replication are message-based, whether two Exchange servers are talking intrasite or intersite.

However, as we've already noted when talking about the directory, Exchange servers in the same site don't use message-based communications to cross-replicate their directories. Instead they communicate more directly with each other. Direct communication is necessary because the servers in a site can't send messages until they have a copy of the directory, so they can't use messages to replicate directories. It's a chicken-and-egg problem.

FIGURE 3.9

FIGURE 3.9

Linking Exchange sites indirectly through foreign e-messaging systems

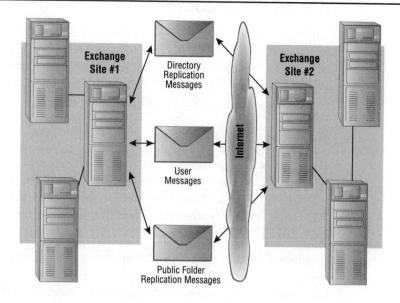

Site Connector

The Site Connector is used for direct links only. It requires synchronous (continuous) connections between sites. The Site Connector is the fastest, least complicated route to intersite connectivity.

X.400 Connector

Despite its name, the Site Connector is not the only way to directly link Exchange sites; the X.400 Connector also performs this function. Again, you need a synchronous network connection for direct links. In addition, the X.400 connector can indirectly link Exchange sites through foreign X.400 systems and it can be used to link Exchange sites to foreign X.400 systems just for user message exchange. Indirect or mail-exchange–only links can be implemented with either a synchronous or an asynchronous (noncontinuous) connection. The X.400 Connector is fully compliant with all of the 1984 and 1988 X.400 transport and message content standards.

Dynamic RAS Connector

You'll learn more about NT's Remote Access Server (RAS) in the next chapter. Exchange's Dynamic RAS Connector (DRASC) lets you set up direct links between Exchange sites in a way similar to the Site Connector, but it operates over cheaper, lower-bandwidth voice, ISDN, and X.25 lines. An asynchronous connection is all you need for a DRAS connection.

Internet Mail Service

The Internet Mail Service (IMS) is your Exchange server's link to SMTP mail systems. It can issue and respond to UNIX Sendmail commands and can do both MIME encoding and decoding and UUencoding/UUdecoding of messages. The IMS can be used only to exchange mail with Internet mail users or to directly or indirectly link Exchange sites.

Microsoft changed the IMS a bit in version 5.0 of Exchange Server. Its original name, *Internet Mail Connector*, was changed along with the way you install the IMS. There are also a number of improvements in the IMS, like its ability to route Internet mail from non-Exchange clients or servers.

Microsoft Mail Connector

You have two post office–wide options for dealing with legacy systems running Microsoft Mail 3.*x* for PC Networks and Microsoft Mail 3.*x* for AppleTalk Networks. Either you can move entire post offices and their user mailboxes to Exchange Server using migration tools that come with Exchange Server, or you can link the legacy systems to Exchange Server, providing recipients on all sides with transparent access to each other. The Microsoft Mail Connector (MMC) supports the latter option.

The MMC creates and interacts with a shadow Microsoft Mail post office on the Exchange server. Exchange sends and receives mail through the MMC using this shadow, which looks like an Exchange server to users on the Exchange side and looks like a Microsoft Mail 3.*x* post office to users on the MS Mail side. Microsoft Mail's EXTERNAL.EXE program or a version of EXTERNAL.EXE that runs as an NT service is used to transfer mail between the shadow and the real MS Mail post office. Connections can be either synchronous or asynchronous. If it can bear the traffic, you need only one MMC to link all of your MS Mail post offices to the Exchange world.

Users of Microsoft Mail 3.*x* for AppleTalk Networks are linked in a similar manner. Once the connection is in place, the MMC gives AppleTalk Mail recipients full access to Exchange recipients, and vice versa.

Before we leave the MMC, I want to be sure you're aware that there is a third option for users of legacy Microsoft Mail for PC networks systems. This one requires neither whole post office migration nor use of the MMC. On a user-by-user basis, you can connect a user's Exchange client directly to both the user's Microsoft Mail and Exchange mailboxes. This lets the user send and receive messages from both the Microsoft Mail and Exchange systems. This option is best when you haven't got the time or other resources to migrate everyone in a Microsoft Mail post office to an Exchange server or to deal with the intricacies of the MMC.

Schedule+ Free/Busy Connector

Microsoft Schedule+ lets users set up meetings with each other. It uses a graphical user interface to show, in aggregate fashion, the times available to users selected for a meeting. This information is available on Exchange servers and in Microsoft Mail for PC Networks post offices. The Free/Busy Connector, which is an extension of the MMC, lets Exchange servers and Microsoft Mail post offices share schedule information. You *can't* use the Free/Busy Connector for Exchange site connections, either direct or indirect.

Exchange Gateways

Exchange Server supports X.400 and SMTP mail natively; to access other systems, you'll need *gateways*. Exchange Server gateways don't resemble the clunky DOS gates used with Microsoft Mail 3.*x*. Like the rest of Exchange Server, they run as processes on NT Server. As long as gateway developers know what they're doing (and that's sometimes a big assumption), gateways tend to be stable, robust, and fast.

Gateways are or will be available for such services as Notes, PROFS, SNADS, fax, and CompuServe, as well as for pagers and voice mail. Microsoft is planning to produce some gateways, and third parties will come out with others. Keep in touch with Microsoft and the trade press for details.

Exchange Client Components

As we've noted before, the real fun of Exchange is on the client side. That's where you get to see the business end of Exchange—from "simple" e-mail to complex, home-grown messaging-enabled applications. Exchange client components include:

- The Exchange client
- Schedule+
- The Outlook client
- The Microsoft Exchange Forms Designer
- Microsoft Exchange Forms Designer forms
- Other client-based applications

Here's a quick look at the Exchange client components from an architectural perspective. Figure 3.10 shows the clients and their functions graphically.

The Exchange Client

You receive, transmit, and access messages in the *Exchange client*. It's your window on your mailbox and on personal and public folders.

FIGURE 3.10

Exchange client components

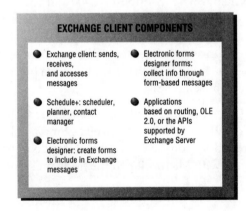

EXCHANGE CLIENT COMPONENTS

- Exchange client: sends, receives, and accesses messages
- Electronic forms designer forms: collect info through form-based messages
- Schedule+: scheduler, planner, contact manager
- Applications based on routing, OLE 2.0, or the APIs supported by Exchange Server
- Electronic forms designer: create forms to include in Exchange messages

Exchange Server ships with clients for Macintosh, Microsoft/PC DOS, Windows 3.1*x*, Windows NT, and with an upgrade for the Exchange client that ships with Windows 95 (aka the Inbox or Windows Messaging). The upgrade adds a range of new features to the Windows 95 Exchange client, including out-of-office messaging, auto-signatures, and free-form rules.

> **TIP**
> Don't try to use the original Windows 95 client to access Exchange Server. It doesn't work. Upgrade to the Exchange Server version of the Windows 95 client. Trust me, it'll save you a lot of grief.

Schedule+

Schedule+ is a messaging-enabled application that includes scheduling, planning, and contact management features. Version 7.5, the version that comes with Exchange Server, is a serious update of the original version, which was labeled "version 1.0" (Microsoft has a knack for skipping version numbers). Most of the improvements lie in the way it handles features such as schedule viewing, printing, and to-do lists, and less in the program's already pretty decent collaborative-scheduling function.

> **TIP**
> Again, don't try to use the 7.0 version of Schedule+ that comes with Microsoft Office 95. Upgrade!

The Outlook Client

Microsoft's Outlook client ships with Microsoft Office 97 and with Exchange Server. Outlook nicely integrates electronic messaging, scheduling, and contact and task management with a whole bunch of other functions like electronic journaling of every message you read or file you open. Take a look at Figures 1.4 and 1.5 for a refresher on Outlook's user interface. Outlook accesses the same directory and information store as the Exchange client. It does modify your Exchange mailbox, adding new folders for things like your schedule, contacts, and tasks; more importantly, it uses a differently structured schedule database, so you have to decide whether you're going to use Schedule+ or Outlook for scheduling and contact/task management.

The Microsoft Exchange Forms Designer

Users and developers can create forms with the Microsoft Exchange Forms Designer, a simple front end for Microsoft's Visual Basic programming language. Forms created with the Designer can be used for a range of tasks, including the collection of data, and can have drop-down pick lists, multiple-choice selections, action buttons, and other useful attributes.

Microsoft Exchange Forms Designer Forms

Forms created in the Microsoft Exchange Forms Designer can be stored on servers and made available to all or select users, who can send them to specific recipients as messages or post them in folders for others to access. Forms users can manually collate data collected in forms; or, with the right programming, data can be automatically extracted from forms and processed. (Look back at Figure 1.10 for a glimpse into the wonderful world of electronic forms.)

Other Client-Based Applications

Aside from the Microsoft Exchange Forms Designer, there are a variety of ways to build client-based applications using Exchange Server's messaging capabilities:

- Microsoft's version 95 and 97 stable of applications (Word, Excel, and so on) include some nice collaborative tools and easy-to-use routing-slip capabilities based on Exchange messaging. Applications from other vendors also incorporate these capabilities.

- You can turn an Exchange message into any OLE 2.0–compliant application just by inserting an object from the app into the message.

- You can write programs that use Simple and Extended MAPI or the X.400-oriented Common Mail Call APIs supported by Exchange Server.

> **NOTE** Exchange is a complex product. The cost of an Exchange installation will, of course, depend heavily on licensing fees imposed by Microsoft. Check with the company for all pricing details.

Conclusion

In this chapter, you got a grounding in the architecture of Exchange. You learned about the core and optional components on both the Exchange server and client sides. You also had a chance to learn how the components interact with each other. The knowledge you've gained here has more than theoretical value: It will help immensely as you move toward installing and managing a real-world Exchange environment.

CHAPTER

FOUR

4

Exchange and Windows NT Server

- Why Exchange Server runs only on top of NT Server

- NT Server is easy to install and use

- Key features of NT Server and their integration with Exchange Server

Exchange Server is part of Microsoft's BackOffice suite of products. Like other BackOffice applications—SQL Server and Systems Management Server, for example—Exchange Server runs only on top of Microsoft Windows NT Server. You can install Exchange Server's very nice Administrator program on an NT Workstation, but not Exchange Server itself. Windows 95? Forget it!

Why NT Server?

NT Server has two key features not available in other Microsoft operating systems. The lack of these features does not make it impossible to run Exchange Server on, say, NT Workstation or Windows 95. Together, however, these features make NT Server the best platform for Exchange Server and Microsoft's other BackOffice products.

The key features? First, NT Server is optimized for lots of users. Second, it has some very nice extended tools for ensuring the integrity of your disk system. Let's look at these features in more detail.

NT Server Can Handle Heavy Multiuser Loads

Servers tend to support lots of users. Server users make major demands on CPU, disk, and network resources. NT Server is optimized to move data within and between these resources even under heavy loads.

Because of this optimization, NT Server can handle a large number of simultaneously connected users—just how many is limited only by your hardware configuration and the number of connect licenses you've bought.

Because it lacks server-oriented optimization and because it *is* optimized for workstation functionality, NT Workstation is limited to a maximum of ten users. Some claim that this limitation is artificially low and designed to force users to buy NT Server so that Microsoft can make more money. I have to disagree. The price difference between NT Server and NT Workstation isn't great enough to justify such an argument.

Windows 95 is also optimized for workstation functionality, but I'm uncomfortable with its continued reliance on MS-DOS to support older hardware technologies.

Windows 95 is great for user workstations running newer hardware and faster, more stable 32-bit applications; however, it doesn't have the stability to function as a platform for critical applications such as e-messaging.

NT Server Supports RAID Levels 1 and 5

Systems using redundant arrays of inexpensive disks (RAID) protect data by writing all or part of it to two or more drives. This ensures that the data can be recovered in case of a drive failure. When the bits in a byte of data are written to two or more drives, data is said to be *striped across* the drives.

There are at least five levels of RAID

- *Level 1* mirrors data stored on one disk onto another disk and provides 100 percent duplication of data. The system usually has to be shut down to replace a failed mirrored drive with the mirroring drive. Shutdown isn't required with NT's level 1 RAID

- *Level 2* uses data disks and extra check drives; data bits are striped across these drives *(bit striped)*, along with information that allows 1-bit data errors to be fixed and 2-bit errors to be detected (though not fixed) on the fly. Level 2 RAID offers the best performance with large data blocks.

- *Level 3* uses a single redundant check disk for a group of data drives. Data is bit-striped across the data disks, and XORed (exclusive ORed) parity information for the data is stored on the check disk. If any drive fails, its data can be reconstructed from the remaining drives and the check disk.

- *Level 4* is similar to RAID level 3, but data is block- or sector-striped—instead of bit-striped—across disks. Level 4 is best for transaction processing.

- *Level 5* doesn't use dedicated check drives; rather, it distributes regular and check data over the drives in the array, based on an algorithm that allows data to be recovered when a failed drive is replaced. Level 5 RAID allows for simultaneous reads and writes of data to disks and is most efficient when handling small amounts of information.

If you show just about anyone these definitions of the various RAID levels, they'll probably tell you I'm all wet. But actually I'm quite dry; the problem is that specific RAID implementations never fully adhere to all the details of these general definitions. Don't worry, though: These definitions are more than adequate to help you understand how NT Server handles RAID.

RAID can be implemented in hardware or software. NT Server supports software-based disk mirroring and disk duplexing (RAID level 1) and disk striping with parity (RAID level 5). NT Workstation supports RAID level 0 only. Other Microsoft operating systems do not support fault-tolerant disk configurations.

Under *disk mirroring* you create a constantly updated copy of all or part of one hard drive on another drive; both drives are connected to the same disk controller. The copy lets you recover from a drive failure. With *disk duplexing* you do the same thing, but the drive being copied is connected to a different disk controller than the drive holding the copy. This eliminates the single point of controller failure you have with disk mirroring.

Disk striping with parity involves creating stripes on up to 32 drives, preferably connected to multiple disk controllers. Data is written in ordered bits across the stripes. Parity information lets you recover data stored on a failed drive using the remaining good drives. Depending on hardware, you can often swap out a bad drive with a good one without even turning off the computer's or drive system's power.

Another benefit of RAID, especially level 5, is better disk performance. A RAID system can improve disk access speeds by splitting reads and writes over multiple drives and multiple disk controllers. (In fact, Microsoft recommends using RAID level 5 disk striping to improve Exchange Server performance. More about this later.)

Consider a Stand-Alone RAID System

You can purchase stand-alone RAID systems for NT from a variety of third-party vendors. Third-party RAID solutions won't let you run Exchange Server on top of NT Workstation or Windows 95, but they might give you better performance than NT Server's built-in RAID functionality. This is especially likely if you run NT Server on a single-processor computer. Stand-alone systems don't eat up your computer's CPU time doing RAID; some even implement RAID in special firmware that further improves their performance.

Exchange is likely to be considered a critical application in your organization. You probably won't want to run it without the benefits of at least RAID level 1.

> **NOTE** You manage NT disks in general and RAID systems in particular using NT's Disk Administrator, which is located in NT's Administrative Tools program group. For more on the Disk Administrator, see the Sybex book *Mastering Windows NT Server 4*. And for more on mastering Windows NT Server 4, see the sidebar in this chapter brilliantly titled—yep— "Mastering Windows NT Server 4."

NT Server Is a Piece of Cake

If you haven't had much (or any) experience with NT Server, don't let that bother you. It is quite simple to install—not much harder than installing Windows, in fact. We'll look at basic NT Server installation in Chapter 6.

Once installed, NT Server is very easy to use. It comes outfitted with the complete Microsoft Windows graphical user interface (GUI) suite that is the spitting image of Windows 95. If you're comfortable with Windows 95, you'll be just fine with NT Server. Trust me.

Applications for NT—Exchange Server included—tend to build on the Windows GUI. Remember the neat GUI administrative front end for Exchange Server we looked at back in Chapters 1 and 2? With their GUI front ends, NT apps let you focus on the substantive task in front of you. That way, you don't have to spend all of your time editing cryptic text files or cobbling together makeshift system monitoring or administration commands in the wide-open spaces of the operating system. (If it's not obvious, that last sentence was referring to UNIX.)

NT Specifics for the Exchange Server Crowd

NT Server is a bundle of nifty components. To understand how NT Server and Exchange Server work together, you'll need a basic grounding in eight of these components:

- NT services
- NT networking

- Microsoft network domains

- NT User Manager for Domains

- NT Server Manager

- NT and multiprocessing

- NT Event Viewer

- NT Performance Monitor

Some of the eight key NT Server components are also available in NT Workstation. That's a nice plus. If you're not already an NT aficionado, by the time you're finished setting up NT Server and Exchange Server, you'll probably be ready to make NT Workstation your desktop operating system. I've even gone a step further. Both my office and home workstations run NT Server. I'll wait while you get back up off your knees after paying homage to yours truly. Anyway, for you NT converts-in-the-making, the following detailed discussion of the eight components is a kind of two-for-one deal: It'll help you get comfortable with both NT Server and your future NT Workstation machine at the same time. And just so you know when a particular component is available only in NT Server, I'll use the words *NT Server* as opposed to *NT* when discussing it. (I'm just loaded with brilliant ideas.)

Mastering Windows NT Server 4

The eight NT Server components discussed in this chapter are far from all you'll ever want or need to know about NT. For the definitive word on NT Server, get a copy of Sybex's *Mastering Windows NT Server 4*. The authors—Mark Minasi, Christa Anderson, and Elizabeth Creegan—manage to make learning about a complex operating system both relatively painless and, believe it or not, fun.

I decided to have Sybex publish my book partly because I liked *Mastering Windows NT Server 4* so much. The deal was cinched when the company assured me that I'd have the same stylistic freedom given to Minasi et al. I got that freedom, and I hope you'll like this book as much as I enjoyed *Mastering Windows NT Server 4*.

NT Services

NT is a full-blown, preemptive, multitasking, multithreaded operating system that's able to run many tasks or processes simultaneously. Many of the processes that run on NT are called *services*. Services can run all of the time the computer is on, or they may be started and stopped manually as needed by those with the appropriate rights. Network protocol services, the computer's login services, and many applications, such as client/server databases and tape backup programs, run as NT services. And—you guessed it—Exchange Server is a set of NT services as well.

The NT Control Panel includes a little Services icon. When you double-click on it, an applet starts up with a window that displays all available NT services. Within this window you can check to see if a service is running, stop and start services, and set a service's default configuration (that is, whether it starts on boot-up, can be manually started, or is disabled). Figure 4.1 shows the Services applet in action on the GerCom Exchange server.

FIGURE 4.1

The NT Services applet is used to monitor and control Exchange Server components.

Don't worry about how services get created or integrated into the operating system; it's the responsibility of the application provider to make sure that this happens. And don't get the idea that the NT Services applet is the only way to monitor Exchange services. No way. As you'll see, Exchange comes with a bunch of its own service monitoring tools.

NT Networking

NT provides support for a range of networking protocols. These include IPX/SPX, NetBEUI, TCP/IP, and (with optional software) SNA networks. Third parties provide other networking protocols for NT Server, including DECnet and XNS.

NT also supports a set of standard remote procedure calls (RPCs) that enable client/server communications between programs running on the same or different computers. RPC-based communications move with equal ease across hardware platforms, operating systems, and networking protocols.

All Exchange client-to-server communications and some Exchange server-to-server communications—intrasite directory replication, for example—are based on the RPCs. The RPCs support only direct links between Exchange servers (as *direct* was defined in Chapter 3). The RPCs can run on top of IPX/SPX, NetBEUI, TCP/IP, or SNA. The RPCs can also work over other network layers that are not transport protocols—for example, Named Pipes or Sockets. In Figure 4.2 you can see how the RPCs work in an Exchange system and use the networking protocols supported by NT. See the sidebar "NT's RPCs and Exchange" for more on this RPC set, which is so central to Exchange.

FIGURE 4.2

How NT's RPCs and Microsoft networking support Exchange Server.

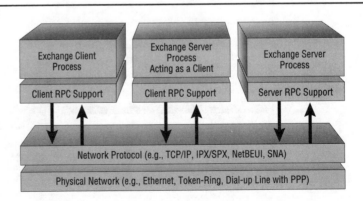

One of the really impressive parts of NT networking is the Remote Access Server (RAS). The RAS supports client-to-server and server-to-server links based on slower connect options. It works with standard phone lines, ISDN, X.25, and RS-232C null modems. Key supported protocols include NetBEUI, TCP/IP, and IPX/SPX—all on top of the Point-to-Point-Protocol (PPP). One NT Server can have up to 256 RAS connections. (For the record, NT Workstation supports only two RAS connections.) As you'll see later, the RAS is a key part of Exchange's connectivity.

NT networking, like Microsoft networking in general, is quite simple. If you've got a network adapter in your computer, you're asked what kind of networking you want when you install NT Server. If you understand basic networking concepts—for example, how to set up a TCP/IP node—you'll have little if any trouble with NT networking. (We'll come back to networking issues constantly throughout the rest of this book.)

Microsoft Network Domains

Microsoft network domains both organize and provide centralized administration and security for groups of resources. Resources include computers, the programs running on them, and, optionally, the peripherals attached to them. Windows and DOS workstations integrate best into Microsoft networks.

Computers in Microsoft networks can include:

- Windows NT servers
- Novell NetWare servers
- Windows NT workstations
- Windows 95 workstations
- Windows 3.11 workstations
- MS-DOS workstations
- Apple Macintoshes

Peripherals include disk drives and the files on them, as well as printers.

NT's RPCs and Exchange

Exchange relies heavily on Microsoft's implementation of the OSF's DCE RPC API. Talk about alphabet soup! Translation: Exchange depends on Microsoft's version of the Open Software Foundation's (OSF's) Distributed Computing Environment (DCE) remote procedure call (RPC) application programming interface (API). That's quite a mouthful, so I'll use the term "OSF RPCs" from here on to avoid drowning you in a sea of acronyms.

In general, remote procedure calls support client-server computing. The OSF RPCs aren't suitable for all client-server applications, because to work they require direct, synchronous (continuous) connections between clients and servers. You can't use the OSF RPCs in a situation where you want to assign a task to a server, disconnect from the server, and then go about your work until the server contacts you to return the results of the task you assigned it. You've got to remain linked to the server during the entire process. So the OSF RPCs are not well suited to things like client-server databases; in fact, Microsoft uses other RPCs to support its SQL Server database.

There are OSF RPCs for clients as well as servers. NT Server, NT Workstation, and Windows 95 support both the client and server RPC sets. The other Microsoft operating systems support only the client RPC sets.

Client and server versions of the OSF RPCs are available for a wide range of operating systems, which means that Microsoft can more easily write Exchange clients and servers for non-Microsoft operating systems. This is key to the company's development of Exchange clients for the Apple Macintosh and a variety of UNIX systems. While Microsoft doesn't appear to have plans for any non-NT Exchange Server implementations at press time, the OSF RPCs keep the company's options open.

Microsoft networks are built around *domains*. A Microsoft network can have one or many domains, each of which is a logically separate entity. A resource in a Microsoft network can belong to one and only one domain.

Generally, domain users log in to domains, not in to the individual machines in a domain. Domains can make life easier both for users and for system managers. Users don't have to remember more than one password to access any resource in the domain (unless it is protected by a special password). System managers can centrally create and administer user accounts for the domain.

Domains also make interserver communications easy. If servers live in the same domain, each has to log in to the domain only once in order to communicate with all other servers in the domain—unless, of course, a special password is required for specific communications.

Domains require *domain controllers,* which is where

- NT administrators:

  - Create and manage accounts for domain users

  - Set access rights for domain resources

- the NT Server operating system:

  - Stores user account information for the domain

  - Stores resource access rights for the domain

  - Authenticates domain users

  - Enforces access rights for domain resources

Of all the resources in a Microsoft network domain, only NT servers can be domain controllers; while every NT server needn't be a domain controller, every domain controller *must* be an NT server. Exchange Server can optionally be installed on an NT server that is a domain controller. That way, you can set up a simple Exchange system using just one NT server.

It's considered good practice to have at least one backup controller in each domain. Backup domain controllers stay in sync with the primary controller and take over if the primary controller fails. They can also perform authentication in parallel with the primary and other backup domain controllers. This helps balance the load in systems with large numbers of users.

As you'll see later, domains are key to using and administering Exchange. Domain and Exchange security are tightly integrated—to see just how tightly, take a look at Figure 4.3, which shows the Exchange Administrator being used to create both a new Exchange mailbox and a new domain user for the mailbox.

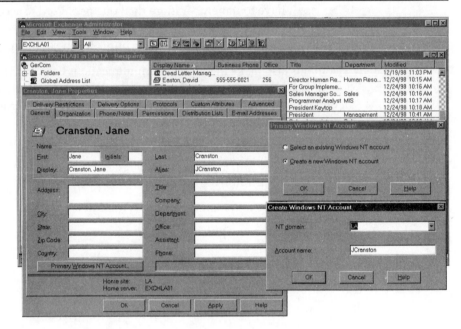

Cross-Domain Trusts

When one domain (called the *trusting* domain) trusts another (the *trusted* domain), it accepts the other domain's authentication of a user or server. The user or server doesn't have to log in to the trusting domain to access its resources; one login to a trusted domain is enough to access all available resources in a trusting domain, unless access to a resource is specifically limited by a special password.

Figure 4.4 shows how cross-domain trust relationships make it easier for users and servers to access resources across a network. The users and servers in domain B (the trusted domain) can access resources in domain A (the trusting domain) without using additional passwords. Note that the figure's arrowhead points to the trusted domain and away from the trusting domain.

Trusts are not only good for users, they're just what the doctor ordered for busy system administrators as well. Trusts expand the reach of administrators in creating and maintaining user accounts. After setting up a trust relationship between domains, an administrator can in one fell swoop create a user in one domain and give that user access to all other trusting domains.

FIGURE 4.4

Trust relationships open a network to users.

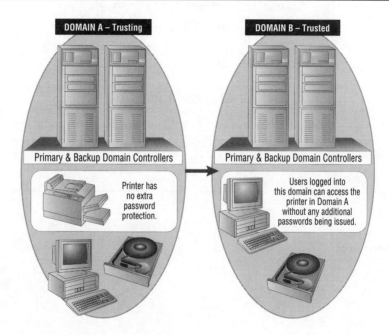

Trust relationships have all kinds of implications for the way users and systems managers operate day to day. For example, with the right kind of trust relationship and security rights you can administer Exchange not on a domain-by-domain basis, but from a multidomain or network-level perspective.

Also, trust relationships are key to cross-domain interaction between Exchange servers. With the appropriate trust relationships and rights in place, Exchange servers in different domains can interact to exchange messages and cross-replicate directories and public folders.

Domain Models

- There are four domain models for Microsoft networks:
- The single-domain model
- The master-domain model
- The multiple-master domain model
- The complete-trust domain model

Let's look at each model in detail.

The Single-Domain Model

Single-domain systems have no need for trust relationships, since there is only one isolated domain. See Figure 4.5 for a graphical depiction of a network with a single domain.

FIGURE 4.5

A network based on the single-domain model.

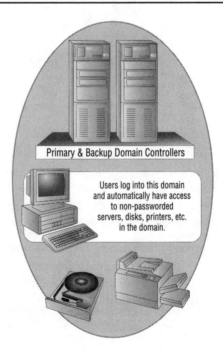

Primary & Backup Domain Controllers

Users log into this domain and automatically have access to non-passworded servers, disks, printers, etc. in the domain.

The single-domain model is best in situations that have no organizational or technical need for a segmented network. The maximum number of users in a domain is limited pretty much by the hardware your domain controller runs on. The more users you have, the larger your domain security tables become; in addition, you'll need more powerful hardware (CPU, RAM, and disks) to plow through the tables when authenticating users. Depending on the hardware you use and based on hardware capabilities current as of January 1997, you can expect to support from 15,000 to more than 40,000 users in a domain.

Once you're running your primary and backup domain controllers on the most powerful hardware you can find or afford, the only way to support more users is by moving either to the multiple-master domain model or the complete-trust domain model. I'll discuss these two in just a bit, but first let's look at the master-domain model.

The Master-Domain Model

Master-domain systems include one administrative domain and one or more resource domains where servers and workstations are located. The master domain handles all security tasks. It is a trusted domain, while all other domains are trusting. See Figure 4.6 for a diagram of a master-domain system.

FIGURE 4.6

A network based on the master-domain model.

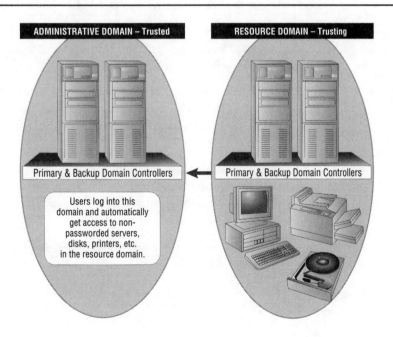

ADMINISTRATIVE DOMAIN – Trusted

RESOURCE DOMAIN – Trusting

Primary & Backup Domain Controllers

Primary & Backup Domain Controllers

Users log into this domain and automatically get access to non-passworded servers, disks, printers, etc. in the resource domain.

The master-domain model is most appropriate in organizations that need to segment resources (say, by department or geographically) and that have a centralized MIS department. Each department or geographical unit can have its own domain, while MIS administers from the master domain. Note that even though this model has multiple domains, there is only one administrative domain—so you're still limited to 15,000 to 40,000 users per domain.

The Multiple-Master Domain Model

Multiple-master domain systems have two or more master domains and two or more resource domains. Each master domain is responsible for some portion of users based on a logical segmenting factor—for example, the first letter of the user's last name, or the geographical breakdown of the company. Each resource domain trusts all of the master domains. Figure 4.7 depicts the multiple-master domain model. Here the master domains trust each other and are trusted by both of the resource domains. This is not required, however; each master domain can be trusted by either one or a set of resource domains. In the figure, for example, Administrative Domain #1 can be trusted only by Resource Domain #1, while Administrative Domain #2 can be trusted by both resource domains.

In many cases, you'll also want two-way trusts between the master domains. That way, system administrators with appropriate rights can create new users, and so on, in any master domain as needed.

The multiple-master domain model works best for larger organizations that need to segment both resources and MIS administration. Resource domains are often based on departmental divisions.

Multiple-master domains are a way around limits on the maximum number of users per domain. So if your domain controller hardware limits you to 40,000 users per domain, *each* master domain can handle up to 40,000 users. With two domains you're up to 80,000 users, and so on.

Multiple-master domains also allow MIS administration to divide the task of managing domains into smaller units. This tends to reduce the likelihood of error and lets large multinational organizations spread the management tasks across geographical and sociopolitical boundaries.

FIGURE 4.7

A network based on the
multiple-master domain
model

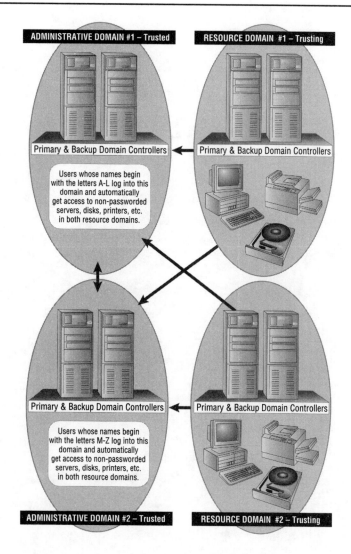

FIGURE 4.7

A network based on the
multiple-master domain
model

The Complete-Trust Domain Model

Complete-trust domain systems consist of several domains; each domain handles
its own security administration. Since this model has no master domains, all
domains must be both trusted and trusting. Figure 4.8 shows a system based on
the complete-trust domain model.

FIGURE 4.8

A network based on the
complete-trust domain
model

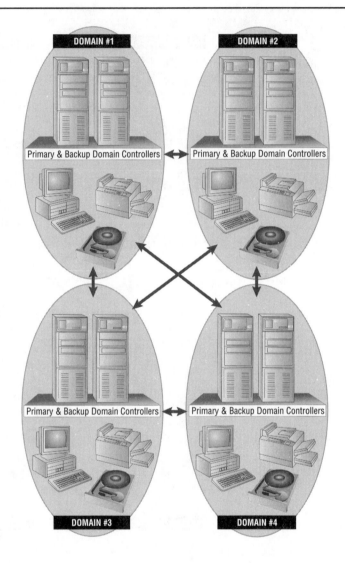

FIGURE 4.8

A network based on the
complete-trust domain
model

Complete-trust domain systems are appropriate when an organization lacks
central MIS administration and is segmented in some way—by department, for
example. Each department is a domain, and control of the domain is in the hands
of the department. Each domain can have up to the maximum number of users
its domain controller hardware will support. The major drawback of complete-
trust domain systems is the number of trust relationships and access rights that
have to be set up and maintained in organizations with lots of departments.

User Manager for Domains and Cross-Domain Trusts

You set up cross-domain trusts in NT's User Manager for Domains. From the Policies menu, select Trust Relationships. From there it's a no-brainer, as long as you've really got other domains and they're on the same continuous local or wide area network. You can set up both trusted and trusting relationships for the domain you're running the User Manager from. We'll get into all of this in hands-on mode later in the book.

The NT User Manager for Domains

So you've got one or more domains—now what? Well, first you'll want to create user accounts and user groups in your domains and give them rights. Even though you can create domain users and Exchange mailboxes with the Exchange Administrator, you'll still need to know how to create and manage domain accounts and groups. For example, as you'll see later—even before you install Exchange Server—you'll want to create a domain-based user group to administer and manage your Exchange servers.

NT Server includes a nice interface, called the User Manager for Domains, for administering and managing domain accounts and groups. Figure 4.9 shows how the User Manager can be used to add a new user account to a domain. Just to prove that the tight integration between NT Server and Exchange security is a two-way street, take a look at Figure 4.10. As soon as I click the Add button in the New User dialog box, Exchange—through User Manager for Domains—brings up a standard set of mailbox-creation property pages. I fill in these pages as needed, then click on OK in the mailbox's Properties dialog box, and I've created a new domain user and an Exchange mailbox all at once.

Though the actual domain account information is stored on an NT server, you can run the User Manager for Domains on an NT workstation as well. (I'm running it on my NT workstation in Figures 4.9 and 4.10.) This is just one of the ways you can manage an NT server remotely. As you'll find out later in this chapter, Exchange Server also supports a lot of remote management functions. In fact, remote management is one of the most impressive features of both products.

FIGURE 4.9

Adding a user to a
domain with the User
Manager for Domains

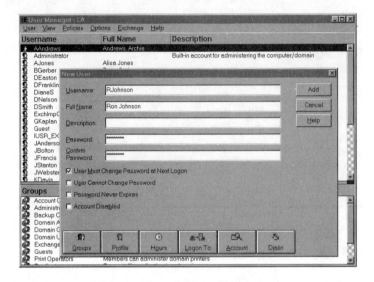

FIGURE 4.10

The User Manager for
Domains lets you set up
an Exchange mailbox for
a new user.

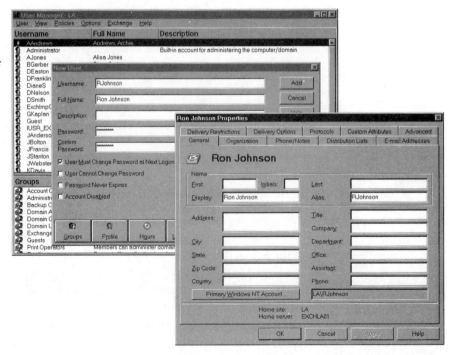

NOTE

Although it runs on NT Workstation machines, the User Manager for Domains comes only with NT Server. You can borrow it from one of your NT servers, or you can use the copy of the User Manager for Domains that's included in Microsoft's optional NT Resource Kit. The kit, worth its purchase price even if you don't need a copy of the User Manager for Domains, is available from a variety of sources. Check with Microsoft for more information.

The NT Server Manager

The Server Manager is another one of those wonderful NT management tools that can run remotely. It lets you see what's happening on other servers and allows you to make certain changes on those servers.

In Figure 4.11, I'm running the Server Manager from my NT workstation. You'll notice that we're looking at the domain LA; the servers and workstations in LA are listed on the upper left-hand side of the screen. Here I'm using the Server

FIGURE 4.11

Using the Server Manager to remotely monitor shared resources

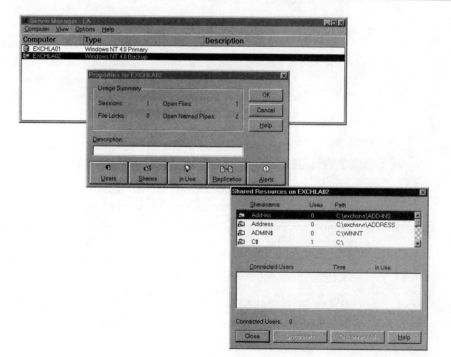

Manager to see what's up resource-wise on my Exchange server, EXCHLA02. You'll notice that I have the option of disconnecting one or more of the shared resources. I might choose to do this if a problem occurred with a resource that I couldn't fix any other way.

Do you remember our earlier discussion of the Control Panel applet for monitoring and administering the services running on an NT machine? Wouldn't it be neat if we could use the applet for remote computers, too? Well, we can't. But not to worry: We can use the Server Manager instead. While at my NT workstation (shown in Figure 4.12), I can stop an Exchange Server process on EXCHLA02. I love it!

FIGURE 4.12

Remotely administering Exchange Server services using the Server Manager

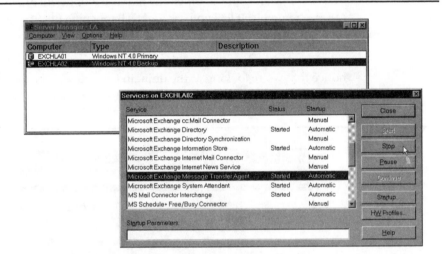

NT and Multiprocessing

As users begin to take advantage of the great features built into Exchange and as you add new users and tasks—an Exchange connector, for example—to an NT/ Exchange server, you'll find yourself scrambling to find the computing horse-power you need to keep everyone and everything happy. You can often pep up a server by adding more RAM and/or a RAID level 5 disk system. If that isn't enough, the next best bet is to add processing power.

When you know that the load on an Exchange server will grow significantly in the span of a year or so, you should seriously consider buying a multiprocessing system, even if you don't outfit it with a full complement of CPUs at the outset. That way, you won't have to upgrade to a whole new machine—you can just add processors when demands increase. A number of vendors now offer computers that support multiple-CPU configurations. To show you that my money or at least my clients' money is where my mouth is, I've taken to insisting on a minimum dual processor Pentium machine for the Exchange Server installations I set up.

The NT Event Viewer

Like all good operating systems, NT logs a variety of things that happen as it runs. In NT parlance, these "things" are called *events*. Event *logging* is just another NT service.

Three kinds of events can occur in NT: system, security, and application. *System events* include activities centering around disk drives, network adapters, serial ports, mice, and other peripheral hardware. *Security events* are attempts by users and NT processes to enter the system. *Application events* can be anything that the authors of an application that runs on an NT machine choose to log.

You use the NT Event Viewer, which you can find in NT's Administrative Tools program group, to look at events. You pick the kind of event—system, security, or application—that you want to look at from the Event Viewer's Log menu. To see details about a particular event, you double-click on the event. Figure 4.13 shows the Application Log for the NT/Exchange server EXCHLA01.

Each event shown in the Event Viewer is given what might be called an "attention level." Events included solely for informational use are flagged with a little blue icon that has a lowercase letter *i* inside it. Events that require some attention are marked with a yellow exclamation-mark icon. Events that have failed or for some other reason require serious attention are flagged with a red stop-sign icon. Events marked with a little key are about application-level security. Figure 4.13 shows the successful loading of a component of Exchange Server's web service, which lets users access their mailboxes and schedules with a web browser.

You can do lots of other useful things with the Event Viewer, such as applying filters to check only some events. For now, though, we'll focus on another of the Event Viewer's great capabilities: You can use it to look at other computers in domains you have access to. In fact, although we're viewing the NT server EXCHLA01 in Figure 4.13, the Event Viewer is actually running on my NT workstation.

FIGURE 4.13

The Event Viewer shows the Application Log for an NT/Exchange server.

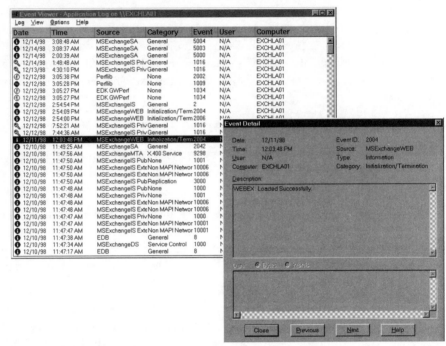

Keep Those Icons in View

I keep shortcuts for User Manager for Domains, Server Manager, Event Viewer, and Performance Monitor on my desktop. A shortcut for Exchange Administrator also occupies a place of honor on my desktop. I use these five apps so often that it's a pain to have to navigate NT 4.0's Start menu to find them.

The NT Performance Monitor

NT's Performance Monitor is a graphically oriented application that lets you monitor hundreds of activities on an NT machine. Like other NT management tools, the Performance Monitor can monitor one or more machines at the same time.

Though you'll find the Performance Monitor useful for a variety of tasks, it's especially helpful in planning and managing your Exchange Server system.

Exchange Server comes with LoadSim, a planning application that simulates various user loads on an Exchange server and a supporting network. The Performance Monitor is one way to measure the impact of these loads. Load-measurement parameters for e-messaging are added to the Performance Monitor when you install LoadSim. Figure 4.14 shows the Performance Monitor and LoadSim in action.

FIGURE 4.14

The Performance Monitor and LoadSim help in planning an Exchange system.

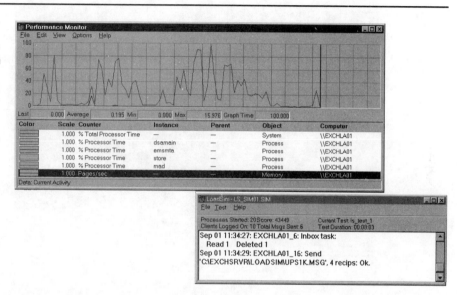

Exchange Server also adds several measurement parameters of its own to the Performance Monitor, letting you monitor certain aspects of the performance and health of an Exchange server. For the record, you'll also use the Exchange Administrator program for some monitoring tasks.

Conclusion

In this chapter you learned why Exchange Server runs only on top of NT Server and how easy NT Server is to install and use. You also had a chance to become familiar with a number of NT Server components and to see how important they are to Exchange Server. This information, combined with what you've learned in previous chapters, will help you in planning and implementing your Exchange system.

CHAPTER

FIVE

5

Designing an Exchange System

- An 11-step process for designing an Exchange system

- Entertaining detailed examples as well as abstract concepts

- Technical details on a number of Exchange components found nowhere else in this book

Whether your system will be based on a single Exchange server in a single site or hundreds of Exchange servers spread out over multiple sites, you need to consider a number of design issues before implementation. This chapter presents a planning model based loosely on an 11-step process developed by Microsoft. Tracking and retracking through these steps will help your organization decide where it wants to go with electronic messaging and how it can get there with Exchange. I can tell you from lots of experience that the 11-step process really works. Generally, I've found I can gather any required information and generate a fairly complex first-draft plan, complete with a most convincing executive summary in a week or less.

This chapter isn't just about design, though. It also offers practical information about Exchange and how it works. Here, for example, you'll find detailed information about Exchange's seemingly endless network connection options: what they do, and which networking topologies and protocols support them. Information like this is central to designing and implementing an Exchange system, and it's not found anywhere else in this book. If you're going to skip a chapter, please—not this one. This is a long chapter covering a great deal of information in detail. Just as you wouldn't try to implement a complex Exchange system in one day, you shouldn't try to plow through this chapter in one hour.

Here, then, with more than a little poetic license, is a list of Microsoft's 11 steps to designing an Exchange system:

1. Assess the needs of users in your organization.
2. Study your organization's geographical profile.
3. Assess your organization's network.
4. Establish naming conventions.
5. Select a Microsoft networking domain model.
6. Define site boundaries.
7. Plan intersite links.
8. Plan servers and internal connections to them.
9. Plan connections to other systems.
10. Validate and optimize your design.
11. Roll out the plan.

Now let's discuss each of these steps in more detail. This discussion builds upon the 11-step process presented by Microsoft in the Exchange docs and other Microsoft publications, but it is very far from a word-for-word regurgitation. Therefore, you should blame me—not Microsoft—if you encounter any problems from following the advice I give in this chapter. (Of course, if this stuff helps in any way, you should send the fruit baskets and such to *me*.)

> **NOTE** Microsoft's documentation for Exchange Server includes a bunch of planning forms that you can use to collect the information you'll need in the various design steps. Because Microsoft's forms cover the bases so well, I decided not to include my own forms in this book.

Exchange Design Is Iterative, Not Linear

Throughout this chapter, remember that designing an Exchange system is not a linear process, it's an iterative one. You'll find yourself coming back to each of the steps to gather new information, to reinterpret information you've already gathered, and to collect even more information based on those reinterpretations. New information will likely lead to design changes and further iterations. Even after you've fully implemented Exchange, you'll return to steps in the design process as problems arise or as your organization changes.

Within reason, the more iterations you go through, the better your final design will be. But take care not to use iteration as a route to procrastination. Whatever you do, start running Exchange if only in a limited test environment as soon as you can.

Assess User Needs

Here you're interested in who needs what, when they need it, and how you'll provide it. You'll want to get a handle on the programming, software, hardware, MIS systems, systems support, and training resources that will be required to satisfy user needs.

Remember that Exchange is an e-messaging package, not just an e-mail product. Users may need specific e-messaging–enabled applications. Depending on what they have in mind, application development can be a real resource hog. Also remember that, in some cases, hardware and software may require new workstations, not just new servers.

Be prepared to give users a clear idea of what Exchange can do. You don't need to get technical with most users; just give them a view of Exchange from the end-user's perspective. Take another look at the first two sections of Chapter 1 to see how you might organize your presentation.

One of the biggest mistakes most people make when implementing a system is to ignore or give only passing attention to the assessment-of-user-needs step. Knowing as much as you can about what the users require up front means you'll have an easier time during implementation.

For example, imagine that you don't know from the get-go that your organization could benefit significantly from a particular custom-programmed e-messaging–enabled application. You'd go ahead and implement Exchange as an e-mail system with only the resources such an implementation requires. You'd get your Exchange system up and it would be perking along just fine when suddenly—maybe three months later—some user comes up with this great idea for an e-messaging–enabled app.

Boink! Suddenly you have to tell management that you need a few programmers and maybe more hardware to implement this—"er, um, idea nobody thought of four or five months ago." I'll leave the rest to your imagination.

> **NOTE** Whatever you find out in your user-needs assessment, add a fudge factor in favor of more hardware and support personnel. Exchange has so many fantastic capabilities that you can be sure your users will find all kinds of ways to challenge whatever resources you make available. Depending on your users and their ability to get away with unplanned demands for resources, fudging by as much as 25 percent is reasonable.

Suffice it to say that a user-needs assessment is the single most important part of the Exchange design process. Because it is, we'll cover it in more detail than the other ten Exchange design steps.

Questions to Ask

There are a number of questions you'll want to answer during your user-needs assessment. Here are the major ones:

1. What kinds of users (for example, managers, salespeople, clerical staff, lawyers, doctors) does my organization have, and what do they think they want from the new Exchange system?

2. What sorts of e-messaging services are different groups of users likely to need (for example, e-mail, calendars and scheduling, public folders, specially designed applications)?

3. Which specially designed applications can be developed by users, and which must be developed by MIS personnel?

4. Do all users need every capability from Day One, or can implementation be phased in—perhaps based on user groupings from question 1, above?

5. What sorts of demands are users (or groups of users) going to put on your Exchange servers? Much of the information in this category can be used with Exchange Server's LoadSim program to simulate expected server load and thus project server hardware and networking requirements.

   - How many users will there be per server?

   - How many sent messages will there be per user per day?

   - How many received messages will there be per user per day?

   - How frequently will users send messages:

     - to others on their server?

     - to others in their site?

     - to others at each of the other sites in your organization?

     - to others outside your organization? Be sure to break this down by the different kinds of external connections you'll have (see steps 7 and 9).

   - How often will users read messages in their mailboxes?

   - How often will users read messages in public folders?

   - How often will users move messages to personal folders stored locally and on the network?

- How often will users move messages to public folders?

- How big will the messages be? What percentage will be 1K in size, 2K, 4K, 10K with attachments, or 100K with attachments?

6. What level of message delivery service will users want and need? This should be stated in hours or minutes between the time a message is sent and received. You'll need to specify this for both internal and external communications.

7. What sorts of hardware and software resources (for example, computers, operating systems, Exchange client licenses) will different groups of users need to implement Exchange on the client side?

8. What kinds of training will be required for users or groups of users?

9. What sorts of MIS resources will be required to support user needs?

An Example: Assessing GerCom's User Needs

Throughout this chapter we'll use a set of examples based on GerCom, the fictitious little company I created for this book. Though the examples are not real, they are based on my own experience in implementing e-messaging systems, including Exchange. The examples are illustrative, not exhaustive; they don't cover every conceivable issue you might encounter in designing your own Exchange system.

Tracking through Microsoft's 11 design steps can be interesting, exciting—even exhilarating. It also can be as boring as watching glue dry. So I'll try to leaven my GerCom examples with a bit of humor. Hey, it's my company; I can do as I like with it, right? Anyway, as you read along, please keep in mind that I'm not making fun of a very important process—I'm just trying to keep an artificial example from becoming dried glue.

What GerCom Users Need to Do

In our user-needs assessment, we at GerCom uncovered several user groups with different needs. Here are some highlights of our assessment.

Our top-level execs, led by little old me, are small in number but big in ideas when it comes to Exchange. We want to do e-mail and apps based on the collaborative tools built into Exchange and both Word and Excel 97. Our controller has this great idea about building a system in Exchange-enabled Excel that lets employees act on their stock options. This system would play against our financials, which run on an Oracle database on a UNIX server. The controller would also like to use an Exchange-Excel system to collaboratively develop annual budgets. And he and I are thinking about more elaborate, custom-programmed Exchange-enabled work-flow apps for things like purchasing. Again, there would be a lot of interaction with our Oracle financials.

Our vice president of human resources is one of those power users—always coming up with ideas that no one else ever thought of. She wants to put, say, the personnel manual and all the forms we use into public folders. Then employees could read the latest copy of the manual or get a form they need. Some forms, like those for our internally administered health insurance, would be full-blown Electronic Forms Designer forms. People would select one of these while in their Exchange client, fill it in, and send it off using the default address built into the form. Forms like all those "W-something" whatsits from the IRS would just be legal electronic copies that people can fill in, print, sign, and return by—gag—our internal snail-mail system.

GerCom execs travel a lot (too much if you ask the board of directors or other employees), so we want to be able to dial in to send and pick up our Exchange mes-sages and use those Exchange-based applications we've come up with. There are several ways to dial into an Exchange server from Microsoft's Exchange client, using either the company's Remote Access Server or the Internet. However, the Exchange client is a bit of a disk- and RAM-resource hog for less well-endowed portable PCs. So for our road warriors, we're strongly considering standardizing on the new Internet-based POP3 and web browser–based clients that come with Exchange 5.

We execs want our clerical staff to do e-mail and to be able to create forms with Electronic Forms Designer. My secretary came up with a great idea for using an e-mailed form to collect personal information about employees. No, we're not one of those super-snooper kind of companies; we just like to recognize things like spouses' and kids' birthdays and such. The clerical staff also came up with the idea of using Microsoft's e-messaging–enabled Schedule+ to do group scheduling and room reservations. They hate the combination of phone tag and written mes-sages now used to set up meetings.

Our systems people expect the executive suite to be a heavy user of Exchange. I haven't seen all the numbers they've come up with from LoadSim yet, but rumor is that they're considering giving us our own Exchange server. Since I know the boss intimately, I'm sure I can get him to sign off on that one.

The salespeople have some big ideas, too. They want in-office and remote E-mail like the top execs, but they also want to use Exchange for customer ordering and to keep copies of our price lists stored on customers' computers automatically updated. We're still not quite sure how we'll do it—heck, this is only Chapter 5—but we do know we'll need some way of linking to those customers. The sales staff also wants to build an e-messaging-based system in which customers can place orders and pay for purchases. That would involve our Oracle-based ordering and payables systems. As president, I like that one, especially the payment part.

GerCom's marketing folks mainly want e-mail so they can send press releases to all those magazine editors who would rather never see another press release. We showed them some of the other stuff you can do with Exchange, but they couldn't seem to come up with any apps. So we told them that unless they could make a good argument for other apps over the next few weeks, they'd have to live with e-mail only for a while. They seem happy.

The manufacturing people are really excited about Exchange. I never mentioned it, but GerCom makes Enter keys—you know, the little key on your computer keyboard marked ↵. (Hey, it's a really specialized world out there.) Anyway, the manufacturing folks figure that Exchange will give them a good way to link their production plans and inventory to the sales department's customer ordering system. Manufacturing wants to be able to send customers automatic updates on shipping dates. A copy will go to sales, of course. Manufacturing figures that this will both keep customers happy and keep our very aggressive salespeople out of their faces. We accepted this proposal, though we know it's going to take some custom programming involving our Oracle data. Of course, manufacturing also wants in-house e-mail.

For some reason, GerCom's engineering department hasn't been able to come up with a use for Exchange other than in-office e-mail. Well, what do you expect from a bunch of people who spend most of their working hours trying to improve the Enter key?

The MIS department wants in-house and remote e-mail, and it has a bunch of ideas of its own about Exchange. For example, it's tired of printing and routing all those Oracle reports that most people ignore. MIS wants to develop an app that downloads electronic copies of those reports to the NT environment, puts them into specific Exchange public folders, and then sends out an electronic form telling recipients that the latest report has arrived.

Why a form and not a message? There'll be a field on the form where recipients can indicate that they don't need the report anymore. The form will be programmed to automatically remove those recipients who don't want the report from its Exchange distribution list. There'll also be a place to put ideas about changing the report or new reports. Pretty neat. The MIS people have not only eliminated a lot of increasingly expensive paper, they've also come up with a way to keep the reporting process alive and responsive to changing needs.

Supporting GerCom's User Needs

Whew! Our users have a lot of great ideas. Now we should begin laying out some specific things we'll need to support their needs. We won't go into detail on things like network connections, server hardware needs, or systems support personnel; those come later. For now, we just need to cover things like acceptable message delivery performance, end-user support personnel, and end-user hardware.

A lot of the apps we're planning are going to be pretty critical to GerCom's bottom line. We've decided we want messages to move between our offices and to our trading partners at a good speed—within ten minutes, if at all possible.

We already know it'll take about six new MIS people just to serve the needs of our 2,500 employees. Two of these will be involved in initial training and then in supporting users who want to develop their own apps. The other four will focus on programming custom apps. We've got plenty of space for these new folks, so we won't have any serious added costs on that front. We will, however, have to buy these new employees some hefty hardware. And we'll have to outfit our training rooms with beefier systems.

We've also decided to hire a corporate Exchange manager who will report to the director of MIS. The six people I mentioned above will report to the Exchange manager, along with any other Exchange-related personnel we add.

We're also trying to decide what to do about user workstations. Someone suggested we cancel all executive travel to pay for new machines for everyone. (I can't imagine where they got that idea.) We probably won't do that, but I'm working with the controller to try to figure out how we can upgrade everyone who needs a new computer (about 75 percent of our employees) in the next year and a half. It will involve lots of bucks, but GerCom's going to gain a great deal from this system, and the Enter key business is really hot right now. That year-and-a-half time frame, by the way, ties in closely with our roll-out plans, which you'll read about at the end of this chapter. Are you beginning to see why I included the sidebar "Exchange Design Is Iterative, Not Linear" in this chapter?

More on User Workstations

"Yes, I know that our users are working on ancient desktop computer systems. But we just don't have the money to buy them what they really need." I wish I had a dollar for every time I've heard that one; why, I'd be able to buy decent systems for most of those poor users. I've always wondered why companies that have money to burn on fancy cars and trips to expensive and often useless meetings and employee seminars can't seem to find the two or three thousand bucks it takes to upgrade a user's workstation.

I limped along for quite some time on a substandard 486 workstation with 8MB of memory. Then I got my NT system with a 200MHz Pentium processor and 128MB of RAM. Yes, 128MB of RAM. When I ran Windows on my old, underpowered sleepwalker, it was all I could do to keep my word processor and e-mail software open at the same time. If I opened anything else, the machine started thrashing around so much between RAM and virtual memory that it slowed to a nearly useless crawl.

With my new system, I can run word processing programs, spreadsheet programs, and Exchange together without wasting precious time to switch between them. And I still have plenty of horsepower left for all those tasks I used to do with paper because I couldn't bring up the applications fast enough when I needed them. At will, I can now simultaneously open (or keep open) such apps as an accounting package, my Exchange client, Schedule+, Microsoft Outlook, a to-do list, specialized address and contact lists, and spreadsheets for tracking the progress of various projects. With all that computer power, I'm also no longer reluctant to run other key programs—say, Internet Web browsers or NT Control Panel applets—at the drop of a hat.

Bottom line: I've had my new system for less than a year; by my estimates, the productivity increase I've experienced in that time has already paid back the cost of the system's purchase.

Maybe all of your users don't need a 200MHz Pentium system with NT and 128MB of RAM. However, as you start assessing user needs, don't let the dismal state of your organization's stable of workstations stop you and your

More on User Workstations (continued)

users from reaching for the stars as you think about potential applications for Exchange. Who knows—you just might come up with a next-generation business-computing model for your organization. And that might get you a corporate car, or a trip to Hawaii for that conference on the role of MS-DOS and the 286 PC in modern corporate computing.

I'm very happy with GerCom's needs assessment. Since we started the process, I've seen the LoadSim numbers for the whole organization. Though they're just rough estimates, they look pretty good; we can refine them later. We're off to a good start.

Study Your Organization's Geographical Profile

You need a list of all the geographical units in your organization. Here you should think not only in terms of cities, states, and countries, but also in-city and even in-building locations. Start at the top and work your way down. At this point, diagrams are very important. Draw maps and building layouts.

This is the time to gather information on the workstations and servers you've got in each location. You'll want to know how many run each of the different kinds of operating systems in your organization. Operating systems you should watch for are Windows NT Workstation and Server, Novell NetWare 3.*x* and 4.*x* Servers and NetWare IPX/SPX workstations, Banyan VINES servers and workstations, Windows 95, Windows 3.1*x*, MS-DOS, Apple Macintosh, UNIX workstations by type of operating system, and workstations used remotely. If you've got hardware and software inventories for these machines, your job will be a lot easier. If you're looking for an automatic inventorying system, check out Microsoft's Systems Management Server. Not only can you use it to gather workstation and server hardware information automatically, it can help you install Exchange clients throughout your organization. You can use all of the information you collect about workstations and servers to determine who's ready for Exchange and who isn't, and how many Exchange client licenses you'll have to buy.

As you gather information in other steps, begin to look at it in the context of your geographical profile. For example, you'll want to meld geographical information with what you've found out about user needs and user groupings.

An Example: GerCom's Geographical Profile

As you can see in Figure 5.1, GerCom has grown by leaps and bounds since earlier chapters. It now has offices in Chicago and New York City—Figure 5.2 shows just how much we've grown. Hey, we've got two buildings in the "City of the Broad Shoulders." Now aren't you sorry you didn't buy stock when you had a chance?

GerCom's top executive staff, marketing, and most of MIS are in Los Angeles; sales has people in all three cities. Manufacturing and engineering are in Chicago, the Enter key capital of the world. We've got 1,500 people in LA, 800 in Chicago, and 200 in New York.

All but two of our network servers run NetWare 3.12. The operating system on the two maverick servers, which support our Oracle database, is Sun Solaris (UNIX). We lucked out when it comes to user workstation types and operating systems: Except for five workstations, they're all Intel-based, almost all run Windows, and all but a few are linked to our NetWare servers using either Novell's ODI or VLM IPX/SPX stack.

FIGURE 5.1

GerCom, an Enter key manufacturer with a national presence

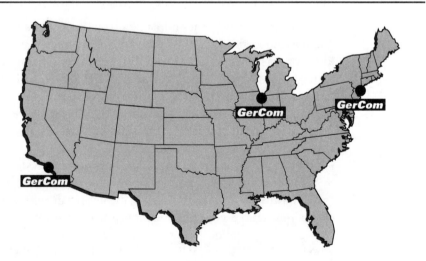

FIGURE 5.2

Two—count 'em, two—
locations in Chicago

California	Illinois	Illinois	New York
1st – 5th Stories	3 Story	3rd and 5th Stories	10th –11th Stories
Downtown	Manufacturing Plant	Downtown	New York City
Los Angeles	Chicago Suburbs	Chicago	

We have five Windows NT workstations, and three are in the executive suite. They belong to me, our controller, and our head of human resources. At my insistence, MIS started learning NT about a year ago. Two of our midlevel MIS staff use NT workstations for everything they do. All five workstations are linked to our Novell servers using NT's built-in IPX/SPX networking capabilities.

Because we're a young company, most workstations are 486-based or better, though a lot of the 486 systems have only 8MB of memory. Still, as I noted in the sidebar "More on User Workstations" in this chapter, we've got a lot of upgrading to do before we can fully implement Exchange.

With information from the first iteration of our user-needs and geographical assessments in hand, GerCom's MIS folks are already beginning to think about who's where, and how to structure the company's NT and Exchange hierarchy. They've also started lobbying me and our controller for user workstation upgrades.

Assess Your Organization's Network

In this step, you just want to know what your network looks like now. This isn't the place to get into what kinds of networking you'll need; that comes later. You need to answer four key questions here: What's connected to what, and how? (If you're counting, that's two questions.) How much bandwidth have we got on each network? And, finally, how reliable are your networks?

What's Connected to What, and How?

Generally, in answering the first question, you should start at the top of your organization and work down to the domain or server level. For each link, name the physical connection, the networking topology, and the networking protocols running on the connection. For example, *physical connection = local hardwire, networking topology = Ethernet, networking protocols = IPX/SPX, TCP/IP, SNA.* This information, especially when combined with the information you've collected in steps 1 and 2, will prove invaluable as you start to plan for the Exchange connectivity you'll need.

In looking at your organization's network, don't forget about connections to the outside world. Do you have connections to the Internet, to X.400 messaging systems, to trading partners? If you've got such connections, pay particular attention to existing naming conventions. They may limit your choices in naming the key entities in the Exchange hierarchy.

How Much Bandwidth Have We Got on Each Network?

To assess the bandwidth on each of your networks, you'll need some help from a network monitoring tool. If your networks are NT-based you can try using NT's Performance Monitor to get a handle on traffic. Microsoft's Systems Management Server has some pretty good network monitoring capabilities, too. For NetWare systems, try one of the many software-based network traffic monitors out there. A lot of modern network hubs, switches, and such also come with excellent network monitoring software. If you're flush with cash, go for a hardware-based monitor, such as Network General's Sniffer.

What you want here is a chart that tells you, on average, how much of a network's bandwidth is available during each of the 24 hours in a day. You'll have to take several samples to get reliable data, but it's worth it. A warning light should go on in your head if you're already using more than, say, 40 percent of the available bandwidth on any network during daytime hours and you're not already running a heavy-duty messaging system like Exchange. With that kind of scenario, you just might have to make some changes in the network before installing Exchange. We'll talk about those changes later; for now, be sure to collect this data on available bandwidth and incorporate it into your organizational maps.

How Reliable Are Our Networks?

Having a reliable network is a really important issue. More and more in corporate America, there is strong pressure to centralize network servers. Centralization makes good economic sense. If all network servers are in one place, one set of staff can support and monitor them, assuring 7-day-a-week, 24-hour-a-day uptime.

That's quite true. However, 7-day x 24-hour server availability is useless if the networks people use to get to the servers are unreliable. I've seen this little scenario play itself out in several organizations: centralize the servers; the network fails; users can't get to their now mission-critical e-mail and other data; responsible IS planners are roundly criticized; lower level IS personnel are even more heavily criticized or fired. Grrr!

Bottom line: don't make your users work on unreliable networks. If your networks can't come close to matching the reliability of your servers, put the servers closer to their users. The little extra it costs to manage decentralized servers is worth the access insurance it buys. Sure, get those networks up to par, but don't risk your Exchange implementation on centralized servers before the reliable network is in place to support them.

An Example: GerCom's Networks

Figure 5.3 shows the GerCom map with some higher-level connectivity information added. In Los Angeles, GerCom has a dedicated T1 TCP/IP link to the Internet. By the way, the registered Internet domain name is "gerberco." GerCom's four office buildings are connected in serial fashion through NetWare servers, using a networking topology consisting of nondedicated, asynchronous dial-up lines and the Point-to-Point Protocol (PPP). We run both IPX/SPX and TCP/IP on the dial-up network.

FIGURE 5.3

GerCom's existing cross-country links

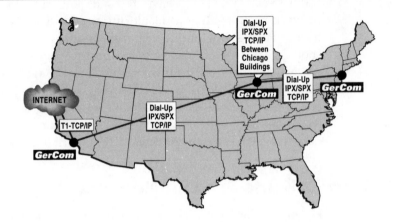

You can see in Figure 5.4 that NetWare servers and user workstations in all Ger-Com buildings are linked by Ethernet and IPX/SPX. We also run TCP/IP to support workstation connections to our Sun UNIX servers, where e-mail and our Oracle databases reside.

FIGURE 5.4

GerCom's existing in-building networks

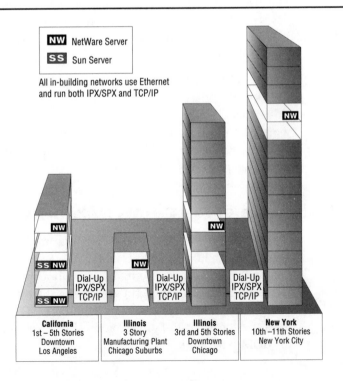

Establish Naming Conventions

It's time to set some criteria for naming the four key elements in your Exchange hierarchy: the organization, sites, servers, and recipients. Your goal here is to establish a logical and consistent set of naming conventions that fit in well with your real-world organizational structure and culture.

As I pointed out in Chapter 2, the choices you make for Exchange organization- and site-naming conventions—at least at the outset—influence both the ease with which you'll be able to manage your Exchange system and the default e-messaging addresses assigned to users. It's true that, at any time, you can change your naming conventions and even the names you've assigned to specific instances of any of the four elements in your Exchange hierarchy. Some of these changes are easy to make, while others are much more difficult. But why put yourself in the position of having to make a bunch of midcourse corrections? Do your best to get things right on take-off.

Naming the Organization, Sites, and Servers

Here's one easy and usually safe naming convention you can use:

- Organization = master company name
- Site = a geographical location
- Server = departmental names

Names for organizations and sites can be up to 64 characters long, but I'd suggest keeping them around 10 characters out of respect for people at "foreign" sites who may have to type in these names as part of a recipient's e-messaging address. Server names are limited to a maximum of 15 characters.

For most names, almost any character is permitted. However, for organization, site, and server names I strongly suggest you use only the 26 upper- and lower-case letters of the alphabet and the numerals 0 through 9. Don't use spaces, underscores, or any accented letters.

If you don't follow this convention, I guarantee that sometime, somewhere, you'll get into trouble. For example, I named a site "LA_HOME" in an early test implementation of Exchange. The underscore became a question mark when the site name was used to construct X.400 addresses. The question mark was technically okay, but it threw users who sometimes had to give their address with an underscore and sometimes with a question mark, depending on the type of address it was. Bottom line: Don't get fancy when naming organizations, sites, and servers.

Naming Recipient Mailboxes

You'll also need some criteria for naming mailboxes. There are four key names for each Exchange mailbox: the first name, the last name, the display name, and the alias name. Exchange administrators create and modify these names in the Exchange Administrator program. You enter the first and last names and, by default, Exchange constructs the display names and alias names from the first and last names. You can change the rules for constructing default display names and alias names, and you can also alter these manually once they've been created. In Figure 5.5 you can see the different names for my Exchange mailbox.

FIGURE 5.5

Exchange creates display and alias mailbox names using first and last names.

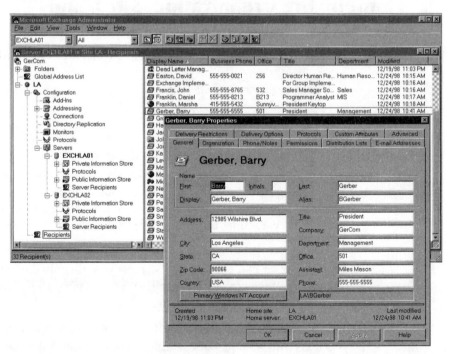

Display Names

The Exchange client global address book shows the display name for each mailbox (see Figure 5.6). You'll need to decide on a convention for display names. You've got two basic options: *first-name-space-last-name (John Smith)* or *last-name-comma-space-first-name (Smith, John)*. You can also set up custom defaults. You can change the defaults at any time, but the change applies only to newly created mailboxes. Fortunately, there's a fairly easy way to automatically change the display names of old mailboxes as well.

Display names can be up to 256 characters long. Display names are only a convenience—they're not a part of the mailbox's e-message address. They are, however, the way in which Exchange users find the people they want to communicate with—so don't scrimp when setting them up. You might even want to include department names and/or titles in display names so that users aren't faced with ambiguous selections, as they might be if they encountered a list of 25 recipients named *John Smith*.

Practically speaking, display name lengths should be limited only by your users' willingness to read through lots of stuff to find the mailbox they're looking for.

FIGURE 5.6

The Exchange client global address book shows each mailbox's display name.

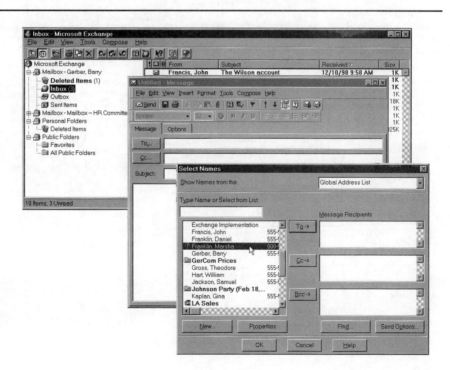

Full-blown religious arguments have sprung up around the metaphysics of display name conventions. I'll leave the decision to you (though, as you'll see, I do have my own preference).

Alias Names

In many e-messaging systems the user's mailbox is identified by an alias name, which is part of the mailbox's address. Either Exchange itself or the gateway for the foreign mail system constructs an address using the alias. Figure 5.7 shows the four addresses that Exchange built for me for cc:Mail, Microsoft Mail for PC Networks, the Internet, and X.400. My MS Mail and Internet addresses use the alias 'bgerber'. cc:Mail and X.400 addresses do not use aliases. Rather, they use the full first and last name attributes of the user.

Aliases can be up to 64 characters long. That's too long, since some people in foreign messaging systems will have to type in the alias as part of an e-messaging address. Try to keep aliases short—10 characters is long enough.

FIGURE 5.7

Exchange Server uses mailbox Alias or the First and Last names to construct e-mail addresses.

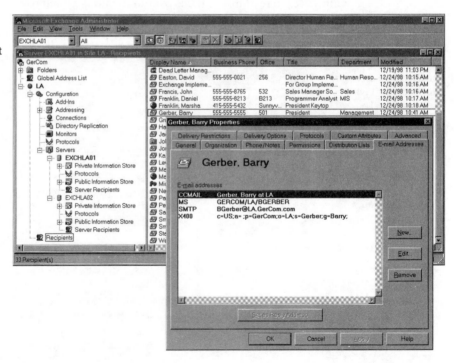

For some foreign messaging system addressing schemes, Exchange must remove illegal characters and shorten the alias to meet maximum character-length requirements. This can result in grief for your users who might have to give out slightly different addresses for different systems, so do what you can to ensure that aliases are constructed using less-esoteric characters.

As with display names, you can set default rules for the aliases that Exchange assigns newly created users. There are several options for these defaults, including *full-first-name-first-letter-of-last-name (JohnS)* and *first-letter-of-first-name-full-last-name (JSmith)*.

Alias naming conventions are a religious issue, too, so you'll get no recommendations from me.

An Example: GerCom's Naming Conventions

GerCom chose to follow the simple guidelines listed above for naming its organization and sites. The organization name is "GerCom." Site naming is based on geography (cities): "LA," "NY," and "Chicago."

We did run into one problem in selecting an organization name: You'll remember from the GerCom network assessment that our registered Internet domain name is "gerberco." My current Internet address for GerCom is bgerber<64>gerberco.com. (Don't try to send anything to that address; remember that all this GerCom stuff is fake.) Given the name I chose for my organization (*GerCom*), the Internet address that Exchange will construct for me by default will be 'bgerber<64>LA.gercom.com'. Take another look at Figure 5.7, if you don't believe me. We could have used "gerberco" for our Exchange organization name, but we like "gercom" too much. We also could have tinkered with DNS MX records on the UNIX side to redirect mail sent to gerberco over to gercom, but since our Internet mail flow is limited right now, we decided to go whole hog and deregister the name gerberco and instead register gercom as our Internet domain name.

We nonconformists at GerCom didn't follow the guidelines for server naming, though. As I mentioned in Chapter 2, rather than create separate departmental servers at each site, my MIS department and I prefer to create one Exchange server, fill it up with users, and then set up a new one. This is a nice approach for smaller organizations that don't want to invest in lots of hardware at the outset. Many large organizations also like this approach, since there's often not much to be gained in identifying different Exchange servers with different departmental units.

GerCom servers get names based on this convention: *EXCH + SITE + an order-ing number.* The first server in the site LA is EXCHLA01, the second is EXCHLA02, and so on.

GerCom display names use the *last-name-comma-space-first-name (Smith, John)* convention. Remember that the display name is what people see when they go looking for a mailbox in the Exchange client. I just think it's easier to find people by their last names (all the Smiths) rather than by their first names (all the Johns). For similar reasons, alias naming at GerCom is based on the *first-letter-of-first-name-full-last-name (JSmith)* convention. Since Exchange and NT security are so tightly integrated, we'll use the same *first-letter-of-first-name-full-last-name (JSmith)* convention for NT usernames. I should note that I had no trouble imposing these conventions on my very compliant and, it should be noted, imaginary MIS department.

Select a Microsoft Networking Domain Model

You've got four networking domain models to choose from. Which is right for your organization? Here you should think about both today and tomorrow, because it's not easy to change a domain model. Moving to a new model often involves changing server and domain names and moving users and resources to different or new domains, and neither of these is pleasant to do with NT. As with Exchange naming conventions, the best way is to get it right the first time.

Go back to Chapter 4 and take a look at the section on the four domain models. Decide how your organization is structured and pick the model that best fits that structure.

An Example: The GerCom Domain Model

At GerCom we've decided on the multiple-master domain model. Look how much we've grown in five chapters: Though we have only 2,500 employees now, we're already in three cities. We're gonna be *big,* and we need to think seriously about exceeding those users-per-domain limits I discussed in Chapter 4.

Figure 5.8 shows how we'll structure the domains. We'll have a master domain for each city, as well as a single resource domain in each of the four buildings we now occupy. Right now only the Chicago master domain will be responsible for multiple-resource domains—one for each of our two Chicago buildings. As we add cities we'll add master domains and appropriate resource domains. As we add buildings in cities we'll add resource domains.

FIGURE 5.8

GerCom's implementation of the multiple-master domain model

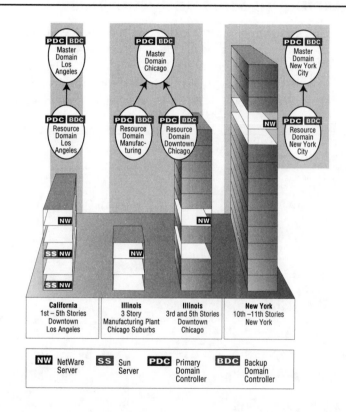

GerCom doesn't have a lot of NT expertise in-house. (I'm probably the most knowledgeable employee right now.) We're planning to hire an NT networking guru right away, and once that person is in place we'll determine how many more NT support staffers we'll need. With the ability to remotely manage NT, we should be able to stay light on the NT support side, at least until we get more deeply into programming Exchange-enabled custom applications. For now, the NT people will report to the Exchange manager we decided on in step 1. That's kind of unusual, but for now we primarily need NT support staff to implement Exchange.

Define Site Boundaries

When defining site boundaries you have to remember a couple of things. First, Exchange sites and Microsoft network domains are related. Second, all of the Exchange servers in a site must have certain networking capabilities.

Exchange Sites and Domains

One domain may include one or more sites. In addition, one or more Exchange sites can cross two or more networking domains (see Figure 5.9). If you want your Exchange system to be easy to administer and manage, I strongly suggest you stay away from multiple sites in a domain and sites that cross multiple domains. Stick with the one-site, one-domain model.

FIGURE 5.9

The three ways that Microsoft networking domains and Exchange Server sites can relate to each other.

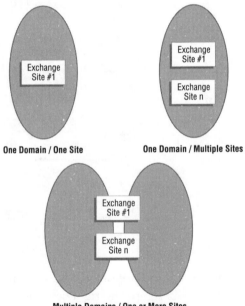

All of the Exchange servers and users in a site must be able to communicate freely, without issuing passwords each time they need to access each other. As I noted in Chapter 4, Exchange server freedom of speech is tightly linked to domain security.

Required Networking Capabilities

With the right security in place, the moment an Exchange server starts running it automatically begins communicating with other Exchange servers in its site. You don't have to do a thing to start these communications—they just happen. The first time this happens, you'll literally jump for joy, especially if you're used to those old fashioned e-mail systems like Microsoft Mail for PCs with all their gizmo gateways, dirsync machines and such.

When communicating with each other, Exchange servers in a site automatically swap user messages and frequently update one another's directory information. Optionally, they can also cross-replicate all or part of their public folders. As noted in Chapter 3, intrasite cross-server directory replication not only helps keep directories up-to-date on all Exchange servers, but it also brings a degree of fault tolerance to Exchange. As long as you have one good copy of the directory on one Exchange server, the others can reconstruct a good portion of their directories from it. Don't let this lull you into thinking you don't need to do regular backups. There is some server-specific information in each server's directory that can only be protected with a backup. It can't be reconstructed from the copies of the directory on other servers.

Frequent intrasite directory replication increases network traffic a bit. Also, since users in a site often have some affinity for each other, you can usually expect higher user messaging and folder replication traffic between servers in one site than between servers in different sites.

All of this intrasite interserver network traffic requires that Exchange servers in a site be connected by a high-bandwidth dedicated network, but high bandwidth isn't absolute. For example, from Exchange's perspective, a 155Mb/sec ATM link isn't high-bandwidth if you're eating up 154.9Mb/sec sending continuous streams of video images. There are no hard and fast rules here, but any physical network that can provide Exchange with 512Kb/sec of bandwidth most of the time should be adequate. Lower bandwidths can work in cases where directories change very little and public folder replication is nonexistent or kept at a bare minimum. Physical networks capable of delivering at least this kind of dedicated bandwidth include (in increasing bandwidth availability) faster Frame Relay and satellite, full T1, microwave, T3, Ethernet, Token Ring, Fast Ethernet, FDDI, ATM, and SONET.

Intrasite communications between servers is based on the remote procedure calls (RPCs) discussed in Chapter 4. Networks must run networking protocols that support the RPCs; these include IPX/SPX, NetBEUI, TCP/IP, SNA, NetBIOS,

Windows Sockets, and Named Pipes. For the best overall performance, I've found TCP/IP is generally the best option, though NetBEUI/NetBIOS can be quite impressive in smaller, non-routed nets.

A good deal of the information that moves between Exchange servers in a site is transmitted in Exchange's native MAPI-based format. As you'll see later, when information leaves an Exchange site it isn't always possible to transmit it in MAPI format.

An Example: GerCom's Site Boundaries

As you'll remember from its geographical assessment, GerCom is located in three cities: Los Angeles, Chicago, and New York. It has more than two physical locations only in Chicago. Though you already know this from GerCom's site-naming conventions, the company will have Exchange sites in each city.

Except in Chicago, our existing Ethernet-TCP/IP-IPX/SPX networks are all we need for intrasite connectivity. We'll have to add a higher-bandwidth connection between our two buildings in Chicago, and we're planning to use a T1 connection for that. Figure 5.10 shows the GerCom building diagram with this new site boundary information imposed on it.

FIGURE 5.10

GerCom's site boundaries

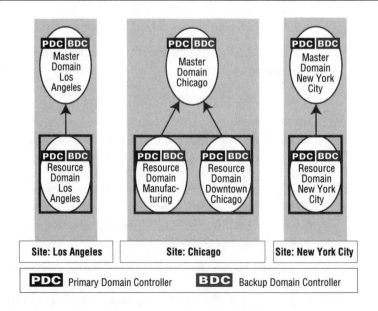

We plan to station an Exchange administrator at each GerCom site. These three MIS employees will be responsible for Exchange installation, testing, implementation, and management. They'll also provide NT system management backup. To do these things, we feel that the three employees must be on-site. We think that one person at each site will be enough, but we're open to adding people if more are needed. The Exchange administrators will report to GerCom's new corporate Exchange manager, mentioned in step 1.

With Exchange Server's great remote management capabilities, the Exchange administrators in each city will be able to help out at other sites when needed without leaving their offices. And when we add administrators, they won't have to be assigned to a specific site—they can remotely go wherever their Exchange administrative skills are required.

The four end-user–oriented Exchange training and app-development staffers mentioned in step 1 will be distributed among the sites as well. Two will be in Los Angeles, one in Chicago, and one in New York. In addition to their main responsibilities, these folks will also back up the Exchange site administrators. Because of the remote management capabilities built into NT Server and Exchange Server, the backup function won't require full knowledge of NT or Exchange Server. These folks will mainly be ready to help when a local hand is physically required.

Plan Intersite Links

As you'll remember from Chapter 3, you link sites by running one or more Exchange connectors on Exchange servers in each site. There's no need for each Exchange server in a site to run its own connectors; one Exchange server can serve all the intersite needs of all Exchange servers in a site. However, if a site has two or more Exchange servers, it often makes sense to run site connectors on multiple servers. This improves performance and, if you use different network links for each connector, allows for redundant links between sites. Figure 5.11 should make this a bit clearer.

Site Link Options

In Chapter 3, I noted that you can connect sites either *directly* or *indirectly*. Direct connections are point-to-point between servers; indirect links pass through foreign e-messaging systems. Both direct and indirect connections use messages to move user communications and directory and public folder replication information between Exchange servers in different sites. With direct connections the servers talk directly to each other. With indirect connections the servers communicate by sending messages through a mediating system, such as a public X.400 service or the Internet.

FIGURE 5.11

Making the Exchange intersite connection.

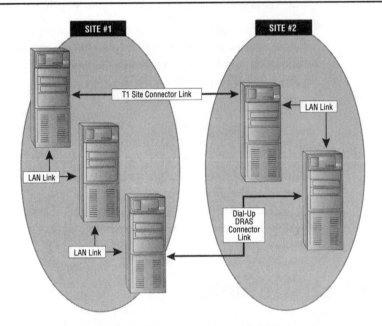

NOTE

I use the terms *connection* and *link* to refer to two very different things. In the paragraph above, they refer to the way in which servers *communicate* with each other, be it directly or indirectly. In other places in this book, *connection* and *link* refer to actual *physical and protocol-level networking options,* such as Ethernet, TCP/IP, and X.400. I tried without success to find another word to modify the terms *direct* and *indirect*.

When connecting Exchange sites, you get to choose between five connector options:

- The Site Connector (direct link only)
- The X.400 Connector (direct and indirect links)

- The Dynamic RAS Connector (direct link only)
- The Internet Mail Service (direct and indirect links)

Let's look at each of these in more detail.

The Site Connector

Of all the Exchange connectors, the Site Connector is the fastest and simplest to set up and manage. And of all the ways to link sites, the Site Connector is most similar to the automatic, built-in links between Exchange servers in the same site. It moves messages and directory and folder replication information between Exchange sites using the Open Systems Foundation (OSF) remote procedure calls. The only difference is that the Site Connector uses standard messages for all three functions, while Exchange servers within a site perform directory replication more directly.

The Site Connector requires a continuous network. It doesn't support dial-up links, and it's best suited to Exchange intersite connections with heavy user loads and directory and public folder replication message duties. If you already have a wide area network with adequate bandwidth in place, the Site Connector can be especially attractive, because you don't need to add any networking infrastructure to support the connector. Of course, if you're expecting heavy cross-site network loads, you'll need high-bandwidth network connections like those provided by topologies such as T1, Ethernet, Token Ring, T3, Fast Ethernet, FDDI, ATM, and SONET. When you begin considering the higher-capacity networking topologies listed here to link sites, you might want to go one step further and merge the sites to take advantage of Exchange Server's higher performance insite communications.

The X.400 Connector

When used for direct site links, the X.400 Connector works a lot like the Site Connector. It sends and receives user communications and directory and public folder replication information as messages. It doesn't use the OSF RPCs, however. The X.400 Connector can move messages between sites in X.400 format or, like the Site Connector, in native MAPI format. If you choose to use the X.400 format, the messages will have to be translated into X.400 before they leave the originating site and then translated back into MAPI after arriving at the receiving site.

The X.400 Connector runs on top of a special physical transport stack that supports TCP/IP, OSI TP0 (X.25), and OSI TP4/CLNP networking protocols. If you're into the OSI world, these protocols will be familiar to you. If not, you can find info on them in any of a number of fine books on OSI-based networking. Like the Site Connector, in direct link mode the X.400 Connector can handle heavy intersite loads given adequate bandwidth.

The X.400 Connector is a bit slower than the Site Connector, both because it has to translate to and from X.400 format when that format is used for intersite communications, and because there's some networking overhead involved in X.400 communications. However, the X.400 Connector gives you more control than the Site Connector over a site link and what passes over it. For example, you can schedule X.400 site connections, restrict the message size, and specify which sites you'll accept messages from. The Site Connector doesn't support restrictions of this sort. The X.400 Connector allows direct server-to-server links over dial-up lines using X.25, for example. The Site Connector doesn't support dial-up links.

You can also use the X.400 Connector for indirect Exchange site links. In this case you connect each Exchange site to a public X.400 provider's network. The sites can be connected to the same provider network or to different ones. Of course, if different providers are used, they must be able to communicate with each other. You can use any of the networking protocols noted above to make these connections.

Cost considerations lead most organizations to opt for lower, sub–local area network bandwidth links to public X.400 providers. That's fine, but it means that indirect site links should be used mostly for low-traffic site connections and to provide redundant links for sites already connected by higher-bandwidth direct links.

The Dynamic RAS Connector

Unlike the Site Connector and like the X.400 Connector, the Dynamic RAS Connector (DRASC) lets you link sites that don't have full-time networks between them. You can use the DRASC for ad hoc asynchronous links using voice, X.25, and ISDN physical connections. Exchange servers talk directly to each other over the DRASC, so DRASC connections support the OSF RPCs. As should be obvious from its name, the DRASC is based on NT's RAS (Remote Access Server), which I talked about in the last chapter. You'll remember that the RAS provides NetBEUI, TCP/IP, or IPX/SPX protocol support on top of PPP.

With the DRASC you get many of the controls that the X.400 Connector delivers without all the complexities of X.400. Exchange data is always moved in native MAPI format, though you won't see any great speed advantage since you're connecting at ISDN bandwidths at best. So, as with low-bandwidth, indirect X.400 site links, use the DRASC for low-traffic or redundant links.

The Internet Mail Service and Other Microsoft Mail Connectors

Both the Internet Mail Service and Microsoft Mail Connector let you link sites directly and indirectly. I won't spend a lot of time on these here; each gets coverage in later chapters. For now, suffice it to say that the caveats about low-speed links also apply to the use of these two connectors.

An Example: GerCom's Intersite Connections

So how about GerCom? What is that paragon of Enter key manufacturers going to do to connect its three sites? Well, as president I've had to swallow hard a couple of times, but we're going to pop for T1 links between our three sites and use Site Connectors. The main reason for this decision is the amount of cross-site traffic we expect our neat but demanding applications to generate in the form of public folder replication and cross-site movement of larger messages. Figure 5.12 shows the GerCom building diagram with our planned intersite connections in place.

Those T1 lines aren't going to be cheap, but we have high hopes that Exchange will revolutionize the way we do business. As you'll see later in this chapter, we're also planning to do some indirect links. These will add important redundancy to our Exchange network.

Plan Servers and User Links to Them

There's quite a bit to do in planning your servers and user links. You need to decide what kinds of hardware to use for each of your Exchange servers. After that you have to figure out how to back up the servers. Then you have to make sure you've got adequate bandwidth on your local networks to keep Exchange happy; if you don't have it, you've got to decide how to get it. Finally, before you go on to the next step in the Exchange design process, you have to think about remote users and how you'll connect them to Exchange.

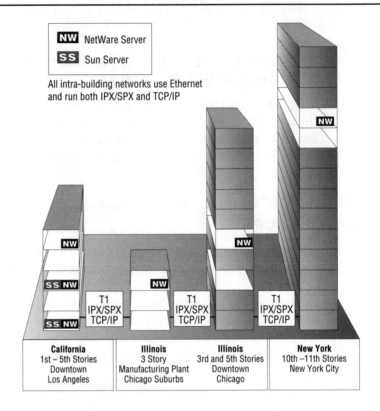

FIGURE 5.12

GerCom's intersite connections.

Designing Your Exchange Servers

The intricacies of Exchange Server design and fine-tuning could occupy a whole book; you'll have to experiment here. Install NT Server and Exchange Server, then run the optimization app that comes with Exchange Server. (We'll talk more about installation and optimization in Chapter 6.) Next, take out that set of user-demand numbers you put together when you did your user-needs assessment. Plug those numbers into LoadSim and run it against a reasonable Exchange server machine—say, a 200MHz Pentium with 128MB of memory and at least two 2GB SCSI hard drives. Don't run LoadSim on your Exchange server. Instead, run it on a separate 166MHz or better Pentium-based NT workstation with at least 64MB of memory. And don't try to simulate more than 200 users on one LoadSim machine. If you don't follow these guidelines, LoadSim may not be able to generate the loads you've asked it to, and you could be led to believe that your Exchange server hardware is adequate when it's not.

SCSI-2, Not Enhanced IDE

Enhanced IDE drives are nice, but unless you know that you'll never need more than 12GB or so of storage (that is, four 3GB drives) on an Exchange server, they're not going to meet your needs. Better to choose SCSI-2 drives. They're fast, with much more lenient maximum drive limits. And SCSI-2 drives can be had in sizes of 9GB or more.

If LoadSim indicates that you've got too little computing power for your needs, start by moving Exchange's transaction logs to another disk drive (this is covered in Chapter 9). If this doesn't solve your problem, you'll need to run NT's Performance Monitor to locate any bottlenecks. (See the Sybex book *Mastering Windows NT Server 4*, by Mark Minasi, Christina Anderson, and Elizabeth Creegan, for more on using the Performance Monitor.)

Look at the obvious culprits: server hard disk capacity, memory, and CPU. Based on the results you get from the Performance Monitor, you can decide what to do. Distributing Exchange databases files differently—for example, putting the server's public folders on a different drive, RAID array, or server—can significantly improve an Exchange server's performance in some situations. Adding RAM to an Exchange server can make a world of difference in performance, because it allows the server to do more work without having to waste time paging RAM segments out to disk. Adding more processors to multiprocessor machines, or moving to more powerful processors like those from Digital Equipment, can be a quick route to improved performance. However, be careful here: Focus on disk capacity and RAM before turning to CPU power. More or faster CPUs can indeed improve performance, but they're not going to fix performance problems originating from poorly optimized disks or too little RAM. If all of this vertical scaling can't solve your problem, consider going horizontal and splitting users across multiple Exchange servers. Exchange makes horizontal scaling very easy.

Server Fault Tolerance

As you're designing your servers, don't forget the whole issue of server fault tolerance. Multiprocessor machines are starting to show up with processors that can back each other up in case of failure. You'll need a version of NT that can handle this sort of processor redundancy. In addition to processor redundancy, look for systems with error-correcting memory. On the disk side, consider multiple controllers and nicely redundant RAID level 5 technologies. Remember, NT Server can do software-based RAID level 5. Many machines are now available with two or more redundant power supplies. Don't forget uninterruptable power supplies (UPSes). More about them later in this chapter. In some cases, you can swap out failed RAID drives and power supplies without even bringing down your system. And, be sure to consider the new technologies that let you set up multiple NT/Exchange servers that mirror each other, with server A able to quickly and automatically replace server B in case server B fails.

You'll need to start thinking now about how you'll manage user storage on each server. Storage management gives you more control over how much of what is stored on Exchange server disks, and it helps you remain within your server disk budget. There are several disk management questions you'll want to answer here, including:

- Do you want some or all of your users to store messages in personal folders on workstation or non-Exchange networked disk drives, instead of in their Exchange server-based mailboxes? (See Chapter 2 for more on these two options.)

- For those who will use their Exchange server mailboxes, do you want to limit the amount of storage they can use?

- Do you want to impose limits on the storage used by public folders?

- If you have public folders containing messages that lose value with time—for example, messages from Internet lists or USENET news feeds—do you want Exchange to automatically delete messages from these folders based on message age?

You can base your answers to most of these questions on the results of your user-needs assessment, though you're bound to make adjustments as you pass through iterations of the design process. And, do note, that while its tempting to force users to store messages in personal folders on local or non-Exchange networked disk drives to save on Exchange server disk, you then run the risk that key user messages won't get backed up. As the ever-present "they" say, "You pays your money and you takes your chances."

Once you're comfortable with the basic design of your servers, you need to plan for uninterruptible power supplies (UPSs). I consider a UPS to be part of a server, not an add-on. UPSs are cheap, given the peace of mind they can bring. You really don't want your NT or Exchange servers crashing because of power losses. Get enough UPSs to serve the power needs of each server, and get a UPS that comes with software to gracefully shut down your servers if power stays off for an extended period.

Backing Up Your Exchange Servers

When you know what your Exchange servers and networks will look like, you can begin thinking about backing up your servers. You need to use backup software that is especially designed for Exchange's client/server architecture. Such software lets you back up an Exchange server's directory and information store without shutting down Exchange processes and, thus, closing off user access to the server. The software communicates with Exchange's directory and information store services to ensure that the databases they are responsible for are fully backed up. I'll talk more about the fine points of Exchange backup in Chapter 10.

NT's own Backup program has been modified to do a proper backup of Exchange servers. Other NT backup vendors, such as Cheyenne Software (ArcServe) and Seagate Software (Backup Exec, Backup Director, and Storage Manager), have released modified versions of their products that can properly back up Exchange Server.

You can back up an Exchange server either locally or over the network. When you back it up over the network, you can run the backup from another NT/Exchange server or from an NT-only server.

For Exchange servers with lots of disk space (5GB or more) and slow network links to potential backup servers (less than 100Mb/sec), I strongly suggest that you bypass the networked server backup option and do the backup locally on and from the Exchange server itself. You'll have to spend some money on a backup device and software for the Exchange server, but you'll get it back in available bandwidth and faster backups. Available bandwidth means that other network-dependent tasks—and there are lots of those on an Exchange network— run faster. And faster backups mean shorter periods of that awful feeling you get when important data is not yet on tape.

Whether you back up over the network or locally, don't skimp on backup hardware. You're going to *add* hard disk storage to your Exchange server, not take it away. Go for high-capacity 4mm or 8mm tape backup systems. Think about tape autoloaders—those neat gizmos that give one or more tape drives automatic access to anything from a few tapes to hundreds of them.

Don't forget those personal folders stored on user workstations. You have to decide who will be responsible for backing them up—Exchange staff, other MIS staff, or users themselves. The technology for centralized workstation backup is readily available. For example, agents are available for most third-party NT backup products that let you back up all or part of specific user workstations.

While you're at it, don't forget NT server backup. If you have NT servers that don't support Exchange, you'll need to back them up, too. You can back up an NT server over the network, but if the servers have lots of disk space, consider the same local backup strategy for non-Exchange NT servers that I suggested for Exchange servers.

Networking Your Exchange Users

Once you've got your server design down, you'll need to think about how to connect users to your Exchange servers. It's usually a no-brainer for local connections, though you'll want to be sure you've got enough bandwidth to move the stuff that Exchange makes available to your users. For example, a message I put together with a very simple embedded color screen capture is 855K. The graphic looks impressive, and it let me make a point that I never could have made without it. Still, I wouldn't want my recipients to get it over a 4Mb/sec Token Ring or 2.5Mb/sec Arcnet link, or even over a very busy Ethernet connection.

If you're concerned about LAN bandwidth, there are a couple of things you can do. First, get rid of those slower networks. Dump 4Mb/sec Token Ring and Arcnet networks. Second, segment your LANs to reduce the number of users on any segment. In this situation you might even put multiple network adapters in your Exchange server, one for each segment or group of segments. And do take a look at faster networking technologies like 100Mb/sec Ethernet and those really neat networking switches that can replace routers and significantly improve network backbone performance. Yes, any of these options will cost your organization some bucks, but they're likely to be bucks well spent. It's just like the way it is with user workstations: Slow technologies don't get used, and the benefits of the applications you're trying to run on top of them are lost.

Don't forget remote Exchange users. Many users need to keep in touch when they're away from the office, whether at home or on the road. Remote users can connect to an NT server by way of its Remote Access Server. The RAS gives users the equivalent of a hardwired connection, so for them it's more or less like being on the office LAN. The major difference is that they probably won't stay connected all the time—they'll connect to send and receive messages, and the rest of the time they'll work offline.

Remote users also can connect to their Exchange servers by way of direct TCP/IP links through an Internet Service Provider (ISP). And don't forget the new Internet-based POP3 and web browser–based client options that are supported by Exchange Server 5. With their lighter weight demands on workstation resources, they could be just what the doctor ordered for your remote users.

We'll talk more about how to implement remote Exchange links in a later chapter. At this point you need to think about how many users will likely need a RAS connection to each site at one time. If it's just one or two, you can set up a couple of modems on an Exchange or NT server and let users dial in to those. If you expect lots of users you might want to consider setting up a separate NT server dedicated to dial-in connections. Remember, one NT server with the right hardware can support up to 256 dial-in RAS connections.

If users will be connecting to their Exchange servers over the Internet, you'll need an Internet connection of adequate bandwidth to support them. Unless you have few users who need Internet access, think T1.

An Example: GerCom's Servers and User Links

With one exception, we GerComites are pretty sure from our LoadSim tests that the "reasonable machine" I described above—a 200MHz Pentium with 128MB of memory and two 2GB SCSI hard disks—will work for now for each of our four Exchange servers. The exception? The LA server. With the heaviest staff load and an Internet connection to boot, we've decided to buy a four-processor capable 200MHz Pentium machine and put 512MB of RAM and 32GB of hardware-based RAID level 5 disk space on the LA server. (We bought the LA machine with only two processors; we'll add more as needed.)

Remember how the GerCom executive suite was possibly going to get its own server? MIS overruled the idea. They really don't want the responsibility of administering two Exchange servers in LA, at least at the outset. Instead they opted for LA's special powerhouse server. Of course, as soon as it looks as if we execs (or any other group, for that matter) need it, we'll get our own Exchange server.

We'll try to limit all but select users to 10MB of mailbox storage. Select users will be those heavily involved in building, testing, or using some of those e-messaging–enabled apps we're planning to do; they'll get as much as 200MB to play with. Since most users won't have write access to public folders, at least at the outset, we're not going to impose any limits on storage there. We will, however, set Exchange to automatically delete messages older than two weeks in those public folders that contain e-mail from Internet lists and older than 5 days for USENET news groups stored in our public folders.

Just from thinking through all the storage issues, there's one thing we know for sure: We won't get far on the 4GB or 32GB of disk space we put in our servers. We're already planning for increased storage needs.

Each server will have a UPS with orderly shutdown software. We'll back up for now with those neat little Hewlett-Packard SureStore 12000 tape autoloader units that let us put six 4mm tapes' worth of storage—up to 48 compressed GB — online. We plan to put one SureStore on each Exchange server. For now, to save some money, non-Exchange NT servers acting as primary or backup controllers will be backed up by the tape units on the Exchange servers.

As you'll remember, all but one of GerCom's networks had adequate bandwidth available; only the Engineering network had less than 60 percent of its bandwidth available during most of the day. We're planning to split the Engineering network into three nets: Two will support our two CAD groups, and the other will be for Engineering's clerical and administrative staff.

For remote users, we'll run the RAS dial-in on all of our servers. To start, there will be two standard voice-line–based RAS links on each server except the one in LA. (The large number of users in LA dictates that we start with six voice–based RAS lines.) In LA we'll also have an ISDN RAS connections for us execs who just can't tolerate those creepy 28.8-kbps modem links. We expect ISDN use at

GerCom to grow considerably over the next few years, unless a better option comes along.

We decided that, for now, we can get the most reliable remote connectivity with RAS, as opposed to TCP/IP or the new Internet-based client connects. However, we'll also test Exchange client TCP/IP links through an ISP and Exchange's new Internet-based web browser and POP3 clients. If they work well, we'll start moving remote users over to them. Heck, if they work well, we might even have some of our users with lower powered workstations use them instead of the resource-hog clients that come with Exchange Server.

Plan Connections to Other Systems

As John Donne almost said, "No organization is an island." In fact, today not only is no organization an island, but no organization can *afford* to be an island. With the e-messaging decade upon us, electronic messaging will increasingly become the primary means of communicating and doing business. Consider connections to systems outside of your organization to be necessities, not niceties.

Connection Options

Exchange sites can be connected directly to foreign X.400 systems, Internet mail systems, and legacy Microsoft Mail for PC and AppleTalk Networks systems and cc:Mail. Legacy system links can include not just message exchange but synchronization of Exchange and legacy address directories as well. With optional gateways from Microsoft and third-party vendors, you can connect to such systems as IBM PROFS, Verimation Memo, MCI Mail, CompuServe Mail, and fax devices. You can even use most of these gateways to link Exchange sites indirectly.

Exchange connections to foreign X.400 systems use the X.400 Connector. Such connections can be either continuous and permanent or dial-up, and they can use any of the X.400 Connector networking options listed above in step 7 (designing site links). The Internet Mail Service can use a continuous and permanent or dial up TCP/IP link to the Internet. Third-party gateways use a range of networking protocols; contact your gateway vendor for specifics. The Microsoft Mail Connector can run on top of almost anything, including TCP/IP, IPX/SPX,

NetBEUI, X.25, voice lines, and the RAS. The Exchange Directory Synchronization Agent mentioned in Chapter 3 lets you keep Exchange and legacy Microsoft messaging systems in sync. It uses the same networking protocols as the Microsoft Mail Connector.

Connect or Migrate?

Now is the time to decide if it's better to migrate users from legacy systems to Exchange Server or to wait and just link them to Exchange Server using various connectors, gateways, or even direct individual workstation connects in the case of Microsoft Mail for PC Networks or cc:Mail. The number of users to be migrated, the kinds of messaging systems they use, and the size of your own technical and training staff will play a big role in this decision. (Migration from Microsoft's and other messaging systems gets a whole chapter of its own later in this book.)

If you do decide to migrate users, you need to determine exactly which messaging systems you'll be migrating your users from: Microsoft Mail for PC Networks and/or AppleTalk Networks, Lotus cc:Mail, IBM PROFS, Verimation Memo, DEC All-in-One, and so on. Next, you need to figure out what kinds of tools, if any, exist that can help you migrate users from each messaging system to Exchange. For example, Exchange includes a nice migration application for Microsoft Mail users. Once you know what kinds of migration tools are available, you have to set a timetable for migration. Finally, you have to determine whether, based on your timetable, you should link other messaging systems to Exchange before you've migrated all users in them over to Exchange.

If you choose to migrate users to Exchange, be aware that Exchange can create new user accounts from text data files. If your legacy messaging system lets you output user information to a file and if you've got someone around who can write a program to assure that all the information Exchange needs is in the file in the right format and order, you should certainly consider using this nice, time-saving Exchange migration option. I'll talk more about migration in a later chapter.

In planning, don't underplay the importance of X.400 connections, especially if your company communicates with organizations outside of the United States. The X.400 suite includes the Electronic Document Interchange (EDI) standard, which supports electronic commerce by providing secure communications when you use your messaging system to, say, purchase products and services. Yes, you can secure your Internet mail communications, but X.400 is catching on, even in the United States. Keep it in mind.

As with intersite links, you need only one Exchange connector to link an entire site to a foreign messaging system. And as long as intersite links are in place, a single foreign messaging system connector can send and receive messages for an entire organization. As with intrasite connections, though, you might want more than one connector to balance network traffic loads and provide redundancy.

An Example: GerCom's External Links

GerCom will stick with its T1 Internet connection, moving management of the e-mail side of its Internet domain from our Sun systems to the Exchange server in Los Angeles. For the time being, at least, domain name service will continue to be handled by GerCom's Sun systems, though we're looking seriously at the DNS software available for NT.

We're also going to set up T1 Internet connections for our other two sites—for intersite redundancy, not direct delivery of Internet mail. Internet mail will still come into the LA Exchange site and be delivered to Chicago and New York through the Exchange system. Those T1s will put us in just the right position bandwidth-wise if our tests of remote access for Exchange users via the Internet are successful and we move most users from RAS to Internet-based Exchange client links.

To support the customer purchasing and payment applications that our salespeople want to build, we'll be using X.400 connections to six of our trading partners—two inside the United States and four outside. This will let us develop the app using the X.400 EDI standard. We'll have one T1 link to a public X.400 provider in Los Angeles. (Yikes, another T1!) Figure 5.13 shows all of GerCom's external links.

FIGURE 5.13

GerCom's connections to the outside world.

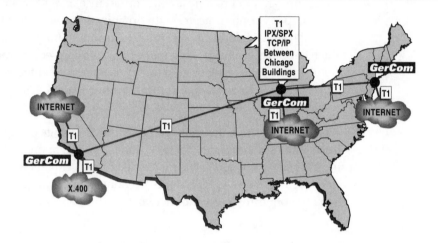

We don't have any legacy Microsoft Mail systems; we've been using our Sun systems to support UNIX Sendmail. Users have a bunch of POP mail clients for e-mail. As indicated above, we want to close down our UNIX-based mail system. So, we'll have to migrate our UNIX mail users to Exchange and deal with that e-messaging address change brought about by changing our registered Internet domain name from "gerberco" to "gercom." We'll use comma-delimited files from the UNIX system to create Exchange user accounts, so we should be able to set up all our user accounts easily. I'm less sure about migrating messages and any storage folders our users may have. We may just leave that up to users; most have reported that much of what's in their folders is no longer of use to them anyway.

Validate and Optimize the Design

Validation means ensuring that you've got a system that guarantees message delivery, integrity, and security. It also means making sure that the system you've designed is versatile enough to handle the range of documents, messaging formats, and applications your organization needs. *Optimization* is a balancing act in which you try to build the fastest, most stable and reliable systems you can while still meeting organizational requirements and keeping costs down.

Guaranteed Delivery

Guaranteed message delivery comes with reliable NT and Exchange servers and reliable internal and external networks. To increase the likelihood of guaranteed delivery, go for as much server fault tolerance and networking redundancy as your organization can afford. Use high-quality server and networking hardware and software inside your organization; buy outside networking services from stable, experienced, and well-established providers. Monitor the health of your networks, and be prepared to fix problems quickly. During the validation phase, send messages of all kinds through all of your connections, and then check to see if they arrive intact. When problems arise, use Exchange's own message-tracking tools to catch up with wayward messages, and take advantage of Exchange's network- and system-monitoring tools to discover why a message didn't get through.

Reliability is only one side of guaranteed message delivery. You also need Exchange servers that are sufficiently fast and networks that have the bandwidth to move messages quickly enough to meet maximum delivery time parameters. If you've specified that all messages should be delivered to all internal users within five minutes, for example, now's the time to see if your Exchange system is capable of performing up to spec. If not, you have to either increase your permissible maximum delivery times or, depending on the source of the problem, come up with speedier servers and/or higher-bandwidth networks.

Message Integrity

Message integrity means that messages arrive in the same form as they were transmitted. Problems with message integrity often can be traced to mismatched binary message-part encoding and decoding. For example, a binary attachment to a message bound for the Internet is UUencoded by the sender, while the receiver expects MIME encoding. As you'll see later, there are lots of ways to set coding parameters in Exchange to help avoid problems like this.

Message Security

Message security is a complex matter. Exchange's support for RSA encryption and public keys works fine for messages sent to other Exchange users inside an Exchange organization. But for messages destined for foreign e-messaging systems, think about add-on security services such as the Internet's SMTP Mail–oriented Privacy Enhanced Mail protocol.

You can try to validate message security on your own or with the help of a certified electronic data processing auditor. If security is important to your organization, I strongly recommend the latter.

System Versatility

Exchange's internal message formatting, along with formatting available in X.400 and Internet Mail, means that you'll be able to send documents of almost any type, containing virtually anything from text to last night's Letterman show. But be sure to validate that everything you need is there and works.

On the applications side, you've got all of the app development environments I mentioned in Chapter 1, as well as applications like Microsoft's Schedule+. Exchange Server is a very popular product, so plenty of Exchange-based e-messaging–enabled applications are already available from third-party vendors and there are many more in development. Keep your eyes open for the latest "killer" Exchange apps.

Optimization

When you've done everything to ensure guaranteed message delivery, message integrity, and security, as well as system versatility, it's time for *optimization*. You optimize your design by checking out alternatives that may help improve your Exchange system. The basic question is: Can you do it better, faster, easier? For example, you might want to consider implementing support for X.400 messaging, even though your organization has no current need for it, simply because competitors are moving toward it.

Optimization can also focus on reducing costs without compromising the quality of your system. For example, you might want to come up with lower-cost options for connecting Exchange sites or for realizing network redundancy.

An Example: Validating GerCom's Design

GerCom's design validates very well. Based on tests we've done, our system seems quite reliable, and we're meeting our ten-minute message-delivery maximum. Our certified data processing auditor says our messaging security looks good, though he did recommend that we adopt Privacy Enhanced Mail for communicating with customers who have Internet-based e-messaging systems.

We've covered the message format bases by including native Exchange, X.400 Mail, and Internet Mail capabilities. We've found nothing that we can't dump into a message and move through and out of our system with integrity. That includes everything from text to a full-color animated "film," complete with sound, showing our exclusive high-end, Fine Egyptian Marble Enter key in action.

On the applications side we've started working with both Schedule+ and Exchange's own Electronic Forms Designer. Both are performing as expected so far. Our development people are quite happy with the custom programming APIs available in Exchange. They're sure they can put together any of the applications our users have requested so far.

We put together and evaluated one alternative networking option, using the Dynamic RAS Connector in place of a Site Connector to link our Exchange sites. I continue to worry about the cost of those T1 connections in our original plans for intersite links, but in our tests the DRASC was just too slow to handle the traffic we expect. So we're now wedded to those T1 lines.

Roll Out the Plan

Rollout doesn't mean dropping a whole Exchange system on your organization all at once. It means making Exchange available to specific systems people and users according to a carefully thought-out schedule. You should also go through a testing phase with specific users.

You might start your rollout in MIS—maybe just with yourself, if you're part of MIS. Next, you might move on to samples of users based on the groupings you uncovered in your user-needs assessment. Then move steadily onward until all users are up and running in Exchange. The key is to get Exchange out to all users as fast as possible without crashing your organization. (Here, I'm referring to your *real* organization, not your Exchange organization.)

Remember that rollout is an integral part of the Exchange design process. As you step through your rollout plans, be ready to change your design. If something doesn't work, change it now. Don't let things pile up to the point that change becomes virtually impossible.

Whether you're in a test or production rollout phase, be sure to keep users in the loop. Get them committed to Exchange. Let them know if and when they're going to see the new Exchange client or other clients supported by Exchange

Server. Explain to them how they can use whatever client you plan to provide them both to do what they're already doing and to get other tasks done. This is where user training comes in.

Keep MIS staff involved and informed as well. An Exchange installation and implementation is a big deal for an MIS department. Over time, I'll bet that just about everyone in MIS will get involved with Exchange. MIS staff should understand and welcome Exchange, not see it as a threat to their jobs. Train MIS personnel as data processing colleagues rather than just end users. You don't have to tell everyone in MIS everything there is to know about Exchange—they can buy this book for that purpose (hint, hint). But be sure to talk to them about both server and client basics from a more technical perspective.

An Example: The GerCom Rollout

The GerCom Exchange rollout is a two-year project, and we're about six months into it. (How time flies when you're having fun.) The rollout is a very detailed and complex process; I can only touch on key highlights here. I've got to keep that glue from drying, you know.

We decided to start with a basic Exchange installation for use by our 11 new Exchange MIS employees and the executive suite. If our executive staffers weren't so computer-literate I'd never have approved this part of the rollout plan, but we execs have all lived with computers and new system rollouts for a long time, and I know we're a good and safe starting point for Exchange. And what better way to get upper management behind Exchange and the rollout?

The first phase of GerCom's Exchange rollout went pretty smoothly, though we were surprised at how poorly the Exchange client performed on anything less than a 486 machine with 16MB of RAM. We're pushing hard to find the resources to upgrade those user workstations.

We allowed two months for phase one of the rollout. As a condition of employment, all of GerCom's new non–Los Angeles Exchange staff had to live in LA for these two months (at great but justifiable expense, I might add). Exchange site administrators participated in the setup of the LA site and then helped bring up the servers for the Chicago and New York sites. The servers were linked by local networks for the test phase, and we were able to proof out the entire GerCom Exchange system right in LA.

During this period our Exchange training and applications development staff went through training of their own. I was happy when, to a person, they came out of training as enthusiastic as I am about end-user and MIS Exchange application development. They did remind us that we had to make a commitment on buying the latest version of Microsoft Word and Excel for our users. We did. Staff also suggested that we buy some evaluation copies of Microsoft's Access database product. We did.

When our trainers finished their own training we had them do some test training with MIS staff. That turned out really well; everyone seemed genuinely enthusiastic. No one openly expressed opposition to Exchange or the kinds of applications we plan to develop with it. I've asked our MIS director to talk to his staff to be sure that what we saw on the surface is real.

At the end of the two-month period the Chicago and New York Exchange staff returned to their respective cities. There they set up their servers and connected them to the T1 lines we had installed. Our LA Exchange site administrator is specially skilled in Internet and X.400 connectivity, so, we sent her to Chicago and New York to help with those connections. Hey, these Exchange folks are traveling as much as we execs are.

Bringing site administrators to Los Angeles worked very well. It concentrated them for training, let them learn from each other as they did real tasks, and helped them build important relationships that would make their jobs both easier and more rewarding. We'll get these folks together on a regular basis, and we'll use this same plan when we implement a new site.

With all sites up and running, the second phase of the GerCom Exchange rollout focused on bringing all of our departments into Exchange for e-mail only. This involved a lot of training and no small amount of Exchange system administration. We were able to create most of our user accounts from comma-delimited files produced on our UNIX system, but that information wasn't enough to fill in all of the blanks on those eleven property pages available in Exchange Administrator's user administration and management tool. We exported more info from our Oracle human resources database in comma-delimited files and imported it into our Exchange servers, but our Exchange administrators still had to fill in information we didn't have in electronic form. They also had to create accounts for employees who didn't have UNIX mail accounts (mostly recent hires).

During phase two we brought the LA and New York sales staffs into the loop first, because they're the biggest contributors to GerCom's bottom line. Then, in order, came Chicago Sales, LA Marketing, Chicago Manufacturing, and Chicago Engineering.

Our Exchange training/end-user application development staff was stretched to the limit a few times during Phase Two of the rollout. The Exchange site administrators also felt a lot of pressure as they worked to add users and tune their systems. Probably at least in part because of the LA training—they all supported each other both technically and emotionally—face-to-face, on the phone, and through our growing Exchange system.

Our hardware and networking projections are holding pretty well, though I have to tell you that our servers' disks are filling up fast. And Performance Monitor tests are indicating that we may soon need to add more processors and memory to our LA machine. (It's either that or cut back on our expectations.)

Phase two lasted four months, though we thought we could finish in three. The final phase of our Exchange rollout involves the creation of end-user and custom-programmed applications. We've allotted 18 months to complete this phase, and we're going to start it now.

We'll work on the two kinds of applications in parallel. We'll start with some of the end-user apps our controller wants to implement, then we'll move on to the human resources apps. Our first custom-programmed application will be the customer notification system that our manufacturing people came up with. Once that's in place, we'll move on to the customer ordering and payment system that sales wants. We figure that we should start easy and work up to the more difficult tasks.

Of course, now that we're into the implementation phase we're hearing new ideas from all quarters. I've asked MIS to work with users to quickly understand what they have in mind and determine if it can be implemented in Exchange— and if it can, what it might cost. The exec staff will look at these proposals with MIS and determine where they should fit into our current implementation plans. Of course, as you might imagine, some of our hotshot users are already coming up with their own Exchange applications based on the user-oriented app tools we've talked about.

Because we execs and MIS worked closely together, there was no finger-pointing when these surprise apps popped up. We gave everyone an opportunity during the early phases of the design process. We told everyone that we couldn't guarantee implementation of ideas that came in late, but we quickly came up with a way to filter new ideas that surfaced during rollout. No one panicked. No one screamed. All is well.

Right now, things look good. A reasonable amount of planning, coupled with an openness to change, has gotten our Exchange rollout off to a very good start. I can't wait to see what the system looks like in 18 months.

Conclusion

In this chapter you learned the 11 steps involved in designing an Exchange system. You also learned that the Exchange design process is an iterative one in which you constantly revisit steps to refine your design. This is true even for the final step—Exchange system rollout, where you test and modify your design in the real world.

Now we're ready to move on to the hands-on part of the Exchange experience. The remainder of this book is devoted to showing you in detail how to bring up an Exchange system. We'll start by installing an NT server and then an Exchange server. Before we finish we'll cover every one of the concepts and realities we've touched on already, and even more. Let's go!

PART II

Installation

Microsoft Exchange Server runs on top of Microsoft's Windows NT Server. In this section, we'll install both products, protect them and their users against hardware crashes, and build a basic networking environment to protect them.

Chapter 6 focuses on installing NT Server, setting up an uninterruptible power supply, backing up, security, and networking. Chapter 7 provides details on Exchange Server installation and security.

Installing Windows NT Server

- Installing Windows NT Server software

- Installing uninterruptible power supplies

- Setting up NT Backup

- Giving domain access to NT servers and workstations

- Setting up NT Server clients

Have you ever gone on the Alice in Wonderland ride at Disneyland? It starts by taking you down a rabbit hole, with Alice saying, "Here we gooooooooooooooooooooooo." That extended "go" fades away toward the end, adding to the ride's excitement and sense of entering the unknown. Like Alice, we're about to embark on a wild and exciting adventure. I promise to do all I can to make our hands-on trip through Exchange interesting, productive, and fun—but a little less bumpy, arbitrary, and confusing than Alice's sojourn in Wonderland. Let's go.

Installation: An Overview

In this chapter, I'm presuming you'll be installing NT Server on a computer with nothing on it that you wish to preserve. For example, I assume you don't need to update a Windows for Workgroups machine to NT Server and preserve the software you've installed under the existing operating system. This seems a reasonable assumption, since you're preparing a machine for Exchange Server and are unlikely to be using an existing workstation or server.

If you're going to install NT Server on top of DOS, Windows 3.1*x*, or LAN Manager 2.2, you should back up your existing system before installing NT Server. If you need help with backing up and restoring or other issues related to installing NT Server over an existing operating system, take a look at *Mastering Windows NT Server 4* (Sybex, 1996), by Mark Minasi, Christa Anderson, and Elizabeth Creegan. It can also help you troubleshoot installation problems, deal with NT Server reinstallations, and handle a host of other things I just don't have the space to cover here. (See the sidebar *Mastering Windows NT Server 4*, in Chapter 4, for more about this book and why I think it's so neat.)

WARNING Microsoft had to do a number of things to NT Server to make it compatible with Exchange Server. Some of these involved new functions required by Exchange Server, while others fixed bugs that emerged when NT Server was stressed to its limits by Exchange Server. These modifications are available in what are called *service packs* for version 3.51 or later of NT Server. You need to install NT Service Pack #5 on version 3.51 or Service Pack #1 on version 4.0 to ensure that all fixes are in place. Even that's not enough, though. As of this writing, if you want to access Exchange Server 5 with an Internet browser, you'll need at least NT 4.0 with Service Pack #2. As I mentioned in Chapter 1, things are likely to change by the time you read this book. The Internet and the high speed, high pressure marketing and software delivery channels it has fostered make unending, unpredictable, and incredibly quick software modification not only possible but economically necessary for vendors. Check the web sites at www.microsoft.com/ntserver and www.microsoft.com/exchange for updates.

NT Server installation is a six-step process. These steps include:

- Setting up the server hardware

- Installing NT Server software

- Installing an uninterruptible power supply

- Setting up NT Backup

- Giving domain access to users and NT systems

- Setting up NT Server clients

Let's look at each of these steps in more detail.

Setting Up the Server Hardware

Setting up the hardware is a pretty straightforward process. First, you pick a server platform and outfit it with various components. Then you test out its memory, disk drives, and other hardware to ensure that everything is working well.

Getting Server Components in Order

In Chapter 5, I wrote of a "reasonable machine" for running Exchange Server: a 200MHz Pentium with 128MB of RAM and two 2GB SCSI hard disks. Let's assume you're starting with this PC or its Digital Alpha, or PowerPC equivalent.

A Lower-Powered Test Machine

If you're just going to test Exchange Server and promise not to put your test configuration into production, you can use a somewhat lesser hunk of hardware than the "reasonable machine" I tout. I'd recommend at a minimum a 166MHz Pentium PC with 32MB of RAM and a 1.6 GB IDE hard disk.

I suggest that you outfit your system with a SCSI-2 peripheral controller, a super-VGA display adapter, at least a 15-inch monitor, an 8x-speed or faster CD-ROM drive, two or more serial ports, a mouse, and one or more network adapters. Let's look at server components in a bit more detail.

Can Your Server See More Than 64MB of RAM?

Not all Pentium-based computers are able to detect RAM beyond 64MB. This limitation is built into the machine's ROM BIOS, which NT Server relies on to know how much memory is available in the computer. If you've installed 128MB of RAM and the BIOS can detect only the first 64MB, then for all intents and purposes you've got only 64MB.

The first time you boot the computer that will become your NT server, you'll know almost immediately whether or not you have a problem. Whatever amount of RAM is reported just after boot-up starts is the amount the BIOS has detected and will report to NT Server.

Can Your Server See More Than 64MB of RAM? (continued)

Some manufacturers with troublesome BIOSs can supply updated BIOS chips without the 64MB limit, while other companies may not have updates available yet. Your best bet is to get a right-to-return guarantee from the vendor that the machine you buy can indeed detect more than 64MB of RAM.

RAM

Make sure that your RAM is fast enough for your server's processor. With a 200MHz Pentium processor, SIMMs with chips rated at 60 nanoseconds or better are fine.

Peripheral Controllers

Peripheral Component Interconnect (PCI) SCSI-2 controllers are the best choice for modern server hardware. Of all currently available controllers, they can move the greatest number of bits in the shortest time. You'll use them to connect both hard disks and tape drives to your server.

You should buy PCI SCSI-2 controllers with a right-to-return guarantee, since not all controllers run properly in all computers with PCI slots. This is due to some vagueness in the Intel PCI spec and to the resulting differences in implementation by various computer and component manufacturers. Things have gotten better over the past year or so, but play it safe; be sure you have that guarantee.

Display Adapters and Monitors

Exchange Server is loaded with applications that use a graphical user interface (GUI). A super-VGA display adapter and a 15-inch or larger monitor let you keep multiple GUI apps open and available.

CD-ROM Drives

NT Server is a software monster, but a fast CD-ROM drive makes NT Server installation and modification almost fun. The NT Server installation program can automatically detect and enable most CD-ROM hardware, including both Enhanced IDE and SCSI devices.

What to Buy

NT Server comes with a little manual titled *Hardware Compatibility List;* it lists the components that work with NT. Before you buy anything, consult this guide. 'Nuff said.

Serial Ports

You'll need one serial port to interface your NT Server to an uninterruptible power supply (UPS). Also, you'll probably want to use a serial port for a mouse. However, if you plan to provide Microsoft's Remote Access Server (RAS) connections for your NT Server users, use a PS/2 or mouse port to free a serial port for RAS.

Mice

Pick either a PS/2 or mouse port or serial mouse depending on serial port availability.

Network Adapters

Based on the Exchange network design you came up with in Chapter 5, you'll need one or more network adapters in your server. Again, PCI adapters are the best choice. As with PCI SCSI controllers, you should buy network adapters with a right-to-return guarantee.

Setting Up Adapters

Be careful how you set up network adapters, especially ISA bus cards. Otherwise, if you get the settings wrong, you may have to reinstall NT Server software all over again. Once you've got an adapter set up the way you want it, write down the settings. You'll need them when you get into the NT Server's network installation.

Setting Up Adapters (continued)

If you use PCI SCSI controllers and network adapters, you shouldn't have to worry too much about setting I/O addresses, DMA channels, or interrupts (IRQs). If you don't use PCI cards, be sure to select IRQs that don't conflict with those of other adapters. Good IRQ options are 5, 10, 11, and 15. If you're using a bus mouse, you'll probably use IRQ 5 for that. So that leaves IRQs 10, 11, and 15 for your controller and network adapter.

Be sure to pick nonconflicting I/O addresses and DMA channels for those adapters that require them. Adapter manuals will give you the basics on configuration methods and parameters. The setup programs that come with individual adapters make it pretty easy to spot conflicts. Don't forget to write down all of the settings you choose. Tape copies of this information both inside and outside the computer.

Testing Key Components

E-messaging is a critical application. As I noted in earlier chapters, you're best off when you run e-messaging on fault-tolerant hardware. But even before you consider this option, you should be sure that everything in your server is working properly. You'll want to test five key components as soon as your server is in-house: memory, hard disks, CD-ROM drives, SCSI controllers, and network adapters.

Good memory and disk tests are time consuming: Testing out the "reasonable machine" I recommended for Exchange Server could take between six and seven days. Don't let that deter you, though. You want to be sure you've got a solid platform under your organization—if for no other reason than you'll sleep better at night.

During NT Server installation, the system is automatically configured for a variety of hardware options. So all of your hardware should be working during the installation process. For this reason, you'll want to test your CD-ROM drive, SCSI controllers, and network adapters before installing NT Server. Be sure to test all of these together to be sure that no IRQ, I/O address, or DMA conflicts occur.

It should go without saying, but I'll say it anyway: Don't consider your testing phase finished until all components pass the tests you set out for them. Now let's start testing.

Testing Memory

Because the quick boot-up memory test on Intel-based PCs cannot find most memory problems, use Touchstone Software's Checkit or QAPlus's DiagSoft to test memory. You should run either of these programs from DOS with no memory manager present, and run the complete suite of tests in slow rather than quick mode. (Similar memory-test products are available for non–Intel-based machines.)

A good memory-test program on a fast machine will take around four hours per 16MB of RAM. So plan to settle in for a long nap after you start testing the 128MB of RAM on your server.

Testing Hard Disks

There are two kinds of software-based hard disk testers: those that write one pattern all over the disk and then read to see if the pattern was written correctly (MS-DOS's SCANDISK is such a tester), and those that write a range of patterns and test to see if each was properly written. You'll want a multipattern tester because it is more likely to find the bit-based problems on a disk. Gibson Research's Spin-Rite is a good multipattern tester that can find and declare off-limits any bad areas on disk that the manufacturer didn't catch. Unfortunately, disk tests are even more of a snoozer than RAM tests. Plan a nap of three days or so around the testing of one 2GB drive.

Cheap Is Cheap

The newspapers in Los Angeles and most big cities are full of ads for what seem to be unbelievably inexpensive components like SIMMs, disk drives, motherboards, and CPUs. Don't bite. Trust me on this one: I've been through the mill with cheap, flaky components. NT Server all by itself can beat the living daylights out of a computer. Add Exchange Server and you'll pay back in your own sweat and time every penny and then some that you saved by buying cheap. Buy from stable, long-lived vendors at reasonable but not fairy-tale prices.

If you've got enough hardware, you might want to run your RAM and disk tests simultaneously. This will cut down on your nap time, but it will get you up and running with Exchange before the dawn of a new century.

Testing CD-ROM Drives

I test my CD-ROM drives in DOS using MSCDEX.EXE and the DOS driver for the drive. If I can do a directory on a CD-ROM in the drive I'm testing and copy a file or two from the CD-ROM, I assume that it's working well enough to move on to NT installation.

Testing SCSI Controllers

If you've tested your hard drives as suggested above, you've also tested their controllers, at least in isolation from other adapters. Just be sure to run your tests again with active CD-ROM drives and network cards to ensure that no adapter conflicts are lurking in the background just waiting to mess up your NT Server installation.

Testing Network Adapters

I never install a machine that will be networked without making sure that it can attach in MS-DOS mode to a server. Because it's easy to make connections in DOS, I tend to use my NetWare server for this purpose. I just load the NetWare Open Data-Link Interface (ODI) stack for the adapter I'm testing and log in to the server. If the login works, everything should be okay. If you're a Microsoft networking type, you can do the same thing with that network operating system's DOS networking drivers.

Installing NT Server Software

As with setting up hardware, installing NT Server is fairly straightforward. If you've read Part I of this book, you should encounter no surprises. We'll go through all the steps you'll take to get NT Server up and running.

I'd love to show you all of the screens you'll see during installation; however, since no operating system is yet in place, there's no way to capture these screens. Rest assured that each step discussed here parallels one or another screen you'll see during installation. Later in this chapter—once we've got NT Server installed—I'll show you enough setup screens to make up for the early deficit.

Starting the Installation

I'll assume from here forward that you're going to install NT Server 4.0, not 3.51. The 4.0 release comes on three diskettes and a CD-ROM. To start installation, put the diskette labeled "Setup Disk 1" into your start-up drive and boot the system. The installation program will start, and you're off to the races. The first thing of note that you'll see is a message telling you that NT Setup is checking out your system's hardware configuration. This will take a while.

In the unlikely event that you have problems at any point during the installation, check out *Mastering Windows NT Server 4*. This wonderful tome also includes information on alternative ways to install NT Server 4.

Once you've gotten through the hardware configuration detection part of the installation process, your screen turns blue and displays in white letters the words Windows NT Setup. At the bottom of the screen you'll see the message Setup is loading files (Windows NT Executive). (What's in the parentheses will change as each new file is loaded.) All of this takes some time, so be patient.

Detecting Mass Storage Devices

Next, you'll be prompted for Setup disk 2; put it in and press Enter. You'll see info about what's being loaded at the bottom of the screen. After a fair amount of time, Setup gives you a list of options. Press Enter to begin installing NT. Setup will then tell you it's ready to begin detecting storage devices like hard disk, CD-ROM, and diskette drives. Detection can be automatic or manual. Unless you've got some pretty weird storage hardware, go ahead and tell Setup to do an automatic detect by pressing Enter.

As soon as you press the Enter key, you're prompted for Setup disk 3. The detection phase won't actually begin until you insert the diskette and press Enter again. Setup now loads a series of device drivers and tests them to see if it can detect a range of popular SCSI controllers, disk drives, and SCSI or IDE CD-ROM drives. The program reports the SCSI and IDE CD-ROM mass storage devices on your system as it finds them. When it finishes, Setup offers you the opportunity to have it load SCSI drivers that you have for devices not supported by NT Setup's repertory of drivers.

If all goes well and Setup has found your SCSI devices and/or IDE CD-ROM drives, press the Enter key to proceed. Don't worry if you don't see your IDE hard disk drives at this point. Setup will take care of them as soon as you press the Enter key.

If a mass storage device in your computer wasn't automatically detected and the NT Server hardware compatibility list says that drivers for it or its controller ship with NT Server, then you've probably got a problem with the hardware itself. Go back and test the device as indicated earlier in this chapter.

If an undetected device isn't supported in the off-the-shelf NT Server package and you have specific drivers for it from the manufacturer, you can manually load them at this point. To do so press the **S** key.

Setup next looks for IDE drives. If it finds any that have over 1024 cylinders, it warns you of this fact and notes that under certain circumstances all of the space on the disk may not be available. If you're using a modern Pentium motherboard with built-in IDE support, you can pretty much ignore this warning. If not, read the warning in full and do as advised; otherwise, press the Enter key to continue the NT installation.

Insert the NT Server CD-ROM Disk

Next, the CD-ROM file system is loaded. Then, if the NT Server CD-ROM disk isn't in the CD-ROM drive already, Setup asks that you insert it in the drive and press the Enter key.

Licenses

When the licensing dialog box pops up, page down through the licensing agreement and then press F8 to agree to the conditions of the license. F8 doesn't show up on the screen until you've paged all the way down to the end of the license.

Checking for Software and Hardware

Setup will look for previous versions of NT on your computer. If it finds one, it will offer you the opportunity to upgrade the existing version or install a new one. That's your call. (If this is a fresh install, you won't see this message.) Setup will also detect other known operating systems and offer you an opportunity to upgrade or install a new version where appropriate. For example, because of differences in the registries of the two operating systems, you can't install NT over Windows 95. However, you can install the two operating systems in parallel on the same machine and Setup will offer this option if appropriate.

If you're installing NT on a computer without a previous version of NT, Setup shows you the basic configuration of your hardware, e.g., PC, keyboard, and mouse type. Change anything that isn't correct and accept the displayed configuration.

What follows assumes you're installing on a fresh computer with no previous version of any operating system installed. If you're upgrading NT Server or installing it over another operating system, you should already know enough about NT installations to handle the minor differences in the installation process from this point on.

Preparing Disk Partitions

At this point, Setup shows you the unpartitioned space on the hard disk drives it detected and asks where you want to install NT Server. If you've worked with DOS disk partitions, what follows should be pretty familiar. You can choose to set up partitions of any size up to the capacity of a disk drive. Assuming you've got two fresh disk drives in your computer, I recommend setting up a partition of around 512MB for the NT Server operating system.

At this point, you only need to worry about the primary partition NT Server is to be installed on. You can take care of other partitions later using NT's Disk Administrator applet. I'll talk more about Disk Administrator later in this chapter.

Now comes the $64,000 question: Do you want to format the partition as a FAT (File Allocation Table) or NTFS (NT File System) partition? FAT partitions are compatible with MS-DOS. You can boot an NT server under DOS and read what's on the server's FAT-formatted partitions. So, you might want to format your operating system in FAT partitions. I myself have pretty much given up on DOS, so I tend to format my NT Server operating system partitions in NTFS format. Choose the format you want and press the Enter key. Setup puts up a little gauge showing formatting progress.

Copying Files from the NT Server CD-ROM Disk

When formatting is finished, Setup asks for the directory that NT should be installed in. Accept the default "\WINNT" by pressing the Enter key.

Setup then asks if you want a basic or a basic and exhaustive examination of your hard disk for corruption. It's best to do the basic and exhaustive test, though it takes a while.

Upon completion of the examination, Setup begins copying files from the CD-ROM to the partition you designated. After copying the files, Setup tells you it has finished this phase of installation and asks you to remove diskettes and CD-ROM disks from their drives so it can reboot your computer. Follow this advice religiously. Leaving even the CD-ROM disk in its drive can mess up the next phase. When you have removed all diskettes and disks, press the Enter key to embark on the next leg of your journey to NT Server.

Setup's Installation Wizard

Upon reboot, NT Setup runs through some basic text startup screens. During this time, it fully formats the disk partition NT server will be installed on and reboots the machine once more. Have patience here; pretty soon Setup goes into graphical user interface mode and asks you to put the NT Server CD-ROM disk back in the CD-ROM drive. Do so and click OK.

Then Setup brings up a Microsoft to guide you through the next phase of NT Server installation. The Wizard looks a lot like the installation Wizards that come with a range of products designed for the Windows 95 operating system. It leads you through further hardware detection, the installation of Windows NT Networking, and a bunch of other housekeeping chores.

The sections below guide you through the various phases of NT Server installation. They're keyed to the installation Wizard. Click Next on the Wizard to move on to the next phase of installation.

Ownership and Licensing

After the hardware detection phase, the Wizard asks you to enter your name and the name of your organization. This is not necessarily the name of your Exchange organization. This information is just used to identify who installed NT Server and the organization claiming ownership of this copy of the product. Enter that information and click Next.

The next wizard screen asks for the CD Key which appears on the back on the jewel case your NT Server CD-ROM came in. Enter the key and click Next.

Next, the Wizard requests licensing information. Select the licensing type you've paid for and enter any required values. Heed the Wizard's warning to use the License Manager in the Administrative Tools program group to set the number of client licenses purchased, once your NT server is up and running. If you don't, users and other systems won't be able to connect to the server.

Naming Your NT Server

The Wizard next asks you to name the NT server. This name should follow the Exchange Server naming scheme you developed based on discussions in the first part of this book. As you'll recall, I named my first NT server EXCHLA01.

Next you're asked whether this NT server is to be a primary or backup domain controller or stand-alone server. If this is the first NT server you're setting up, make it the primary domain controller. If not, select one of the other options. Because of the load domain controller status tends to put on an NT server, it's best not to make your Exchange servers do double duty as NT domain controllers. However, in the early phases of Exchange server installation, testing, and evaluation, you should be able to get away with assigning domain controller and Exchange server status to a single computer.

Creating an Emergency Repair Diskette

The NT emergency repair diskette is used to recover operating system information in case of a partial hard disk failure. The Wizard next offers you a chance to make such a disk. Jump at it. I can't tell you how many times I've been able to recover a seemingly dead server by using its emergency repair disk.

Selecting Components for Installation

The good old Wizard now offers you a list of components you can install. Decide what you want. Don't bother to install Windows Messaging. It'll be wholly over-written later when you install an Exchange client on the server.

Also, don't bother with the fancy graphically based screen savers. They just eat up CPU. It's better to use NT Server's console-lock command for security, rather than a screen saver. Once you've got NT Server running and you're logged in, you can activate the command by simultaneously pressing the Ctrl, Alt, and Delete keys and clicking Lock Workstation in the Windows NT Security dialog box that pops up. While the screen is locked, press the Ctrl, Alt, and Delete keys for a password-prompt dialog box. Enter the password for the administrator or your own password, and you're back in business.

Installing Windows NT Networking

NT Server is nothing without networking. The Wizard now takes you into the network installation portion of the Setup process. When the Wizard shows you a dialog box with *2) Installing Windows NT Networking* highlighted, click Next.

First, the Wizard asks if you're wired to the network or will connect by a Remote Access Server dialup connection. Though you can connect Exchange servers using dialup connections, any Exchange server's primary connection should be through a hardwired, permanent link. So, select that option and click Next.

Installing Internet Information Server

The Wizard's next question is key to your Exchange server installation. You're asked if you want to install Microsoft's Internet Information Server (IIS). If you want Exchange users and/or anonymous individuals to access your Exchange server using a web browser, you'll need an Internet Information Server somewhere on your network.

The IIS doesn't have to be installed on an Exchange server. Again, if you're in the early installation, testing, and evaluation stage with Exchange Server, go ahead and install the IIS on this soon-to-be Exchange server. Later you can set up a separate server to support web access for all of your Exchange servers.

Installing Network Adapters

The Wizard will now offer to auto-detect any network adapters in your computer. Automatic detection is generally pretty reliable, so I suggest you click Start Search and let Setup find your adapter or adapters. However, Setup can't detect information about I/O addresses, Interrupts, and DMA channels for a lot of older ISA bus cards, so verify what Setup says about these settings and enter the correct information, if necessary.

If Setup is unable to detect your adapter or adapters, click Select from list and find your adapter or adapters on the list that the Wizard brings up. You may have to use a diskette from your adapter's manufacturer, if drivers for the adapter aren't included with NT Server. NT Server's hardware compatibility list can help you here.

Selecting Networking Protocols

Life is full of choices and so is NT Server installation. Your next set of choices is extremely important. The Wizard presents several networking protocol options. TCP/IP protocol installation is selected by default. If you've got Novell NetWare users, you'll also want to install IPX/SPX protocols. If you can at all avoid it, don't install NetBEUI. With your NT network properly setup, you'll have no need for it.

When you've finished selecting networking protocols, click Next. The Wizard next presents you with a list of requested and suggested networking services.

Unless you have a strong reason for doing otherwise, accept the suggestions and click Next. If you want to get more deeply into networking options, click Select from list and make still more choices. For more details on networking protocols, see *Mastering Windows NT Server 4*.

Installation at Last

The networking installation portion of the Wizard next warns you that it's about to actually install something. If you're ready, click Next. If not, move back through the Wizard's screens to correct or change anything that needs to be altered.

Installation begins, and you're almost immediately offered a dialog box with such things as the I/O port address, interrupt number, and transceiver type (e.g., 10BaseT) that will be assigned to your network card or cards. Select the default settings or, if offered, change the parameters as needed. Remember what I said above about problems Setup has auto-detecting these parameters on ISA bus adapters; the Wizard will warn you about this. Make sure these settings are correct. If they're not, you're going to have to do quite a bit of manual configuring of your server later on.

The Wizard next asks if there is a DHCP (Dynamic Host Configuration Protocol) server on your network. If there is and you answer yes, the DHCP server will assign an IP address to your computer automatically and give it other information necessary for TCP/IP networking. Unless you instruct otherwise, DHCP will usually give the server a different IP address every time the server's old IP address expires (every three days by default). That can wreak havoc on Internet mail and other TCP/IP related services on your server. So, even if you've got a DHCP server, it's best to assign a permanent IP address to the computer.

The Wizard next brings up a TCP/IP networking dialog box. For details on configuring TCP/IP networking, check out *Mastering Windows NT Server 4*. It's chock-full of useful stuff on the subject.

One thing to be sure to look into is Microsoft's Windows Internet Name Service (WINS). WINS lets you automatically or manually associate an NT networking computer name like EXCHLA01 with an IP address. Then, when a workstation or server comes looking for another workstation or server with a specific NT networking name, the WINS server tells it the associated IP address. With that address in-hand, the workstation or server is able to quickly establish communications without the aid of slower, more limited protocols like NetBEUI.

When you've finished setting up TCP/IP networking, click OK. The Wizard next presents a dialog box that lets you review the binding of the networking services, protocols, and adapters that will be set up on your NT server. You can disable some of these if you wish, but for now I suggest you let them be.

Finally, the Wizard tells you that it is ready to start the network so you can continue configuring the network. Click Next to move along.

Welcome to the Network

Assuming you're installing this server as a Primary Domain Controller, if all goes well network-wise, the Wizard asks you to specify the name of the domain you want to create and the administrator name and password for the domain. Since you're creating a new domain, you'll be creating a new administrator name and setting a password for it. Enter this information and click Next. In my case I entered, *LA* as my domain name. Remember from Chapter 5 that this is the name of the Exchange site this server will support. I entered the name *administrator* and a password of my choice in the administrator name and password fields presented by the Wizard.

If you don't get the dialog box discussed in the paragraph above and you're using an ISA network adapter, it's most likely because one or more of the default parameters offered by the Wizard for your adapter—the I/O address port, interrupt, or DMA channel—is incorrect. In such a case, NT Server is unable to talk to the network adapter and set up network communications. Verify these parameters and rerun NT Server installation. Remember how I noted the importance of getting those adapter parameters right? Now you know why.

NT Servers and Workstations Need Special Rights to Enter a Domain

NT is very security-conscious. NT servers and workstations can't enter a domain unless they've been given permission to do so by an NT account with sufficient rights. This permission is given using an NT application called *Server Manager*. When you first set up a domain, you obviously can't get permission to enter it from anywhere. So entering an administrator name and password creates the first account in your NT domain and gives that account the rights to enter your server into the domain. You can then use Server Manager with that same account or another account that is granted similar rights to grant other servers and workstations permission to enter the domain. I'll talk more about all of this later in this chapter.

Installing Internet Information Server

After Setup does its thing for a bit, the Wizard presents you with a dialog box with one option remaining, Finish. Click on Finish to complete the NT Server installation.

If you've asked to install the Internet Information Server, you're next presented with a list of IIS options. At this point, just accept them all and click OK. Answer the typical installation questions that come next and when you're finished, IIS installation begins. For help installing the IIS see Sybex's *Mastering Windows NT Server 4* and Peter Dyson's *Mastering Microsoft Internet Information Server* (Sybex, 1996).

Finishing Up

To complete NT Server installation, you're asked to set the correct time, time zone, and date and to configure your display adapter. When you've finished with these, Setup copies files from the CD-ROM disk to your hard disk drive and then prepares your computer to run NT. If you asked to create an emergency repair disk, you'll be offered the opportunity to do so now.

When all else is done, Setup brings up a dialog box that lets you reboot your computer and start NT. Do it! NT Server boots up and asks you to log into your newly created DOMAIN. Enter the administrator name and password you provided during installation; you're now running NT Server.

At this point, you can fiddle with your display adapter's video resolution, if necessary, and do any other housekeeping chores you'd like. To play with the display adapter resolution, right-click on the desktop and choose properties.

At last, you get your reward. It may seem anticlimactic, however. All that work and what do you get? Microsoft Windows, that's what! Heck, you've probably seen that a hundred times. No bells? No whistles? No dancing bears? Nothing—just plain-vanilla Windows front-ending one of the most powerful multitasking, multi-threaded operating systems in the world. Enjoy!

Oh yes, if you're offered the opportunity to back up the previous version of NT so you can recover in case the Service Pack install doesn't work, jump at the chance. I can't tell you how many times some little thing went wrong in an upgrade and how returning to the previous service level saved my life.

Upgrade Time

Now that you've installed NT Server 4.0, don't forget to bring it up to at least Service Pack 1, if you're going to run Exchange Server without Internet browser access. If you want Internet browser access, install at least Service Pack 2. To keep it simple, just install Service Pack 2 or greater on your server, whatever you plan to do with Exchange. NT Service Packs are cumulative, so installing Service Pack 2 assures that all Service Pack 1 changes have been installed as well.

Service pack installation is easy. Get the Service Pack off the Internet or from Microsoft on a CD-ROM disk. Unpack the Service Pack software if it's compressed into a self-executing file. Before running a Service Pack update, be sure to shut down all running programs. Then run the UPDATE.EXE file that comes with the Service Pack software. When the update is finished, your computer is rebooted and you're good to go.

WARNING
As of this writing at least, Microsoft's Internet Information Server is one of the most volatile pieces of software in the world. If you have an earlier version of NT Server 4.0, IIS version 2.0 is included. You need at least version 3.0 of IIS and an IIS component called "Active Server Pages" to access Exchange servers through the Internet, for example, to see your mail with a web browser. So, after installing IIS, check its version number. If it's less than 3.0, get your hands on and install IIS 3.0 or greater. If you aren't offered the option of installing Active Server Pages when you install IIS 3.0, get and install them, too.

Setting Up and Formatting Other Disk Partitions

If you installed more than one hard disk drive in your computer or if the partition you installed NT Server on is smaller than the disk drive the partition resides on, you're not quite done yet. You'll need to use NT Server's Disk Administrator applet to set up and format one or more additional disk partitions. Here's how to do it.

To get to the applet, click on the Start menu icon on the NT Server Task Bar at the bottom of your screen. Next select Programs from the Start menu; then select Administrative Tools from the Programs menu and finally select Disk Administrator from the Administrative Tools menu. (See Figure 6.1.)

FIGURE 6.1

Starting NT Server's Disk Administrator applet

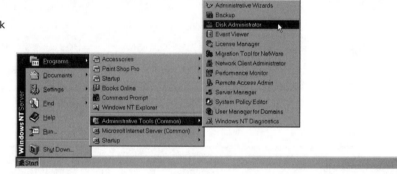

In Figure 6.2 you can see that half of Disk 0 in my server is formatted NTFS style. That happened when I installed NT Server. The other half hasn't been partitioned or formatted. Disk 1 is totally unpartitioned and unformatted. To partition a drive, click on it in Disk Administrator's graphic presentation of your disk drives. Then select Create from the Partition menu. This brings up a dialog box like the one in Figure 6.3. Set the partition size you want in MB. When you're done, click OK.

Disk Administrator's graphic presentation of your disk drives now changes to show that the partition exists, but isn't yet formatted. To format the partition, select Format from the Tools menu. Use the Format dialog box that pops up to select such things as NTFS or FAT formatting and click Start. You'll next see a little dialog box warning you about all the terrible things you can do to your drive by formatting it. Click OK and formatting begins.

FIGURE 6.2

Disk Administrator ready
for some disk partition-
ing and formatting

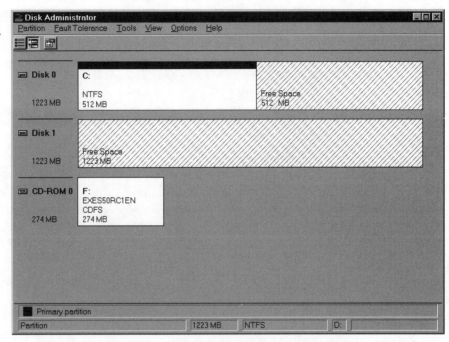

FIGURE 6.3

Using Disk Administrator
to set the size of a disk
partition

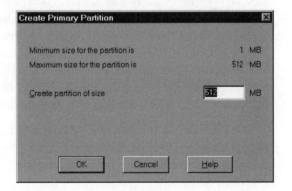

After a partition is formatted, Disk Administrator's graphic presentation of it changes. In Figure 6.4 I've formatted the rest of Disk 0 as a FAT partition and all of Disk 1 as an NTFS partition. Why? Glad you asked.

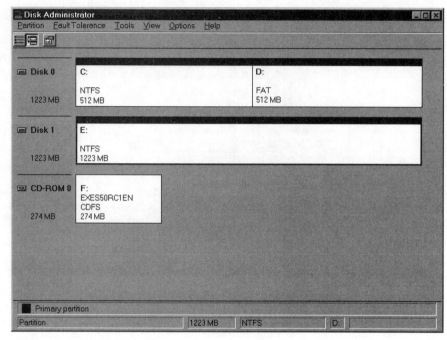

Access to FAT partitions is quick and dirty. Access to NTFS partitions is a bit slower. Because of the higher speed of access to FAT partitions, Microsoft advises putting Exchange Server's temporary transaction logs on a FAT partition. We'll talk more about these logs later. Put simply, these logs hold data that Exchange Server must quickly dump from memory when it's too busy to write the data to its permanent directory and information store databases. Later, at its leisure, Exchange Server moves data from its transaction logs to the databases. That 512MB FAT partition on Disk 0 will be reserved for the transaction logs.

Though they're a bit slower to access, NTFS partitions are more fault tolerant than those of the FAT persuasion. Microsoft strongly suggests that you put your Exchange Server databases on NTFS partitions. That's why the NTFS Disk 1 has one NTFS partition.

We've only touched the surface of Disk Administrator in this section. Take a look at *Mastering Windows NT Server 4* for more on this very useful NT Server applet.

Don't Forget Shutdown

Like all good operating systems, NT Server must be shut down; you should never just turn off an NT server. NT Server buffers a lot of data to RAM before writing it to disk. Though the writes from RAM are done quickly, on a busy server there's always data waiting in the buffers. A graceful shutdown ensures that this data is all written out to disk. To shut down a server, click on the Start menu icon and select Shutdown. You can select from three options: Shutdown the computer, Restart the computer, or Close all programs and log on as a different user. If you pick Shutdown the computer, don't turn off the computer until you see a message telling you that it's okay to do so.

Installing an Uninterruptible Power Supply

An uninterruptible power supply (UPS) takes power from the wall socket and feeds it to a battery to keep it charged. The UPS continuously feeds power from its battery to your computer through internal power-conversion circuitry. When power from the wall socket fails, the UPS battery continues to supply power to your computer, letting it run at least until the battery is exhausted and, if so configured, shutting down the computer before UPS battery power is exhausted.

As I noted in Chapter 5, a UPS should be considered part of your NT Server installation. Let's install one right away.

The UPS Itself

Buy a UPS with "online" circuitry; these tend to be the best and most responsive in power outages. Also, it should be one that can be controlled by an NT server, so it should be equipped with an RS-232 port that you connect by a cable to one of the server's serial ports. Get the RS-232 cable from the UPS's vendor if at all possible; then you won't have to mess with that old devil known as RS-232 interfacing.

NT Server's built-in UPS software talks to the UPS and can shut down the server gracefully, just as if you'd done it manually. Get a UPS that can detect and signal both a wall socket power failure and a low battery (which usually means about two minutes of power left in the battery). With low-battery information available, NT Server doesn't have to begin a shutdown immediately on power failure. If wall-socket power returns before the low-battery signal, no shutdown needs to occur at all.

For more on selecting a UPS, see *Mastering Windows NT Server 4*.

Configuring UPS Support

Figure 6.5 shows NT Server's UPS setup screen; to get to it, just double-click on the UPS icon in the Control Panel. To get to the Control Panel, click on the Start menu icon at the bottom of the screen, then point to Settings on the Start menu and finally point to Control Panel. In the figure, the UPS is connected to the second serial port. I've told the setup program that my UPS sends positive voltages to indicate power failure, low battery, and remote UPS shutdown, as indicated on the screen under UPS Configuration. (The best source of information as to whether your UPS's signaling voltages are negative or positive is the UPS's manual or manufacturer.)

FIGURE 6.5

NT Server's UPS setup screen

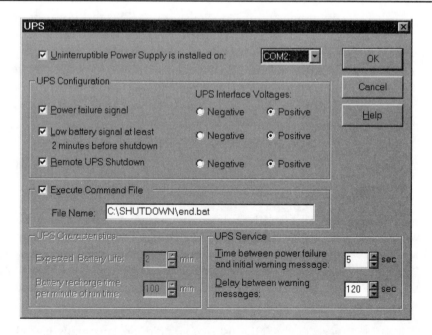

By checking the Remote UPS Shutdown box, I'm telling NT that it can shut off the flow of power to the server. NT would take this action if it detected very erratic power-failure or low-battery signals, which can indicate battery problems and the need to devote all power in the UPS to recharging the battery.

Under Execute Command File, I've told NT to execute a batch file, END.BAT, on shutdown. This particular file deletes some temporary files that one of my applications writes and closes but leaves on disk until the application itself is closed. This ensures that the files are cleaned off the disk, even though the application will remain open if the server is shut down due to a power outage.

I've accepted the default values in the UPS Service area located in the lower right corner of the configuration window. This means that when a power failure occurs, the UPS service will send a message to users five seconds after it happens and then every 120 seconds thereafter until power is restored or the server is shut down.

The UPS Characteristics area in the lower-left corner of the window applies to UPSs that don't provide a low-battery signal. Since you'll be sure to buy a UPS with such a signal, you won't even get an opportunity to fill in this information, right?

Testing the UPS

Of course, you need to test your UPS regularly. Do the tests during off-hours and warn users that you'll be taking the system down. Testing is simple: Just cut power to the UPS and make sure that everything goes as expected. Be sure to let the test go far enough for battery power to run out and for the UPS service to shut down the server.

UPSs with Special Software

Most good UPSs come with special software for NT. This software replaces the basic UPS software that comes with NT, providing such enhanced features as scheduled periodic testing of the UPS and monitoring of power quantity and quality over time. This software doesn't add much to the cost of a UPS, and it's well worth having.

Setting Up NT Backup

As I mentioned in Chapter 5, a variety of products are available for backing up NT. NT comes with its own backup software, which is quite functional if you're not using a tape autoloader. It's important to get some sort of backup going immediately on your NT server, so let's get NT's own backup program up and running right now.

Hardware

Okay, let me say it right at the start: Please don't use anything other than 4mm or 8mm SCSI-2–compatible tape drives. Forget those awful third-floppy minicartridge thingies that take forever to back up a byte of information to low-capacity tape cartridges. And don't mess with those fancy new units that use gigantic but relatively low-capacity (and high-priced) 3M cartridges. Stick with the proven, working, relatively inexpensive 4mm or 8mm tape technologies. If you go with 4mm, be sure to get a DDS2 unit that can handle larger-capacity 4GB tapes.

Installing a SCSI-2 tape backup unit is easy. Just plug it in and be sure that your SCSI chain is terminated at both ends. You can use the same SCSI controller you use for your disk drives, though you'll get better backup throughput if you use a separate controller for the tape drive. Also be sure to use the shortest SCSI cables you can: When a SCSI cable chain (including the cable inside your computer that supports internal disk drives) gets too long, you'll start experiencing some pretty crazy data glitches on your disks and tape drives.

Installing Tape Device Drivers

NT comes with device drivers for a wide range of tape drives. To install the driver you need, find the Tape Devices icon in the Control Panel and double-click on it. This brings up the Tape Devices dialog box shown in Figure 6.6. Click on the Drivers tab to move to the Drivers property page and click Add. (See Figure 6.7.) Select the driver you want and click OK. The driver will then be installed.

If you're using a SCSI-2 4mm tape drive, your life should be quite easy. The generic driver for 4mm devices (shown in Figure 6.7) will work with any SCSI-2 4mm drive, unless the drive's manufacturer has done something weird with the unit's interface. Even if this is the case, drivers for those units are either included in NT Server or are available from the tape unit's vendor. NT Server comes with drivers for Exabyte 8200 (SCSI-1) and 8500 (SCSI-2) 8mm drives, which are also quite generic.

FIGURE 6.6

Add a new tape device driver using Windows NT Tape Devices applet.

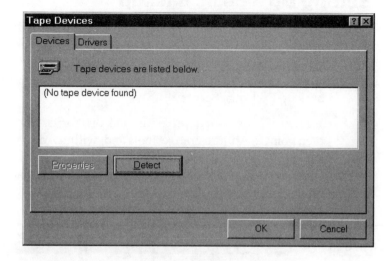

FIGURE 6.7

Select the right driver from the Install Driver dialog box.

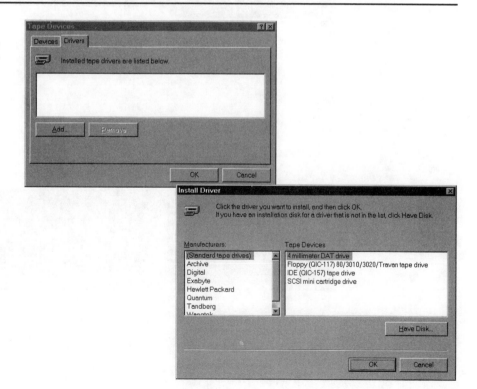

Setting Up a Basic Backup

The real lessons we can learn about backups have to do with Exchange Server—but we're not ready for such a lesson right now. Nevertheless, you should have a backup in place immediately. So right now I'll take you through a simple backup scenario using NT's Backup program. In a later chapter, I'll show you how to back up Exchange Server.

To open NT's backup program, click on the Start menu icon, point to Programs, then point to Administrative Tools and, within Administrative Tools, point to Backup. This opens a window like the one in Figure 6.8. In the Drives window, click on the little box next to the drives you want to back up. I've chosen to back up both the C and D drives on my computer.

FIGURE 6.8

The start-up window for NT Server's Backup application

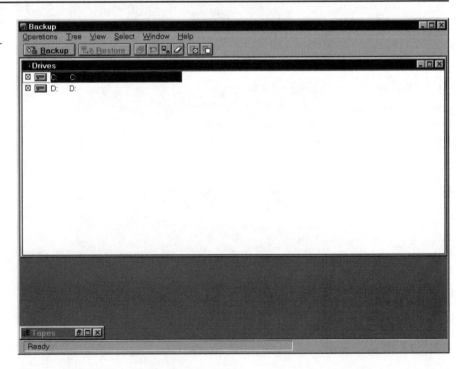

Selective Backups

If you want to back up only some directories or files on a disk drive, double-click on the icon for the drive. This opens a typical directory tree from which you can choose what you want to back up.

Next, double-click on the Tapes icon at the bottom of the Backup window to open the Tapes window. If you've put a blank cartridge in your tape drive, your Tapes window will look like the one in Figure 6.9. The only time the window *won't* look like this one is when you've cheated and installed one of those infernal minicartridge tape units. In that case, you'll see something—though I have no idea what, because I refuse to get mixed up with the things—telling you the tape isn't formatted. To format it, click on the Operations menu and select Format Tape from the menu.

FIGURE 6.9

Backup's Tapes window indicates that a blank tape is installed in the drive.

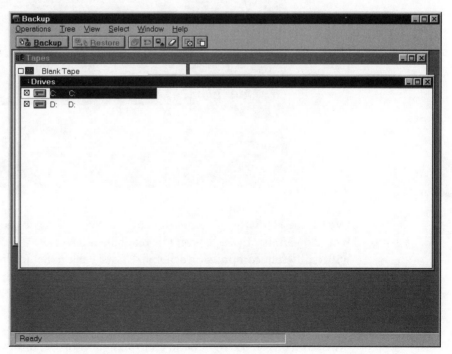

When everything is ready, with your blank tape in the drive, click on the Drives window. Then, click the Backup button located on the toolbar (in the top left-hand corner of the Backup window). This brings up the Backup Information dialog box (see Figure 6.10). In the figure, I've left the default Tape Name intact. I've also instructed Backup to verify the backup and to back up the server's Registry—which, among other things, replaces such files as SYSTEM.INI and WIN.INI on NT servers.

FIGURE 6.10

Setting up a backup using the Backup Information dialog box

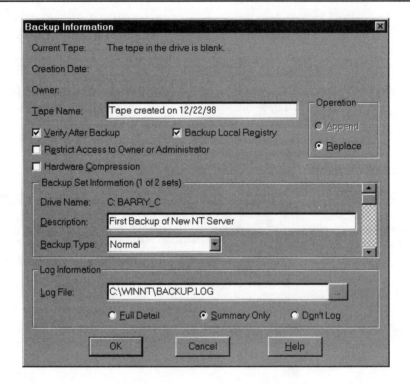

I've left the Hardware Compression box unchecked, since choosing that option would mean that the tape won't be readable if I ever use a piece of equipment with a different compression scheme. Under Backup Set Information, I've added my own description for the backup. I'll hold on to this backup for a while, since it will let me restore my system to the pristine way it was just after I installed NT Server. I'm doing a normal (full) backup as opposed to a differential or incremental backup, and I've accepted the default Log Information parameters. The little scroll bar on the right hand side of the Backup Set Information area of the

Backup Information dialog box indicates that I'm backing up more than one disk drive. Scrolling down lets me put in backup set information for my D drive. That's it. Now just click on the OK button to start the backup.

Restoring files is just as easy—you use the same interface. And as with backing up, you can restore all or only some files. I could say a lot more about backups, but I'll save it for a later chapter when I discuss backing up Exchange Server.

Giving Domain Access to Users and NT Systems

You can log into a domain on any Windows-based computer simply by entering a valid domain user name and password. As noted previously, Windows NT workstations and servers can enter a domain only after they've been given explicit permission to do so. Here's how to create domain users and permit NT systems to join a domain.

Creating Domain Accounts and Groups

An NT/Exchange user must log in to a domain using an NT security account. Each account is created in a specific domain and may be given rights in other domains through trust relationships. Each Exchange user has a mailbox on a specific Exchange home server. Though there are some exceptions, which I'll discuss in a later chapter, to access their Exchange home server, users must be logged in to the same domain as the server or into a domain that is trusted by the home server's domain.

You'll remember from Chapter 4 that you can set up an NT security account at the same time you create a new Exchange mailbox. Unless you have a specific reason for doing otherwise, you're best off letting Exchange create new NT security accounts. It will give users the rights they need in the domain and configure them properly for Exchange.

Though you'll often create Exchange mailboxes and NT security accounts at the same time, there will be times when you'll have to create new accounts or groups outside of Exchange. Since we'll need to set up a new account and group before we install Exchange Server in the next chapter, here's a brief, basic tutorial on creating accounts and groups in a domain.

Figure 6.11 shows the User Manager for Domains, which you use to create and modify domain users and groups. You'll find this app in the Administrative Tools program group on your NT server.

FIGURE 6.11

The User Manager for Domains

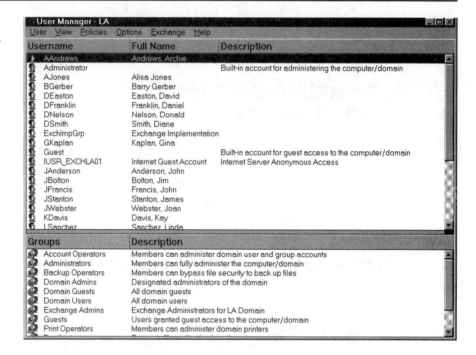

Make sure you're working in the right domain. The domain name appears at the top of the dialog box, right next to the words "User Manager." (Notice that in Figure 6.11 I'm in my LA domain.) If you've got more than one domain and you're not in the right one, click on the User menu and then choose Select Domain. You'll see a little dialog box like the one shown in Figure 6.12. Click on the domain you want, then click on OK to return to the User Manager screen. The domain you chose will now be listed at the top of the screen.

To add a new user, select New User from the User Manager's User menu; the New User dialog box will pop up (see Figure 6.13). Here you'll give the user a Username (alias), a full name, and a password, and you'll set rules about passwords.

FIGURE 6.12

Selecting the correct
domain

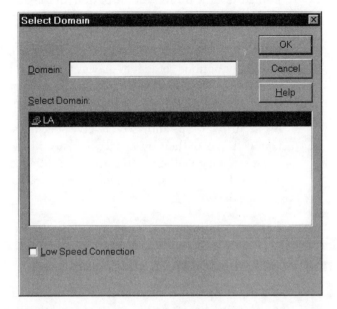

FIGURE 6.13

Creating a new
domain user

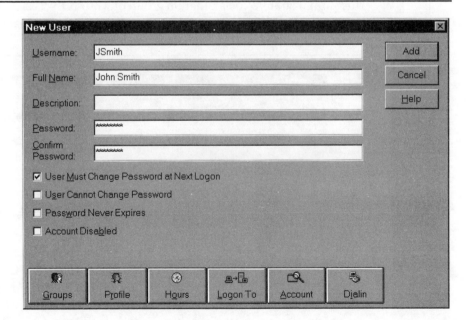

Using the large buttons at the bottom of the dialog box, you can add a user to different user groups, specify a script that runs on login, set valid domain login hours for the user, specify whether the user can log in to all workstations or just specific ones in the domain, and specify the type of account being used. These custom user options come into play as you begin to implement a range of applications in your domain. For more on these options and creating domain users in general, see *Mastering Windows NT Server 4*.

NT security groups allow you to give specific rights to a set of NT security accounts. Think of them as shortcuts. Instead of assigning rights to each account separately, you give them to the group, and then all members of the group inherit the rights. I'll save the specifics for the next chapter, when we'll set up a group for Exchange Server administrators.

Giving Domain Access to NT Servers and Workstations

You'll need to grant an NT server or NT workstations access rights to a domain in two situations: before you install them and if you need to move them to a new domain. You grant access rights using the Server Manager program, which is in the Administrative Tools program group on your NT server. Select the Server Manager icon to get started. Figure 6.14 shows the Server Manager dialog box.

FIGURE 6.14

The Server Manager

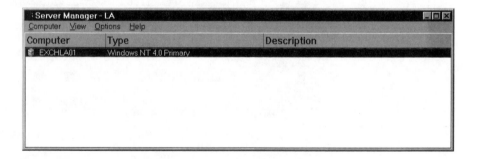

Once you've opened the applet, if the right domain isn't already selected, select it as you did with the User Manager for Domains (using the Computer menu instead of the User menu). Then, from the Computer menu, select Add to Domain. Use the Add Computer To Domain dialog box to add a new workstation, server, or backup domain controller to the domain (see Figure 6.15). Click on Add when you're done. Now, when that new or wandering NT server or workstation shows up, the domain will welcome it with open arms. As you'll remember from my NT Server installation instructions, if you forget to grant domain rights prior to installation, you can actually grant them during an NT server or workstation installation. Microsoft put this capability into the installation program for those of us who can't remember what we ate for dinner last night.

FIGURE 6.15

Using the Server Manager to give domain access to an NT system

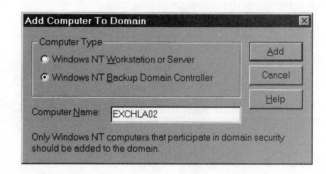

Setting Up NT Server Clients

I'm going to cover Windows 95 networking in a fair amount of detail, and I'll give less attention to networking the other Windows-based operating systems. When push comes to shove, Windows networking is pretty much the same no matter which flavor of the OS you're using—Windows 95, Windows NT Server or Workstation, or Windows for Workgroups. There are minor differences in the graphical interfaces for each OS, but that's about it.

Windows 95

During installation of Windows 95, if the computer you're setting up has a network adapter, you'll have the option to set up networking components. You'll go through a process very similar to the one for setting up NT Server networking at the product's installation.

To install and configure networking after a Windows 95 installation, start by double-clicking on the Add New Hardware icon on the Windows 95 Control

Panel. This brings up a Wizard that will attempt to detect anything new you've put into the computer since installing the OS. Track through the Wizard's screens; if the adapter is detected (and it very likely will be), the Wizard will install the proper driver for it. If the adapter isn't detected, you can either try adding it manually using the Wizard or wait until the next step.

When the Wizard is finished, double-click on the Network icon in the Windows 95 Control Panel. This brings up the Network dialog box (see Figure 6.16). Here's how to set up the Network dialog box.

FIGURE 6.16

Windows 95's Network dialog box

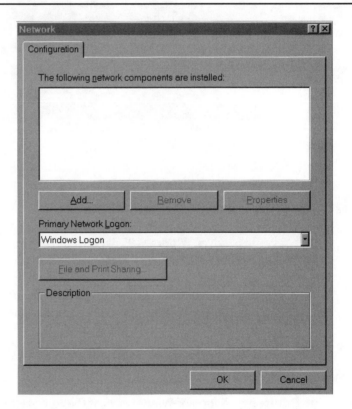

Configuration

Configuration includes the installation and setup of network adapter drivers, Windows network client software, network protocol support, and network-oriented services.

Installing Adapter Drivers If you weren't able to install a driver for the computer's network adapter, you'll need to do it here. Click on Add in the Network dialog box, then double-click on Adapter in the resulting Select Network Component Type dialog box. This brings up the Select Network adapters dialog box (see Figure 6.17). If your adapter is listed, double-click on it. If it isn't listed, then you'll need a driver on diskette from the manufacturer. Click on Have Disk and tell Windows 95 which drive the disk is in. Once the driver is installed, click on OK to return to the Network dialog box.

FIGURE 6.17

Setting up a network adapter

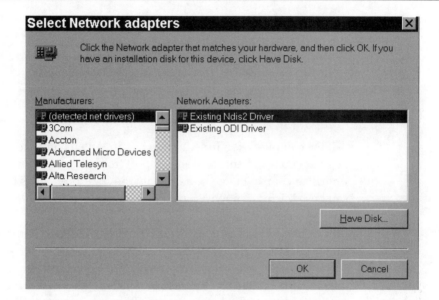

Installing Windows Client Software Next, you'll install one or more Windows clients. Click on the Add button in the Network dialog box and then double-click on Client in the resulting Select Network Component Type dialog box. As you can see in Figure 6.18, you can install clients for Microsoft and other network manufacturers. Install the Microsoft network clients by clicking on 'Microsoft' in the Manufacturers area of the screen and then double-clicking on 'Client for Microsoft Networks' in the Network Clients area. Repeat this to install each of the client types needed on the computer.

FIGURE 6.18

Selecting the network
clients to install

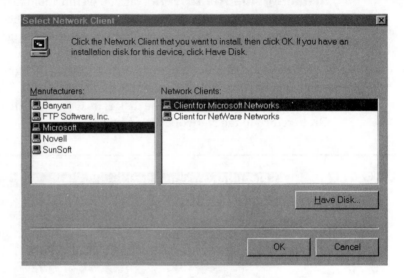

If the computer you're setting up needs Novell NetWare 3.*x* support, I strongly suggest you use client NetWare support from Microsoft rather than from Novell—unless, of course, there's some reason the computer needs Novell's ODI stack or can't use Microsoft's substitute. If the computer needs NetWare 4.*x* support, you'll have to use Novell's own shell support. Novell's and Microsoft's support for each other's networks is constantly changing; stay in touch with the vendors for news on the latest and greatest.

Installing Network Protocols   When you finish adding clients, you're ready to add any network protocols the computer needs. Back in the Network dialog box, click on Add, then double-click on Protocol. This brings up the Select Network Protocol dialog box shown in Figure 6.19.

Depending on the clients you've added, you will already have installed some protocols. For example, if you've added Microsoft's support for its and Novell's networks, you've already installed the NetBEUI and IPX/SPX protocols. In the Select Network Protocol dialog box, add TCP/IP support. I prefer Microsoft's implementation of TCP/IP. To install it, just select 'Microsoft' from the list on the left and 'TCP/IP' from the list on the right. You'll be taken through a standard TCP/IP installation process.

FIGURE 6.19

Selecting the network
protocols to install

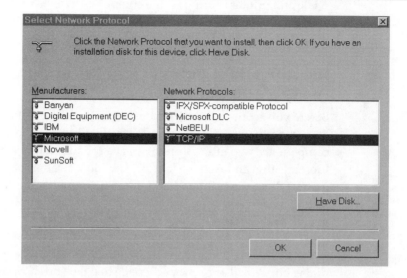

Installing Network Services   You can add some special network-oriented services to the computer you're setting up. From the Network dialog box, click on Add, then double-click on Service in the resulting Select Network Component Type dialog box. This brings up the Select Network Service dialog box shown in Figure 6.20. Services include file and printer sharing for Microsoft and NetWare networks, as well as some backup agents.

FIGURE 6.20

Selecting which network-
ing services to install

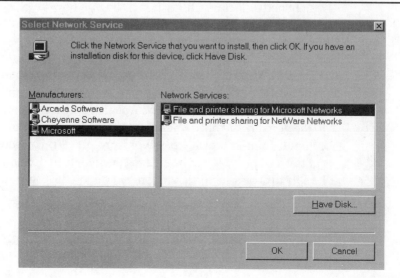

File and printer sharing let the computer share its resources with others in its domain. The agents allow backup software that's running on another computer to back up all or part of the machine you're setting up.

Identification, Domain Log On, and Access Control

Before you set up any networking parameters, the Network dialog box has only one property page, Configuration (see Figure 6.16). Once you've added network components, two more property pages are added to the Network dialog box: Identification and Access Control. The Identification page lets you enter information about the computer and the login domain. The Access Control page is for setting resource-sharing security options for the computer. Let's take a brief look at each of these pages.

Identification   Click on the Identification tab at the top of the Network dialog box. You'll see a property page like the one shown in Figure 6.21. Type in the name you want to give the computer you're installing. You can optionally type in a description of the computer.

Domain Log On   Now you need to set up for the domain you want to access. Click on the Network dialog box's Configuration tab (see Figure 6.22). Then double click on Client for Microsoft Networks to bring up the dialog box shown in Figure 6.23. Select Log on to Windows NT domain. Type in the name of the domain you want to log into; in my case, LA. Select 'Quick logon' or 'Logon' and restore network connections, depending on how much network traffic you want to generate at initial logon and whether you want users to wait a bit when they connect to a network resource for the first time.

Access Control   Next, click the Access Control tab in the Network dialog box to bring up the Access Control property page (see Figure 6.24). Here's where you set security for the computer. With share-level access control, anyone who logs in to the domain will have full access to any disk files or printers shared out on the computer, unless they are password-protected. If you select the 'User-level access control' option, you will be able to specify which domain users and groups will be able to access each resource shared out on the computer.

FIGURE 6.21

Identifying the computer

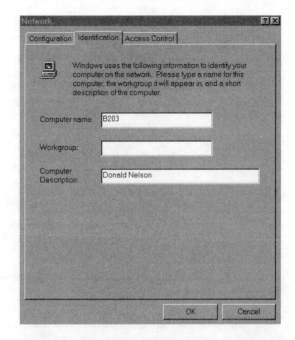

FIGURE 6.22

Preparing to configure
the Client for Microsoft
Networks

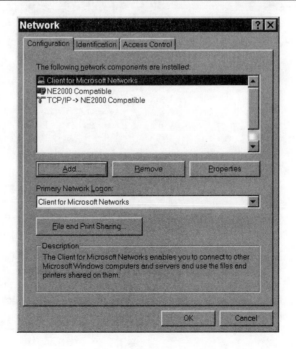

FIGURE 6.23

Setting domain log on
information for the Client
for Microsoft Networks

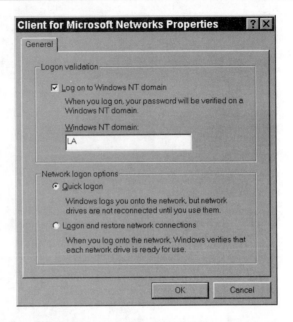

FIGURE 6.24

Setting access para-
meters for shared
resources

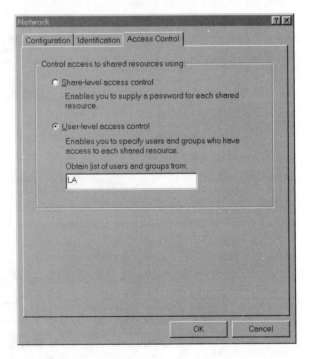

Rebooting to Implement Changes

When you're done with network configuration, click on OK in the Network dialog box. You'll be told to reboot your computer for the changes you've made to take effect; go ahead and reboot now. When the Windows 95 screen comes back up, you should be able to see your NT server when you double-click on your desktop's Network Neighborhood icon.

Windows NT Workstation

Like NT Server, NT Workstation lets you do network configuration at the time you install it. And as with NT Server, if you need to do a network configuration after installing NT Workstation, you can do it by double-clicking on the Network icon in the NT Workstation Control Panel. This brings up the Network dialog box shown in Figure 6.25. You may have to fish around a bit, but you should be able to find the NT Workstation equivalents of all the buttons and pick lists we just covered for Windows 95.

FIGURE 6.25

NT Workstation's Network Settings dialog box

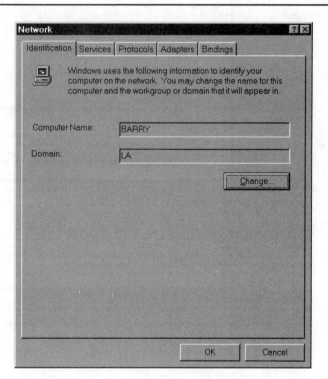

Windows for Workgroups

I won't even mention Windows 3.1. In my opinion, Windows for Workgroups is *the* only choice if you want to network Windows and you're not ready for Windows 95 or NT Workstation. You can upgrade existing Windows 3.1 installations to Windows for Workgroups for a modest sum, then use Windows for Workgroups for all new installations.

As with the other Windows operating systems, you can do a networking setup when you install Windows for Workgroups, as long as the computer has a network adapter. If you need to mess with networking after installation, click on the Network Setup icon in the Network program group; this opens the Windows for Workgroups Network Setup dialog box (see Figure 6.26). As with NT Workstation, you should be able to determine very quickly how to do all of the network setup tasks I've already discussed in detail for Windows 95.

FIGURE 6.26

Windows for Workgroups' Network Setup dialog box

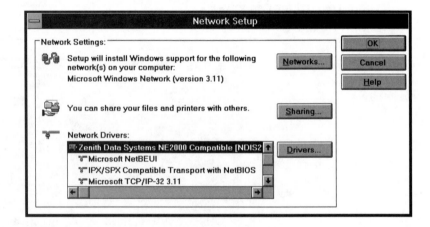

Novell NetWare and Other Clients

If you have clients that run NetWare drivers, there are a couple of ways you can give them general access to NT servers. You can read about these in *Mastering Windows NT Server 4*. I'll talk a bit about NetWare–to–Exchange Server connectivity in Chapter 11. In addition, if you need to link DOS or OS/2 workstations to NT Server, check out *Mastering Windows NT Server 4*.

Conclusion

In this chapter you learned how to install a Windows NT server: preparing hardware, installing software, hooking up and configuring UPS and backup protection, giving domain access to users and NT systems, configuring networking, and setting up different kinds of clients.

With NT Server in place, we can now move on to installing Exchange Server itself. Here we goooooooooooooooooooooooo [fade toward the end]. You didn't think our trip to Wonderland was over, did you?

CHAPTER

SEVEN

7

Installing an Exchange Server

- Getting ready

- Installation

- Preparing to run Exchange Server

This will be a fun chapter because, after all the theory and planning and installation of NT Server, we're actually going to get an Exchange server up and running. Installing an Exchange server is a three-step process. First, you go through several operations to prepare for the installation. Second, you run the Exchange Server Setup program. And third, you do a few minor housekeeping chores once installation is complete. Let's get to work.

Getting Ready

Before installing an Exchange server, you'll need to ensure that your hardware is properly set up. Then you'll have to pull together some key information about your NT server, a couple of user accounts, and your soon-to-be Exchange server. Finally, you'll set up security for your Exchange server.

Verifying Server Hardware Setup

If you've read the previous chapters, you're more than ready now. Unless you're running a really basic test machine, I'm assuming you've got that 200MHz Pentium system with 128MB of RAM and two 2GB SCSI-2 drives that I recommended back in Chapter 5. You should also have installed a good UPS and a 4mm or 8mm SCSI-2 tape backup device.

Gathering NT Server Information

You'll need to assemble information on the domain system that Exchange Server will be installed into, as well as the type of NT server you'll be installing it on.

The Domain Model

If you're installing Exchange Server in a single-domain system as defined in Chapter 4, you won't have to take any special steps before installation. If Exchange Server will operate in domain systems based on any of the other three domain models defined in Chapter 4, or if your Exchange site will cross domains, I assume you've already set up the required cross-domain trusts.

The NT Server's Role

As I suggested earlier in this book, you'll normally want to run Exchange Server on an NT server that is neither a primary nor backup domain controller. This is to ensure that Exchange Server and domain-controller functions, both of which can place a heavy load on your server, won't have to compete with each other on the same server.

This, of course, is the ideal. Since this is your first Exchange server installation, you'll probably use the NT server you set up in the last chapter. And since it's probably the first NT server you've set up, it's also acting as a primary domain controller. Not to worry—just don't expect to run a monster production Exchange server on this kind of setup.

All of the above goes double for the Internet Information Server (IIS). If you want to access your Exchange Server from the Internet, for example, to work with mail in your Exchange mailbox, you'll need to be running IIS. IIS can be an even bigger resource hog on an NT Server than domain controller support. For early testing and learning it's fine to run Exchange Server and IIS on an NT server that is also a domain controller. I do strongly suggest, however, you use that 200MHz Pentium jobbie I've been touting.

The NT Server Name

Be sure you've set the NT server computer name to the name you want Exchange Server to use when referring to the third item in the Exchange hierarchy, the server. If it's not set to the desired name, *change it now*. To change the name after Exchange installation is difficult to impossible.

Gathering Account Information

To install Exchange Server, you'll need info about the NT server's Administrator account. You'll also have to come up with names for an NT account and group you'll create later in this chapter.

The Administrator Account for the NT Server

When you installed NT Server you created an account (probably named "Administrator") and entered a password for it. Be sure you've got the password at hand.

The User Name and Password for the Site Services Account

In a minute, you'll create a special domain-based Windows NT security account that will be used by all Exchange servers in a site to run Exchange Server processes. Without this account, Exchange Server processes can't run—which means that Exchange Server itself can't run. The account also ensures that unauthorized Exchange servers can't be introduced into an Exchange site.

Pick a user name and password for this account (the name "Services" is a good if unimaginative choice). You'll create the Site Services account very shortly.

The Name of the Exchange Server Administration Group

It's a good idea to set up a domain-based group that has specific rights to administer an Exchange server. Then, when you need to give someone these rights, all you have to do is add them to the group.

You'll create the Exchange Server administration group in just a bit. Right now, you just have to pick a name for it. A good choice is "Exchange Admins." My creativity zooms.

Gathering Exchange Server Information

The Exchange Server Setup program will give you a number of options. To respond to some of these options, you'll need some specific information, including the names of your organization and site, the path where Exchange Server is to be installed, and a list of the Exchange Server components you want to install.

The Organization and Site Names

The organization and site names represent the top two items in the Exchange hierarchy. You should have these ready from Chapter 5.

The Installation Path

The Setup program defaults to the path C:\EXCHSRVR. Unless there's some reason that you can't use this path, accept the default.

What Will Be Installed?

As with most programs installed in Microsoft Windows environments, you'll be able to choose which Exchange Server components you want to install. Options include Exchange Server itself and the Exchange Administrator program. Within these options you can choose whether to install specific subsets of components. For your first installation, you'll probably want to install everything—which is *a lot* of stuff; that's one reason for the high-capacity drives.

NOTE   Exchange client software can be set up so that users can install it from a server. This is done in a separate step that we'll cover in Chapter 11.

Setting Up Security

As I noted earlier, Exchange security is based on an NT security account (Site Services) and administration group (the Exchange Server administration group). We're now ready to set these up.

Creating the Site Services Account

To set up the Site Services account, log in to the domain in which you'll be installing Exchange Server. Log in as Administrator, then open the User Manager for Domains in the Administrative Tools program group. (Go back to Chapter 6 if you need background on the User Manager for Domains.)

From the main User Manager for Domains window, click on the User menu and select New User. Next, fill in the New User dialog box that pops up (use Figure 7.1 as a guide). Be sure to deselect the 'User Must Change Password at Next Logon' box and to select 'User Cannot Change Password' and 'Password Never Expires.' When you're done, click on Add and then click on Close. (The Cancel button turns into a Close button after you click on Add.) On installation, Exchange Server Setup will grant any required rights to the account you've just created.

FIGURE 7.1

Setting up the Site Services account

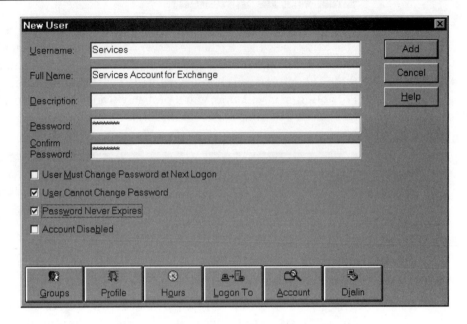

Remain in the User Manager for Domains for the next step.

If you haven't already done so, create an account for yourself. We'll use the account in just a second.

> **WARNING** Be sure to record the user name and password for the Site Services account; you'll need them when you install Exchange Server.

Creating the Exchange Server Administration Group

From the User menu in the User Manager for Domains, select New Global Group and enter a group name and description in the dialog box that pops up (see Figure 7.2). Then, from the Not Members box, select the users to be added to the group and click on Add. (Add the account you created for yourself to the group.) Finally, close the User Manager for Domains applet by clicking on the close button.

After Exchange Server has been installed, you'll be able to grant your group the proper permissions. I'll cover that process later in this chapter.

FIGURE 7.2

Setting up the Exchange Server administration group

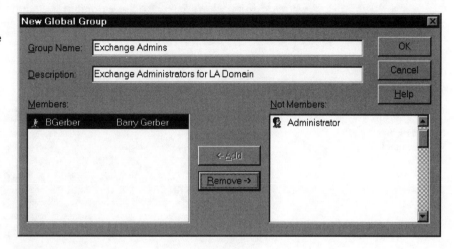

Running the Exchange Server Setup Program

At last! Be sure to pick the directory on the CD-ROM with the correct processor version (Alpha, Intel 386, or PPC) and language (English, French, and so forth) for your installation environment. Remember, you're choosing the language that such things as event logs will appear in—not the languages Exchange clients will support.

Use Windows NT Explorer to find the Exchange Server Setup program for your processor. You'll find it under the SETUP directory on the Exchange Server CD-ROM. When you've located the program, double-click on its name to start it up. Let's discuss some of the screens you'll see once Exchange Server's Setup program is up and running.

WARNING The first thing you'll see when the Setup program starts running is a dialog box like the one in Figure 7.3. If any programs are running on the server, close them. Lots of stuff gets updated by Setup, so take this warning seriously. When you're done reading the information in the dialog box, click on OK.

FIGURE 7.3

Setup's technical and legal warnings

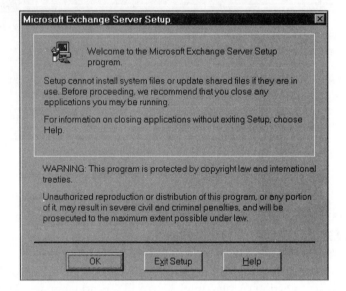

Selecting Installation Options

Setup will now tell you that it's searching for installed Exchange Server components. When the search is done, you'll need to pick the installation mode you want and set the directory in which Exchange Server will be installed (see Figure 7.4). Again, I suggest accepting the default directory for this first Exchange Server installation.

Batch Mode Installation

You can actually install Exchange Server in a noninteractive batch mode, which can be especially useful when you're installing remotely. You'll need a program that lets you do software distribution, such as Microsoft's NT Server-based System Management Server.

Check out the Exchange Server documentation and the sample batch files on the Exchange Server CD-ROM for more on batch installations.

Next, click on Complete/Custom for the type of installation. This brings up a dialog box like the one in Figure 7.5, which offers you the option of installing four sets of Exchange Server components: Microsoft Exchange Server, Microsoft Exchange Administrator, Books Online, and Active Server Components. By now you should be pretty clear on what the Server and Administrator components are. Books Online are Exchange Server's online documentation. Active Server Components support Internet browser access to Exchange Server for such things as reading mail and looking up addresses.

FIGURE 7.4

Choosing installation options

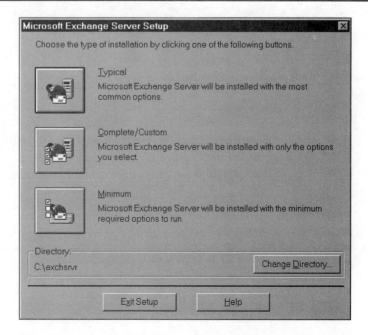

FIGURE 7.5

Selecting the Exchange
Server components to
be installed

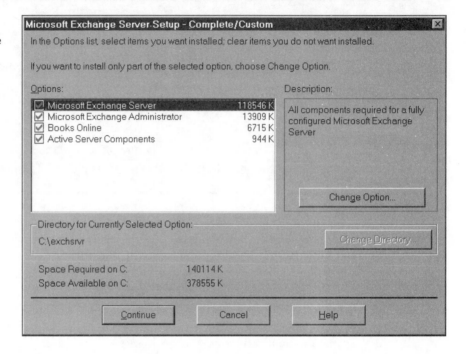

Refining Installation Options

If the Change Option button is highlighted when you click on one of the
options in the Complete/Custom dialog box shown in Figure 7.5, you can
specify which subcomponents under that option are to be installed. For
example, you can choose which specific server components you want to
install by selecting Microsoft Exchange Server and then clicking on Change
Option. See Figure 7.6.

You'll find this capability useful when installing additional Exchange servers in
a site. For example, you may not need to install certain Exchange connectors
in a site. You can deselect their installation with the Change Option button.

FIGURE 7.6

Selecting Additional Exchange Server components for installation

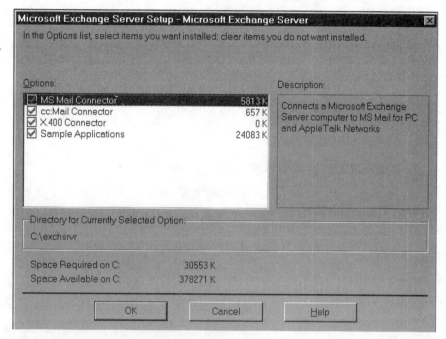

> **Microsoft Exchange Server Setup - Microsoft Exchange Server**
>
> In the Options list, select items you want installed; clear items you do not want installed.
>
> Options:
> - ☑ MS Mail Connector   5813 K
> - ☑ cc:Mail Connector   657 K
> - ☑ X.400 Connector   0 K
> - ☑ Sample Applications   24083 K
>
> Description:
> Connects a Microsoft Exchange Server computer to MS Mail for PC and AppleTalk Networks
>
> Directory for Currently Selected Option:
> C:\exchsrvr
>
> Space Required on C: 30553 K
> Space Available on C: 378271 K
>
> [OK]   [Cancel]   [Help]

For the first Exchange Server installation in a site, it usually makes sense to install all components. So be sure that all boxes are checked and click on Continue to move on. If you've already installed Microsoft Internet Information Server, Setup will tell you at this point that it's temporarily stopping the World Wide Web Publishing Service. Click on OK and you're on to licensing.

WARNING

You can install Active Server Components on your Exchange server or on another machine. At least to begin with, I suggest you install them on your Exchange server. Active Server Components do their thing in consort with Microsoft's Internet Information Server (IIS). To install Active Server Components on any machine, the machine must be running NT Server 4.0 with Service Pack 2 or greater. Additionally, it must be running Internet Information Server 3.0 or greater. Finally, IIS's Active Server Pages must be installed. Whew! See Chapter 6 for more on all of this. If the prerequisite software isn't installed and running, Exchange Server Setup won't even let you think about installing Active Server Components.

> **NOTE**
>
> If you're an old hand at Exchange Server installation, you may be wondering where the Internet Mail Connector is in the installation options list. Well, as noted in earlier chapters, the IMC has been renamed the "Internet Mail Service," or IMS. But don't go looking for the IMS on the installation options list, because it isn't installed when Exchange Server itself is installed. You install it later using the Exchange Administrator program. More about all of this in Chapter 15.

Selecting a Licensing Mode

As you can see in Figure 7.7, there are two ways to license client access to Exchange Server: per server or per seat. Choose the appropriate mode and fill in the number of concurrent connections if you choose Per Server (according to the licenses you purchased) and click on Continue.

FIGURE 7.7

Inputting client licensing information

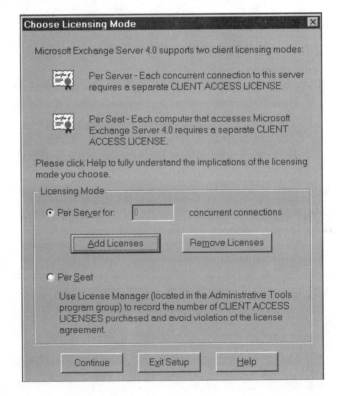

Entering Organization and Site Names

Here's another point at which to shout, "at last!" You can finally use that organization and site-name information you put together back in Chapter 5. (In Figure 7.8 I've entered the info for my fake company, GerCom.) When you're finished, click on OK. When prompted, click on OK a second time to confirm that you want to create a new site.

FIGURE 7.8

Inputting Exchange
Server organization and
site names

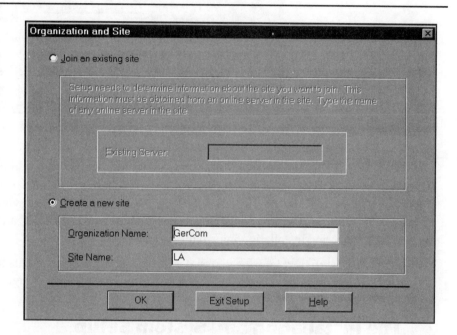

Specifying a Site Services Account

Now give Setup the name and password for the Site Services account you created a while back. (Figure 7.9 shows the dialog box for doing this.) Be careful here; you want to use the Site Services account you created, *not* the Administrator account you're logged in to right now.

FIGURE 7.9

Entering Site Services
account information

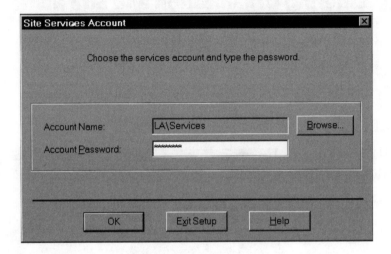

Find the account by clicking on Browse. The Add User or Group dialog box
pops up. Find the Site Services account you created earlier in this chapter—it'll be
called "Services" if you used the account name I suggested. Click on the name,
then click on Add, and finally click on OK. This will return you to the Site
Services Account dialog box. Enter the password, click OK, and you're done
entering installation information.

Setup next informs you that it has granted a series of rights to the Site Services
account. Click on OK to acknowledge the dialog box message.

File Installation and System Setup

Setup now begins copying files to your server. It then adds objects such as organization and site to the Exchange Server directory. Finally, it installs Exchange services such as the Message Transfer Agent (MTA), information store, and directory
service and modifies the registry on your NT server.

After installation is finished, you're offered an opportunity to run the Exchange
Server Performance Optimizer, which is a Microsoft Wizard. If you have only one
drive in your server, don't bother running the Optimizer. If you have more than
one drive, go ahead and run it. The Optimizer can improve the performance of
your Exchange server by moving Exchange Server database files to other hard
drives on the server. You can run the Optimizer now or as often as you want later.
Its first page is shown in Figure 7.10.

FIGURE 7.10

The first page of the Exchange Performance Optimizer

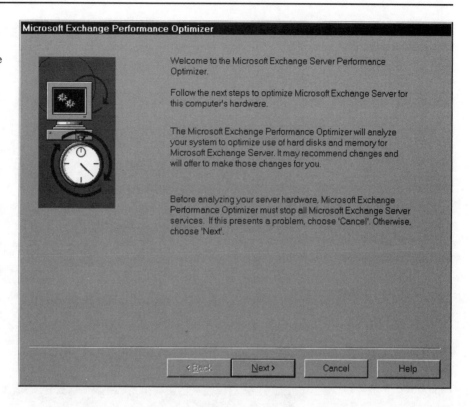

Click on the Next button on the first page, and the Optimizer stops all currently running Exchange Server services. You're then taken to the second Optimizer page (see Figure 7.11). Type in the appropriate information for your Exchange server. The only item that might give you some trouble is the one labeled 'Limit memory usage to.' If you select this item, Exchange Server will use no more than the amount of RAM memory indicated in the MB field when it runs. This is useful if you're using the server to run other programs such as Microsoft SQL Server, or if the server is acting as a primary or backup NT domain controller. If you choose to use this option, allow at least 32MB for Exchange Server. The default value of zero gives Exchange Server access to all server memory.

When you're done filling in the fields on the second Optimizer page, click on Next. The Optimizer will now begin analyzing your hard drives to determine the best location for various Exchange files (see Figure 7.12).

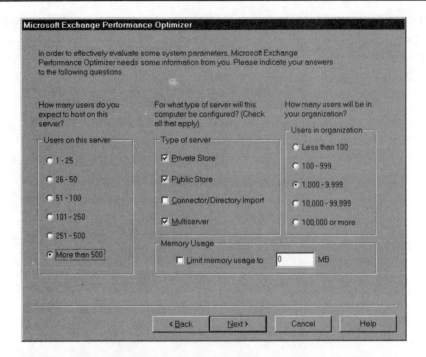

FIGURE 7.11

Entering information to be used by Exchange Performance Optimizer

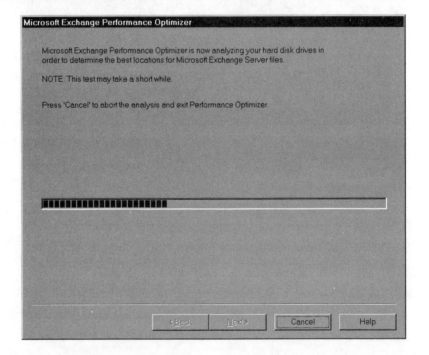

FIGURE 7.12

The Exchange Performance Optimizer analyzes server hard disks to determine where to put Exchange Server database files.

After the Optimizer has finished its analysis, it asks you to click on Next to continue. Do so and you're presented with suggested locations for the various Exchange Server databases. If you don't like any of the suggestions, change them and then click on Next.

Figure 7.13 shows the suggestions that the Optimizer came up with for my Exchange server. The Optimizer suggests putting the Exchange transaction logs on drive C and the database files on drive D. Remember in the last chapter I created a FAT partition for the transaction logs (D:) and a NTFS partition for the databases (E:)? So, before accepting the Optimizer's suggestions, I'll replace C: with D: for the two transaction logs, and D: with E: for the four databases. The Optimizer next asks if you want it to automatically move the database files it suggested should be moved (see Figure 7.14). Though there is a way to move these files yourself, it's best to let the Optimizer do the moving. So leave the 'Move files automatically' option selected and click on Next. Since you're running the Optimizer right after installing Exchange Server, don't worry about the warning to back up your database files. If you run the program after you've created Exchange recipients and such, then for added safety be sure to back up those files before letting the Optimizer move them.

FIGURE 7.13

The Exchange Performance Optimizer suggests new locations for some Exchange databases.

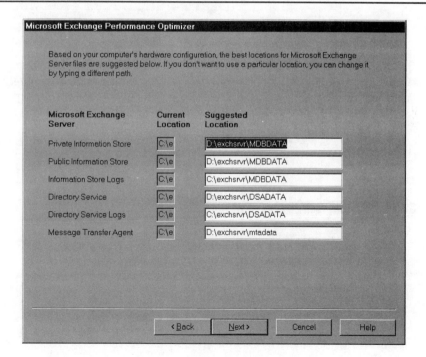

FIGURE 7.14

The Exchange
Performance Optimizer
is ready to move certain
Exchange Server
database files.

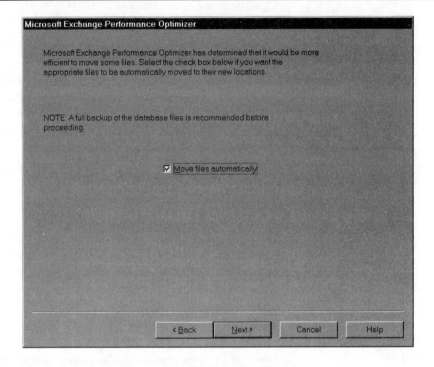

After the Optimizer has churned away for a while, you'll see the last Wizard page telling you that optimization is finished and that a log of the optimization process will be written to disk. The Optimizer will also tell you that it's ready to restart the Exchange Server services it stopped. Click on Finish, and the program will save some parameters and restart the services.

When the Optimizer is finished, Exchange Server will be up and running.

Postinstallation Activities

You'll need to complete a series of tasks immediately after installation:

- Check out Exchange Server's Windows program group
- Ensure that all required Exchange Server processes are up and running

- Ensure that Exchange communications are working properly (by starting up the Administrator program)

- Set up permissions for the Exchange Server administration group

You do these tasks while logged in to your Exchange server as the domain administrator. Since you installed your Exchange server under that login, you should be ready to go.

Exchange Server's Windows Program Group

The first thing you'll see after successfully installing Exchange Server is a new Windows program group called 'Microsoft Exchange.' Figure 7.15 shows the group as it appears just after completion of Exchange Server installation. To get to this program group under normal circumstances, click on the Start button on NT Server's Task Bar, select Programs, and then select Microsoft Exchange. (See Figure 7.16.)

FIGURE 7.15

The Microsoft Exchange program group just after Exchange Server is installed

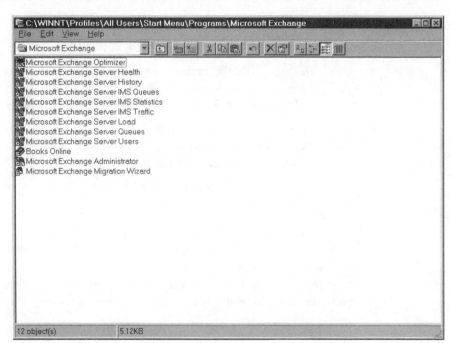

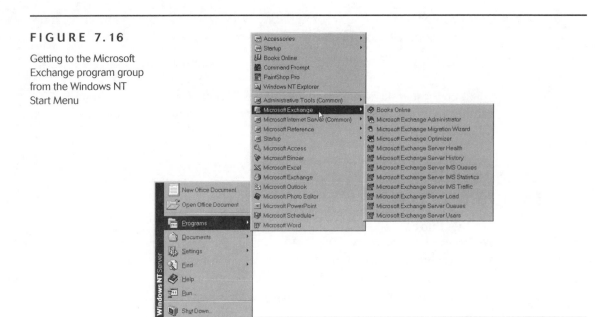

FIGURE 7.16

Getting to the Microsoft Exchange program group from the Windows NT Start Menu

The Microsoft Exchange program group initially contains three key applications:

> *The Exchange Administrator.* This application is used to do just about everything, from adding users to setting up links with other Exchange servers and foreign messaging systems. You'll use it extensively from here on.

> *The Exchange Migration Wizard.* The Migration Wizard moves users from various mail systems (for example, Microsoft Mail for PC Networks, cc:Mail, and Novell GroupWise) to Exchange; I'll go over it in Chapter 17.

> *The Microsoft Exchange Optimizer.* Use this icon to run the Performance Optimizer anytime you want.

Microsoft has also included icons in the Microsoft Exchange program group for a set of preconfigured, Exchange Server–oriented NT Performance Monitor runs. (I talked about the Performance Monitor back in Chapter 4.) These icons let you keep an eye on some key Exchange Server components and can warn you about problems before they get to the trash-your-system stage.

Verifying That Exchange Server Processes Are Running

Now you need to make sure that all Exchange Server processes are running. If they're not, you'll have to do some troubleshooting.

Are the Services Running?

Open the Start menu by clicking on the Start button on NT Server's Task Bar. Select Settings and then select Control Panel. In the Control Panel, double-click on the Services icon. This brings up the NT Services monitoring and control dialog box that I first discussed in Chapter 4. A typical NT server has a number of services, so you'll probably have to scroll down to see the services that are specific to Microsoft Exchange. Your Services dialog box should look pretty much like the one shown in Figure 7.17.

FIGURE 7.17

The Services dialog box with Exchange Server processes displayed

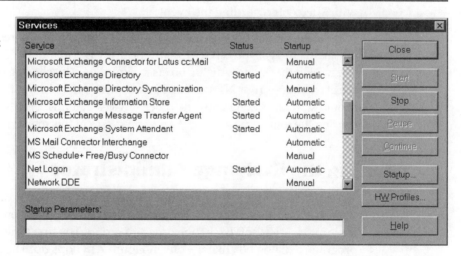

Make sure that the Exchange directory, information store, MTA, and System Attendant are up and running. Remember: Exchange Server doesn't even exist if these four core components aren't running.

Don't try to start any Exchange Server services that aren't running, even if the service applet says they are to start up automatically. If a service other than one of the four core components isn't running at this time, it shouldn't be running at all.

For example, notice in Figure 7.17 that the service MS Mail Connector Interchange isn't running on my server. That's because I haven't yet entered the parameters required to run it.

If all is well, click on Close and move on to the next section, which deals with the Exchange Administrator.

Troubleshooting Problems with Services

If some or all of the Exchange Server processes that should be running aren't, first take a look at the NT Event Log using the Event Viewer, which I discussed back in Chapter 4. The Event Viewer is in the Administrative Tools program group. The Event Viewer can display three logs: System, Security, and Application. If the Application Log isn't being displayed, select Application from the Event Viewer's Log menu. Look for events related to Exchange Server that are marked with a red stop-sign icon—these indicate serious problems such as failure to start a service. If you find a problem that you think you can handle, try to fix it; otherwise, check with Microsoft regarding the event.

In the meantime, you can try shutting down the server and rebooting it. If that doesn't fix things, you can try to start the processes manually. To do this, highlight a service in the Services dialog box (see Figure 7.17) by clicking on it, then click on the Start button. Your NT server will chug away for a bit, and then the service should start up—along with any other services that this service depends on. Try starting the four core Exchange Server processes in this manner.

Starting the Exchange Administrator

To set permissions for the Exchange Server administration group you created a while back, you'll use the Exchange Administrator application. The Administrator is in the Microsoft Exchange program group. The first time you run the program, a dialog box like the one in Figure 7.18 pops up. The Administrator is a client to Exchange Server, so you have to tell it which server to connect to. Type in the name of your server (or click on Browse to bring up a tree with the Exchange hierarchy on it, then find your server on the tree and double-click on it). Select the Set as default checkbox so that the Administrator will always go to this server on start-up, then click on OK.

After a bit of churning, the Administrator window should open—proof that Exchange client/server communications are working. The Administrator (the client) was able to talk to your Exchange server (the server). Note that in this case both the client and server parts of the application are running on the same computer, your NT/Exchange server. Figure 7.19 shows my Exchange Administrator window.

FIGURE 7.18

Selecting a default Exchange server for the Administrator program

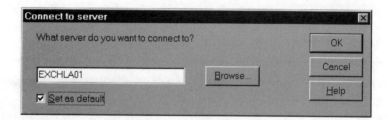

FIGURE 7.19

The Exchange Administrator window

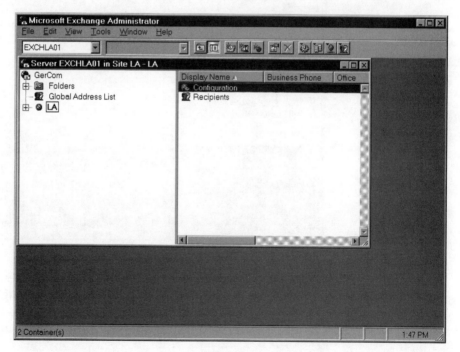

You've seen the Administrator in earlier chapters; now you'll actually start using it. Just to get a feel for how it works, double-click on the name of your site in the Administrator window; mine's called "LA." Your window should look similar to the one in Figure 7.20. By double-clicking on the LA site object, I opened it and displayed the other objects it contains. There's another way to display the objects an object contains. If there's a little plus sign to the left of an object, it contains other objects. Click on the plus sign to display the objects. (All of this probably reminds you of the Windows 95 and NT Explorers' display.) Incidentally, this same tree interface is used in the Exchange client.

FIGURE 7.20

Displaying objects contained in the site object

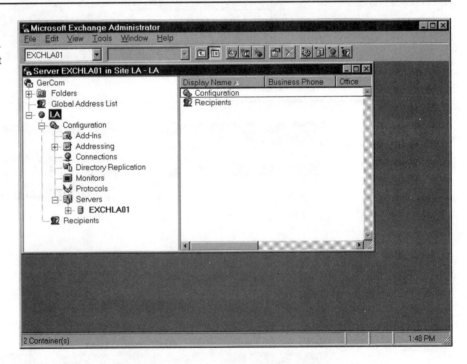

Go ahead and play around with the Administrator's objects; you've earned some rest and relaxation time. Just don't try to delete anything. When you're done, leave the Administrator window open and join me in setting up some key access rights for your Exchange server.

Running Administrator Remotely

As long as you have the right security permissions, you can run the Exchange Administrator program from any networked NT workstation or server. This is convenient, since you won't have to keep running to an Exchange server to administer it.

To install the Administrator on any other NT computer, just run the Exchange Server Setup program from that machine, select the Complete/Custom installation option, and select only the Microsoft Exchange Administrator for installation. Once the Administrator is installed, start it up and run it just as you did on the Exchange server.

Setting Permissions for the Exchange Server Administration Group

By setting the appropriate permissions, you'll fix it so that users who are put into the Exchange Server administration group can access your Exchange server. Assuming you're still in the Exchange Administrator, click on the site name in the hierarchy tree, then from the Administrator's File menu select Properties. A dialog box like the one in Figure 7.21 pops up.

Select the Permissions property page tab to bring up a dialog box like the one shown in Figure 7.22. Notice that the Administrator account you created when you installed NT Server and the Services account you set up earlier are the only ones with rights to administer in your Exchange site.

Next, click on the Add button in the Permissions property page to open up the Add Users and Groups dialog box (see Figure 7.23). Select the Exchange Server administration group you created earlier, then click on the Add button in the dialog box.

Before you click on OK, take a look at the top of the Add Users and Groups dialog box. The little List Names From drop-down menu at the top lets you give users or groups in trusted domains permission to administer your Exchange server. It's a pretty powerful menu, because it makes possible remote administration from anywhere you've got a network connection to any available domain. We'll use it quite a bit in later chapters.

FIGURE 7.21

The General property
page of the site proper-
ties dialog box

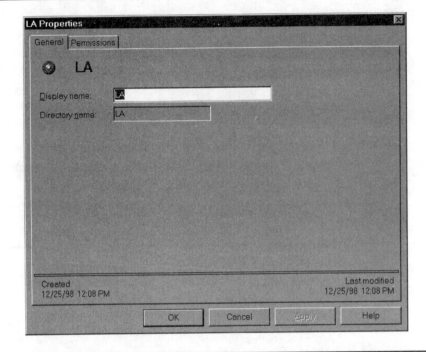

FIGURE 7.22

The Permissions
property page of the site
properties dialog box

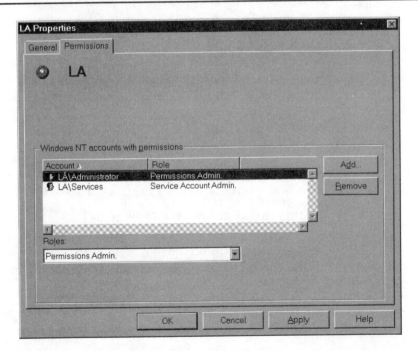

FIGURE 7.23

Granting administrative permissions to an Exchange Server administration group.

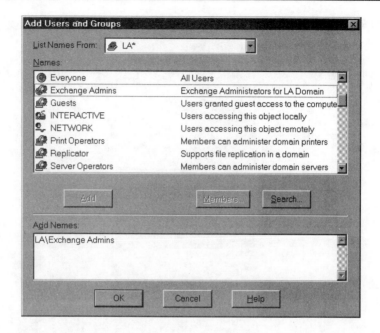

After you click on OK in the Add Users and Groups dialog box, you'll see that anyone who belongs to the Exchange administration group now has basic administrative rights for the site (Role = 'Admin'). (See Figure 7.24.) If you want the group to have full control over the site, assign it the role Permissions Admin. I strongly suggest that you give Permissions Admin. rights to the administration group, unless you and others plan to administer your Exchange server while logged in as NT administrator. The NT administrator account has full control over the site because when you installed Exchange Server it was assigned Permissions Admin. rights for the site by default.

To assign the role Permissions Admin. to your Exchange administration group, open the Roles drop-down list in the Permissions property page by clicking on the down arrow on the right-hand side of the list. This opens the list (see Figure 7.25). Click on Permissions Admin. in the drop-down list.

Your Exchange adminstration group now has the rights associated with the role Permissions Admin. (see Figure 7.26). Click OK on the site Properties dialog box and you're done.

FIGURE 7.24

The Exchange adminis-
tration group now has
basic administration
rights for the site

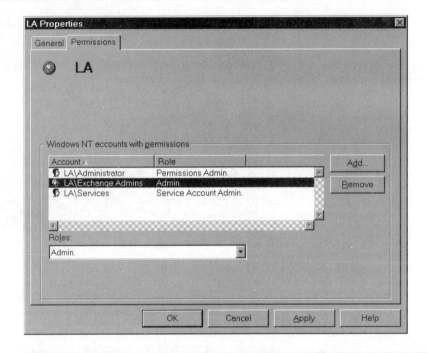

FIGURE 7.25

Granting Permission
Admin. rights to the
Exchange administra-
tion group

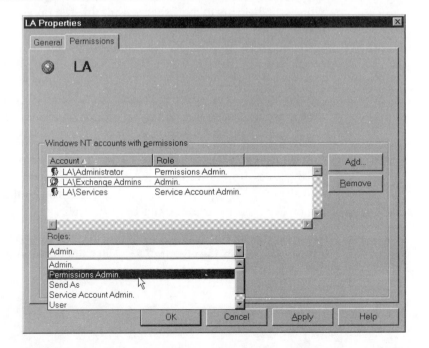

FIGURE 7.26

The Exchange administration group now has Permission Admin. rights for the site.

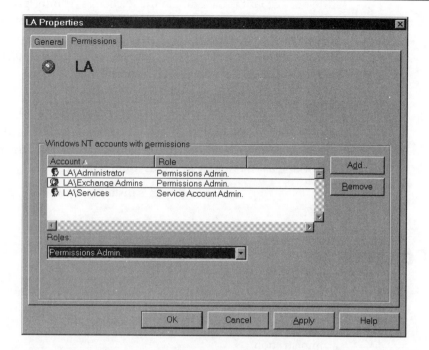

In order to complete the exercises in the rest of this book, you'll need to give Permissions Admin. rights to the Exchange administration group at both the site and Configuration container levels.

Accounts and groups with permissions at the site level inherit rights to the site recipients container, but they do not inherit rights to the Configuration container. So you also need to give the Exchange administration group the rights to the site's Configuration container. To do so, just click on the container name (see Figure 7.20 for the location of the Configuration container). Then select Properties from the Administrator's File menu and click on the Permissions property page on the resultant Configuration properties dialog box. Finally, repeat the steps you just completed for the site, and you're done.

If your account is included in the Exchange Admins group, you no longer have to log into NT as Administrator to administer any Exchange server in the site. Just to test things out, log out of your NT server. To log out click on the Start button, select Shut Down, click on Close all programs and log on as a different user, and then click on Yes. When asked, simultaneously press the Ctrl, Alt, and Delete keys to log back in using your own NT account.

To be sure that the Exchange Server administration group is set up properly, double-click on the Exchange Administrator icon. If the Administrator runs and you're able to fiddle around in the hierarchy tree, your membership in the group is working as it should. Close the Administrator.

That's it. Your Exchange server is installed, optimized, and ready to use.

Conclusion

In this chapter you learned how to prepare for an Exchange Server installation, install Exchange Server, and take care of some postinstallation housekeeping chores. In the next couple of chapters, I'll introduce you to basic Exchange Server administration.

PART III

Basic Exchange Server Administration and Management

So you've got Exchange Server up and running; now you need to get comfortable with its Administrator program. The next three chapters deal with the basics of Exchange Server administration and management. In Chapter 8 we'll focus on the Exchange Administrator and how you use its menus to do a wide range of useful system administration and management tasks. You'll learn everything from creating new Exchange mailboxes for users to setting up monitors that help keep Exchange servers up and running. In Chapter 9 we get into administering and managing Exchange Server's hierarchy and core components. You'll use the skills you gain to configure and maintain such things as Exchange information stores, message transfer agents, and public folders. And in Chapter 10 we tackle backing up and restoring Exchange servers. This process is as important for a stable and reliable Exchange system as carefully planned, well-administered, and efficiently managed Exchange servers.

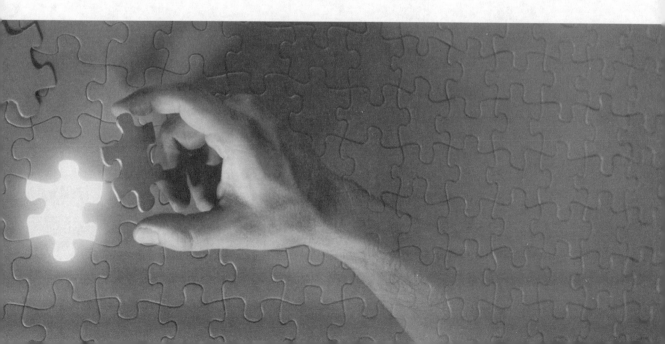

CHAPTER

EIGHT

8

The Administrator and Its Menus

- Administration and management defined

- Exchange Administrator basics

- The Exchange Administrator File menu

- The Exchange Administrator Edit menu

- The Exchange Administrator View menu

- The Exchange Administrator Tools menu

This chapter and the next walk you through lots of menus and pages for setting properties of one kind or another. I think you'll find it useful to track through everything once and set some specific Exchange Server parameters when appropriate. When you need to come back to a particular section, it should be relatively easy to find. Just remember that Chapter 8 deals with basic Exchange Administrator program menus, while Chapter 9 covers objects in the Exchange hierarchy, including the four core Exchange components.

Administration and Management

Notice that this section of the book deals with Exchange Server administration *and* management. There's a real and sharp difference between the two terms. In a nutshell, *administration* is everything you do to set up Exchange Server, while *management* is what you do to keep the server running and its users happy.

Administration includes tasks like creating Exchange recipients such as mailboxes and distribution lists; setting up Exchange server backups; and configuring Exchange components such as sites, servers, Message Transfer Agents (MTAs), and connectors. Management covers tasks like monitoring Exchange servers and ensuring that they keep running, backing up and restoring a server, tracking mail messages to find out why they weren't delivered, and keeping address book information current as people change offices and phone numbers.

You use the Exchange Administrator program to do both administration and management, so "Administrator" might seem like a less-than-comprehensive name for the program. But when I consider the alternatives—the sexist "Admin-Man," for example—the name seems just fine.

Administrator Windows

The Exchange Administrator takes advantage of several Microsoft Windows capabilities. For example, it lets you use multiple windows for views of one or more Exchange servers, and each window has two variable-size panes.

Multiple Windows

Figure 8.1 shows the Administrator window. Inside the window are two additional windows, both labeled in part 'Server EXCHLA01 in Site LA.' This tells you that you're looking at two views of the server EXCHLA01, which resides in the Exchange Server organization GerCom and the site LA.

You may recall from earlier chapters that Exchange Server is object-oriented and that the Administrator is the tool you use to manipulate its objects. Also, remember that some Exchange Server objects are containers—that is, they hold other objects. Not all objects are containers, but all containers are objects.

The lower window in Figure 8.1 shows the Recipients container for the LA site, hence the name 'Server EXCHLA01 in Site LA—Recipients.' Notice that the word "Recipients" in the left-hand pane is highlighted, telling you that the container is selected. The objects in the Recipients container—Exchange recipients—are shown in the right-hand pane.

FIGURE 8.1

Two views of the same Exchange server

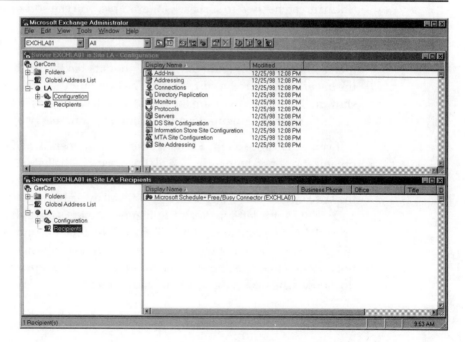

Because I just finished setting up EXCHLA01 and have created no recipients yet, the only recipient is the Schedule+ Free/Busy Connector. This connector is used to exchange Schedule+ information between Exchange sites and MS Mail post offices. This allows users in both systems to set up meetings using Microsoft Schedule+ while taking into account the schedules of potential meeting participants.

Notice the scroll bar at the bottom of the lower window. It's showing because there are more columns for the list of recipients than can be displayed, given the window's current width. Two columns aren't displayed in the lower window; these are labeled 'Department' and 'Modified.' Respectively, they show the recipient's department and the date and time when a recipient was last modified. To see columns that aren't displayed in a window, you can either resize the window or scroll over until the columns are visible.

While I'm talking about columns, note that you can re-sort the rows in certain lists. If a list has column title bars like the ones in the two windows in Figure 8.1, you can click on some of the bars to re-sort the list by the column. Not all column title bars can be used to sort lists, for example, you can sort recipients lists only by display name and the date an object was last modified.

The upper window shows the Configuration container within the LA site container. The term 'Configuration' isn't highlighted in the left-hand pane because the lower window is the current one. The Configuration and Recipients objects show in the LA site; these are the two second-level objects in the LA container. As you can see, the Configuration object contains a number of other objects.

If you want to see all the Exchange Server containers available in your organization, just double-click on all the objects in the left pane until there are no objects with plus (+) signs in front of them. Or you can click on all plus signs until they become minus (–) signs. At this point all available containers will be open and visible in the left-hand pane. In Figure 8.2 there's enough screen real estate to open all but two containers, OFFLINE ADDRESS BOOK and SCHEDULE+ FREE BUSY. There will come a time when you'll have so many sites and servers in your organization that opening all containers may give you repetitive-strain injury, so do it now, while you've got just one site and server.

FIGURE 8.2

Almost all of the containers in a new Exchange organization are displayed in the left-hand pane.

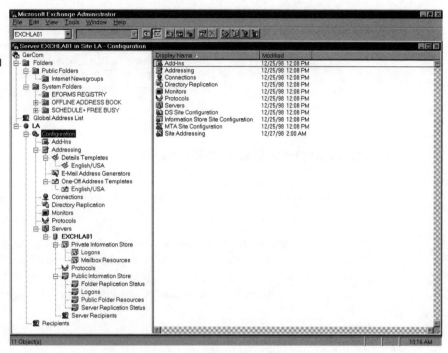

Now it's your turn. Open the Exchange Administrator. If you completed the exercises in the last chapter, one Exchange server view window opens automatically. You can see what's inside any object in the Exchange hierarchy—in the left-hand pane—by clicking on the object. Open your site by double-clicking on its name or by clicking on the plus sign to the left of the site's name. Then open another window by selecting New Window from the Windows menu. Now play with the two windows, getting each to display whatever you'd like. You can open more windows or close any of them at any time.

The neat thing about these multiple windows is that you can easily have different servers or sites open in different windows. This lets you manage multiple servers in multiple sites simultaneously (if, of course, you've got the necessary rights to those servers).

> **NOTE**   Try to start thinking of the collection of objects you see in the Adminis-
> trator as the *Exchange Directory*. A copy of the directory for an entire
> Exchange organization is stored on each Exchange server in the organi-
> zation. As you'll see later, the directory is automatically updated and
> replicated across the organization. This is what makes centralized man-
> agement of Exchange servers possible and extremely easy.

Manipulating the Splitbar

The left and right panes of the two windows in Figure 8.1 are divided by a
splitbar—a bar that lets you adjust for the amount of screen real estate used by the
two panes in a window.

To move the splitbar, just move your Windows pointer so that it's touching any
part of the splitbar and the pointer will turn into a crosshair. Then press and hold
down the left mouse button. While still holding down the left mouse button,
move the splitbar until you're happy with the size of the right and left panes.

Preliminary Settings

We're going to cover the Administrator's menus pretty much sequentially. Before
we start, however, you'll need to set a few parameters in a dialog box that you
access from a menu appearing later in the sequence.

Setting Auto Naming Options

Open the Administrator's Tools menu and click on Options to bring up the
Options dialog box (see Figure 8.3). Remember when I talked about the near-
religious issues surrounding Exchange Server display names and aliases earlier
in this book? Well, here's where you get to choose your religion and set the
default for the way display names are shown and aliases are created. You use
the Auto Naming property page to do this.

Pick your poison. Custom options let you use the variables *%First*, *%Initials*,
and *%Last* to construct a name. You can display selected characters from one of
the variables by placing a number after the percent sign in the variable name. (For
example, %1First displays the initial character in each first name—so the first
name *Barry* displays as *B*.) Click on Apply, but don't close the Options dialog box.

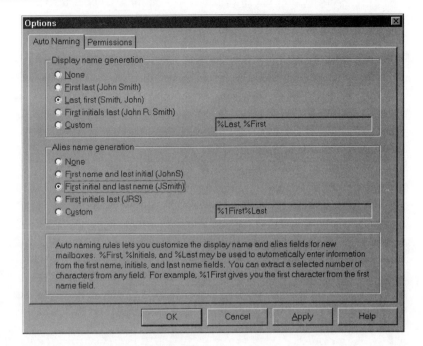

Setting Permissions Options

As you'll remember, Exchange Server security is based on NT Server security. You can give an NT account or group the permissions (rights) to administer and manage all Exchange servers in a site, as you did with your Exchange administration group in the last chapter. You can also permit different users or groups to administer different pieces of Exchange Server—even different Exchange servers. For example, you might give one group permissions to administer a specific site's recipients, while permitting a different user to administer each of the Exchange servers in a site.

With a few exceptions, if an NT account or group has permissions to an Exchange Server container, these permissions automatically extend to all objects in the container, including nested containers. Objects within the container automatically inherit the permissions that were granted to the account or group at the master container level. For example, when we gave the Exchange administration group (Exchange Admins) permissions in the site container, those permissions were inherited by objects in the site's Recipients container. As you'll discover in Chapter 9, permissions granted at the site level are not inherited by objects in the Configuration container which is also a subcontainer of the site container. I'll explain this apparently incongruous state of affairs in Chapter 9.

As we go through the Administrator's menus, you should see all of the permissions options for all objects, so you need to ensure that some general Administrator parameters are properly set. Click on the Permissions tab in the Options dialog box. Make sure your computer account's domain is showing and that 'Show Permissions page for all objects' and 'Display rights for roles on Permissions page' are selected (see Figure 8.4).

Don't worry about the whys and wherefores of these options right now; I promise that by the end of this chapter you'll be on intimate terms with both. If you've changed either of the two options, click on Apply, but don't close the Options dialog box yet.

> **NOTE** You might not want to set separate access permissions for every little piece of Exchange Server. If not, you can go back and deselect 'Show Permissions page for all objects' after we've gone through this chapter.

FIGURE 8.4

The Options dialog box shown with its Permissions property page

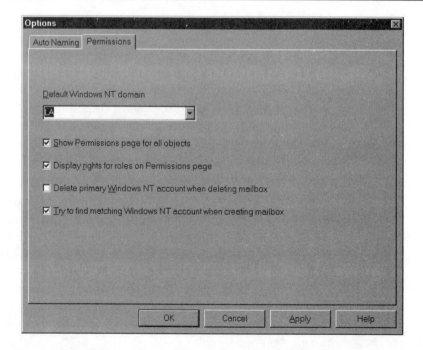

Setting the NT Account Deletion Option

Keep an eye on Figure 8.4 as we move along. Recall that you can create NT accounts while creating Exchange mailboxes, and vice versa. When you delete an NT account in the User Manager for Domains, you're asked if you want to delete the mailbox associated with the account as well. When you delete a mailbox in the Exchange Administrator, the NT account associated with it is deleted only if you select the option 'Delete primary Windows NT account when deleting mailbox.' If you select this option, you are alerted before the deletion and offered the opportunity to not delete the mailbox.

Setting the Option to Find a Matching Windows NT Account

As you'll soon see, when you create a mailbox you will usually assign an NT account to it. If the account doesn't exist, you can create a new one on the spot. If you want to assign the mailbox to an existing NT account, you can either search for it manually while creating the mailbox or select 'Try to find matching Windows NT account when creating mailbox.' If you check this option and, while you're creating a new mailbox, the Exchange Administrator finds an NT account with a user name that matches the alias you've given the mailbox, you'll be offered the option of assigning the account to the mailbox.

This can save a bit of manual searching time on already-established NT systems, so I suggest you accept the default check for the option. When you're finished, click on OK.

> **WARNING** The settings you established above apply to the copy of the Administrator program you're running now and to the account you are logged into now. If you install and run the program on another computer or log into the same computer under a different account, you'll need to modify these settings for that computer or account. Be very careful here. If your naming conventions aren't the same as Administrator's default, the recipients you create will be misnamed until you properly set auto-naming properties in the Options dialog box.

WARNING The setting we're about to make applies to your Exchange site. Once set, it stays in effect for the site until changed—no matter which copy of the Administrator you use to view the setting.

Changing Site Addresses

When you installed your Exchange server, at least four special site addresses were created for your site: cc:Mail, Microsoft Mail, SMTP (Internet), and X.400. These addresses are appended to Exchange Server recipient alias names to create full MS Mail and SMTP addresses. Exchange Server uses First and Last Names along with the site addresses to create full cc:Mail and X.400 addresses. For example, as you can see in Figure 8.5, the SMTP site address for the GerCom LA site is @LA.GerCom.com. My alias name is BGerber, and my SMTP address is BGerber@LA.GerCom.com.

You can change any of the four site addresses. Use caution here, however, because any changes you make should be based on addresses you have or expect to get in the real world. For example, if you've already got an Internet domain name, you'll want to change the site's SMTP address to reflect that name.

SMTP, cc:Mail, and X.400 addresses are modified in one way (which I'll talk about in a minute). Microsoft Mail addresses are modified using the Microsoft Mail Connector dialog box, which we'll cover in a later chapter. To change a cc:Mail, an SMTP, or an X.400 address, click on the Configuration container for your site in the left-hand pane of an Administrator window. Then double-click on the Site Addressing object, which is in the right-hand pane of the window, and click on the Site Addressing tab. (See Figure 8.2 for help in locating these objects.)

In the resultant Site Addressing dialog box, click on the address you want to change, then click on Edit (see Figure 8.5). Edit the address using the cc:Mail, SMTP, or X400 dialog box that pops up, then click on OK to close each dialog box.

We're done with the preliminaries. Now we're ready to move on to the first menu of the Administrator: the File menu.

FIGURE 8.5

The Site Addressing dialog box is used to change the base e-messaging address for a site.

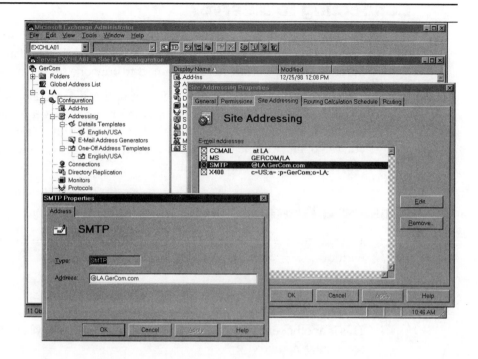

FIGURE 8.5

The Site Addressing dialog box is used to change the base e-messaging address for a site.

The File Menu

As you can see from Figure 8.6, the File menu is pretty important. You use it to connect to new servers and create new recipients and other objects, as well as to view and set object properties and duplicate certain objects, such as mailboxes.

FIGURE 8.6

The Exchange Administrator's File menu

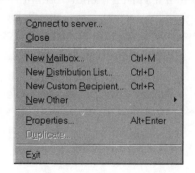

Connecting to a Server

You use the File menu's Connect to Server option to link to a server and open a new window on it. Since all servers in a site contain copies of all information for the site, you'll generally need to connect to only one server in a site.

As we'll see later, the Connect to Server option is most useful when you have multiple sites; you'll then establish a connection to a server in each site that you need to administer and manage. Remember from our little exercise above that you can open multiple windows in any site by using the New Window option in the Administrator's Window menu.

Closing a Window

The File menu's Close option is used to close any selected Administrator window.

Creating a New Mailbox

This is another exciting milestone: You're going to create your first Exchange recipient, a mailbox.

From here on, I'll assume you've already opened the Administrator. Click on your site (mine is LA); your Administrator screen should look like the one in Figure 8.7. Next, from the File menu choose New Mailbox. A dialog box like the one shown in Figure 8.8 pops up to tell you that you must create new recipients in a *site-based recipients container*—in my case, the LA site Recipients container, since I have no other sites. I've played a nasty trick on you by having you first click on your site. There is a method to my madness, however. The first time I saw the dialog box shown in Figure 8.8, I thought that something had broken. Now you know that it's just a friendly reminder and that the Administrator will take you to the right container. To avoid the dialog box, just click on the site-based Recipients container you want to use before selecting New Mailbox. Go ahead and click on OK in the warning box.

The next thing you'll see is the mailbox's Properties dialog box, shown in Figure 8.9. Note the eleven tabs on the dialog box; each lets you set a different group of attributes for a mailbox. Let's take a look at each of the eleven property pages used to administer and manage mailboxes.

FIGURE 8.7

The Administrator with a site selected

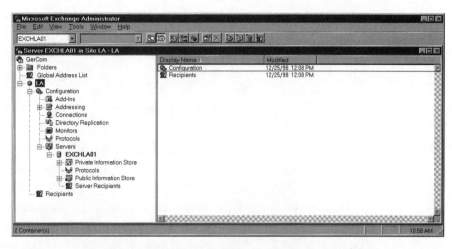

FIGURE 8.8

The Administrator's wrong container warning

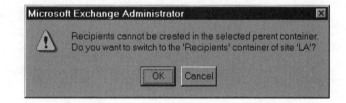

General Properties

As you can see in Figure 8.9, you use the General property page to fill in all the information about a mailbox and its user. This is also the place where you grant the right to use the mailbox to a specific NT account.

Filling in General Information   In Figure 8.10 I've already filled in information to create a mailbox for myself on the General property page. As I noted in an earlier chapter, the Display and Alias names are created automatically; the ones for your site may look different, depending on how you set your options earlier in this chapter. Now fill in the information for your first mailbox (you'll probably want to make it your own). *Don't* click on OK or Apply yet.

> **NOTE**
>
> When creating a new mailbox, you don't have to fill in every last lovin' field on every property page—only the display and alias fields on the General property page must be filled in.

FIGURE 8.9

The mailbox's Properties dialog box

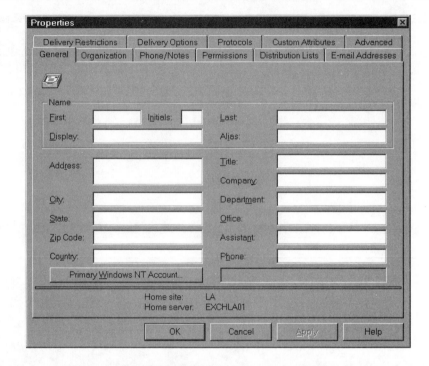

FIGURE 8.10

Filling in the General property page of the mailbox's Properties dialog box

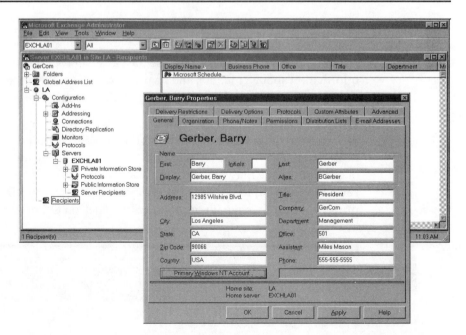

Granting an NT Account the Rights to a Mailbox To grant an NT account the rights to a mailbox, click on Primary Windows NT Account on the General property page to bring up the dialog box shown in Figure 8.11. You can grant rights to an existing NT account or create a new account.

FIGURE 8.11

Granting mailbox access rights to an existing or new NT account

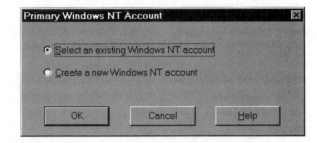

If access rights are to be granted to an existing NT account, click on 'Select an existing Windows NT account' and then click on OK. This brings up the Add User or Group dialog box shown in Figure 8.12. Making sure you're in the right domain, find and click on the account you want to give rights to, click on Add, and then click on OK.

FIGURE 8.12

The Add User or Group dialog box lets you assign rights to a mailbox to an existing NT account.

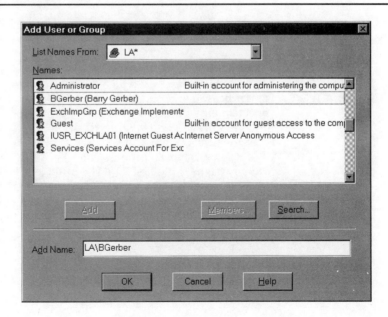

If you selected 'Try to find matching Windows NT account when creating mailbox' when you set the Tools/Options/Permissions options discussed above, the Administrator will look for an NT account with the same name as the alias. If one is found, you'll be given the option of using that account here. If you accept the option, you're done. If you don't, you can either locate an account with the Add User or Group dialog box or create a new account.

If you need to create a new NT account and give it rights to the mailbox you're creating, select the 'Create a new Windows NT Account' option from the Primary Windows NT Account dialog box (see Figure 8.11) and then click on OK. The Create Windows NT Account dialog box pops up (see Figure 8.13). Be sure the domain is correct, then either accept the default NT account name offered or type in a name of your choice and click on OK.

FIGURE 8.13

Creating an NT account to be assigned rights to a new mailbox

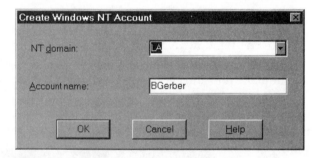

> **NOTE**
>
> As you can imagine, based on the limited information Exchange Administrator has when it creates a new NT account, many of the attributes you might enter for an NT account are blank. Still, Exchange Administrator does a pretty good job. The NT account's username defaults to the Exchange mailbox's alias. The account's full name is set equal to the mailbox's display name and the password is set to blank so the user will have to change it the first time she or he logs in. If the account will be used only to access the Exchange mailbox, don't worry; this automatically set information is sufficient. If, on the other hand, you need to further configure the account for NT access, you can do that in NT's User Manager for Domains.

Organization

Use the Organization property page to record information about the mailbox user's status in your organization's hierarchy (assuming, of course, that the mailbox will be used by one person and not by a group of people or a custom-programmed application). Here you can set the names of the mailbox user's manager and the names of those who report directly to the user. You can view this information in other places in Exchange; for example, the user of an Exchange client can open and view an Organization property page for any unhidden mailbox in the Exchange Global Address List.

The Mailbox User's Manager   To add information to the Organization property page, first click on the Organization tab. Then, to add information about the mailbox user's manager, click on Modify in the Manager box. A dialog box showing a list of valid Exchange recipients pops up (see Figure 8.14). This dialog box is called the *address book*. It lists all unhidden Exchange recipients: mailboxes, distribution lists, custom recipients, and public folders. Find the manager's name in the address book, click on the name, and then click on OK in the address book. (In the figure, I've selected myself as the manager of my Administrative Assistant, Miles Mason. I created a mailbox for Miles while you weren't looking.)

FIGURE 8.14

Setting the name of the Exchange recipient who manages a mailbox user

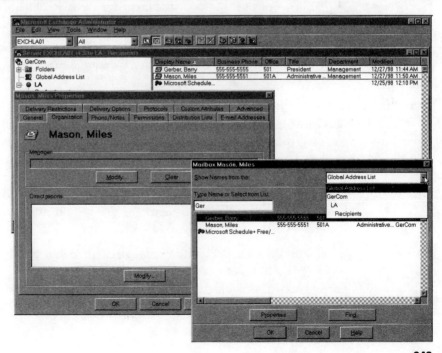

The Address Book Dialog Box

You'll be seeing the address book dialog box shown in Figure 8.14 a lot throughout the rest of the book, so I want to talk a bit more about how to use it.

Notice in Figure 8.14 that I found myself in the address book by typing in the first three letters of my last name. As the number of recipients in your organization grows, this is a way to quickly find the one you're looking for.

Another way to narrow down a search is to use the drop-down menu for the 'Show Names from the' option. The menu is open in Figure 8.14; as you can see, it lets you walk down your Exchange hierarchy and pick the specific site and Recipients container to search in.

Finally, you can use the Find button. It brings up a template with fill-in-the-blank fields for things like first and last name, title, and department.

NOTE   When you're working in the Exchange client, you'll tend to think of entries in the address book as individuals, groups of individuals, or public folders. When you use the address book in the Exchange Administrator program, try to think of these real-world entities as recipient objects. Doing so will make your life as an Exchange administrator/manager easier—I guarantee.

Recipients Managed by the Mailbox User   To add information on recipients who report directly to the mailbox user, click on Modify in the Direct Reports section of the Organization property page. The address book dialog box pops up. From the address book, select and add each of the recipients reporting to the mailbox user. When you're done, click on OK in the address book. (In Figure 8.15, I've added three recipients—which I again created while you weren't looking—who report directly to Miles Mason.)

In Figure 8.16, I'm using my Exchange client to look at the Organization property page for Miles Mason. As you can see, all of the organizational information I entered above is visible to the client.

FIGURE 8.15

Setting the recipients who report directly to a mailbox user

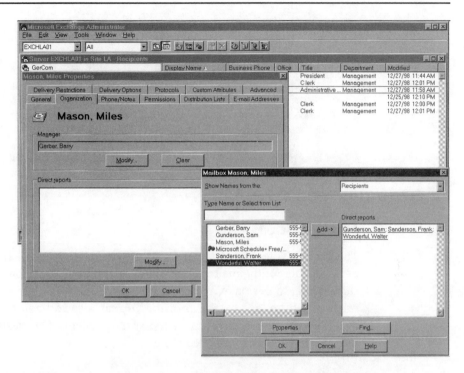

FIGURE 8.16

An Exchange client user views a mailbox's Organization property page

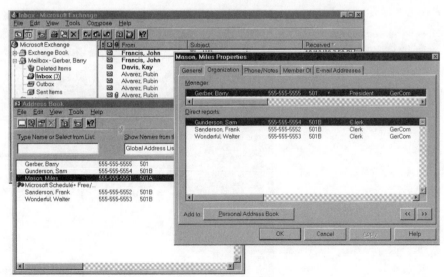

NOTE Before viewing Miles Mason's Organization property page with the Exchange client, I had to use the Exchange Administrator program to apply the changes I made to his mailbox. If I hadn't done this, the changes would not have been available for viewing by the Exchange client. Remember this when you change mailbox attributes on any property page: Until you apply changes you've made to a mailbox (by clicking on Apply or OK in the mailbox's Properties dialog box), any changes you make will not be available to the Administrator program or to Exchange client users. This rule applies to modifications you make to any Exchange Server object. When you apply a change, you are saving it to the Exchange directory, where the Administrator program or an Exchange client can access it.

Phone/Notes

The Phone/Notes property page is pretty basic (see Figure 8.17). The phone number you enter for the mailbox user on the General property page is automatically carried over to this page. You can add a range of other telecommunications-oriented information for the user, and you can also add notes about the user. All of this information will be visible to Exchange clients. Go ahead and fill in the page for the mailbox you're creating.

FIGURE 8.17

Entering telecommunications and other information for a mailbox user

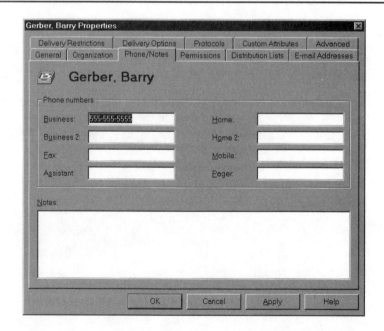

246

Permissions

You use the Permissions property page to establish or change rights for the mailbox.

> **NOTE**
>
> If you don't see the Permissions property page, or you don't see the Roles and Rights boxes at the bottom of the page, you've been messing with those options we set back at the beginning of the chapter. To make things right, close the mailbox's Properties dialog box by clicking on OK; then open the Tools menu, select Options, tab to the Permissions property page, and be sure that 'Show Permissions page for all objects' and 'Display rights for roles on Permissions page' are selected. Click on OK in the Options dialog box, then reopen the Properties dialog box for the mailbox you were creating by double-clicking on it in the Recipients container. Whew!

Accounts with Inherited Permissions   Notice in Figure 8.18 that the permissions of two Windows NT accounts (LA\Administrator and LA\Services) and one NT group (LA\Exchange Admins) have been inherited by mailbox objects. The accounts and the group have permissions at the site level. These permissions are inherited by the Recipients container and all objects in it—individual mailboxes, in this case.

FIGURE 8.18

Controlling access to a mailbox

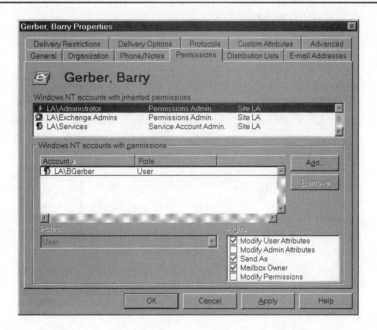

LA\Administrators is the account I used when I installed Exchange Server, so it was granted organization-wide rights by default. I gave permissions to run Exchange services in the LA site to the LA\Services account. Like LA\Administrators, it got organization-wide permissions when I installed Exchange Server. LA\Exchange Admins is the group I granted site-management rights to in Chapter 7. If you followed the instructions in Chapter 7, your 'Windows NT accounts with inherited permissions' box should look very similar to mine, except for the site name.

You can't remove permissions on a mailbox from accounts and groups listed in the 'Windows NT accounts with inherited permissions' box; you have to remove the permissions for these accounts or groups at the appropriate container level. (All of this container-level stuff will become clearer as we move along.)

Granting Permissions to Other Accounts or Groups   When an NT account is made the Primary Windows NT account for a mailbox on the General page, it is automatically given permissions on the mailbox. As you can see in the 'Windows NT accounts with permissions' box in Figure 8.18, BGerber was given default permissions for the mailbox.

You can add to this list of NT accounts or groups with permissions on a particular mailbox. You can also limit the role that any account or group with permissions can play. This lets you do a number of things, including creating multiuser mailboxes or assigning a group to perform certain administrative tasks on one or more mailboxes without giving the group full administrative rights or access to all mailboxes.

To give an NT account or group permissions on a mailbox, click on Add in the Permissions page and use the Add Users and Groups dialog box that pops up to choose an account or a group. You've used this dialog box before, so I'll let you take it from here.

Each account or group with permissions on a mailbox must have a *role*. Essentially, roles expand or limit what an account or group can do to a mailbox. There are five role types for mailboxes:

- Admin
- Permissions Admin
- Send As
- User
- Custom

Notice that BGerber's role is that of User. You use the Roles drop-down menu to pick a role for an account or group (see Figure 8.18). You won't see the Custom role here, and I'll explain why in just a bit.

Each role type is defined by the rights it has. These rights are listed in the lower right-hand section of the Permissions property page (see Figure 8.18). There are five mailbox rights:

- *Modify User Attributes* permits changes to the mailbox's user-modifiable attributes ("attributes" is another name for properties). For example, in an Exchange client a user can delegate to other NT accounts or groups certain access rights to his or her mailbox.

- *Modify Admin Attributes* permits changes to any mailbox attribute that is modifiable in the Exchange Administrator. For example, those manager and direct-reports attributes you set on the Organization property page can be modified by those with Modify Admin rights. You certainly wouldn't want users to change their place in the organizational hierarchy, even if it's only in Exchange, would you?

- *Send As* allows the NT account or group granted the right for a mailbox (Mailbox A) to send a message from another mailbox (Mailbox B) that appears to have come from the mailbox on which the right was granted (Mailbox A). This right can be useful when *A* wants *B* to send messages that appear to have come from *A*. However, it should be granted with great care, because it can be very dangerous in the wrong hands, like when a disgruntled employee sends out a nasty message that appears to come from some innocent person's mailbox.

- *Mailbox Owner* can log in to the mailbox and send, receive, read, and manipulate messages.

- *Modify Permissions* can change permissions for the mailbox—that is, the entries on the mailbox's Permissions property page.

If the box in front of a particular right is checked in the Rights area of the Permissions property page, the role includes that right. Take a look at the rights for the different roles by selecting each role from the drop-down Roles menu.

There is no preset Custom role. To set up a Custom role, just check off the boxes for the rights you want an account or group to have. If the rights you choose don't match those for a particular role, Custom shows in the drop-down menu as the role type for that account or group.

Distribution Lists

You can add mailboxes to distribution lists using the Distribution Lists property page (see Figure 8.19). You don't have any distribution lists yet, so you can't do it now, but I'll add my mailbox to a distribution list I sneakily created while you were otherwise occupied.

FIGURE 8.19

The Distribution Lists property page

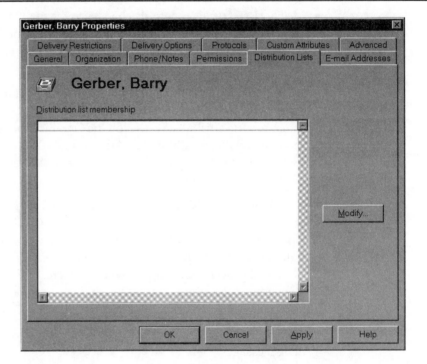

To do this, I click on Modify in the Distribution Lists property page to bring up the dialog box shown in Figure 8.20. Then I click on the distribution list to which I want to add my mailbox (LA Sales, the only list I have) and click on Add. Finally, I click on OK in the dialog box. My mailbox has now been added to the LA Sales distribution list.

You can also add a mailbox to a distribution list by using the configuration dialog box for a particular distribution list. This method is easier, since you don't have to open every mailbox you want to add to the list. I'll show you how to do this when we get to distribution lists.

FIGURE 8.20

Adding a mailbox to a
distribution list

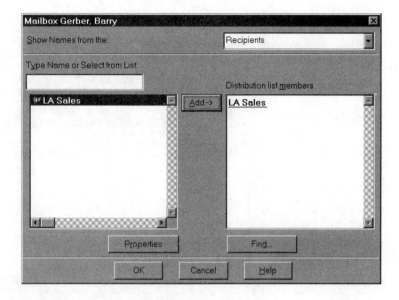

E-Mail Addresses

You've seen the E-mail Addresses property page in earlier chapters. It shows a mailbox's addresses for different types of E-messaging systems. Four addresses are created by default: cc:Mail, MS Mail, SMTP, and X.400 (see Figure 8.21). You can add new addresses and modify or remove existing ones.

Using this property page, you can manually change a specific user's address or add a new address for a user. For example, I sometimes give certain users a second SMTP address that includes their specific department. Adding or changing addresses manually is fun, but not for those new to Exchange Administrator, because it's usually not enough to just change the address. You'll also have to do some things in other areas in Exchange Administrator and maybe even in external systems. I'll talk about all of this stuff in a later chapter.

If you wish, Exchange Administrator can regenerate addressing entries on this and all other recipient property pages when you change an e-mail addressing default for an entire site. If you add a gateway for another e-messaging system (CompuServe, for example) and gateway includes the logic to generate addresses for existing recipients, the appropriate new gateway address can be added automatically to each recipient's E-Mail Addresses property page.

FIGURE 8.21

Use the E-mail Addresses property page to display, create, and modify addresses for a mailbox.

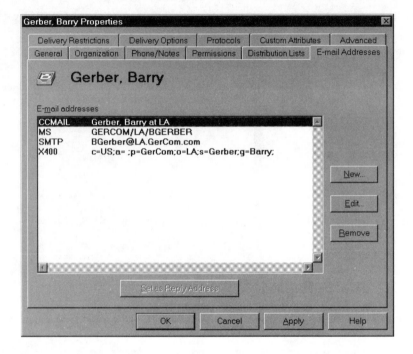

Delivery Restrictions

If, for whatever reason, you want to let only certain recipients send messages to a particular mailbox, you use the Delivery Restrictions property page. As you can see in Figure 8.22, you can specify who can and who can't send messages to the mailbox.

You add recipients to the Accept Messages From or Reject Messages From lists by clicking on the appropriate Modify button; you'll see the address book dialog box shown back in Figure 8.14. Select the recipients you want to add or exclude and then click on OK in the Recipients list dialog box. To record your restrictions, click on either OK or Apply on the Delivery Restrictions property page.

When a restricted recipient tries to send a message to an off-limits mailbox, the system will return the message (see Figure 8.23).

(I love the Send Again button; you can send the message again until you're blue in the face and you'll keep getting these rejection notices.)

FIGURE 8.22

Use the Delivery Restrictions property page to specify which recipients can send messages to a mailbox.

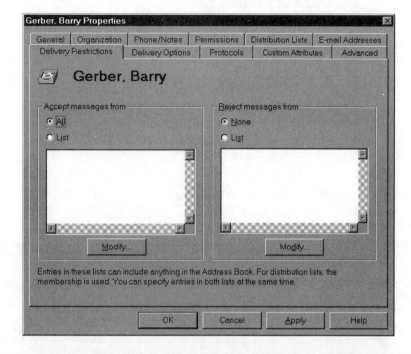

FIGURE 8.23

A system message tells restricted recipients when they've tried to send a message to an off-limits mailbox.

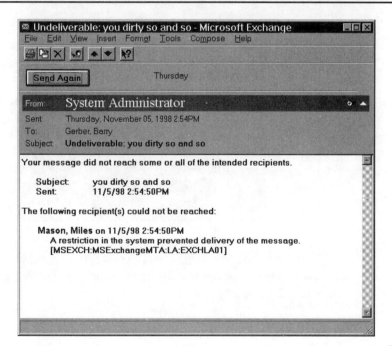

Delivery Options

You use the Delivery Options property page to give other recipients rights to the mailbox. You do this when a mailbox owner wants another mailbox owner or group to manage his or her mailbox—for example, when a secretary is assigned to watch a boss's mail, or when people go on vacation and need their mailboxes monitored.

In Figure 8.24 I've given Send On Behalf Of permissions to my mailbox to Miles Mason, my Administrative Assistant. This lets Mason send new messages and reply to messages for me using my mailbox as the return address. The From field in Send On Behalf Of messages identifies both the person sending the message and the individual on whose behalf the message was sent.

FIGURE 8.24

Use the Delivery Options property page to give other recipients special rights to a mailbox.

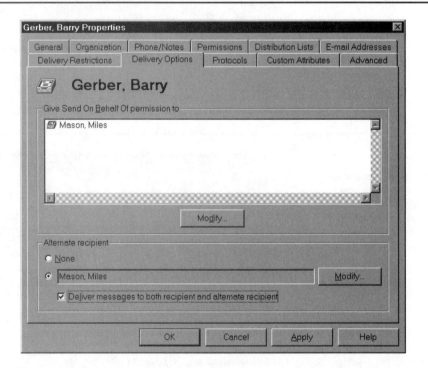

Can you imagine going through and setting Send On Behalf Of options for each user? Whew! But not to worry: Users can do it for themselves using their Exchange clients.

NOTE   The Send On Behalf Of permission is different from the role right Send As, which you set on the Permissions property page for a mailbox. Remember, Send As lets the user of one mailbox send a message as though it came from another mailbox, without any hint that the other mailbox didn't send the message itself. If you worry about users sending embarrassing messages that look like they came from another user, then Send On Behalf Of is a far safer option than Send As. If both options are granted to a user, Send As will override Send on Behalf Of.

At the bottom of the Delivery Options property page, I've indicated that messages to me should be delivered to an alternate recipient, Miles Mason. If I hadn't selected the 'Deliver messages to both recipient and alternate recipient' option, messages would have been redirected to Mason without a copy being sent to me.

The Alternate recipient option can be used in league with Send on Behalf Of to keep up with incoming mail when an employee is out of the office for one reason or another, or when she or he stops working for the organization. It can also be used to monitor an employee's use of Exchange messaging, since mailbox owners have no idea that messages for their own mailbox are also being sent to another mailbox.

Protocols

As I noted in earlier chapters, Exchange 5.0 comes with a bunch of new Internet-oriented features. You use the Protocols property page to enable four of these features for a mailbox. I've devoted a whole chapter to these new features. So here I'll give you the most basic of introductions. Follow along, referring to Figure 8.25 as I discuss the Protocols page.

The four new protocols supported by Exchange Server are:

- *HTTP (Web)* lets mailbox users access their Exchange server with an Internet browser, for example, to read their e-mail. "HTTP" is an acronym for Hypertext Transfer Protocol.

- *LDAP (Directory)* allows a mailbox user to access the Exchange directory (e-mail addresses, phone numbers, etc.) using a Lightweight Directory Access Protocol (LDAP) compliant client. This is a neat way to get e-mail addresses when using a non-Exchange client such as a POP3 client or to find information about an Exchange user with an LDAP client.

- *NNTP (News)* gives a mailbox user access to USENET newsgroups stored in Exchange server's public folders. "NNTP" stands for Network News Transfer Protocol.

- *POP3 (Mail)* support lets a mailbox user read and send mail through their Exchange server using a Post Office Protocol version 3 (POP3) compliant client like Qualcomm's Eudora.

FIGURE 8.25

Using the Protocols property page to enable and modify the Internet-oriented features available to an Exchange mailbox user

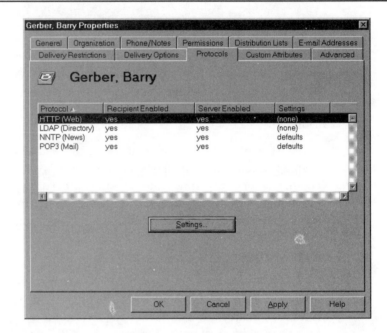

Each of the four protocols can have up to three sets of attributes. These are represented by the columns in the table in Figure 8.25: Recipient Enabled, Server Enabled, and Settings. If 'yes' appears in the Recipient Enabled column for a particular protocol, the protocol service is available to the user of the mailbox you're working on. If the Server Enabled column is marked 'yes,' then you know that support for the protocol has been enabled on your Exchange server. The Settings column tells you if there are parameters you can set for a protocol and, if there are parameters, whether the current settings are defaults or custom.

We will cover this much more thoroughly later on.

Custom Attributes

In the next chapter you'll learn how to create up to ten custom fields to hold information about recipients. For example, you could create a custom field to hold an employee ID number for each recipient. Custom fields are created at the site level and apply to all recipients in the site.

Use the Custom Attributes property page to fill in custom fields for a mailbox. For example, imagine that you've created a custom attribute called Employee ID for all recipients. You enter the specific Employee ID for the user of a specific mailbox on that mailbox's Custom Attributes property page. Since we haven't yet created any custom attributes, there's nothing much we can do here. (If you find all of this still a bit murky, don't worry. Things will clear up in the next chapter.)

Advanced Properties

The Advanced property page is fun (see Figure 8.26). It's where you can do a lot of interesting but often esoteric things.

Figure 8.26 shows the Advanced property page for my mailbox. I've filled in a few fields, but your page should look pretty similar. Starting at the top left-hand corner of the property page, we'll move more or less from left to right, inching our way downward as we go.

FIGURE 8.26

The Advanced property page for a mailbox

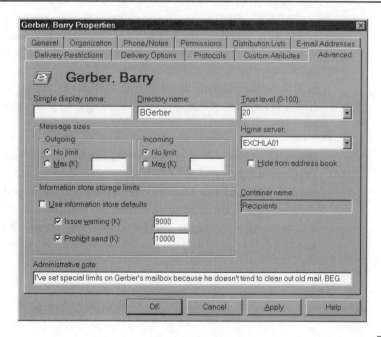

The Simple Display Name   The Simple Display Name field is especially useful in certain multilingual Exchange environments. Exchange clients and the server's copy of the Administrator program show the simple display name when the full display name can't be properly displayed. For example, if a full display name is stored in a double-byte character set like Kanji, and a particular copy of the client or the Administrator program isn't set to display the character set, the simple display name is shown in place of the full display name.

The Directory Name   Directory names are unique identifiers for objects stored in the Exchange directory. Generally, you're offered a default directory name for any kind of object, and although you can change the name while creating the object, you can't change it afterward.

For a mailbox, the default directory name is the alias constructed by Exchange Server when you filled in the new mailbox's General property page. In Figure 8.26, the alias for my mailbox, BGerber, is offered as the default directory name. You can change the directory name while creating a mailbox, but you can't change it after you've clicked on either OK or Apply in the mailbox's Properties dialog box. The only way to change a directory name after you've gone this far is to delete the object and re-create it, so name with care.

Trust Level   Use the Trust Level field to tell Exchange Server whether it should include the mailbox when it does directory synchronization with cc:Mail, Microsoft Mail 3.2, or compatible systems. We'll talk about this in a later chapter.

Message Sizes   The Message Sizes field lets you set maximum sizes for outgoing and incoming messages from and to a mailbox. In the next chapter you'll learn how to set site-based default sizes for outgoing and incoming messages; with Message Sizes, you can refine that setting for an individual mailbox. Use the Max (K) field for either incoming or outgoing messages, and type in the message size limit in kilobytes.

Home Server   The Home Server field is where you specify which server the mailbox is to be created on; it's the place where messages for the mailbox are stored. If you change the home server on the Advanced property page, Exchange Administrator asks if you want to move the mailbox to the server you've just chosen. Answer yes, and the mailbox is moved. (There's another way to move a mailbox to another server. We'll get into that method in a later chapter.)

Hide from Address Book   Select Hide From Address Book to prevent a mailbox from showing up in the various address lists in Exchange address book (not just Global Address List). Generally, you'll want to hide a mailbox from the address book to protect a particular mailbox's privacy or when it is used by custom-programmed applications rather than by human users.

Information Store Storage Limits   Use the Information Store Storage Limits options to either accept the mailbox's default maximum size limits that were set elsewhere—you'll learn how to do this in the next chapter—or set your own maximum limits for the mailbox. As shown in Figure 8.26, you can use either or both of two options when setting your own limits. The mailbox user gets a warning when the first limit is reached, and then at regular intervals thereafter until storage drops below the limit. When the second limit is reached, the mailbox can no longer send mail. It still can receive mail, however, since you don't want those who send messages getting a bunch of bounced message notifications just because a mailbox user is a resource hog.

Container Name   Use the Container Name option to set the name of the Recipients container that will hold the mailbox. As you'll see soon, you can have multiple Recipients containers in a site. To change the name of the Recipients container, click on Modify; this brings up a little tree that shows you the Recipients containers available in the site where you're creating the mailbox. You can't pick a container outside of this site, and once you've clicked on Apply or OK for the mailbox you're creating, you can't change the Recipients container assigned to it. After that point, you won't even see the Modify button.

Reconfiguring an Existing Mailbox

To reconfigure an existing mailbox, just locate it in the Recipients container and double-click on it. You'll get the same Properties dialog box you've been using to create new mailboxes. Now just edit as you wish and click OK or Apply to save your changes.

Follow these same directions to modify any existing recipient, whether mailbox, distribution list, custom recipient, or public folder.

Administrative Note   The Administrative Note field is a place where you can type in up to 1,024 characters of descriptive text about the mailbox or its user. This information is visible only in the Administrator program.

That covers as much about mailboxes as we need to for now. Let's continue with the next option on the Administrator's File menu, New Distribution List.

Creating a New Distribution List

As you'll remember, distribution lists are another form of Exchange recipient. To create a new distribution list, click on New Distribution List in the Exchange Administrator's File menu. This pops up the Distribution List Properties dialog box shown in Figure 8.27.

FIGURE 8.27

The General property page of the Distribution List properties dialog box

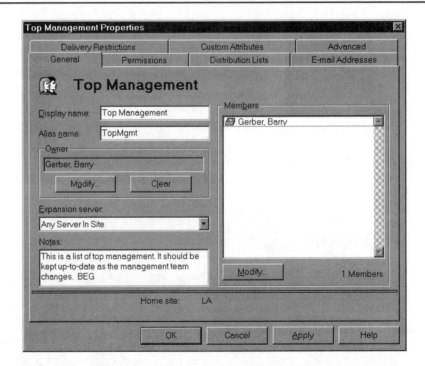

An Exchange Server distribution list has most of the properties of a mailbox, except four property pages are missing—Organization, Phone/Notes, and Delivery Options, none of which would make much sense for a distribution list. The

other seven pages are either exactly like or very similar to their mailbox-based cousins. I'll emphasize the differences here and refer you back to the mailbox property pages for the similarities.

General Properties

Let's look first at the items on the left-hand side of the General property page, then at the items on the right.

Display and Alias Names   You need to fill in a Display name and an Alias name. The Display name will show in the address book; the Alias will be used in creating e-mail addresses for the address list.

Owner   The name in the Owner field is the person to whom users should forward requests to be added to or removed from a distribution list. By default the list owner is given rights to add and delete users from within an Exchange client. Since my GerCom list will include the company's top management, and since I'm the president of this mythical company, I've assumed ownership responsibilities. (I don't want anyone but a top exec involved in decisions about whom to admit to this list.) To set an owner for a distribution list, click on Modify in the Owner box to bring up a standard address book dialog box like the one shown back in Figure 8.14. Select the owner and click on OK.

> **NOTE**   Only one Exchange recipient can own a distribution list. A distribution list cannot own another distribution list.

Expansion Server   Distribution lists must be *expanded*—that is, the members of the list must be identified and an efficient route to each member must be determined. Expansion is done on an Exchange server in a site; if a distribution list is large (with thousands of users), you may want to specify an expansion server for it that is less busy. For smaller lists, you don't have to change the Any Server in Site default.

Notes   Put anything you like in the Notes field of the distribution list. This information will be displayed for users when they look at the properties of the list using their Exchange clients.

Members   Finally, add list members. Click on Modify in the Members area and select members from the address book dialog box that pops up. Click on OK when you're done.

Click on Apply if you want to record your work so far, but don't close the distribution list's properties dialog box yet.

Permissions

The distribution list's Permissions property page looks and behaves almost exactly like the one for a mailbox—the only thing missing is the Mailbox Owner right, which is irrelevant for a distribution list. So, refer to mailbox permissions if you have any questions about the Permissions page for the distribution list.

Those No Account Distribution Lists

Unlike mailboxes, distribution lists don't have Primary NT accounts. You can see this by comparing Figure 8.10 (for a mailbox) with Figure 8.27 (for a distribution list). Figure 8.10 includes the Primary Windows NT Account button, while Figure 8.27 doesn't.

NOTE   If you want to take away a distribution list owner's right to add and remove the list's members while using an Exchange client, remove the Modify User Attributes right from the owner's role. Similarly, if you want to give other users the right to modify a distribution list, add their NT Accounts to the Permissions page for the list and assign their accounts the Modify User Attributes right.

Included Distribution Lists

Distribution lists can include other distribution lists. You use the Distribution Lists property page to optionally add your new list to selected existing distribution lists. Click on Modify in the Distribution Lists property page to bring up a dialog box showing existing distribution lists (see Figure 8.28). Use the dialog box to add your new list to existing lists and click on OK when you're done.

FIGURE 8.28

Adding a new
distribution list to existing distribution lists

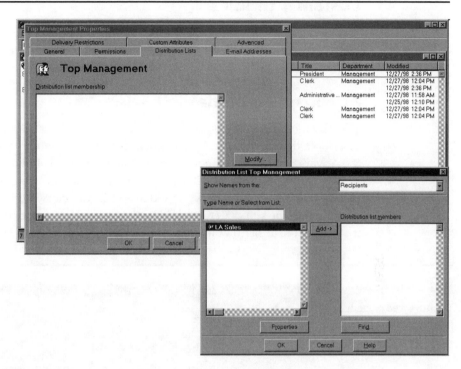

E-Mail Addresses

Exchange Server distribution lists have their own e-mail addresses. Among other benefits, this allows users of foreign e-messaging systems to send messages to the distribution lists. Except for different addresses, the distribution list's E-mail Addresses property page looks exactly the same as the one for mailboxes.

Delivery Restrictions

The Delivery Restrictions property page for distribution lists is a carbon copy of the one for mailboxes, pure and simple. You'll probably use this page more often than the one for mailboxes because it lets you specify which mailboxes, additional distribution lists, and custom recipients can easily send one message to large groups of users. For example, you can prevent a slew of mass mailings—those advertising everything from cars for sale to apartments for sublet—by giving only a narrow set of mailboxes the rights to send messages to large distribution lists such as those containing all recipients in a department, a site, or an entire Exchange organization.

Custom Attributes

The distribution list's Custom Attributes property page is identical to the one for mailboxes. As I noted above, I'll cover custom attributes in more detail in the next chapter.

Advanced Properties

The Advanced property page for distribution lists differs enough from the one for mailboxes that it's worth taking a quick look at the differences. Figure 8.29 shows the Advanced property page. First note that there is no Home Server field as there is for a mailbox (see Figure 8.26). Distribution lists live only in sites and their attributes (names, members, etc.) are stored in the site directory. While mailbox attributes are stored in the site directory, mail itself is stored on a specific home server, so it's reasonable to say that mailboxes live both in sites and on servers.

FIGURE 8.29

The Advanced property
page for distribution lists

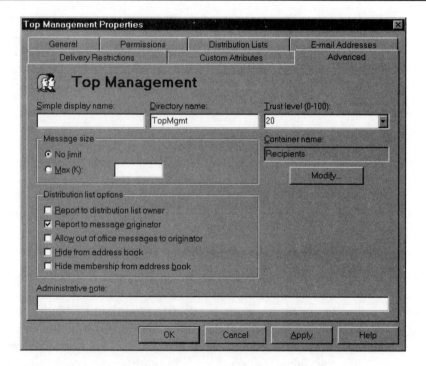

Message Size Limit   You'll notice that, unlike the Advanced property page for mailboxes, distribution lists don't have size-limit options for both incoming and outgoing messages; instead they have a Message Size Limit setting. Distribution lists receive messages, they usually don't send them, though by giving a list Send As rights, you can use it to send messages. The limits you set on the Advanced property page are for incoming messages only.

Distribution List Options   Let's look at Distribution List Options in the Advanced property page one at a time. I've already talked about the Hide from address book option, so I won't cover it again.

- *Report to distribution list owner* sends notification to the owner of the distribution list when message-delivery problems occur.

- *Report to message originator* sends notification to a message's originator when the message is undeliverable because it exceeds the specified size limits.

- *Allow out of office messages to originator* sends to the originator of the message individual out-of-office messages from all list members who have active out-of-office messages.

- *Hide membership from address book* protects the privacy of the members of a distribution list. Even if the list itself isn't hidden, users can't tell whose names are on it.

Now that you are familiar with distribution lists, you're ready to move on to the next option on the Administrator's File menu, New Custom Recipient. Refer back to Figure 8.6 for a view of the File menu.

Creating Custom Recipients

You'll remember that custom recipients are essentially aliases for recipients in foreign e-messaging systems. They're helpful when a lot of people in your organization need to communicate with users of non-Exchange systems.

Setting Type of Address

To create a custom recipient, click on New Custom Recipient in the Exchange Administrator's File menu. This brings up the dialog box shown in Figure 8.30. Select the type of address for the custom recipient and then click on OK. (In the figure, I've chosen to create a custom recipient with an Internet address.)

FIGURE 8.30

Selecting the type of
address for a new
custom recipient

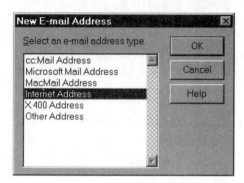

The E-Messaging Address Properties Dialog Box

The next thing you'll see is a dialog box for entering the custom recipient's
e-messaging address. Figure 8.31 shows the dialog box for the new Internet-
based custom recipient I want to create. If you're creating a custom recipient for
a different type of messaging system, you'll see a dialog box with fields appropriate to that system. When you're done entering the address, click on OK.

FIGURE 8.31

Entering the address for
a new custom recipient

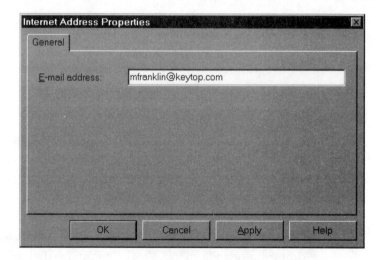

Standard Property Pages

Next you'll see the Properties dialog box for custom recipients. It looks very much like the one for mailbox configuration, except that it's missing the Delivery Options property page, which is not of much use here anyway (see Figure 8.32). If you think of a custom recipient as a sort of mailbox–distribution list hybrid, nothing in these property pages should surprise you. That said, I'll leave the rest of custom recipient configuration to you.

FIGURE 8.32

The Properties dialog box for custom recipients

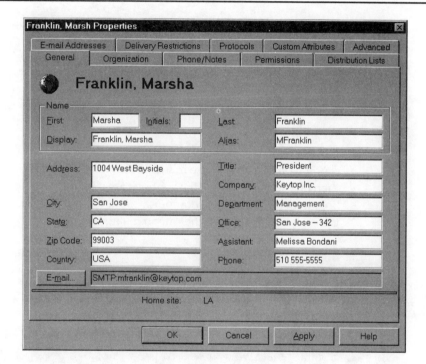

New Other Options

Figure 8.33 shows the menu that pops up when you select New Other from the Exchange Administrator's File menu. You can use this submenu to create a variety of objects and services. For instance, this is where you create new monitors that watch the health of Exchange servers and links to other sites and systems. This is also where you establish new recipients containers for a site and new information stores, as well as where you create Exchange Server connectors and set up directory synchronization with other systems.

FIGURE 8.33

The New Other
options menu

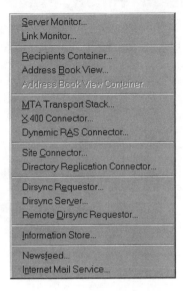

FIGURE 8.33

The New Other
options menu

You won't be able to use many of the New Other options until you've got more than one server or site. Other options are a bit advanced for our needs right now. So, I'll focus here on server monitors and recipients containers. I'll cover everything else on the New Other menu in later chapters.

Public Folders Are Recipients, Too

As you'll remember from earlier chapters, public folders are the fourth type of recipient. However, they're created by users, not by Exchange Server administrators; that's why there's no New Public Folder option on the Exchange Administrator program's File menu. We'll discuss the administration and management of public folders in the next chapter.

Configuring a Server Monitor

Server monitors are really impressive. They watch over Exchange servers, their clocks, and the services running on them. One server monitor can operate on one or more of the servers in a site. You can set up multiple monitors in a site or even in an organization. You can also set up a monitor so that it notifies you if a service shuts down or never starts, if clients can't connect to the server, or if the server disappears from the network. Server monitors are also able to restart computers or services and synchronize server clocks.

Server monitors are important; you should get comfortable with them right away. Let's create one for your server. From the Administrator's File menu, select New Other, then select Server Monitor. Since monitors are created in the Monitors container for a site, Exchange will warn you if you're not in one of these and will offer to take you there, just as it does if you're not in a site recipients container when you create a mailbox.

General Properties   When you see the server monitor's Properties dialog box shown in Figure 8.34, you're ready to go. I've already filled in the General property page for my server EXCHLA01.

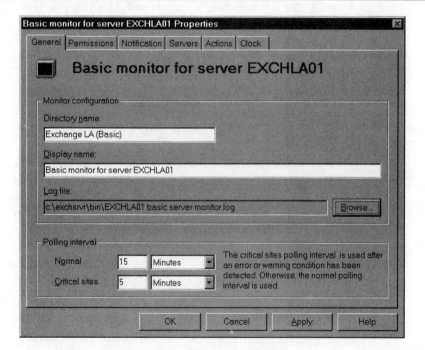

FIGURE 8.34

Configuring the General property page for a Server monitor

You can set several options on the General property page. These include:

- *The Directory Name.* As with all standard directory names, you won't be able to change it after creating the server monitor.

- *The Display Name.* This is what you see when you look into the Monitors container. It can be up to 256 characters long.

- *The Log File.* This specifies the file in which the server monitor puts information about its activities. Even if a monitor can watch over many servers, I generally store its log file on the server that the monitor will run on (the one it was created on). That way, if the network goes down, the monitor will still be able to write to its log file. Click on Browse to set the directory and file name.

- *The Normal Polling Interval.* This is the time period the monitor waits before checking to see that all is running properly on the server. The default is fifteen minutes, which is just about right in most situations.

- *The Critical Sites Polling Interval.* This is the time period the server monitor waits before checking servers that are in trouble and that it is trying to fix. ("Sites" in this context actually refer to Exchange servers, not Exchange sites.) The default polling interval is five minutes. As you'll see in a bit, reviving a dead service or server can involve two or three cycles, each of which will require a wait equal to one critical sites polling interval. You'll have to decide on the best interval for each server monitor you create. For now, accept the default setting.

Permissions   The list of role rights is a bit different on the server monitor's Permissions property page than on other permissions pages you've worked with. The only right you haven't seen before is Delete, which is the right to delete the server monitor. If you give monitor access rights to other accounts or groups, grant the Delete right with caution.

Notification   Use the Notification property page to tell the server monitor whom to contact (and how to do it) when a problem arises. Click on New and the New Notification dialog box opens (see the lower right-hand corner in Figure 8.35). You're offered three options in the New Notification dialog box:

- *Launch a Process* starts a program. For example, it can start a program that sends information about the problem to an alphanumeric pager.

- *Mail Message* sends a mail message about the problem to a specific recipient.

- *Windows NT Alert* sends a standard network message about the problem to a specific computer.

FIGURE 8.35

The New Notification
dialog box

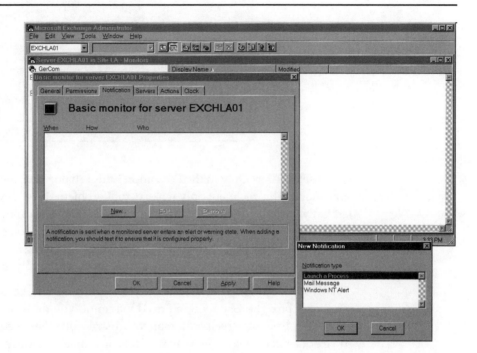

Click on the Notification option you want and then click on OK in the New Notification dialog box. The Escalation Editor dialog box for the option you've chosen pops up. This dialog box looks pretty much the same for all three options; Figure 8.36 shows how it looks when the Mail Message option is chosen. For the other two options, the Mailbox to Notify field is replaced by other fields appropriate to the particular notification action you're setting up.

To fill in the Escalation Editor dialog box for mail message notification, enter the time interval that the monitor should wait before issuing notification when it detects a problem. (The default is fifteen minutes, but in many cases you'll want more immediate notification.) As you can see in Figure 8.36, you can set the time unit to minutes or hours.

FIGURE 8.36

Using the Escalation Editor (Mail Message) box to configure notifications

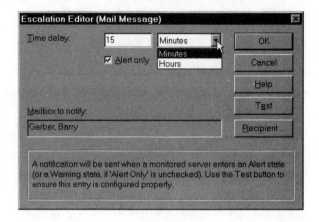

If you select Alert Only in the Escalation Editor dialog box, the monitor sends notification to this recipient only when actual problems exist. If you *don't* select Alert Only, then the monitor notifies the recipient about warnings and potential problems, as well as actual problems. This is a nice option: You can tell the monitor to notify certain people both when a problem starts brewing and when it reaches a critical level, while notifying others only when things actually go wrong.

Finally, click on Recipient to select any recipient from the resultant address book dialog box. (I probably don't need to remind you that the recipient here can be any valid Exchange recipient, mailbox, distribution list, or custom recipient.) If you've got a fax or pager gateway in place, of course, you can send the message to recipients accessible through the gateway as well.

When you've finished selecting a recipient, click on Test. Exchange will run a check to ensure that you've picked a valid and reachable mailbox. If you don't get an error message, click on OK in the Escalation Editor dialog box. You'll get a warning telling you that notifications will not be sent until the next polling interval after the notification time (the delay you just entered) has passed. Click on OK again and you'll now see your notification listed on the Notification property page.

With all of this mail message notification experience behind you, you should have no trouble setting up one of the other two notification processes. So let's move on to the next property page for the server monitor.

NOTE You can set up as many kinds of notifications as you want. Just click on New in the Notification dialog box and fill in the New Notification and Escalation Editor dialog boxes with your information.

Servers You use the Servers property page to choose the servers and services you want monitored (see Figure 8.37).

FIGURE 8.37

Selecting a server to monitor

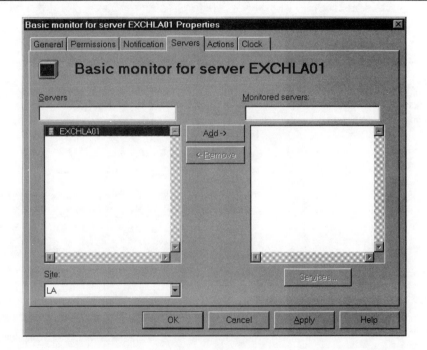

Click on the name of your server and then click on Add to put it into the Monitored Servers scroll box. If you want to include more than one server in this monitoring operation, add it here. If you have access to other sites, you can add servers from them by choosing another site from the Site drop-down menu in the lower left-hand corner of the Servers property page.

Now select your server in the Monitored Servers scroll box and then click on Services, just below the right-hand scroll box, to bring up the dialog box shown in Figure 8.38. By default, three of the four core Exchange services are listed in the

Monitored Services scroll box: the directory, the information store, and the MTA. (The System Attendant isn't automatically included because it's largely responsible for all monitors; if it dies, active monitors die with it.)

Leave the default settings for now and click on OK in the Services dialog box. You can come back later and add any service you'd like, whether it's an Exchange Server service or not.

NOTE As should be pretty obvious from what we've just done, a server monitor can watch different services on each of the servers it monitors.

FIGURE 8.38

Selecting services to be monitored on a server

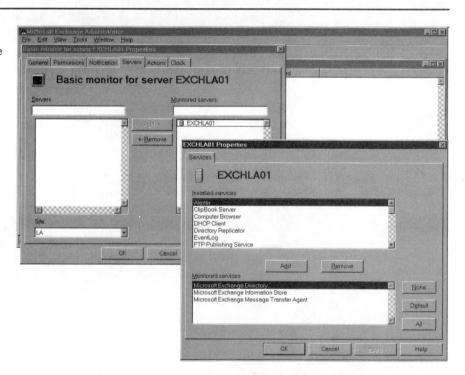

Actions You use the Actions property page to tell your server monitor what to do when a service is not running (see Figure 8.39). What you put on this page applies to all of the servers being monitored. In the figure, I've already selected options and filled in fields on the page.

FIGURE 8.39

Setting options for
actions to be taken when
a service is not running

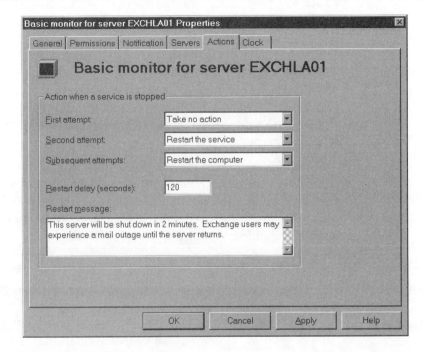

You have three options when a service is not running: Take No Action, Restart the Service, or Restart the Computer. As you can see, I've instructed the monitor to do nothing on the first attempt, to restart the service on the second attempt, and to restart the computer on subsequent attempts. Timing for these actions is based on the polling intervals that were set on the General property page. When you request a computer restart, you can set a delay time before it restarts and include a message that will be sent to users logged in to the computer. I've selected a 120-second delay. The default is 60 seconds.

NOTE Exchange clients should generally be able to survive the disappearance of their Exchange server whether due to a server outage or network problem, though they won't be able to access any messages stored on the server until the server is back up and functioning properly. If you're responsible for an MS Mail installation or any of the other file-based e-messaging systems out there, I bet you'll consider this little feature of client/server messaging alone to be worth the price of an Exchange system.

Clocks   The Clock property page deals with keeping Exchange server clocks synchronized. We'll come back to it later when we have more than one installed Exchange server.

Starting a Server Monitor   When you're through setting parameters, click on OK in the server monitor's Properties dialog box. You'll see your monitor in the Monitors container for your site. Double-clicking on the server monitor reopens the Properties dialog box, which you can use at any time to change the monitor's properties.

Now you have to start the server monitor. Click on the monitor name and then select Start Monitor from the Tools menu. Next, you're asked what server you want to run the monitor on. After you answer, the monitor's window opens, indicating that your server monitor is now up and running and ready to act as you instructed should anything go wrong (see Figure 8.40).

FIGURE 8.40

A server monitor up and running

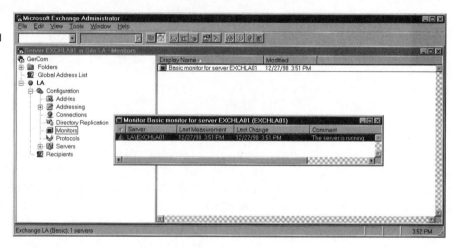

If you double-click on the line in the monitor that displays the monitor's name (see Figure 8.40), a dialog box pops up that lets you see how things are going. Try it. When you no longer need to see the monitor, minimize its window for better access to other Administrator windows.

Server monitors continue running when you exit the Administrator and resume when a server is rebooted. To stop a server monitor, close its window.

To test your server monitor, double-click on the Services applet in your Exchange server's Control Panel, then halt a core Exchange Server service, such as the MTA. The monitor should restart the service just fine.

For a really serious test, disable the service by clicking on Startup in the Services dialog box and selecting Disabled. The monitor will now be unable to restart the service—so if you've specified a computer restart, your Exchange server will be rebooted after any polling and service restart intervals have passed. Since you've disabled it, of course, the service won't start on reboot, either, so change the service's start-up status back to Automatic after the reboot. The monitor will now be able to restart the service. (Remember to give the monitor enough time to go through the polling and restart delays you've set.)

Creating a New Recipients Container

You can put all the recipients in a site into one container—the default container named Recipients—or you can create separate containers to hold specific kinds of recipients. You can use multiple recipients containers to more easily manage different types of recipients. For example, you could set up separate containers to hold the recipients used by specially programmed messaging-enabled applications or put all distribution lists in a single container.

You can't move existing recipients once they've been created in a specific recipients container, so plan additional recipients containers carefully before you start adding recipients to one container or another.

You can create a new recipients container in a site or in an existing recipients container. First highlight either the site or an existing recipients container, then select Recipients Container from the New Other options menu under the Exchange Administrator's File menu. A Properties dialog box like the one in Figure 8.41 pops up.

General Properties　On the General property page for the recipients container, fill in the display and directory names and add an administrative note if you want, as shown in Figure 8.41.

Permissions　The Permissions property page for the new recipients container has one new role right on it: Add Child. An NT account or group with Add Child rights can create subcontainers under the master container. You'll see this right frequently on Permissions property pages for the various containers I'll discuss in the next chapter. For now, accept the defaults and click on OK in the Properties dialog box for the container.

FIGURE 8.41

The Properties dialog box for a new recipients container

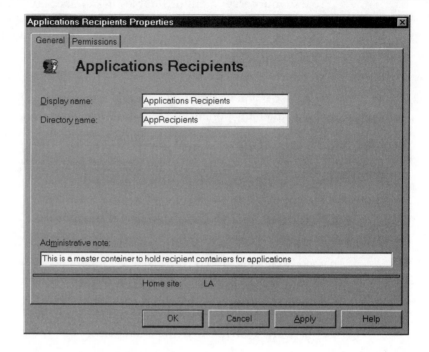

The New Container   In Figure 8.42 you can see the new recipients container I created to hold recipients containers for different custom-programmed messaging applications. Because I created it while the Recipients container was selected, the new container is a subcontainer of the Recipients container.

That's it for the New Options menu for now. Let's move on to the remaining options on the Administrator's File menu. Refer back to Figure 8.6 for a reminder of the File menu.

Properties

Properties, of course, are what you've been setting on all those property pages. You can view the properties of any Exchange object either by clicking on the object and then selecting Properties from the Exchange Administrator's File menu or by holding down the Alt key while pressing the Enter key. For objects other than containers, you can also see properties by double-clicking on the object in the right pane. However, this won't work with containers since clicking once, twice, or a million times on a container only shows you what's inside.

FIGURE 8.42

A container to hold other recipients containers for custom-programmed messaging enabled applications

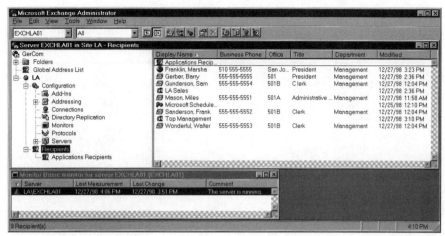

Duplicating Objects

You can duplicate any non-container object. For example, you can duplicate a mailbox and then use the copy to set up a new mailbox with similar properties.

To duplicate an object, click on it and select Duplicate from the Administrator's File menu. This brings up a standard Properties dialog box for the object with all the properties of the original intact, except that blanks replace the information that makes the original object unique. For example, all four fields are blank in the Name area on the General property page for a duplicate mailbox. (Look back at Figure 8.10 for the location of the Name area.)

The Edit Menu

The Exchange Administrator's Edit menu is pretty plain-vanilla. It includes all of the usual items: Undo, Cut, Copy, Paste, Delete, and Select All. 'Nuff said.

The View Menu

Figure 8.43 shows the Exchange Administrator's View menu. Use this menu to indicate which Exchange objects are to be shown and how the views of Exchange's hierarchy are to be formatted. You can also use it to move the splitbar and to toggle on and off both the toolbar (below the menu bar on the Administrator window) and the status bar (at the bottom of the Administrator window).

FIGURE 8.43

The Exchange Administrator's View menu

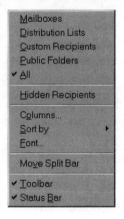

What to View

Most of the time, I like to see all recipients in the Administrator, so I select All on the Administrator's View menu. To view only certain recipients, select the ones you want using the View menu; to view recipients you've hidden, select Hidden Recipients.

You can also select the recipient types you want to view from the drop-down menu in the toolbar, as shown in Figure 8.44. Notice that hidden recipients aren't listed in the drop-down menu; the only way to view hidden recipients is by using the View menu.

Recipient Attributes and Views

Exchange recipients can have a plethora of attributes or properties; Figure 8.45 shows some of these. A number of recipient attributes are used for column heads when you view a list of recipients in a recipients container. Note that the attributes shown in the right-hand scroll box in Figure 8.45 are the titles of the column bars for the recipients listing in Figure 8.46.

FIGURE 8.44

Selecting recipients to
view using the Exchange
Administrator's toolbar
drop-down menu

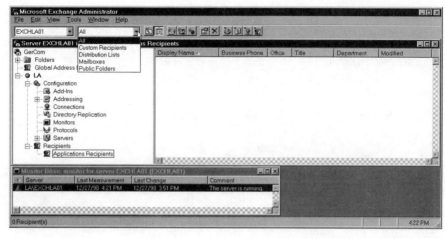

FIGURE 8.45

Some of the attributes of
Exchange recipients

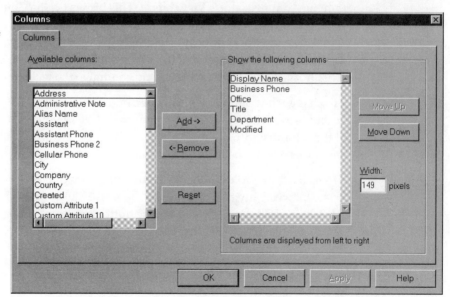

FIGURE 8.46

Recipient attributes are displayed as column heads in a recipient listing.

To change the attributes (columns) used in a display of recipients, select Columns from the Administrator's View menu. This brings up the Columns dialog box shown in Figure 8.45. Use the dialog box to add and remove attributes to be displayed. The topmost attribute in the right-hand box in Figure 8.45—Display Name—is the leftmost column in the recipients list in Figure 8.46. The second attribute, Business Phone, is the second column in the recipients listing, and so on.

To change the column display order, highlight a column title and use the Move Up and Move Down buttons to position the title as you wish (see Figure 8.45). To set the column width for an attribute, click on the attribute and enter the measurement (in pixels) in the Width box. Each column has its own width setting.

To resize the recipients display columns, place your Windows pointer on the little line between any two column title bars (see Figure 8.46). The pointer turns into a crosshair. Hold down the left mouse button and move the crosshair until you're happy with the real estate that each column occupies.

Sorting Lists

You can sort certain Exchange Server lists—recipients lists, for example—by column headings. The Sort By option on the View menu lets you select a default sort column. There are two options: Display Name (the default) and Last Modified Date.

Remember, you can change the sort order for any list by clicking on the column title bar you want to sort by. If you're permitted to sort by that column, the list will be resorted.

Fonts

Use the Font option on the View menu to change the display font used by the Exchange Administrator.

Move Splitbar

The Move Splitbar option on the View menu is another way to set the splitbar on an Administrator window. Select it and your Windows pointer is automatically placed on the splitbar of the current Administrator window. At that point, you can move the splitbar as you wish, changing the real estate occupied by the two panes in the window.

The Toolbar

As you already know, you can use the toolbar, which is located below the menu bar, to set the type of recipients you want to view. The toolbar also lets you select the Exchange server you want to focus your attention on. More about this capability later.

Finally, the toolbar contains buttons for performing various Administrator functions. You can see these in Figure 8.46. Here's what the buttons do in the order they appear from left to right:

- move up one level in the Exchange hierarchy
- show or hide the container tree view in the left-hand pane of an Administrator window
- create a new mailbox
- create a new distribution list
- create a new custom recipient
- show the properties of an object
- delete an object
- move to Configuration container
- move to Servers container
- move to Connections container
- move to Recipients container

You don't have to worry about memorizing these functions. Just hover over the button you're interested in with your mouse pointer and in a second a standard Windows tooltip will pop up telling you the button's function.

The Status Bar

The status bar is in the bottom area of the Administrator screen. In Figure 8.46, the status bar displays "9 Recipient(s)" to tell you that there are nine objects (recipients) in the currently selected container. Keep the status bar turned on—it doesn't cost you anything.

The Tools Menu

The Exchange Administrator program's Tools menu is chock-full of interesting functionality (see Figure 8.47). The first four items on the menu make it easier to create mailboxes en masse. The items fit nicely into the category of advanced Exchange Server administration, so I'll cover them in later chapters.

FIGURE 8.47

The Exchange Administrator's Tools menu

Finding Recipients

The Find Recipients option gets more and more valuable as the number of recipients and servers in your Exchange organization grows. To search for a recipient, select Find Recipients from the Tools menu. If you're asked which server you want to connect to, click on Browse, find your server, and click on OK in the Connect to Server dialog box. The Find Recipients dialog box will pop up (see Figure 8.48).

FIGURE 8.48

Finding specific
Exchange recipients

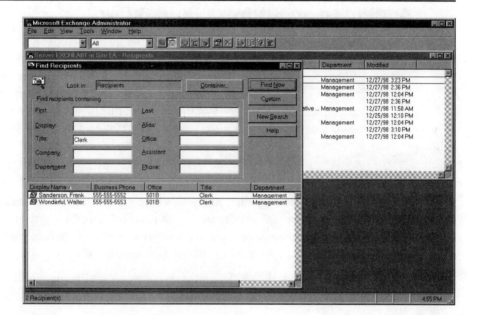

You can search on attributes such as first name and last name, as shown in Figure 8.48. And by clicking on the Custom button, you can search on those custom attributes I'll talk about in the next chapter. Clicking on Container brings up a dialog box that lets you select the site and recipients container to search in.

When you've filled in the appropriate fields in the Find Recipients dialog box, click on the Find Now button. When the searching is finished, you'll see a list of all recipients that meet the criteria you entered. (In Figure 8.48 I searched for all of the recipients in GerCom's LA site with a title of Clerk.)

Recipients are listed by the columns set under the Columns option of the Administrator's View menu (see Figure 8.45). You can use the list of found recipients pretty much as if it were a recipients container. For example, you can double-click on any found recipient to edit its Properties dialog box.

Moving a Mailbox

When users move to new locations, or when you need to move a mailbox for administrative reasons, it's nice to be able to move mailboxes from one Exchange server to another. The Tools menu's Move Mailbox option makes this easy. You can move mailboxes only within a site, however. Since we'll need at least one additional Exchange server to move a mailbox, I'll talk about mailbox moves in a later chapter.

Adding to an Address Book View

You might have noticed that the New Other menu includes an option that lets you create different views of the Exchange address book. (Refer back to Figure 8.33.) The address book is used to find e-mail and other information stored in the Exchange directory. Having various views of the address book can make it easier for users to find specific addresses or other information. I'll talk about address book views and the various options associated with them in Chapter 17.

Cleaning Mailboxes

Users tend to fill up their mailboxes at breakneck speed, so Exchange Server provides a number of ways to deal with this problem. One way is to set limits on the amount of storage available to mailboxes; another is to remove messages from any or all recipient mailboxes based on specific criteria.

To set up criteria for cleaning mailboxes, select the recipients whose mailboxes you want to clean. You can select any or all recipients in the following:

- In the Global Address List

- In any site's or server's recipient containers, including those you've created yourself

- In a found recipients list created using the Find Recipients option on the Tools menu

Use Windows' standard list-selection keys to select the recipients. For example, to select a noncontiguous group of mailboxes, hold down the Ctrl key while clicking on each mailbox you want to clean. Once you've selected the recipients, click on Clean Mailbox on the Tools menu; this brings up the dialog box shown in Figure 8.49.

Everything in the dialog box should be pretty easy to figure out except for Sensitivity, which is a privacy-based attribute that's set by the person sending a message. Select all of the criteria you want and click on OK to start the mailbox-cleaning process immediately. This is a powerful little tool; use it with care.

Starting a Monitor

You've already used the Start Monitor option to start the server monitor you created earlier in this chapter, so you already know what this option is for and how it works.

FIGURE 8.49

Specifying criteria for cleaning mailboxes

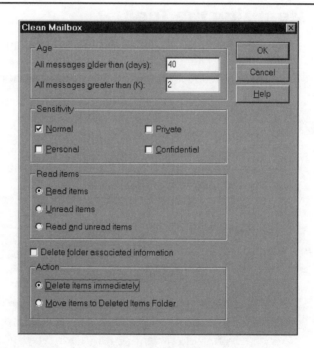

Tracking a Message, Administering Forms, and Working with Newsgroup Hierarchies

You'll learn how to track a message, administer forms, and deal with newsgroup hierarchies in later chapters. Tracking messages is much more fun when you have more than one server. The last chapter of this book deals exclusively with Microsoft

Exchange Forms Designer. We'll cover newsgroups and their hierarchies in the chapters on the new Internet-oriented services that come with Exchange 5.0.

Saving Connections

You can save the Administrator's connections to Exchange servers upon exiting from the Administrator or at some other time. When you come back into the Administrator, the connections are automatically reestablished. To save connections upon exit, select that option. To save connections at any time, select Save Connections Now.

Customizing the Toolbar

You can add to or subtract from the Administrator's toolbar. Just select the Customize Toolbar option from the Tools menu and use the very friendly interface to tailor the toolbar to your own special needs.

Options

You already used the Options option way back at the beginning of this chapter, so we've now covered everything in the Tools menu.

Raw Properties

I can't resist showing you a well-hidden little capability of the Exchange Administrator. It lets you start up Administrator in such a way that you can examine and modify every last bloody property available for any object. When you start the Administrator this way, you're in what Microsoft calls "raw mode." Even if you never use raw mode, you should check it out to see how absolutely detailed the object properties can get.

To start the Administrator in raw mode, open a DOS Command Prompt window. At the command prompt, go to the disk drive where you installed Exchange Server. Then change to the directory C:\exchsrvr\bin and type `admin/raw`.

That's it. When the Administrator starts, highlight any object and open the File menu. You'll find a new option on the menu, Raw Properties, located just below Properties. Click on it and play to your heart's content. One warning: Use your

Raw Properties (continued)

mouse, and keep your hands off your keyboard so there's no chance you'll change anything. You're not ready for that kind of stuff yet.

The graphic enclosed in this sidebar shows some of the raw properties or attributes for the mailbox I created earlier in this chapter.

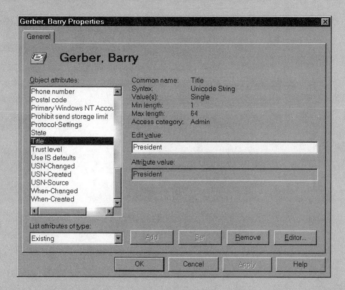

The Title attribute is selected, and my title—President—is listed and can be edited in the Edit Value box. Notice that the Access category for Title is Admin. This means that only NT accounts or groups with Admin role permissions for the mailbox can change this property.

Conclusion

In this chapter you learned about the Exchange Administrator program and how to use it and its menus to do a number of administrative and management tasks. In the next chapter we'll continue using the Administrator to configure Exchange Server's hierarchy and core components.

The Exchange Server Hierarchy and Core Components

Basic administration and management of:

- **The Exchange Server hierarchy**

- **The directory service**

- **The information store**

- **The system attendant**

After plowing through the last chapter, you're probably beginning to appreciate at least some of the effort that Microsoft put into developing Exchange Server to achieve such a high level of flexible, easy-to-implement functionality. This and coming chapters will add to that appreciation—I guarantee it.

Now that you're comfortable with Exchange Server's Administrator program, its menus, and a number of its functions, I want to show you how to use it to administer and manage the Exchange Server hierarchy and core components. As in the last chapter, I'll focus mainly on the basics here, saving advanced administration and management for later chapters.

> **NOTE** As you've probably already discovered, some types of property pages are very similar, no matter where you encounter them. The Permissions page is a good example. So, from this point on, if we've already covered the subject matter of a particular property page, I'll skip over it without comment. I'll still let you know when we're bypassing material we'll cover in later chapters. Therefore, if I don't say anything at all about a specific property page or property, I'm assuming that you already know how to deal with it. Check back to earlier discussions for specifics.

The Exchange Server Hierarchy

You'll remember from Chapter 2 that the Exchange Server hierarchy includes the organization as well as its sites, servers, and recipients. In the last chapter, we talked a good deal about three kinds of recipients: mailbox, distribution list, and custom. Here we'll focus on the organization, sites, and servers. We'll also cover the last of the four recipient types: public folder.

Let's see what tools are available for administering and managing the hierarchy. Open the Administrator program and make the left-hand pane look like the one shown in Figure 9.1. As we move along, refer back to this figure if you need help in finding a particular object in the Exchange hierarchy.

FIGURE 9.1

The Exchange Administrator, ready to administer and manage the Exchange hierarchy

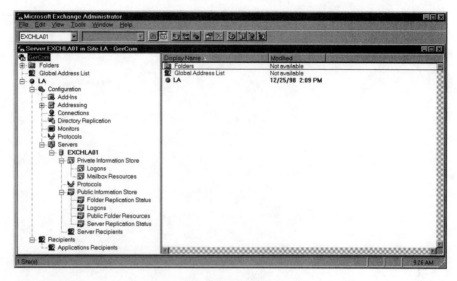

The Organization

Click on the name of your organization in the left-hand pane of the Administrator window, and then open the File menu and click on Properties. This brings up the Properties dialog box for the organization (see Figure 9.2).

General Properties

Talk about starting off easy! There's only one thing you can change on the General property page—the display name for your organization.

The *display name* is what you see when you look at the Exchange Server hierarchy in the Administrator; it's also the organization name that Exchange client users see in their address books. The default display name, which can be up to 256 characters long, is the organization name you entered when you installed the first server in your Exchange organization. You can change the display name to make the organization's name more meaningful to those who administer and use your Exchange system. For example, I could change "GerCom" to "Barry Gerber's Wonderful Enter Key Company" (but I won't).

FIGURE 9.2

The Properties dialog
box for an organization

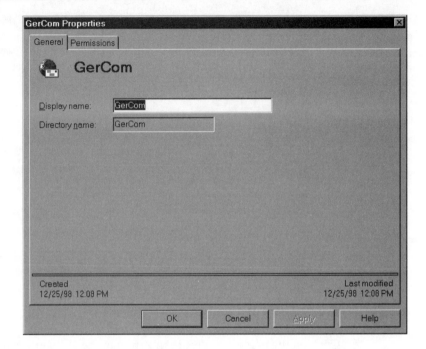

Changing the display name doesn't change the *directory name* (shown below the display name in Figure 9.2). Like the display name, the directory name defaults to the organization name you entered when you installed the first server in your Exchange organization. Unlike the display name, however, the directory name can't be changed with the Administrator program; that's why it's grayed out. The only way you can change the directory name is by reinstalling Exchange Server on every server in the organization!

NOTE Remember that an object's directory name is used to identify the object within your organization's Exchange Server directory, so the directory name for each object must be unique. Also, remember that once a directory name has been created, it can't be changed.

Permissions

The Permissions property page (shown in Figure 9.3) is pretty similar to the ones you saw in the last chapter, but it includes one right you've never seen: Replication. An NT account or group with Replication rights can administer and manage Exchange Server directory replication. I've popped down the Roles menu in Figure 9.3 so you can see the roles. There's nothing you weren't exposed to in Chapters 7 or 8.

FIGURE 9.3

The Permissions property page for an organization

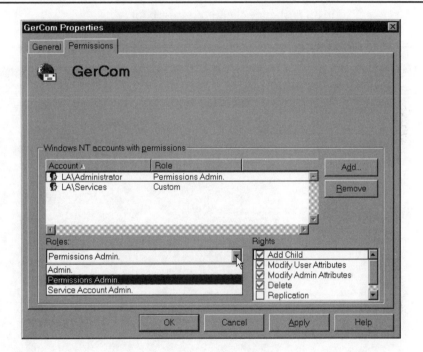

Notice that only the NT domain Administrator account (LA/Administrator) and the account we designated to run our Exchange server's services (LA/Services) have permissions at the org level. The two accounts received these permissions by default when we installed Exchange Server. The Exchange Admins group we created back in Chapter 7 isn't here, because we gave the group permissions at the site level. You'll see the Exchange Admins group in a bit when we look at site-level permissions.

Sites

To bring up the Properties dialog box for your site, click on the site name and select Properties from the Exchange Administrator's File menu (see Figure 9.4).

General Properties

As with the organization's General properties page, you can change a site's display name. And as with an organization, changing a site display name affects only what you see on the hierarchy tree in the Administrator and what users see in an Exchange client's address book.

FIGURE 9.4

The Properties dialog box for a site

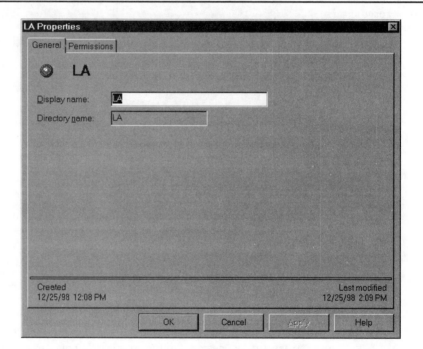

Permissions

As you can see in Figure 9.5, the Exchange Admins group we gave site permissions to back in Chapter 7 does indeed have those permissions. Also, notice that the Services account has permissions at the site level. As with organization-level permissions, these were granted by default upon installation of our Exchange server.

FIGURE 9.5

The Permissions
property page for a site

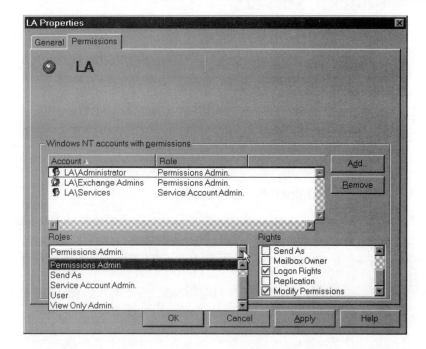

The Sites Permissions page has one new right, Logon Rights, as well as one new role, View Only Admin. Logon Rights allow an NT account or group to log on to any server in the site with the Administrator program. Logon Rights let a user view objects but not change them. Beyond that, once they are logged on to a server, what an account or group can do is controlled by other rights granted at the site level and lower levels in the Exchange hierarchy. View Only Admin gives an NT account Logon Rights to the site and nothing more. Go ahead and browse through the roles and rights on the site's Permissions page to see how things hang together.

Servers

The Servers' General and Permissions property pages are very much like those for the organization and site. We'll talk a bit more about permissions at the Servers-container level in a bit. For now, let's move on.

Specific Servers

The Organization, Site, and Servers Properties dialog boxes sport only two property pages. Individual servers, on the other hand, have Properties dialog boxes with a number of pages, so there are lots of things you can do in their administration and management.

Let's look at the Properties dialog box for a specific server right now. Click on the name of your server in the left-hand pane of the Administrator window (mine is named EXCHLA01). Then select Properties from the File menu. This brings up that server's Properties dialog box, as shown in Figure 9.6.

General Properties

You can enter information on the server's physical location in the Server location field. You can create as many different locations as you'd like. Think of locations as sub-sites that you can use to improve Exchange client-server performance and control network traffic. Locations are clusters of Exchange servers that are linked by higher capacity networks. Then, when an Exchange client or server needs to access information that is stored on multiple servers, it will go to servers in other locations only if it can't get the information from a server in its own location. In Exchange 5, locations are used to control public folder access.

If a public folder is replicated across two or more locations and the location contains a replica of the folder, any access to it will be within the accessing client's or server's location. If the location doesn't contain the replica, then a replica will be accessed in another location.

The only other thing you can do on the General property page is to add an administrative note.

Services

Back in the last chapter you set up a server monitor, which among other things involved selecting the specific services to be monitored on each server. The Services property page is just another place to select those services. The page looks and acts just like the one shown back in Figure 8.38; refer to the figure and its related text if you need to modify the services being monitored for a specific Exchange server.

FIGURE 9.6

The Properties dialog box for a server

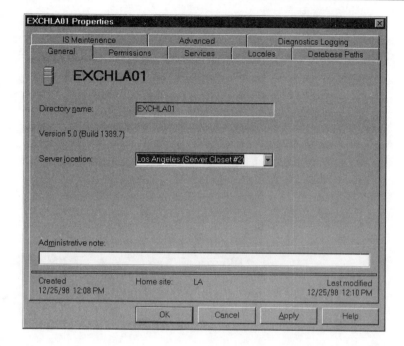

Locales

If you need support for languages other than English on an Exchange server, you use the Locales property page to select the languages. As you can see in Figure 9.7, a wide variety of languages is available. To select one, highlight it and click on Add. You can add as many languages as you like.

Language support is more important than you might expect. Even if your users only work in English, there are times when you may need language support just to allow an Exchange server to receive certain messages. For example, one Exchange site I set up had difficulty receiving mail from someone in Northern California. It turned out that the person was using a recent flavor of Netscape Navigator with support for Korean. After we installed support for Korean on the servers in the site, the messages came through just fine.

NOTE Exchange Server's support for locales requires support by NT Server for each selected language. Check with Microsoft for more information on availability and licensing issues.

Use the Locales property page to select language support for an Exchange server.

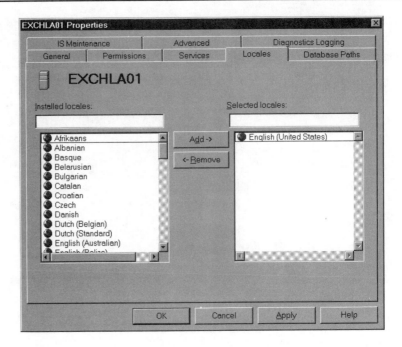

Database Paths

You'll remember that I advised you to put multiple disk drives in your Exchange server. If you did, you can improve the performance of your server by moving key files to other drives. Here's a quick look at the path-change options on the Database Paths property page, which is shown in Figure 9.8.

- *Directory Database* holds the copy of the Exchange Server directory stored on this server.

- *Directory Transaction Logs* are used by Exchange to improve database fault tolerance and performance.

- *Directory Working Path* is where temporary files related to the Exchange directory are stored.

- *Private Information Store Database* holds user mailboxes (the ones stored on an Exchange server).

- *Public Information Store Database* holds public folders.

- *Information Store Transaction Logs* perform the same function for the information store as the directory transaction logs do for the directory.

• *Information Store Working Path* performs the same function as the directory working path does for the directory.

> **NOTE**
>
> You can (and usually should) let Exchange Server's Performance Optimizer program, discussed in Chapter 7, take care of modifying database paths. The Performance Optimizer runs a set of built-in tests to determine whether changing the path of a particular database is likely to have a positive effect on performance. If the tests indicate that a database path change makes sense, the Performance Optimizer then moves the database and makes the required system changes automatically.

FIGURE 9.8

Use the Database Paths property page to change NT directories for key Exchange files.

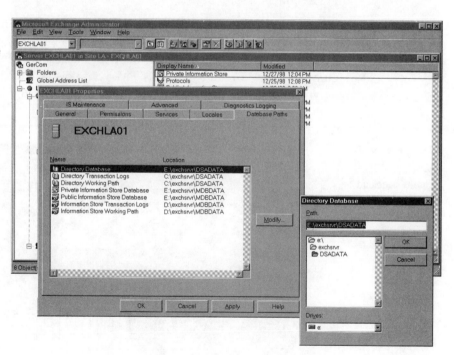

To change a database path, first create the directory on any drive you wish. Next, click on the existing path in the list of database paths and then click on Modify. You'll get a standard Windows NT directory walker, as shown in the lower right-hand corner of Figure 9.8. Find the drive and directory you want and click on OK. Moving a database using the Database Paths property page not only moves files, but also changes system parameters. That's why you should never move databases without using the Database Paths page.

IS Maintenance

The IS Maintenance property page is used to set up a schedule for all maintenance functions—such as defragmentation of public and private information stores, and how frequently Exchange Server is to check for and delete messages in public folders that are past their age limits—on an Exchange server's private and public information stores (ISs).

As you can see in Figure 9.9, you have two general options for scheduling: Always and Selected Times. If you pick Always, the IS maintenance is done every 15 minutes. That's much too frequent, especially for a new Exchange server, so I don't recommend selecting Always.

If you choose Selected Times, you can set up a custom maintenance schedule using the little day/time table on the IS Maintenance property page. You can look at the Selected Times schedule table in one-hour increments—the default shown in Figure 9.9—or in 15-minute intervals. Pick your poison in the Detail view box. For now, you can't go wrong if you accept the daily 1 A.M. to 6 A.M. default.

FIGURE 9.9

The IS Maintenance property page and its default schedule

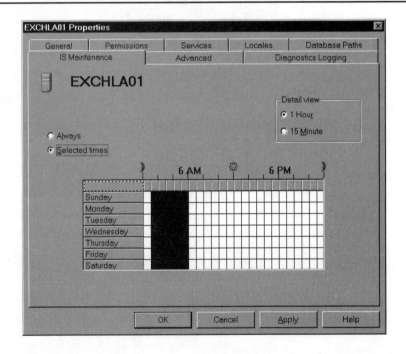

Advanced Properties

Check out Figure 9.10 as we look at the Advanced property page for a server. Those directory and information-store transaction logs I talked about earlier can get pretty humongous. As you'll see in the next chapter, they're deleted when you back up the Exchange directory or information store. If you don't do a backup—and for the life of me I can't figure out why you wouldn't—the logs just accumulate.

FIGURE 9.10

Setting Advanced properties for a server

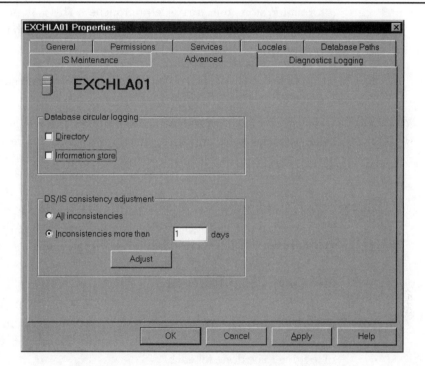

If circular logging is turned on for the directory and information store, Exchange Server continually overwrites earlier transaction logs. By default, circular logging for both the directory and information store is turned on. However, since I'm such a backup nut, I strongly suggest that you turn these options off and instead rely on NT's Backup program to prune your server's transaction logs.

In certain situations, the information store and directory on an Exchange server can get out of sync. For example, when you restore an Exchange server from a backup tape, you may wind up with mailboxes in the private information store that aren't represented in the directory, or vice versa.

You can adjust for these inconsistencies on the Advanced properties page. If a mailbox is found in the private information store without a directory entry, Exchange creates the directory entry. In such a case, you'll have to reenter any information for the mailbox using the Properties dialog box for mailboxes you worked with in the last chapter. The same rules apply for public folders.

If a directory entry is found without a corresponding mailbox in the private information store, the entry is left untouched. This is done because a new mailbox gets a directory entry immediately upon creation in Exchange Administrator, but the mailbox isn't created in the private information store until its user logs into it for the first time or the mailbox is sent its first message. When a public folder is found in the directory, but not in the public information store, the directory entry is deleted.

As Figure 9.10 shows, the Advanced properties page lets you adjust for all inconsistencies or for only those of a certain age. If you're adjusting for a certain age, run the check once to mark inconsistencies, and then run it again n days later, where n is greater than the number you enter in the dialog. Then only the inconsistencies older than the number of days you entered will be reconciled. This way adjustments will not be made for inconsistencies that may be fixed in the normal course of directory replication. Click on the Adjust button to start an inconsistencies reconciliation.

Diagnostics Logging

Exchange Server can write diagnostic information to NT Server's Event log. As I noted in Chapter 4, some of this logging happens automatically. You use the Diagnostics Logging property page to specify additional items to log and the depth of logging to be done for each.

Most of the time, you'll do diagnostics logging when you've got a problem. In many cases, knowledgeable technical support folks at Microsoft or another group will tell you what they want logged and then ask you to turn it on. However, it's still worth knowing how to use the Diagnostics Logging page, so let's try it.

When you first tab over to the Diagnostics Logging property page, it looks pretty sparse. All you see are the name of the server; a tree listing several cryptic names that you might correctly assume represent Exchange Server objects; and, at the bottom, some unselected logging-level options.

You can set diagnostic logging options for most services at the root level, except for the information store, MSExchangeIS. Double-clicking on MSExchangeIS opens a list of public and private information store subservices as well as system and Internet protocol services (see Figure 9.11).

When you click on a service in the left-hand Services pane, the right-hand pane shows the specific items within the service that can be logged. Figure 9.11 shows some of the diagnostic items for MSExchangeDS, the directory service.

You can set a logging option for any item in the right-hand box by clicking on the item and then selecting an option in the Logging Level area at the bottom of the property page. (In Figure 9.11 I've chosen a medium level of logging for directory service security.)

FIGURE 9.11

The Diagnostics Logging property page

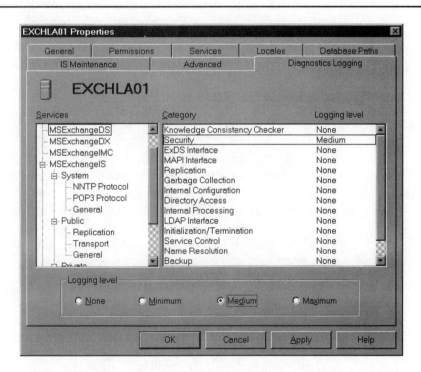

To set the same logging level for a group of items, just use the standard Microsoft Windows selection options: Ctrl+mouse-clicks for noncontiguous items and Shift+mouse-clicks for contiguous items.

Recipients: A General Overview

There are four types of recipients containers in the Exchange hierarchy: server recipients containers, site recipients containers, the Global Address List (GAL), and the Public Folders container. Exchange Server uses recipients containers to construct address books, and the Exchange Administrator program uses them to organize access to recipient objects when they are administered and managed. Each recipient is represented in multiple containers. (It's best to think of recipients as being *represented* in containers, rather than being *stored* in containers.)

From our discussion of them in Chapter 7, you already know a little about site recipients containers. We'll talk more about them in just a bit.

The GAL is the master recipients container for an organization. It contains all of the recipients in all sites in the organization, except for hidden recipients. The GAL is near the top of the Exchange hierarchy (see Figure 9.1).

The recipients container for each server holds the mailboxes that have their homes on the server (see Figure 9.1, lower left-hand corner). You'll remember from the last chapter that you set a mailbox's home server while creating it, but this can easily be changed to another server in the site by using Move Mailbox. Remember too that you set a mailbox in motion by changing the mailbox's home server on its Advanced property page.

The other three types of recipients—distribution lists, custom recipients, and public folders—are not represented in server recipients containers. As noted in the last chapter, distribution lists and custom recipients are represented in site recipients containers. As you'll soon see, public folders are represented in both site recipients containers and in the Public Folders container near the top of the Exchange hierarchy and in the Global Address List if they're not hidden (see Figure 9.1).

Of the four types of recipients containers, only site recipients containers have revisable properties. So let's spend a bit of time exploring these properties.

Site Recipients Container Properties

As you know, each site starts with one default recipients container called *Recipients*, and you can create more containers as needed. What I say here about the default Recipients container applies to any other recipients containers you create.

To display the Properties dialog box for Recipients, select the container by clicking on it. Then select Properties from the Exchange Administrator's File menu. As you can see from Figure 9.12, the Properties dialog box for Recipients looks similar to the ones for the organization and sites.

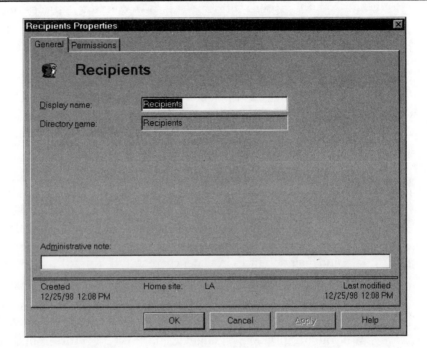

General Properties

The only addition to the General property page for Recipients is an Administrative Note field. Like all such notes, this one is visible only to NT accounts and groups with Exchange administrative rights for the recipients container.

Permissions

The rights and roles on the Permissions property page for Recipients are mainly a combination of what makes sense from the property pages for the mailbox (see the last chapter) and the site (see above). There are no rights here that you haven't seen before.

> **NOTE** If an NT account or group has permissions at the site level, these permissions are inherited by all recipients containers in the site. So, for example, if an account has Mailbox Owner rights at the site level, it also has those rights for any recipients containers in the site. Take a look at the permissions for your Recipients container. You'll see that the permissions of your Administrator and Services accounts and your Exchange Admin group have been inherited by the container.

Administering and Managing Public Folders

In the last chapter on Administrator menus, we covered most of the basics of recipient administration and management. However, one type of recipient isn't created using Administrator menus: public folders. Users—or more correctly, *Exchange mailbox users*—create public folders while in their Exchange clients. Folder creators and their designees and Exchange Server administrators share the role of administering and managing public folders. In this section, we'll cover the role of administrators; we'll deal with the administrative and management role of public folder creators and their designees in a later chapter.

As you probably haven't installed an Exchange client yet and thus don't have any public folders, I'll walk you through this section using one of mine. To administer and manage a public folder, locate it in the Public Folders container under your organization, highlight it, and select Properties from Exchange Administrator's File menu. This brings up a Properties dialog box for the folder; see Figure 9.13 for the location of the Public Folders container and a view of the dialog box.

> **NOTE** The organization-level Public Folders container isn't the only place you can access public folders. In each site, you designate a recipients container to hold your public folders. (We'll talk later about how you do this.) This can be the default Recipients container or any other recipients container you create. Public folders created by mailbox owners in a site reside in this recipients container.

FIGURE 9.13

The Properties dialog box for a public folder

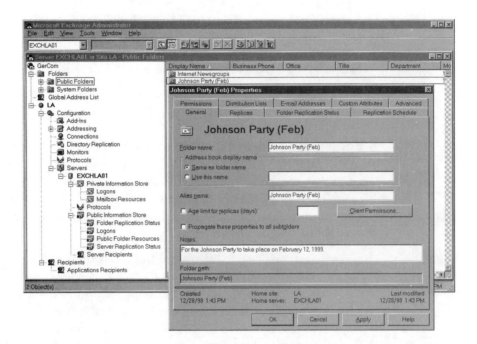

NOTE

By default, public folders are marked as hidden when they're created. A hidden public folder can't be seen in its site recipients container, and—because Exchange address books are constructed using the unhidden recipients in recipients containers—a hidden recipient does not show up in the address book. Public folders are hidden by default because, except for very specific applications, there's no reason for users to mail messages to public folders instead of directly posting to them. It's better not to clutter the address book with addresses that won't be used—or, worse, might be used by accident.

NOTE

If you want to see hidden public folders, select Hidden Recipients from the Administrator's View menu. You don't need to worry about all of this too much, though. Just work on public folders in the organization's **Public Folders** container, which shows all such folders, hidden or not.

A number of the properties for public folders have to do with cross-server public folder replication. We'll cover those properties in a later chapter that deals specifically with public folder replication.

General Properties

Among other things, the General property page is used to set some names, give Exchange client users rights to the folder, and enter notes.

Folder and Address Book Display Names   The folder name is displayed in Exchange client folder hierarchy trees; the address book display name is what an Exchange client sees in the address book when a public folder isn't hidden. By default, the folder name and address book display name are the same. You can override the default by entering a different address book display name in the Use This Name field.

You'll want to use the different address book display name option when you have subfolders with the same name. In the Exchange client folder hierarchy, these will make perfect sense. For example, say you have master folders with the names *Windows NT* and *Exchange Server,* and under each master folder you have a *Specs* subfolder to hold specification information for each product. In the Exchange client folder hierarchy, it will be clear which Specs folder is for each product, since it will be shown as a subfolder of the product.

However, in the address book—which is a flat alphabetical listing—you'll just see two folders named *Specs* next to each other and far removed from the names of their parent folders. Giving address book display names like *Windows NT Specs* and *Exchange Server Specs* to the Specs folders helps alleviate this confusion.

Alias Name   The alias name can be up to 64 characters long and is used to construct E-mail addresses for the folder. In addition, as with other recipient aliases, an Exchange client user can type in all or part of a public folder's alias when addressing a message to the folder. When the user sends the message, the user's client finds the alias's real e-mail address and sends the mail.

If you change the name, keep it simple; otherwise, people outside your organization who address messages to the folder will have to type in a long name—and that can lead to addressing errors, not to mention outright anger for those with short tempers.

Age Limits for All Replicas   Replica age limits are used when public folders are replicated between Exchange servers. We'll cover them in a later chapter.

Client Permissions   Clicking on the Client Permissions button lets you assign specific folder rights to recipients who can then work with a public folder using their Exchange clients (hence the term *Client Permissions*). Figure 9.14 shows the Client Permissions dialog box. As the folder's creator, I'm given the role of Owner. As you can see, the Owner has complete control over the folder.

FIGURE 9.14

The Client Permission dialog box

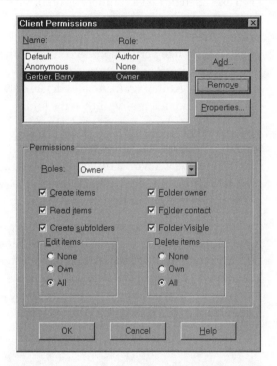

NOTE   In Figure 9.14, the mailbox used by Barry Gerber—*not* the NT account used by Barry Gerber—is given Owner permissions for the folder. This is an important distinction. As you'll see in a later chapter, the creator of a public folder can also give out client permissions to other recipients. All of this is also done at the Exchange recipient level rather than the NT account level. Users don't have to worry about NT accounts; Exchange server makes the links between recipient mailboxes and the Exchange accounts that are granted permissions to them.

There is a default group that includes all Exchange recipients not separately added to the Name list box. When the folder is created, this group is automatically given the default role of Author (see Figure 9.14). Authors don't own the folder and can't create subfolders. Users falling into the default group (because they aren't listed separately) cannot serve as folder contacts. A folder contact receives notifications about the folder (for example, a warning that the folder's storage limits have been exceeded or that a conflict has occurred in folder replication). A folder contact is also the person whom users should ask for access to the folder. The contact may or may not have permission to change permissions on the folder. Only a folder owner can change permissions. A contact without owner permissions can receive requests for access, but has to ask someone with owner permissions to actually set up the access. Authors can edit and delete only their own folder items, while owners can edit and delete anything in the folder.

Microsoft has come up with several interesting roles—including Owner, Publishing Editor, Editor, Publishing Author, Author, Non-Editing Author, Reviewer, and Contributor—each with a different combination of client permissions. I'll leave it to you to check out the specific permissions assigned to each of these roles when you've got some public folders to work with.

One way to control access to a public folder is to edit the default group's permissions. You can also control access to a public folder by adding recipients with permissions on it. To do so, click on the Add button in the Client Permissions dialog box and select the recipient you want from the standard recipients list dialog box that pops up. You can then assign a role to the added recipient. Click on OK in the Client Permissions dialog box when you're done.

> **NOTE** Wondering about that Anonymous user in Figure 9.14? You set access rights to a public folder for users who don't have Exchange mailboxes through the Anonymous user. When such users access a public folder, for example, with an Internet browser, the rights granted to the Anonymous user control what they can do with the folder. More about this neat little user in Chapter 17.

Notes Let's go back to Figure 9.13. The notes you enter in the Notes field of a folder's Properties dialog box can be used for administrative purposes. They also show up as a property of the folder in the address book used by Exchange clients. So be careful what you put in this field.

Folder Path   The folder path is the location of the folder in the public folder hierarchy. This path will change if a user moves a public folder—say, into another public folder.

Skipped Property Pages

The Replicas, Folder Replication Status, and Replication Schedule property pages deal with public folder replication. I'll talk about them in Chapter 14.

The Permissions, Distribution Lists, E-mail Addresses, Custom Attributes, and Advanced property pages are pretty much like the ones you've seen for other recipients. So we'll skip them here; you can check Chapter 8 for information on these property pages.

> **NOTE**   As I mentioned above, public folders are by default hidden from the Exchange address book when they're created by Exchange clients. Only an Exchange Server administrator can "unhide" a public folder from the address book. To do this, deselect Hide from Address Book on the Advanced property page for the folder.

Exchange Server Core Components

That's it for the Exchange hierarchy. Now let's move on to the core components. As you'll remember from Chapter 3, there are four core components: the directory service (DS), the Message Transfer Agent (MTA), the information store (both private and public), and the System Attendant.

Let's discuss how to administer and manage the four core components. You deal with core components at two different levels: the site and the server.

At the site level, you work in the Configuration container. Before we actually deal with the core components, I need to tell you a bit about permissions at the Configuration-container level and below.

Notice in Figure 9.1 that the Configuration and Recipients containers are at the same level in the Exchange hierarchy: They're both second-level objects in the site. You'll remember from our discussion earlier in this chapter that site-level permissions for NT accounts or groups are inherited by recipients containers in the site.

The same rule doesn't apply to the site Configuration container, even though it's at the same level in the Exchange hierarchy as recipients containers. Except for the Administrator and Services accounts, which get their usual default permissions for the Configuration container when your Exchange server is installed, you have to specifically grant accounts or groups permissions for a site's Configuration container. So, for example, the permissions of the Exchange Admins group aren't inherited by the Configuration container, even though you gave the group permissions at the site-container level.

You have to add permissions at the Configuration-container level for the Exchange Admins group or any other NT accounts or groups that should have access to the Configuration container. To do this, click on the Configuration container and select Properties from the Administrator's File menu. Then use the Permissions property page in the resultant Configuration Properties dialog box to add NT accounts or groups and to set appropriate permissions, which in most cases means assigning the permissions role Permissions Admin to the account or group.

There's a good reason for the different inheritance rules that apply to the Configuration container and recipients containers. Site configuration is a complex task that requires a clear understanding of the complexities of Exchange Server. On the other hand, while recipient administration and management is not for the technically unaware, it doesn't take the same level of Exchange Server mastery as site configuration does. By limiting site-based inheritance only to recipients containers, Microsoft has ensured that you will never accidentally assign site-configuration permissions to people who aren't trained to do it.

The buck *does* stop at the Configuration-container level. Once you've granted an NT account or group rights at the Configuration container level, all objects in the Configuration container (including subcontainers) inherit those rights. For example, once you've granted site Configuration-container level permissions to your Exchange Admins group, individual servers in the site inherit those permissions.

Okay, let's get going. If it's not already open, start up the Exchange Administrator and make it look like the window shown in Figure 9.15. Be sure you've clicked on the site's Configuration container in the left-hand window pane. Notice the three core component configuration options in the right pane: DS Site Configuration, Information Store Site Configuration, and MTA Site Configuration. Let's walk through each of these options.

FIGURE 9.15

Finding the site con-
figuration options for
Exchange Server's
core components

NOTE You can manage the System Attendant only at the server level. That's
why it doesn't show up in the site's Configuration container.

Administering and Managing
the Directory Service

As you'll remember, the directory contains all of the objects for a site. Much of
directory service (DS) administration and management is for multiserver sites,
which we'll cover in Chapter 13. For now, we'll look at those directory service
properties that are useful in sites with only one server.

Administering and Managing the DS at
the Site Level

You use the DS Site Configuration Properties dialog box to set some of the system
maintenance and offline address book parameters. This is also the place to create
those custom attributes for recipients that I wrote about in the last chapter.

To open the dialog box, click on the Configuration container for your site. Then either double-click on DS Site Configuration or click on DS Site Configuration and select Properties from the Administrator's File menu. This pops up a dialog box like the one in Figure 9.16.

General Properties

We'll cover General properties, such as *tombstones* and *garbage collection*, when we talk about public folder replication in a later chapter.

FIGURE 9.16

The DS Site Configuration
Properties dialog box

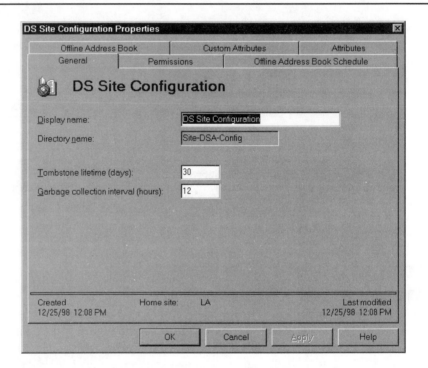

Offline Address Book Schedule

You use the offline address book when you're not connected to your Exchange server—for example, when users are away from the office and connecting to the server only to send and receive new messages. When users compose messages offline, the offline address book lets them address the messages.

Generally, just before users leave the office they'll download an updated copy of the offline address book or they'll download it when remotely connected. Exchange Server constructs the address book from the recipients container you specify (see the next section). You use the offline Address Book Schedule property page to set the schedule used to update the offline address book to reflect new and recently deleted recipients in your site or organization.

The offline Address Book Schedule property page looks almost exactly like the IS Maintenance property page in Figure 9.9. Take a look at Figure 9.9 and its associated text for details on setting the schedule.

How frequently you should schedule updates to your offline address book depends on how often you add and delete recipients for your site, how many addresses are in the recipients container used to generate the address book, and how busy your Exchange server is. You might want to start with a single daily update at around midnight.

Offline Address Book

Only one recipients container can be used as the source for a site's offline address book. The site's Recipients container is the default. In most cases, the best recipients container to use for the offline address book is the Global Address List. That way, all of the addresses in your Exchange organization will be available to offline users. If you use the GAL to generate your offline address book, be sure that your users have sufficient disk space to hold what can be a pretty large file.

Select the recipients container you want using the Offline Address Book property page (see Figure 9.17). Click Modify on the property page to bring up a little Offline Address Book Container dialog box. Use it to walk through the Exchange hierarchy and find the site and recipients container you want; then click on it and click on OK in the Offline Address Book Container dialog box.

You can regenerate the offline address book any time you need to. Just click on the Generate Offline Address Book Now button on the Offline Address Book property page.

In multiserver sites, you can change the Server that is responsible for generating the offline address book. Select it from the Offline Address Book Server dropdown menu.

FIGURE 9.17

Selecting the recipients container used to generate the offline address book

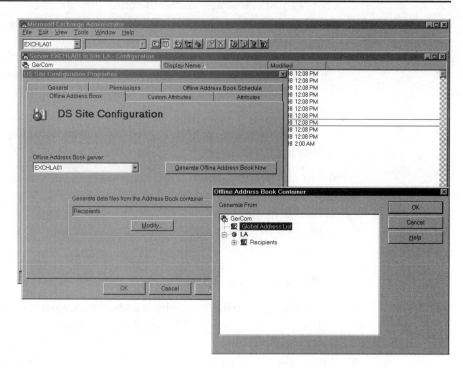

Custom Attributes

You use the Custom Attributes property page to create up to ten of those custom fields I talked about in the last chapter. In Figure 9.18, I'm creating a new custom field called Employee ID. As soon as I click on Apply, that field will show up on the Custom Attributes property page of *every* old and new recipient in the site; in fact, even public folders will get the field.

Figure 9.19 shows the Custom Attributes property page for my mailbox. The newly created field is right up at the top; someone is typing in my employee ID right now.

FIGURE 9.18

Creating a new custom attribute field, Employee ID, for all recipients in a site

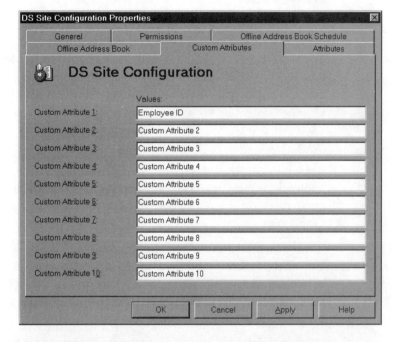

FIGURE 9.19

The new Employee ID field appears on the Custom Attributes property page of all recipient objects, including this mailbox.

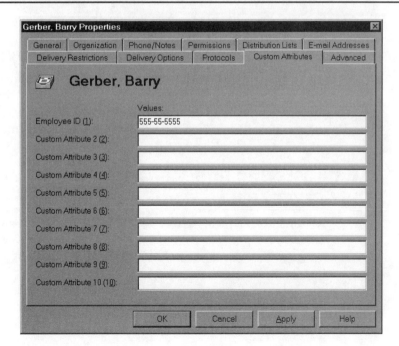

Attributes

The Attributes property page lets you restrict access to specific recipient attributes for Lightweight Directory Access Protocol (LDAP) client access and controls what gets replicated between sites. For example, you may want fully authenticated Exchange mailbox users—those who log in using NT account security—to see the phone numbers connected with a mailbox or custom recipient. However, you may not want anonymous users who you permit to browse your Exchange directory using a Lightweight Directory Access Protocol client to be able to see phone number attributes.

As Figure 9.20 shows, you can set attribute access parameters at four levels: anonymous requests, authenticated requests, intersite replication, and system attributes. You already know what the first two of these are from the paragraph above.

Intersite replication is the process by which the directories in one Exchange site are replicated to another site. If you don't want some directory attributes to be replicated to other sites, here is where you specify which attributes aren't to be replicated. This option has no effect on directory replication between the servers in a site. All attributes are replicated within a site.

System attributes have no function in Exchange 5. Though they existed in earlier versions of the LDAP specification, they were eliminated from the spec with the promulgation of LDAP version 3. Due to these changes, system attributes may not be present in the version of Exchange Server you're using.

The drop-down menu in Figure 9.20 lets you select the recipient type you wish to change access parameters for. The default is All Mail Recipients. The drop-down menu lets you select a specific recipient type: mailbox, distribution list, public folder, or 'remote address' (another name for 'custom recipient').

Administering and Managing the DS at the Server Level

All server-level directory service administration and management focuses on multi-server, multisite Exchange systems. We'll get into this whole can of spaghetti in later chapters.

FIGURE 9.20

Restricting access
to specific directory
attributes

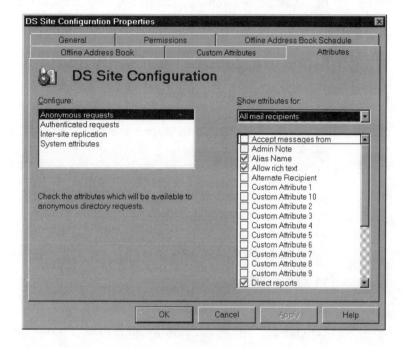

Administering and Managing the MTA

Because the Message Transfer Agent moves messages in and out of an Exchange
server, it's too early to discuss it at this time, when we've got only one server up
and running. We'll devote lots of time to MTA administration and management
in later chapters.

Administering and Managing the Information Store

As you'll remember from earlier chapters, the Exchange Server information store
includes both a private and public segment. At the site level, you administer and
manage the information store, not its two component parts. At the server level,

however, administration and management of the private and public information store are done separately.

Administering and Managing the Information Store at the Site Level

You use the Information Store Site Configuration Properties dialog box to set a variety of properties for mailboxes and public folders. To open the dialog box for site-level administration and management of the information store, double-click on the Information Store Site Configuration object in the Administrator's right-hand pane. (Take a look back at Figure 9.15 if you need help in finding the object.) When you've found and double-clicked on the appropriate object, you'll see a Properties dialog box like the one in Figure 9.21.

General Properties

Like all recipients, every public folder is represented in multiple containers. At the site level, public folders are represented by default in the site container named Recipients. The Public folder container field is blank if the default is selected. You can change the default public folder container on the General property page; however, I suggest you leave it as is, unless you have strong reasons for using another container. To change the container, click on Modify and pick a container from the Public Folder Container dialog box that pops up.

> **NOTE**   As I advised earlier, even though public folders are represented in the site's Recipients container (or whatever alternative you choose), you should view and work with them in the organization-level container called Public Folders. This will help keep your attention focused on the fact that, due to replication, public folders often live in an organization, not just a site.

If the 'Enable Message Tracking' check box is selected, a daily log file is kept on all messages that the information store handles. Exchange Server's Message Tracking Center (which I'll talk about in Chapter 17) uses these log files to help you figure out what might have happened to wayward messages. I suggest that you enable message tracking right now and start building the log files. If you want to play with the Message Tracking Center once something is in the log files, select Track Message from the Administrator's Tools menu.

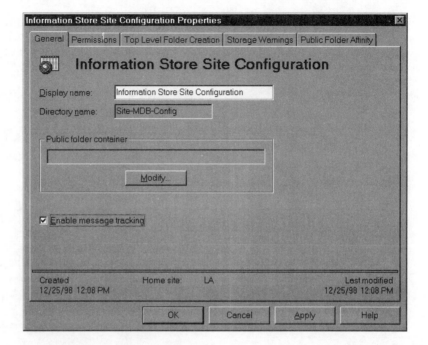

FIGURE 9.21

Setting sitewide parameters for information stores

Top-Level Folder Creation

As I noted above almost too many times, public folders are created by Exchange users working in their Exchange clients. You use the Top Level Folder Creation property page to specify which recipients can create public folders at the top (or root) level of the public folder hierarchy. Until a top-level folder is created, it's not possible to create subfolders below it.

By limiting top-level public folder creation to specific recipients, you ensure that public folders won't multiply out of control—at least at the root level. Recipients with top-level folder creation rights can give other recipients the rights to create subfolders. This lets you distribute responsibility for public folder administration and management.

As you can see in Figure 9.22, the default is to allow all recipients to create top-level public folders. You should change this default quickly. Remember: For this property page, recipients includes all recipients. Use your imagination, but get some kind of controls in place right away.

FIGURE 9.22

Top Level Folder Creation property page settings determine which recipients can create top-level public folders.

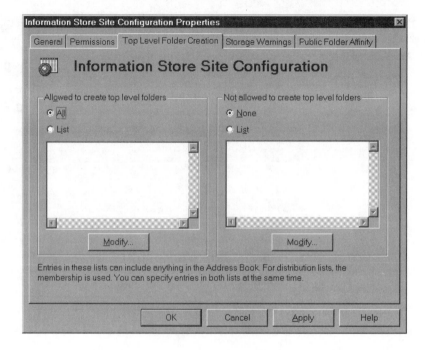

To specify which recipients are allowed to create top-level public folders, click on the Modify button on the *left-hand* side of the Top Level Folder Creation property page. A standard address book dialog box opens; use it to select which recipients can create top-level public folders. To specify which recipients aren't allowed to create top-level public folders, click on Modify on the *right-hand* side of the property page and select from the address book dialog box that pops up.

NOTE   If you grant top-level public folder creation rights to one or more recipients and leave the None option selected on the right-hand side of the property page, only those recipients who have been granted the rights will be able to create top-level public folders. In other words, you don't have to create a specific list of *excluded* recipients. You can give a subset of a distribution list rights by including the distribution list in the allow list and including the users in the distribution list that you don't want to give rights to in the not allowed list.

Storage Warnings

You can set maximum size limits for mailboxes and public folders. When these size limits have been exceeded, Exchange can send warning messages to users responsible for the offending mailboxes or public folders. You use the Storage Warnings property page to set the schedule for issuing these warnings.

This page looks and behaves almost exactly like the IS Maintenance schedule page shown back in Figure 9.9. The only addition is a Never option to accompany the Always and Selected Times options. Select Never if you don't ever want to warn users when they've exceeded message size limits. If you want to issue warnings, the default Selected Times schedule should be fine.

Public Folder Affinity

You use the Public Folder Affinity property page when you have multiple sites, and users in one site need to access public folders in another. We'll cover this page in Chapter 14.

Administering and Managing the Private Information Store at the Server Level

Because this is the first time we'll actually do some administering and managing at the server level, here's how you get to and open the Private Information Store properties page. First, be sure your server is visible in the left-hand pane of the Administrator window; then click on it. Your Administrator window should look something like the one in Figure 9.23.

As you can see in the figure, your server contains a number of objects. Focus on the five objects for administering and managing core components that are listed in the right-hand pane of the window: Private Information Store, Public Information Store, Directory Service, Message Transfer Agent, and System Attendant. As I noted earlier, we'll deal with directory service and MTA administration and management in later chapters.

Let's get started with the private information store. Click once on Private Information Store and select Properties from the Administrator's File menu to bring up the Properties dialog box shown in Figure 9.24.

FIGURE 9.23

Selecting server-level
core component admin-
istration and
management options

FIGURE 9.24

Setting server-specific
parameters for the
private information store

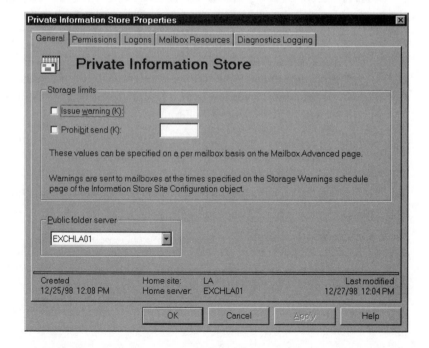

WARNING If you double-click on Private Information Store, you'll be taken to the Private Information Store container just below your server's name. (See Figure 9.23 where the Private Information Store container is shown right under my server's name, 'EXCHLA01'.) More about this in a bit.

An Exchange server's private information store holds the contents of mailboxes. Because it contains user and application folders and messages, it can grow to immense proportions in the twinkling of an eye. So managing and administering the private information store often focuses on controlling mailbox storage.

General Properties

As Figure 9.24 shows, the General property page starts you right off with a storage control opportunity. In the last chapter you learned how to set specific storage limits for a mailbox; here you set the default limits for *all* mailboxes stored on the server. You can set two parameters. With the first, a mailbox user is warned per the Storage Warnings schedule until the storage space consumed falls below the total kilobyte value set. With the second parameter, the mailbox can no longer send messages when storage reaches this limit. Messages are still received, but none can be sent.

Public folders created by users of mailboxes on a specific server don't have to be stored on the same server as the mailboxes—they can be stored on any server in a site. You can use the Public Folder Server drop-down list on the General property page to change the default (which is to use the same server, if it has a public information store; if not then the first server in alphabetical order with a public information store is used). Because we have only one server right now, this option isn't of much use. It can, however, be a nice way to balance loads when you've got multiple servers.

Logons

The Logons property page shows you which mailboxes are linked to the server as clients. Both user and system client connections are displayed. Figure 9.25 shows logon information for a range of mailboxes on my server. A single mailbox usually has many logons because the mailbox connects to a variety of Exchange Server services. Each logon is a connection to a different service. Sometimes the same user name will appear as having multiple mailboxes open. This happens when a person has rights to open multiple mailboxes as, for example, when a secretary has rights to open a boss's mailbox to read and printout the boss's mail. Yes, there are still such bosses in the world.

FIGURE 9.25

The Logons property page shows client connections to a server

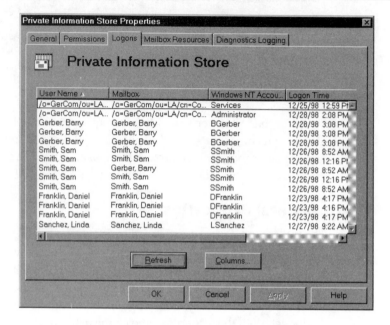

You can use the Columns button to change the columns included in the Logons list. In the last chapter, when I talked about the Administrator's View menu and recipient attributes, I showed you how to change display columns. (Refer back to Figure 8.45 and its related text for more information.) You can sort the rows in the Logons list by any column simply by clicking on the title bar at the top of the column.

> **NOTE**
>
> A page or so back, I noted that double-clicking on Private Information Store in the container for your server takes you to the Private Information Store container just below your server's name. You'll notice in Figure 9.23 that the Private Information Store container has a couple of sub-containers: Logons and Mailbox Resources. Instead of opening the Private Information Store properties dialog box shown in Figure 9.24 to see the logon information shown in Figure 9.25, you can just click on the Logons container and see the same info. This is a pretty neat time saver that also applies to Mailbox Resources, discussed immediately below and, as you can see in Figure 9.23, to a number of the properties of the public information store.

Mailbox Resources

The Mailbox Resources property page provides another tool for controlling mailbox storage. As you can see in Figure 9.26, when you sort the mailbox resources list by Total K, you can quickly spot the disk resource hogs on a server. The list shows only the names of mailboxes that have been logged into at least once or that have received at least one message.

FIGURE 9.26

Use the Mailbox Resources property page to determine which mailboxes use a lot of disk storage.

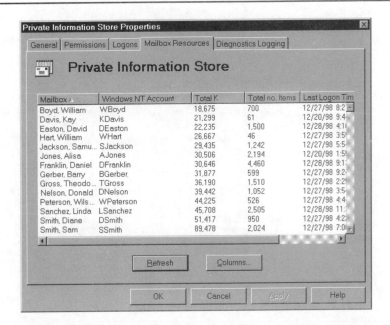

Private Information Store Properties

| General | Permissions | Logons | Mailbox Resources | Diagnostics Logging |

Private Information Store

Mailbox △	Windows NT Account	Total K	Total no. Items	Last Logon Tim
Boyd, William	WBoyd	18,675	700	12/27/98 8:2
Davis, Kay	KDavis	21,299	61	12/20/98 9:4
Easton, David	DEaston	22,235	1,500	12/28/98 4:1
Hart, William	WHart	26,667	46	12/27/98 3:5
Jackson, Samu...	SJackson	29,435	1,242	12/27/98 5:5
Jones, Alisa	AJones	30,506	2,194	12/20/98 1:5
Franklin, Daniel	DFranklin	30,646	4,460	12/28/98 9:1
Gerber, Barry	BGerber	31,877	599	12/27/98 9:2
Gross, Theodo...	TGross	36,190	1,510	12/27/98 2:2
Nelson, Donald	DNelson	39,442	1,052	12/27/98 3:5
Peterson, Wils...	WPeterson	44,225	526	12/27/98 4:4
Sanchez, Linda	LSanchez	45,708	2,505	12/28/98 11:
Smith, Diane	DSmith	51,417	950	12/27/98 4:2
Smith, Sam	SSmith	89,478	2,024	12/27/98 7:0

Refresh   Columns...

OK   Cancel   Apply   Help

> **NOTE** Wouldn't it be lovely to have a printout of this report, which you could use to clean out the worst storage hogs? Well, you can have just that and a number of other useful stats on your Exchange Servers. Check with Seagate Software and Microsoft for various Exchange Server–oriented tools available for Seagate's Crystal Reports report generation software.

Administering and Managing the Public Information Store at the Server Level

To open the Public Information Store Properties dialog box, click on your server in the Administrator window, and click on Public Information Store in the right-hand pane, then choose File ➤ Properties. This opens the dialog box, shown in Figure 9.27. Many of the property pages for this dialog box—including Instances, Replication Schedule, Age Limits, Folder Replication Status, and Server Replication Status—are used for public folder replication. I'll talk about them in a later chapter. For now, we just need to look at the General property page.

FIGURE 9.27

Setting server-specific parameters for the public information store

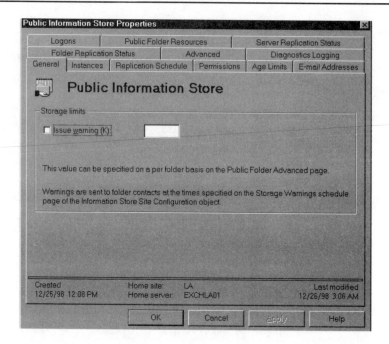

The General property page lets you set storage limits for all public folders created on the server. You can override this setting from the Advanced property page of any public folder.

Administering and Managing the System Attendant

The System Attendant performs lots of functions on an Exchange server—from watching for and fixing inconsistencies in server-based copies of site directories to enabling and disabling certain aspects of Exchange security. You can manage the System Attendant only at the server level. As you'll see, there's not much you need to do there.

Click on your server name in the left-hand pane of the Administrator window, then double-click on System Attendant in the right-hand pane. This brings up the System Attendant Properties dialog box shown in Figure 9.28. We need to look only at the General property page.

FIGURE 9.28

Setting parameters for a server's System Attendant

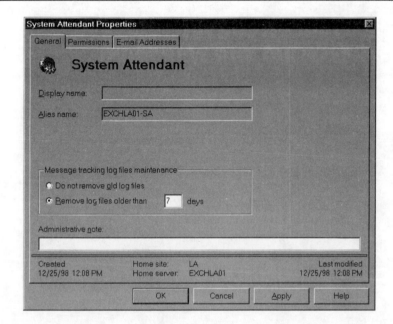

Right now, it's pretty safe to accept the default and let the System Attendant delete message-tracking log files more than seven days old. Later, when you've got multiple servers and sites, you might want to extend the number of days. However, if you back up your server regularly using the backup cycle I suggest in the next chapter, seven days should be fine. You'll always be able to restore recent log files from your backup if you need them.

Conclusion

In this chapter you learned how to do a range of basic administrative and management tasks for objects in Exchange Server's hierarchy and for its core components. At this point, you've got a lot of practical knowledge under your belt. The coming chapters will add significantly to that knowledge.

CHAPTER
TEN

10

Backing Up an Exchange Server

- Backup basics

- The role of Exchange Server transaction logs in backup

- How to set up an Exchange Server backup

- How to restore from an Exchange Server backup

- How to automate an Exchange Server backup

In Chapter 7 you learned how to use NT Server's Backup utility to back up an NT Server. Backup includes special features for protecting the two key Exchange Server databases—the information store and the directory. When you use these features, you can back up the databases without shutting down your Exchange Server and without denying Exchange clients access to the server. In this chapter you'll learn how to use these features.

We'll cover five topics here:

- Some backup basics
- Exchange Server transaction logs and backup
- Setting up an Exchange Server backup
- Restoring from an Exchange Server backup
- Automating a backup

Some Backup Basics

Before we get into Exchange Server backups, let's make sure you're comfortable with some backup basics. First, we'll go through a brief tutorial on the archive bit. Then we'll do a quick overview of the types of backups supported by NT's Backup program. Finally, I'll talk briefly about basic backup strategies.

The Archive Bit

Every NT file has a bit called the *archive bit,* which is set to "on" by the operating system when a file is created and when anything is written to the file. As you'll soon see, certain types of backups turn the bit to "off" to indicate that a file has been backed up. This makes the archive bit a great tool for determining when a file needs to be backed up. If the bit is on, a backup is required. If it's off, the file has already been backed up.

Backup Types

NT's Backup program lets you do five types of backups:

- *Normal:* All selected files are backed up irrespective of their archive bit settings. After backup, the archive bit for each file that has been backed up is turned off.

- *Copy:* All selected files are backed up irrespective of their archive bit settings. After backup, the archive bit for each file that has been backed up is *not* changed.

- *Incremental:* All files with their archive bit turned on are backed up. As with a normal backup, the archive bit for each file that has been backed up is turned off.

- *Differential:* All files with their archive bit turned on are backed up. The archive bit for each file that is backed up is *not* changed.

- *Daily:* All files that have changed on the day of the backup are backed up. The archive bit for each file that is backed up is *not* changed.

General Backup Strategies

Standard backup practice is to do a normal backup once a week and incremental or differential backups every other day. Because a differential backup doesn't change the archive bit, every differential backup covers all new files, as well as files that were changed since the last normal backup. To recover a failed server when you do differential backups, all you have to do is recover the last normal backup and the last differential backup. For this reason I prefer differential backups over incremental ones.

If you perform incremental instead of differential backups, to restore a failed server you have to recover the last normal backup and then, in order, all of the incremental backups since the last normal backup. That's not only more work, it also leaves more room for error: Imagine what a mess you could have if you were to restore those incremental backups even slightly out of order.

Differential backups use more tape, since they tend to back up more stuff every day. But tape is cheap compared to the lost time—not to mention the potential for error—that comes with incremental backups.

Whatever basic backup strategy you choose, be sure to protect your backup tapes in some way. Store them in a fireproof safe and/or off-site. If your company has a disaster-recovery plan, Exchange Server and its backups should be included in it.

Exchange Server Component Backup Strategies

You need to come up with a plan for backing up Exchange Server components. Here are some thoughts and ideas that might prove helpful.

I considered presenting some of this section's material later in the book, when you'll have more than one server up and running in your site. However, I've decided to include it here, both because it's interesting and because I think you're ready for it.

You'll remember that Exchange Server automatically maintains a copy of its directory on each server in a site. This is done through a process called *directory replication*. In directory replication, Exchange Servers in a site check with each other to ensure that their directories are up to date. If a server determines that its directory is out of sync with the others, it gets updates from one or more servers in the site.

Because of directory replication, if you have to restore a server's directory it doesn't matter whether the backup contains the absolutely most current copy of the directory. Once the restore is complete, the other servers in the site will quickly update the newly restored directory through the replication process.

I prefer to do a normal backup of the directories on all servers every Sunday at midnight, followed by a differential backup of each server's directory at midnight on each of the other six days of the week. I use a four-week cycle, holding the fourth week's tape as an archive for a year.

I suggest using the same backup strategy for the private and public information stores on a server. Keep the directory and information store backups as closely synchronized as you can to ensure the least amount of difference between the two.

WARNING If e-messaging is particularly critical to your organization, you might want to do more than one differential backup of Exchange Server directories and information stores per day. Certain situations might even require you to do a backup every two hours.

Exchange Server Transaction Logs and Backup

Like all good client-server database systems, Exchange Server uses *transaction logs* to improve server fault tolerance. All changes to a server's directory and private and public information stores are written first to files called *transaction log files*. Different sets of log files are used for the directory and information store.

Once the directory or information store service has written data in RAM to a transaction log file, it then writes the data to the database itself. Writing to a database entails lots of overhead, including indexing and other tasks. Writing to a transaction log file requires no such overhead, so data moves quickly from RAM to the log files, reducing the likelihood that a specific transaction will be lost if a server crashes. In the event of a crash, the database can be recovered back to currency using the transaction log files.

When you use the Backup utility to back up Exchange Server's directory or information store, you can use all of the backup types except daily. A normal backup backs up the databases and associated transaction logs; when it's finished, Backup then deletes the transaction log files that have been backed up.

When you do an incremental directory or information store backup, only the transaction log files are backed up. Nothing in the actual directory or information store databases is, or needs to be, backed up, because all changes since the last backup are contained in the transaction log files. Once the transaction log files are incrementally backed up, the Backup program deletes them, leaving you ready for the next full or incremental backup.

When you do a differential or copy backup, transaction log files are not deleted.

WARNING   If you don't routinely do normal or incremental backups of a server's directory and information store, the transaction log files—which can become gigantic—will accumulate quickly. You can use circular logging, which you'll remember we discussed in the last chapter. But for my money, you're better off backing up and letting the Backup program delete those transaction log files.

Setting Up an Exchange Server Backup

I'll assume that, following the instructions back in Chapter 7, you've installed a tape drive on your Exchange Server and are backing up from that server.

The Backup utility interacts with the Exchange Server directory and information store services to back up the directory and information store as objects. Before you can back these up, the Directory and Information Store processes must be up and running on your Exchange Server.

Also, to back up any server you must be a member of the NT Backup Operators group on the server. This group is automatically created when NT is installed. As NT administrator, you can use the User Manager for Domains to add yourself to this group. If you're logged in as NT administrator, you've already got these rights.

Selecting Exchange Servers and Components

To start, you need to open Backup. You'll find the utility in the Administrative Tools program group on your NT server. Find the Backup icon and click on it to bring up the program (see Figure 10.1). If it's not open already, you'll need to open the Microsoft Exchange backup window. Open the Operations menu and click on Microsoft Exchange. Then tell Backup which Exchange server you want to work with using the little Microsoft Exchange dialog box that pops up.

Next, you need to select the server or servers that you want to back up from the left-hand pane in the Microsoft Exchange window. As you can see in Figure 10.1, you can choose to back up anything—whether it's all of the servers in an organization or a single server—just by clicking the box next to the organization, site, or server name.

If you want to refine your backup, move to the right-hand pane of the Microsoft Exchange window. There you can select the Exchange Server components you want to back up. When you first open the Microsoft Exchange Window, you'll see your Exchange site or sites in the right-hand pane. To open a site, double-click on the site name. Now the server or servers in the site become visible. Next, double-click on the server you want to focus on and you'll see two icons representing the server's directory and information store. (Refer to Figure 10.1.) You can select the Directory or the Information Store or both for backup. You must back up both the private and public segments of the Information Store. As you'll see later in this chapter, you can restore either or both of the information stores.

For now, just click on your server name in the left-hand pane. Your Backup window should now look like the one in Figure 10.1.

FIGURE 10.1

Selecting Exchange Server components for backup

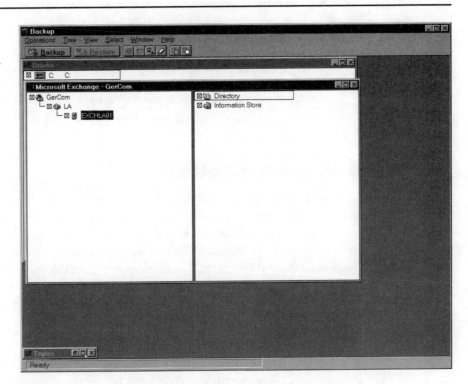

Backing Up NT Server Drives

If you prefer, you can use Backup to simultaneously back up Exchange Server components and other files on your NT server. Here's how to add one or more drives to your backup.

Select the drives you want to back up from the left-hand pane of the Drives window. In Figure 10.1, the Drives window is just peeking out over the top of the Microsoft Exchange window. As you can see, I've selected my C: drive for backup, along with the directory and information store on my Exchange Server.

I won't go into details here, but you can also back up selected files on any drive. Just double-click on the drive letter in the Drives window; this pops up a window with a directory tree for the drive you selected. Then simply click on the directories and files you want to include in your backup.

> **NOTE**   If you're already using another program for general NT Server backup, you can continue to use it. If the program has a module specifically designed to back up Exchange Server, you can use that too. But, don't try to back up your Exchange Server databases and logs with a standard backup utility while they're online. It won't work. You can use a standard backup program, if you shut down Exchange Server before beginning the backup.

Selecting Backup Options

Now click on the Backup button right under the Operations menu. This brings up the Backup Information dialog box, shown in Figure 10.2. The figure shows that I accepted the default Tape Name and Operation parameters. (*Append* means that the backup you're setting up will be added to the tape after the last backup. *Replace* means that this backup will overwrite everything already recorded on the tape. Use the Replace and Append options as you wish, depending on how many normal, incremental, or differential backups you prefer to put on a single tape.)

You should always verify a backup. If a backup doesn't run properly, your data isn't protected. Backup verifies ordinary NT files based on a file-by-file comparison. This is not possible with Exchange Server components, since they can change from moment to moment. So verification for these components is based on a simple checksum test to ensure that the data written to tape is readable.

Since I'm backing up the drive that contains the NT Registry for EXCHLA01, I've selected the Backup Registry option. Remember that the Registry is a storage place for all of the key information about the NT server itself as well as the NT/Windows 95–compatible applications installed on the server. The Registry is the equivalent of Windows 3.*x*'s WIN.INI and SYSTEM.INI files and much, much more. You should therefore back up the Registry with great regularity.

I haven't marked the Restrict Access to Owner or Administrator option, though this is a good way to increase security. To access a backup set with this option

FIGURE 10.2

Providing information about the backup

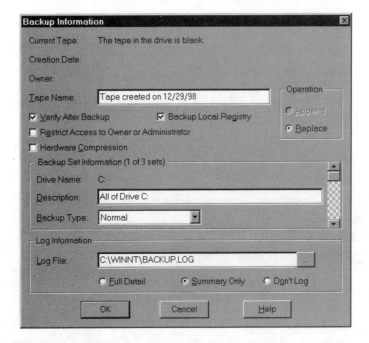

selected, you must be logged on as the owner (the person who created the backup) or a user who's a member of the administrators or backup operators groups.

I also haven't selected Hardware Compression. As I mentioned in Chapter 6, hardware compression saves tape, but tapes created with it are readable only in drives that use the same hardware compression algorithm. Different manufacturers tend to use different compression algorithms—so you're up a creek if your current drive breaks and can't be repaired, and the manufacturer no longer makes a drive using the same algorithm. Uncompressed tapes, on the other hand, are pretty much readable in drives of the same type regardless of manufacturer. I want the freedom to use anyone's tape drive, hence my choice of options.

Right below the Hardware Compression option is a box named 'Backup Set Information (1 of 3 sets)'. Notice that the box has a scroll bar on it. You enter specific information for each of the backup sets you're creating in this box, using the scroll bar to move through the different backup sets. As Figure 10.2 shows, my first backup is of my C: drive. I've described this backup set as "All of drive C:," and I've told Backup to do a normal backup.

Once you've finished with the first backup set, use the scroll bar to move to the next backup set information box. Figure 10.3 shows my second backup set, which is for the Exchange directory. Again, I've chosen a normal backup, though I could have chosen a different backup type for this set if I had wished. Notice that the Backup Registry option is now grayed out: I can back up my NT server's Registry only when I'm backing up files on the disk that contains the Registry. Backing up Exchange Server components, even if they're on the disk with the Registry, doesn't count.

In Figure 10.4, I've entered information for my third and final backup set; it's for the information store.

> **NOTE**
>
> Only the Description and Backup Type fields can be unique for each Backup Set Information box. When you set anything else in the Backup Information dialog box, it applies to all of the backup sets you're creating. So, for example, if you change the Operation mode from Replace to Append, all of your backup sets will use the Append option.

FIGURE 10.3

Entering information for an Exchange Server directory backup

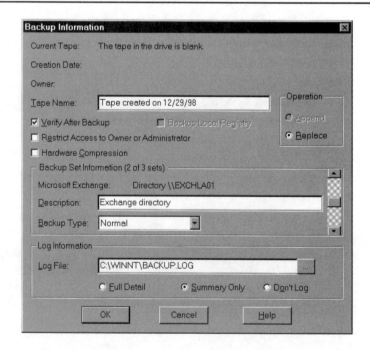

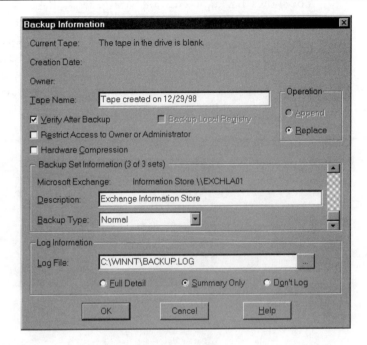

FIGURE 10.4

Entering information for
an Exchange Server
information store backup

Seeing Replace as the Operation option for all three of my backups gave me a
bit of a scare the first time. Was Backup going to back up my C: drive in its
entirety, write the directory backup over the first backup set, and then write the
information store backup over the directory backup set? Not to worry. The first
backup set overwrites whatever is on the tape. The remaining backup sets in the
group are appended to the ones that come before.

When you've finished entering information about your backup sets, the only
thing left to fill out before you start the backup is the Log Information box just
below the Backup Set Information box. For now, leave the settings at their default
values. The default log file directory and file name are fine, and most of the time
you don't need to gather more than summary information in your tape log files.
Click on OK to begin your backup.

Monitoring Backup Progress

Once your backup starts, you'll see a Backup Status dialog box like the one in Figure 10.5. You can use this dialog box to monitor backup progress. As the Summary

343

box shows, Backup is creating backup set #1, the backup of my whole C: drive. The Summary box shows that drive C: is being backed up and that this is the first backup set on the tape; in the figure, the file \EXCHSRVR\BIN\EMSMTA.EXE is currently being backed up. So far, the backup has been under way for 37 seconds, during which 3 directories, 49 files, and 12,346,253 bytes have been backed up in those 37 seconds. The Backup program has encountered no corrupt files, nor have any files been skipped up to this time.

FIGURE 10.5

Backup status for the C: drive

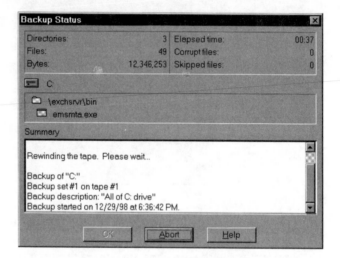

When Backup moves on to the Exchange Server directory database, the Backup Status dialog box will look like the one shown in Figure 10.6. Notice that this figure shows backup set #2. After backing up the directory, Backup turns to the information store and backs it up to backup set #3 (see Figure 10.7).

When it's finished backing up the information store, Backup begins its verification of each of the three backup sets. You'll see a dialog box much like the Backup Status dialog box, except that it's named Verify Status.

When Backup is done verifying all the backup sets—assuming everything went well (and it usually does)—it tells you that it has successfully finished its work. Click on OK in the Verify Status dialog box, and you're done with the backup.

FIGURE 10.6

Backup status for the Exchange Server directory

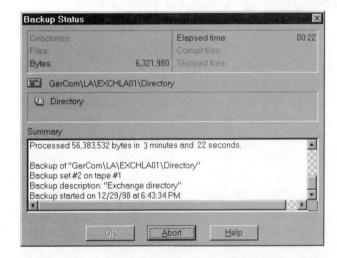

FIGURE 10.7

Backup status for the Exchange Server information store

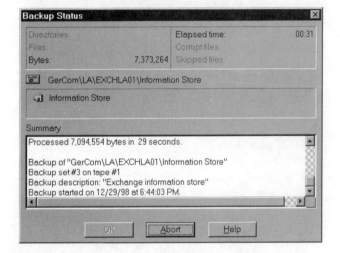

Restoring from an Exchange Server Backup

To restore from an Exchange Server backup, you first need to tell Backup what you want to restore. Then you need to tell it how to do the restore.

Specifying What to Restore

To restore from a backup set, start the Backup program. Maximize the Tapes window, which you'll find down in the lower left-hand corner of the Backup window. In Figure 10.8, I've told Backup to restore both the Exchange Server directory and information store databases (see the right-hand pane of the window). If you don't see the detailed information on your backup sets, double-click on the drive letter in the right-hand pane of the Tapes window. This will cause Backup to read backup set information from the tape and display it.

You can also use the Tapes window to restore other files that were backed up. Just double-click on the drive letter in the right-hand pane of the Tapes window. This opens up a window with a directory tree for the drive. Use this directory tree to choose files for restoration.

FIGURE 10.8

Specifying Exchange
Server components to
be restored

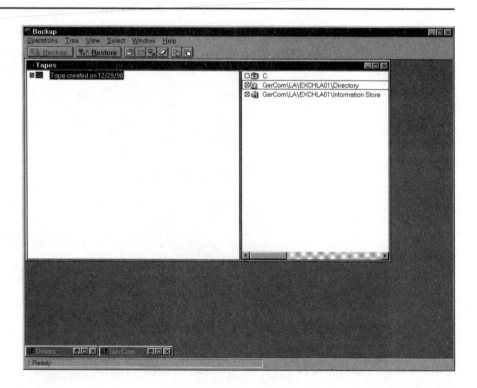

> **WARNING**
>
> If you need to restore these other files as well as the Exchange Server directory and information store, always restore the other files **first**. Otherwise, you could overwrite directory or information store data when restoring the other files.

Specifying How to Restore

After you've told Backup what to restore, click on the Restore button in the upper left-hand corner of the Backup window. This brings up a Restore Information dialog box. Figure 10.9 shows the dialog box for restoring the Exchange Server directory. Figure 10.10 shows the dialog box for restoring the information store.

You use the scroll bar on the Restore Information dialog box to move between dialog boxes for each of the backup sets from which you've chosen to restore. You set restore parameters for a specific backup set after scrolling to the dialog box for that backup set.

FIGURE 10.9

The dialog box for restoring the Exchange Server directory

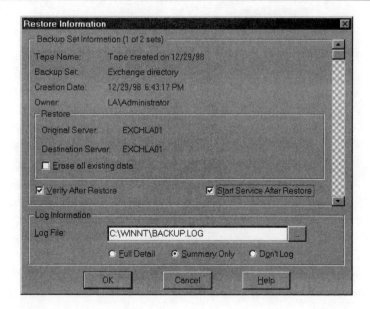

FIGURE 10.10

The dialog box for restoring the Exchange Server information store

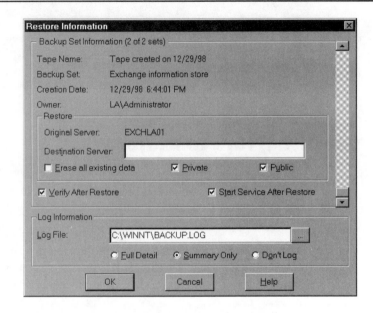

Restoring the Exchange Server Directory Database

Keep your eye on Figure 10.9 as you move through this section. The Erase All Existing Data option is important: If you *don't* check it, Backup tries to restore the directory database using the directory database already on the server and whatever directory information is stored on tape. This is the first thing to try if your Exchange Server's directory database is in trouble. It's faster and less messy, because it doesn't delete the directory database (as does the Erase All Existing Data option). If this method doesn't work, repeat the restore with the Erase All Existing Data box checked.

Of course, you'll want to verify after restoring, and you'll generally want to start the directory service after restoring the directory. Leave the Log File information as is, unless you have a problem restoring; if you do have trouble, select Full Detail from the three options just below the Log File name field. Those details might help you figure out why you're having trouble.

Restoring the Exchange Server Information Store Database

As you can see in Figure 10.10, the Restore Information dialog box for the information store looks pretty much like the one for the directory. There are two differences, though: You can modify Destination Server, and you can choose to restore the private information store, the public information store, or both.

Depending on where your problem lies, decide whether to restore one or both of the information stores. If you're having trouble with mailboxes, restore the private information store. If the problem is with public folders, restore the public information store.

You can restore one or both of the information stores either to the original server you backed up or to another destination server. Most of the time you'll do the former. The only time you'd restore to another server would be to recover information for a user or a set of users without changing the contents of the original information store. You'd need a spare off-line Exchange Server with the same organization and site names as the original for this sort of restore. Microsoft has said it will, at some unnamed date, modify Exchange Server to allow for selective restoration of data directly to Exchange's databases. Until that happens, you'll have to restore to a spare off-line server and then manually move restored data to the in-service Exchange Server.

Make your selections, then click on OK in the Restore Information dialog box. When the backup starts, you'll see a Restore Status dialog box that looks pretty much like the Backup Status dialog boxes in Figures 10.6 and 10.7. From here on, it's just a matter of waiting for the restore to finish.

> **WARNING** Good backup practice requires that you test your backups regularly. That spare off-line server I talk about in this section is a great place to test. Test at least once a month; more frequently if you consider e-messaging mission critical.

Automating a Backup

You can create batch files to automate backups of your NT/Exchange Server, including its directory and information store databases. Then you can use NT Server's built-in scheduler to automatically run these batch files when you want.

Creating a Batch File for Backup

In addition to running Backup by double-clicking on its icon in the Administrative Tools program group, you can start it at DOS command prompt; the program is called NTBACKUP.EXE. It has a number of command-line switches that you can use to specify just what you want backed up and how the program is to proceed. The syntax of an NTBACKUP.EXE command is as follows:

```
ntbackup operation path [/DS server /IS server][/a][/v][/r]
[/d "text"][/b][/hc:{on / off } ]   [/t {option}][/1 "filename"]
[/e][/tape:{n}]
```

operation: Specifies the operation: `backup` or eject.

Path: When backing up a drive, specify one or more directory paths to be backed up. When backing up Exchange Server components, specify the component and the server as follows:

DS *server*
IS *server*

where *server* is the name of the server you're backing up in Uniform Naming Convention format. (For us mere mortals, that means the server name with two backslashes in front of it; for example, \\EXCHLA01. `DS` requests a directory backup. `IS` requests an information store backup.)

Each path specified creates a separate backup set.

`/a` adds the backup set or sets following the last backup set already on the tape. Without `/a`, this backup overwrites whatever is on the tape.

`/v` verifies the backup.

`/r` restricts access to the Owner or NT Administrator account.

`/d "text"` is a description of the backup contents.

`/b` requests a backup of the Registry.

`/hc:on` or `/hc:off` turns hardware compression on or off.

`/t {`*option*`}` selects the backup type; options are Normal, Copy, Incremental, Differential, and Daily. (Daily doesn't apply to Exchange Server component backup.)

`/1 "`*filename*`"` requests logging to *filename*, including any path you specify. If you don't include the `/1` option, no log will be created.

/e requests that only exceptions be written to the log. This is equivalent to selecting Summary Only in the Log Information area of the Backup Information dialog box. If you leave out /e, your log will include full details.

/tape:{n} specifies which tape drive to use for the backup when you have multiple tape drives, where n is a number from zero to nine. Tape drive numbers are listed in the Registry. See *Mastering Windows NT Server 4*, by Mark Minasi, Christa Anderson, and Elizabeth Creegan, (Sybex, 1996) for help on accessing the Registry.

Here's the NTBACKUP command that does pretty much what we did in the nonautomated backup we did a few sections back. The only thing we can't do is specify different descriptions and backup types for each backup set.

```
ntbackup backup E:\ DS \\EXCHLA01 IS \\EXCHLA01 /v /d "Backup of
EXCHLA01-Exch. Srvr. Components + dirs" /b /hc:off /t Normal /l
"C:\WINNT\BACKUP.LOG" /e
```

To do a differential backup, the only thing you'd change is the option for /t *from Normal to Differential.*

Next, save the normal backup command to a batch file called NORMAL.BAT and the differential backup command to a batch file called DIFFERNT.BAT. To run either backup, just type the batch file name at the DOS command prompt. Or you can create a new Windows desktop shortcut that links the batch file to an icon. You can then run the backup just by double-clicking on the appropriate icon.

Using NT's Scheduler to Automate Backups

A lot of really useful applications for NT and NT Server are available in Microsoft's Windows NT Resource Kit. (Contact Microsoft for information on availability and cost.) One of these is a little GUI-based program called WINAT.EXE in the NT 3.51 Resource Kit and just WINAT in NT 4.0 kit. You can use it to schedule other programs and batch files to run at specific times on specific days on specific computers.

To install WINAT.EXE or WINAT, you'll need to install the NT 3.51 or 4.0 Resource Kit, following the directions that come with the kit. You'll find a new program group called Resource Kit. In the group, you'll find a subgroup called 'Configuration' and, in that group, an icon with a clock on it labeled Command Scheduler. Click on the icon and you're off.

WINAT.EXE places schedule entries into an NT service called Schedule. If that service isn't running, WINAT.EXE informs you and then asks if you want to start it. Click on Yes to start the service.

Next, the Command Scheduler dialog box pops up (see Figure 10.11). To schedule a command, click on Add. This brings up the Add Command dialog box, shown in Figure 10.12 (which shows that I've scheduled my normal backup to take place every Sunday starting at midnight). When you're done filling in the Add Command dialog box, click on OK. The scheduled event is now listed in the Command Scheduler.

FIGURE 10.11

The NT Command Scheduler's GUI interface

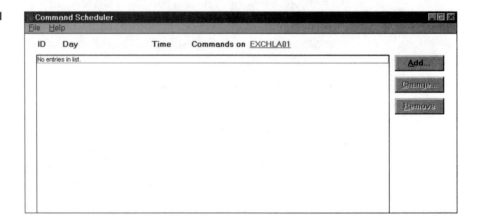

FIGURE 10.12

Using the Add Command dialog box to schedule a normal backup

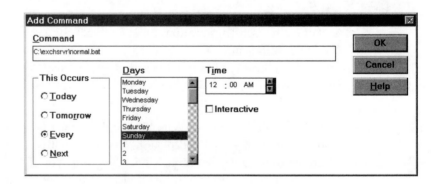

> **WARNING**
>
> If your backup will require more than one tape or if there's any other reason why someone will have to interact with the backup process, be sure to select the Interactive option. This assures that NT Backup's GUI interface will be on screen while the scheduled backup is running. If you don't select this option and interaction is required, your backup will fail.

To schedule your differential backups, repeat the Add Command process. As you can see in Figure 10.13, I've scheduled my differential backups for midnight on every day of the week but Sunday. (To select more than one day, hold down the Ctrl key and click on each day you want.)

When you've finished with the Command Scheduler, select Exit from the File menu. You can always come back to edit any scheduled event. Just open the Command Scheduler, select the event you want to change, and click on the Change button, which shows up only when events are scheduled.

> **WARNING**
>
> The Schedule service never forgets the events you've scheduled, so you want to make sure the service is always running. When WINAT.EXE starts the schedule service for the first time, it doesn't set it to start automatically on reboot. You definitely want the service to start up automatically when you restart your server. So run the Services applet in the control panel and change the Startup option for Schedule to Automatic.

FIGURE 10.13

Using the Add Command dialog box to schedule a differential backup

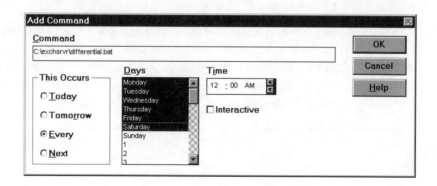

Did That Backup Work?

You should always monitor backup logs to be sure that a backup has been completed successfully. One easy way to do this is by using a little utility that comes with the Exchange Server Resource Kit. (Contact Microsoft for details on obtaining this free collection of useful programs.) There is a utility called 'sendmail', not to be confused with the Unix sendmail service. The Resource Kit's sendmail utility lets you send a message to any Exchange mailbox and even attach a file. Using sendmail and Command Scheduler, I've set up a little batch file that sends me Backup's log file after my nightly backups have completed. My backups start at midnight and I have sendmail send the log file to me at 6am.

My batch file follows below. I've also included a second version of the batch file where explanatory information in square brackets replaces the actual parameters shown in the first version of the file. Armed with the two files and what you already know about Command Scheduler, you should have no trouble setting up an automated mailing of the backup log each day.

```
c:\exchsrvr\sendmail -u [name of the Exchange client MAPI
profile you want to use] -p [password for the MAPI profile] -r
[Exchange mailbox to receive the message] -m [text to include
in the message] -s [subject of the message] -f [file to attach
to the message]

c:\exchsrvr\sendmail -u "Barry Gerber" -p secret -r bgerber -m
"EXCHWW01 Backup Log" -s "Backup Log" -f c:\winnt\backup.log
```

It's wonderful to be able to check the backup log each day, right from my Exchange Inbox. Most of the time everything is just fine. However, I have discovered a few backups gone wrong and fixed them quickly. I can even check things out when I'm away from the office, using one of the many clients available for my Exchange mailbox. Yep, it's wonderful!

Conclusion

In this chapter you learned a bit about backups in general, and NT and Exchange Server backups in particular. You also learned how to manually and automatically back up an Exchange Server using NT Server's Backup program.

PART IV

Exchange Clients for Windows

Exchange Server is a pretty nifty little gadget. But without clients, it's nothing more than fancy technology. Though this is a book on Exchange Server, we need to spend a little time talking about Exchange clients. This section is devoted to that discussion.

In Chapter 11 we'll focus on the Windows Exchange client from an administrative perspective. We'll cover installation of the Windows client both on a server and, from the server, onto user workstations. Then we'll talk a bit about running Exchange clients on top of Novell's NetWare networking software. In Chapter 12 we'll take a look at the Windows Exchange client from the user's perspective. We'll take a quick tour of Windows client menus to get comfortable with the impressive functionality that Microsoft has built into the client.

Installing Exchange Clients
for Windows

■ Installing Exchange client software on a server

■ Installing an Exchange client on a workstation

■ Notes for NetWare administrators

We'll start this section by installing Exchange client software for Windows on a server so that users can install it on their workstations. Then we'll actually install a client. Finally, I'll talk briefly about running Windows clients in a Novell NetWare environment. In the next chapter, we'll focus on the basics of Windows client use.

We'll save some topics for later chapters. These include support for remote (dial-up) client access.

Installing Exchange Client Software on a Server

As the administrator of a new Exchange site, you have to do a couple of things before you or your users can install the Exchange client software. First, you have to copy the client software to a server where users can then run a setup program to install it on their workstations. Then you have to do a bit of preliminary setup work on the client software to customize it. Let's get to it!

We're going to install the Exchange client software on a server. Users will then install Exchange clients on their workstations using this software. We'll use our Exchange server, though we could install the software on any NT server. We'll use a special setup program that comes with Exchange Server to install the clients.

Exchange clients come in versions for several computer operating systems, including MS-DOS, 16-bit Windows, Windows 95, Windows NT, Macintosh, and the Microsoft Outlook client. Using the client installation program, you can choose which clients to install; the program will create an *installation point*—a standard Microsoft networking disk share—for each client version. Users then connect to the installation point for the client software version they need and install the appropriate software.

> **WARNING** The Outlook client is a pretty hefty baby. It comes with lots of graphic images and such. The version I installed took up over 235MB on one of my Exchange server's hard-disk drives.

Let's do the installation. Put the Exchange client CD-ROM in your server's CD-ROM drive, and then select the language version of the client you want to install. (English-language clients are in the ENG subdirectory.) Go to the directory for the appropriate language and run the SETUP.EXE program. Setup first tells you to close all programs so that it can update any files it needs to. Do so and click on Continue. Next it provides default Name and Organization information for licensing purposes. Accept the default or change it, click OK, and click OK again to verify this information. Setup then offers you an opportunity to select the disk drive and server directory you want to install the clients in. Accept the default or enter a new drive and directory option.

Next, Setup asks if you want to do a complete or custom installation (see Figure 11.1). If you want to install all of the Exchange clients, select Complete. Be careful here! In Complete mode, Setup installs Exchange clients for other hardware platforms that run Windows, such as the NT client for Digital Equipment's Alpha chip–based line of computers. To choose which clients are installed, select Custom and pick your clients from the Microsoft Exchange Custom dialog box that pops up.

Setup now installs the clients and sets up installation points for them. When it's finished and the installation points are in place, users can easily find the client they need by finding its installation point. In Figure 11.2, for example, I've found the installation point for the Intel version of the Windows NT Exchange client, and I'm about to install it on my workstation.

FIGURE 11.1

Selecting a complete or custom installation

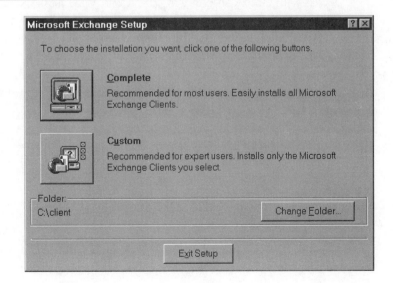

FIGURE 11.2

Getting ready to install the Exchange Windows NT client

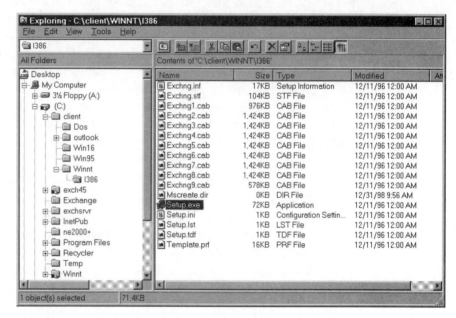

Preparing Exchange Client Software for Installation

As with almost all Windows programs, you install Exchange clients for Windows by running the standard SETUP.EXE program. Preparing client software for installation involves setting default parameters that will apply when a user or systems-support person runs SETUP.EXE to install a client.

> **NOTE**
>
> If you're willing to accept the defaults that Microsoft has set up for client installations, you don't have to do any of what follows in this section. I do, however, suggest that you at least take a look at the options to see if there are any that you'd like to change.

You prepare the Exchange client software for each operating system—for example, Windows 16-bit, Windows NT, or Windows 95—separately. We'll work with the Exchange client for Windows NT, but the procedure is pretty much the same for all Windows clients.

You need to run a program called STFEDTR.EXE. If it's in your Microsoft Exchange program group, find and click on the Microsoft Exchange Setup Editor icon. If STFEDTR.EXE isn't in your Microsoft Exchange program group, find it on the Exchange client CD-ROM. Using NT Explorer, look in the appropriate language directory under the directory STFEDIT, under the appropriate hardware platform, for example: \ENG\STFEDIT\I386. When STFEDIT.EXE is up and running, you'll see a dialog box like the one shown in Figure 11.3.

FIGURE 11.3

The Microsoft Exchange Setup Editor dialog box

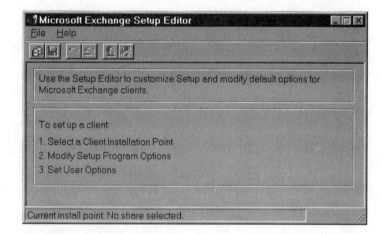

Preparing client software for installation is a three-step process:

1. Select a client installation point

2. Set user options

3. Modify Setup program options

NOTE

As you move through the last two of these three steps, be aware that there are a couple of escape hatches if you need them. You can return to Microsoft's preset user and Setup program defaults by selecting Restore Defaults from the Setup Editor's File menu. If you want to return to the last-saved options set, select Undo All Changes from the File menu. Just remember that you can't apply the Setup program and user options selectively; if you revert to the preset defaults, you do it for both options.

Selecting a Client Installation Point

To set the client installation point for a particular operating system version of the Exchange client, open the File menu in the Microsoft Exchange Setup Editor dialog box and click on 'Select Client Installation Point'; the Select Client Installation Directory dialog box pops up (see Figure 11.4). Select the appropriate disk drive and walk through the directory until you've selected the operating system for which you want to set up—I've selected the Intel (I386) processor version of the Windows NT Exchange client—and click on OK.

FIGURE 11.4

Selecting a client installation point

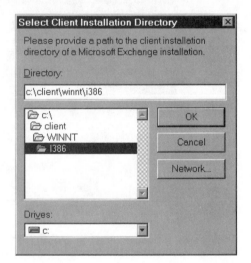

Modifying User Options

Once you've set a client installation point, you're ready to view and change the defaults for certain user options available in the client. Remember, if you change the defaults here, you change them for all future installations of this particular client from this particular client installation point. (Users can still change these options if they need to once they've installed their clients.)

Select Set User Options from the Setup Editor's File menu. This brings up the User Options dialog box (see Figure 11.5). Most of these options are pretty self-evident, but let's look at them quickly.

FIGURE 11.5

Setting default general
options for an Exchange
client installation

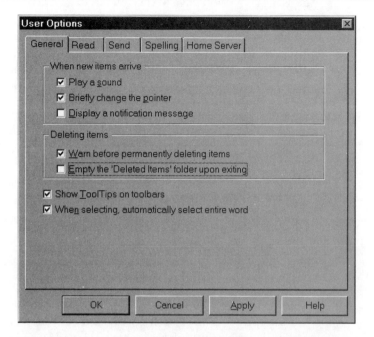

NOTE

> Though it doesn't show in Figure 11.5, because the latest user interface wasn't available at the time of this writing, you have one more option on the page. You can choose to make the Exchange client a newsreader for Internet newsgroup articles. As I mentioned in an earlier chapter, Exchange 5 comes with support for Internet newsgroups at the server level. Now you can see that the Exchange client offers newsgroup client support as well.

General Defaults   As we move through this section, keep an eye on Figure 11.5. A change in the pointer and a sound such as a tone or a bell are usually enough to let a user know that a new message has arrived. Displaying a notification message can be helpful for those who work in noisy environments or have hearing impairments. However, unless most of the users for this client installation point need an on-screen notification message, don't check that option under 'When new items arrive' on the General property page. The one drawback of the notification message is that you have to click on OK to get rid of it. Sounds and pointer modifications, on the other hand, just happen and terminate all by themselves.

I like the Deleting Items defaults: When a message or folder is deleted, it's automatically moved into the Deleted Items folder. When items are subsequently deleted from the Deleted Items folder, they're gone for good—or, in Exchange parlance, "permanently deleted." So you should be sure that users are warned before any permanent deletions occur.

You also don't want a Deleted Items folder to be emptied when users exit from their clients, which is the default, because it means that every message and folder in there is wiped out upon exiting. Better to leave deleted items in the folder and to urge users to clean out older messages in their Deleted Items folders on a regular basis. If that doesn't work, you can remove items from the Deleted Items folder using the Clean Mailboxes option in Exchange Server's Administrator.

The next option pertains to ToolTips, those little boxes that pop up when your mouse pointer touches a button on a Windows toolbar. Because the icons on toolbar buttons aren't always great communicators, I suggest you accept the 'Show ToolTips on toolbars' default.

If the option 'When selecting, automatically select entire word' is selected, if you're dragging through text, once you pass a word separation boundary (a space), when you select or deselect a letter of each additional word, the whole word will be selected or deselected.

Read Defaults   You set read defaults from the Read property page (see Figure 11.6). The default for the 'After moving or deleting an open item' option causes the client to return to a view of the folder and a list of the items in it. The other two options open the item that's either above or below the moved or deleted item; I prefer to have the next item below opened, because I like to sort items in my folders in descending order by date so that the latest messages are always at the top of any folder. If I then delete an item while it's open, the next item in the folder opens. This is especially helpful when I'm reading new messages in my Inbox. I delete the message I've just read, and the next one— usually an unread message—pops open. This works very nicely for me; however, selecting anything other than the default presumes a lot about how a user works. So it's best to take the default and let users make their own changes.

When users reply to a message, it's a good idea to include and indent the text of the message they're replying to. Including the original message ensures that the person or persons receiving the reply will better understand why the reply was made, and indenting the text sets the old message off from new text. Whether the original message should be closed when a user is replying to it is a choice best left to the user, so I've deselected the default 'Close the original item' option.

FIGURE 11.6

Setting default read options for an Exchange client installation

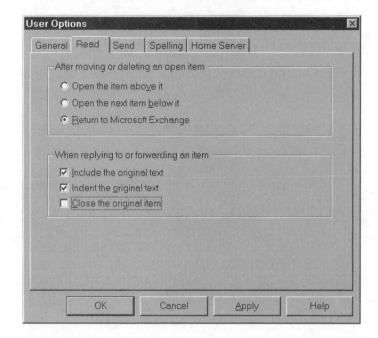

Send Defaults   Use the Send property page to set default send options (see Figure 11.7). Generally, you don't want to encourage automatic requests for return receipts for every read or delivered message because return receipts can generate a lot of unnecessary message traffic and essentially bogus demands for messaging storage. When users need to be sure that a message was delivered or accessed, they can request a delivery receipt or read receipt while composing the message. The defaults are fine here.

The *sensitivity* level of a message is its degree of privacy. Sensitivity options include Normal, Personal, Private, and Confidential. In most organizations, the default of Normal should be adequate. (You might remember that sensitivity level is one of the criteria you can use to clean mailboxes in the Exchange Administrator program.)

Importance is a priority level; defaulting clients to Normal is fine.

FIGURE 11.7

Setting default send options for an Exchange client installation

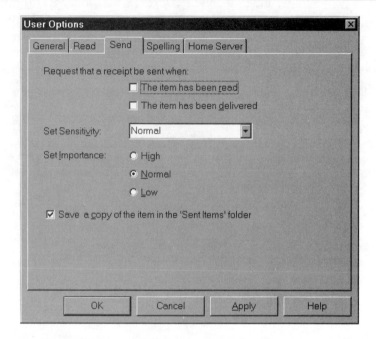

A copy of sent messages should always be saved in the Sent Items folder. This helps users keep track of messages and gives them the option of resending any messages that don't get delivered for one reason or another. As with Deleted Items folders, users should be encouraged to clean out their Sent Items folders on a regular basis.

Spelling Defaults   Unless your users are particularly poor spellers, leave the General Options boxes in the Spelling property page unchecked (see Figure 11.8). The 'When checking, always ignore' defaults should be okay, too.

Home Server Default   You enter the name of a default Exchange home server on the Home Server property page (see Figure 11.9). If you don't type in a default, the user will be prompted for a server name the first time he or she runs the client.

FIGURE 11.8

Setting default spelling options for an Exchange client installation

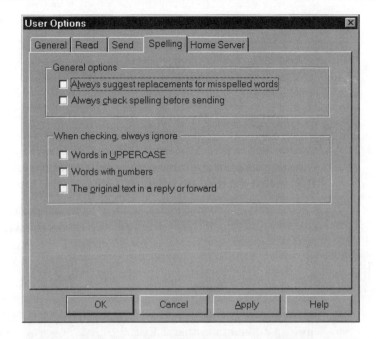

FIGURE 11.9

Setting the default home server options for an Exchange client installation

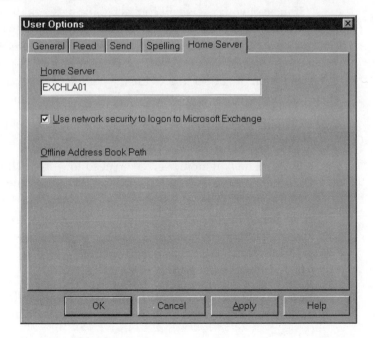

Exchange Server directory replication ensures that the home server for a user's mailbox is recorded not only on the home server, but also on all servers in the site. So when a user installs an Exchange client, the name of the user's home server can be automatically obtained from any Exchange server in a site. This means that you can enter the name of any Exchange server in your site in the Home Server field. The folks at Microsoft think this is a pretty nifty feature. I have to agree.

When users are logged into a Microsoft network (using their NT account user names and passwords), they're automatically authenticated for use of the Exchange mailbox tied to their NT account. When they open their Exchange client, it opens without asking for any additional security information. That is what it means to "Use network security to logon to Microsoft Exchange."

If a user wants to connect to Exchange over a non-Microsoft network—for example, over the Internet using an account obtained from an Internet Service Provider (ISP)—network security is not used. When users attempt to start their Exchange clients in this situation, a little dialog box pops up asking them to enter their NT account user name, their password, and the NT domain they are registered in. If the correct information is entered, the user's Exchange mailbox is opened. This method also works for users who are logged into an NT network under a different user name than their mailboxes are tied to.

If most of your users will connect to the network through ISPs, then you might want to deselect 'Use network security to logon to Microsoft Exchange.' If you have a number of Microsoft networking and ISP users, you might want to create two separate installations of the Exchange clients on your Exchange server. One installation can be set to provide the default network security setting, while the other provides the do-not-use-network-security setting.

I'll talk more in Chapter 18 about using the Internet to access your Exchange server with an Exchange client.

Users, usually remote users, who need to work with their Exchange clients while not connected to their Exchange server, can download an offline address book that can be used to address messages. We talked about this address book a bit in an earlier chapter. You can enter a default path where the offline address book will be stored on the disk drives available to the user.

Modifying Setup Program Options

Now you need to decide if you want to change default options for the SETUP.EXE program when it installs the client. Unlike user defaults, what you select here could be central to specific realities or policies in your organization, so at least take a quick look at this section. To get started, select Modify Setup Program Options from the Setup Editor's File menu. This opens the dialog box shown in Figure 11.10.

FIGURE 11.10

Setting general defaults for Setup to use during an Exchange client installation

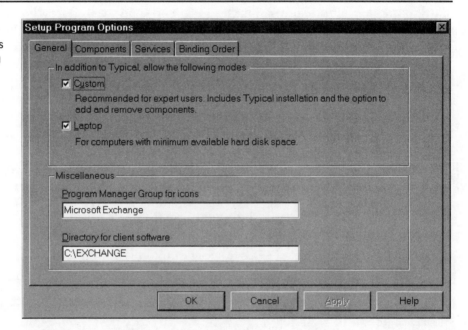

General Defaults　You may want to deselect the Custom mode option check box on the General property page (see Figure 11.10). This gives users the option to add or remove Exchange client components during an installation. (Having access to the Custom mode could lead to some problems for inexperienced installers, however.) If you don't support laptops for this particular installation group, deselect that option, too. If both options are deselected, the person doing the installation won't be presented with mode choices, making the installation experience lighter and just a little less intimidating.

You might want to change the 'Program Manager Group for icons' default to something as simple as "E-Mail" or "E-Messaging," or, for example, "GerCom E-Mail." (Well, you wouldn't use "GerCom," but you get the point.)

You can change the default installation directory as needed.

Components Defaults   The Components property page is pretty basic (see Figure 11.11). If you want to offer users the option of installing both the Exchange client and Schedule+, leave the default as is. As with installation modes, if only Exchange is selected, users won't even get an option here.

Services Defaults   Exchange services include things like a server-based mailbox (Microsoft Exchange Server), a personal address book, personal folders, and access to legacy Microsoft Mail 3.x post offices. You use the Services property page to specify the services options that will be offered to those who install this client (see Figure 11.12).

Select the service you want to add from the 'Available on the server' box and click on Add. To remove a service, select it and click on Remove.

Binding Order Defaults   You'll remember from earlier chapters that Exchange clients talk to Exchange servers using a set of remote procedure call (RPC) Application Programming Interface (API) options based on Open Systems Foundation specs. You'll also remember that these RPCs can ride on top of a variety of networking protocols, including Named Pipes, Novell SPX, TCP/IP, NetBEUI and Banyan's VINES IP. You use the Binding Order property page to specify the networking protocols to be used and the order in which clients should attempt to bind RPCs to specific protocols (see Figure 11.13).

FIGURE 11.11

Setting Exchange components defaults for Setup to use during an Exchange client installation

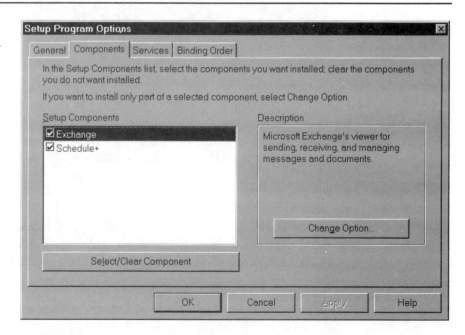

FIGURE 11.12

Setting services defaults for Setup to use during an Exchange client installation

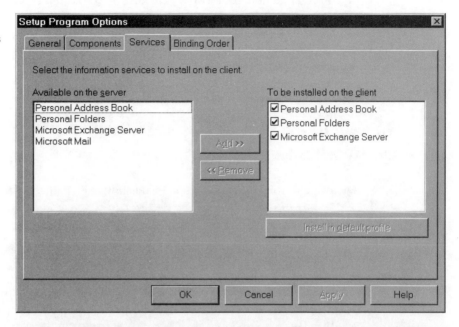

FIGURE 11.13

Setting binding order defaults for Setup to use during an Exchange client installation

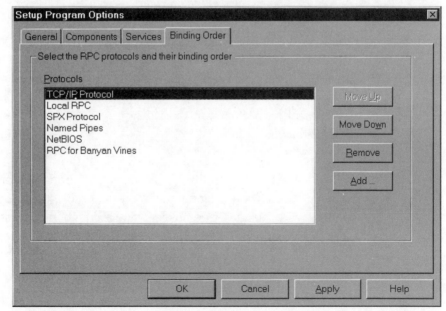

You can add new protocols by clicking on the Add button. A dialog box pops up and asks for the name of the Exchange server to be checked for available protocols. Accept the default server, or change the name when you've got more than one server; then click on OK. The protocols available on that server will be added to the Protocols list.

Installing Exchange Client Software in Network Share Mode

In a standard Exchange client installation, all of the software required is copied to the user's workstation. The DOS- and Windows-based Exchange clients can also be installed so they run from a shared network directory. This saves disk space on user workstations and allows for greater control over Exchange client environments.

To set up Exchange for a shared installation, first open a DOS command prompt window. Next, move to the appropriate client directory—CLIENT\WIN16, for example. Then run SETUP.EXE with the command-line switch /A. The specific client software, as well as SETUP.EXE and the configuration files it needs, are copied to the shared directory you specify. You can then perform individual shared-workstation installations of the client by running this copy of SETUP.EXE. If you want to modify default installation parameters for a shared-client installation, run the Microsoft Exchange Setup Editor with this directory as the client installation point. To set up a shared DOS client installation, run the DOS client Setup program and choose the Shared option.

Remember, you have to do a separate SETUP /A for every operating system version of the client you wish to make sharable from the network. Also keep in mind that network sharing gets more and more complicated as you add more applications and when users share a common operating system directory (only Windows 3.x and Windows 95 allow this). Don't forget that sharing operating system and application software can put heavy loads on your networks. Check with Microsoft for more on the rewards, punishments, and how-to's of network sharing.

You can remove protocols to help enforce network policies on permitted protocols. Then, even if someone installs a prohibited protocol on a workstation, it won't be used for RPC bindings.

Use protocol ordering to ensure that multiprotocol clients bind first with specific protocols. For example, if TCP/IP is the preferred protocol in your organization or if TCP/IP RPC bindings deliver the fastest Exchange client/server communications on your network, you might want to move TCP/IP up to the top of the Protocols list as I did for the GerCom NT client installs. Also, be aware that Named Pipes is the slowest transport for RPC communications. Unless you absolutely have to, avoid using it or give it a lower priority in the Protocols list.

WARNING Make sure you don't include protocols that aren't generally available on workstations and Exchange servers on your site. It can take several minutes before an Exchange client times out when a particular protocol fails. Clients can't move on to try the next protocol in the list until they time out on a failed one. So if a lot of unavailable protocols are at the top of the Protocol list, the Exchange client start-up will be seriously delayed.

Okay, you're done setting installation options for one of your clients. Click on OK in the Setup Program Options dialog box to apply your changes, and then exit from the Exchange Setup Editor. To configure clients for other operating systems, repeat the steps outlined above.

Installing an Exchange Client on a Workstation

At last! Let's get right to installing a client. We'll install the Windows NT client on our Exchange server.

Open the NT Explorer on the Programs menu, open Network Neighborhood, and find your Exchange server. Then find the share where the clients were installed. It's called Exchange on my Exchange server. (See Figure 11.14.) Work your way through the Explorer tree and find SETUP.EXE for the NT client and double-click on it.

FIGURE 11.14

Installing the Exchange
client for Windows NT
from an Exchange server's
client installation share.

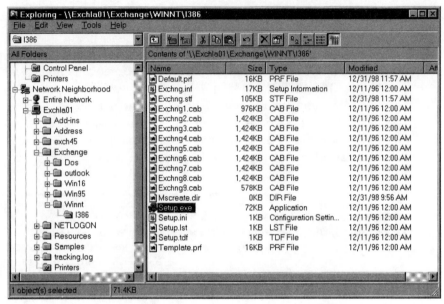

The first thing you'll see is a warning to close down all applications. Do so.
Because you're installing on your Exchange server, you should even shut down
the Exchange Server services running on it. When you're done, click on OK in the
warning dialog box.

Next, if they're not offered by default, enter your name and the name of your
Exchange organization, and click on OK (see Figure 11.15). Then you'll be asked
to confirm that what you've just entered is correct. If it is, click on OK again. If it's
not correct, click on Change to go back to the dialog box shown in Figure 11.15.

Now accept the default path (folder) or set a new one for the Exchange client
installation (see Figure 11.16). To change the path, click on the Change Folder button, type in the new path, and click on OK. If the path doesn't exist, Setup will
create it. Click on OK to move on.

Unless you removed the installation mode options when you changed the
Setup options, next you'll see a Microsoft Exchange Setup dialog box like the
one shown in Figure 11.17; click on Custom to bring up the Microsoft Exchange—
Custom dialog box (see Figure 11.18). If both Exchange and Schedule+ are not
checked, click on Select All and then click on Continue.

At this point, Setup will begin copying files to your client directory and will then set up your client and report a successful installation. That's it—your client's installed.

In the next chapter we'll talk a bit about using the client.

FIGURE 11.15

Entering your name and Exchange organization

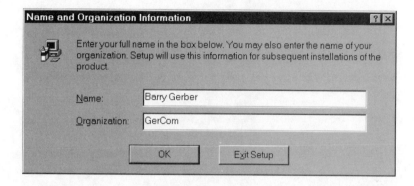

FIGURE 11.16

Changing the Exchange client installation path

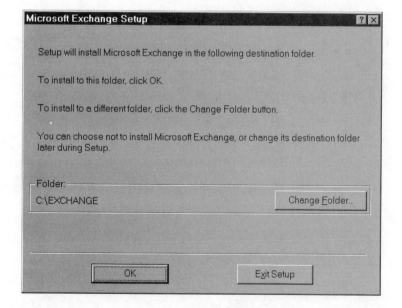

FIGURE 11.17

Choosing the installation mode and an opportunity to change the Exchange client installation path

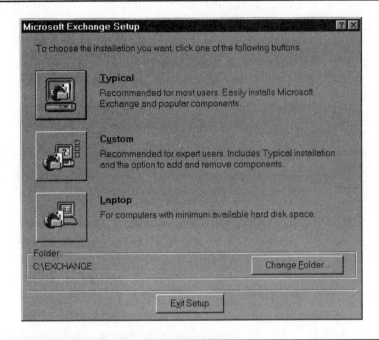

FIGURE 11.18

Selecting specific Exchange client components for installation

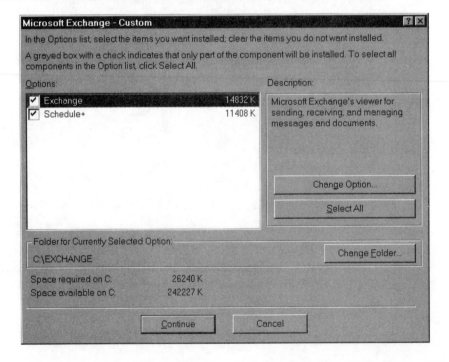

Notes for NetWare Administrators

If you don't have any Novell NetWare clients on your networks, take a look at the Conclusion section and you're out of here. If, on the other hand, you have NetWare clients that need to access an Exchange server, you may need to turn on the Service Advertisement Protocol (SAP) Agent on your Exchange server and ensure that routers are passing certain NetWare-specific packets. After we go over all of this, I'll conclude this chapter with a brief discussion and some tips about NetWare clients and Exchange Server.

SAP Agents

NetWare servers use the Service Advertisement Protocol (SAP) to communicate with each other. In certain circumstances, NetWare clients can't see NT servers unless the NT server is running a SAP emulator called the *SAP Agent*.

Do You Need a SAP Agent?   You'll need to run the SAP Agent on your NT/Exchange server in either of the following two situations:

- If your Exchange server is not on the same network segment as a NetWare server

- If a Windows for Workgroups client is running only the Microsoft IPX–compatible transport and is not on the same network segment as your Exchange server

With any other NetWare client setup you don't need to worry about the SAP Agent. If you fall into that lucky category, move on to the section on installing NetWare clients and Exchange Server.

Starting the SAP Agent

To turn on the SAP Agent, choose Network from your NT/Exchange server's Control Panel. Then from the Network Setting dialog box, choose Add Software. Select SAP Agent from the drop-down list of software on the resultant Add Network Software dialog box and click on Continue. When prompted, let NT restart the computer; when the computer comes back up, the SAP Agent will be running. (Check the Control Panel's Services applet if you're skeptical.) That's it.

Ensuring Proper Routing

All of the work you just did won't amount to a hill of beans unless your routers are doing their thing. The SAP Agent uses SAP 0x640 to let NetWare servers know that your Exchange server is there. So make sure that SAP 0x640 is being passed by any routers that sit between the NetWare servers and your Exchange server. Routers from different manufacturers are configured differently; if you're not the routing guru in your organization, check with someone who is for help with this one.

NetWare Clients and Exchange Server

When you install a current edition of Windows 95, Windows for Workgroups, or Windows NT Workstation, everything you need is installed to let you run Exchange clients in a Microsoft networking or Novell NetWare environment. If you're running older versions of Windows or DOS, you can modernize them by using updates that come with NT Server 3.51 and later.

> **NOTE**
>
> Remember, each NetWare user must have an NT account as well as an Exchange mailbox. It's best to use the same user ID and password for both NetWare and NT. You can manually set up the account and mailbox, or—as you'll learn in a later chapter—you can automate the process by importing NetWare account information into NT/Exchange.

To conclude this section, here are a few tips about NetWare-based Exchange clients:

- Be sure that your NT server's Ethernet frame type matches the frame type being used by NetWare clients.

- Be sure to set different NetWare Internal Network Numbers if you have multiple network adapters in your NT server or if you're using NT's NWLink protocol with multiple frame types.

- Add the following lines to your NET.CFG file if you want to run both the Exchange client and Schedule+:

  Protocol IPXODI

  ipx sockets = 50

Conclusion

In this chapter you learned how to set up Exchange client software so it can be installed from a network server onto user workstations. You also installed a client on your Exchange server. Finally, you NetWare types learned a bit about IPX/SPX-based Exchange clients.

CHAPTER

TWELVE

Exchange Clients for Windows 101

- Starting up an Exchange client for the first time

- Sending and receiving messages

- Creating a public folder

- Working with shared mailboxes

- Using Exchange client menus

Because the focus of this book is on Exchange Server, I really don't have a lot of time for the client side of things. So my goal here is to provide you with enough information to use an Exchange client in your explorations of Exchange from this point forward. Elizabeth Olson has written a nice book—*Microsoft Exchange Plain & Simple* (Sybex, 1996)—that focuses on Exchange clients. Check it out for more client information.

In spite of the limited time we can devote to Exchange clients, we're still going to cover quite a bit of territory in this chapter. We'll start up a new client for the first time, send and receive a message with our client, create a new public folder, create and access a shared mailbox, and take a quick tour of some client menus. I'll close with a few comments on Microsoft's Outlook client. That's quite a handful, so let's get started.

Starting Up a Newly Installed Client

In the last chapter, you installed an Exchange client on your Exchange server. Find the icon for your Exchange client—for Windows 95 and NT 4.0, it's the desktop icon labeled 'Inbox'—and double-click on it.

If you created an Exchange mailbox for yourself back in chapter 8 *and* you installed the Exchange client while logged in as yourself *and* you're now logged into your NT domain as yourself *and* you modified your NT Exchange client as I suggested in the last chapter, the Exchange client should open right up with no further action on your part.

If any of the above is not the case, when you double-click on the Inbox icon, the Exchange installation Wizard should start up. (See Figure 12.1.) Let's track through the Setup Wizard's pages, so that you're aware of the manual setup process for Exchange clients.

> **NOTE**
>
> As you go along, remember that this is exactly the experience an end user will have when starting an Exchange client for the first time. Try to think like a nontechnical user during this procedure; this will help you come up with ideas for special instructions or other help you might want to give your users. As will become more and more obvious as you move through the rest of this chapter, it's much easier on your users if you do some of the preliminary setup work I discussed in the last chapter and referred to by inference in the second paragraph of this section.

FIGURE 12.1

The first page of the
Microsoft Exchange
Setup Wizard

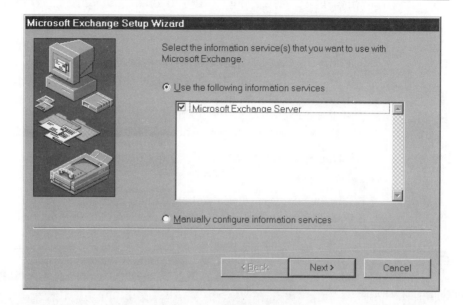

WARNING

I'm assuming that you've been using the NT account you created for yourself. If you expect to have new users who will be logging into their NT accounts for the first time to set up and use their Exchange clients, remember to tell them their password. If you created a user's NT account while creating someone's mailbox with the Exchange Administrator program, the default password is blank. If you created the NT account using the User Manager for Domains, then depending on the options you select when creating accounts, you'll need to provide the user with whatever password information will be needed to log in.

I'm also assuming that you've added your personal NT account to the Exchange Admins group you created back in Chapter 7. If you didn't, you should now, since you won't be able to do some of the tasks discussed here unless you are a member of that group.

On the first page of the Setup Wizard, you select from among the information services available to your Exchange client. If you included only Microsoft Exchange Server when setting up your Exchange client installation in the last chapter (see Figure 11.12 and related text), the first page of your Wizard should look like the one in Figure 12.1. If, on the other hand, you included other services, such as Microsoft Mail, you'll see those services on the first page of the Wizard.

Under 'Use the following information services', select Microsoft Exchange Server. If other services are displayed and you want your Exchange client to connect to them, select them too. If you select other services, be sure you have the information required to set them up. For example, if you want to connect to both your Microsoft Mail and Exchange Server mailboxes, you'll need to know the drive and directory or the NT share where your Microsoft Mail post office is loaded.

Don't choose the 'Manually configure information services' option. Click on Next when you're finished.

In the next Wizard dialog box, shown in Figure 12.2, you specify the names of your Exchange server and your mailbox on the server.

FIGURE 12.2

Entering Exchange
server and mailbox
names

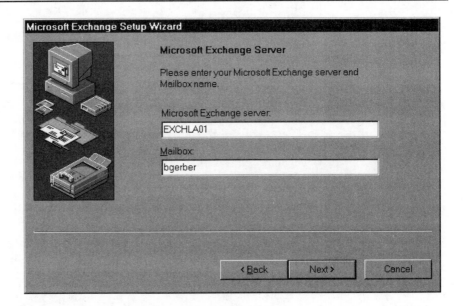

When you're through entering this information, click on Next. The Wizard page lets you specify whether the computer you're setting up will be doing remote as well as local Exchange server access (see Figure 12.3). If you answer Yes, Exchange will set you up for remote access. For now, answer No; you can always add remote services later if you need them. Click on Next when you're finished with this dialog box.

The next Setup Wizard page lets you specify a location for your Personal Address Book (see Figure 12.4). As you'll see in a bit, all unhidden Exchange Server recipients are available to Exchange clients when they create new messages—these are held in *public* address books. You can also have a Personal Address Book (PAB), into which you can put a copy of any address in any Exchange public address book. You can also create addresses for recipients in foreign e-messaging systems and store them in your PAB. This is often a better option than creating Exchange Server custom recipients when only one or two users need to use an address.

FIGURE 12.3

Specifying whether this computer will be used for remote access

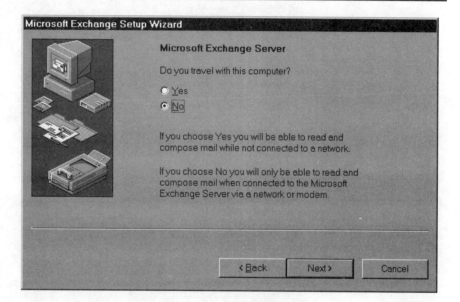

Generally, each PAB should be stored on the user's own personal disk space. If you wish to allow it, however, PABs can be stored on network servers. Accept the default directory and file name, or enter your own path name and click on Next.

On the next Wizard page, shown in Figure 12.5, you are offered the option of having Exchange start up when Windows starts up. Select 'Add Exchange to the Startup group' if you wish to accept this option and have your Exchange client run when Windows starts up. If not, select 'Do not add Exchange to the Startup group'. Click on Next when you're done.

That's it. As you can see in Figure 12.6, you're done setting up your initial Exchange client. Click on Finish and your Exchange client will start up for the first time.

FIGURE 12.4

Choosing a location
for the Personal
Address Book

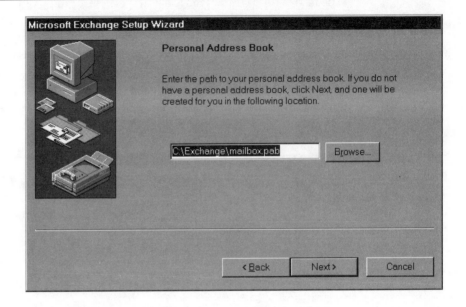

FIGURE 12.5

Telling Windows whether
to run Exchange on
startup

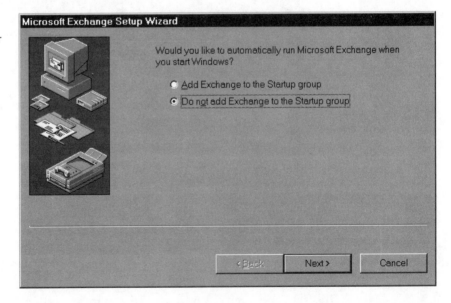

FIGURE 12.6

Setup is done.

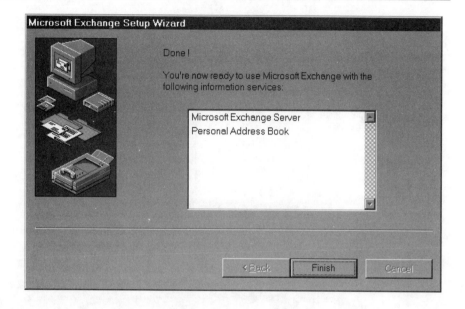

Sending and Receiving a Message with an Exchange Client

As soon as your client is finished logging in to your Exchange server, you'll see a window similar to the one in Figure 12.7. To open the left-hand pane that shows you folders, select Folders from the View menu. If you can't see the toolbar just under the client's menu bar, select Toolbar from the View menu. The client window is kind of small and scrunchy, so you'll want to enlarge it until it looks like the one in Figure 12.8.

Now you should be able to see all seven of the client's default column titles. Like the Exchange Administrator, Exchange remembers the window size you've set when you exit. Every time you run the client, the window will be set to that size. Also like the Exchange Administrator, the client is divided into two resizable panes. The left-hand pane contains mailboxes and public and personal folders in a hierarchical arrangement. The right-hand pane displays the messages contained in the folder that has been selected in the left-hand pane.

FIGURE 12.7

The Exchange client window must be resized after it starts up for the first time.

The Compose Icon

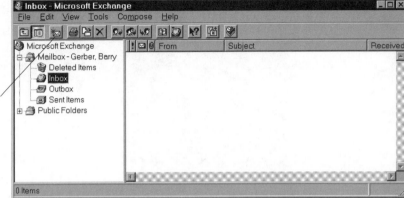

FIGURE 12.8

The client window after it has been enlarged to a comfortable working size

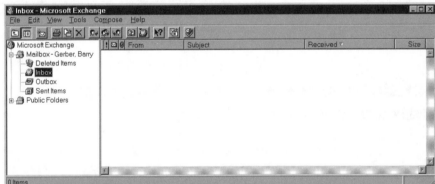

Sending a Message

Let's start by sending ourselves a message. Click on the Compose icon in the toolbar just below the client's menus (see Figure 12.7 for the icon's location). This opens a New Message window like the one in Figure 12.9. If you don't see the standard toolbar for managing messages in the New Message window, select Toolbar from the message's View menu. If the text-formatting toolbar isn't visible in the New Message window, select Formatting Toolbar from the message's View menu. Your client will remember that you've turned on these toolbars and present them on every new message window.

FIGURE 12.9

An Exchange client's
New Message window

envelope   diskette   printer

The Toolbar
The Formatting
Toolbar

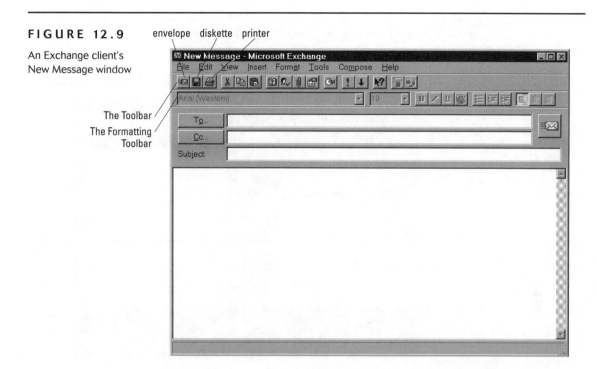

If you didn't know you were in an Exchange client, you just might think you were running a word processing application. The top of the screen includes drop-down menus and a number of icons that you've probably seen in your Windows-based word processor. These allow you to produce very rich messages that can include text in different fonts, sizes, formats, and colors, as well as variously formatted paragraphs and lists.

The New Message window starts to look more e-messagy just below the formatting toolbar. This is where you enter the address of the recipient(s) of your message. Click on To; this brings up our old friend the Address Book dialog box (see Figure 12.10).

Notice in Figure 12.10 that I've clicked open the drop-down list of address lists. The default is the Global Address List—which, of course, is the same Global Address List you encountered in the Exchange Administrator. It holds addresses for all unhidden recipients in your Exchange organization. The Recipients list is the address list only for GerCom's LA site. You'll remember that we created the recipients container 'Application Recipients' back in Chapter 8 when we were experimenting with the Exchange Administrator. I talked about the Personal Address Book earlier in this chapter, so I'll say no more about that here. Stick with the Global Address List for now.

FIGURE 12.10

The Exchange address book as viewed from an Exchange client

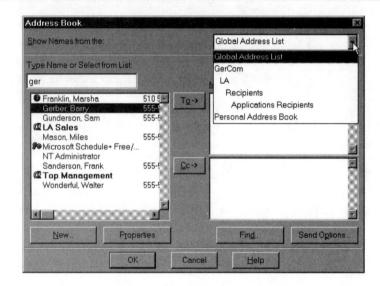

Since you'll be sending this message to yourself, click on your name in the Global Address List, then click on To and OK in the Address Book dialog box. This returns you to your message (see Figure 12.11). Now use your mouse to place the text cursor in the 'Cc' (carbon copy) field of your message (or you can tab to the field). Type in the first few letters of your first or last name, depending on how you chose to show display names back in Chapter 8. If you chose the First_Name Last_Name option, type in the first few letters of your first name. If you selected Last_Name, First_Name, type in the first few letters of your last name. Don't do anything else in the 'Cc' field. You'll see why we did all of this in just a bit.

Now move to the Subject field (again using either your mouse or the Tab key). Type in some text for a subject title.

Next, move to the message field and type in a message. When you're done, click on the Send icon (on the upper right-hand side of the dialog box) to send your message to the Exchange server. In a second or two, the message should show up in your Inbox (see Figure 12.12).

FIGURE 12.11

Composing a new
Exchange message

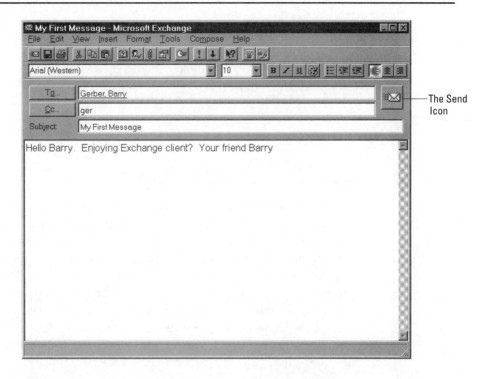

The Send
Icon

FIGURE 12.12

The new message shows
up in the Exchange
client's Inbox.

Show/Hide Folder List

Show Address Book   Go To Inbox

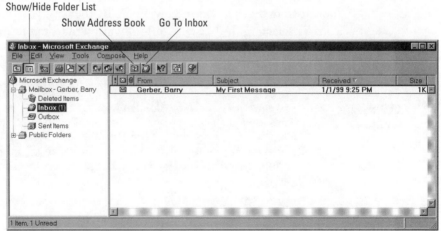

NOTE   A few of the icons on the main Exchange client window in Figure 12.12 are labeled for your information. The rest of the icons are either identified in Figure 12.13 or not terribly important right now. Anyway, as with most Windows apps, you can always find out what an Exchange client icon is for just by putting your mouse pointer on it and waiting a second for a tiny information box to show up.

Reading a Received Message

Let's take a look at your newly received message. Double-click anywhere on the message line in the Inbox window (see Figure 12.12) to open it. Figure 12.13 shows the open message. Take a look at the 'Cc' field—notice how your Exchange client figured out your name from the few letters you typed in while composing the message? Entering partial names into message address fields can save time compared with clicking on the To button and finding names in the Address Book. Separate a list of partial names with semicolons. If you enter a partial name that's not in the Address Book, or one that appears in more than one display name or alias name, the client will offer you a chance to change what you've entered or to pick from a list of all recipients containing the partial name.

I won't go into detail about the message's toolbar icons here; check out Figure 12.13 for specifics. If you don't see the toolbar in your message, select Toolbar from the message's View menu. By the way, you can alter the toolbar icons by selecting the Customize Toolbar option from the Tools menu on any received message. The changes you make apply to all received messages.

NOTE   You can also customize toolbars for the main client window and for new messages. Just select the Customize Toolbar option from the Tools menu while the main client window or a new message is open. Changes you make take effect from the time you make them, and they apply to all folders and messages in the main client window as well as to all new messages.

FIGURE 12.13

A received Exchange
message

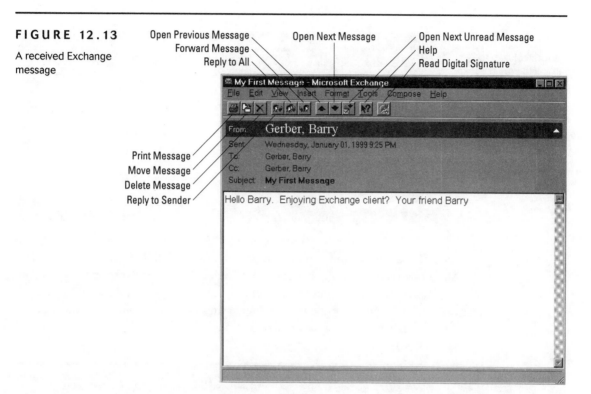

Open Previous Message
Forward Message
Reply to All

Open Next Message

Open Next Unread Message
Help
Read Digital Signature

Print Message
Move Message
Delete Message
Reply to Sender

Creating a New Public Folder

Remember that Exchange public folders are created by mailbox users in
Exchange clients. For coming chapters we're going to need a public folder or two,
so I want to show you how to create one now.

Open your Exchange client and double-click on Public Folders in the left-hand
pane of the client's window, or click on the plus-sign icon just in front of Public
Folders. Your client window should look something like the one in Figure 12.14.
(Notice that the little plus sign becomes a minus sign when the master Public
Folders folder is open.)

You've opened the master folder for public folders, which contains two subfolders: Favorites and All Public Folders. If your Exchange organization has a large
number of public folders, you can drag the ones you use a lot to your Favorites subfolder. This makes them easier to find. Folders in the Favorites folder are also the
only ones that are available when you work offline without a connection to your
Exchange server.

FIGURE 12.14

The master folder for public folders and its two default subfolders

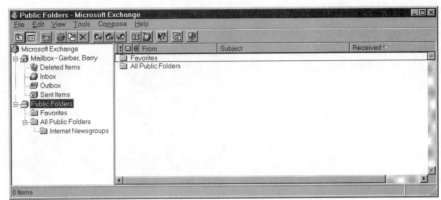

You can create new public folders only in the folder 'All Public Folders.' So click on All Public Folders and then select New Folder from your Exchange client's File menu. This brings up the New Folder dialog box (see Figure 12.15). Enter a name for the folder; I've given mine the somewhat unimaginative name Barry's First Public Folder. When you're done, click on OK.

> **NOTE** Notice that public folder 'Internet Newsgroups'? It was created when I chose to install nesgroup services as part of the Exchange Server installation. It'll hold USENET newsgroups and their messages when I turn on newsgroup services in a later chapter. If you chose not to install newsgroup services, you won't see this folder.

The new public folder now shows up under the All Public Folders hierarchy (see Figure 12.16). If you can't see the full name of your new folder, use the split-bar (which I discussed in Chapter 8) to make the left-hand pane of your client window a little larger.

FIGURE 12.15

Naming a new folder

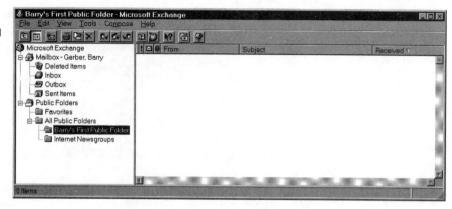

FIGURE 12.16

The new folder in the All Public Folders hierarchy

Now click on your new folder so that it is highlighted, then select Properties from your client's File menu or right mouse click on the folder and select Properties from the pop-up menu. This brings up the Properties dialog box for the folder, shown in Figure 12.17.

We're not going to spend a lot of time with this dialog box. Mailbox owners use public folder Properties dialog boxes to:

- Add a description for other mailbox owners who access the folder
- Set up views of the folder based on specific column title bars
- Set up some administrative rules on folder characteristics, access, and such
- Manage those neat electronic forms I talked about earlier
- Set permissions for using the folder
- Make folders available to users of Internet newsreader software

Go ahead and look around in the Properties dialog box. When you're done, click on Cancel, unless you've made some changes. If you have, then click on OK to save your changes.

NOTE You create and manage private folders inside of mailboxes in the same way you create and manage public folders. 'Nuff said.

FIGURE 12.17

The Properties dialog
box for a public folder

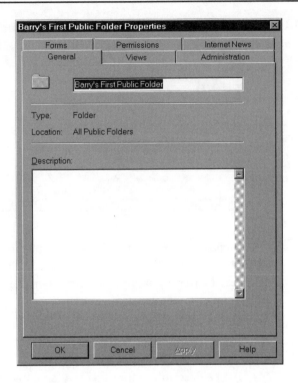

Now let's take a look at our new public folder from an Exchange administrator's point of view. Open the Exchange Administrator, then open the Folders container just under the organization container, and finally open the Public Folders container. Your Administrator screen should look pretty much like the one in Figure 12.18, and you should see the folder you just created in the Public Folders hierarchy.

Next, click on your new public folder and select Properties from the Administrator's File menu. This brings up a dialog box you've seen before: the Administrator's Properties dialog box for a public folder—in this case, your new public folder (see Figure 12.19). The last time you saw this dialog box, back in Chapter 9, we were working with one of my public folders, since you didn't have any at the time. Now that you've got your own folder, you might want to go back over Chapter 9's section on public folder management. Go ahead. I'll wait. I promise.

FIGURE 12.18

Finding a public folder
in the Exchange
Administrator

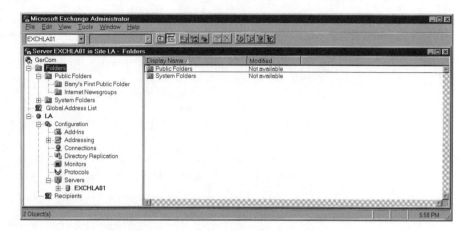

FIGURE 12.19

The Properties dialog
box for a public folder

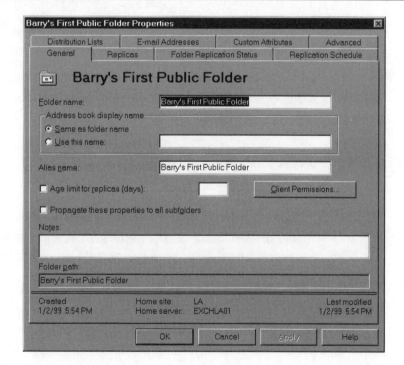

NOTE

Remember how public folders are hidden from the Address Book when they're created? That means they're also hidden from the container that holds them. Check it out. Look in the recipients container your public folders are stored in. (Unless you've changed the default, it's the Recipients container for your site.) The folder is nowhere to be seen. And because your public folder isn't visible in the Recipients container, it's also not visible in your site address list or in the Global Address List, which is based on the contents of site-level recipients containers.

To make your public folder visible, tab over to the Advanced property page on the Properties dialog box for your folder and deselect 'Hide from address book'. Now you'll see it in the Global Address List and the Recipients container.

Though it's hidden from the Address Book, the folder is still visible to all in the Exchange client Public Folder hierarchy. While in an Exchange client, the folder owner can use the Permissions property page (on the folder's Properties dialog box discussed above) to limit access to the folder. Those who don't have access to the folder can still see it, but they can't access items in the folder or put new items into it. Those with no access to a folder's contents also can't see subfolders within the folder. You can hide the folder from the public folders list by deselecting the Folder Visible property on the folder's permissions tab. Then only users you've specifically given access can see the folder from their Exchange clients.

Creating, Accessing, and Using a Shared Mailbox

As I mentioned in Chapter 2, you can create special mailboxes to support the activities of small groups of people who work together. Such mailboxes are especially useful when you don't need or want the potentially wide exposure of public folders.

Say a small local committee is set up to recruit a new plant manager to replace the old manager. By setting up a mailbox that all members of the committee can access and then hiding that mailbox from Exchange address books, the group can work together assured of a fair amount of privacy.

Shared but unhidden mailboxes can work well for other applications. For example, users could send questions to a mailbox that help-desk personnel shared.

To organize the help-desk function, subfolders could be created in the mailbox to hold each person's active and inactive items. A help-desk coordinator could even be made responsible for assigning questions to different personnel. An assignment would be as easy as dragging a new message into a specific user's subfolders. Public folders also can be used to implement these sorts of applications, especially if you make use of the Folder Visible property.

Creating a Shared Mailbox

You create a shared mailbox in Exchange Server's Administrator program and access it through your Exchange client. Open the Administrator and select New Mailbox from the File menu. (By now you should be quite familiar with the Properties box for mailboxes.) Fill in a name for the mailbox. As you can see in Figure 12.20, I'm calling mine HR Committee #1.

FIGURE 12.20

Creating a shared mailbox

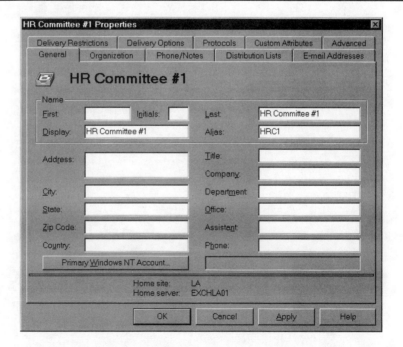

You don't have to associate a primary Windows NT account with this new mailbox, since it will be used by people who already have NT accounts. You just have to give those accounts User permissions for the new mailbox. You do this on the new mailbox's Permissions property page (see Figure 12.21). When you click on either Apply or OK to record your new mailbox entry in the Exchange directory, the Administrator program gives you the opportunity to associate an NT account with a mailbox. Just click on Cancel in the 'Primary Windows NT account' dialog box to skip this option and create the mailbox without associating it with a primary NT account.

FIGURE 12.21

Giving NT users and groups access to a shared mailbox

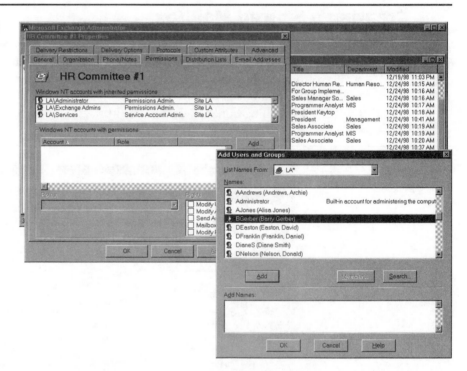

NOTE

Depending on the option you've chosen for creating display names and aliases, you may have to alter the default names that the Administrator suggests to get the display name or alias you want. That's quite easy to do: Just delete the suggested name you don't like and then type in the name you want.

> **WARNING**
>
> Don't take on the management role for every shared mailbox you create; let the mailbox users do this collectively or by assigning the responsibility to one of their number. Users can grant various levels of access permission for the mailbox, and they can remove these permissions as well. I'll show you how this is done a little later in this chapter.

That's it. You've created a mailbox that can be shared by a group of users. Now you need to tell your Exchange client to open the mailbox when it starts up and add its address to your Personal Address Book. After we do that, I'll show you how to hide the mailbox from the address book for privacy.

Accessing a Shared Mailbox

Now go to your Exchange client. As you go along, keep an eye on Figure 12.22.

From the Tools menu in the Exchange client's main window, select Services. Be sure that Microsoft Exchange Server is selected in the Services dialog box, then click on the Properties button in the Services dialog box.

FIGURE 12.22

Telling an Exchange client to open additional mailboxes when starting up

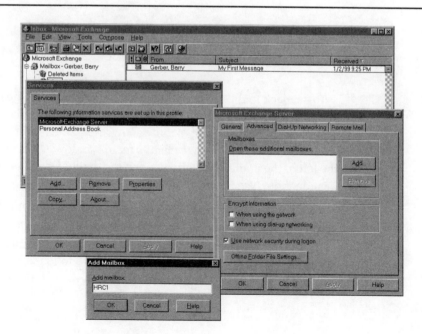

Select the Advanced property page tab on the dialog box labeled Microsoft Exchange Server. In the Mailboxes area, click on Add to add another mailbox to be opened. Enter the mailbox's name in the Add Mailbox field in the Add Mailbox dialog box. Click on OK when you're done, and the mailbox's display name will be added to the 'Open these additional mailboxes' window (see Figure 12.23). If you try to open the mailbox in an Exchange client but don't have the correct permissions, you'll get an error.

FIGURE 12.23

A shared mailbox will now be opened when an Exchange client starts up.

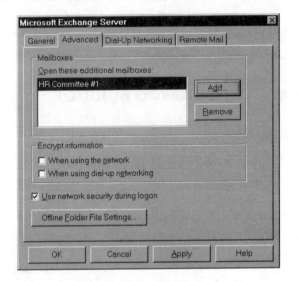

To get back to the Services dialog box, click on OK in the Microsoft Exchange Server dialog box and then click on OK in the Services dialog box to complete your work. The new mailbox now shows up in the folder hierarchy on the left-hand side of your Exchange client's main window. Click on the plus-sign icon to the left of the mailbox's name to open the mailbox and see the standard folders included in it (see Figure 12.24).

Now let's add the mailbox to your Personal Address Book. Click on the Address Book icon in your Exchange client's main window (the icon looks like a little book, as shown in Figure 12.24). This brings up the address book. Find the mailbox, click on it, and then click on the 'Add to Personal Address Book' icon (see Figure 12.25). That's it. The mailbox is now in your Personal Address Book.

NOTE

To grant other recipients access to your shared mailbox, click on the shared mailbox when you're in your Exchange client and then select Properties from the File menu in the client's main window. This brings up a Properties dialog box for the mailbox. Tab over to the Permissions property page and click on Add. You'll get a standard Address Book dialog box. Pick the recipients you want to add from the dialog box, such as a distribution list, custom recipients, or a public folder, then click on OK. Once you've added a recipient to the Permissions property page, you can grant it many different roles—ranging from None, which allows no access to the folder at all; to Reviewer, which allows read access to the folder but not write access; to Owner, which gives full read, write, and permissions control over the mailbox.

FIGURE 12.24

A new shared mailbox shows up in an Exchange client's folder hierarchy.

Address Book

New Shared Mailbox

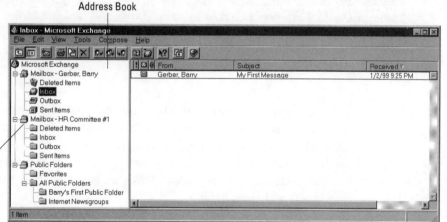

FIGURE 12.25

Adding a shared mailbox to your Personal Address Book

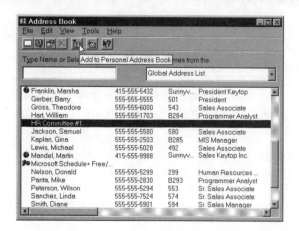

Hiding a Shared Mailbox from the Address Book

You don't have to hide a shared mailbox from the Address Book. You certainly wouldn't want to hide the help-desk mailbox I talked about above, for example. However, if you've created the mailbox for a sensitive purpose like that of our human resources mailbox—and there's no reason for others to see it—you're better off hiding it. That way others won't even know of its existence, and they won't be able to send messages to it either purposely or unintentionally.

Once you and any other users have added the shared mailbox to your Personal Address Books, you can go ahead and hide the mailbox from the address list.

WARNING If you hide the mailbox before trying to add it to Personal Address Books, you won't be able to select it from the Global Address List or the site's Address Book. You'll have to add the address manually using the little Rolodex-card icon on the Address Book toolbar.

Here's how to hide the mailbox. In the Exchange Administrator, find the mailbox in the Recipients container and double-click on it to bring up its Properties dialog box. Tab over to the Advanced property page and select 'Hide from address book' (see Figure 12.26). When you're done, click on OK. Now, in your Exchange client, open the Global Address List or the site's Address Book. The mailbox is no longer there.

Sending a Message to a Shared Mailbox

Okay, let's send a message to the shared mailbox. Click on the Compose icon. This brings up a New Message window. Click on the To button, then click on Show Names from the dialog box and select Personal Address Book. Double-click on the shared mailbox's name and click on OK. Add a subject and some text for the body of the message, then click on the large envelope icon on the right-hand side of the New Message window to send the message.

Within a second or two, the message is delivered to the shared mailbox. Click on the mailbox's Inbox and you should see the message. Double-click on the message to read it. That's it. Pretty neat, huh?

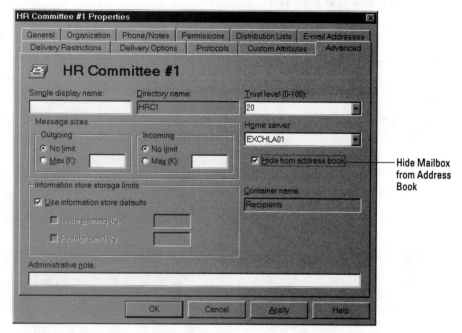

FIGURE 12.26

Hiding a shared mailbox from the Address Book

A Quick Tour of the Exchange Client's Main Window Menus

To conclude this chapter, we'll take a very quick tour of the menus for the main window of an Exchange client. My goal here is merely to highlight the capabilities of the client, not to teach you how to use all of them. I'll skip over obvious items such as the File menu's Open and Save As options. And I won't be discussing the menus for new and received messages here—partly because some of what's in them will be covered as we look at the client's main window menus, and partly because I don't want to turn this into a full-blown tutorial on Exchange clients. As with everything in this chapter, check out Elizabeth Olson's *Microsoft Exchange Plain & Simple* if you need more details on Exchange clients.

The File Menu

The Exchange client's File menu is shown in Figure 12.27.

FIGURE 12.27

The File menu of an
Exchange client's main
window

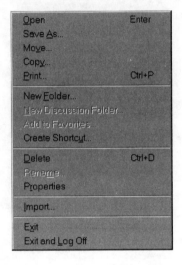

Open	Enter
Save As...	
Move...	
Copy...	
Print...	Ctrl+P
New Folder...	
New Discussion Folder...	
Add to Favorites	
Create Shortcut...	
Delete	Ctrl+D
Rename...	
Properties	
Import...	
Exit	
Exit and Log Off	

New Folder

To create a new folder, highlight the private or public container you want to create the folder in, then click on New Folder. This brings up a New Folder dialog box.

New Discussion Folder

Discussion folders are public folders. They are very similar to regular public folders created with the New Folder option on the File menu. However, by default messages in them are organized by conversation threads, which makes sense for a folder where several people converse about a set of topics.

Add to Favorites

The Favorites folder is great when there are many public folders and you want to easily find those that you use a lot, or when you want access to a folder offline. To add a public folder to Favorites, select the folder and click on Add to Favorites. The selected folder shows up as a subfolder of the Favorites folder. (This is only a pointer to the folder. The actual folder remains in its place as a subfolder of the All Public Folders folder.)

Create Shortcut

Create Shortcut is a pretty nice feature: It lets you create a pointer to a public or private folder or even a whole mailbox and then drag and drop that pointer into a message, put it into a word processing document, or even add it to your Windows 95 or NT 4.0 desktop. When the message's recipients open the icon of the pointer, they open that folder. Of course, recipients must have been granted access to the folder or mailbox.

Highlight the folder you want to create a shortcut for and then click on Create Shortcut. This brings up a dialog box for naming the file that the shortcut will reside in.

Delete

To delete folders or messages, select them and click on Delete. They're gone. (Well, private folders and the items they contain are actually put into the Deleted Items folder, from which you can retrieve them if needed. However, once an item is deleted from the Deleted Items folder, it's gone forever, unless you've backed it up.)

Rename

Rename is for folders. Select the folder you want to rename and click on Rename to bring up the Rename dialog box. Type in the new name and click on OK.

Properties

Mailboxes, folders, and messages all have properties. Select the message or folder whose properties you want to see and then click on Properties.

NOTE
If you use Windows 95 or NT 4.0 you can bring up a pop-up menu containing some of the options found on the File and other menus. Right mouse click on any object in the left- or right-hand pane of your Exchange client to pop up the menu. In fact, you should get comfortable with right mouse clicking all over your Exchange client. There are tons of neat timesaving capabilities built into Exchange client's right mouse menus.

Import

You can import messages, folders, and address lists from a Microsoft Mail 3.x for Windows mailbox (.MMF file) or Personal Address Book (.PAB file). This is useful for moving from MS Mail to Exchange or merging PABs. Click on Import and tell the Exchange client where to find the .MMF or .PAB file it is to import.

Exit and Exit and Log Off

Select Exit to leave Exchange while remaining logged in to all information services. You'll use this option when you want to close your Exchange client but still want to run other applications that use your information services, such as Microsoft Schedule+. Choose Exit and Log Off to leave Exchange and log off of all information services.

The Edit Menu

The Exchange client's Edit menu is shown in Figure 12.28.

FIGURE 12.28

The Edit menu of the Exchange client's main window

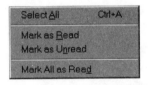

Mark as Read, Mark as Unread, and Mark All as Read

When a message has not been read, its subject line as seen in a folder appears in bold type. When a message has been read, its subject line is in plain type. Select the messages for which you want to change the read status, then click on any of these three options as appropriate. Choosing Mark All as Read will mark all messages in the open folder as having been read, regardless of which lines are selected.

The View Menu

The Exchange client's View menu is shown in Figure 12.29.

FIGURE 12.29

The View menu of the Exchange client's main window

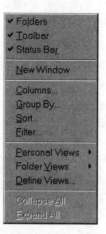

Folders, Toolbar, and Status Bar

If the Folders, Toolbar, and/or Status Bar items are checked, they'll show up on your Exchange client. The status bar is at the bottom of the Exchange client's main window; back in Figure 12.18, the status bar reads '2 Object(s).'

New Window

Selecting New Window gives you a whole new additional Exchange client main window.

Columns, Group By, Sort, and Filter

Use this set of items to view the messages in a private or public folder organized in different ways. This can be very useful when you need to use the messages in a folder for different purposes. For example, you may at times want to look at only those messages in your Inbox that are from your boss, and you may want those messages sorted in descending order by date. At other times you may need to see all of your Inbox messages sorted in ascending order by sender or by conversation thread.

Folder views created with this set of options remain in effect until you create another view, even if you exit and log off of your Exchange client. The next section covers the creation and selection of permanently saved views.

Personal Views, Folder Views, and Define Views

You can create and save instructions for organizing and displaying your messages in a private or public folder. These instructions are based on the same information given for Columns, Group By, Sort, and Filter.

Personal views are available only to the mailbox user. You can apply them to any private or public folder, but only you see the messages organized in this way. The Exchange client includes a set of default personal views that organize messages by such criteria as From and Subject. You can create other personal views by selecting the Define Views option from the View menu.

When you click on Personal Views, you'll be offered the default views that come with the Exchange client along with any you've created. Select one of the personal views to apply it to the open folder.

Folder views apply to a specific private or public folder. If you have the rights to do so, you can create views for a public folder. Users of a public folder can select any available view for a folder; the owner of a public folder can set a default view by choosing from among the existing ones. To create a new view for a folder, select the folder and then click on Define Views.

The same Define Views dialog box works for both personal views and folder views. Just select the kind of view you want to create and go to it.

When you select a folder and click on Folder Views, you're offered a list of existing views. Click on the one you want to apply to the folder.

Collapse All and Expand All

If you're using a folder view that collapses messages into groupings by sender, subject, or some other attribute, you can use Collapse All and Expand All to hide or display groups of messages. To hide all but the main group categories in the folder, select Collapse All. To display all of the messages under all of the group categories in the folder, select Expand All.

The Tools Menu

The Exchange client's Tools menu is shown in Figure 12.30.

FIGURE 12.30

The Tools menu of the
Exchange client's main
window

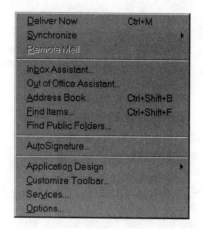

Deliver Now	Ctrl+M
Synchronize	▶
Remote Mail	
Inbox Assistant...	
Out of Office Assistant...	
Address Book	Ctrl+Shift+B
Find Items...	Ctrl+Shift+F
Find Public Folders...	
AutoSignature...	
Application Design	▶
Customize Toolbar...	
Services...	
Options...	

Deliver Now

Select Deliver Now (or press Ctrl+M) to send messages waiting in your Outbox
and check for new messages.

Synchronize

When you work offline with your Exchange client, you can have an image of
your online Exchange client environment. That image is stored in what is called
an *offline folder*. What's included in that environment is determined by your folder
synchronization setup. You keep this image up-to-date by synchronizing it with
your online environment.

You can synchronize when connected remotely or when connected directly
to the network, as you might do with a portable PC. If connected remotely by
modem and your connect isn't too expensive, you can fire off a synchronization
nightly as I do with my home Exchange client. If you're using a portable on the
road, when you return to the office with your offline folder full of new items
you can update your online environment by synchronizing it with the offline
folder. If there are any messages waiting to be sent in your Outbox, they're sent
out through your server and any messages waiting for you on the server are
delivered to your Inbox.

NOTE The following instructions don't make much sense for the permanent, LAN-connected workstation that you use to run your Exchange client. Synchronization is for that computer you use at home or on the road when you're going to be disconnected from your Exchange server.

First, you must set up your offline folder. Now I'll show you the easiest way to do this. Because you'll certainly want to synchronize your mailbox, select your primary mailbox by clicking on it while running Exchange client, and then select Properties from the client's File menu. Tab over to the Synchronization property page in the resultant Properties dialog box, then select 'When offline or online' from the page (see Figure 12.31). This ensures that you'll be able to access your Deleted Items, Inbox, Outbox, and Sent Items folders whether you're connected to your Exchange server or not. You also need to do this same operation for every other folder in your mailbox that you want to have available when offline.

FIGURE 12.31

Setting up synchronization for an Exchange mailbox

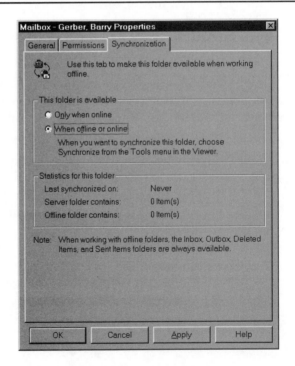

Next, click on OK. You'll be told that you need an offline folder and will be offered the opportunity to create one. Accept the offer, and in a flash the offline folder is created and ready to hold an offline image of your mailbox. You can add any other private folders and public folders in your Favorites folder to your offline folder in the manner outlined above.

Then use the Synchronize option on the Tools menu to ensure that your online and offline Exchange client environments are the same. The menu includes a small submenu that lets you synchronize all folders or only the currently selected folder. This submenu also allows you to download the current copy of the offline address book, which we discussed in Chapter 9.

> **TIP**
>
> When setting someone up to use an Exchange client at home, I often have them bring their workstation to the office. I connect the workstation to the network and set up and perform a synchronization of all folders. For users with big mailboxes, this method is especially nice, because they don't have to run the first and most time-consuming synchronization when connected at home at 28.8Kbps. And don't forget those public folders. Any public folder you drag into the Favorites folder under Public Folders will be copied during the synchronization if you've turned on the 'when online or offline' property on the folder's Synchronization property page.

Remote Mail

Remote mail lets you set your client to do such things as periodically dial up your Exchange server to pick up message headers or messages. The interface is pretty self-explanatory. So have fun.

Inbox Assistant

The Inbox Assistant is a very nice rules-based agent with a helpful graphical user interface. It can perform a wide range of functions with mail that comes into your Inbox—for example, putting the mail into another folder, forwarding a message to another address, or performing a custom action that deals with the message. All of these tasks can be based on various properties of the messages, from the sender to the occurrence of specific text in the subject line or body of the message.

Out of Office Assistant

The Out of Office Assistant is another neat GUI agent that you can use to send an auto-reply message telling people you're out of the office—and letting them know what the consequences might be (for example, that you won't be getting to your mail until a specific date). The Out of Office Assistant generates only one message to a specific message originator during the time you're away from the office. If the original message is sent to an Exchange Server distribution list, the Out of Office Assistant generates out-of-office messages for the list's members, provided the option has been selected in Exchange Administrator on the Advanced property page of the list. The services of the Inbox Assistant are also available as you set up out-of-office message scenarios.

Address Book

Select the Address Book menu item to see and work with the Exchange Address Book. Because you can easily access the Address Book when composing a message, you're most likely to select it from here when you want to add an item to your Personal Address Book. (You can also bring up the Address Book by pressing Ctrl+Shift+B or by clicking on the Address Book icon in your Exchange client's main window.)

Find Items

Select Find when you want to locate a message or messages that contain, for example, specific text in the subject line or body of the message. This item also has a really impressive GUI.

Find Public Folders

Use Find Public Folders if you're looking for a public folder with specific characteristics, for example, with specific text in its name or description.

AutoSignature

With AutoSignature, your Exchange client can append a standard text message to your outgoing messages. You can create one or more such messages and set one as the default. People often use autosignatures to give their name or phone number or even to make spicy comments about themselves or life itself.

Application Design

The Application Design item contains some nifty tools to help you design private and public folders. These can be especially helpful for nontechnical users. You can also launch the Forms Designer from here (discussed in a later chapter).

Customize Toolbar

With the Customize Toolbar item, you can add lots of icons to the main window's toolbar. These icons give you quick access to menu options. If you find yourself using a particular menu item a lot, think seriously about adding an icon for it to your toolbar. Select Customize Toolbar to see the range of options available.

Services

You use the Services option to add, modify, or delete information services. (You've already used Services to access that shared mailbox you created earlier.)

Options

The Options item is where users can override many of the default settings you established with the Exchange Setup Editor in the last chapter. It's also the place to give permission to other recipients to send messages on behalf of yourself, as well as a myriad of other neat functions.

The Compose Menu

The Exchange client's Compose menu is shown in Figure 12.32.

FIGURE 12.32

The Compose menu of the Exchange client's main window

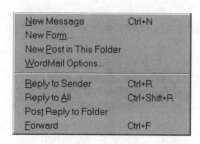

New Message

Select New Message to compose a message in a new message window. Clicking on the New Message icon in the main window, or pressing Ctrl+N, has the same effect.

New Form

Use the New Form option to access one of those electronic forms I've discussed before. You can put a form into a folder for others to fill in. (I'll talk more about forms in Chapter 18.)

New Post in This Folder

You can post a new message directly to a folder. To do so, select a private or public folder by clicking on it, then select New Post in This Folder. This brings up a fairly standard window for composing a message. This window, however, has a field for entering keywords that you can use to search for the message. Type in your message, add attachments, embed objects, and so on, then enter any keywords and click on the icon that looks like a little note with a thumbtack in it to post the message to the selected folder.

WordMail Options

You can use Microsoft Word as the editor for your Exchange client. Word itself doesn't open. You just have all the capabilities of Word available to you in your Exchange client, courtesy of OLE2. That's pretty neat, but, if you send mail to Exchange users who don't use WordMail, they're not going to see all those fantastic special thingies Word lets you do. Frankly, I prefer to use the Exchange client's already pretty nifty built-in editor.

Reply to Sender and Reply to All

Use the Reply to Sender or Reply to All option to answer a selected or open received message. You can reply either just to the person who sent the message or to all its recipients. When working with an open received message, you'll find it far easier to use the message's own Reply to Sender and Reply to All icons, which appear on the message's toolbar (see Figure 12.16). You can also use keyboard alternatives: Ctrl+R for Reply to Sender, or Ctrl+Shift+R for Reply to All.

Post Reply in This Folder

Instead of mailing a reply to a message, you can post your reply in the folder where the message resides using the Post Reply in This Folder option. Posted replies work especially well in folders designed to support ongoing discussions. A user posts or sends a message to the folder, and other users respond to the original message or to replies to it by posting their own replies in the folder. This option works pretty much like New Post in This Folder.

Forward

The Forward option sends a copy of a received message to one or more other recipients; Ctrl+F is the keyboard alternative. As with replies, it's easier to use the Forward icon on the toolbar of an open received message (see Figure 12.13).

Conclusion

In this chapter you learned how to set up your Exchange client when running it for the first time. You also learned how to compose, send, and read a message; create a new public folder; and create and access a shared mailbox. Finally, you took a quick tour of your Exchange client's main window.

This concludes the part of this book dedicated to the Exchange client. Now we're ready to expand our Exchange environment to include additional servers and to administer and manage those servers using the Exchange Administrator program. See you in the next section.

PART V

Expanding an Exchange Organization

In Chapter 13 we'll install a second Exchange server in our site. Then we'll look at the tools that the Exchange Administrator program provides for administering and managing sites with multiple servers. In Chapter 14 we'll add a third Exchange server. This time, however, we'll install it in a new site in our organization. Then we'll focus on administering and managing a multisite Exchange organization.

CHAPTER

THIRTEEN

Administering and Managing Multiserver Exchange Sites

- Adding an Exchange server to a site

- Using the Exchange Administrator in multiserver sites

- Administering and managing multiserver sites

- Exchange Administrator menu items useful in multiserver sites

- Administering and managing the directory service in multiserver sites

- Administering and managing the Message Transfer Agent in multiserver sites

Okay, we're finally ready to add a second Exchange server to our site and to start administering and managing it and its older sibling. Generally, you add new servers in a site to handle the load created by additional users or to provide local area network connectivity for a group of users with slower wide-area links to other Exchange servers in the site. We'll be moving pretty fast in this and the following chapter, so fasten your seat belts.

Installing an Additional Exchange Server in a Site

You've already installed one Exchange server in your site, and installing another is a pretty basic task since it will be almost a carbon copy of the first installation. (You will need a second NT server on which to install Exchange Server.) Instead of going through the second installation in detail, I'll just call your attention to any differences you'll encounter in installing another server in your site. You'll find full details on installing NT Server in Chapter 6 and Exchange Server in Chapter 7.

Installing an Additional NT Server

For our purposes here, you should install your second server in your existing domain—the one you used for your first installation. (For me, that's my LA domain.)

Unless you have a good reason not to, let the second NT server act as a backup domain controller. And don't forget to name the server according to the naming conventions you've set up. (Mine will be called EXCHLA02.) When you're done and your new NT server is up and running, be sure you can see it from your first server. Try connecting to one of the second server's drives from your first using NT server's Network Neighborhood.

WARNING It can take a while before your two servers see each other, so wait 15 minutes or so before trying this. At a more basic and immediate level, if you've installed support for TCP/IP, try pinging your new server from your first. (You can run ping from a command prompt. Just type 'ping ip_address', where ip_address is the IP address you assigned to the new server when configuring it for networking.) A successful ping means that at least your adapter and TCP/IP services are working.

Installing an Additional Exchange Server

Run SETUP.EXE from the Exchange Server CD-ROM. When you get to the Organization and Site dialog box, select 'Join an existing site' and enter the name of your existing Exchange server. The Setup program will use this information to contact the server and gather information on the site you want to join (see Figure 13.1).

FIGURE 13.1

Exchange Setup's Organization and Site dialog box

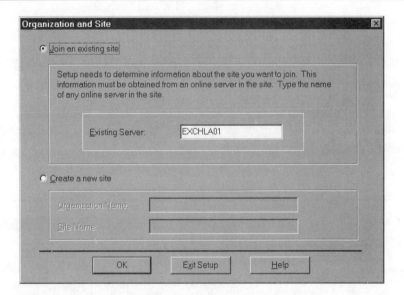

After a short wait, Setup shows you the organization and site information it has found (see Figure 13.2). If the information is correct—and it should be in this case—click on Yes to continue.

Next, Setup presents you with the name of Exchange's Site Services account—whichever account you gave as the Services account when you installed your first Exchange server—and asks you to enter its password (see Figure 13.3). Do so and click on OK to continue.

Installation will now begin, and it will take a bit longer than your first Exchange server installation. Among other things, once your new Exchange server is up and running, Setup automatically configures directory replication between your two servers and then starts it up. From this point on, the two servers will cross-replicate directory changes automatically. Ain't computers wonderful?

FIGURE 13.2

Confirming Exchange
organization and site
information

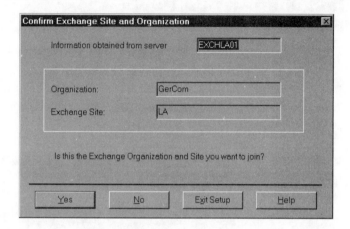

NOTE

You don't need to reinstall the Exchange client files. Users of the new
Exchange server can install them from your first server.

FIGURE 13.3

Entering a password for
the Exchange Site
Services account

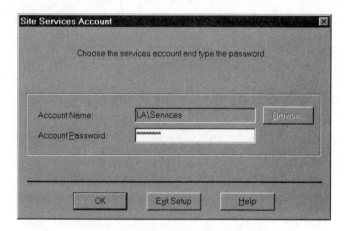

To prove that the installation is working, open the Exchange Administrator
program on your first server. You should now see two servers under your site
(see Figure 13.4). Now go over to your new server and open its copy of the

Administrator. You should see the same two servers, although things will look a little different from how they appear on the first server (see Figure 13.5). I'll talk about the differences very shortly.

FIGURE 13.4

The newly installed Exchange server, viewed through the Administrator program running on an already-installed Exchange server

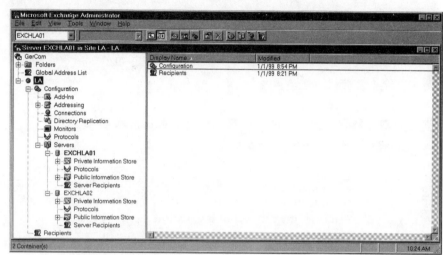

FIGURE 13.5

The newly installed Exchange server, viewed through the Administrator program running on the new server

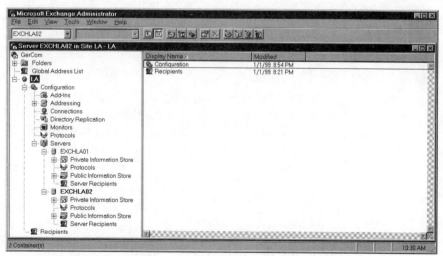

WARNING Whichever server you run the Administrator from, you won't see all the details about the other server until directory replication has finished. The replication can take up to an hour—and sometimes even longer—to complete, depending on the size of your first server's directory, the computing power available in each server, and network load. So if you can't see everything, don't assume that something is wrong right off the bat. As long as your two Exchange servers are talking over the network, the core component services are running, and your servers are installed in the same site, in time everything should work fine.

Using the Exchange Administrator in Multiserver Sites

The Exchange Administrator was designed to let you manage a whole Exchange organization from one workstation or server. In this section we'll focus on understanding the concept of the default server, connecting to multiple Exchange servers, and navigating a multiserver site hierarchy.

The Default Server

In any Exchange server window, one server is the default server. The Administrator program lets you know which one is the default in three ways: The name of the server is displayed in the drop-down list at the top of the Administrator window; the title of the server window shows the server's name; and it's also displayed in bold in the hierarchy tree of the window's left-hand pane.

In Figure 13.4 the server name 'EXCHLA01' appears in the drop-down list on the Administrator's main window, which means EXCHLA01 is the default server. Also indicating the name of the default server are the server window title 'Server EXCHLA01 in Site LA—LA' and 'EXCHLA01' in boldface type on the Exchange hierarchy tree.

Figure 13.5 shows the Administrator running on my new server, EXCHLA02. Here the default server is EXCHLA02, as you can see from the drop-down list, the server window title, and the boldface name in the left-hand pane.

Using just the window shown in Figure 13.4 or Figure 13.5, you can administer and manage either of your Exchange servers. Just remember that during some Administrator operations, you'll have to specify an alternative server if you don't want to work with the default. For example, if I'm running the Administrator on my first server (EXCHLA01) and want to add a new mailbox to my second server (EXCHLA02), I would have to override the default home server setting, EXCHLA01, by selecting the new server's name, EXCHLA02, from the Home Server drop-down list on the Advanced property page of the new mailbox's properties dialog box. In Figure 13.6, I've popped down the Home Server list so I can make EXCHLA02 the home server for the new mailbox I'm creating for John Lewis.

FIGURE 13.6

Setting the home server for a new mailbox when the home server is to be different from the default server

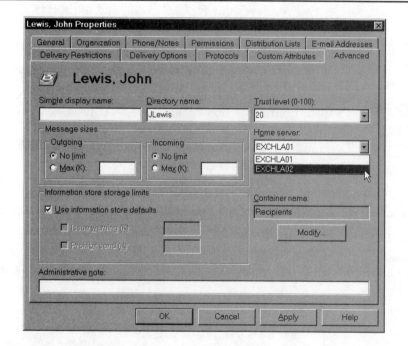

Connecting to Multiple Exchange Servers

If you need to create a lot of mailboxes, you might find it easier to physically go to your other server (EXCHLA02 in my case), rather than changing the home server while you create each new mailbox. That's no problem if the other server is nearby. But if it's not, there's a much easier solution: By opening a window connected to your second server, you can administer and manage your Exchange system with the second server as the default server.

To open additional server windows, select the 'Connect to server' item from the Administrator's File menu. This brings up the Connect to Server dialog box . Type in the name of the Exchange server you want to connect to, or click on Browse to open the Server Browser dialog box and find the server in your Exchange hierarchy (see Figure 13.7). If you use the Server Browser, click on OK when you're done and then click on OK again in the Connect to Server dialog box. (In my case, I'm on EXCHLA01 and I'm opening a connection to EXCHLA02.)

A new window now opens on the server you choose; in Figure 13.8, it's the lower window. Notice that the Administrator's server name drop-down list, the server window's title for EXCHLA02 and the boldface name in the hierarchy tree tell me that my default server is EXCHLA02.

If I now attempt to create a mailbox in the new window, all is well. The default home server is my second server, EXCHLA02 (see Figure 13.9).

This game of "musical windows" may be interesting, but what you should take away from this section—above all else—is the sense that you can administer and manage your Exchange servers from anywhere within your site. "Anywhere" means from any Exchange server or even from an NT workstation that has network connectivity to your Exchange servers, because, remember, you can install the Administrator on your NT workstation and access all the servers in your site from there.

FIGURE 13.7

Opening a new window on an Exchange server

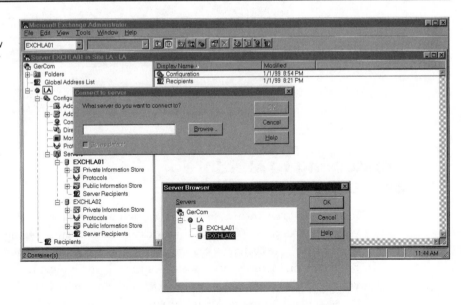

FIGURE 13.8

The Exchange Administrator with a new server window opened

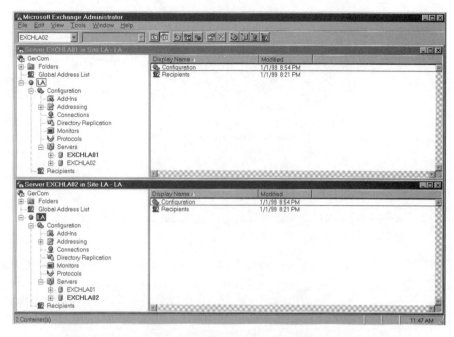

FIGURE 13.9

When a mailbox is created in the second Exchange server's window, that server is offered as the default home server.

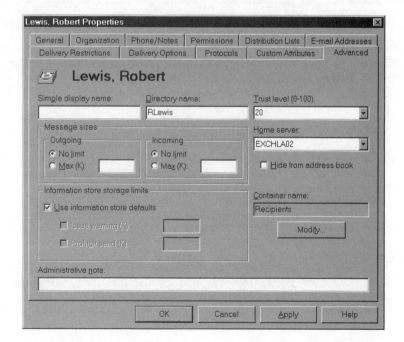

NOTE

I hope you've noticed that you didn't have to grant any special rights to your new server before you could access it with the Administrator, and that your two servers were able to talk to each other and replicate their directories without receiving such rights. That's because of three things: Both servers are in the same NT domain; the Exchange Admins group (which you created back in Chapter 7) has permissions to administer and manage all Exchange servers in the site; and, the servers share a common Site Services account. It works differently when your servers are in different domains and sites, as we'll see in the next chapter.

Navigating the Site Configuration Hierarchy

As I'm sure you realized back in Chapter 9, administering and managing Exchange servers is largely a matter of finding the correct configuration tool in the hierarchy of the Administrator window's left-hand pane. Figure 13.10 shows some of the site-relevant configuration options you have with Exchange Server.

FIGURE 13.10

Site-based configuration options displayed by Exchange Server's Administrator program

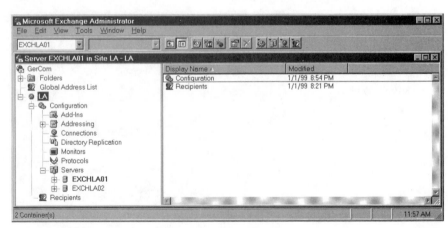

To see some configuration options, you have to select the container that holds them. For example, selecting the Configuration container shows you all the options it contains (see Figure 13.11).

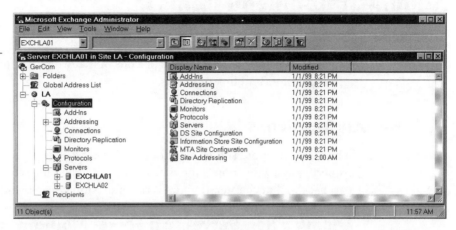

FIGURE 13.11

A closer look at the options in the Configuration container

Because some of the options in the Configuration container are suboptions—Addressing, for example—they are shown in the tree below the Configuration container (in the left-hand pane) as well as in the Configuration container (right-hand pane). Other options such as DS Site Configuration, have no suboptions, so they show up only in the Configuration container itself (in the right-hand pane).

Administering and Managing Multiserver Sites

Remember all the times we bypassed an item in the Administrator program's menus or skipped an opportunity to configure one of Exchange's core components? Well, now we can turn our attention to some of these items—the ones that are relevant to multiserver sites. We'll also look at some stuff I haven't talked about yet. When we're done here, you'll at least know what every site-relevant configuration item is all about.

> **NOTE** As in earlier chapters, when we've already beaten a particular property page to death, I'll generally bypass the page silently.

Administrator Menu Items in Multiserver Sites

Right now we need to discuss two options in the Administrator's File menu: server monitors and link monitors.

Server Monitors

When I talked about server monitors in Chapter 8, we passed over the Clock property page. Well, now's the time to get to it, using the server monitor we created back in that chapter. If yours is running, stop it by closing its window.

Adding a New Server to a Server Monitor

Before you can make use of the Clock property page, you've got to add your new server to your server monitor. So let's open the monitor now; you'll find it in the Monitors container in the left-hand pane of the Administrator window. Click on the Monitors container, double-click on your monitor to open its Properties dialog box, and then tab over to the Servers property page. Click on your new server and then click on Add to move the server to the Monitored Servers box (see Figure 13.12).

The Server Monitor's Clock Property Page

The clocks on the Exchange servers in an Exchange organization should be kept as closely synchronized as possible. Among other things, good clock synchronization means that sent and received messages will be stamped with accurate times; it also helps ensure accurate replication of directories and public folders.

A server monitor can watch the clocks of the Exchange servers that it's responsible for and keep their clocks in sync with the clock on its own server. It can even take time-zone differences into account, using NT's time-zone information.

FIGURE 13.12

Adding an Exchange server to a server monitor

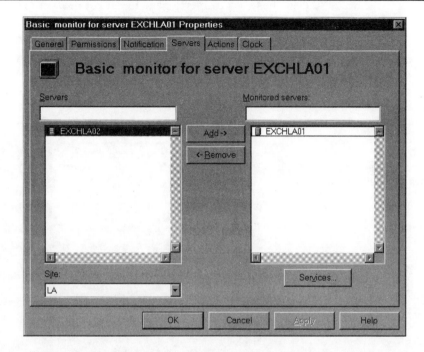

Synchronizing Lots of Clocks

As your Exchange network grows, think about running secondary or backup server monitors for redundancy. On the other hand, try not to assign clock synchronization responsibilities for the same Exchange server to too many monitors. If you do, you'll wind up with an unmanageable plate of server-monitor spaghetti.

Hey, this is starting to sound pretty complicated. The best way to get a handle on clock synchronization is to lay out a diagram on paper. You can start with those server location and connectivity diagrams from Chapter 5; they'll give you a good sense of the way your servers cluster and communicate. From there you can select your monitoring and monitored servers and determine which are the best candidates to run primary and backup monitors.

You use the Clock property page to tell your server monitor what to do if a monitored server's clock deviates from the monitoring server's clock by a specific number of seconds. As you can see in Figure 13.13, you can ask a server monitor to issue warnings and alerts at specific levels of clock deviation. You can also choose to have the monitor synchronize the errant clock with its own clock. It's usually best to select the Synchronize option for both warning and alert states.

FIGURE 13.13

Setting parameters to keep Exchange server clocks in synchronization

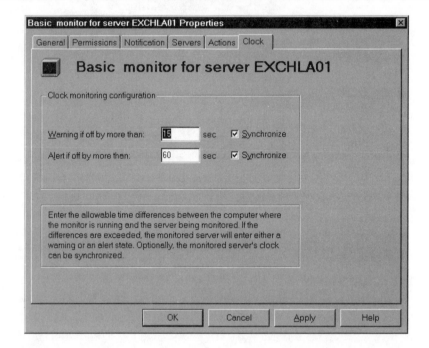

Be sure that your Clock property page looks like the one in Figure 13.13 and click on OK in the monitor's properties dialog box. Then restart your monitor by selecting Start Monitor from the Administrator's Tools menu. Your server monitor should look something like the one in Figure 13.14. This monitor has been running for about 30 minutes. Notice that the clocks on the two servers are in perfect synchronization. Though you can't see it on the monitor, they started out about 10 minutes out of sync.

FIGURE 13.14

A server monitor keeps clocks synchronized.

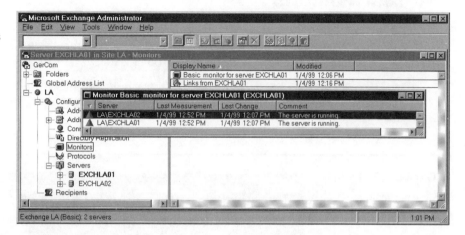

Of course, you should keep the clock on the monitor's host server synchronized with a reliable time source. You can manually keep the clock in sync with an external source, such as the time provided by your telephone company or, if you're a real stickler for accuracy, the atomic clock maintained by the United States Bureau of Standards. Alternatively, you can synchronize the clock with another server monitor whose host server's clock is in sync with an external time source.

Synchronizing Clocks to a Standard Time Source

To assure that the clocks are accurate on my clock-monitoring Exchange servers, I use the program TIMESERV.EXE that comes in the NT Resource Kit. Using NT's Command Scheduler (see Chapter 10), I schedule TIMESERV.EXE to run daily on the clock-monitoring servers and, voila, no more time-drift problems across my Exchange system. Check the Resource Kit for more info on TIMESERV.EXE.

Link Monitors

Link monitors watch connections between multiple Exchange servers as well as between Exchange servers and foreign e-messaging systems. Like server monitors, they can notify you of problems in a variety of ways.

To set up a link monitor, select Link Monitor from the New Other submenu of the Administrator's File menu. This opens the link monitor's properties dialog box (see Figure 13.15).

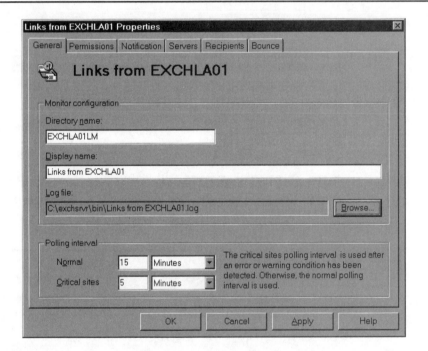

Fill in the Directory Name and Display Name fields. It took me a while to come up with a naming convention for this. Here's my logic for choosing the display name 'Links from EXCHLA01': I'll be running this monitor from the EXCHLA01 server. The monitor will check all links from EXCHLA01 to other servers and foreign e-messaging systems. For redundancy, I'll also run monitors on other servers in my LA site. The one I run on EXCHLA02 will be called 'Links from EXCHLA02.' Make sense?

Set a log file name. It's a good idea to give it the same name as the monitor itself. Then set the polling interval—that is, how frequently the monitor will check links. You can leave the default settings for now. (For more on monitor polling intervals, see Chapter 8.)

When you're done with the link monitor's General property page, tab over to the Notification page, which will look something like the one in Figure 13.16. This property page works just like the Notification page for a server monitor. Let's quickly set up a mail notification. Click on New, select Mail Message from the New Notification dialog box, and click on OK (see Figure 13.17).

FIGURE 13.16

The link monitor's Notification property page

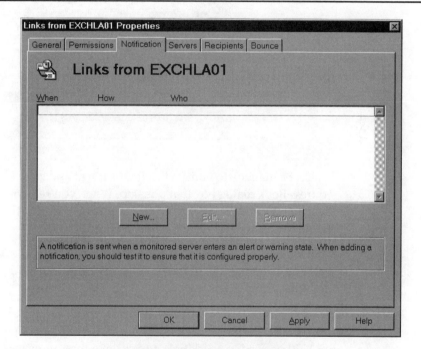

FIGURE 13.17

Selecting a notification type in the New Notification dialog box

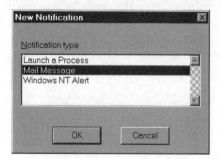

Next you'll see the Escalation Editor dialog box shown in Figure 13.18. Deselect the Alert Only check box if you want messages to be sent when the link monitor enters both warning and alert states.

FIGURE 13.18

Setting rules for escalation upon a link failure

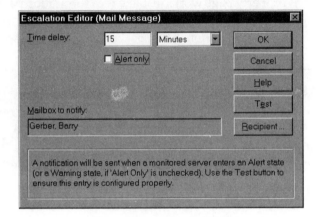

To select a mailbox to notify, click on Recipient and choose a mailbox from the Address Book dialog box that pops up. When you're done, click on OK in the Escalation Editor dialog box. At this point your Notification property page should look something like the one in Figure 13.19.

Now tab over to the Servers property page (see Figure 13.20). Highlight each server link you want monitored, then click on Add to add the server(s) to the Monitored Servers list.

Link monitors are able to automatically check connections to other Exchange servers in an Exchange organization. The Recipients property page, shown in Figure 13.21, is used to check links to foreign e-messaging systems, including other Exchange organizations. Basically, the link monitor sends a message to a valid or invalid address in the foreign system. Then it waits for an automatically generated reply from a valid recipient in the foreign system or, if the message was sent to an invalid address, for a nondelivery message from the foreign system. Either response can be taken as proof that the foreign system is up and running.

FIGURE 13.19

A completed Notification property page

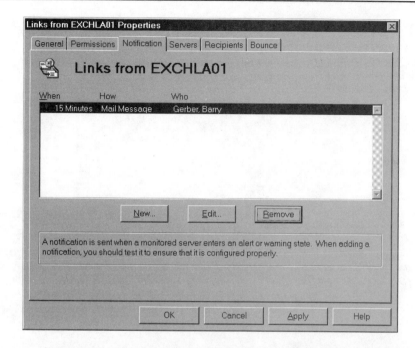

FIGURE 13.20

Selecting server links to be monitored

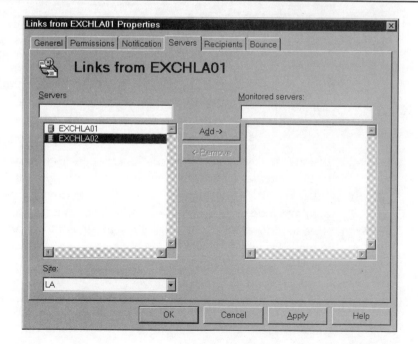

FIGURE 13.21

The Recipients property page is used to check links to foreign e-messaging systems.

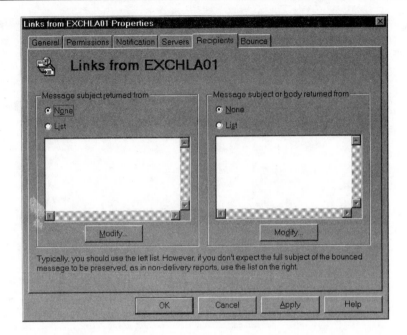

NOTE

Although the Recipients property page is intended for foreign e-messaging systems, you can test it out inside your Exchange system. Just set up a link monitor on your first server that sends a periodic link-check message to a mailbox on the new server you just installed. Then, as a client logged into the mailbox, use the Inbox Assistant to generate a blank reply to any messages from the System Attendant.

Finally, tab over to the Bounce property page (see Figure 13.22). Here you set the time interval for how long the monitor should wait before entering warning and alert states when it doesn't receive a reply from a server. You can set a link monitor's time units in seconds, minutes, and hours. Accept the defaults for now. Later, for critical links, you'll want to experiment to determine the shortest bounce-message return times you can set without causing the link monitor to generate false failed-link results.

FIGURE 13.22

The link monitor's
Bounce property page

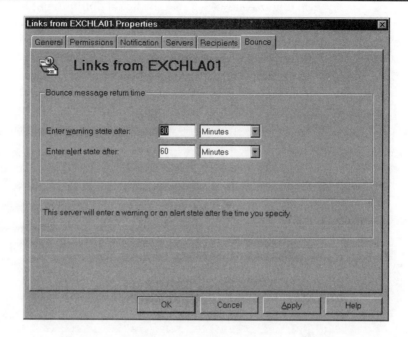

When you're done with the Bounce property page, click on OK in the link monitor's properties dialog box. The new link monitor will show up in the Monitors container for your site (see Figure 13.23). To start the new monitor, click on it, select Start Monitor from the Administrator's Tools menu, and specify the server on which to run the monitor. Within a few seconds a new window for the link monitor opens, and the monitor is up and running.

FIGURE 13.23

A new link monitor
appears in the Monitors
container and is soon
running.

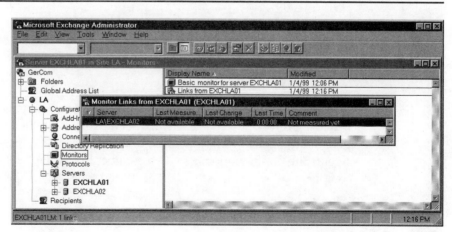

You'll notice, however, that the link monitor in Figure 13.23 shows the link to EXCHLA02 as unavailable. As noted in the Comment column, that's because the monitor hasn't even checked the link. As soon as the monitor takes its first measurement (assuming that the link is up), the monitor changes to show that the link is operational (see Figure 13.24).

FIGURE 13.24

A link monitor indicates that a server link is operating.

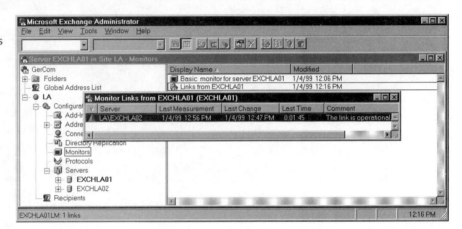

If you're an e-messaging veteran, you've got to be thinking, "Wow! Why did it take so long to come up with these sorts of goodies? The only other thing I could ask for is that the monitor tells me which component is responsible for the failed link." I agree—and I'd bet that Microsoft or third-party companies will do something about this in the not-too-distant future. For now, of course, you can always use third-party monitoring systems to deal with general network failures.

Exchange Core Components in Multiserver Sites

The Site Configuration container offers you tools for administering and managing three of the four Exchange Server core components: DS Site Configuration, Information Store Site Configuration, and the MTA (Message Transfer Agent) Site Configuration. As you remember from Chapter 9, the fourth core component, the System Attendant, is configured solely at the server level.

We covered DS Site Configuration in its entirety in Chapter 9—remember all that stuff about offline address books and custom attributes? We'll talk a bit more about Information Store Site Configuration in the next chapter. And although we bypassed MTA Site Configuration in Chapter 9, we're ready for most of it now.

As you'll remember from Chapter 9, some site-relevant administration and management of Exchange Server's core components is done at the server level. We finished with the private information store and the System Attendant back in Chapter 9. We'll cover server-level Directory Service and MTA administration and management here.

Because you can replicate public folders across Exchange servers in a site, we could also get into server-level public information store administration and management in this chapter. However, I want to wait until the next chapter, where I'll be able to talk about both intrasite and intersite folder replication.

Whew! Got all that? Let's go.

Administering and Managing the DS in Multiserver Sites

Because we've already covered site-level directory service (DS) administration and management, we'll focus on the server level here.

Server-Level DS Administration and Management in Multiserver Sites

As you'll remember, the directory is a site-based database that holds detailed information about all Exchange Server recipients. The directory is automatically replicated between all the servers in a site.

There's very little we need to deal with here. Figure 13.25 shows the properties dialog box for server-level administration and management of the directory service. You use the General property page to force intrasite directory replication and to ensure that the information required to carry off directory replication is in order.

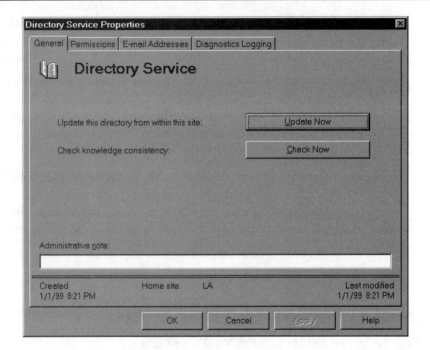

FIGURE 13.25

The directory services properties dialog box

Through automatic directory replication, each server in a site has a copy of the directory for the site—not just for its own directory objects. Generally, automatic directory replication keeps directory copies on all servers in sync. When you add a new server to a site or recover a server from a backup, you can force a replication update for your default server by clicking on the Update Now button on the directory service's General property page.

Normally, a server checks once a day to see if its knowledge about new servers that have come online is consistent with reality. If new servers are found, automatic replication starts between existing servers and the new servers. You can force this process by clicking on the Check Now button on the directory service's General property page. As with the Update Now button, you'll find the Check Now button most useful when a new server is added to a site or when a server is restored from a backup.

We won't get into the details of the other three property pages on the directory service's properties dialog box—Permissions, E-mail Addresses, and Diagnostics Logging—because they should already be quite familiar to you at this point.

Administering and Managing the MTA in Multiserver Sites

The MTA is primarily responsible for routing messages to other Exchange servers and—with help from various connectors and gateways—to foreign e-messaging systems. The MTA also converts messages to and from X.400 format. It has little to do with messaging between recipients on a single server.

First, let's focus on site-level tools for MTA administration and management. Then we'll deal with the server-level tools.

Site-Level MTA Administration and Management in Multiserver Sites

Among other things, you use the MTA Site Configuration properties page to enable message tracking and to set a number of key parameters that govern the behavior of MTAs in the site. Click on the Configuration container in the left-hand pane of an Exchange Administrator window, then double-click on MTA Site Configuration in the right-hand pane. This opens the MTA Site Configuration properties dialog box (see Figure 13.26).

General Properties

If the 'Enable message tracking' box is checked, a daily log file will be created and the MTA will log all of its message transactions to the file. As with log files for the information store (which we covered in an earlier chapter), the MTA's log files are used by Exchange Server's Message Tracking Center to help you ride herd on stray messages. As with the information store, I strongly suggest that you enable MTA message tracking right now.

Messaging Defaults

Messaging defaults define and control communications for the MTAs on a site's servers. As you can see in Figure 13.27, the Messaging Defaults property page is loaded with options. Generally, you can accept the default values you see when you tab over to the page. As you work with your Exchange servers and their links to each other and to the outside world, you'll come up with your own values for some or all of the parameters.

FIGURE 13.26

Setting sitewide parameters for Message Transfer Agents

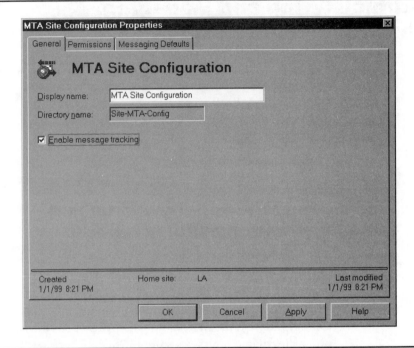

FIGURE 13.27

Setting sitewide default parameters for extra-server MTA message transfers

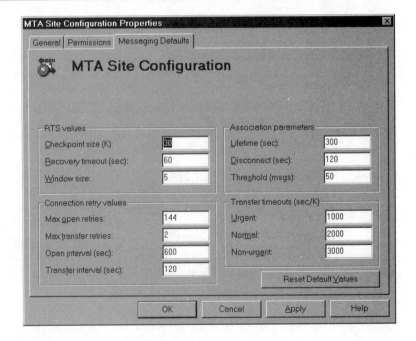

Here's a quick overview of the options on the Messaging Defaults property page.

RTS Values   *RTS* stands for "Request to Send." It's part of the Open Systems Interface spec for electronic mail, which is based on CCITT X.400 mail recommendations. RTS is responsible for preventing the loss of mail sent between two MTAs, even in the face of repeated connection crashes.

- *Checkpoint size (K)*: Checking if a message has been received correctly at given points in the transmission—say, after the transmission of each 30K—eliminates the need to resend the whole message in case of a crash; upon reconnection, sending can begin just after the last successful checkpoint.

- *Recovery timeout (sec)*: If restarting a connection takes more than this number of seconds, checkpoint information is deleted and the entire message is sent again.

- *Window size*: This is the number of checkpoints (also called *window slides*) that are sent before the server hears from the receiving side. For best performance, the more window slides sent the better; increase or decrease the window size until an optimum is reached.

Connection Retry Values

- *Max open retries*: This is the number of times an MTA attempts to open a connection to another system before it tries to find another route for the message. If the MTA can't locate an alternate route, the message is returned to the sender.

- *Max transfer retries*: This is the number of times an MTA attempts to send a message when it has actually established a connection to another system before attempting to reroute the message. If the MTA can't locate another route, the message is returned as undeliverable.

- *Open interval (sec)*: This is the time interval in seconds that the MTA waits before attempting another connection to a system when the last attempt failed.

- *Transfer interval (sec)*: This is the time interval in seconds that the MTA waits to resend a message once a connection is open.

Association Parameters   An *association* is created when an MTA opens a connection to another system. While the association is open, the MTA can send any number of messages destined for the other system. Once the association is closed, another one must be opened before new messages can be sent.

- *Lifetime (sec)*: This is the time interval in seconds that an association remains open if there is no activity on the association (connection).

- *Disconnect (sec)*: If an MTA sends a disconnect request to a remote system and gets no response, the MTA waits this number of seconds before terminating associations and the connection on its side.

- *Threshold (msgs)*: When the number of messages queued for another system exceeds this threshold, the MTA opens another association and sends multiple streams of messages to the system to speed up message transmission. Whatever the value set for this parameter, the MTA automatically opens additional associations for messages marked by their senders as "high priority."

Transfer Timeouts (sec/K)   Each Exchange message has an importance (priority) level of high, normal, or low that is set when the message is composed. The default importance level is Normal. The values assigned to Urgent, Normal, and Non-urgent determine the total amount of time that can pass before the MTA gives up and returns the message as undeliverable.

That's it for site-level MTA administration and management.

Server-Level MTA Administration and Management in Multiserver Sites

To get to the MTA properties dialog box for a server, find the server's name in the left-hand pane of an Exchange Administrator window and click on it. (You may have to double-click on the Servers container in the pane to see the specific servers in it.) Next, double-click on Message Transfer Agent in the right-hand pane of the window. The properties dialog box for the MTA pops up (see Figure 13.28).

As we move through the property pages for the MTA, don't change anything. This will be a hands-off sightseeing trip.

FIGURE 13.28

The Server-Level Message Transfer Agent Properties dialog box

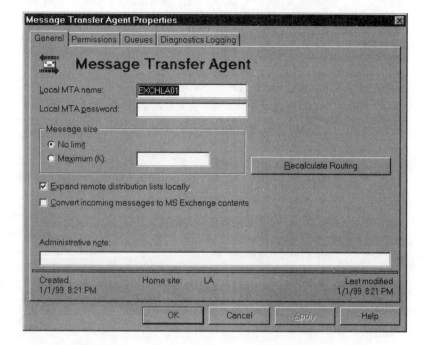

General Properties

You use the General properties page for the MTA, as shown in Figure 13.28, to set a variety of parameters.

Local Name and Password The local name is used to identify the MTA to foreign e-messaging systems. The password is used by foreign e-messaging systems when they connect to the MTA.

Maximum Message Size If you've set a maximum message size, the MTA returns any messages larger than the maximum to the sender. This maximum applies to both outgoing and incoming messages.

Recalculate Routing Remember that the MTA is responsible for keeping the message routing table up-to-date. Whenever you do something that might change a routing table (such as adding a gateway or reconfiguring a connector), you're asked whether you want to rebuild the table. You can do this immediately or, since rebuilds take at least a few minutes, wait until you're all done reconfiguring and then rebuild it manually. To do this, click on Recalculate Routing.

Expand Remote   Distribution Lists LocallyA remote distribution list is one that is created in one site and made available to other sites by way of directory replication. When a message is sent using any distribution list, the list has to be expanded—that is, the addresses of its individual members must be found—before the message can be sent to list members. Messages using remote distribution lists can be expanded at the local site or sent to the remote site for expansion.

Local expansion is more efficient if you have a lot of distribution lists that include members from different sites. When a list is expanded locally, the message is delivered to local members immediately, and a single copy of the message—along with a list of recipients—is sent to each site with list members.

Convert Incoming Messages to MS Exchange Contents   When the 'Convert incoming messages to MS Exchange contents' option is selected, the MTA converts messages in X.400 format to Exchange's MAPI format.

Queues

An Exchange server sets up a different queue for each server in a site, as well as queues for connectors and gateways. You can view messages in queues and manage them from the Queues property page. Tab over to the Queues property page (see Figure 13.29) and open up the Queue Name drop-down list to see which queues your server's MTA supports. In addition to the private and public information stores, at the very least you'll see your other Exchange server.

When a queue has messages, you can get detailed information on them (select the message and click on Details); change the priority of messages in the queue to reorganize the order in which the MTA will send them (select the message and click on Priority); and delete messages (select the message and click on Delete).

FIGURE 13.29

Managing MTA queues using the Queues property page

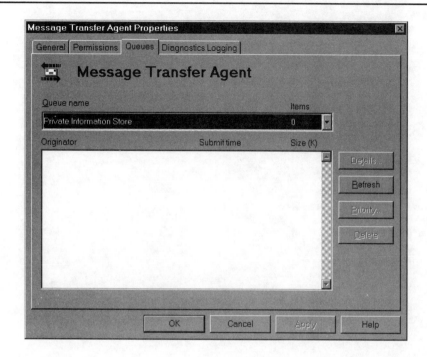

Conclusion

In this chapter you installed an additional Exchange server in an Exchange site. You then learned how to use the Exchange Administrator program to administer and manage multiserver sites—including building multiserver server and link monitors, as well as administering and managing the directory service (at the server level) and the MTA (at both the site and server levels).

Now let's hurry on to the next chapter, where we'll work with multisite Exchange organizations.

Administering and Managing Multisite Exchange Organizations

- ■ Installing an Exchange server in a new domain and site

- ■ Connecting domains and sites

- ■ Setting up directory replication between two sites

- ■ Adding servers to server and link monitors

- ■ Giving users access to public folders stored in other sites

- ■ Using tools for administering and managing intersite routing

Now that you know how to install and deal with new Exchange servers in a site, you're ready to tackle something new: the installation, administration, and management of new sites in an Exchange organization. There's lots to do, and this is a long chapter. Take it in small, easy bites and keep your seat belts fastened.

Installing an Exchange Server in a New Site

Back in Chapters 6 and 7, you already did almost everything you need to do to establish a new server in new site. So I'm going to take you through the steps very quickly, adding anything you need to do to make your multisite Exchange system work.

Installing an NT Server in a New Domain

In this section we'll get a new NT server up and running in a new Windows NT domain. Then we'll set up some trusts that let one domain's resources (such as Exchange servers) interact freely with resources in our other domain. Finally, we'll establish some permissions that let NT administrators in each of our two domains administer and manage users, groups, and so forth, in the other domain.

Installing the NT Server

You'll install this NT server just as you installed the one in Chapter 6. Remember to create a new domain for the server (mine will be 'NY', for GerCom's New York City offices). Go to it! I'll see you in the next section, after you've finished installing your new NT server.

Setting Up Cross-Domain Trusts

Since your new NT server is in a different domain from your old server, you must set up trust relationships between your two domains for Exchange to work properly. Cross-domain trusts also let users in your two domains share resources. And, with the addition of some cross-domain permissions, you'll be able to administer and manage your first domain from your second domain, and vice versa.

In the following two subsections, I'll show you how to set up cross-domain trusts. Then, in the next section, I'll help you establish cross-domain administrative permissions.

You'll be physically switching back and forth between your two domains a couple of times in this section, so work with care here. Of course, if your domains are separated by miles, rather than steps, you'll have to work cooperatively with someone in the other domain.

Setting Up Trust Permissions in Each Domain   Let's start in the first domain you created (mine is LA, remember?). Log in to the domain as Administrator. Then, from an NT server or workstation in the domain, open the User Manager for Domains, which is in the Administrative Tools program group. From the program's Policies menu, select Trust Relationships. The Trust Relationships dialog box pops open (see Figure 14.1).

FIGURE 14.1

The NT Server Trust
Relationships dialog box

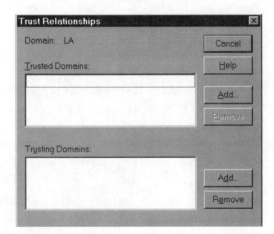

First we need to let your new domain trust your first domain. So click on Add for the 'Trusting Domains' box. This pops up the Add Trusting Domain dialog box shown in Figure 14.2.

FIGURE 14.2

Allowing one domain to
trust another

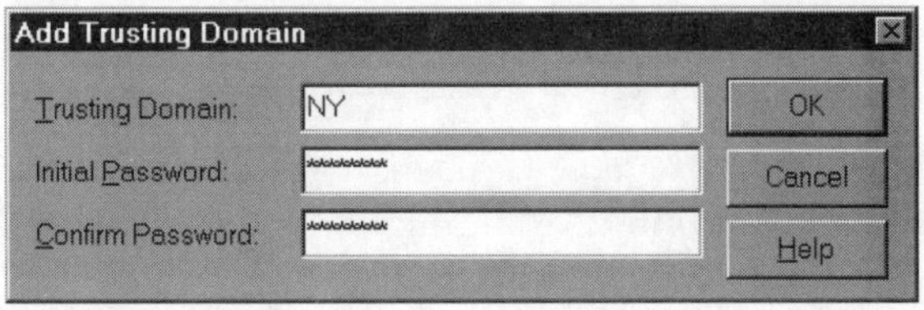

Enter the name of your new domain (mine is NY). Then type in the password that the new domain must give when setting up a trust relationship with your first domain. Type in the password again to confirm, then click on OK. Be sure to write down the password, unless it's one you can easily remember. Leave the User Manager's Trust Relationships dialog box open.

Now you need to work in your new domain. So, while logged in to your new domain as Administrator, open the User Manager for Domains. At this point, it's probably easiest to run the User Manager from your new NT server, though you could run it from a workstation in your new domain (if you've installed one). Once the program is running, do exactly what you just did for your first domain, but enter the name of the first domain here, to give it permission to trust your new domain. (For example, I'd enter "LA".) You can enter the same or a different password. Click on OK when you're done, and leave the Trust Relationships dialog box open.

Adding Trusted Domains   At this point we need to add the trusted domains on each side. So go back to the User Manager for your first domain. In the Trust Relationships dialog box (Figure 14.1) click on the uppermost Add button; the one for Trusted Domains. The Add Trusted Domain dialog box opens (see Figure 14.3).

FIGURE 14.3

Adding a trusted domain

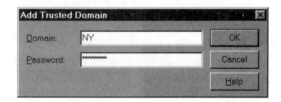

Enter the name of your new domain and the password you set for it in the last step, then click on OK. After a bit, you should see a message telling you that the trust relationship has been established, and the Trust Relationships dialog box should look something like the one shown in Figure 14.4.

NOTE   The domain name is the same in both boxes. This makes sense since you've given your new domain the rights to trust your first domain, and you want your first domain to trust the new domain. (I won't hold it against you if you go back and reread the last two sentences.)

FIGURE 14.4

One side of a cross-domain trust relationship is established.

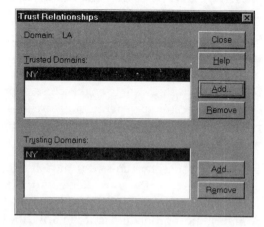

If you have any problems, repeat the process outlined above. Be sure you're logged in to both domains as Administrator and that you enter the correct domain name and password. If that doesn't work, make sure that your network is running properly and that your NT servers are communicating with each other. When everything is the way it should be, click on Close in the Trust Relationships dialog box for your first domain.

Now you've got to set the trusted domain for your new domain. Go back to the User Manager for your new domain and do the same thing you just did in your first domain, substituting the name of your first domain. When you're all done, the Trust Relationships dialog box should look like the one in Figure 14.5, except that the name of your first domain should appear in both boxes. When everything is okay, click on Close in the Trust Relationships dialog box and you're done.

FIGURE 14.5

The other side of a cross-domain trust relationship is established.

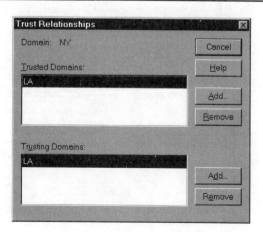

Setting Cross-Domain Administrative Permissions

You can remotely administer one domain from another. This lets you create new users, groups, and so on, for the second domain from the comfort of your first-domain easy chair. You don't *have* to do this, and in some cases for security reasons, you won't want to enable cross-domain NT administrative rights. However, in most cases such permissions are most welcome, because they not only make administration easier, they also let administrators at different locations help each other out remotely.

Here's how to set up cross-domain NT administrative permissions. If it's not already open, open the User Manager for Domains on a workstation or server in your first domain (again, mine is LA). In the Groups pane of the window, find the Administrators group; in Figure 14.6, it's the second group.

The Administrators group is created by default when NT is installed. It has full rights to administer and manage users, groups, and the like in a domain. Any

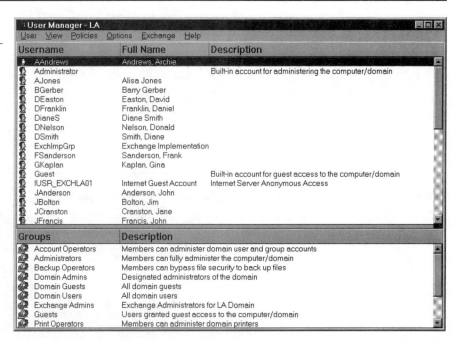

FIGURE 14.6

Locating the Administrators group in the User Manager for Domains user or group added to this group gets full administrative rights for the domain. The user 'Administrator' becomes a member of this group when NT is installed.

> **NOTE**
> If you had added your NT account to the Administrators group, you could be doing all of the cross-domain trust setup while logged in to that account instead of the Administrator account. But be careful here: you may not want to do this, because when you do, anyone who gains access to your account has full administrative rights.

> **NOTE**
> If you do add your account to the Administrators group, be sure to take precautions to keep others out of your account. For example, when logged in with your own account, always lock your NT workstation when you go away from your computer. To do that, simultaneously press the Ctrl, Alt, and Delete keys and then select Lock Workstation from the resultant Windows NT Security dialog box. To unlock your workstation, enter your password. Heck, it's OK with me if you lock your workstation even if your account isn't in the Administrator's group.

We need to add the Administrator account from our new domain to the Administrators group for our first domain, and vice versa. As we proceed, follow along using the figures as a guide. Double-click on the Administrators group, or select it and then click on Properties from the User Manager's User menu. This opens the Local Group Properties dialog box (see Figure 14.7). (For more on NT's local and global groups, see *Mastering Windows NT Server 4*, by Mark Minasi, Christa Anderson, and Elizabeth Creegan (Sybex, 1996).) Click on Add in the Local Group Properties dialog box to open the Add Users and Groups dialog box shown in Figure 14.7. Then click open the List Names From drop-down list and select the name of your new domain (mine is NY).

After a bit of churning, the Add Users and Groups dialog box will list the users and groups in your second domain (see Figure 14.8). Select the user 'Administrator' and click on Add; the Administrator user will appear in the Add Names pane at the bottom of the Add Users and Groups dialog box. Click on OK to add the Administrator user from your new domain to the Administrators group in your first domain (see Figure 14.9).

FIGURE 14.7

Selecting the domain whose Administrator account will have cross-domain administrative permissions

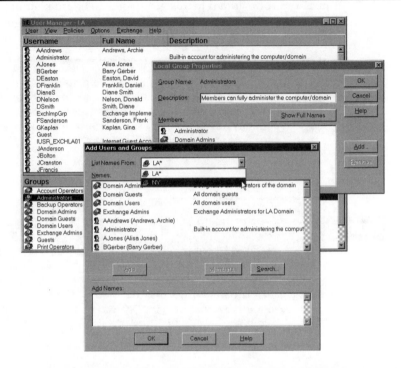

FIGURE 14.8

Giving permission to the NY domain administrator to administer and manage the LA domain

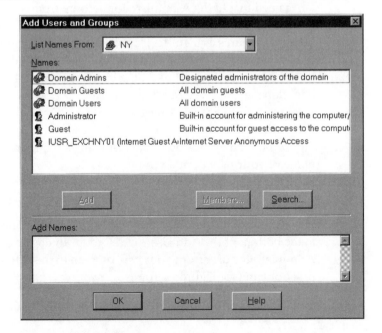

FIGURE 14.9

The NY Administrator has permission to administer and manage the LA domain.

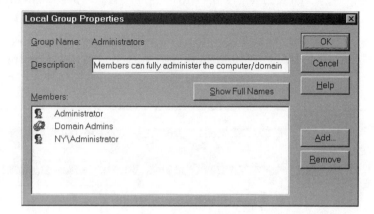

That's it for one side of the cross-domain relationship. Now you need to go to your new domain, run the User Manager for Domains, and repeat the steps above. When you're done, the Administrator in one domain will be able to remotely administer and manage the other domain, and vice versa. If you want to give any other users cross-domain rights, just add them as we did above.

Installing an Exchange Server in a New Site

In this section we'll get a new Exchange server up and running and set up cross-site permissions that let you administer each site from the other. After we get these permissions in place, we'll be able to link the servers so that they can replicate directories and public folders.

Installing the Exchange Server

You can go ahead and do your new Exchange site/server installation just as you did your first one back in Chapter 7. Just be sure your organization and site names are set correctly (mine are GerCom and NY). And be sure to set up an Exchange Server administration group for your site, just as you did the first time in Chapter 7; for ease of administration later on, I suggest that you give your new group the same name as your first Exchange Server administration group. (Remember, I suggested the name 'Exchange Admins.') And don't forget to assign this group the role Permissions Admin for both the site and Configuration container; check back to Chapter 7 if you need help doing this. When you're done with the installation, we can rendezvous in the next paragraph.

All done? Good. Just to make sure everything worked properly, open the Exchange Administrator program on the new Exchange server in your new site. It should look something like mine, which is shown in Figure 14.10.

FIGURE 14.10

A new Exchange site as viewed from the Administrator program

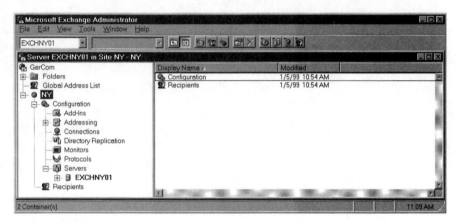

Setting Up Required Cross-Site Permissions

We're now ready to link our two sites. First, however, we have to set up some cross-site permissions. These are the basic permissions you need for cross-site administration and management.

To begin, open the Exchange Administrator in your first site; select your site name—LA in my case—by clicking on it (see Figure 14.11). Next, select Properties from the Administrator's File menu to bring up a properties dialog box for the site. Tab over to the Permissions property page (see Figure 14.12).

FIGURE 14.11

Selecting the site name

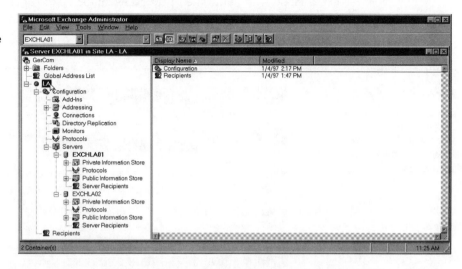

FIGURE 14.12

The Permissions page of the site's properties dialog box

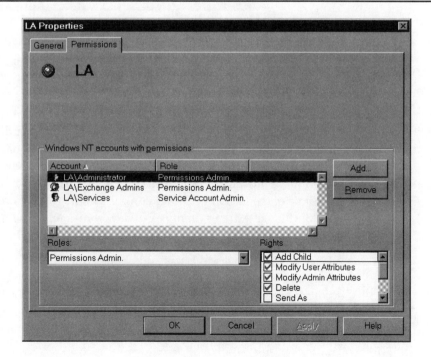

Next, click on Add in the site's properties dialog box to open the Add Users and Groups dialog box (see Figure 14.13). Select your other domain—mine is NY—from the List Names From drop-down list.

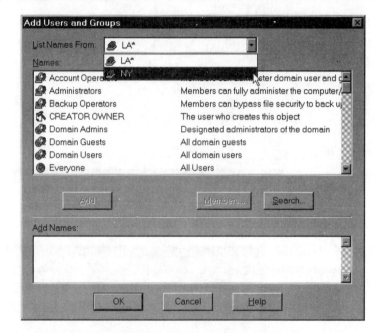

Now you should see the users and groups in your other domain (see Figure 14.14). Select Exchange Admins (or whatever you named your Exchange Server administration group when you installed your new NT and Exchange servers just a bit ago) and click on Add in the Add Users and Groups dialog box. The name of the Exchange Server administration group in your other site ('NY\Exchange Admins' in my case) now shows up in the Add Names pane at the bottom of the Add Users and Groups dialog box (see Figure 14.15).

Click on OK in the Add Users and Groups dialog box. The Exchange Server administration group from your other site now appears in the Windows NT accounts with the Permissions box. Change the group's role from the default 'Admin' to 'Permissions Admin' so that it can fully administer this site (see Figure 14.16). Finally, click on OK in the properties dialog box for your site.

FIGURE 14.14

Finding the Exchange Server administration group from another site that will have administrative permissions in this site

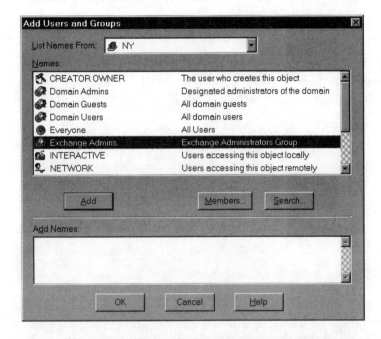

FIGURE 14.15

Giving the Exchange Server administration group from another site administrative permissions in this site

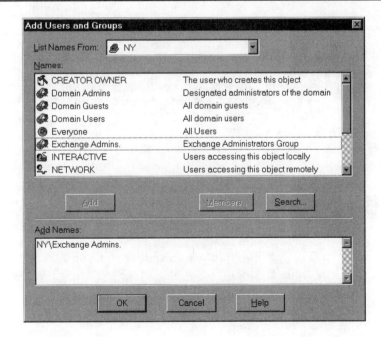

FIGURE 14.16

The Exchange Server administration group from another site is given administrative permissions in this site.

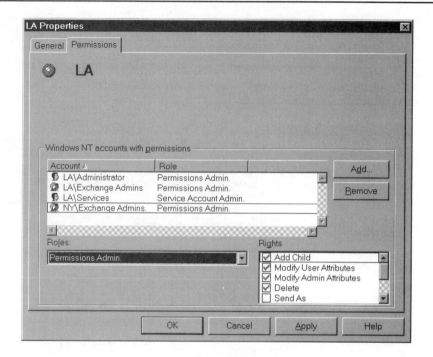

NOTE

There's nothing magic about your Exchange Server administration group. You can create other groups or assign permissions to any existing NT account or group. I'm using the Exchange Admins group because it contains the users whom I trust to administer across these two sites.

WARNING

You're not finished yet. Now you need to go to your new Exchange site and give the same site-level permissions to the Exchange Server administration group in your first site. This is exactly what you just did—only this time you'll do it from your new site, and you'll give permissions to the first site's administration group.

You're still not finished. Now you need to add some permissions at the Configuration container level. Because you're fresh from adding permissions, I'll just give you general directions for completing this task.

Select the Configuration container in your first site by clicking on it, and then select Properties from the Administrator's File menu. Next, tab over to the Permissions property page in the resultant Configuration Properties dialog box. Add the Exchange administration group (probably called 'Exchange Admins') from your other site and assign it the role Permissions Admin. Then add the Site Services account (probably called 'Services') from your other site and assign it the role Service Account Admin.

When you're done, your Configuration dialog box's Permissions property page should look something like the one in Figure 14.17.

You're almost done—but not quite. Now you've got to repeat the tasks outlined above for your other site. Go to it!

FIGURE 14.17

The Configuration dialog box's Permissions property page with cross-site permissions properly set

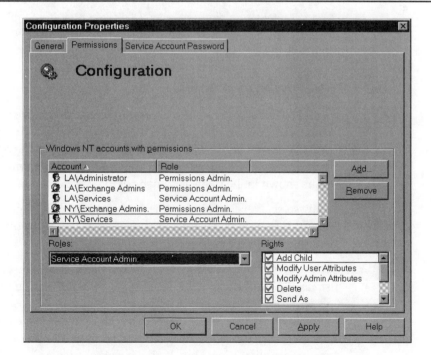

Setting Up a Site-to-Site Link

Exchange sites, as you'll recall from Chapter 3, are linked by connectors; they're also linked in pairs. You set up a connector in each of two sites and configure them to talk to each other. If you have multiple sites, you need one pair of communicating connectors for every pair of sites you want to link. Connectors carry information about user communications, directory replication, and public folder replication between sites in the form of messages.

Now we're ready to set up our first site connection. We'll use the Exchange Site Connector. It's going to be quite easy for two reasons: the Site Connector is the simplest of the Exchange site connectors to implement, and we've set up the proper cross-site permissions.

> **NOTE**
>
> From here on, I'll use the term *site connector* to refer to site connectors in general and *Site Connector* to refer to the specific connector we're about to install. It would have been better if Microsoft had given the Site Connector a different name to distinguish it from the collective group of site connectors. That didn't happen, hence my naming conventions.

Setting Up the First Site

You can begin setting up a Site Connector from either of the two sites you're going to connect. Let's start in your first site. Open the Exchange Administrator, then select the Connections container (see Figure 14.18). Depending on the options you chose when installing the two Exchange servers in your first site, you may not see all of the connectors shown in the right-hand pane of the Administrator window in Figure 14.18.

Now select New Other from the Administrator's File menu, then select Site Connector from the New Other submenu (see Figure 14.19). This brings up the New Site Connector dialog box.

In the New Site Connector dialog box, type in the name of the new server you just installed and click on OK (see Figure 14.20). The Exchange Administrator now looks for this site. When it finds the site, the Administrator checks to see if you have the proper cross-site permissions. The cross-site rights you just granted to the Exchange Admins group and the Services account in each of your two NT domains are what's key here. If all the rights are in order, Administrator opens the Site Connector Properties dialog box shown in Figure 14.21. This is a Site Connector from your first site to your second site. The Site Connector is for the second site—hence its default name ('Site Connector (NY)' in my case).

FIGURE 14.18

The Connections container is selected.

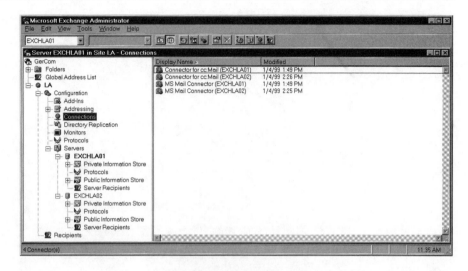

FIGURE 14.19

Selecting Site Connector on the New Other submenu

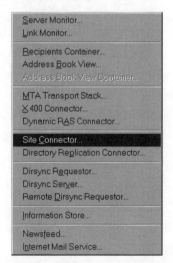

FIGURE 14.20

Specifying a server in the site to which to connect

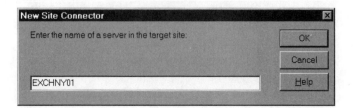

FIGURE 14.21

The Site Connector Properties dialog box

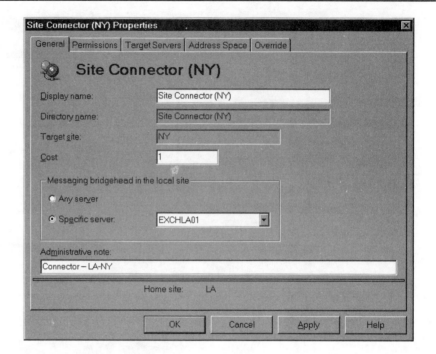

> **NOTE**
>
> If you're told that you don't have permission to contact the other site, be sure that the NT user account you're working from in your first site is a member of the Exchange Server administration group (probably Exchange Admins) for your first site.

General Properties

Accept the default display and directory names in the Site Connector Properties dialog box. (The target site will be automatically chosen for you; it's NY in Figure 14.21.) Cost is a number from 1 to 100 that's used when you're running more than one connector to a site. When messages need to be sent between sites, the available site connector with the lowest cost is used. This is very useful if, for example, you have a fast link like the Site Connector running as your primary connection and a slower link such as the Dynamic Remote Access Service

Connector (DRASC) running as a backup. When setting up the DRASC, give it a higher cost number than the Site Connector's; that way, messages will always be sent between your sites using the Site Connector except when it is down.

The 'Messaging bridgehead in the local site' option defaults to any server, meaning that any server in the local site can send messages to the other site. If you choose a specific server, as I have in Figure 14.21, then only that server can send messages to the other site. All other servers in the site must send messages to the bridgehead server, which then sends out all messages over its Site Connector.

A bridgehead server can help reduce network traffic a bit when your two sites are connected by a wide area network. This is so because with a bridgehead server only one Exchange server needs to open and maintain communications sessions across the WAN. And because the Message Transfer Agents (MTAs) on servers other than the bridgehead server don't have to transfer messages between sites, you'll save a little processing power on those servers.

The administrative note I entered in Figure 14.21 helps me remember the direction of the connection—from LA to NY.

Target Servers

The Target Servers property page is shown in Figure 14.22. 'Target servers' are the servers in the remote site that will handle messages sent from this site to the remote site. By default the name of the server you typed in the New Site Connector dialog box (shown in Figure 14.20) is selected as a target server. If other servers are listed in the Site Servers box on the left-hand side of the Target Servers property page, you can add one of these to the Target Servers box (on the right-hand side of the property page) by selecting it and clicking on Add. To delete a server from the right-hand Target Servers box, select it and click on Remove.

'Target server costs' are used by servers in the local site to determine which target server to communicate with. As with the Site Connector cost parameter on the General property page, target server costs can range from 1 to 100, and you can set a different cost for each target server. You use target server costs to control message transfer loads—giving higher costs to target servers that you want to receive messages less frequently. To set a cost parameter for a specific target server, select the server by clicking on it, enter a value in the 'Target server cost' field, and click on the Set Value button. When messages are transmitted, target servers with higher costs will have messages sent to them only when servers that have lower costs associated with them are unavailable.

FIGURE 14.22

Selecting target servers
for a Site Connector

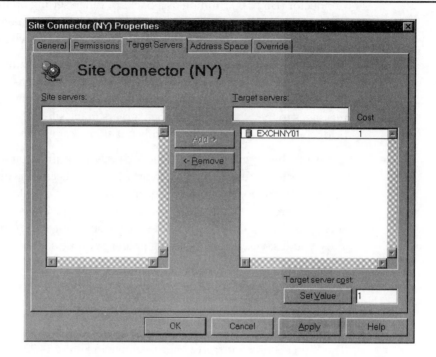

Address Space

You use 'address spaces' to direct messages with specific addresses to and
through Exchange connectors, for connections between Exchange servers, and
for connections between Exchange servers and foreign e-messaging systems. For
now, you don't have to worry about address spaces. The Exchange Administrator creates one default X.400 address space that is sufficient to move all messages
in and out of the site you're working in (see Figure 14.23). Notice that the X.400
address covers my entire NY site, GerCom NY.

Override

If you can establish cross-domain trusts and the specific Exchange Server permissions we set up above, you won't need to use the Override property page (see
Figure 14.24). However, for political or other reasons, this sometimes isn't possible. In such cases, you can use the Override page to provide the security information required to create and operate a Site Connector.

FIGURE 14.23

The Address Space property page with its default X.400 address

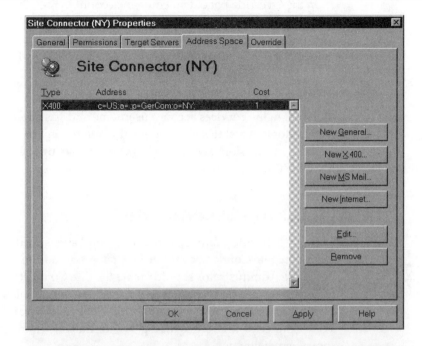

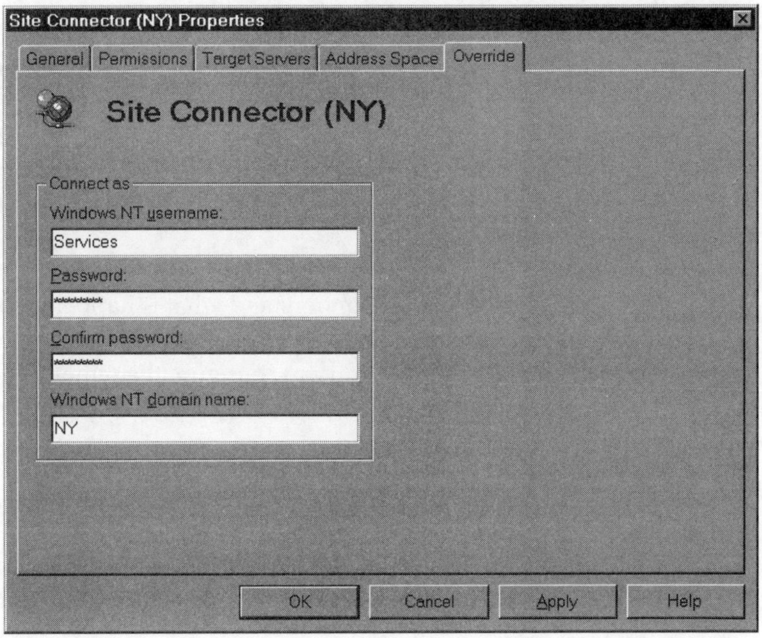

FIGURE 14.24

The Override property page is used when cross-domain trusts and liberal Exchange Server permissions can't be set.

On the Override page, you enter an account in the other site, along with its password and the name of the domain where the other site resides. To avoid permissions problems, use the Exchange Site Services account for the other site (named 'Services', if you used the naming conventions I suggested). Of course, your counterpart in the other site has to do the same thing using your Site Services account name, password, and domain name.

I typed in the Services account username and password as well as the name of my NY domain just to show you what would go in this space, if I didn't have the required permissions set up. Unless you can't set up these permissions, you can leave the Override property page blank.

Setting Up the Second Site

Setting up the Site Connector in your second site is really easy. After you click on OK on the Site Connector Properties dialog box, a little box pops up and asks you if the Administrator should create the Site Connector in your remote (second) site (see Figure 14.25). If you click on Yes—which you should—the Site Connector for the second site is created automatically, and you're presented with a Site Connector Properties dialog box for that site (mine is NY). Figure 14.26 shows the dialog box.

FIGURE 14.25

A chance to create the Site Connector for the second site

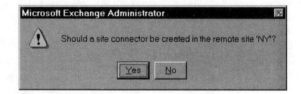

Now, make sure you understand what is happening here. You're still using the Exchange Administrator in your first site. Because of the permissions you set up earlier in this chapter, you can configure the remote site connector without changing servers or doing anything other than answering Yes when presented with that little box in Figure 14.25.

General Properties

Look closely at Figure 14.26, which shows a site connector to your first site from your second site. The name of my connector is 'Site Connector (LA)', and it has been created in my NY site. That's why when I pick a specific bridgehead server, I'm offered EXCHNY01. You'll also notice that the administrative note I entered recognizes that this is the NY-to-LA connector.

FIGURE 14.26

The Site Connector Properties dialog box for the second or remote site

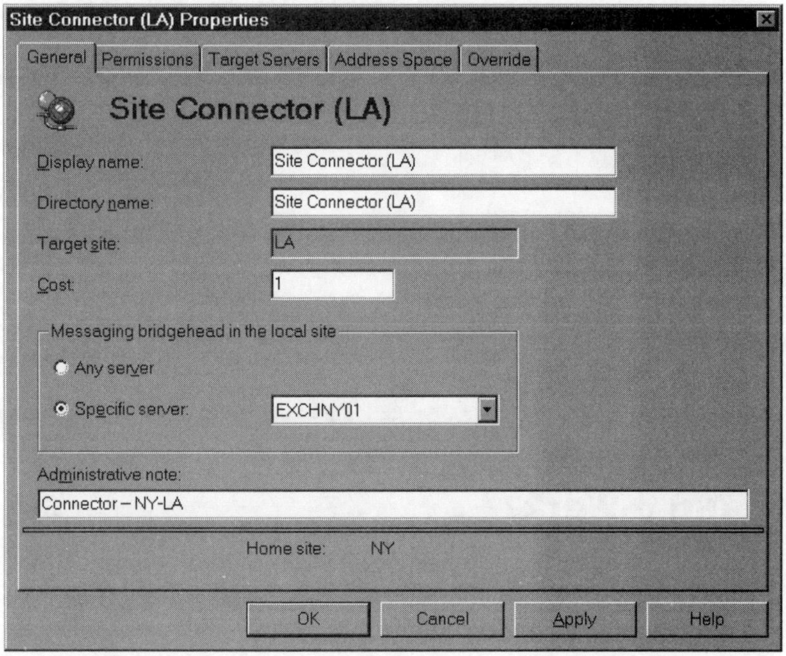

Target Servers

Because we have two servers in our first site and because we want only one (EXCHLA01 in my case) to be the bridgehead server, we need to be sure that the other server is not in the Target Servers box on the right, since we don't want our NY bridgehead to contact it. If it does appear in the Target Servers box, select it and click on Remove. In Figure 14.27, I'm about to remove my second LA server, EXCHLA02, from the Target Servers list.

When you're finished, click on OK in the Site Connector Properties dialog box and you're done. Your sites are now connected and talking to each other at a basic level.

FIGURE 14.27

Removing a server from the Target Servers list

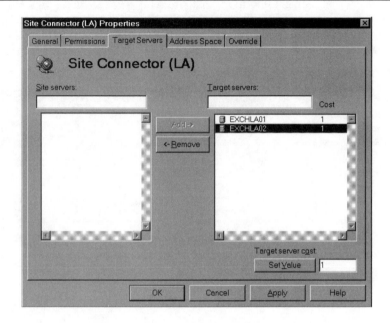

Did It Work?

You should now see the Site Connector to your second site in the Connections container for your first site (see Figure 14.28). And you—or whoever is stationed at your second site—should see the Site Connector to your first site in the Connections container for your second site (see Figure 14.29).

FIGURE 14.28

The Site Connector from the first site to the second site

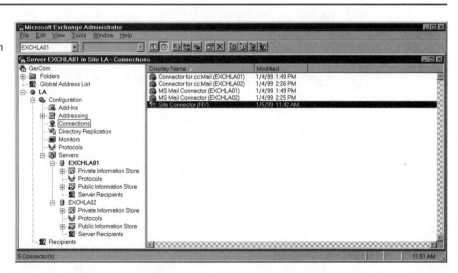

FIGURE 14.29

The Site Connector from the second site to the first site

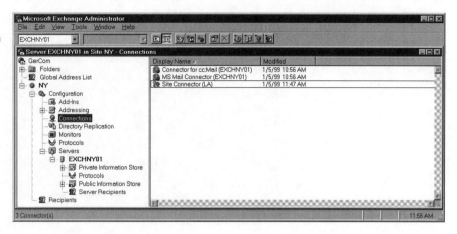

Setting Up Directory Replication between Sites

Okay, our two sites are connected for messaging. Now we need to set up directory replication between them.

Setting Up Directory Replication in the First Site

From the Exchange Administrator, select the Directory Replication container for your first site. Then select the Directory Replication Connector item from the New Other submenu in the Administrator's File menu (see Figure 14.19). This brings up the New Directory Replication Connector dialog box shown in Figure 14.30. We're setting a Directory Replication Connector from our first site (mine's LA) to our second site (mine's NY).

Make sure the name in the 'Remote site name' field is correct and enter the name of a server in the site. Because the site is available on the same network, be sure to select the 'Yes, the remote site is available on this network' option. And, of course, let the Administrator configure replication on both sides. When you're done, click on OK.

Next you'll see the Directory Replication Connector Properties dialog box shown in Figure 14.31. We need to look only at the General and Schedule property pages right now.

FIGURE 14.30

The New Directory
Replication Connector
dialog box

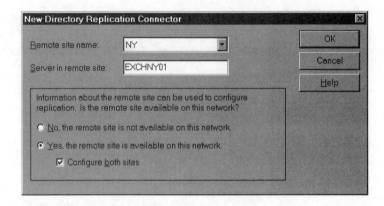

FIGURE 14.31

The Directory Replication
Connector Properties
dialog box

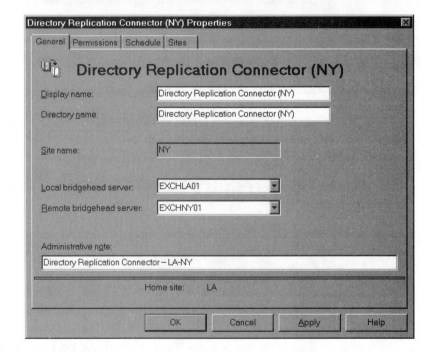

General Properties

Accept the default Display and Directory names. Be sure that local and remote
bridgehead server choices are as you want them to be, and add an administrative
note if you wish.

Schedule

The default schedule is the one set in the Selected Times calendar; it allows for directory replication every three hours (see Figure 14.32). Using the default should be fine in most cases; if the two sites are connected by a low-bandwidth network or one with very high traffic, you may want to do replication even less frequently. If you add and delete recipients at a breakneck pace throughout the day, every day, then more frequent directory replication might be necessary. (The Always option means replication every fifteen minutes.)

FIGURE 14.32

Setting the cross-site directory replication schedule

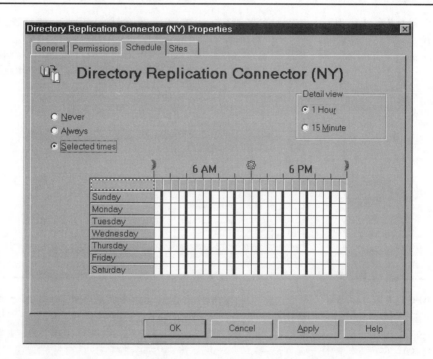

Setting Up Directory Replication in the Second Site

Things just don't get any easier than this. When you're done with the Schedule property page, click on OK in the Directory Replication Connector Properties page. Remember how, back on the New Directory Replication Connector dialog box (Figure 14.30), you asked to have the other side of the Directory Replication Connector automatically configured? Well, that's what happens. The Connector in your other site is configured without any action on your part and directory replication begins.

Did It Work?

First, use the Exchange Administrator at each of your two sites to see if the directory replication connectors have been created; they'll be in the Directory Replication container for each site. Figures 14.33 and 14.34 show my two sites with the directory replication connectors created in each.

While you're in your second site, create an Exchange mailbox or two. If you need to refresh your memory about this, go back to Chapter 8.

FIGURE 14.33

The directory replication connector for the first site

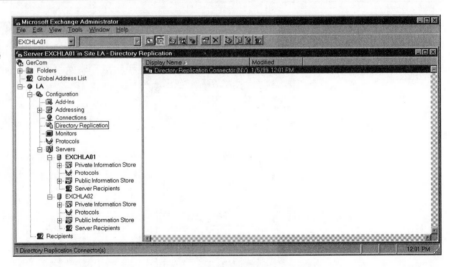

FIGURE 14.34

The directory replication connector for the second site

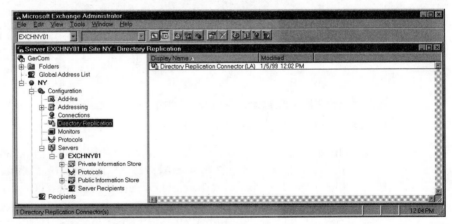

Next, after 10 or 20 minutes, depending on server and network performance, take a look at the Exchange Administrator in each site. You'll find that you can now see all the objects for both sites from either site. Your directories have been fully replicated across your two sites (see Figures 14.35 and 14.36).

FIGURE 14.35

An Exchange Administrator view from one site (LA) shows the objects in both sites (LA and NY)

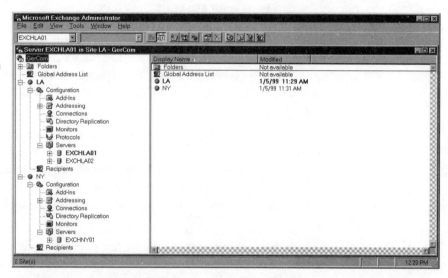

FIGURE 14.36

An Exchange Administrator view from one site (NY) shows the objects in both sites (NY and LA)

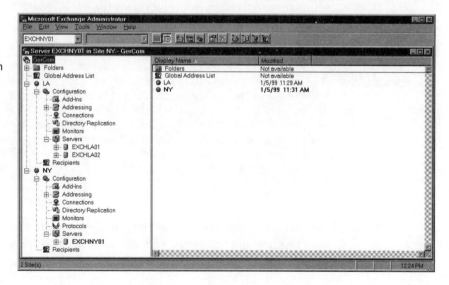

If what you have isn't what the figures show, there are a few things you can do to speed up directory replication. Everything you're going to do here is done automatically by Exchange Server over the course of a day—you're just forcing these actions so you can assure yourself that it's all happening as advertised.

Perform the following steps in each of your two sites. If you need more info about the first two dialog boxes discussed here, see Chapter 13.

- Double-click on Directory Service in the container for the default server. Then, on the General property page of the resultant Directory Service dialog box, click on Check Now. This forces the server to discover information about new sites in your organization. Close the dialog box.

- Double-click on Message Transfer Agent in the container for the default server, then click on Recalculate Routing on the General property page of the resultant Message Transfer Agent dialog box. When you do this, the server updates its routing tables and creates an MTA queue for the new site. Tab over to the MTA dialog box's Queues property page to see the queue created for the server in the other site. Close the dialog box.

- Double-click on the Directory Replication Connector in the site's Directory Replication container. Next, on the Sites property page of the resultant Directory Replication Connector dialog box (see Figure 14.37), click on the name of your inbound site and then on Request Now to force an update of directory replication information for the site. Close the dialog box.

NOTE As you create and tear down Exchange connectors in the sections below, follow the above three steps any time you need to force a quick update of the Exchange directory database. This lets you see the fruits of your work more immediately than if you wait for your Exchange servers to do these tasks automatically. When you're running a production Exchange environment, you'll rarely if ever need to track through these steps; Exchange Server's automated processes will take care of everything in more than enough time.

To further confirm that all is well, look in the organization-wide Global Address List container in one of your sites. You should see the addresses for both sites in the list (see Figure 14.38).

FIGURE 14.37

The Sites property page allows for selective directory replication updates.

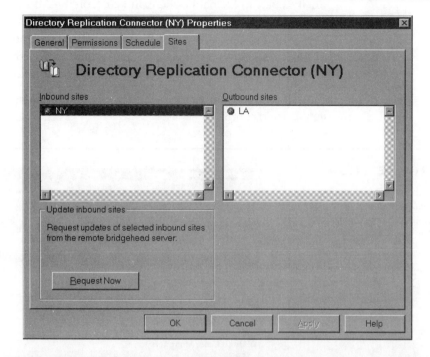

FIGURE 14.38

Addresses for both sites are visible in either site's copy of the Global Address List.

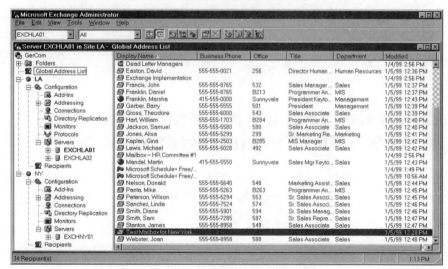

Finally, open an Exchange client and click on the Address Book icon on the toolbar (you'll remember that it looks like a little open book). Click open the 'Show Names from the' drop-down list. You should now see your second site along with your first, as shown in Figure 14.39. Take a close look at the Global Address List. You should see addresses from both your first and second sites in the book.

Congratulations! You've managed to get a pretty sophisticated Exchange system up and running.

FIGURE 14.39

Both the first (LA) and second (NY) sites are available in the client Address Book.

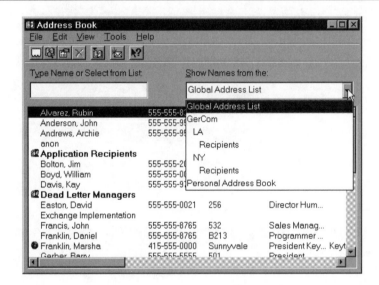

Using the Exchange Administrator in a Multisite Organization

What you learned in the last chapter about using the Exchange Administrator in multiserver sites should help you here. Using Figure 14.40 as a guide, notice that:

- The default server in the currently selected site/server window shows in the drop-down list near the top of the main Exchange Administrator window ('EXCHLA01' in Figure 14.40).

- The title bar for each site/server window includes the site name to help you know which site and server are your defaults ('Server EXCHLA01 in Site LA - LA' for the first window and 'Server EXCHNY01 in Site NY - NY' for the second window in Figure 14.40).

- The default site and server in each site/server window are bolded ('LA' and 'EXCHLA01' in the first window; 'NY' and 'EXCHNY01' in the second window in Figure 14.40).

FIGURE 14.40

Administering and managing two sites from the same Exchange Administrator program

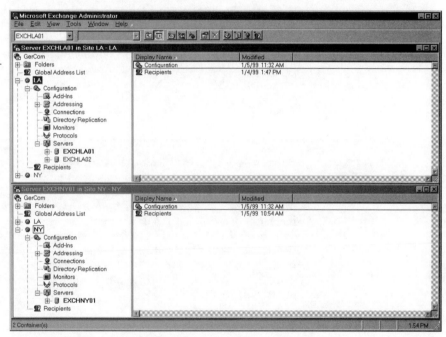

You can open additional windows on either your default site or your other site; just select 'Connect to server' from the Administrator's File menu, click Browse, and then select the site and server you want to connect to from the Server Browser dialog box that pops up.

Because of the cross-site permissions you gave the Exchange administration group in each of your two sites earlier in this chapter, you have tremendous control over your entire Exchange system. From this point on, you can administer and manage your first site from your second site, and vice versa. Just select the

'Connect to server' option from the File menu of the Exchange Administrator in one site and use the Server Browser dialog box to connect to a server in the other site. Then use the new Administrator window to administer and manage that site (see Figure 14.40). It's as easy as pie. If you need a refresher on connecting to servers, check out Chapter 13.

WARNING You can't fully administer and manage a site if you're not connected to a server in it. For example, from the first site/server window in Figure 14.40, I can view, create, and edit all objects in my LA site. Because I am not directly connected to a server in my NY site in this window, I can only view objects in the NY site from this window; I can't create or modify them. To fully administer and manage NY site objects, I must work in the second site/server window in Figure 14.40, which is directly connected to the server EXCHNY01 in the NY site.

TIP If those two windows in Figure 14.40 tend to overload your personal information processing circuits, here's how you can cut the visual stimulation a bit. Just drag one of the windows on top of the other so that the other window is covered. Resize the windows and the main Exchange Administrator window to your aesthetic preferences. Then, when you need to work with the window that's hidden, select its default server from the drop-down default server name list at the top of the Exchange Administrator's main window. The hidden window instantly comes to the top of the window stack, and the other window is hidden until you call it up with the drop-down list. Neat!

Setting Up Direct Site-to-Site Links Using Other Exchange Connectors

You'll remember from Chapter 5 that you can link Exchange sites using a variety of connectors other than the Site Connector: the X.400 Connector, the Dynamic Remote Access Service Connector (DRASC), the Internet Mail Service (IMS), and the Microsoft Mail Connector (MMC). We'll cover the X.400 and DRAS Connectors here, saving the IMS and MMC for later chapters.

Remember that the X.400 Connector can do both direct (point-to-point) and indirect (via foreign e-messaging systems) site links. Here we'll deal only with direct X.400 site connections; I'll talk about indirect links in a later chapter. The DRAS allows only for direct site-to-site links; we'll cover it in this chapter.

As with the Site Connector, you set up like connectors in each site and point them at each other. Each connector supports communications between two Exchange servers.

> **NOTE** Before we can install our connectors, we need to set up a network transport stack for each connector. As we go along, remember that transport stacks live on Exchange servers, while connectors live in Exchange sites.

Setting Up an MTA Transport Stack

Exchange connectors ride atop MTA transport stacks. Site Connectors automatically take care of transport stack issues. You have to install transport stacks for other connectors. A number of MTA transport stack options are available, including:

- *Protocol:* X.25 using Eicon Technology Corporation's X.25 port adapter hardware. *Prerequisite:* Eicon X.25 networking support must be installed (comes with Eicon hardware).

- *Protocols:* asynchronous, ISDN, and X.25 using NT Server's Remote Access Server. *Prerequisite:* Remote Access Server must be installed (comes with NT Server).

- *Protocol:* TCP/IP. *Prerequisite:* TCP/IP networking support must be installed (comes with NT Server).

- *Protocol:* Open Systems Interface (OSI) TP4. *Prerequisite:* TP4 networking support must be installed (comes with Exchange Server).

Except for the Eicon MTA transport stack, you can install only one of each MTA transport stack per Exchange server. You can install multiple Eicon port adapters in an Exchange server and set up one transport stack per adapter. All MTA transport stacks can support multiple Exchange connectors. So, using one MTA transport stack on one server, you can connect to any number of Exchange servers—the only requirement being that those servers are reachable on the same network.

By way of example, we'll set up TCP/IP and Remote Access Server (RAS) MTA transport stacks. (You'll find detailed instructions for setting up the Eicon and OSI stacks in the Exchange documentation.) For the TCP/IP stack, you'll need to have the TCP/IP protocols installed on the server in each site that will house the connector. For the DRASC, NT Server's RAS must be installed on the servers in each site that will house the DRASC. (For help installing and configuring these, see Sybex's *Mastering Windows NT Server 4*.)

Setting Up a TCP/IP Transport Stack

In your first site, open the Exchange Administrator's File menu. Select New Other and then select MTA Transport Stack from the New Other submenu (see Figure 14.19). This pops up the New MTA Transport Stack dialog box (see Figure 14.41). Select TCP/IP MTA Transport Stack, select the server you want to install the stack on (I've chosen EXCHLA01), and click on OK.

FIGURE 14.41

Selecting the networking protocol and server for a new MTA transport stack

The next thing you'll see is the TCP Properties dialog box shown in Figure 14.42. Unless you have a strong reason for doing otherwise, accept the default Name; you need to enter OSI address information only if other applications or services that communicate with an X.25 service are installed on the server. The OSI address information ensures that the existing X.25 service and the TCP/IP transport stack you're creating don't clobber each other.

For all intents and purposes, you're now finished. The Connectors property page simply shows the Exchange connectors that are riding atop the MTA transport stack. Since you haven't created your connector yet, you won't find anything on that page right now. After your connector is in place, come back to the Connectors page; the connector you linked to this MTA transport stack will appear.

Click on OK in the TCP Properties dialog box, then look in the container for your server. Your MTA transport stack should show up in the right-hand pane (see Figure 14.43).

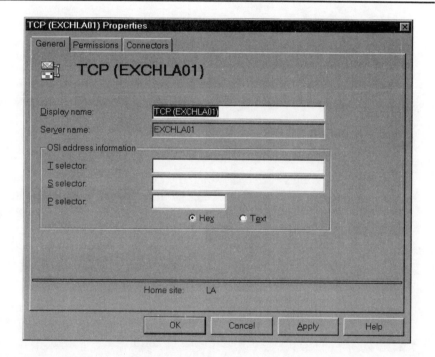

Now you need to set up a TCP/IP MTA transport stack in your other site. To do this, just repeat the process outlined above for a server in your other site. If the Site Connector and directory replication connector we created in the last section are in place (or even if they aren't in place, but the cross-domain, cross-site permissions I discussed earlier are), you don't have to actually visit the other site. Just connect to a server in the other site and use the new Exchange Administrator window for that connection to add the MTA transport stack.

FIGURE 14.43

A new TCP/IP MTA transport stack in its home server container

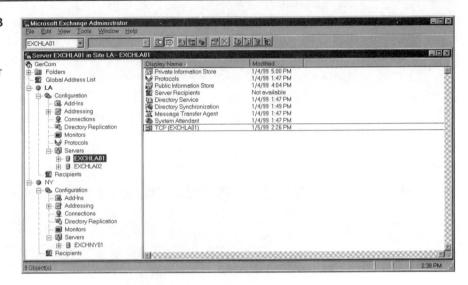

Setting Up a RAS MTA Transport Stack

This one's even easier than the TCP/IP MTA transport stack. In your first site, select MTA Transport Stack from the New Other submenu in the Exchange Administrator's File menu. Then, from the New MTA Transport Stack dialog box that pops up, select RAS MTA Transport Stack and the server you want the transport stack installed on. (Refer back to Figure 14.40 for a view of the New MTA Transport Stack dialog box.) This brings up the RAS Properties dialog box (see Figure 14.44).

You can optionally enter the telephone number used to make a dial-up connection to the server on which you're installing the RAS MTA transport stack. This security-enhancing feature allows RAS MTA transport stacks in other sites to call back to this server upon being contacted by it. As with the TCP/IP MTA transport stack, the Connectors property page for the RAS Properties dialog box is useful only after you've created at least one Exchange connector and assigned it to this transport stack. So click on OK in the RAS Properties dialog box when you're done.

The RAS MTA transport stack now joins the TCP transport stack in the container for the server it was installed on (see Figure 14.45).

FIGURE 14.44

The RAS Properties dialog box is used to configure a RAS MTA transport stack.

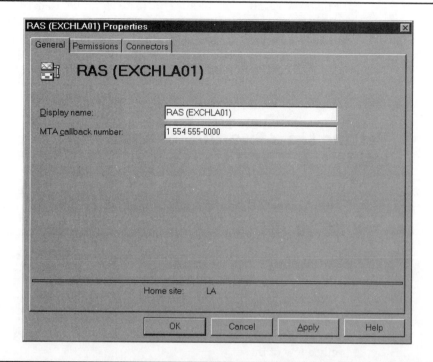

FIGURE 14.45

A new RAS MTA transport stack appears in its home server container.

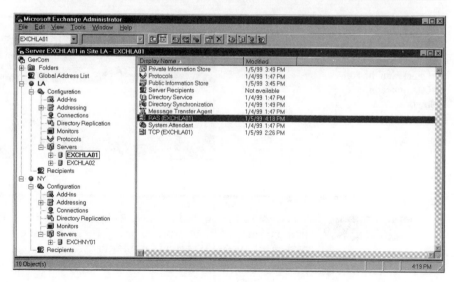

Before you move on, be sure to create a parallel RAS MTA transport stack in your other site. Again, if your sites are already connected by some sort of site connector and a directory replication connector, or if the correct permissions are in place, you can do this from your first site. Just open a server in the other site and use the new Administrator window for the site to create your RAS MTA transport stack.

Setting Up a Site-to-Site Link Using the X.400 Connector

To set up a site connection using the X.400 Connector, first open the File menu on the Exchange Administrator for your first site. Select New Other from the File menu, and then select X.400 Connector from the New Other submenu. The New X.400 Connector dialog box pops up (see Figure 14.46). Since only your TCP/IP MTA transport stack can support the X.400 Connector, it will be the only one listed in the Type box. Click on OK.

Next you'll see the dialog box for your new X.400 Connector (see Figure 14.47). The dialog box contains a lot of property pages, but don't worry. At least when the X.400 Connector is used to directly link Exchange sites, you need to deal with only a few of these.

FIGURE 14.46

Selecting an MTA transport stack with the New X.400 Connector dialog box

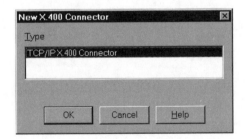

> **NOTE**
>
> We won't talk about the Delivery Restrictions property page here, even though you can use it productively for site-to-site connections. We already discussed it back in Chapter 8.

FIGURE 14.47

The dialog box for an X.400 Connector

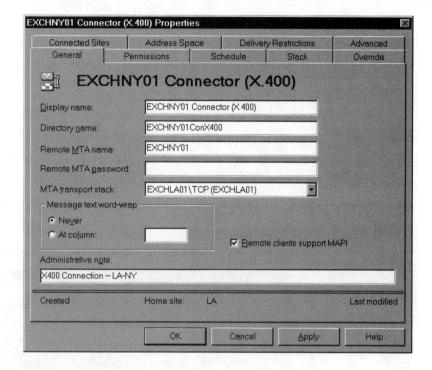

General Properties

Give the connector a name; *Remote_Server_Name + Connector + (X.400)* is a good model. Because I'm setting up this connector in my LA site and the target site is NY, I've named the connector 'EXCHNY01 Connector (X.400)' to clearly indicate that communications are from LA to NY by way of X.400. As you'll see in a bit, this name makes it really easy to find the right connector when you've got more than one in a site.

The 'Remote MTA name' field contains the name of your remote Exchange server (EXCHNY01 in my case). For greater security, you can set passwords for X.400 MTAs. You'd enter the password for the remote MTA here, if it had one. You set the password for the local MTA—the Exchange server you're working on right now—from the server's MTA General page or optionally, from the Override property page of the X.400 Connector dialog box you're working on right now.

Leave the 'Message text word-wrap' and 'Remote clients support MAPI' options set to their defaults. You may need to change one or more of these defaults when using the X.400 Connector to link to foreign e-messaging systems.

Add an administrative note if you'd like. When you're finished, tab over to the Schedule property page.

Schedule

The Schedule property page is shown in Figure 14.48. Leave the Always default as is; since your sites are directly connected, there's no reason to change the default, other than a need to control really heavy traffic.

When you're finished with the Schedule page, tab over to the Stack property page.

FIGURE 14.48

Setting a schedule for X.400 connections

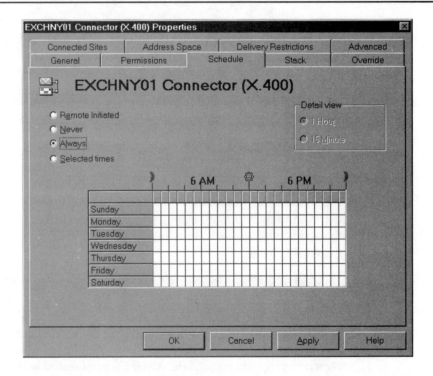

NOTE

You may have noticed that the X.400 Connector has a Schedule property page, while the Site Connector has none. You can't schedule links with the Site Connector—they're continuous by definition. "But," I can hear you thinking, "didn't I encounter a schedule recently?" You sure did, but it was for the directory replication connector you created. Put simply, directory replication can always be scheduled. Connections between sites using the Site Connector can't be scheduled, but connections between sites using other site connectors can. Eee-aye-eee-aye-oh.

Stack

See Figure 14.49 for the Stack property page. Since we're running our X.400 Connector on top of a TCP/IP stack, all we need to do here is enter an Internet domain name for the other Exchange server or its IP address. (I entered the IP address of my Exchange server in New York, EXCHNY01.) When you're done, tab over to the Address Space property page.

FIGURE 14.49

Providing stack addressing information

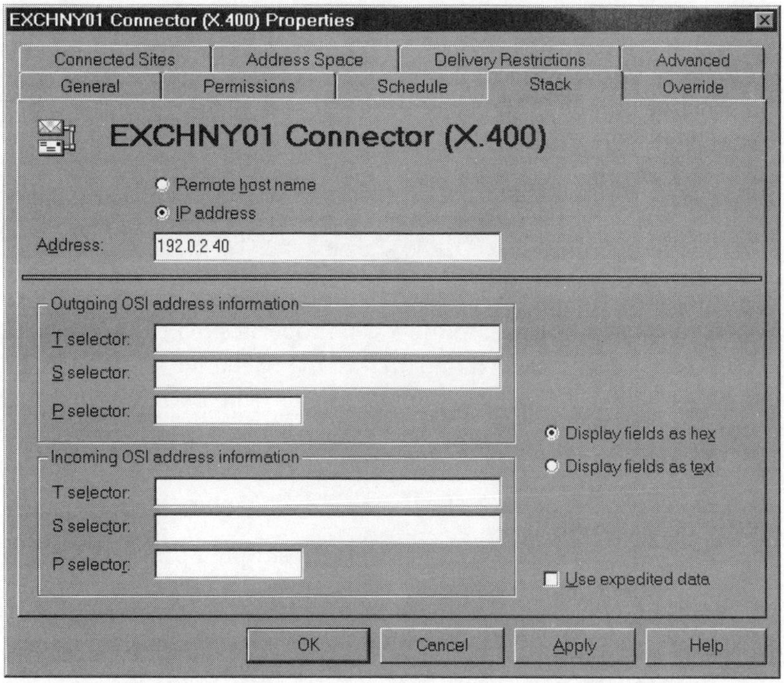

EXCHNY01 Connector (X.400) Properties

Connected Sites | Address Space | Delivery Restrictions | Advanced
General | Permissions | Schedule | Stack | Override

EXCHNY01 Connector (X.400)

○ Remote host name
◉ IP address
Address: 192.0.2.40

Outgoing OSI address information
T selector:
S selector:
P selector:

◉ Display fields as hex
○ Display fields as text

Incoming OSI address information
T selector:
S selector:
P selector:

☐ Use expedited data

OK | Cancel | Apply | Help

Address Space

Figure 14.50 shows the Address Space property page as you'll first see it. You need to add an address space for your other server. It should be an X.400 address space, so click on the New X.400 button on the right-hand side of the page.

FIGURE 14.50

The Address Space property page

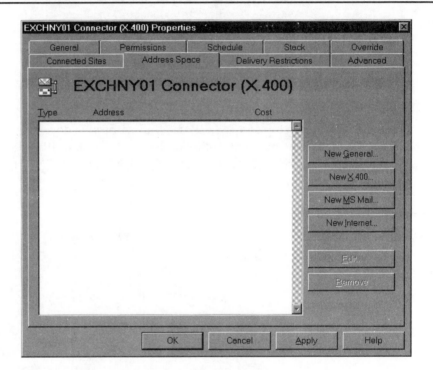

This brings up the X.400 Properties dialog box shown in Figure 14.51. Fill in the Organization name (that is, the Exchange site you're connecting to) and the 'Private management domain name' (the Exchange organization). Hey, we're talking apples (Exchange) and oranges (X.400) here, so don't expect a one-to-one parallel in terminology. Leave the other parameters as they are. When you're done, click on OK in the X.400 Properties dialog box.

You're returned to the Address Space property page (see Figure 14.52). The new X.400 address should be in place.

FIGURE 14.51

Entering an X.400 address for the other site

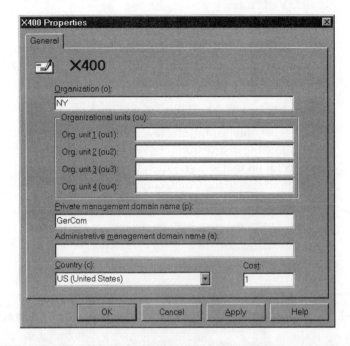

FIGURE 14.52

The Address Space property page with the X.400 address entered in Figure 14.51

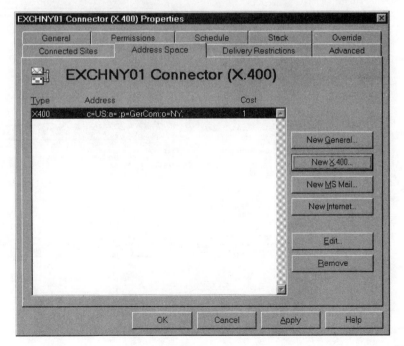

Override

If you need to, you can use the Override property page to set up an MTA name and a password that are different from your Exchange server's own MTA name and password. You can also use the Override page to set alternate messaging parameters from those of your server's MTA's defaults.

You're now done with this site; click OK on the dialog box to create the connector.

Now you need to create a parallel X.400 Connector on your other server. Just follow the instructions above, adjusting for the fact that you're setting up the connector on that server. When you're done with both sites, you should see the new connectors in the Connections container for each site (see Figure 14.53).

Notice in Figure 14.53 how the names of the connectors—EXCHNY01 Connector X.400, for example—make it very easy to see not only the target Exchange server, but also the type of connection being used. As you'll soon see when we add our next connector, the names can really help.

FIGURE 14.53

The X.400 connectors are in place in each site.

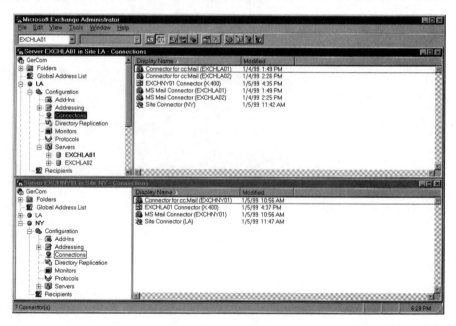

Connecting Sites

You need to do one last thing before your sites can communicate. For each site, double-click on your new X.400 Connector and tab over to the Connected Sites property page in the resultant Connector Properties dialog box (see Figure 14.54).

FIGURE 14.54

The Connected Sites property page

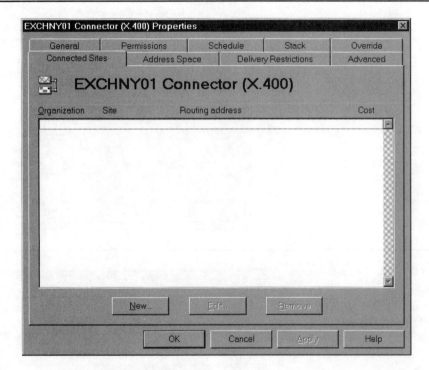

While in your first site, you need to add a connection to your other site. Click on New on the Connected Sites Properties dialog box to bring up a site-selection Properties dialog box (see Figure 14.55). Be sure the Exchange organization name is correct, then type in the name of the site you want to connect to. When you're done, click on OK.

The Properties dialog box closes and the connection shows in the list box in the Connected Sites property page (see Figure 14.56). You're now done with this page. Click on OK.

FIGURE 14.55

Entering site connection
information

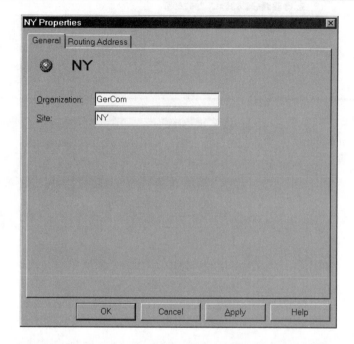

FIGURE 14.56

The Connected Sites
property page containing
the specified connection
information

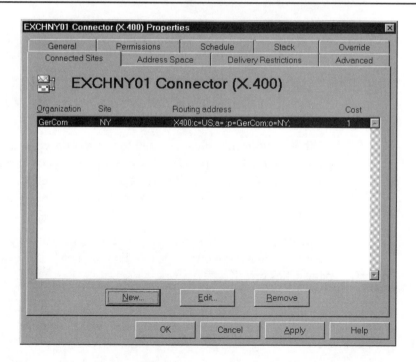

Now do the same thing with your other server. Your sites are now linked by X.400 Connectors.

> **NOTE**
>
> If you haven't installed a directory replication connector between your two sites yet—which would be the case if you didn't track through the installation process for the Site Connectors and directory replication connector detailed above—you need to do that now. Refer to the section earlier in this chapter on setting up a directory replication connector.

Did It Work?

If you've got Site Connectors in place, you might want to delete them from both sites, just to be sure that your X.400 connectors are working. Now that you know how easy it is to re-create your Site Connectors, this shouldn't phase you at all.

For a quick test, create a new mailbox in one of your sites. Then follow the three steps outlined earlier in this chapter for manually forcing directory replication. If everything is working, you should see the new mailbox in the Global Address List from each site. If this isn't the case, go back and retrace your steps in creating your MTA transport stacks and X.400 connectors.

Setting Up a Site-to-Site Link Using the Dynamic RAS Connector

We'll cover this process more quickly, depending on a lot of things you learned in the last section.

Select the Connections container in your first site, then select Dynamic RAS Connector from the New Other submenu of the Exchange Administrator's File menu. This opens up the Dynamic RAS Connector Properties dialog box (see Figure 14.57).

General Properties

Name the connector using the conventions I suggested for the X.400 Connector, changing (X.400) to (DRAS). Enter the name of the remote server—EXCHNY01 in my case—which is the Exchange server in your other site—NY in my case. Select the MTA RAS transport stack from the RAS stacks that exist in the site.

FIGURE 14.57

The Properties dialog box for a Dynamic Remote Access Service Connector

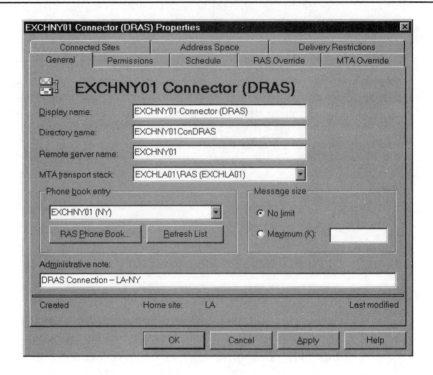

In the 'Phone book entry' field, choose the RAS phone book entry that will dial up your other server with a Dynamic Remote Access Service connector (DRASC).

> **NOTE**
>
> You can add phone numbers to a RAS phone book only while locally logged in to the server running the RAS—you can't, for instance, add numbers to a phone book on Server B while administering Server B from Server A. You'll have to add the numbers while locally logged in to the server running the RAS (Server B).

If you wish, you can set a maximum size for messages transmitted over this connector. Generally, I suggest that you not set a limit. If your DRAS Connector is being used as a backup to another site connector that goes down, you might want to temporarily set a maximum message size limit. This would ensure that your slower DRAS Connector doesn't spend its time delivering one or two large messages while many smaller messages go undelivered.

When you're finished with the General property page, tab over to the Schedule page.

Schedule

The default schedule is Always, which for some dial-up connections may be too frequent. I like the schedule shown in Figure 14.58: one contact at midnight and subsequent contacts every other hour from 9 a.m. to 11 p.m.

FIGURE 14.58

Scheduling site links for a Dynamic Remote Access Service Connector

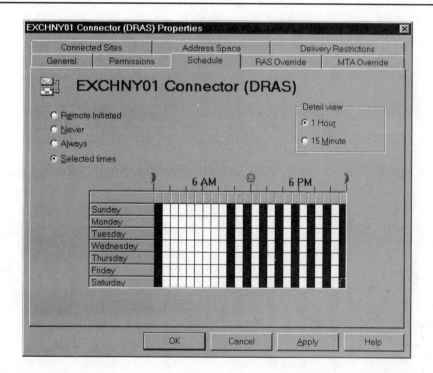

Other Property Pages

You probably didn't need to enter any account or domain information into the Override page of your Site or X.400 Connector Property dialog boxes. However, you do have to do this on the RAS Override page of the DRAS Connector

Property dialog box. Enter the name of the account you want to connect to in the other site (usually the Exchange services account) along with the account's password and the NT domain in which the account is located. Check Figure 14.24 for a specific example. The RAS Override property page includes two items not relevant to the Site Connector Override page, the MTA callback number, and the overriding phone number. The remote MTA uses the callback number to contact your Exchange server's MTA after contact by your server. The overriding phone number is used instead of a phone number listed in the RAS phone book.

On the Address Space property page, create an address for your other site as you did for your site and X.400 connectors. Then, on the Connected Sites property page, set a routing link to your other site. Just click on New, enter the name of your other site in the resultant Site Properties dialog box, and click on OK there when you're finished.

You know what to do with the Delivery Restrictions property page. When you're done, click on OK in the Dynamic RAS Connector Properties dialog box, and your DRASC is all set up.

The Next Steps

Now create a DRAS Connector in your other site.

NOTE If you haven't yet installed a directory replication connector between your two sites—which would be the case if you didn't track through the installation procedures for the Site Connector/directory replication connector and the X.400 Connector as detailed above—you'll need to do that now. Refer to the section on setting up a directory replication connector earlier in this chapter.

When everything is set, you'll see two functioning DRAS Connectors—one in the Connections container for each site (see Figure 14.59).

Now notice how smart we were to have named the connectors as we did. You can immediately tell which is the DRAS Connector, the X.400 Connector, and the Site Connector. Double-click on the one you want; the appropriate connector dialog box pops up and you're ready to administer and manage the connector. What could be easier?

FIGURE 14.59

DRAS Connectors in place for each site

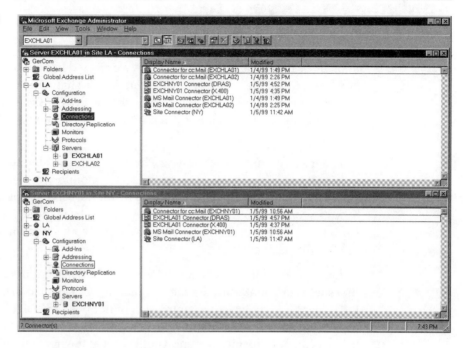

Some Clarifying Comments on Site-to-Site Connections

Before we move on to monitors and public folder replication, I want to make sure you understand a couple of things. You can set up only *one* directory replication connector for each unique pair of sites. If you tried right now to create another directory replication connector (assuming you have only the two sites you've already connected for directory replication), the Exchange Administrator program wouldn't let you do it. If you have more sites and you create connections between them, then the Administrator would happily let you create another directory replication connector.

It's important to note, however, that for purposes of redundancy your single directory replication connector can run on top of multiple site connectors. That's why you should keep both your DRASC and either your Site Connector or X.400 Connector in place. Keeping both your Site Connector and X.400 Connector in place—assuming that both use the same physical network, as ours do in the previous examples—doesn't make much sense, since there's no redundancy advantage.

Adding New Servers to Server and Link Monitors

Remember the server and link monitors we created in previous chapters? Well, now we can add the new server we set up in this chapter to those monitors. (If you need more information while doing the next two tasks, refer to the sections on server monitors in Chapters 8 and 13, or to the section on link monitors in Chapter 13.)

If your server monitor is running, close it. Select the Monitors container for your first site, then double-click on the server monitor you set up back in Chapter 8. When the Properties dialog box for the server pops up, tab over to the Servers property page and add your new server from the site drop-down list. Click on OK in the Properties dialog box. Open your server monitor and you'll see that the new server is now being monitored.

If your link monitor is running, close it. Select the Monitors container for your first site, then double-click on the link monitor you created in Chapter 13. When the Properties dialog box for your link monitor pops up, tab over to the Servers property page and add your new server. Click on OK in the Properties dialog box. Open your link monitor and you'll see that the new server has been added. After several minutes, the monitor tells you that the link to your new server is working correctly.

Figure 14.60 shows my server and link monitors with my new server added to each.

Setting Up Cross-Site Public Folder Access

The only issue we haven't covered in the area of information store administration and management is cross-site public folder access. This is the perfect time and place for that, so let's get going.

FIGURE 14.60

A new server is added to the existing server and link monitors.

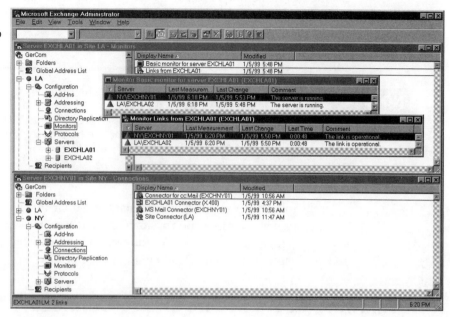

If a site is included in directory replication, users at any site in the Exchange organization can see its top-level public folders and all levels of subfolders from their Exchange clients. However, a user (for example, an Exchange mailbox user) at one site (Site A) can access a specific public folder that lives at another site (Site B) *only* if the user has permission to access the folder *and* if one of the following criteria is met:

- *Option 1:* Users from Site A are permitted to connect directly to all of the public folders in Site B.

or

- *Option 2:* Public folders from Site B are replicated in Site A.

In the following two sections, you'll learn how to set up both cross-site direct access to public folders and public folder replication. Before we start, you should have at least two public folders on each of the servers in each of your sites. If you've been paralleling my examples, you should now have three servers. Be sure there are at least two public folders on each server. Put a couple of messages in each folder. (If you need a refresher on public folder creation, refer back to

Chapter 12. Remember, Exchange clients create public folders, so you'll need to install clients in your sites, if you haven't already done so. Check out Chapters 11 and 12 if you need help installing clients.)

> **NOTE**
> As you may remember from earlier chapters, in the simplest model public folders are stored on the home server of the mailbox used to create them. However, this does not have to be the case. You can designate any Exchange server in a site to hold public folders created by users with mailboxes on any other server in the site.

For the following exercises, be sure that any public folders created on the second server in your first site are stored on that server. Use the Private Information Store Properties dialog box for the second server to check this setting. Refer back to Chapter 9 if you need help with this dialog box.

Allowing Users in One Site to Connect to Folders in Another Site

Let's start with Option 1 in that little list above detailing cross-site connections to public folders by users. This option has one prerequisite: Users must have a direct network link to the site whose public folders they will connect to. An indirect link through a foreign e-messaging system isn't enough.

Setting Up Public Folder Affinity

In the Exchange Administrator, select the Configuration container for your first site, then double-click on Information Store Site Configuration. This brings up the Information Store Site Configuration Properties dialog box. Back in Chapter 9, we covered everything about this dialog box in detail, except the Public Folder Affinity property page. And are we ready for that page now!

You use the Public Folders Affinity property page to give users in one site the ability to connect directly to all public folders in another site (see Figure 14.61). The page shows the sites for which you can set affinity in the Sites box on the left-hand side. Select your site and click on Add to create an affinity in your first site for public folders in your second site. The selected site then appears in the 'Public folder affinity' box on the right-hand side of the property page. In Figure 14.61, you can see that I have only one choice from my first (LA) site—and that's my NY site.

FIGURE 14.61

Permitting users in one site to access all public folders in another site

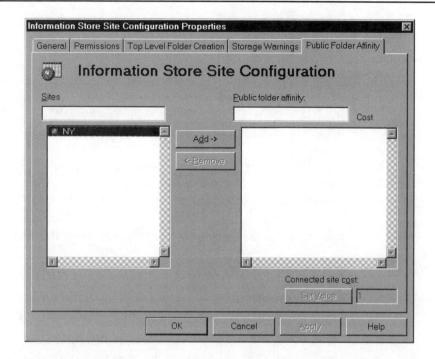

You set a cost for each site for which you have an affinity in the 'Connected site cost' field in the lower right-hand corner of the Public Folder Affinity property page. Costs are used to determine which site to connect to when a specific public folder exists in more than one external site. This can happen when you replicate one site's folders to two or more other sites. (We'll get to public folder replication in just a bit.) You should set costs based on the available network bandwidth between your site and the other site. When a user needs to connect to a public folder in another site, the link is made to the site with the lowest cost. For now, accept the default cost value.

Now click on OK in the Information Store Site Configuration Properties dialog box, and you're done.

Did It Work?

To test out the affinity you set, open a client at your first site and then select a public folder from your second site. You should be able to open any of the messages in the folder. Select another public folder from your second site. Again, you should be able to view any of the folder's messages.

NOTE

Remember that although user mailboxes have home servers, they really live in sites, and public folders are stored on specific servers but really live in sites as well. This means that a user whose mailbox is in a specific site can access all unrestricted folders in that site without your having to do anything at all as an Exchange administrator. It's only when you want users in one site to access public folders in another site that you have to consider public folder affinity or replication.

At this point, if you were to open a client in your second site, you would see top-level public folders and all levels of subfolders from your first site, but you wouldn't be able to access the items inside those folders. That's because you didn't set public folder affinity with the first site at your second site. To do that, you'd have to repeat the process we just finished, except this time in your second site.

Benefits and Costs

As you've seen, setting up public folder affinities is really easy. In one fell swoop you give all users in a site access to any unrestricted public folders in another site.

Another advantage of public folder affinity is immediacy. When you want to be sure that users are working with the latest view of a public folder, you'll usually want to pick affinity over replication. If all users connect to the one and only copy of a public folder, they know that whatever they (or others) put into or take out of the folder will be seen immediately by anyone connected to the folder. As you'll see in a bit, public folder replication is by contrast usually subject to at least small delays.

Nonetheless, two problems can occur with public folder affinity. First, users have to connect to extrasite public folders across the network to access them. If sites are connected by higher-bandwidth networks, that may be no big deal, depending on how many users try to access public folders at any given time. If network bandwidth is low or if cross-site public folder access is heavy, users connecting to extrasite public folders can bring a network to its knees.

The second problem with public folder affinity is that you can't select which public folders will be accessible. By default, all folders are available to users. If you want everyone in a public folder's home site to have access to the folder, but you don't want users in other sites to have such access, you have to remove any default access rights to the folder and assign such rights to a distribution list that includes all users in the home site. That's a lot of work, especially if you have more than a few public folders whose extrasite access you wish to restrict.

Both of these problems can be avoided with public folder replication. Let's move on to that option right now.

Cross-Site Public Folder Replication

Public folders can be replicated between servers within a site as well as between servers in different sites. With public folder replication, users don't need to be directly connected to another site to access its public folders. Instead, they access synchronized replicas of the folders, which are stored on their home servers or at their home sites. Generally, you replicate public folders to make them available to users in other sites, to reduce cross-site network traffic, to distribute the load for heavily accessed folders across multiple servers in a site, and to create redundant copies of folders in one or more sites in case any single copy becomes unusable.

Public folder replication can be done at two levels: the server level and the folder level. Server-level replication lets you bring one or more folders *from* other sites *to* your site; you might want to think of it as a sort of *pull* process. Folder-level replication lets you replicate one folder at a time *from* your site *to* one or more sites; thus, you can think of it more as a *push* process. Regardless of which level you use, once replication is set up, all replicas of a given folder are automatically kept in sync with each other.

NOTE Before we start, remove any public folder affinities you may have set up in the last section. There may be times when you want to set up affinities between two sites and at the same time replicate specific public folders between them; for the following exercise, however, we just want to replicate.

Setting Up Public Folder Replication at the Server Level

Though public folders are treated as belonging to sites and even to an entire Exchange organization, their physical home is on Exchange servers. As you'll soon see, whether you replicate at the server level or folder level, there are times when you have to think in terms of servers.

In the left-hand pane of an Exchange Administrator window, select the container for the server to which you want to replicate public folders; let's call it the *target server.* I'm going to replicate a folder in my NY site (my *source site*) over to my LA site (my *target site*). The physical home for the folder will be the target server EXCHLA01. In other words, I'll pull a folder from my source site (NY) to my target server (EXCHLA01). Unless it carries specific restrictions, once the public folder has been replicated to EXCHLA01, it will be available to all users in my target site, LA. So I'll select the container for EXCHLA01 in the left-hand pane of the Administrator window.

Next, click once on Public Information Store in the right-hand pane of the Administrator window and select Properties from Exchange Administrator's File menu. This brings up the Public Information Store Properties dialog box for the target server (see Figure 14.62).

I already talked about the General property page of this dialog box back in Chapter 9. This is where you can enter serverwide parameters for maximum public folder size.

You set up public folder replication from the Instances property page. Tab over to it and you should see a page that looks something like the one in Figure 14.63.

FIGURE 14.62

The Public Information Store Properties dialog box

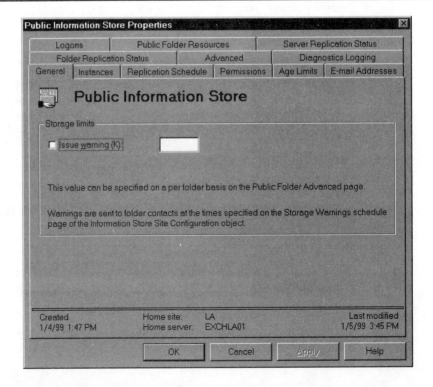

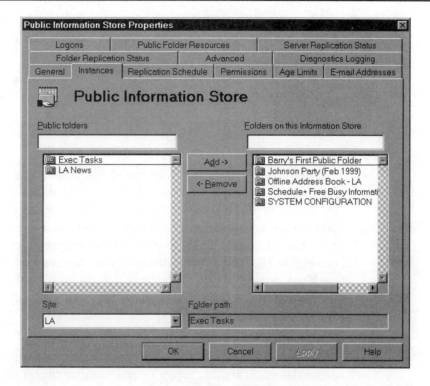

FIGURE 14.63

The Instances property page of the Public Information Store Properties dialog box

Some Basics   You're looking at information about public folders in the home site of the target server you just selected. (In my case, the site is LA and the target server is EXCHLA01. We know that it's LA because 'LA' shows in the Site drop-down menu in the lower left-hand corner of the Instances property page. And we know that it's EXCHLA01 because that's the target server we selected earlier.)

Before I set up the replication of a folder in my NY site, we need to talk a bit about the Instances property page as it looks when you first tab over to it; that is, when it focuses on your target site and server. That'll put some basics under your belt that will come in handy as we actually replicate a folder in the next section.

First, let's look at the right-hand side of the Instances property page. The 'Folders on this Information Store' box shows public folders and other items already in the target server's public information store. The folders 'Barry's First Public Folder' and 'Johnson Party (Feb 1999)' reside on my target server, EXCHLA01.

NOTE   Also on the target server are items that aren't public folders in the classic sense. Each is sitewide, as opposed to being only for the server you're working on at the time. The Offline Address Book and Schedule+ Free/Busy Information support, respectively, remote Exchange client access and cross-site Schedule+ appointment scheduling. The SYSTEM CONFIGURATION public folder holds information about public folders in the site. For now, don't mess with these.

Now let's turn our attention to the left-hand side of the Instances property page. The Public Folders box shows this site's public folders that are available for replication to the target server's public information store. The two folders in my example are Exec Tasks and LA News. These folders reside on the other server in my LA site, EXCHLA02. If I wanted to replicate the folder LA News to my target server, EXCHLA01, I'd select it and click on Add, which would move it over to the 'Folders on this Information Store' box. Remember, users in my LA site can open and use the folders on EXCHLA02, even if their mailboxes are on EXCHLA01. So, I'd only replicate folders from EXCHLA02 to EXCHLA01 to lighten network traffic or to improve folder access performance for users on EXCHLA01.

The Remove button is used here to turn off replication of public folders whose original home is another server in the site or another site altogether. Though the Remove button is highlighted in Figure 14.63, I actually can't remove any of the five items in the 'Folders on this Information Store' box, since this *is* their current physical home and replication to this information store is, thus, a physical impossibility.

Replicating a Public Folder at the Server Level   We're now ready to replicate a folder in our other site. Open the Site drop-down menu in the lower left-hand corner of the Instances property page and select your other site from it (mine is NY). Your Instances page should now look something like the one shown in Figure 14.64.

I want to replicate the public folder Jolly Elves to my target server, EXCHLA01. To do so, I select the folder and click on Add. As you can see in Figure 14.65, the folder moves over to the 'Folders on this Information Store' box, indicating that it will be replicated to EXCHLA01 when you click on OK.

That's it. It's that easy.

FIGURE 14.64

Using the Instances property page for another site to set up public folder replication

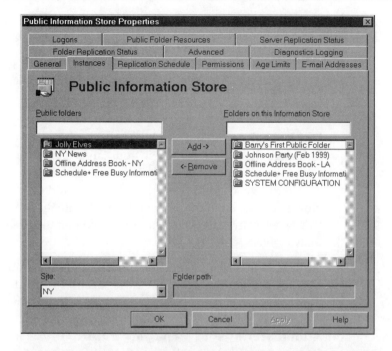

FIGURE 14.65

The public folder will now be replicated.

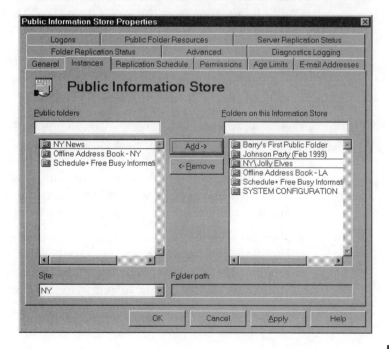

NOTE

I really don't want users in LA wasting their (and GerCom's) time reading the news meant for NY. By not replicating the folder NY News to my LA site, I ensure that LA users won't be able to open the folder and access items in it. If public folder affinity were in effect, I'd have to play with the folder's permissions to accomplish the same end.

Did It Work?　To find out whether the replication worked, simply open an Exchange client for a mailbox in your target site (LA in my case), then find the folder you set replication for (mine is Jolly Elves). Select the folder. You should be able to see what's in the folder, and you shouldn't be told that you can't access it. Now select the other folder in your second site that you didn't set replication for (NY News in my case). You should be told that the contents of the folder are unavailable.

Replication doesn't happen immediately. If everything isn't as expected, wait a reasonable time, depending on the replication schedule you set. If things still don't go as advertised, retrace your steps, following the example above.

Administering and Managing Public Folder Replication at the Server Level　Let's take a quick look at some of the other property pages in the Public Information Store Properties dialog box. These pages let you administer and manage public folder replication at the server level.

- *Replication Schedule* (Figure 14.66): You use this property page to set timing for replications from the selected server to other servers. Generally, the preferred setting is the default, Always.

- *Advanced* (Figure 14.67): The Advanced property page allows you to set a time in minutes for the Always option in the Replication Schedule page and to specify the maximum size for each individual replication message the IS sends during public folder replication. The IS will not, however, break up a single message, so if it has to replicate a message larger than this size, it will surpass this limit and the message will not be replicated.

- *Age Limits* (Figure 14.68): Use the Age Limits property page to set the number of days after which messages in public folders that haven't been modified are deleted. Ages can be set for all folders in a public information store, as well as for specific folders (select a folder and click on Modify).

FIGURE 14.66

The Replication Schedule property page

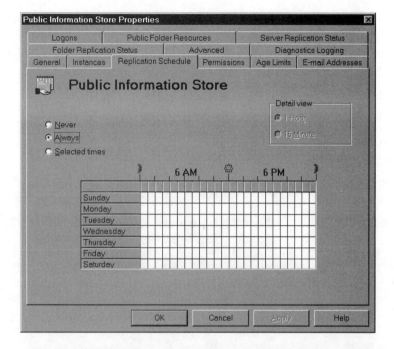

FIGURE 14.67

The Advanced property page

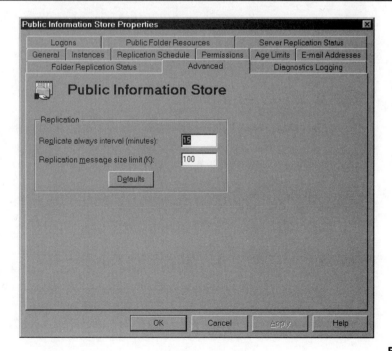

FIGURE 14.68

The Age Limits property page

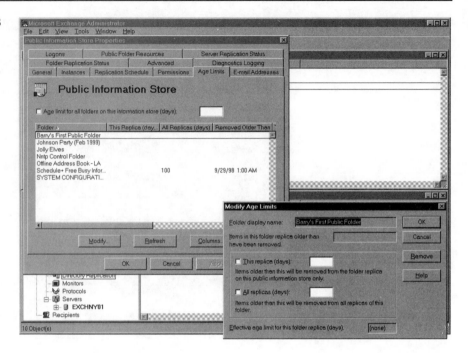

- *Folder Replication Status* (Figure 14.69): Use this property page to monitor the replication process for public folders and their hierarchy for the organization. (Monitoring the hierarchy gives each site a view of the public folder tree structure. Only folder affinity settings or replication, however, give users in one site access to the folders.) Notice in the figure that my folder replicas are in sync.

- *Server Replication Status* (Figure 14.70): Use this property page to monitor the replication process for specific servers. The status 'Local Modified' means that there have been changes in the public folders that are to be replicated to EXCHLA02 and EXCHNY01. If all changes had been replicated, 'In Sync' would be displayed in the Replication Status column for each server. 'Average Transmission Time' is in seconds. It tells how long, on the average, it takes to complete a replication cycle for the server in that row. Hidden off to the right of the property page is another column, 'Last Transmission Time', which reports the time in seconds required for the last replication cycle. You can use these times to gauge the performance of your server. If replications are taking too long to or from a particular server, you might want to look into solutions like a faster site connector.

FIGURE 14.69

The Folder Replication
Status property page

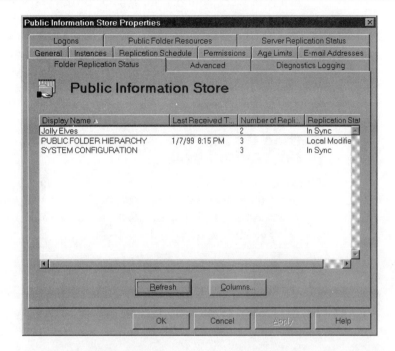

FIGURE 14.70

The Server Replication
Status property page

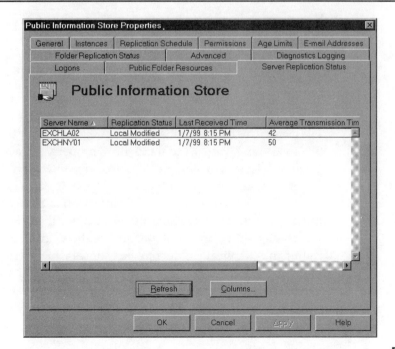

From your work with previous dialog boxes, you should be familiar by now with the remaining property pages in the Public Information Store Properties dialog box. The Logons page shows who's connected to the selected server's public information store, just like the Logons page for the Private Information Store dialog box that we discussed in Chapter 9. And based on our discussions in earlier chapters, you should have no problems with the Permissions, E-mail Addresses, and Diagnostics Logging property pages.

Setting Up Public Folder Replication at the Folder Level

Remember that replication at the folder level is a *push* process. You replicate a public folder *from* one site (the *source* site) *to* a server (the *target* server) in the same or another site. When the folder has been replicated to a server in another site, it is available to users in that site—the target site.

> **NOTE** You don't need to remove the server-level folder replication you set up in the last section. It will have no effect on what we do here.

Replicating a Public Folder at the Folder Level   In the Exchange Administrator, find one of the public folders in your first site. Look for the folder under the organization-level Public Folders hierarchy near the top of the tree in the left-hand Administrator pane. (I'll use the folder Barry's First Public Folder; see Figure 14.71.)

Click once on the folder and then select Properties from the Administrator's File menu. This brings up the Properties dialog box for the folder (see Figure 14.72). Since we already discussed the General property page for this dialog box back in Chapter 9, let's tab over to the Replicas page so we can set up replication for this folder. As you can see from Figure 14.73, the Replicas property page looks a lot like the Instances page in the Public Information Store dialog box we looked at in the last section. The rules here are pretty much the same as for the Instances page, too. The Servers box on the left-hand side shows available target servers, while the right-hand 'Replicate folders to' box shows which servers currently are receiving replicas of the folder. In the figure, we're looking at my source site, LA. If I wanted to replicate this folder to EXCHLA02 (the second server in my LA site), I would select it and click on the Add button.

FIGURE 14.71

Finding a public folder to replicate

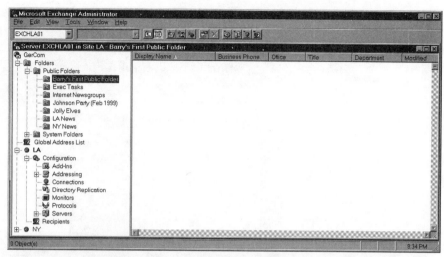

FIGURE 14.72

The Properties dialog box for the public folder to be replicated

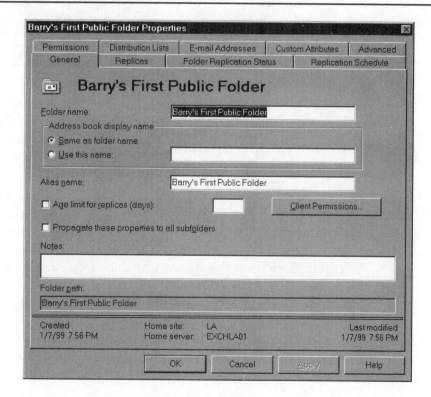

FIGURE 14.73

The Replicas property
page showing the
source site

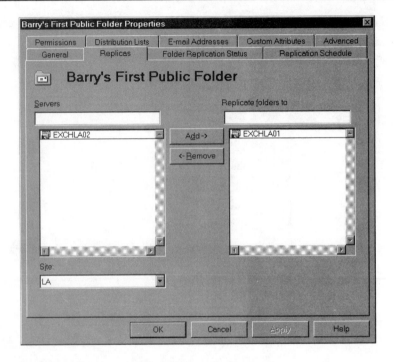

Use the Sites drop-down menu to move to your other (target) site, NY in my
case; see Figure 14.74. To set up replication of Barry's First Public Folder from my
LA site to the server EXCHNY01 in my NY site, I would select the server in the
Servers box and click on Add.

This places the server in the 'Replicate folders to' box, indicating that the folder
will now be replicated to the target server. As you can see in Figure 14.75,
EXCHNY01 in my NY site will now receive a replica of Barry's First Public
Folder. That's it.

Did It Work?   Let's see if the replication worked. After waiting long enough
to allow replication—15 minutes if you chose the default replication schedule—
open an Exchange client whose home server is in your second site. (In my case,
that would be EXCHNY01.) Select the folder you chose to replicate. You should
be able to see what's in the folder, and you should not be told that the folder is
unavailable. If you can't access the folder, retrace the steps outlined above.

FIGURE 14.74

The Replicas property page showing the target site

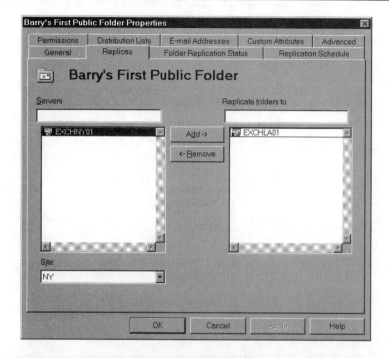

FIGURE 14.75

The public folder will now be replicated to the target server.

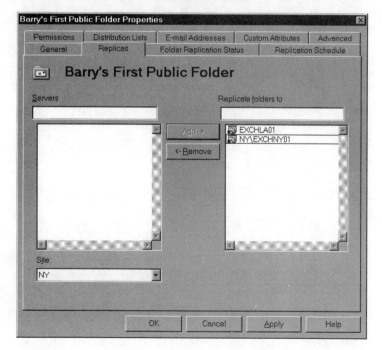

Administering and Managing Public Folder Replication at the Folder Level Two property pages in the Properties dialog box for a public folder can help you administer and manage that folder's replication: Folder Replication Status and Advanced. Let's briefly look at these two pages.

- *Folder Replication Status* (Figure 14.76): Use this property page to monitor folder replication. The page works much like the same property page for server-level replication described above; however, since this page is for a single public folder, it shows status in terms of servers instead of specific public folders. As shown in Figure 14.76, my folder is in sync on both servers.

- *Advanced* (Figure 14.77): Use the Advanced property page's Trust Level list box to control whether the folder's address is included when the Exchange directory is sent to foreign e-messaging systems during directory synchronization. (We'll talk about directory synchronization in a later chapter.) Use the 'Replication msg importance' list box to set a priority for replication of the folder. Use 'Public folder store storage limits' to override—for this folder only—the limits set on the General property page of the Public Information Store Properties dialog box.

FIGURE 14.76

The Folder Replication Status property page

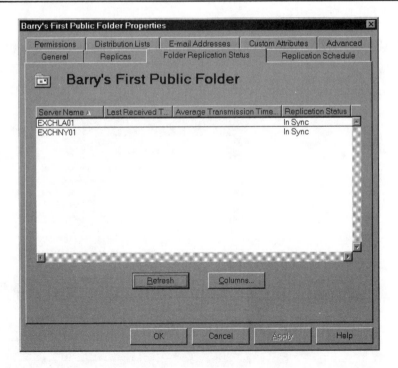

FIGURE 14.77

The Advanced prop-
erty page

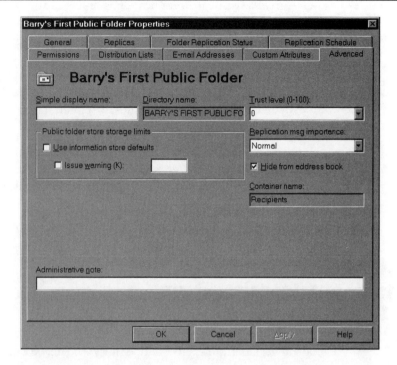

The rest of the fields on the Advanced property page—as well as the Permissions, Distribution Lists, E-mail Addresses, and Custom Attributes property pages—should be old hat from your experience with other dialog boxes.

Benefits and Costs

You have to set up public folder replication between each pair of sites on a folder-by-folder basis. This is more work than is required for setting public folder affinity, which lets users in one site connect to all unrestricted public folders in another site. However, replication is generally lighter on network bandwidth, since users access a local replica rather than connecting to the one and only copy of a public folder stored somewhere out there on a wide area network. With replication, bandwidth is required only to keep replicas in sync.

It's also somewhat easier to exclude public folders from extrasite access with replication rather than with affinity. With replication, you replicate the folders you want people to see. With affinity, you have to mess with permissions on folders you don't want people to see.

One great advantage of replication is online redundancy. Even with just one replica of a public folder (that is, there are two instances of that folder), your risk of losing important information in the event of an Exchange server crash is cut in half. With two replicas (three instances), your risk is cut by two-thirds, and so on. And best of all, the public folders on a server will be automatically rebuilt when a crashed server comes back online. Sure, you should still back up your servers, but unless you back up every 15 minutes or so, you'll never capture that piece of newly folderized information to tape.

Replication does have one drawback: Each replica of a folder takes up disk storage space. Among the other issues mentioned above, in deciding whether to use affinity or replication, you should also consider the cost of bandwidth versus disk storage space.

Site-Level Addressing and Routing Administration and Management

Look in the Configuration container for your site. Notice the Site Addressing object. This is where you deal with site addresses themselves and with message routing between sites. Since we already covered site addresses back in Chapter 7 when we installed our first Exchange server, we'll talk about intersite routing here.

Click on the Configuration container in the left-hand pane of an Administrator window, then double-click on Site Addressing. This opens up the Site Addressing Properties dialog box shown in Figure 14.78.

General Properties

The 'Routing calculation server' option on the General property page plays an important role in Exchange Server. One Exchange server in each site is designated as the routing calculation server, and the System Attendant on that server creates a routing table and replicates it to the other servers in the site. This table is used to send messages outside the site through Exchange connectors and gateways. A new routing table is calculated every time a change occurs that affects routing—for example, when a new connector is installed.

FIGURE 14.78

The Site Addressing
Properties dialog box

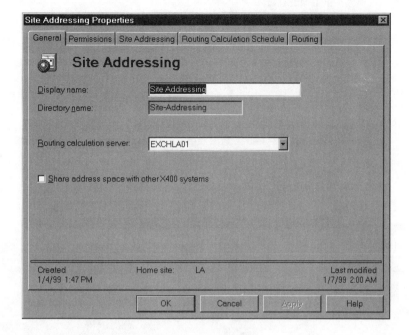

You can assign the task of calculating the routing table to any server in a site using the 'Routing calculation server' drop-down menu. Though routing calculation requires little CPU time, you might want to assign this task to the least busy of the servers in a site.

Use the 'Share address space with other X.400 systems' option to let an Exchange server pick up and route messages for another system. It's most useful when you're making the transition from an X.400 system to Exchange. The other system doesn't need to be connected to the outside world; instead, it can send and receive messages through the Exchange server.

Routing Calculation Schedule

Settings on the Routing Calculation Schedule property page determine when a new routing table is calculated. You've seen this page lots of times before, so I'll say no more about it here.

Routing

The Routing property page shows all current routing table entries and lets you manually force a recalculation for the site's routing (see Figure 14.79). You can also save the routing table to disk as a comma separated values (CSV) file and view routing details for an entry. Routing 'Details' include any connections (hops) between your site and the remote node; such information can be useful in tracing a downed link.

In Figure 14.79, you can see the routes in place from my LA site to my NY site. Each of my three Exchange connectors (DRAS, X.400, and Site) uses a standard Exchange-type address (/O=GERCOM/OU=NY) and a standard X.400 address (c=US;a= ;p=GERCOM;o=NY) to communicate with my NY site.

FIGURE 14.79

The Routing property page shows routing addresses for all connectors in a site.

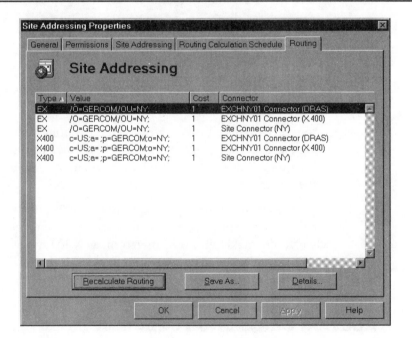

Conclusion

You learned a lot in this chapter, including how to install an Exchange server in a new domain and site; how to connect two domains and sites; how to set up directory replication between two sites; how to add new servers and links to existing server and link monitors; how to give users access to public folders in other sites; and how to use tools for administering and managing intersite routing.

Now that you're an Exchange server connection wizard, you're ready to tackle connections to foreign e-messaging systems. Onward!

PART VI

Connecting to Other
E-Messaging Systems

Now that you're an Exchange intrasite and intersite communications expert, it's time to focus on linking Exchange systems to other e-messaging systems. In Chapter 15 we'll talk about linking Exchange organizations to foreign X.400, Internet, and legacy Microsoft Mail systems and to Exchange gateways. We'll also cover indirect links between Exchange sites using X.400 and Internet mail.

In Chapter 16, we'll cover the synchronization of directories between Exchange and Microsoft Mail systems. At this point, you are pretty much an expert on a major portion of Exchange Server and Administrator. Given all of this, I'll move through the remaining chapters of this book at a significantly greater speed. You're really ready to fly on your own at this stage, and this chapter is a good first step out of the nest.

External Links Using Exchange Connectors

- Using the X.400 Connector

- Using the Internet Mail Connector

- Using the Microsoft Mail Connector

- A brief overview of the cc:Mail Connector

- A quick look at Exchange gateways

One of the most exciting things about e-messaging is the ability it gives you to communicate with people outside your organization. Whether it's a friendly hello to a customer or a transfer of funds between trading partners, e-messaging makes interaction quick and easy.

Though the options for external connections have narrowed significantly over the last year or so, many remain. Exchange comes with four connectors for external systems:

- *The X.400 Connector,* which we put to use for site-to-site links in Chapter 14

- *The Internet Mail Service,* which supports the Internet's Simple Mail Transport Protocol (SMTP) and MIME message-encoding standards

- *The MS Mail Connector,* which links Exchange and older Microsoft mail systems and lets you keep using MS Mail 3.*x*–compatible gateways with Exchange Server

- *cc:Mail Connector,* which links Lotus's cc:Mail Connector to Exchange Server

We'll cover each of these options in order in this chapter.

The X.400 Connector

As you'll remember from Chapter 14, an X.400 Connector must ride on top of a Message Transfer Agent (MTA) stack; check back there for your stack options. Either use an existing stack or create a new one, depending on how you'll make this X.400 link.

Next, select the X.400 Connector option from the New Other menu on the Exchange Administrator's File menu. Fill in the General property page in the Properties dialog box that pops up for the new connector. You'll notice in Figure 15.1 that I've followed the naming conventions for Exchange connectors that I discussed in Chapter 14. Here, I'm setting up a link to a public X.400 service provider, Public X.400 Corp. Connecting to this provider will give GerCom's Exchange users direct access to external users of X.400 systems.

FIGURE 15.1

Filling in the General property page for a connection to a public X.400 service provider

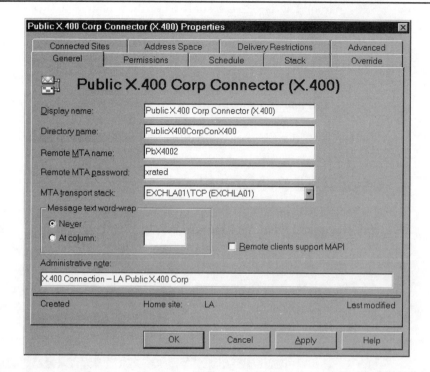

General Properties

I obtained the correct MTA name and password for the target system from the X.400 service provider. I'm running my connection on top of a TCP/IP stack. I could have run it on top of any of the X.400-appropriate MTA stacks we discussed in Chapter 14. Because I can't be sure that users on the other side of GerCom's link to Public X.400 Corp will have MAPI-capable clients, I've deselected 'Remote clients support MAPI'.

Both your server and the foreign system can contact each other to exchange messages, or one system can contact the other at all times for message exchange. If your server will be contacting the foreign X.400 system, then use the Schedule page to set that schedule. If the foreign system will contact your server exclusively, set the schedule frequency to Never.

Use the Override property page to enter an MTA name and password for your Exchange server. The name you enter overrides the MTA name specified on the General page of the server-level MTA object (which defaults to the Exchange server name). This is necessary only when the foreign X.400 system you're connecting to can't handle a name as long as the Exchange server's. We discussed the other Override page parameters in Chapters 13 and 14. Don't change any of these settings unless it is absolutely necessary for connecting to the X.400 site. Work with the manager of the foreign system to determine whether changes are required.

You'll need to get pertinent X.400 addressing information from the manager of the target system. Enter that information on the Address Space property page. (Check out Chapter 14 if you need a refresher on using the page.)

Advanced Properties

The Advanced property page is used mostly to set parameters for X.400 conformance and links, message size, message body part, and the global domain identifier (GDI) for the foreign system. Follow along with Figure 15.2 as we cover the parameters on this page.

The default, '1988 normal mode', should work with most foreign X.400 systems; see the Exchange documentation for details on these options.

FIGURE 15.2

Selecting X.400 parameters on the Advanced property page

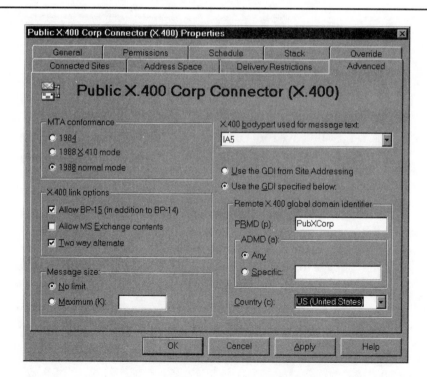

Choose from among the X.400 link options. Conformance with 1988 normal mode supports the Body Part-15 (or BP-15) standard, which includes specifications for such things as the encoding of binary message attachments and the handling of Electronic Data Interchange (EDI) body parts. The more limited BP-14 standard is specified in the 1984 X.400 standard, and is supported in the 1988 X.400 standard. If you're sure the foreign system supports BP-15, then select this link option. If you don't select BP-15, binary parts will be sent in BP-14 format, which can still be handled by any X.400 system that conforms with 1988 normal mode.

Select 'Allow MS Exchange contents' if you're using this connection exclusively to link two Exchange sites indirectly or if you know that all users at the receiving foreign system (or systems) have Extended MAPI–compliant clients. (Check to be sure about the latter condition—you don't want those foreign users to be confused by an extra body part containing Exchange stuff that doesn't map to the X.400 standard.)

Under the 'Two-way alternate' option, two X.400 systems take turns transmitting and receiving messages, speeding transmission somewhat. The X.400 Connector supports this option; if the foreign system also does, select the option in the 'X.400 link options' area of the Advanced property page.

The Message Size option is just like similar options we've covered before. Use it to set the maximum size for messages that the connection will send or receive.

Leave the 'X.400 bodypart used for message text' option set at IA5, unless you're communicating with systems that support foreign languages and their accents and other special characters. Other options on the drop-down list include versions of IA5 that are specialized for languages such as German, Norwegian, and Swedish, as well as some other standards.

The global domain identifier (GDI in Figure 15.2) is a portion of the X.400 address of the target system. It is used to prevent message transfer loops that involve outgoing messages. Check with your X.400 provider for help with these settings.

Setting Up an Indirect Site Link

Indirect site link setup is a piece of cake: Just tab over to the Connected Sites property page and click on New to bring up the Properties dialog box shown in Figure 15.3. (You saw this one back in Chapter 14, when we directly linked two sites with the X.400 Connector.) Type in the name of the site you want to link to—I'm linking to my Chicago site in Figure 15.3—and then tab over to the Routing Address property page, which is shown in Figure 15.4.

FIGURE 15.3

Setting the name of another Exchange site for an indirect X.400-based link

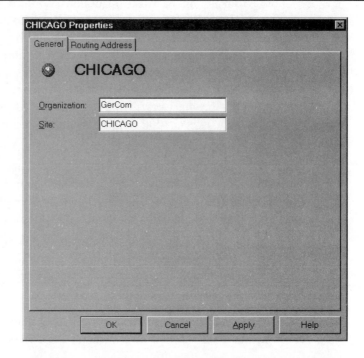

FIGURE 15.4

Setting X.400 addressing information for the other site

By default, the X.400 organization name—the name of the Exchange site you want to connect to—is filled in, along with the 'Private management domain name' for your Exchange organization and the Country setting. As long as you created (or plan to create) a parallel X.400 Connector in your other site using default naming conventions, you can accept the defaults. The only thing you might have to change is the Country setting—and that's required only if the other site is located in another country.

Be sure to set the Cost parameter appropriately. If you've linked two sites with more than one connector pair, set the cost of this connection higher or lower, depending on the amount of bandwidth it has compared to the other links you've set up between the two sites. For example, if this is a low-bandwidth link based on an X.25 connection, set its cost higher than that of a full T1-based site link. If you set the cost of this link equal to the cost of one or more other connectors, the messaging load to the site will be balanced between the connectors with the same cost.

That's it. With the parallel X.400 Connector set up and running in the other site, your two sites will exchange user messages as well as directory and folder replication information through standard X.400 messages. The two sites don't even have to connect to the same public X.400 service provider. As long as the providers they connect to can communicate with each other, everything should work fine.

Did It Work?

If you're establishing a link to a foreign e-messaging system, test the link first by sending a message to a user in an X.400 system. Then have the same user send a message back to you. If this link supports an indirect Exchange site link, first try the message exchange suggested above. Then add a mailbox at one site and see if it is replicated at the other site. If that works, try the same thing from the other site.

The Internet Mail Service

In Exchange 4.0, the connector that linked an Exchange server to the Internet was called the 'Internet Mail Connector' or IMC. For Exchange 5.0, Microsoft decided to rename the IMC, calling it the 'Internet Mail Service,' or 'IMS' for short. The name was changed because the IMS does more than connect an Exchange server to Internet mail resources. For example, it can route mail from non-Exchange clients—like the POP3 mail client Eudora—to the Internet. As with the X.400 Connector, you can use the IMS to connect an Exchange site or a whole organization to foreign e-messaging systems, as well as to link Exchange sites in the same organization.

The IMS and TCP/IP

The IMS supports the Internet's Simple Mail Transport Protocol (SMTP). It runs on top of TCP/IP. You don't have to create an MTA stack for the IMS; it uses NT's built-in TCP/IP networking.

The IMS is an SMTP mail host. A mail system must have access to an SMTP mail host to participate in the Internet mail system. The IMS communicates directly with other SMTP mail hosts to send and receive Internet mail.

The IMS can be used with a continuous or noncontinuous connection to the Internet or to your organization's own TCP/IP local- or wide-area network. In continuous connect mode, the IMS assumes that any other SMTP mail host it needs to send mail to is available all the time. The IMS attempts to send outgoing messages whenever it has a spare moment. There is no fixed delivery schedule. If the receiving SMTP host isn't available, the IMS keeps trying to send a message until a preset timeout period is reached. If the message hasn't been delivered by the end of the timeout period, the IMS returns it to the sender as undeliverable. Other SMTP hosts treat the IMS in the same way when sending messages to it.

In noncontinuous connect mode, the IMS sends and receives mail through a specific SMTP mail host, which might best be called an "Internet mail gateway." The gateway queues up messages for the IMS and the IMS queues up messages for the gateway. The IMS connects to the gateway by dialing up to it on some fixed schedule. Another IMS can serve as a gateway, as can an SMTP mail host supported by an Internet Service Provider (ISP). The IMS supports noncontinuous connections using NT's Remote Access Service (RAS). If a dial-up-enabled IMS is unable to reach its gateway to send a message within the preset timeout period (after retrying several times at specified varying intervals), it returns the message to the Exchange user. Similarly, if the IMS doesn't contact the gateway to receive a message within the timeout period, the gateway returns the message to its sender.

In just a bit, I'll show you how to configure both continuous and noncontinuous Internet connections.

Setting Up TCP/IP

If you haven't already done so, you'll need to set up TCP/IP on your Exchange server. This entails installing the TCP/IP software that comes with NT Server, assigning an IP address to your Exchange server, and providing information to your network's Domain Name Service (DNS)—which among other things equates hard-to-remember numeric IP addresses with the more common text-based host and Internet domain names.

TCP/IP setup is pretty simple. Be sure to set a domain name while installing TCP/IP. Mine's gercom.com. If you're going to use RAS for a noncontinuous Internet link, don't forget to set up RAS with dial-out capabilities. Also, remember to create a RAS phone book entry for the ISP you'll be connecting to.

NOTE You don't need to run DNS to run a TCP/IP network. However, if you're going to send SMTP mail to the outside world, your life will be far easier if you set up DNS. We mere mortals address SMTP mail using text-based host/Internet domain names ('gercom.com', for example). But SMTP servers must send mail to IP addresses (such as '192.0.2.148'), not to domain names. Without DNS, you'd need to manually maintain a "HOSTS" table of all the domains you want to communicate with, as well as their respective IP addresses. Without DNS or a HOSTS table, the IMS would have no way of translating domain names into IP addresses.

DNS is a client/server application. DNS client support is part of the TCP/IP services that come with Windows for Workgroups, Windows 95, and Windows NT. DNS server support comes with NT Server 4.0. There are some third-party vendors that sell NT DNS products. DNS services can also be provided by a UNIX system.

I don't have the space here to go into too much detail on TCP/IP or DNS, so I'll point you once again to the Sybex book *Mastering Windows NT Server 4*, by Mark Minasi, Christa Anderson, and Elizabeth Creegan. You can also take a look at the NT Server and Exchange Server manuals. Other sources of DNS information include the documentation that comes with your DNS software; and the book *sendmail*, by Bryan Costales, Eric Allman, and Neil Rickert (O'Reilly & Associates, 1993) and *DNS and BIND in a Nutshell* by Paul Albitz & Cricket Liu, same publisher, 1992.

Creating Key DNS Records for Exchange

Let's assume that your Exchange server is outfitted with TCP/IP and an IP address, and that you've got DNS running in your organization. You need to enter a record in DNS for the Exchange server that's running the IMS. This is called an *address record*, or simply an *A record*. Now let's say I want to do this for my LA Exchange server. Imagine that I've given the server the Internet host name EXLA01IP for DNS purposes, that my Internet domain name is gercom.com, and that the IP address of EXLA01IP is 192.0.2.148. The A record would look like this:

```
exla01ip.gercom.com.  IN A 192.0.2.148
```

> **WARNING** The period after 'com' in 'exla01ip.gecom.com.' is *required*, as are all of the periods in the DNS records listed in this chapter.

You don't have to give your server a different name for DNS purposes than for NT networking; I just did it to show you that you can. You also need to set up at least one *MX* (*Mail Exchanger*) record to tell DNS which computer (or computers) process SMTP mail for your system. To keep with the naming conventions I used for SMTP mail, my subdomain name here must be my site name—LA—and my domain name must be gercom.com. Given all of this, the MX record would look like this:

```
la.gercom.com. IN MX 10 exla01ip.gercom.com.
```

This record says that mail bound for the domain address la.gercom.com should be sent to the DNS-defined host exla01ip.gercom.com. The *IN* means that this is an Internet record, and the number *10* is a preference value. If there are multiple MX records for mail delivery to a given domain, the delivering SMTP server will first attempt a delivery to the host with the lowest preference value.

You can also use A records to have mail for all your Exchange sites sent to the same SMTP host. In my case, I would just add a record like the one above for each site, substituting the name of the site for *la*.

There's one neat thing you can do with MX records: You can set up domain aliases. For example, if people in GerCom's LA sales department want to use the domain name la.sales.gercom.com on their business cards (instead of the simple la.gercom.com), you can add an MX record to direct mail sent to la.sales.gercom.com to exla01ip.gercom.com. The record would look like this:

```
la.sales.gercom.com. IN MX 10 exla01ip.gercom.com.
```

This record says that mail bound for la.sales.gercom.com should be sent to exla01ip at gercom.com.

Installing the IMS

In Exchange Server 4.0, you installed an Internet Mail Connector when you installed Exchange Server. With Exchange Server 5.0, you install an IMS using the New Other submenu of the Exchange Administrator's File menu. See Figure 15.5. Selecting this option brings up the Internet Mail Wizard (Figure 15.6), which helps you through IMS installation.

FIGURE 15.5

Starting installation of the Internet Mail Service

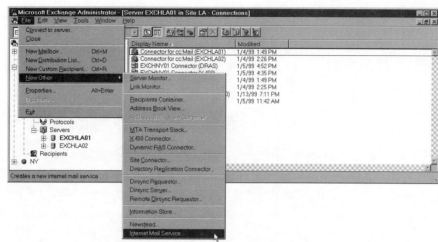

FIGURE 15.6

The Internet Mail Wizard makes it easier to install the Internet Mail Service.

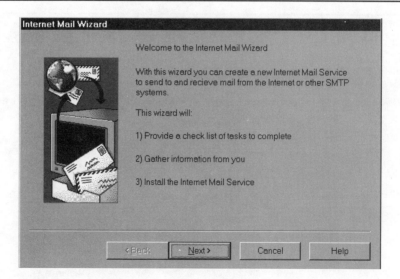

Click on Next to display the next wizard page (Figure 15.7). This page reminds you to do the tasks we just discussed. Assuming you've completed these tasks, click on Next to bring up the wizard's first configuration page. See Figure 15.8. Use this page to specify the Exchange server the IMS is to be installed on and to indicate whether the IMS will support dial-up noncontinuous links.

FIGURE 15.7

The Internet Mail Wizard lists tasks to be completed before moving on.

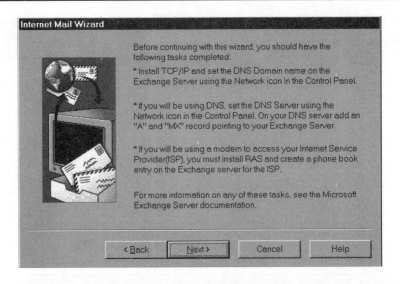

FIGURE 15.8

Selecting the Exchange server to host the Internet Mail Service and the dial-up option

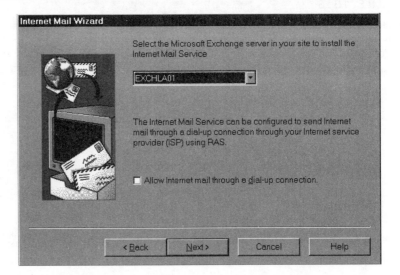

If you indicate that you want dial-up (noncontinuous) connects, the next wizard page you'll see looks like the one in Figure 15.9. Here's where you tell the IMS where to get the telephone number and networking information it needs to access the dial-up SMTP mail host that will serve as your Internet mail gateway. The dial-up information is entered into the RAS phone book. Use the Dial-up Networking program in the Accessories program group to set up the phone book entry.

FIGURE 15.9

Telling the IMS where to find information for a RAS dial-up (noncontinuous) connection

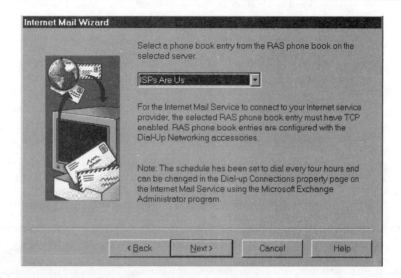

Arranging for Dial-Up Internet Mail Gatewaying

Basically, whoever operates the SMTP mail host that will serve as your gateway will have to tell the world, through its Domain Name Service, that your domain can be reached for mail purposes through the gateway mail host. If you don't already have a domain name, you can work with the provider of gateway services to get one. Commercial Internet Service Providers (ISPs) are usually well set up to do this.

When all is set up, your IMS will connect to the gateway at set intervals. While connected, it will send outgoing Internet mail and pull down any incoming mail that is queued up on the gateway machine. After installation of the IMS, you'll need to make a few settings to assure that all of this happens. I'll talk about these later in this chapter.

Figure 15.10 shows the next wizard page. This is where you tell the IMS whether you want it to send Internet messages to any and all SMTP mail hosts using your network's Domain Name System or to route outgoing messages through one SMTP mail host that will take care of sending them out to all other hosts. Choose the first option when you want to hide (firewall) your mail system from the outside world. You'll also find the first option attractive when your Exchange server is relatively low-powered and you've got a monster UNIX machine already functioning as an SMTP mail host. In this case, the monster will handle outgoing mail traffic far better than your Exchange server. In Figure 15.11, I've chosen to have the IMS ship all of its outgoing mail to GerCom's UNIX server, BIG'UN. Choose the second option if you don't need a firewall and have an adequately powered Exchange server.

FIGURE 15.10

Setting the IMS to send messages directly to other SMTP mail hosts

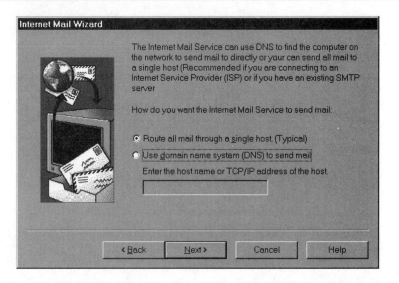

Use the next wizard page (see Figure 15.12) to tell the IMS whether you want it to send messages to all or selected Internet addresses. You can use the second option to distribute the load of sending mail over multiple IMSs on your Exchange servers, assigning responsibility for different sets of addresses to different IMSs. If you select the second option, you'll get a message warning you to configure the addresses after IMS installation is finished. (See Figure 15.13.)

FIGURE 15.11

Setting the IMS to send messages through another SMTP mail host

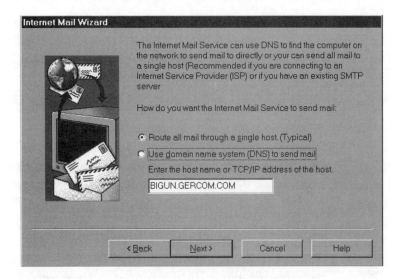

FIGURE 15.12

Telling the IMS to send messages to all or selected Internet addresses

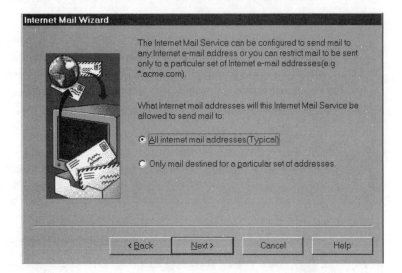

FIGURE 15.13

A warning to configure the specific addresses the IMS will handle after installation is finished

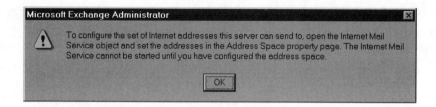

Next the Internet Mail Wizard asks you to enter the Internet address to be used for your Exchange site. The default is the address constructed from your site and organization name plus "com". As you can see in Figure 15.14, the default address offered by the wizard for GerCom is "@LA.GerCom.com". You can change the default here or later by opening the site addressing object in the Exchange Administrator's Configuration container.

After you finish with your Internet site address, click on Next to enter the name of a mailbox or distribution list that is to receive reports about non-delivered messages. See Figure 15.15. This is an important step. Non-delivery report notifications are one of the key ways you can monitor the health of your Exchange Internet link and, most importantly, keep your users happy.

Hold on, we're almost done. On the next wizard page you enter the NT account and password for your Exchange Service Account. This is the account you set up and used when you installed your first Exchange server in the site. See Figure 15.16. Like all other Exchange services (the MTA, Information Store, Directory, etc.), the IMS will be installed to run under the authority of your Exchange Service account.

Finally, click on Next and you'll see the final page of the wizard (see Figure 15.17). Click on Finish and after a minute or so, you'll see the dialog box in Figure 15.18, telling you that the IMS has been installed and started. If you don't get that message, check out your TCP/IP configuration and take a look at the Application log in the NT Event Log for any IMS errors.

> **NOTE**
>
> Just before releasing Exchange Server 5.0, Microsoft changed the look and some of the text in the wizard pages shown in Figures 15.17 and 15.18. I didn't have time to include the revised pages here. So, your wizard pages will look a bit different than the ones shown in the two figures. I'll call your attention to any differences.

FIGURE 15.14

Setting the Internet address for the Exchange site

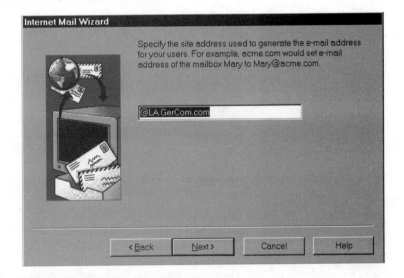

FIGURE 15.15

Specifying a mailbox or distribution list to receive non-delivery report notifications for messages handled by the IMS

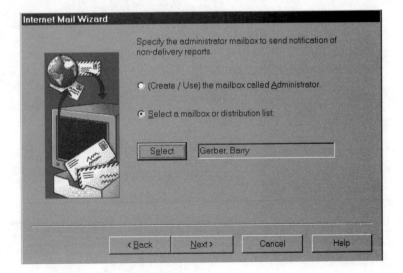

FIGURE 15.16

Entering information on the Exchange Services account

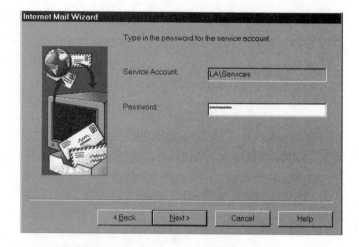

FIGURE 15.17

Finishing IMS installation

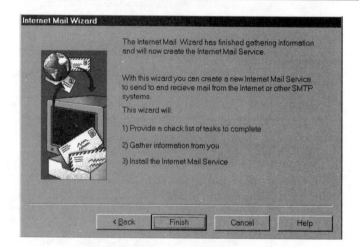

FIGURE 15.18

The IMS has been successfully installed and started.

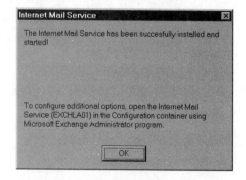

Setting IMS Properties

At this point, your Internet Mail Service is ready to receive mail on a continuous Internet link without any special fancy settings like sending to only specific Internet addresses. To set your IMS to do more than the basics, you have to open and use the IMS Properties dialog box. You know I'm not going to let you off without a thorough lesson in this handy-dandy little gizmo, so let's go. Find the Internet Mail Service in your Connections container and double-click on it. This brings up the Internet Mail Service Properties dialog box shown in Figure 15.19.

FIGURE 15.19

The Internet Mail Service Properties dialog box

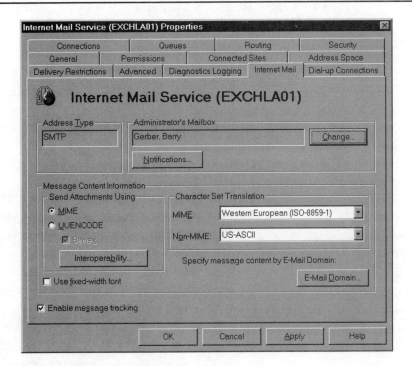

Internet Mail Properties

The Internet Mail Service Properties dialog box is a bit unusual in one regard: It opens on the Internet Mail property page rather than the General page. See Figure 15.19. Otherwise, it behaves pretty much like other Properties dialog boxes. Let's look at the Internet Mail property page in more detail. Follow along on Figure 15.19.

Address Type   When an Exchange user sends a message, it is directed to one or more e-mail addresses. Each of these addresses must be of an address type that has been defined in the Exchange system. Messages of a specific address type are handled by specific Exchange Server components. For example, messages with X.400-type addresses are handled by X.400 connectors. Messages with SMTP-type addresses are handled by IMSs with SMTP in the Address Type field of the Internet Mail property page (see Figure 15.19). The address type SMTP is entered in this field when you install the IMS with the wizard. The address type cannot be changed.

The Administrator's Mailbox   When you ran the IMS installation wizard, you selected an Administrator's mailbox (or distribution list) to receive non-delivery report notifications. You can choose a different mailbox or list at any time by clicking on the Change button.

Notifications   Click on Notifications to set up the kinds of notifications that should be sent to the IMS administrator's mailbox; you can see the options in Figure 15.20. When I first set up an IMS, I like to see notifications for all non-delivery reports. Later, when I'm more comfortable with the way the IMS and addressing are set up, I select the option 'Multiple matches for an E-Mail address occurred'.

FIGURE 15.20

Selecting the NDR notifications to be sent to the IMS administrator's mailbox or distribution list

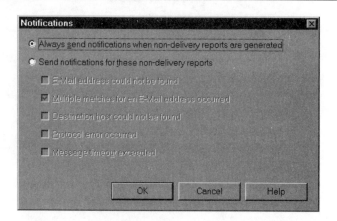

Send Attachments Using   In order to travel through the Internet, messages with binary attachments must be encoded to remove any 8-bit characters. Two encoding schemes are popular on the Internet: the newer MIME (Multipurpose Internet Mail Extensions) and the older UUencode (UNIX-to-UNIX Encode).

The Send Attachments Using area (see Figure 15.19) is where you set the default encoding method for messages outbound from the IMS. As you'll see in just a bit, you can actually set different defaults on an outbound-domain-by-outbound-domain basis. Because it nicely supports a variety of message types and allows for the invocation of a supporting helper application, MIME is your best bet, unless you know you'll be sending exclusively to foreign systems where only the UUencode scheme is in use. Encoded message parts are decoded automatically by either the receiving SMTP host or by the user's e-messaging client. With some systems, automatic decoding isn't available. In this case, the recipient must manually decode the encoded message parts.

NOTE Here's another change that came too late for me to include it in this edition. In the final release version of Exchange Server 5.0, the 'Send Attachments Using' area on the Internet Mail property page is called "Message Encoding". This newly named area includes not only options for message encoding, but also, under MIME, options for how text in messages should be sent. These options are: Send message body as plain text and Send message body as HTML. Plain text is straight 7-bit ASCII text, which is recognizable by any SMTP mail client. HTML encoded text includes any formatting information required to display such things as bold, italic, and colored text as well as different fonts. I'll talk more about HTML encoding in Chapter 18.

Interoperability Click the Interoperability button to set message content parameters to ensure that your IMS sends messages in a format that is compatible with the SMTP hosts it will communicate with (see Figure 15.21).

FIGURE 15.21

Selecting settings to ensure compatibility with other SMTP hosts

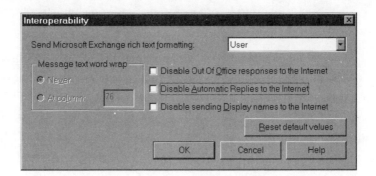

Rich Text Formatting   You don't want to send messages in Exchange's rich text (bold, italic, underline, color fonts, etc.) to people who can't take advantage of it, because they'll often see a lot of meaningless junk when they open a message. Options for the 'Send Microsoft Exchange rich text formatting' field include User, Always, and Never. Unless you know for sure that all or no recipients in a foreign e-messaging system can handle rich text, User is usually your best option. When User is selected, the IMS sends in rich text only if that option has been enabled for the individual recipient. Administrators can enable rich text for custom recipients—the only Exchange Server recipients who might not be able to handle rich text—on the Advanced property page of the custom recipient's Properties dialog box. Users can do the same for addresses they create in their Exchange client personal address books.

Word Wrap   The proper word-wrap settings let recipient clients format message text into nice, word processor–like paragraphs. The default should work fine in most cases. You cannot alter this setting if you've selected MIME encoding.

Disable Options   You can disable the delivery of out-of-office messages and automatic replies to recipients reached through your IMS. You can also do the same for Exchange display names, which can be used by many SMTP systems to show more information about you than your simple Exchange Server alias name. Unless you've got some technical or policy reason for doing so, don't disable any of these options.

Character Set Translation   Now let's go back to the Internet Mail property page (see Figure 15.19). Accept the Character Set Translation defaults; other options are for certain foreign languages.

Fixed-width Font   If you want the IMS to convert all inbound messages into a non-proportional font, select this option. This is a useful option if the bulk of your inbound Internet mail depends on characters being aligned properly, e.g., tables and reports.

E-Mail Domain   You use the E-Mail Domain button to set different message-content parameters for specific domains with which your IMS will exchange mail. In Figure 15.22, I'm telling the IMS to UUencode messages with binary attachments that are sent to the domain msmail.davis.com. That's because Davis's Microsoft Mail SMTP gateway can decode only UUencoded messages. As you can see in the figure, you can set all of the content parameters for the domain, including those for interoperability.

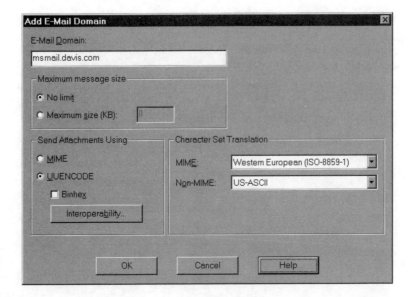

FIGURE 15.22

Setting message size and content information for a specific domain

Enable Message Tracking   As you did in past chapters with your MTAs and information stores, you should enable message tracking here. This will let you check the status of messages sent out through and coming in from the IMS.

General Properties

Use the General property page to set default message-size limits for the IMS; you can also enter an administrative note (see Figure 15.23). Notice that you have no control over the computer name given to the IMS; it's preset to the name of the Exchange server it runs on.

Address Space

As with the X.400 Connector, you use the Address Space property page to set addresses that the IMS will send messages to (see Figure 15.24). These can be as specific as the address of a single recipient or as general as all SMTP recipients. If you have multiple IMSs, you can use the Address Space page to control which addresses a specific IMS sends messages to. For redundancy and load balancing, you can set up the same address space definitions on multiple IMSs.

The simplest approach is to create one address—a general SMTP address space for all recipients. The IMS installation wizard does this for you. So, if that's all you need, you're all set as far as the Address Space page is concerned.

FIGURE 15.23

The General property page of the IMS Properties dialog box

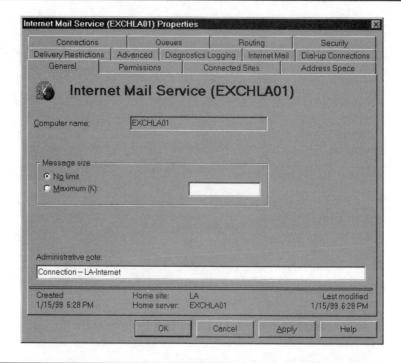

FIGURE 15.24

Setting the addresses to which the IMS will deliver messages

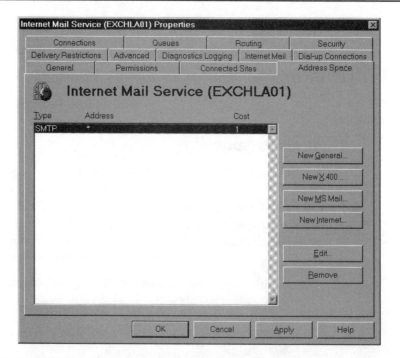

Let's say you want this IMS to handle only messages to the 'com' and 'gov' Internet subdomains. Instead of the address space created by the IMS installation wizard, you'd create two Internet address spaces—one for *.com and one for *.gov. You don't have to limit yourself to these higher level subdomains: You can set up an IMS that just delivers mail to a specific company, university, or even individual.

Advanced Properties

You use the Advanced property page shown in Figure 15.25 to set a number of parameters for individual messages.

Message parameters are used to control the interaction between the outgoing message queue for the IMS and the IMS itself. The settings are:

- *Unread limit:* When the number of unread messages in the queue exceeds this limit, no more messages are accepted into the queue.

- *Back-off interval:* At the end of this period of time, a check is made to see if the number of messages in the queue has dropped below the unread limit.

- *Max unread time:* Messages that remain in the queue beyond this period of time will be returned to the Exchange sender as undeliverable.

FIGURE 15.25

The Advanced property page of the IMS Properties dialog box

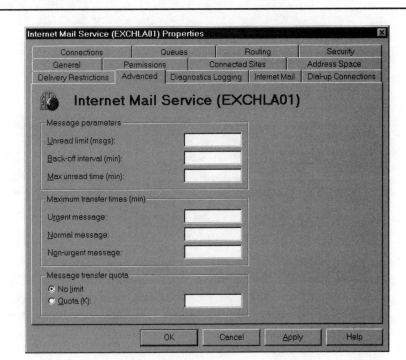

- *Maximum transfer times:* Outgoing messages that aren't delivered within the periods of time set are returned to the sender as undeliverable; different times can be set for messages of different delivery priority.

- *Message transfer quota:* When the combined size of the messages in the outgoing IMS queue exceeds this parameter, outgoing messages will queue up in the MTA.

Dial-up Connections

Here's where you set up a noncontinuous connect to another SMTP mail host—called an "Internet mail gateway" above—which your IMS will send and receive messages through. Generally, this will be an SMTP mail host operated by an Internet Service Provider. If you told the IMS installation wizard that you wanted to do a dial-up connection, the wizard partially completed the entries on the Dial-up property page. If not, you can set up a dial-up connection from scratch on this page.

Let's take a closer look at the options on the Dial-up Connections property page. Track along on Figure 15.26.

FIGURE 15.26

Setting the IMS for dial-up connections

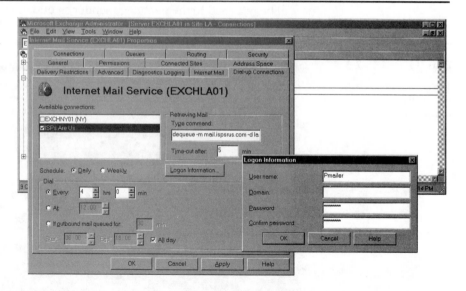

Available Connections   Make sure you pick the correct dial-up entry in your Remote Access Service (RAS) phone book. If you need to add a new entry, use the Dial-Up Networking program that's in the Accessories program group on your Exchange server. Then come back to the Dial-up Connections page. Of course, you must have the proper modem and RAS installed and enabled for dial-out calls before you do all of this.

Logon Information   Click the Logon Information button and add the necessary user name, domain, and password information for logging onto the SMTP mail host that will act as your gateway. You won't need domain information, unless you're going to connect to another NT server that provides the gateway service.

Retrieving Mail   This is probably the most complex part of dial-up gatewaying. The IMS will send mail as soon as it connects to the gateway. But, to receive mail, you may need to make an entry in the Type Command field. Whatever command you type in the field is executed on your Exchange server after the connection is made to the provider's network. What you enter in this field depends on the kind of Internet mail gatewaying technology your provider has in place.

You can get up-to-date status reports on various gateway mail retrieval options for Exchange from a web site operated by Simpler Webb Inc. Check it out at www.swinc.com. This site not only discusses the options, but it gives you specific instructions for retrieving mail using each option.

In Figure 15.26, I entered the command dequeue, which is actually a program for Intel processor–based machines (DEQUEUE.EXE) that you can download free from the Simpler Webb site. This program works with Internet mail hosts running the program sendmail 8.8 or greater.

You can't see the full command I entered because the field window is too small. For the record, here it is: dequeue -m mail.ispsrus.com -d la.gercom.com. As you'll learn at the Simpler Webb site, typing dequeue -? gives you a list of command line options for the program. The name of the mail server acting as your gateway is -m. The name of the domain you want to retrieve mail for is -d.

For sites not running sendmail 8.8 or greater or using other Internet mail server packages, the Simpler Webb's web site discusses a range of options other than the preferred DEQUEUE.EXE. These include the UNIX commands rsh, rexec, and finger.

All of the command options require some level of cooperation from your provider. To the end of rewarding nice folks, www.swinc.com includes a list of Internet Service Providers who've gotten the message re: dial-up connect.

Schedule   As you can see in Figure 15.26, you have a wide range of options for scheduling connects to your gateway. What you set here depends on your organization's need for immediacy in its Internet mail communications. The default of every four hours is a good starting point. Adjust it as you work with the dial-up connect.

Be careful with the 'If outbound mail queued for X min' option. The IMS will not contact the gateway unless there is at least one message in its outbound queue and the last dial up was X minutes or more ago. So, if no one tries to send a message for three days, incoming messages awaiting pickup at your gateway will just sit there. If your users send a fair number of outgoing messages through this IMS, this setting is fine. If not, stick with an hourly schedule.

Connections

The Connections property page provides a lot of tools for controlling your links to other SMTP systems (see Figure 15.27).

Transfer Mode   You set the send-receive functionality for the IMS in the Transfer Mode area of the Connections property page. Will your IMS both send and receive messages, only send or only receive messages, or do neither? You can accept the default to have the IMS both send and receive, or you can balance loads by having it send messages while another IMS receives them.

FIGURE 15.27

Using the Connections property page to set several parameters that control links with other SMTP systems

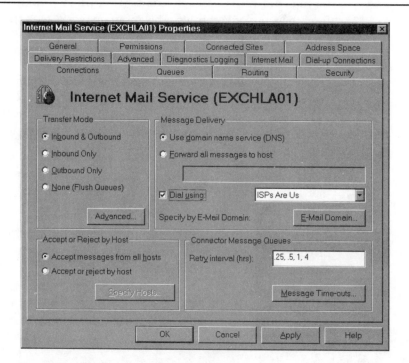

Select the None (Flush Queues) option to stop the IMS and have it deliver all messages in its queues. This is useful when queues are temporarily laden with messages due to such things as heavy internal message creation or when the IMS receives a lot of messages.

If queues back up regularly, then it may be time to change some Connections parameters or take even more drastic steps. You make parameter changes in the Advanced dialog box; to open it, click on the Advanced button on the Connections property page. Here you can set the maximum number of inbound and outbound connections to the IMS, as well as the maximum connections to a single host and the maximum number of messages sent during one connection (see Figure 15.28).

FIGURE 15.28

Setting advanced parameters for IMS connections to other SMTP hosts

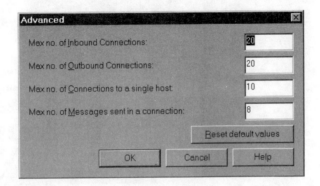

Normally, sticking with the defaults is fine; you'd generally change them to fine-tune the IMS's message I/O performance. For example, if outbound message queues get backed up regularly, you might want to increase the number of outbound connections and reduce the other three parameters. The key to good performance is CPU power and the amount of memory in the Exchange server supporting the IMS. So if parameter adjustments don't help, consider adding another IMS or beefing up processing power and/or RAM.

Message Delivery   Now we're back on the Connections property page (see Figure 15.27). You can use DNS to resolve (that is, convert) text-based addresses into IP addresses or you can forward messages to another SMTP host for handling. Unless you're running a very small system, I strongly suggest that you develop and use DNS. If you want to forward messages to another host that handles DNS, specify the name of the host or enter its IP address.

Dial Using   Check Dial using to indicate that the IMS should connect by dialing to an SMTP mail host. Select the specific RAS phone book entry to be used when dialing from the drop-down list.

E-mail Domain   If you wish, you can click on the E-Mail Domain button and set different message-delivery parameters for different domains. See Figure 15.29.

FIGURE 15.29

Setting specific message-delivery parameters for a domain

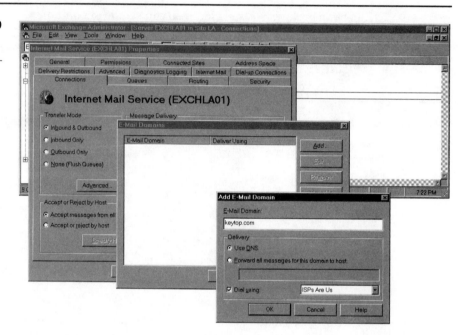

Accept or Reject by Host   If you have a reason for doing so, you can specify only those SMTP hosts you'll accept mail from or those hosts you won't accept mail from. Select 'Accept or reject by host' to bring up a dialog box that lets you enter specific host addresses. This is a nice way to restrict access to your Exchange system for security purposes or to prevent distracting messages from users of certain external e-messaging systems.

Retry Interval   As I noted back at the beginning of this section, the IMS continues trying to send a message until a timeout period is reached. Set the retry intervals in the 'Retry interval (hrs)' field of the Connections property page's Connector Message Queues area. In Figure 15.27, the defaults—.25, .5, 1, and 4—are in effect. So when the IMS first attempts to contact a host to send a message, if the connection is not made, it waits .25 hour for a reply. If it receives no reply on the second try, it tries to connect again. If the third attempt fails, the IMS waits for .5 hour, and so on.

When it reaches the end of the string of retry wait times, the IMS retries connections at the last interval of time. It continues trying to send the message until a specific length of time passes. This time is set using the Message Timeouts dialog box that pops up when you click on the Message Timeouts button on the Connections property page (see Figure 15.30). Timeouts are set for Urgent (24 hours), Normal (48 hours), and Non-urgent (72 hours); the default settings are in parentheses.

Another nice feature: There are also timeouts after which the sender is notified that a message is still waiting to be sent. These too are based on message urgency. Defaults are four hours (Urgent), 12 hours (Normal), and 24 hours (Non-urgent). However, notifications are only sent for Urgent mail by default. To send notifications for Normal or Non-urgent mail, select the checkboxes next to those options.

FIGURE 15.30

Setting timeout parameters for messages to other SMTP hosts

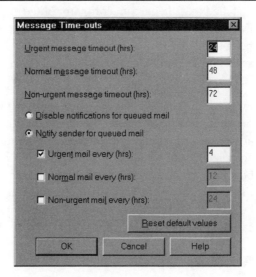

Queues

You can check on and manipulate messages in the IMS's various queues. You can also watch over the IMS and other Exchange queues with the pre-set Performance Monitor applications that are installed when you install Exchange Server. You'll find these in the Microsoft Exchange program group on your Exchange server. For more on NT's Performance Monitor application, see Chapter 4.

Routing

The IMS can route certain incoming SMTP messages back out to the Internet. Why, you might ask, would I want to do that? A good question, I might respond.

Let's say you've set up your Exchange server to support POP3 mail service. (We'll get into that can of spaghetti in Chapter 18.) So now your users can get to their Exchange mail using a POP3 client like Qualcomm's Eudora. Great, that only lets them get their mail. How do they send it out? The POP3 protocol requires that, in addition to setting an incoming POP3 mail host for your POP3 client, you also set a specific SMTP mail host to handle outgoing mail from the client.

The same host can support both incoming and outgoing mail, but if your IMS is going to take outgoing POP3 client mail and ship it on to the Internet, you may have to set it up to do so. You don't want messages to Exchange users to be routed back to the Internet. You want them to be delivered into the Exchange system where they will be processed and sent to users. By default, incoming IMS messages addressed to the Internet domain name of the site where the IMS is installed (e.g., la.gercom.com) are routed right into the Exchange system. If your IMS supports other Exchange sites with their own Internet domain names, you'll need to tell the IMS to route messages addressed to those domains into the Exchange system. Here's how you do that.

Tab over to the Routing property page on your IMS properties dialog box. See Figure 15.31. Click on the Add button. In the Edit Routing Table Entry, type in the name of the domain, other than the default. That is, a domain that represents addresses inside your Exchange site or organization. Then check the Should be accepted as "inbound" option and click OK on the Edit Routing Table Entry dialog box. Repeat the above steps for each domain in your organization. In Figure 15.31, I'm adding my New York site to the list of domains for which incoming mail is to be accepted as inbound to my Exchange system. There are lots of other things you can do with this routing capability. I'll leave all of that to your imagination.

Security

You use the Security property page (see Figure 15.32) to set up NT security for connections to other IMSs or other SMTP hosts on NT systems.

Secure Outbound Connections   Here you can set NT account information for all connections to IMSs or other SMTP hosts on other NT systems. When this information is provided, sessions to NT systems are encrypted. Use the E-Mail Domain button to set up different NT security information for different SMTP mail domains.

FIGURE 15.31

Setting up inbound message routing for POP3 clients

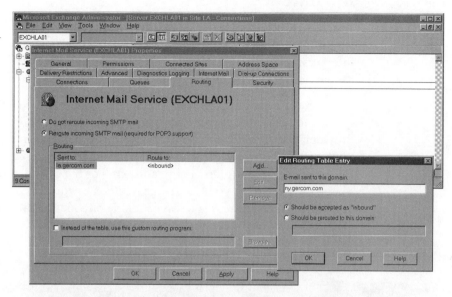

FIGURE 15.32

The Internet Mail Service's Security property page

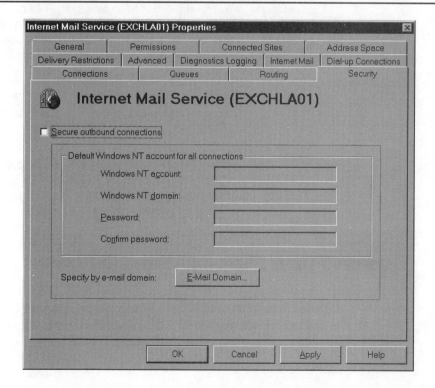

Did It Work?

That's it—you're done. Click OK on the IMS Properties dialog box. Assuming that your TCP/IP and DNS configurations are set and you've got a connection to the Internet in place, your IMS will start working as soon as you start it up using the Services applet in the Control Panel.

Try sending mail to your Exchange mailbox from outside of your Exchange system, for example, from an account you've set up with an Internet Service Provider. Use a POP3 mail client such as Eudora or the ones provided by Microsoft or Netscape. Next, ask someone on the Internet to send mail to your Exchange mailbox's Internet mail address. For the record, it does no good to send a message from your Exchange mailbox to your Exchange mailbox's Internet address. The address is resolved inside of your Exchange server and delivered. The message never gets out to the Internet.

> **TIP**
>
> I have an account with an Internet Service Provider. One of the main things I do with it is to test new IMSs. I use a POP3 mail client connected to the ISP's network to send messages to myself on a new IMS and to receive messages I send through the new IMS from an Exchange client. For more on using POP3 clients, see Chapter 18.

If everything works, you're home free. If you have problems, take a look at your DNS entries. If they look OK, be sure you've allowed enough time for those entries to find their way out to other DNS servers on the Internet. It can take several days before new DNS information is fully distributed across the worldwide hierarchy of DNS servers. If someone tries to send messages to your announced Internet address, and the DNS that person uses hasn't acquired your DNS information yet, the messages will be returned to the sender with a note indicating that your address couldn't be found.

Setting Up a Site Link Using the IMS

As you did with the X.400 Connector, you can use the Connected Sites property page on the Internet Mail Service Properties page to start both direct and indirect links to other Exchange sites. You can even connect to sites running X.400 connectors, since you can specify an X.400 address in SMTP format.

A link is direct if the IMS talks to another Exchange server over the Internet or to your own internal TCP/IP network without the intervention of intermediate SMTP or X.400 systems. If intermediate systems are involved, then the link is indirect.

Did It Work?

Take a look at the "Did It Work?" section for the X.400 Connector. You can perform the same tests here as I laid out there to determine if your IMS is functioning properly.

The MS Mail Connector

If your organization is using Microsoft Mail (MS Mail) for PC Networks or Apple-Talk Networks, you can transparently link MS Mail and Exchange users with the MS Mail Connector (MMC). Exchange also comes with software for migrating (moving) MS Mail users to Exchange; we'll discuss this software in a later chapter.

Migration is a pretty big move. As you start building your Exchange system, the MMC lets you maintain communications between Exchange users and MS Mail users. With Exchange-MMC links in place, you can then take a more leisurely approach to migration.

You can also use the MMC to let Exchange users take advantage of gateways not yet available for Exchange Server and to give MS Mail users access to Exchange's more powerful and stable connectors and gateways. For example, you can use Exchange's Internet Mail Service and the MMC to move SMTP mail in and out of MS Mail environments, dumping Microsoft's weak SMTP gateway for Microsoft Mail for PC Networks (MS Mail PC) in the process.

Because MS Mail PC is the more widely used of the two MS Mail products, I'll cover connectivity to it in detail here. I'm also assuming that you are familiar with the concepts and software behind MS Mail PC. (See the Exchange documentation for more information on using the MMC for linking Exchange systems and MS Mail for AppleTalk Networks.)

Whichever of the two MS Mail products you're connecting to, the MMC works in pretty much the same way. A shadow MS Mail PC network and post office are created on the Exchange server running the MMC. Then an NT service runs on the Exchange server that essentially emulates the functions performed by MS Mail PC's EXTERNAL.EXE program. This service moves messages between the Exchange shadow post office and the MS Mail PC post office, just as EXTERNAL.EXE does for a group of real MS Mail PC post offices. (For MS Mail for AppleTalk Networks, you connect the Macintosh mail side to the shadow post office and then run a connecting service on the Exchange server running the MMC.)

The MMC runs on top of standard NT local area network protocols or using NT's Remote Access Service (RAS) asynchronous or X.25 connections. You can use one or all of these links; network links should be set up before you configure the MMC. You can run only one instance of the MMC per Exchange server, but you can connect to multiple MS Mail PC post offices through a single MMC. And one MMC can serve some or all of the sites in an Exchange organization.

WARNING   You have to install the MMC before you can use it. If you installed it when you installed Exchange Server, you're ready to go. If not, you'll need to run the Exchange Server setup program and install the MMC. After that, you can move on to the configuration discussion below.

To start configuring the MMC, find and double-click on the MS Mail Connector you want to run in the appropriate Connectors container of your Exchange Administrator. If you have multiple servers in a site and you've installed the MMC on each, you'll see multiple instances of the MMC, each marked for the server it resides on; make sure to pick the one for the server you want. The MS Mail Connector Properties dialog box will pop up (see Figure 15.33).

Interchange

The MMC opens on the Interchange rather than the General property page. The first thing you need to do is add an administrator's mailbox. Click on Change and select an Exchange recipient from the resultant address list dialog box.

If the primary language for clients isn't English, select the correct language from the drop-down list. Select the Maximize MS Mail 3.x Compatibility checkbox to let MS Mail users view and save OLE-embedded objects sent from Exchange clients. When this option is selected, the MMC creates a second version of the embedded object that's compatible with the earlier version of OLE supported by the MS Mail PC Windows client. Compatibility is costly in terms of storage, because the second version can be quite large—up to 1MB—so choose this option with care and forethought.

FIGURE 15.33

The MS Mail Connector
Properties dialog box
opens on the Interchange
property page.

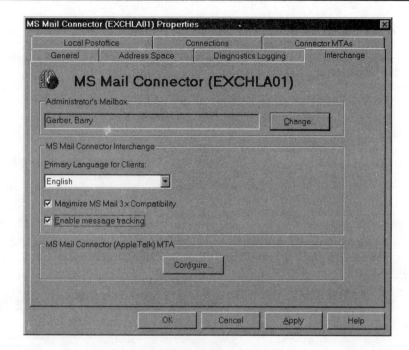

As usual, I strongly suggest that you enable message tracking. Though we're
not going to get into it here, you use the Configure button to set up the MS Mail
Connector for AppleTalk Networks.

General Properties

Use the General Properties page shown in Figure 15.34 to set message-size limits
and to enter an administrative note for the MMC. Notice that the note entered in
Figure 15.34 follows the syntax I recommended earlier for Exchange connectors.

Connections

Tab over to the Connections property page (see Figure 15.35). This is where you
add and maintain the MS Mail PC post offices serviced by the MMC. Notice in
the figure that the connection to the Exchange shadow MS Mail PC network and
post office—GERCOM/LA in my case—is already there; the link is created automatically. By the way, the MS Mail PC network is GERCOM and the post office is
LA, both of which, of course, parallel the names of my Exchange organization
and the Exchange site in which I'm creating the MMC.

FIGURE 15.34

The General property
page of the MS Mail
Connector Properties
dialog box

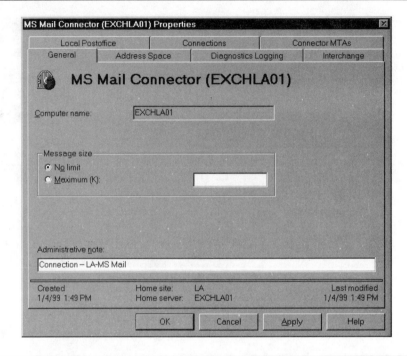

FIGURE 15.35

The Connections prop-
erty page of the MS Mail
Connector Properties
dialog box

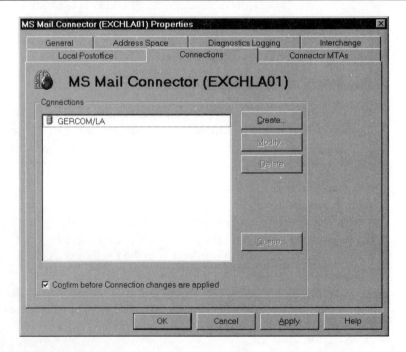

Now we have to create links to other real MS Mail PC post offices. From the Connections property page, click on Create to bring up the Create Connection dialog box shown in Figure 15.36. We're going to create a local area network–based link, so be sure that 'LAN' is selected under Connection Parameters. Next, we have to tell the MMC where the post office is located on the LAN.

FIGURE 15.36

Setting up a new connection to an MS Mail PC post office

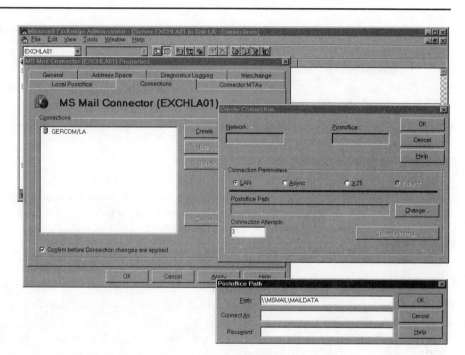

NOTE If we'd chosen the Async or X.25 option, we would have been asked for appropriate information to make the connection. If you've set up a modem connection between two MS Mail PC post offices, you should have no trouble filling in the info for Async or X.25 connections.

Click on Change to enter the post office location. This brings up the Postoffice Path dialog box shown in the lower right-hand corner of Figure 15.36. The path must be entered in Universal Naming Convention (UNC) format, which doesn't use disk drive letters and allows computers to connect without drive mappings. Generically, the UNC format is *Computer_Name**ShareName.* My MS Mail PC post office is on the NT computer named MSMAIL in the share MAILDATA. (MS Mail PC administrators will immediately recognize MAILDATA as a standard data directory for MS Mail PC post office installations.) So the path shown in Figure 15.36 is \\MSMAIL\MAILDATA.

NOTE

If your MS Mail PC post office is on a NetWare server, you must run the NT service Gateway Service for NetWare. The UNC syntax for a Net-Ware server is

```
\\NetWare_Server_Name\NetWare_Volume_Name\
Directory_Path.
```

Use the Connect As field to enter a network logon account name for the server that's holding the MS Mail PC post office. Enter the password for the account in the Password field. You need to fill in these fields only if the service account for the MMC doesn't have standard domain-based security access to the MS Mail PC post office server.

NOTE

For NetWare-based post offices, create a NetWare user with the same name and password as the NT service account for Exchange. This is the account that will run the services that support the MMC on your NT/Exchange server. If you do this, you don't have to enter the Net-Ware account name and password in the Postoffice Path dialog box. The MMC will be able to connect to the post office just by virtue of the matching NT and NetWare account names and passwords.

Once you've entered the path to the MS Mail PC post office, click on OK in the Postoffice Path dialog box. If you've entered the correct path and if security is properly set, you're returned to the Create Connection dialog box (see Figure 15.37). If something doesn't work, make sure that the path and security are set correctly.

Notice that I didn't have to manually enter the names of the MS Mail PC network (GCMSMAIL) or post office (LA)—the Exchange server automatically retrieved this information from the post office.

Change the Connection Attempts default if you want the MMC to attempt to deliver messages more than three times before returning them to the sender on the Exchange side. Click on the Upload Routing button to get routing information on MS Mail PC *indirect* post offices. These are post offices that have mail routed to them by the MS Mail PC post office you're connecting to now. This routing is set up at the MS Mail PC post offices. The MMC can reach indirect post offices through its connection to the routing post office. With routing in place, you don't have to create an MMC connection to each of the indirect post offices.

FIGURE 15.37

The connection to the MS Mail PC post office has been established.

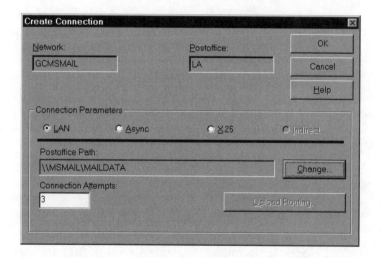

Click on OK in the Create Connection dialog box when you're done, then click on OK in the Apply Changes Now dialog box that pops up next. This finalizes the creation process and adds the newly created MS Mail PC post office link to the Connections area of the Connections property page.

Tab over to the Address Space property page. Notice that an MS Mail address type has been automatically added to the list for the MS Mail PC post office (see Figure 15.38).

FIGURE 15.38

A new address space
is added for the MMC
connection

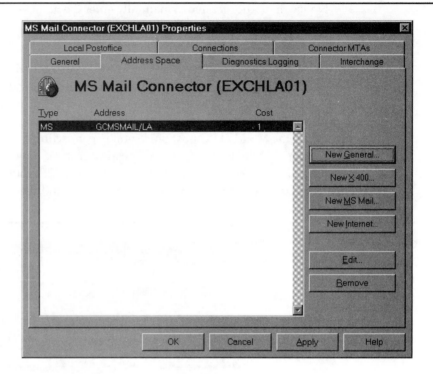

Connector MTAs

An MTA must be created to serve your newly established MS Mail PC post office connection. The MTA is an NT service. You manage it just like any other NT service—for example, the services for the four Exchange key components.

Tab over to the Connector MTAs property page and click on New. This brings up the New MS Mail Connector (PC) MTA Service property page (see Figure 15.39). Give the service a name. You'll see this name when you run the NT Control Panel's Services applet.

Log Messages

Indicate whether you want message traffic logged. Log files will be put into the shadow post office's LOG directory.

FIGURE 15.39

Setting up an MTA to
support connections to
MS Mail PC post offices

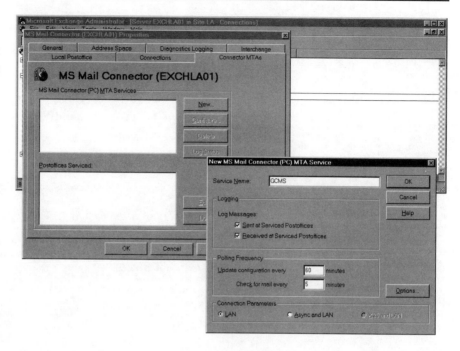

FIGURE 15.39

Setting up an MTA to
support connections to
MS Mail PC post offices

Polling Frequency

Leave the polling frequency settings at their default levels. The value you set in
the 'Update configuration every' field determines how fast the MTA will get
changes in parameters set in the Options dialog box. Remember, the default is 60
minutes. You can change the frequency at which the PC MTA checks for mail in
the 'Check for mail every' field.

Connection Parameters

Use the Connection Parameters area to select the means by which the MTA will
connect to the real MS Mail PC post offices it supports. Three options are
available: LAN, Async and LAN, and X.25 and LAN. The Async and LAN option
supports both asynchronous-modem and LAN connections, and the X.25 and
LAN option supports LAN as well as X.25 connections. Put another way, all three
options support LAN connections. More on this in a bit.

Options

Click on Options to bring up the MS Mail Connector (PC) MTA Options dialog box (see Figure 15.40). If you wish, you can use the Maximum LAN Message Size field in the Options dialog box to set a maximum size for messages moved in both directions by this MTA over a LAN-based link. If the space on a target MS Mail PC post office falls below the value in the 'Close postoffice if' field, the MTA will stop transmitting messages to the post office until the available disk space reaches the value set in the 'Open postoffice if' field.

FIGURE 15.40

Setting options for the MS Mail Connector (PC) MTA

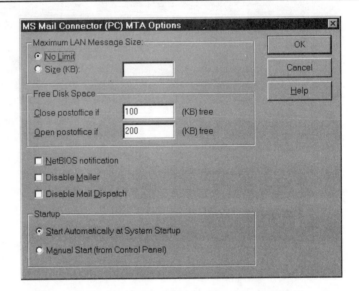

Select 'NetBIOS notification' to have the MTA notify MS Mail PC users on the same LAN that they have new mail. Check 'Disable Mailer' if you want to stop the MTA from distributing messages to the LAN-connected post offices it serves. Selecting 'Disable Mail Dispatch' stops the MTA from distributing directory synchronization messages to LAN-connected post offices. (We'll discuss MS Mail PC directory synchronization in the next chapter.)

Finally, select the start-up mode for the MTA service from the Startup area of the Options dialog box. The default starts the service when NT starts. This is usually the appropriate choice. If you want to start the service manually using the Services applet on NT's Control Panel, choose that option.

When you're done configuring options, click on OK to return to the New MS Mail Connector (PC) MTA Service dialog box shown in Figure 15.39.

Close the New MS Mail Connector (PC) MTA Service dialog box by clicking on OK. Your Connector MTAs property page should look something like the one in Figure 15.41.

Now you can assign the post office you set up on the Connections property page to your new MS Mail Connector MTA. Click on List in the MTA Service dialog box to bring up the Serviced LAN Postoffices dialog box (see Figure 15.42).

FIGURE 15.41

A new MS Mail Connector MTA service has been created.

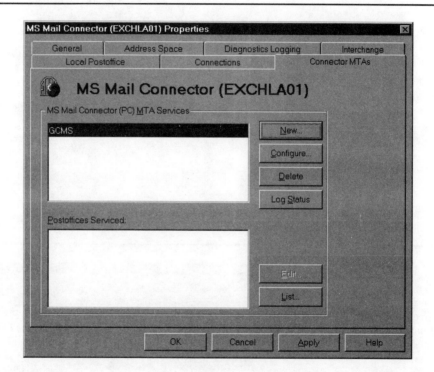

Select the post office you wish to service. Click on Add and then click on OK. Your Connector MTAs property page should look like the one in Figure 15.43.

If an MMC will be handling a lot of message traffic and will be using multiple connection methods (LAN, Async and LAN, X.25 and LAN), it's best to create at least one MMC MTA for each method. Just be sure to assign LAN-linked post offices only to the MTAs that support such links exclusively, not to MTAs that support Async and LAN or X.25 and LAN. This will leave the MTAs connected by the latter two methods free to handle only the message traffic that isn't based on LAN links.

FIGURE 15.42

Adding a LAN-linked post office to the list of serviced LAN-linked post offices

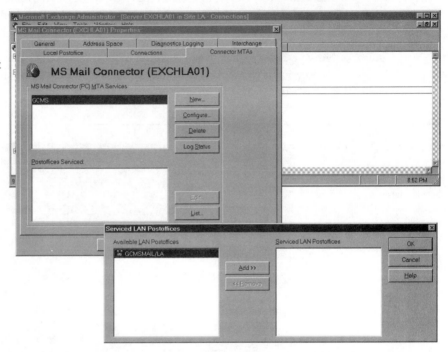

FIGURE 15.43

The post office will now be served by the newly created MS Mail Connector MTA service.

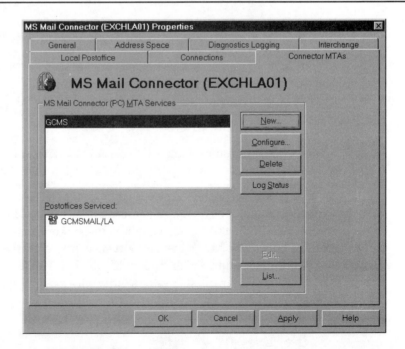

Local Postoffice

The Local Postoffice property page shown in Figure 15.44 is for the MMC shadow post office. You can change the Sign-on password as well as the network and post office names. You need a password for Async or X.25 connections only. If you change the shadow's network or post office name on this page, click on the Regenerate button to re-create the site's MS Mail addresses to reflect your changes. Unless you have an excellent reason for doing so, don't change the network or post office name.

You'll need information on the Local Postoffice page when you set up one or more real MS Mail PC post offices, so that they can access the shadow post office. Write down the network and post office names as well as the Sign-on ID and, if you entered one, the Sign-on Password.

FIGURE 15.44

The Local Postoffice property page shows information about the MMC shadow post office.

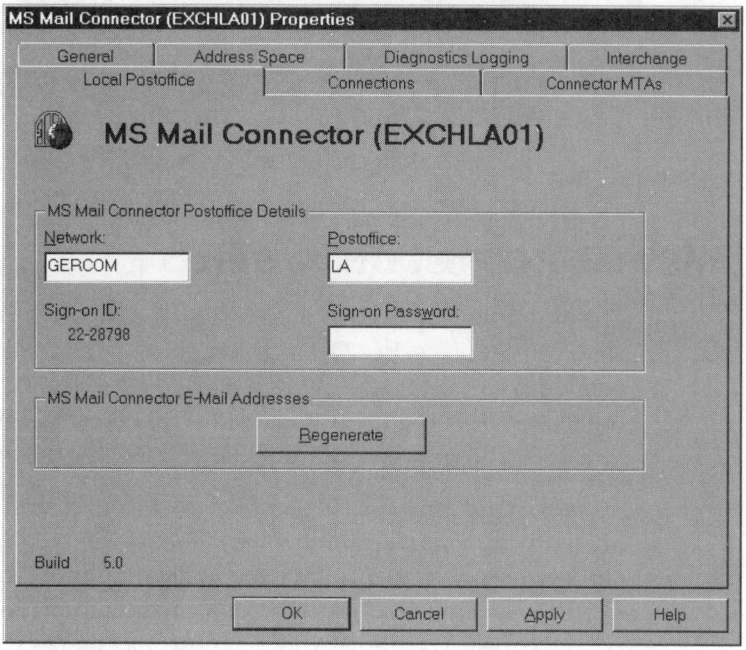

Starting the MTA Service

Open the Services applet on the NT Control Panel. Find the new MMC MTA service you created. As you may remember, the service I created is called GCMS (for

GerCom MS Mail). In Figure 15.45, you can see that I've located it on the Services applet. If you've indicated that you want the MMC MTA service to start automatically in the future, you won't have to do this again.

Click on Start to bring up the service. Also, make sure the MS Mail Connector Interchange service is running.

FIGURE 15.45

Starting an MMC MTA service

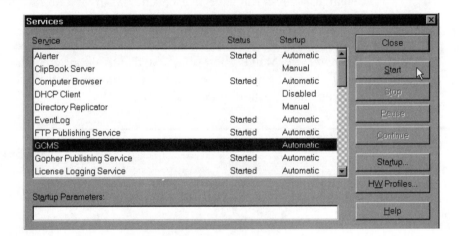

MS Mail PC Post Office Setup

The next thing you need to do is tell the real MS Mail PC post offices about the shadow post office. In a DOS session, start up MS Mail PC's ADMIN program and log in as someone with MS Mail PC Admin rights. You or someone in your organization should know how to do this. When ADMIN is up and running, you'll see a DOS screen that looks something like the one in Figure 15.46.

Use the right arrow key to select External-Admin, then press the Enter key. This brings up the External-Admin screen shown in Figure 15.47. Make sure that the Create option—on the menu at the top of the screen that starts out 'Create Modify Delete'—is selected and press Enter. Fill in the information about the MMC shadow post office here. Use the network and post office names you wrote down just a bit ago.

The route type should be Direct. Be sure to pick a connection type—MS-DOS Drive, Modem, or X.25—that matches the LAN, Async, or X.25 configuration for this post office on the MMC MTA that serves it. When you're finished entering the configuration information, you're asked if you want to create the post office. Be sure that Yes is selected and press Enter.

FIGURE 15.46

MS Mail PC's ADMIN program is up and running.

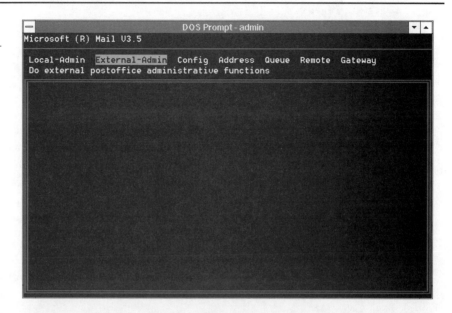

FIGURE 15.47

Creating an external post office entry for the MMC shadow post office

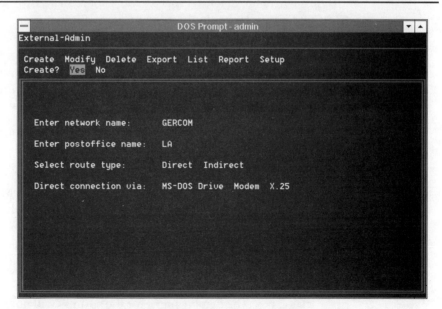

Your MMC's shadow post office and your real MS Mail PC post office(s) are now communicating with each other through the MMC MTA. All we need to do now is test the link.

Did It Work?

You test the MMC link by sending messages from the MS Mail PC side to the Exchange side, and vice versa. Addressing these messages will be a bit primitive, since we haven't yet synchronized directories between our MS Mail PC and Exchange systems. We won't be able to select the addresses from the address list, so we'll have to enter them manually.

Let's start on the MS Mail PC side. The following example assumes that you're using the MS-DOS MS Mail PC client. With the To field selected as you compose a new message, press Enter. This brings up the Postoffice Address List. Press the left arrow key to bring up the list of Address Lists, from which you select Postoffice Network List and press Enter. The Network List now pops up. Select the name of your MMC shadow post office's network (GERCOM in my case) and press Enter.

If there is more than one post office (that is, Exchange site) in your network (Exchange organization), a list of post offices will be presented. Pick the post office you want to send test mail to; you'll then see a little box for entering the mailbox's name (see Figure 15.48).

Here's where the magic happens. Notice that I'm addressing mail to GERCOM/LA, which is both the name of my Exchange organization and site and the name of the MMC shadow post office. The mailbox name I type in at this point is that of an Exchange mailbox, so the mail will be sent to that mailbox. To an MS Mail PC user, it looks as if the message will be sent to a real MS Mail PC post office on a real MS Mail PC network. Once we've got directory synchronization going, the illusion will be even better.

After you type in the Exchange mailbox name, press Enter, then compose the message and send it off. In a few minutes, the message will show up in the Inbox of the mailbox owner's Exchange client.

To send a test message from an Exchange client to an MS Mail PC network mailbox, start composing a new message. Click on To and then click on New in the Address Book dialog box. Select Microsoft Mail Address from the resultant New Entry dialog box and click on OK. To enter the address, use the New Microsoft Mail Address Properties dialog box that pops up (see Figure 15.49).

When you're finished, click on the little To button in the lower left-hand corner of the dialog box. The display name for the address will now appear in the To field of your new message. Complete the message and send it off. After the MMC MTA has done its thing, the owner of the MS Mail PC mailbox can access the message using any of the MS Mail PC clients.

If your test fails, go back and be sure you've done everything I've indicated above. This is one of the more complex Exchange connectors to set up, so it's not inconceivable that everything won't work the first time.

FIGURE 15.48

Addressing an MS Mail PC message to an Exchange mailbox

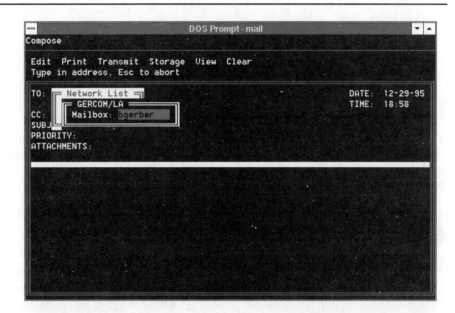

FIGURE 15.49

Entering a new MS Mail PC address while composing an Exchange message

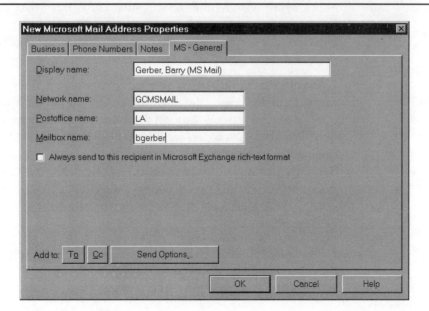

The cc:Mail Connector

If your legacy system is Lotus's cc:Mail, Microsoft has a way for you to link your users to Exchange Server. The cc:Mail Connector links cc:Mail post offices and Exchange Server sites. Like the MS Mail Connector, it passes messages between cc:Mail and Exchange Server and it synchronizes addresses between the two systems.

Conceptually, the cc:Mail Connector works similarly to the MS Mail Connector. Some of the terminology is different for cc:Mail, as are some of the tasks you must complete to install and use the cc:Mail Connector. However, with a quick read of the previous section on the MS Mail Connector, you should be well prepared for the cc:Mail Connector. The Exchange Server documentation for the cc:Mail Connector should fill in any informational gaps. That said, I'll leave it to you to set up any cc:Mail Connectors you need.

Exchange Gateways

Gateways link dissimilar e-messaging systems to each other. Though they're all built into Exchange, the X.400 Connector, Internet Mail Service, and Microsoft Mail Connector are gateways. A wide variety of vendors provide gateways for e-messaging systems and devices such as PROFS, SNADS, CompuServe, fax machines, pagers, and voice mail. Check with Microsoft for information on products and vendors. You install, administer, and manage these gateways pretty much like the connectors we covered in this chapter.

As you plan for links to other e-messaging systems, keep in mind the wide range of connectivity options available via the Internet. You can reach a number of e-messaging systems through the Internet—CompuServe and MCI Mail are two examples. So you don't really need special gateways to these systems. You can even reach X.400 systems through the Internet, making the X.400 Connector desirable only if you need to support functions like the X.400 flavor of electronic data interchange. You can, of course, reach the Internet through most X.400 systems. So if X.400 is your e-messaging protocol of choice, you can pretty much get along on it alone.

Exchange's Internet Mail Service is a powerful, robust, and stable link to the Internet. As a general rule, don't add gateways you don't need. Every gateway is another administrative and management headache. Save the gateways for e-messaging systems you can't readily reach through the Internet, such as fax, pagers, or voice mail. Even in this area, things are changing everyday. For example, faxing and paging are getting more Internet capable every day. Can voice mail be far behind?

Conclusion

In this chapter you learned how to connect Exchange sites to foreign X.400, Internet, and MS Mail PC e-messaging systems to exchange messages and, where possible, to indirectly link Exchange sites. You also learned how gateways fit into the Exchange environment. Now you're ready to tackle directory synchronization between Exchange and Microsoft Mail PC systems.

CHAPTER
SIXTEEN

Directory Synchronization with MS Mail PC Systems

■ **Understanding Dirsync**

■ **Adding an Exchange organization to a Dirsync System**

■ **Building a new Dirsync system that includes an Exchange organization**

■ **Administering and managing the Exchange Server directory synchronization service**

In the last chapter, using the Microsoft Mail Connector (MMC), we enabled mail interchange between our Exchange and Microsoft Mail for PC Networks (MS Mail PC) systems. As you'll recall, when we tested the MMC we had to enter addresses for the other system manually. In this chapter we'll use directory synchronization (*Dirsync*) to remove that annoying inconvenience. Using Dirsync, we'll import Exchange addresses into MS Mail PC, and vice versa. Then, when they compose messages, users of Exchange and MS Mail PC will be able to pick addresses for the other system from address lists just as they do for their own system.

NOTE You can also exchange addresses with Microsoft Mail for AppleTalk Networks systems and with any other e-messaging system that supports the Dirsync protocols. I won't cover these topics here because of the relatively limited installed base of the AppleTalk product and lack of demand for Dirsync with other systems. (See the Exchange Server docs for more on using Dirsync with MS Mail for AppleTalk Networks and other e-messaging systems.)

Understanding Dirsync

Let's start by talking about Dirsync, which is a component of MS Mail PC. Each MS Mail PC post office has a directory database that includes those recipients whose mailboxes reside in the post office. *Dirsync* is the name of the process that keeps the recipient directories in a group of MS Mail PC post offices synchronized. This ensures that the address lists for any post office will include the current recipients at all of the post offices that participate in the Dirsync process.

One MS Mail PC post office is set up to be a *Dirsync server*. All other post offices that participate in the Dirsync process are set up to act as *Dirsync requestors*.

The Dirsync requestor in each post office sends directory change updates for its post office to the Dirsync server. Each Dirsync requestor asks the Dirsync server for directory updates for all of the other post offices, and the server sends them out. Requests and their responses are moved between MS Mail PC post offices as messages.

WARNING The Dirsync server performs the equivalent of the Dirsync requestor functions for its own post office. So a post office that is a Dirsync server *cannot* also be a Dirsync requestor. This is a key piece of the Dirsync puzzle. Forget it and you'll do an Escheresque meltdown trying to figure out how the Dirsync server gets updates from and sends them to its own post office.

Dirsync is amazingly simple, yet when I incorporated my Exchange system into an existing MS Mail PC Dirsync process, I managed to do just about everything wrong in spite of having been involved with MS Mail PC and Dirsync for years and years. Why did I screw up? I had set up the Dirsync process on the MS Mail PC side eons ago, and I thought I remembered how it worked. I didn't. The consequences? The Dirsync-Exchange link failed, and it took hours to fix it.

To save you from the miseries I suffered, here's a list of several key rules of the Dirsync road, some of which I repeat for emphasis from the Dirsync basics above.

- A single MS Mail PC post office—including an Exchange Server shadow MS Mail PC post office—can function as either a Dirsync server or a Dirsync requestor. It *cannot and need not* function as both. The Dirsync server performs requestor duties for its own post office.

- There can be only *one* Dirsync server for a group of Dirsync requestors. One Dirsync server can serve multiple MS Mail post offices, whether they are on the same or different MS Mail PC networks. Here's where I went wrong in my first effort to include my Exchange system in the Dirsync process I'd already established on the MS Mail PC side. My one and only Dirsync server was already running on one of my MS Mail PC post offices. I then created a Dirsync server on one of my Exchange servers and all hell broke loose—or, more precisely, *nothing* broke loose. Trying to keep the requestors happy, the two Dirsync servers got into deadlock battles of epic proportions, and I never saw an updated address list on either side. Things returned to normal once I got rid of the Exchange Dirsync server.

- There can be only one Dirsync requestor per MMC and, you'll remember, only one MMC per Exchange server.

- Because Dirsync uses messages to exchange requests for updates and the updates themselves, the MMC must be installed and running between your Exchange and MS Mail PC systems.

- As is true without Exchange in the mix, you must run DISPATCH.EXE on the MS Mail PC side to perform whichever Dirsync server or requestor tasks are assigned to real MS Mail PC post offices. There is no need for (or equivalent of) DISPATCH.EXE on the Exchange Server side; these tasks are performed by the Exchange Server's directory synchronization service.

Adding an Exchange System to Dirsync

Throughout this section, I'll assume that you've got Dirsync running on the MS Mail PC side. If not, the MS Mail PC *Administrator's Guide* provides detailed instructions. The Microsoft application note on Dirsync (WA0725.DOC) is also very helpful. You can view it at Microsoft's Knowledge Base web site or download it from one of the company's many online libraries.

Since the Dirsync system is up and running on the MS Mail PC side, a Dirsync server is already in place. That means we need only to install a Dirsync requestor on the Exchange side.

To set up a Dirsync requestor on one of your Exchange servers, select Dirsync Requestor from the New Other submenu on the Exchange Administrator program's File menu. This brings up the New Requestor dialog box, where you select the Dirsync server that the requestor will use (see Figure 16.1). My Dirsync server is on the MS Mail PC network GCMSMAIL in the post office named LA, so I've selected the only MS Mail PC network/post office option, GCMSMAIL/LA.

Click on OK in the New Requestor dialog box when you've chosen the Dirsync server post office. Next you'll see the properties dialog box for the requestor (see Figure 16.2).

General Properties

The requestor is treated by Exchange Server as a connector, so I've named it EXCHLA01 Connector (Dirsync) GCMSMAIL. (You can't see the whole name in Figure 16.2, because the field box is too small.) If you want the name of the requestor to be appended to each imported MS Mail PC display name, check the box next to the Name field. Generally, however, you won't want to do this. It's usually better if MS Mail PC addresses look just like standard Exchange addresses.

FIGURE 16.1

Selecting the Dirsync
server post office

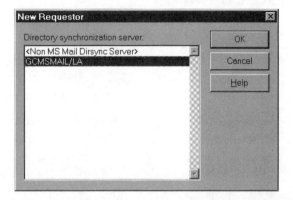

FIGURE 16.2

The Dirsync requestor's
Properties dialog box

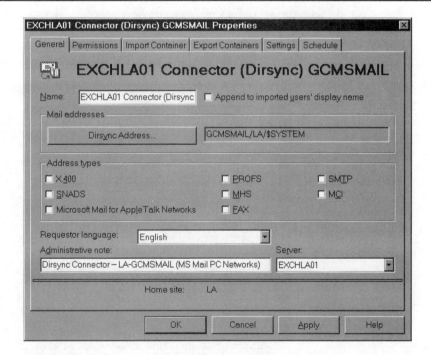

The Dirsync address is set automatically, based on the choice you made in the
New Requestor dialog box; don't change it. Use the Address Types box to select the
types of addresses you want to request from the Dirsync server. The Requestor Language drop-down list contains the primary language used on your mail system. Use
the Server drop-down list box to select the server that the requestor is assigned to.

Import Container

Use the Import Container property page to tell the requestor where to put incoming address updates (see Figure 16.3). Click on Container and pick the container you want from the list of Exchange Server recipients containers that pops up (see Figure 16.4). If you've added no new recipients containers, select the container Recipients, which holds all recipients for the site.

As you know, the contents of recipients containers in one site are replicated to other sites. Therefore, once MS Mail PC updates have been imported into a recipients container at one site, they will be replicated—along with whatever else is in the container—to all other sites. The addresses also get incorporated automatically into Exchange's Global Address List. Because MS Mail PC addresses are custom recipients, you can do anything with them that you can do with other custom recipients. For example, you can hide any address from the address book.

FIGURE 16.3

The Import Container property page

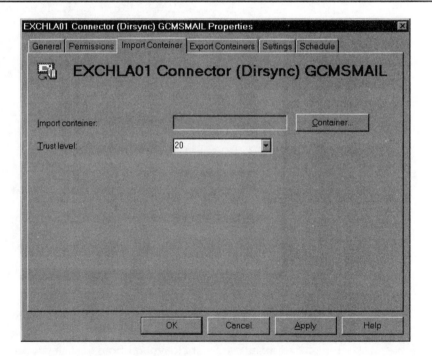

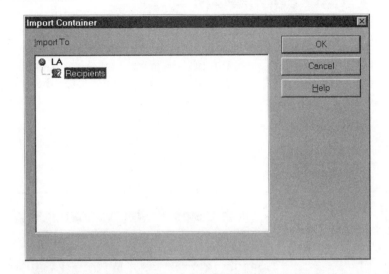

FIGURE 16.4

Selecting the recipients container to receive incoming MS Mail PC addresses

Eliminating Your MS Mail SMTP Gateway

When it imports MS Mail mailbox addresses, Exchange treats them as custom recipients. An Exchange custom recipient for an MS Mail mailbox is assigned MS Mail, cc:Mail, Internet, and X.400 addresses by default. So, using my fake company GerCom as an example, a person with the MS Mail mailbox name bgerber will get an SMTP address of bgerber@la.gercom.com. If someone on the Internet sends a message to bgerber@la.gercom.com, the Microsoft Mail Connector is running on my LA server, and I've set my DNS to point to the Exchange server with the Internet Mail Service for all mail to la.gercom.com, the mail will be received by the la.gercom.com IMS and magically transferred to bgerber's MS Mail mailbox. In one fell swoop you've eliminated your pesky MS Mail SMTP Gateway.

Export Containers

Select the Exchange recipients containers whose addresses will be exported to the MS Mail PC system using the Export Containers property page (see Figure 16.5). The neat part of this process is that you can add any or all containers at any or all of your sites. (Notice the Site drop-down list in the lower left-hand corner of the page.) Thus, through one requestor, you can export all of the addresses in your Exchange organization.

Select the recipients containers you want to export from each site, then click on Add for each one to add it to the export list.

FIGURE 16.5

Selecting the recipients containers whose addresses are to be exported to the MS Mail PC side

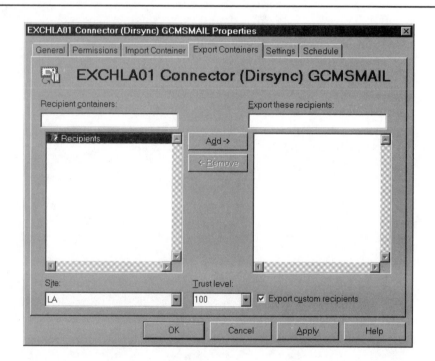

The Trust Level field controls which Exchange recipients—mailboxes, distribution lists, custom recipients, and public folders—get exported. On the Advanced property page of the dialog box for every Exchange recipient, you'll find a trust-level field. If the trust level set there is higher than the one set on the Export Containers property page, the recipient won't be exported. If the trust level set for the recipient is lower than or equal to the level set on this page, the recipient will get exported. Trust-level values can range between 0 and 100.

Because the trust level that's set on the Export Containers property page shown in Figure 16.5 is 100—the highest possible level—all recipients will be automatically exported, no matter what their trust-level setting.

If you want to exclude specific recipients from the export process, set the trust level on the Export Containers property page at a lower level—say, 80. Then set the trust level for those recipients you don't want exported to a value higher than the Export Containers page trust level—90, for instance.

Exchange's custom recipients are exported by default. You can deselect the 'Export custom recipients' box to prevent custom recipients from being exported.

Settings

If you want to add security to your Dirsync process, enter a password on the Settings property page (see Figure 16.6). This password is unique to Dirsync and has nothing to do with other passwords used with the MMC. In just a bit, we'll tell the Dirsync server about this password.

FIGURE 16.6

The Settings property page

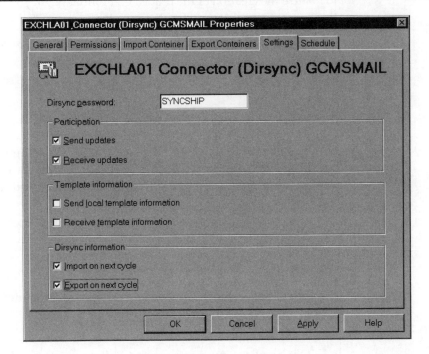

597

If you expect really heavy Dirsync traffic, you can set up two Exchange-based Dirsync requestors to the same Dirsync server. Each requestor must be on a different server and use a different MMC. If you do this, select Send Updates for one requestor and Receive Updates for the other. If you're going to have only one requestor, select both options.

If your MS Mail PC post offices use address templates, you can select to send Exchange templates to MS Mail and receive MS Mail templates in Exchange here. Check both 'Import on next cycle' and 'Export on next cycle' to force the requestor to perform both tasks on its next scheduled run.

Schedule

Set the schedule for the requestor using the Schedule property page (see Figure 16.7). Notice that the page has no Always or Never options. This is because directory synchronization is generally run once a day; in fact, on the MS Mail PC side you can't schedule it to run more often than once a day. Leave the default scheduled time as it is.

When you've finished setting the requestor schedule, you're done. Click on OK to finalize the creation of the requestor. From now on, you'll find the requestor in the Connections container for the site where you created it.

Now you need to start the directory synchronization service using the Services applet on the Control Panel for the server on which you installed the requestor. While you're at it, be sure that directory synchronization is set to start automatically.

Dirsync Server Settings

Now you need to tell the Dirsync server, which I'm assuming is already running on the MS Mail PC side, that it will be contacted by the Dirsync requestor you just set up. This is a security measure. Using MS Mail PC's DOS-based ADMIN.EXE program:

- Select Config from the first menu you see and press Enter.
- Select Dirsync from the next menu and press Enter.
- Select Server from the next menu and press Enter.
- Select Requestors from the next menu and press Enter.
- Select Create from the next menu and press Enter.

Use the resultant input screen to add the name of your Exchange MS Mail PC shadow network and post office (see Figure 16.8). If you've included a password in the Settings tab of the Dirsync Requestor object in Exchange for extra security, enter the same password you set up when creating the requestor.

Now simply restart DISPATCH.EXE. That's it.

FIGURE 16.7

Setting a schedule for the Dirsync requestor

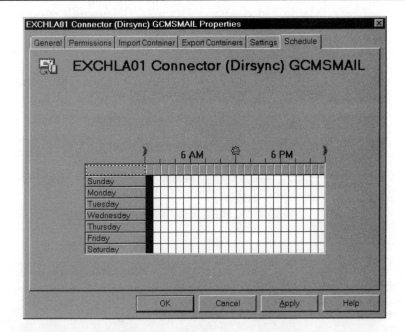

FIGURE 16.8

Giving an Exchange Server–based Dirsync requestor access to an MS Mail PC-based Dirsync server

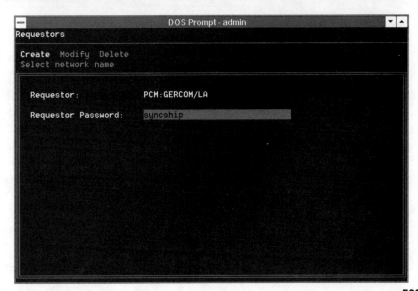

Did It Work?

You'll have to wait until a full Dirsync cycle has completed to find out whether the process was successful. This can take a day or so. You'll know that everything worked as advertised when your Exchange recipients show up on the MS Mail PC side, and vice versa. Figure 16.9 shows the Open Directory and Address dialog boxes as they appear in the MS Mail PC client for Windows. In the Open Directory dialog box, my GerCom sites look like any other MS Mail PC post office. Note that the directory for LA (shown in the Address dialog box) even includes unhidden public folders, so MS Mail PC users can send messages to those folders just as Exchange users can. I turned on the Global Address List option on the MS Mail PC side (in MS Mail PC's ADMIN.EXE). So if we were to select the Global Address List from the Open Directory dialog box, shown in Figure 16.9, we'd see all of the MS Mail PC *and* GerCom addresses, just as we do on the GerCom side.

After the first Dirsync cycle, create a few new test mailboxes on both sides. If everything is okay, Dirsync will update the directory databases on the Exchange and MS Mail PC sides to reflect these additions.

FIGURE 16.9

An Exchange site address list as it appears in an MS Mail for windows client

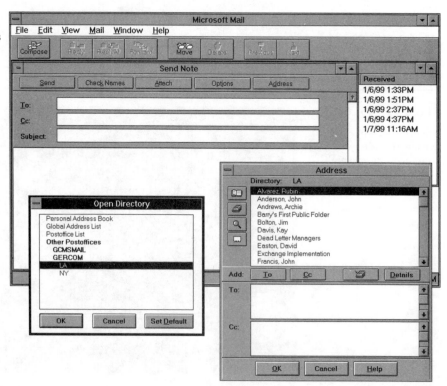

NOTE

When testing, you can speed up the Dirsync process on the MS Mail PC side by running a bunch of programs normally handled by DISPATCH.EXE. The *Administrator's Guide* for Microsoft Mail for PC Networks includes detailed instructions for doing this. On the Exchange side, you can schedule the requestor to run hourly (using the requestor's Schedule property page) and then select both the Send Updates and Receive Updates options on the requestor's Settings property page. This will force a full Dirsync cycle on the Exchange side at the top of the hour. If you don't want to wait until then, just reset the server clock to the top of the hour.

Building a New Dirsync System That Includes an Exchange Organization

If, for whatever reason, you have one or more MS Mail PC post offices and have never installed Dirsync in the past but wish to add it now, you have two options. You can set up your system exactly as we did above, running your Dirsync server on the MS Mail PC side and running Dirsync requestors on all other MS Mail PC post offices, including any shadows on the Exchange side. Alternatively, you can run your Dirsync server on an Exchange server and run Dirsync requestors on all other post offices (and, if you have them, shadow post offices). Here's how to do the latter.

I'm assuming throughout the following discussion that you've already read the sections above that deal with setting up and running a Dirsync requestor on an Exchange server. I'm also leaving most of the setup on the MS Mail PC side to you. For help, check out the Microsoft Mail for PC Networks documentation.

Setting Up a Dirsync Server on an Exchange Server

To begin setting up a Dirsync server on an Exchange server, select Dirsync Server from the New Other submenu on the Exchange Administrator's File menu. This brings up the Dirsync Server Properties dialog box (see Figure 16.10).

FIGURE 16.10

Setting up a Dirsync
server on an
Exchange server

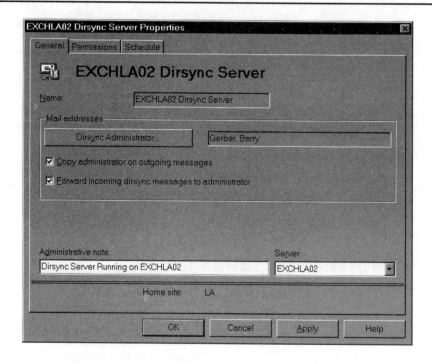

As you can see, Dirsync server setup is very easy. At this point you should be able to do it without any coaching from me. Go to it.

When you've finished setting up the Dirsync server, be sure to start the directory synchronization service on the Exchange server that the Dirsync server is running on. You'll find the service in the Control Panel's Services applet on the Exchange server. Also make sure you set the directory synchronization service to start automatically when your Exchange server is rebooted.

NOTE   Remember, just as with a Dirsync requestor running on the Exchange side, the Microsoft Mail Connector must be running on the Exchange server supporting the Dirsync server. Remember, too, that you don't need a Dirsync requestor on the Exchange server running your Dirsync server. The Dirsync server handles requestor functions for its shadow post office.

Setting Up a Remote Dirsync Requestor

Once you've set up the Dirsync server, you need to tell it which requestors will be contacting it, just as we did a bit ago for our MS Mail PC–based Dirsync server. (Refer back to Figure 16.8.) To do this, you must create a *remote Dirsync requestor* for each requestor that will contact the Dirsync server.

Things can get a little confusing here because, in spite of its name, a remote Dirsync requestor is *not* a requestor. Rather, it's two things:

1. An authorization for a real Dirsync requestor to contact the Dirsync server

2. A set of specs on, among other things, which Exchange Server recipient containers should be used for addresses imported from and exported to the real requestor's post office

So based on the terminology that's implied if not specifically used on the MS Mail PC side, a better name for the remote Dirsync connector would have been *requestor definition.*

To create a remote requestor, select Remote Dirsync Requestor from the New Other submenu. Select the Network/PO from the New Requestor dialog to get to the new Remote Dirsync Requestor's property page dialog box. The dialog box, which is shown in Figure 16.11, looks a lot like the one we used earlier to create an Exchange-based Dirsync requestor. For that reason, I won't go into any more detail here.

When all is set up and running on the Exchange side, you next have to set up Dirsync requestors in your other post offices. (See the Microsoft Mail for PC Networks *Administrator's Guide* for help on the MS Mail PC side.) If for some reason you have other Exchange-based shadow post offices, refer to the first section of this chapter for instructions on creating Dirsync requestors on the Exchange side.

Now start up DISPATCH.EXE on the MS Mail PC side; again, see the Microsoft Mail for PC Networks docs for details.

When everything is running properly, test your Dirsync setup by ensuring that addresses from the Exchange side show up in the appropriate MS Mail PC address lists, and vice versa. (For more on testing, see the "Did It Work?" section earlier in this chapter.)

FIGURE 16.11

Creating a remote
Dirsync requestor

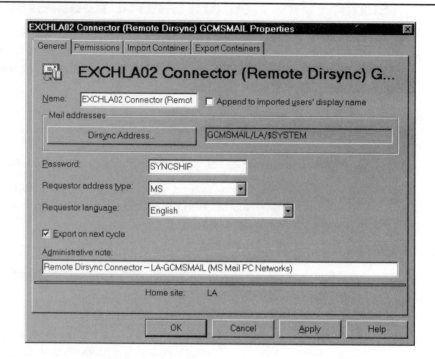

**Administering and Managing
the Exchange Directory
Synchronization Service**

Whether you've installed a Dirsync requestor or server on your Exchange server, I've asked you to start the directory synchronization agent (DXA) service. The DXA is the real power behind Dirsync. It's similar to the program DISPATCH .EXE on the MS Mail PC side because it does a lot of the real work of directory synchronization.

You don't have to worry much about the DXA. Still, because the service is an Exchange object, there is a dialog box you can use to administer and manage it. The DXA object you want is in the container for the server on which you installed your Dirsync requestor or server. When you install the MS Mail Connector on a server, the DXA service is also installed; you need to use the one on the server that supports your Dirsync requestor or server. (In my case, it's EXCHLA01.)

Find the directory synchronization object in the correct server container and double-click on it. You'll see a dialog box like the one in Figure 16.12.

FIGURE 16.12

The dialog box for administering and managing the Exchange Server directory synchronization service

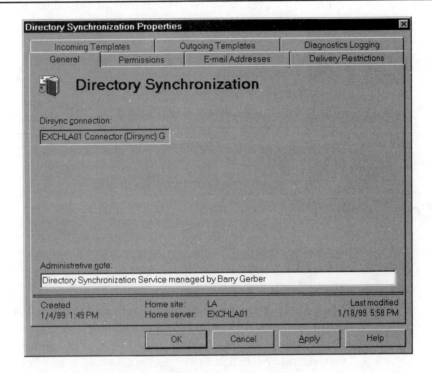

The only property pages that won't be familiar to you are those pertaining to Incoming Templates and Outgoing Templates. By default, only two pieces of information about each recipient are included in the Dirsync process: mailbox name or alias (JSmith, for example) and display name (Smith, John). As you'll remember, Exchange Server provides a large number of additional recipient information fields—including home address, office phone, fax, and department—and it lets you define up to ten additional custom attribute fields. To add recipient information fields on the MS Mail PC side, you must define a template that will hold that information.

Exchange users can view Exchange recipient information fields when running an Exchange client, and MS Mail PC users can see MS Mail PC recipient information when running an MS Mail PC client. So how do you allow users on one system to see information about recipients on the other system? You use the Incoming Templates and Outgoing Templates property pages.

Each Exchange Server recipient information field has a name, as does each field in an MS Mail PC template. You set up mappings or links between Exchange Server's and MS Mail PC's field names on the Incoming Templates and Outgoing Templates property pages. Mapped fields are exchanged along with the two standard recipient information fields and, voilà, information about recipients on both systems is available to users of either system.

Mapping is easy as long as you have the field names for your MS Mail PC template in hand. Setting up MS Mail PC templates is also a breeze; the Microsoft Mail PC *Administrator's Guide* provides very clear instructions. I'll leave the rest to you.

Conclusion

In this chapter you learned how to synchronize addresses between Exchange and MS Mail PC systems. Specifically, you learned about MS Mail PC's Dirsync process and how to add an Exchange organization to an existing Dirsync system.

You also were exposed to enough information about MS Mail PC–based Dirsync and Exchange-based Dirsync to build a new Dirsync system around your Exchange system. Finally, you learned a bit about the directory synchronization service and how to administer and manage it.

Now we're ready to move on to some heavy-duty advanced topics. First we'll explore all of those Exchange Administrator menu items we bypassed in earlier chapters. Then we'll tackle all those neat advanced Internet protocol-based goodies that come with Exchange 5.0. Finally, we'll build an Exchange electronic form and make it available to Exchange users.

PART VII

Advanced Topics

With this section, our tour of Exchange Server comes to an end. We've been over a lot of flat and gently sloping territory in the past 16 chapters. Now it's time to head up into the mountains for a look at some of the advanced features of Exchange Server. In Chapter 17 we move into the heights of advanced Exchange Server administration and management. We'll cover all of those topics I earlier promised to get to. You're ready now, and we're gonna have fun! Chapter 18 takes us up pretty high into the world of some special Internet protocols that support web browser access to Exchange Server mailboxes, POP3 mail clients, Internet newsgroups, and LDAP access to Exchange Server's directory. In Chapter 19 we'll reach for the peaks of Exchange application development, focusing on one of the easier and most interesting options—Exchange Server's Forms Designer package.

Advanced Exchange Administration and Management

- Advanced information store administration and management

- Advanced Exchange security

- Migration of foreign e-messaging system users to Exchange

- Advanced Exchange directory administration and management

- Remote Exchange and NT Server administration

- Advanced Exchange client support

- A quick look at Schedule+

As you've probably realized, Exchange Server is loaded with fancy and fantastic features. Although we've covered a lot of these already, a rather diverse set of Exchange Server's more advanced features remains to be explored. We'll tackle these features in this chapter. Here's what we'll be covering:

- Creating new information stores
- Moving mailboxes
- Tracking messages
- Setting up advanced security
- Migrating users from other e-messaging systems
- Importing information into the Exchange directory
- Extracting information for the Exchange directory from other sources
- Exporting directory information from Exchange Server
- Moving mailboxes between Exchange sites
- Working with Address Book Views
- Other advanced Exchange Administrator options
- Remotely administering Exchange and NT servers
- Supporting remote users
- Supporting roving users
- A quick look at Schedule+

I think you'll be pleased to see that a number of these features are really quite easy to use. As with the last chapter, I'll respect your Exchange Server expertise and skip the detailed hand-holding of earlier chapters.

Creating New Information Stores

There can be *one and only one* private information store and *one and only one* public information store on each Exchange server. These stores were created when you installed the server. Either, but not both of them, can be deleted at any time by locating the store in the appropriate Exchange Administrator server container and pressing the Delete key.

Why would you delete an information store? There are several reasons. To devote maximum computing resources to public folders on a server, you can delete the private information store on that server. Conversely, you can delete the public information store to increase the resources available for the support of private information store access.

To reduce the number of public folder servers and the amount of replication required, you can eliminate the public information stores on some servers, then have users access public folders on the remaining public information store servers. Do this with care, however, because the amount of traffic related to cross-network public folder access could be worse than that generated by public folder replication.

To make more computing resources available for Exchange connectors, delete the public information store from servers running connectors. Be careful about deleting private information stores on servers running connectors, though; except for those with X.400 and MS Mail connectors, servers running Exchange connectors (including the Internet Mail Service and any third-party gateways developed with the Exchange gateway development kit) must have a private information store.

But what if you later need to reinstall a deleted private or public information store? No problem. Let's say you need to add back the public information store on one of your Exchange servers. Just select Information Store from the New Other submenu on the Exchange Administrator's File menu. The New Information Store dialog box pops up (see Figure 17.1). Notice that the dialog box starts up assuming you want to create a new private information store. As you can see in the figure, I have private information stores on all of the Exchange servers in the LA site I'm running from, so I'm not offered an opportunity to create private stores.

However, when I select Public under 'Information store type' in the New Information Store dialog box, the server in my LA site that doesn't have a public information store—EXCHLA02—is shown (see Figure 17.2). To create the store, all I have to do is click on the server name and click on OK. That's it. The information store is automatically created.

FIGURE 17.1

The New Information
Store dialog box

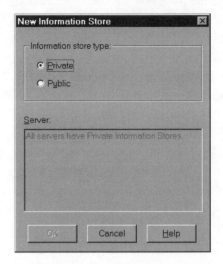

FIGURE 17.2

Creating a new public
information store

WARNING Now that you know how easy it is to delete information stores, be careful before taking that big step and make sure to preserve anything in the stores you want to keep. For public information stores, create a replica of the public folders you're going to delete on another public information store server. For private information stores, use the Move Mailboxes option on the Administrator's Tools menu to move mailboxes to another private information store.

Moving Mailboxes

You can change the home server of a mailbox, although the changes are limited to other Exchange servers in a site. In other words, you can't move a mailbox to an Exchange server in another site. I'll talk about how to move mailboxes between sites later in this chapter.

Why would you want to move a mailbox? One reason, as noted above, is you need to move mailboxes before deleting a private information store. Also, you can balance the loads on different servers in a site by moving mailboxes between them. And, of course, when you consolidate two or more servers, you'll need to move their mailboxes to your new megaserver.

To move a mailbox, select it in the Global Address List, site, or server recipients container using the Exchange Administrator on the mailbox's current home server. Next, select Move Mailbox from the Administrator's Tools menu and then select the server you want to move the mailbox to (see Figure 17.3). That's it. After a little cooking time, the mailbox is moved to the private information store on the selected server. You can select and move multiple mailboxes using the standard Windows item selection keys.

FIGURE 17.3

Moving a mailbox to another server in a site

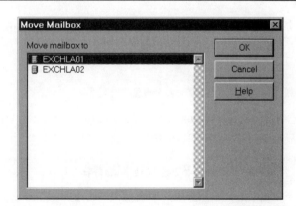

Once a mailbox has been moved, neither the Exchange administrator nor the mailbox's user has to do a thing. The Exchange system knows where the new home server is, and the Exchange client can find the mailbox without any alteration in the user's profile. Also, no mail is lost that comes in during the actual move—even if the user is connected to the mailbox when it is moved. In the latter case, the user does have to stop and restart the client, but that's it. All else is totally transparent, thanks to client/server technology and the creative way it was implemented by the Exchange development team.

Tracking Messages

One of the biggest pains in the management of e-messaging systems comes from lost (or *allegedly* lost) messages. With Exchange Server's message-tracking capability, you can get information on the status of messages in your Exchange system. This includes those between Exchange users, those generated by Exchange system components, and those originating in or destined for foreign e-messaging systems.

You'll remember that in earlier chapters I always suggested that you turn message tracking on for whatever information store or Message Transfer Agent we were working with. This is because Exchange Server's message tracking system relies on logs created when tracking is turned on. So if you haven't already done so, I suggest you go back and turn tracking on. The following objects can generate tracking logs:

- The information store in the site Configuration container
- The Message Transfer Agent in the site Configuration container
- The Internet Mail Service in the site Connections container
- The MS Mail Connector in the site Connections container
- The cc:Mail Connector in the site Connections container

You can track both user messages and system messages. Let's begin with user messages.

Tracking User Messages

You can track user messages using two search modes: basic and advanced. We'll start with the basic mode.

The Basic Search Mode

Start up Exchange's Message Tracking Center (or, as we'll call it here most of the time, the *tracker*). To do so, select Track Message from the Administrator's Tools menu. You'll first be presented with a standard server browser that allows you to select a server to connect to. Select the server where the message originated—the home server of the user who sent the message—and click on OK.

Next, the Message Tracking Center dialog box shown in Figure 17.4 pops open. A second or two later, the Select Message to Track dialog box opens (see Figure 17.5). This is where you enter criteria for the messages you want to track.

FIGURE 17.4

The Message Tracking
Center dialog box

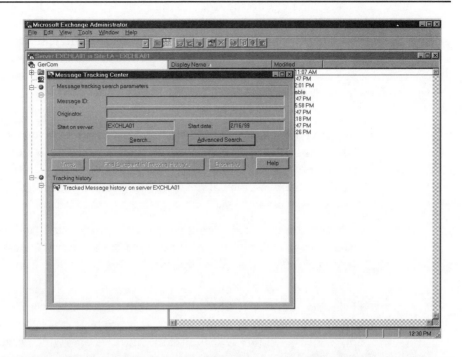

FIGURE 17.5

Looking at messages
found after search crite-
ria have been set

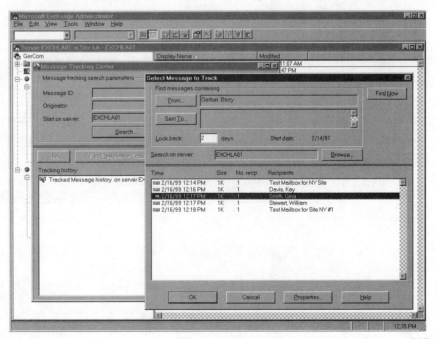

You can put information into the From field and/or the Sent To field in the Select Message to Track dialog box. Clicking on either button brings up a standard address book dialog box. You can select a single sender and multiple recipients. In Figure 17.5, I've asked the tracker to find messages sent by me (my home server is EXCHLA01 in my LA site) over the last two days. For the record, I know that these messages were received without incident.

You use the Look Back field to tell the tracker how far back to search in the logs; an entry of 0 means to search the last 24 hours of logs. Click on Browse to change the server whose message tracking logs will be searched. If you've selected a sender in the From field, the default search server is set to the home server of the sender. Otherwise, the default is the one you connected to with the server browser just before the tracker started up.

When you're done entering your search criteria, click on Find Now in the Select Message to Track dialog box. When the tracker has finished searching, it lists the results of its search in the dialog box.

As you can see in Figure 17.5, the tracker found five messages sent by me on February 16, 1999. To find out more about a message, double-click on it or highlight it and click on Properties. This brings up the Message Properties dialog box shown in Figure 17.6. Notice that the message, which I sent at 12:17 p.m. on February 16, 1999, was transferred into the private information store on the Exchange server EXCHLA01.

FIGURE 17.6

Viewing specific information about a message

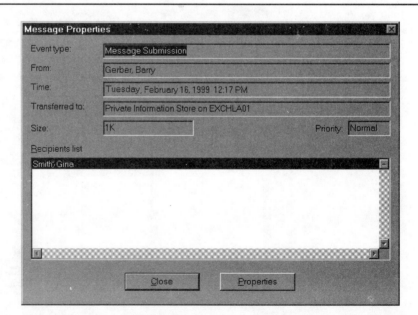

If you double-click on a recipient listed in the Message Properties dialog box or click on Properties while a recipient is selected, you'll see the full Properties dialog box for the recipient. So, for example, if I were to double-click on 'Smith, Gina', I'd get the full Mailbox Properties dialog box for Gina Smith's mailbox, complete with all of its property pages. This is the dialog box you use to administer and manage a mailbox in Exchange Administrator. Sometimes you'll find it useful to look at information in this dialog box; for example, you might want to check out the recipient's e-mail addresses (on the E-Mail Addresses property page) when trying to figure out why a message was lost.

Now let's look at the tracking history for a message. Select a message and click on OK on the Select Message to Track dialog box (Figure 17.7). Now you're returned to the Message Tracking Center dialog box (see Figure 17.8). Click on Track, and the tracker goes to work. Soon you'll see a tracking history for the message (as shown in Figure 17.8). You can look at the properties of any item in the tracking history list. Notice in the figure how the message is fully tracked across my Exchange system right up to its delivery to Gina Smith's mailbox.

FIGURE 17.7

Selecting a message for a detailed tracking history

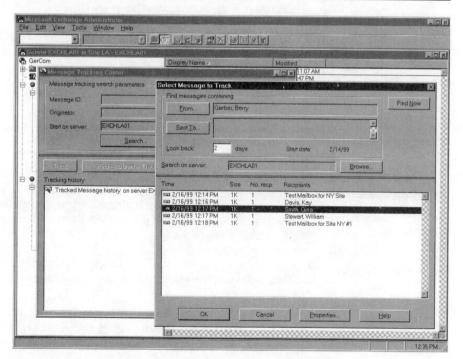

FIGURE 17.8

Viewing the tracking history for the message selected in Figure 17.7

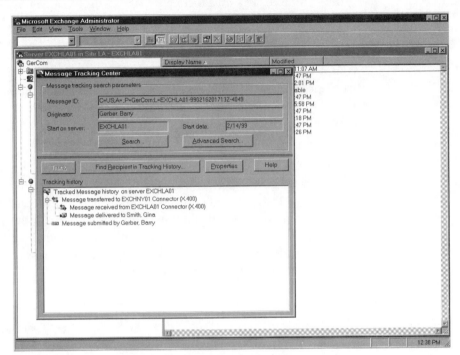

When you're done with the results of your search, close up all of the windows related to the Select Message to Track dialog box; only the Message Tracking Center dialog box remains open. To do another basic search, click on Search in this dialog box (see Figure 17.4).

NOTE

The message queues for such Exchange Server objects as Message Transfer Agents (MTAs), Internet Mail Services, and Microsoft Mail Connectors can also be useful in tracking a message. Even before you bring up a message tracker, check the queues for the appropriate servers in the site originating the message. If the message remains in a queue beyond a normally scheduled cycle of the MTA or connector, check to ensure that links and services in your messaging network are up. If they are, then be sure the receiving server or Internet mail host is running.

You can take a more proactive approach to link and server availability problems by running the Exchange link and server monitors we talked about in earlier chapters. You can also use NT Server's Performance Monitor (discussed back in Chapter 4) and the specific Performance Monitor setups that are installed with Exchange Server to warn you when queues exceed a specified length.

The Advanced Search Mode

To track user messages using the advanced search mode, click on Advanced Search in the Message Tracking Center dialog box (see Figure 17.4). The resultant Advanced Search dialog box, shown in Figure 17.9, gives you three search options. Only two of these—'Transferred into this site' and 'By Message ID'—apply to user messages. The third option, 'Sent by Microsoft Exchange Server', is used for tracking system messages; we'll get to it in just a bit.

The 'Transferred into this site' option lets you track messages that came into the site through a particular Exchange connector or gateway—for example, an X.400, Internet Mail, or Microsoft Mail connector. The 'By Message ID' option allows you to track messages by a unique system ID.

Select one of these two search options and click on OK in the Advanced Search dialog box. You'll then see a dialog box that lets you set up and execute the option you chose.

'Transferred into this Site'   Let's start with the 'Transferred into this site' option. Figure 17.10 shows the Select Inbound Message to Track dialog box used for this option. As you can see, I've asked the tracker to find all messages that were transferred into my LA site (my search server is EXCHLA01) through the X.400 Connector that links my LA and NY sites. I've requested information only for the last twenty-four hours.

Since I entered no specific sender or recipients, the resulting list includes all messages transferred through the connector. This includes a system attendant message, directory update information from my NY site to my LA site, and one visible message from someone in the NY site to me.

FIGURE 17.10

Tracking messages sent through an X.400 Connector from another site

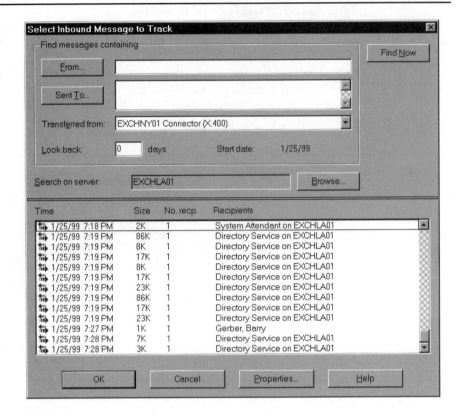

At this point, I could double-click on any message to see some basic information about it. (See Figure 17.6.) I can also do a tracking history on any message, just as I did in the last section. (See Figure 17.8.) These options are available for any message search. So, I'll mention them from here on only when its absolutely necessary.

'By Message ID'   Every Exchange message has a unique identifier that includes the address of the originating organization, the name of the originating Exchange server, the date, and a series of digits. When you track a message by its ID, you get the most complete and useful history of the message's progress through your Exchange system.

Here's an example of an Exchange message ID:

```
c=US;a= ;p=GerCom;l=EXCHLA01990110144428FK004600
```

Can you pick out the date '01/10/99' in the digits just after the server name?

The ID is one of the properties of a message; you use it to track a message using the Message Tracking Center. But how do you find the ID? First you have to find a copy of the message. If you're trying to figure out why a message never arrived at its intended location—which is generally why you'd use the tracker—you'll want the copy of the message stored in the Sent Items folder for the originating mailbox.

Using an Exchange client, find and open the message. Then select Properties from the message's File menu. Tab over to the Message ID property page in the resultant New Message Properties dialog box for the message. There in all its lengthy glory is the message ID (see Figure 17.11).

FIGURE 17.11

Finding an Exchange message's ID

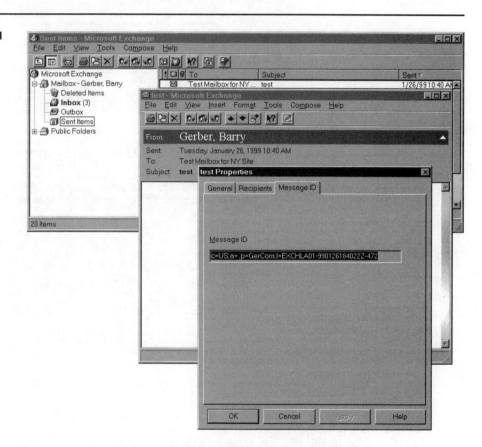

Once you have the message ID, go to the Exchange Administrator and select Advanced Search from the Message Tracking Center dialog box (see Figure 17.4).

Then select 'By Message ID' from the Advanced Search dialog box (see Figure 17.9). Next you'll see the Select Message to Track dialog box shown in Figure 17.12. Enter the message ID, set the search server and Look Back options, and click on OK.

When the message is found, you're returned to the Message Tracking Center. Click on Track to view the message history. (See Figure 17.13.)

FIGURE 17.12

Entering the ID of a message to be tracked

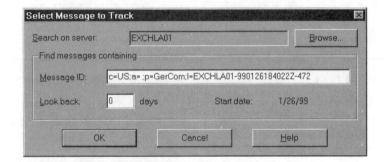

FIGURE 17.13

The results of a tracking history request for a message found by its message ID

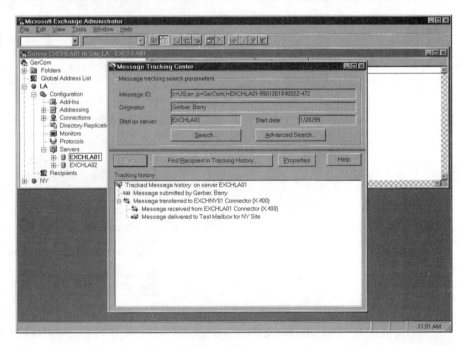

> **NOTE**
>
> Worried about accurately typing in that long message ID? Relax. If you're running the Exchange client and the Administrator on the same machine, you can use Ctrl+C to copy the ID from the Message ID property page and then Ctrl+V to paste it into the Message ID field.
>
> If you're running the client and the Administrator on different servers, you can paste the ID into a message and send it to yourself. Or you can drag the original message into a new message and send it to yourself as an attachment to the new message. When you open the new message, you can look at all the properties, including the ID, just as if it were the original message. If you need to track the message for a user, this last approach is especially useful. Users don't have to know anything about message IDs—all they need to do is send you the message that needs to be tracked.

Tracking System Messages

If you're interested in messages generated by key Exchange Server components such as the directory, information store, System Attendant, or directory synchronization, select 'Sent by Microsoft Exchange Server' from the Advanced Search dialog box and then click on OK (see Figure 17.7). This brings up the Select System Message to Track dialog box (see Figure 17.14). Use the 'From' drop-down list box to select the Exchange Server component you're interested in, then set the search server and the number of Look Back days and click on Find Now. Found messages will be listed in the box in the lower part of the dialog box.

Figure 17.14 shows the results of a search I did for the information store on the server EXCHLA01 in my LA site. As you can see, three messages were generated by EXCHLA01: two addressed to the EXCHLA02 server in my LA site, and one for the server EXCHNY01 in my NY site. These are public information store messages that contain info used in public folder replication. Wow! Remember way back when we talked about how cross-site public folder replication was based on messages? Well, here they are.

As usual, you can see more detail about a message by double-clicking on it in the list box or by selecting it and clicking on Properties.

FIGURE 17.14

FIGURE 17.14

The Select System Message to Track dialog box

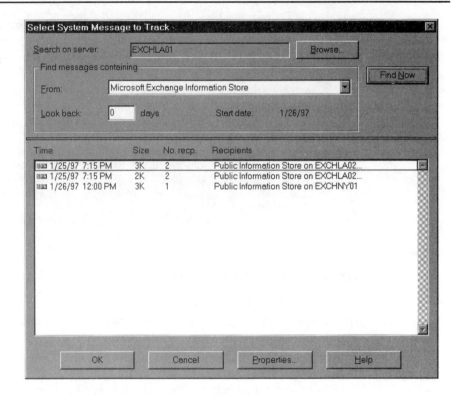

Setting Up Advanced Security

Exchange Server is pretty secure in and of itself. User message stores and the use of the Exchange Administrator are protected by NT security. Also, the remote procedure calls (RPCs) that support some Exchange communications can be set to encrypt message data as it crosses network wires.

In addition to all of the above, a level of advanced security is available in Exchange: digital signatures and data encryption based on the RSA public key cryptography system. A digital signature assures a message's receiver that the contents of the message haven't been altered since it was digitally signed and that the message was truly sent by the indicated originator. Data encryption with public and private keys virtually guarantees that only authorized recipients can read a message.

You have to enable advanced security on a mailbox-by-mailbox basis. Each enabled Exchange mailbox has two pairs of keys, each consisting of a public and a private key. One pair of keys is for digital signing, and the other is for encryption.

When a user chooses to sign an outgoing message, the user's Exchange client uses the private signing key of her or his mailbox to add a digital signature to the message. The message recipient's Exchange client verifies the signature using the public signing key of the sender's mailbox.

To encrypt an outgoing message, the Exchange client uses the unique public encryption key for the mailbox of each recipient of the message. When a user receives an encrypted message, the user's Exchange client uses the private encryption key for his or her mailbox to decrypt the message.

Public keys are stored in the Exchange directory as attributes of each advanced security–enabled mailbox. Private keys are stored on each user's private disk space in an encrypted file with the extension .EPF.

To run advanced Exchange Server security, you'll need to install a special *Key Management Server* program, or simply *KM Server.* Among other things, KM Server does the following:

- Certifies public signing and encryption keys to ensure their authenticity.

- Creates public and private encryption keys. (Public and private signing keys are created by Exchange clients.)

- Holds backups of private encryption keys and public signing keys.

- Generates tokens that are used only once to enable digital signatures and encryption or to recover lost or forgotten keys for a user.

- Maintains the original copy of the list of users whose rights to advanced security have been revoked.

The KM database itself is encrypted for additional security.

NOTE Generally, the first release of Exchange Server's advanced security cannot be used for messages sent to foreign e-messaging systems, nor can Exchange automatically handle messages with similar advanced security features that are received from foreign e-messaging systems. The standards for cross-system advanced security aren't quite ready for prime time.

> **NOTE**
> The one exception to this rule is other Exchange organizations. Users of Exchange 5.0 clients in different Exchange organizations can exchange security keys. This, at least, breaks down the no-advanced-security barrier between Exchange organizations.

No digital signature or data encryption system is perfect. However, the systems included in Exchange are about as good as they get. You have a choice of three encryption algorithms: DES (Data Encryption Standard), CAST-40, and CAST-64. (*CAST* stands for the initials of Carlisle *A*dams and *S*tafford *T*avares, who developed the algorithm at Northern Telecom.)

Both DES and CAST-64 use 64 bits for keys, while CAST-40 uses only 40 bits. Because it produces a shorter and more easily broken key, CAST-40 is less secure than either CAST-64 or DES. Because the U.S. government does not allow the exportation of 64-bit encryption technologies to countries other than those in North America, however, only CAST-40 encryption is available for Exchange Server software shipped elsewhere. You can set the encryption algorithm used for each site separately, so if you have sites both inside and outside North America, you won't have to use the less-secure CAST-40 algorithm across your entire organization.

Installing the Key Management Server

The KM server software is installed on an Exchange server. For maximum security, the server should be set up to use the NT File System (NTFS).

> **WARNING**
> You must install **only one** KM Server for each Exchange organization. If you don't heed this warning, be prepared for authentication and encryption errors.

You can administer and manage all aspects of advanced security from any Exchange site in your organization. If you want to do it from a site other than the one where KM Server is installed, you must install certain KM Server components on an Exchange server in that site. We'll do a full first-site installation of the KM Server software in this section, and in the next section we'll do a follow-up installation of selected components in another site.

KM Server is at the heart of your advanced Exchange security system. Be sure to locate it in a physically secure place.

KM Server access doesn't generate much network traffic, so it doesn't really make much difference where the server is located. I chose to install KM Server in my GerCom LA site on the Exchange server EXCHLA01.

KM Server is an NT service. Every time you start up KM Server, you need to enter a special password that it uses for a number of operations. You can type in the password manually or have it entered automatically from a floppy disk. You're given both options during installation.

If you choose manual entry, the installation program will give you the password before it terminates. Be sure to write the password down and keep it in a safe place.

If you decide to go the password-to-floppy route, put a blank disk in the A: drive of the Exchange/KM server before starting the KM Server installation process. From now on whenever you need to start the service, the floppy must be in the KM server's A: drive. Be sure to treat the disk with respect, and keep it under lock and key when it's not in use. The password is stored in nonencrypted format and can be read or copied by anyone. You should make your own copies of the disk and store them in a safe and secure place.

The KM Server software is installed from the Exchange Server CD-ROM and is located in the EXCHKM subdirectory for your operating system. Log in as NT administrator for the domain in which you're doing the installation, then run SETUP.EXE from the EXCHKM subdirectory.

Most of the installation process for KM Server is pretty standard; Figure 17.15 shows the only unusual dialog box you'll see. The country code is used to ensure that certain names used in the advanced security system conform to X.500 standards. Just be sure the Country Code field is set to the country where the site is located. If you want to create that floppy disk I talked about just above, be sure there's a blank disk in drive A: of the machine you're installing on and that you've selected 'Create KM server startup floppy disk'.

FIGURE 17.15

The Key Management
Server Setup dialog box

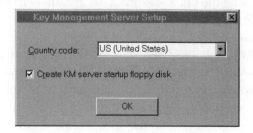

When installation is finished, start up the Key Management service using the NT Services applet. Then take a look in the Configuration container for the site where you just installed KM Server. You'll see two new objects—one called CA and one named Encryption. We'll talk about these in just a bit.

Advanced Security Administration and Management in Other Sites

This section shows you how to add advanced security administration and management capabilities to other sites. If you're eager to start using KM Server, I suggest that you bypass this section and proceed to the next one, which focuses on the ins and outs of actually administering and managing advanced security.

As soon as KM Server installation is finished—assuming you're logged in as NT administrator for the domain where KM Server was installed—you can administer and manage advanced security for all sites in your organization. However, at that time you can do this only from the site where KM Server was installed. To enable advanced security administration and management in other sites, you have to install selected KM components on a server in each of those sites.

> **NOTE**
>
> You're not enabling advanced security for these other sites—it was enabled for all sites when you installed KM Server in the first site in your organization. You're just making it possible to administer and manage advanced security from these other sites.

You can install the advanced security administration and management components only in sites that are continuously and directly linked to the site where KM Server was installed; a Dynamic RAS connection or indirect link through a foreign e-messaging system isn't enough. The advanced security administration and management components in your site must be able to talk in real time to KM Server using the RPCs we discussed in earlier chapters. The real-time link is necessary both for general KM Server administration and management and when mailboxes are enabled for advanced security. This means that sites without continuous RPC links to the KM Server site cannot administer and manage their own advanced security. Instead, they must rely on the services of KM administrators in sites where advanced security administration and management has been installed.

To enable advanced security administration and management in a site other than the one where you installed KM Server, log in to an Exchange server in the new site as NT administrator and run the same KM Server SETUP.EXE program you ran in your first site. This time SETUP.EXE checks to see if KM Server is already installed in your organization. How does it do this? It looks into each site's Configuration container for an object with the directory name CA. When it finds the object, it knows not only that the full KM Server has already been installed, but also *where* it was installed.

> **WARNING**　Because the SETUP.EXE program looks for the CA object in the directory replica of the server it is running on, be sure to allow enough time for the CA object to be replicated to that directory. When you can see it there, it's safe to run SETUP.EXE.

When SETUP.EXE finishes, it puts up a little dialog box telling you to contact the Key Management administrator in the site where KM Server was installed regarding enabling security on individual mailboxes. Though it doesn't read that way, the developers at Microsoft say that the dialog box is to remind you that you need the direct RPC-based link to KM Server I discussed just a bit ago.

Next we have to ensure that the proper security permissions are set so that KM Server can be administered and managed from all sites where the KM administration and management components are installed. We crack that little nut in the next section.

Let's turn for a moment to the example we've been using throughout this book. In addition to installing KM Server on EXCHLA01 in my LA site, I installed KM Server administration and management components on the EXCHNY01 server in my NY site. Once the security permissions are properly set, I'll be able to administer and manage KM Server from either site.

Administering and Managing the Key Management Server

There are three distinct KM Server administration and management tasks:

- Setting encryption algorithms

- Setting KM Server's own security

- Enabling advanced security for mailboxes

We'll cover each of these tasks in order below. To start, be sure you're logged in as NT administrator for the domain where you installed KM Server. Then open the Exchange Administrator for the site where KM Server was installed.

Setting Encryption Algorithms

You use a site's Encryption object to administer and manage KM Server settings. You can set the algorithm used when encrypted messages are sent from the current site to other Exchange sites in North America. To do this, open the Encryption Properties dialog box by double-clicking on the Encryption object in the Configuration container for the site. The General property page contains one alterable field, the display name, and you already know how to use the Permissions page if you need it. So tab over to the remaining property page, Security (see Figure 17.16).

FIGURE 17.16

The Security property page of the Encryption Properties dialog box

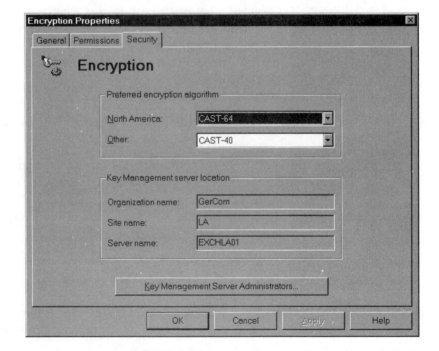

Use the top drop-down list to change the encryption algorithm used at the current site for Exchange messages addressed to other North American Exchange sites in your organization. Your two options here are CAST-64 and DES. If you change the encryption algorithm after enabling advanced security for specific mailboxes, the users of those mailboxes will still be able to read messages created under the previous algorithm. However, some reconfiguring will be required to enable the new algorithm for those mailboxes.

You can't change the encryption algorithm for messages addressed to Exchange sites in your organization that are outside North America. Even though a drop-down list is present for "other" sites, there is only one option on the list: CAST-40.

Setting KM Server's Own Security

If you have standard Exchange Permissions Admin rights on a site's Configuration container, you can change encryption options using the Encryption Properties dialog box shown in Figure 17.16. However, to use the rest of the options in this dialog box, you must have some very special rights. You must be a Key Management Server administrator (KMSA).

As a KMSA, you can change the KM Server password and add and remove other KMSAs. You can also enable and disable advanced security for mailboxes. Once you've enabled advanced security for a mailbox, the mailbox's owner can use digital signatures and data encryption. As you can see, KMSAs are very powerful, so you should assign KMSA rights with great care. To start with, the default KMSA is the NT administrator account for the domain where KM Server was installed.

To modify KM Server's own security for the first time, be sure that you're logged in as NT administrator for the domain containing the site where KM Server was installed. Then open the Encryption Properties dialog box (see Figure 17.16). In addition to changing encryption algorithm options, you can use this dialog box to change the Key Management Server password or to add or remove KMSAs. To do either of these tasks, click on the button labeled Key Management Server Administrators. Next you'll be asked for the KM Server password (see Figure 17.17); the default is PASSWORD, but you can and should change it in just a bit. Every time you do an advanced security function, you're asked for that danged password. However, if you check 'Remember this password for up to 5 minutes', you can work for at least a little while without bother.

When you're done with the Password dialog box, click on OK to open the Key Management Server Administrators dialog box shown in Figure 17.18. To change the password, click on Change Password and fill in the resultant dialog box labeled 'Change The Password For The Key Management Server'. To add a KMSA, click on Add Administrators and select one or more NT accounts from the Add Users dialog box that pops up. To remove a KMSA, click on Remove Administrators, select the KMSA you want to remove, and click on Done.

FIGURE 17.17

Entering the Key Management Server password

FIGURE 17.18

Change the KM Server password and add or remove KMSAs using the Key Management Server Administration dialog box.

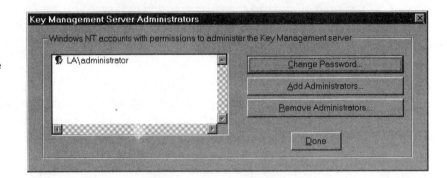

In Figure 17.19, running from my LA site, I've added the NT administrator for my NY site to the list of KMSAs. Now the NY administrator can change the KM Server password, add and remove KMSAs, and enable advanced security for all mailboxes in my Exchange organization.

FIGURE 17.19

Adding a new Key Management Server administrator

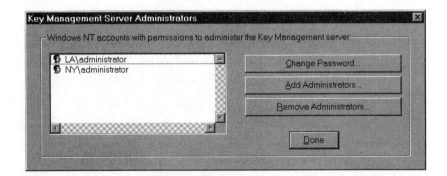

Enabling Advanced Security for Mailboxes

Now we're ready to actually enable advanced security for mailboxes. This is a two-step process that's done partly on the Exchange Server side and partly on the Exchange client side. We'll start with Exchange Server.

Enabling Advanced Security for Mailboxes: The Exchange Server Side

As a KMSA, you have two options when enabling advanced security for mailboxes: the mailbox-by-mailbox option and the bulk automated option. If you need to enable advanced security on only a few mailboxes, the mailbox-by-mailbox method is adequate. However, if you've got a bunch of mailboxes that need enabling, the bulk option is a better choice. We'll start with mailbox-by-mailbox, because it'll help you better understand the enabling process and the tools used in it.

You can work on mailboxes in any recipients container, from the Global Address List to a server's recipients container. Locate the mailbox for which you want to enable advanced security, and double-click on it. This opens the standard mailbox properties dialog box. The box has a new tab on it named Security; tab over to it. The Security property page is protected by the KM Server password, which you'll be prompted for (see Figure 17.20).

FIGURE 17.20

Entering the KM Server password to gain entry to a mailbox's Security property page

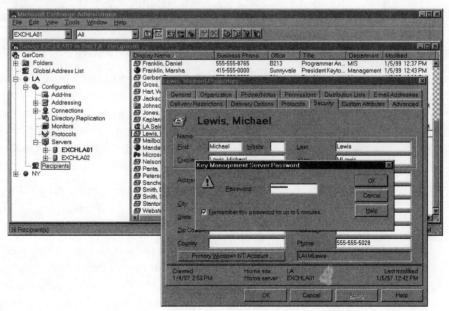

Once you've entered the correct KM Server password, you'll see the Security property page for the mailbox (see Figure 17.21).

FIGURE 17.21

The Security property page

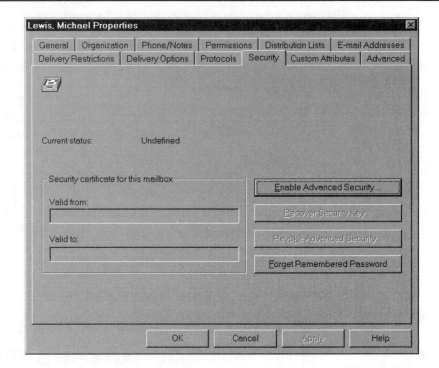

At this point, you can enable advanced security by clicking on—you guessed it—Enable Advanced Security. Besides turning on advanced security, this option creates public keys for the mailbox and generates a code called an *advanced security token*. In a second or so, you'll see a dialog box labeled 'Microsoft Exchange Administrator' (see Figure 17.22). Write down the advanced security token and give it to the mailbox owner for use in setting up advanced security on the client side.

Click on OK in the Microsoft Exchange Administrator dialog box. The Security property page now looks something like the one in Figure 17.23. You're through enabling advanced security for the mailbox.

Don't worry about the Recover Security Key and Revoke Advanced Security options right now; we'll talk about them later in this chapter. If you checked 'Remember this password for up to five minutes' when entering the KM Server password (see Figure 17.20), clicking 'Forget Remembered Password' forces the Exchange Administrator program to forget the password before those five minutes pass.

FIGURE 17.22

An advanced security token has been generated for the mailbox.

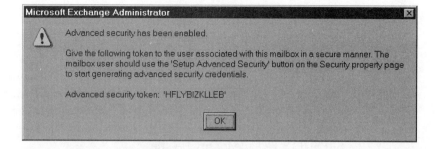

FIGURE 17.23

The Security property page after advanced security has been enabled

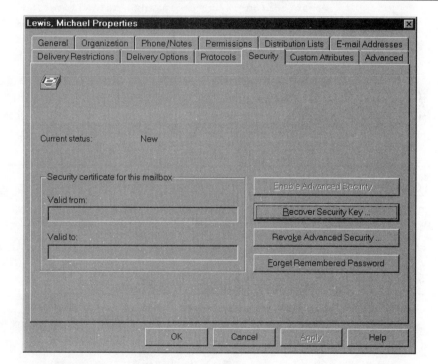

If you need to enable advanced security for several mailboxes at once, there's an alternative to the manual process I just described. Run the DOS program SIMPORT.EXE, which is located in the \Security\Bin directory on all servers where you ran KM Server's SETUP.EXE. The SIMPORT.EXE program requires access to a file called SECADMIN.DLL, which is in the \EXCHSRVR\BIN directory. To access the file, you need to include this directory in your path. If you don't know how to do this, check out the Windows NT docs for more information.

From the command line for SIMPORT.EXE, enter the Exchange organization, site, and recipients container(s) you want to run against as follows:

```
simport /o=organization /ou=site /cn=recipients container
[/cn=recipients container]
```

SIMPORT.EXE asks you to enter the KM Server password and the name of the Exchange server that KM Server is installed on. The program generates a text file named SRESULTS.TXT that lists each mailbox by organization, site, and recipients container, and also lists the token generated for each mailbox. Here's a bit of an SRESULTS.TXT file for my LA site:

```
/o=gercom/ou=la/cn=recipients/cn=AAndrews,LNOBWFUD
/o=gercom/ou=la/cn=recipients/cn=AJones,HJVGKEQC
/o=gercom/ou=la/cn=recipients/cn=AStone,YDARYKQX
/o=gercom/ou=la/cn=recipients/cn=BGerber,ELCNMADV
```

Enabling Advanced Security for Mailboxes: The Exchange Client Side   Open a client for the mailbox for which you want to enable advanced security. Select Options from the client's Tools menu to open the Options dialog box, then tab over to the Security property page (see Figure 17.24).

FIGURE 17.24

Use the Options dialog box to enable advanced security for a mailbox.

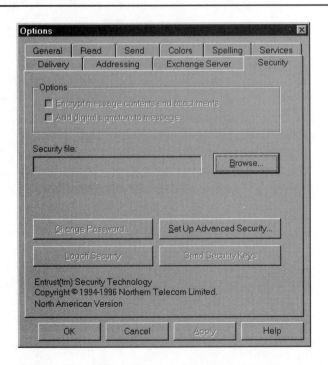

Next, click on Set Up Advanced Security to bring up the Setup Advanced Security dialog box (see Figure 17.25). Type in the token for the mailbox that was generated by the KMSA, then enter and confirm an advanced security password that will be used when you generate or try to open a digitally signed or encrypted message. (The password must be at least six characters long.)

FIGURE 17.25

Entering the security
token and advanced
security password

Don't worry about the Security File field: If it's filled in, fine. If it isn't, your client will automatically select a name for the file. When you're done, click on OK.

Next you'll see a dialog box telling you that your request for advanced security was sent to KM Server and that you'll be notified when the request has been processed (see Figure 17.26). This feature is pretty impressive. Communications between clients and KM Server are all by e-messages, so the client can be linked to the Exchange server environment by anything from a dial-up connection to a hard-wired WAN or LAN link.

After the time required for a round-trip mail cycle, a message from the System Attendant will appear in the client's Inbox. The subject of the message will be 'Reply from Security Authority'. This is a very special message. When you open it, you won't see a standard message window. First, you're asked for the advanced security password you entered a few paragraphs above (see Figure 17.27). Type in the password and click on OK.

FIGURE 17.26

The client has sent a message asking that advanced security be enabled for its mailbox.

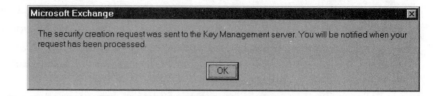

FIGURE 17.27

Entering the mailbox's advanced security password

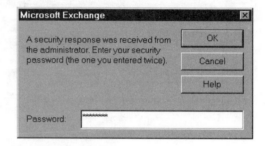

Next you'll see a little dialog box telling you that security has been successfully enabled (see Figure 17.28). When you click on OK to acknowledge that you've read the notice, you're done. The message from the System Attendant is gone.

FIGURE 17.28

Advanced security has been successfully enabled.

NOTE After you've enabled advanced security for a mailbox, you can tell Exchange to digitally sign and encrypt **all** messages by selecting the two respective options on the Options dialog box (see Figure 17.24).

After a while, in the Exchange Administrator take a look at the Security property page of the mailbox for which you just enabled advanced security. Because the mailbox is now fully security-enabled, the Valid From and Valid To fields will be filled in (see Figure 17.29). By default, security keys are valid for a year and a half. New keys will be automatically generated at the end of this time period.

FIGURE 17.29

The valid life span of a mailbox's security keys has been set.

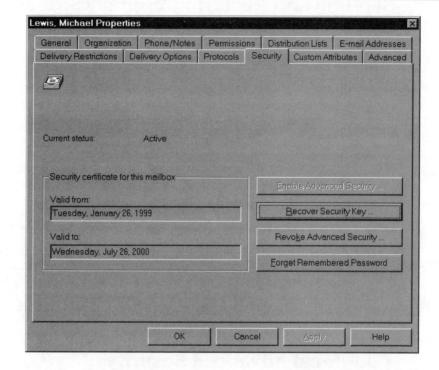

When a mailbox's Security property page looks like the one in Figure 17.29, advanced security is fully enabled, and the mailbox user can send and receive digitally signed and/or encrypted messages. The mailbox's public keys are part of the mailbox definition in the Exchange directory. Therefore, mailbox users in other sites will not be able to communicate with the mailbox using advanced security until a fully security-enabled replica of the mailbox has reached their sites.

NOTE You can keep track of advanced security activity in Exchange by keeping an eye on NT Event Viewer's Application log. You'll find the Event Viewer in the Administrative Tools program group.

Sending and Receiving Digitally Signed and Encrypted Messages

Since this book doesn't focus on the Exchange client, I'll just give you a quick overview on the topic. If, when using the Options dialog box, you asked to have all messages digitally signed and encrypted, then you'll be led through any required steps for each message. If you've chosen to sign or encrypt messages individually, then while composing a message select Properties from the message's File menu. Tab over to the Security property page and from the Options area select 'Encrypt message contents and attachments' and/or 'Add digital signature to message' (refer to Figure 17.24). When you send the message, you'll be led through the steps required to give it advanced security.

> **TIP**
>
> There is an easier way to request that a message be digitally signed and/or encrypted. Once advanced security is enabled, you'll find a couple of new little buttons on each message you compose. One requests a digital signature for the message. The other asks for encryption.

Additional Advanced Security Administration and Management Options

The Security property page for a mailbox has two options that we didn't talk about earlier: Recover Security Key and Revoke Advanced Security (see Figure 17.23). We're now ready to tackle these options.

Recovering a Security Key

The Recover Security Key option on the Security property page is useful in the following situations:

- Users lose their token before using it to set up advanced security on the client side.

- Users lose their advanced security password (more on this later).

- Users corrupt or remove the local security file for their mailbox.

- You've changed the encryption algorithm for a site and need to update mailboxes that were enabled for advanced security before the change took effect.

Click on Recover Security Key to start the recovery process. When it's finished, the Microsoft Exchange Administrator dialog box shown back in Figure 17.22 pops up. The token will be different than the original one; when the user reinstalls advanced security, whichever of the first three problems needed fixing will be fixed, or the new encryption algorithm will be enabled for that user.

Revoking Advanced Security

Click on Revoke Advanced Security to remove advanced security rights for a mailbox. If you ever want to re-enable these rights, just generate a token for the mailbox and ask the mailbox user to enable advanced security on the client side.

Migrating Users from Other E-Messaging Systems

You can move users from foreign e-messaging systems to your Exchange system. In some cases, Microsoft provides specific migration tools, while in others no tools are available. Even if there are no tools for migration, you can still automate at least part of it on your own.

Migration is a complex process. Rather than describe it here in detail, I just want to make sure you know that it's available. Most of the documentation for migration is provided only on the Exchange Server CD-ROM, in the 'Migrate' directory. Let's take a quick look at your options.

Exchange Server ships with migration tools for the following e-messaging systems:

- Microsoft Mail for PC Networks
- Microsoft Mail for AppleTalk Networks
- Lotus cc:Mail
- Novell GroupWise
- Collabra Share

- DEC All-In-1

- IBM PROFS

- Verimation Memo (for Memo/MVS only)

MS Mail for PC Networks and Lotus cc:Mail migrations are both done entirely using the Microsoft Exchange Server Migration Wizard, which is installed along with Exchange Server. Both migrations move most available directory and message data to the Exchange environment, and both also assume a live network link between your Exchange system and your MS Mail PC or cc:Mail system. If everything is running properly, these two migrations are a piece of cake.

Migrating from the other four systems supported by Microsoft is a little more difficult. First you run what Microsoft calls a *migration source extractor*, which takes directory and message data from the foreign e-messaging system and writes it to a file that can be imported into Exchange. Once you have this file, you can import it into your Exchange environment using the Migration Wizard's Import from Migration Files option.

If Microsoft doesn't support migration from your current e-messaging system, you can still automate at least part of the process. If your e-messaging system lets you export directory and/or message data, and if you can get the data into a format acceptable to Exchange Server, you can then import it into Exchange Server using the Import from Migration Files option of the Migration Wizard.

If that's not possible, Microsoft provides information on building your own migration source extractor to produce data that can be imported into your Exchange Server directory using the Migration Wizard. And if you don't want to get that fancy, you can build user information files that can be imported into Exchange Server using the Administrator program's Directory Import option, which I'll discuss in a moment.

NOTE	Whichever route you take, be sure that someone on your migration team fully understands both the foreign e-messaging system you're working with and the computer operating system that it runs on top of. Without this expertise, you can get into some very hot water. If no one in your organization qualifies for this distinction, consider getting help from the vendors of your e-messaging system and operating system, or think about hiring a knowledgeable consultant or two.

Importing Information into the Exchange Directory

As I noted previously, you can build user information files that can be imported into an Exchange Server's directory. You create directory import files either manually or, preferably, using one or more computers. Let's start with a brief discussion of a directory import file's structure. Then we'll talk a bit about how to do a directory import.

The Structure of an Exchange Directory Import File

Here's a portion of a simple directory import file:

```
Obj-Class,Common-Name,Display-Name,Home-Server,Comment
Mailbox,AAndrews,Archie Andrews,~SERVER,Comic Book Character
Mailbox,BGerber,Barry Gerber,~SERVER,
Mailbox,CPumpkin,"Pumpkin\, Charles",~SERVER,
Mailbox,Services,Exchange Services Account for Domain NY,
~SERVER,
```

The first line in a directory import file lists the names of the fields that are to be imported. Each following line lists the values of the import fields for a specific object. These must be listed in the same order in which the field names of the items themselves are listed in the first line of the file. A variety of field separation options can be used; the default is the very standard comma-delimited mode.

The object class (*Obj-Class*) is set to *Mailbox*, meaning that, upon import, Exchange Server should create a new mailbox object for the row entry. Common object classes include *Mailbox* (mailbox), *dl* (distribution list), and *Remote* (custom recipient). *Common-Name* is the new object's name in the Exchange Server directory. Because Common-Name will become the mailbox's directory name, it must be unique from all existing directory names in the site. Common-Name also will become the new object's alias name.

You already know what *Display-Name* is. *Home-Server* is the Exchange server on which the new object should be created, and *Comment* is any text you want to add for the object.

~SERVER tells the Exchange directory import utility that the account should be created on the Exchange server on which the import is run. (I could just as well have replaced each instance of *~SERVER* with the name of a specific Exchange server.) And that backslash in old Charlie Pumpkin's name tells the directory import option that the comma is part of Charlie's display name, not a field separator.

645

The import file listed above will create four new mailbox recipient objects in an Exchange directory. If you just want to change some attributes of one or more existing recipients, you need to add a field called *Mode* and set the mode for any row with changes to Modify.

You can see how Mode is used in the import file below, which changes Charlie's display name from *Pumpkin, Charles* to *Pumpkin, Charlie*. Big deal, huh? Well, it's important to Charlie. Note that I've included Charlie's Common-Name; without it, the import option wouldn't know which recipient to modify. I deleted the Home-Server entry, since that was set when I ran the directory import file listed above.

```
Obj-Class,Mode,Common-Name,Display-Name
Mailbox,Modify,CPumpkin,"Pumpkin\, Charlie"
```

You may be wondering how to find the names of the fields you want to include in an import file. Short of asking Microsoft, there are four ways, which are listed below in increasing order of risk. The option is for *certified* Exchange Server directory experts only.

- Use the Exchange Administrator's Export Directory option (discussed later in this chapter), which outputs a directory import file whose first line includes the names of several directory objects. This file also helps you become familiar with the general structure and format of import files.

- Check out the directory import and export documentation that comes with Exchange Server.

- Use the HEADERS.EXE utility that comes with the Exchange portion of the Back Office Resource Kit.

- Run the Exchange Administrator program in raw mode: Open a DOS command prompt, move over to the directory where the Exchange Server executables are stored (usually \EXCHSRVR\BIN), and type admin/raw. Once the Administrator is running, select an instance of the object you're interested in—say, a mailbox—and then select Raw Properties from the Administrator's File menu. Use the resultant dialog box to find the object names you need.

Importing Directory Information

Once you've got a file to import, directory import is a piece of cake. Select Directory Import from the Exchange Administrator's Tools menu. Using the resultant Directory Import dialog box shown in Figure 17.30, select the NT domain, Exchange server, and recipients container you want to import to.

FIGURE 17.30

Importing information to
an Exchange Server
directory

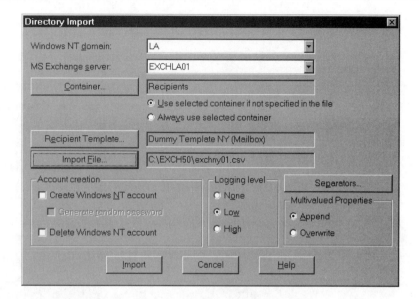

The Recipient Template is a useful gizmo—it's just an Exchange recipient that you create with some fields filled in. When recipient information is imported, Exchange Server uses the template to add any standard information for those recipients. For example, I created a mailbox in my NY site that I called 'Dummy Template (Mailbox)' (see Figure 17.31). Into that mailbox I put such standard information as GerCom's New York address and company name. Now when I import directory information and specify the template, this information is automatically added for each recipient in the file. (Unique information like first name and last name is taken from the file, not the template.)

NOTE Notice in Figure 17.31 that my dummy mailbox has been associated with no NT account. This is perfectly permissible. There's no need for an NT account here, because the mailbox will never be opened by anyone. Similarly, when multiple Exchange users share a mailbox, while they all need permissions to use the mailbox (granted on the mailbox's Permissions property page), the mailbox doesn't have to have a *Primary* NT account.

You can get really fancy creating templates. For example, you can make a template for each department—or even for each supervisor in a department—because even information such as Manager (supervisor of the mailbox owner) on the Organization property page can be templated into a group of mailboxes.

FIGURE 17.31

A "dummy" mailbox template for GerCom's NY site

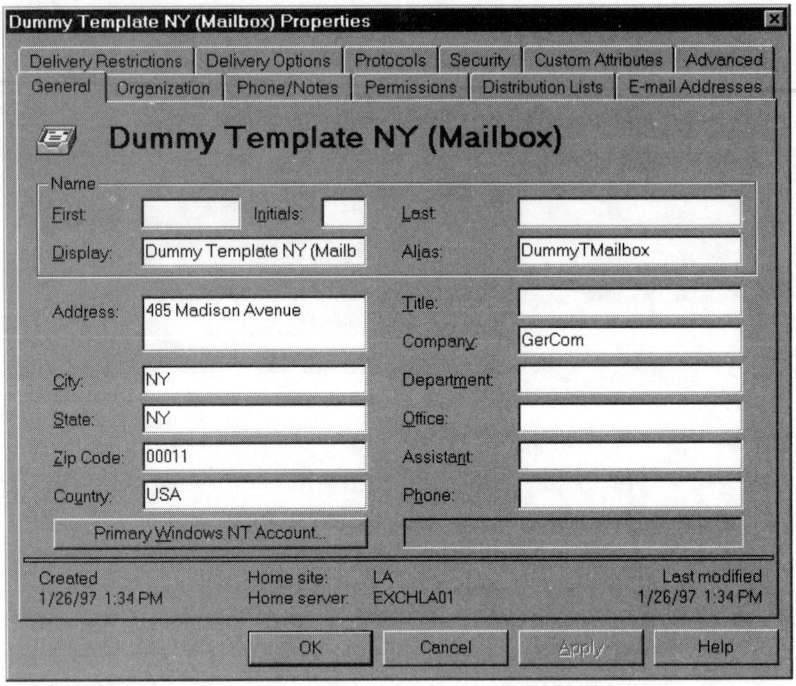

Of course, you'd have to set up a different directory import file for each template, but it might be worth it in terms of the hours of manual input saved. And remember, by using the Modify mode in a directory import you can change any templated information you want for a group of recipients. (For more about the Modify mode, see the section above on the structure of an Exchange directory import file.)

If you want to create an NT account for each newly created mailbox, check that option in the Directory Import dialog box, shown back in Figure 17.30. Select a logging level—Low is a good choice unless you are having trouble importing a file.

If your import file uses standard comma-delimited separators, don't worry about the Separators button. If it doesn't, use the button to set the correct separators.

The Multivalued Properties area of the Directory Import dialog box is very useful. If a directory import file contains values for an existing object—for example, recipients for a specific distribution list—and you select Append, the new values are appended to the old values (that is, the new distribution list recipients are added to the old ones). If you select Overwrite, the new values replace the old values (that is, the new recipients for the distribution list become the only recipients for that list).

When you've finished filling in the dialog box, click on Import and the file will be imported.

Extracting Information from Other Sources for the Exchange Directory

Often, migration isn't the problem—or at least it isn't your *only* problem. Perhaps you need to, say, pull information from some nonmessaging source and use it to create a new directory or enhance one that already exists. Or maybe you want to grab users from your operating system's security database, or even from some totally non-MIS database such as the one for your organization's human resources data.

If you can get the information into a format acceptable to the Exchange Administrator's Directory Import option, the rest is easy. The Administrator provides two operating system account-extraction options: one for NT systems and the other for NetWare systems. Let's look at these and then touch briefly on the extraction of directory data from non-MIS databases.

Extracting a Windows NT Account List

Select the Extract Windows NT Account List option from the Exchange Administrator's Tools menu, then fill in the resultant Windows NT User Extraction dialog box. As you can see in Figure 17.32, you extract the accounts one domain at a time. When you're finished filling in the dialog box, click on OK to begin the extraction.

The following is a portion of a file produced by an extraction from my NY domain:

```
Obj-Class,Common-Name,Display-Name,Home-Server,Comment
Mailbox,AAndrews,Archie Andrews,~SERVER,Comic Book Character
Mailbox,BGerber,Barry Gerber,~SERVER,
Mailbox,CPumpkin,"Pumpkin\, Charles",~SERVER,
Mailbox,Services,Exchange Services Account for Domain NY,~SERVER,
```

Surprise! You've seen this file before. It's the example I used earlier in this chapter when talking about the structure of Exchange directory import files. So it should be no additional surprise when I tell you that this file is ready to be imported into Exchange Server using the Directory Import option. If I wanted, I could enhance the individual data items or even add items; I just have to be sure that the file retains Exchange Server's directory import format.

FIGURE 17.32

Preparing to extract a list
of Windows NT accounts

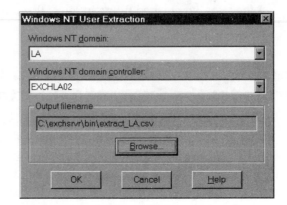

Extracting a NetWare Account List

Select Extract NetWare Account List from the Administrator's Tools menu, then fill in the NetWare User Extraction dialog box that pops up (see Figure 17.33). Be sure to enter the name and password of a NetWare user with NetWare supervisory rights. When you're done, click on OK to extract the user information.

FIGURE 17.33

Preparing to extract a list
of NetWare accounts

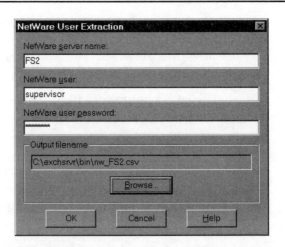

Here's the file I got when I extracted the four users on my test NetWare server:

```
Obj-Class,Common-Name,Display-Name,Home-Server
Mailbox,SUPERVISOR,,~SERVER
Mailbox,GUEST,,~SERVER
Mailbox,BARRYGNW,,~SERVER
Mailbox,ADMINISTRATOR,,~SERVER
```

In the revised export file listed below, I added "FS2" to Common-Names to ensure uniqueness. I also added display names for the four NetWare users. To indicate that a comma should be included in the display name for 'Gerber, Barry', I put a backslash before the comma. The file retains the Exchange Server directory import format.

```
bj-Class,Common-Name,Display-Name,Home-Server
Mailbox,SUPERVISORFS2,"Administrator (On FS2)",~SERVER
Mailbox,GUESTFS2,"Guest (On FS2)",~SERVER
Mailbox,BARRYFS2,"Gerber\, Barry (On FS2)",~SERVER
Mailbox,ADMINISTRATORFS2,"For NT Administrator",~SERVER

Extracting from Non-MIS Databases
```

If programming resources are available, you can pull information from non-MIS databases and put it into Exchange Server's directory import format. This can be useful both for creating basic Exchange directory entries and for enhancing already existing entries.

For example, you could extract basic user-name information from your organization's human resources database and incorporate it into a directory import file. Or you could pull such items as the home address, fax and phone numbers, and even supervisor's name and put them into a directory import file.

Exporting Directory Information from Exchange Server

Let's start by looking at the reasons you might want to export Exchange Server directories. Then we'll look at the structure of an export file. Finally, we'll talk about how you do an export.

Why Export?

There are a number of reasons why you might want to export your Exchange Server directories into files:

- When moving an Exchange Server mailbox to another site. (Remember, you can use the Move Mailbox option only within a site.) You can use directory export only to transfer Exchange directory information for the user; to move the actual mailbox, the user must temporarily move the contents of the server-based mailbox to a locally stored mailbox.

- To create a text file with selected properties for mailboxes, custom recipients, and distribution lists for some administrative use, such as generating a printed list of e-mail addresses of all or selected recipients for distribution to customers.

- To export all or part of a directory to another e-messaging system.

- To create a backup of at least a portion of the directory to be used in case of a catastrophic system crash in which—perish the thought—all tape backups of the directory are lost.

The Structure of a Directory Export File

The following fields are included in an Exchange Server directory export:

- Obj-Class
- First Name
- Last Name
- Display Name
- Alias Name
- Directory Name
- Primary Windows NT Account
- Home-Server
- E-mail Address
- E-mail Addresses
- Members
- Obj-Container
- Hide from AB

This list doesn't represent everything, but it's certainly adequate for most of the reasons you might want to export a directory.

Recipient types are grouped in this order: distribution lists, mailboxes, custom recipients. So don't assume that custom recipients haven't been exported just because they don't show up in alphabetical order among the mailboxes (as they do in the recipients container). The following segment of a directory export file has been reformatted to make it easier to read:

```
Obj-Class,First Name,Last name,Display Name,Alias Name,
Directory Name,Primary Windows NT Account,Home-Server,E-mail
address,E-mail Addresses,Members,Obj-Container,Hide from AB
dl,,,LA Sales (Distribution List),LASales,LASales,,,,
MS:GERCOM/LA/LASALES%SMTP:LASales@LA.GerCom.com%
X400:c=US;a=p=GerCom;o=LA;s=LASales;,Recipients/cn=BGerber%
Recipients/cn=RAlvarez%Recipients/cn=MLewis%
Recipients/cn=WPeterson,Recipients,0

Mailbox,Archie,Andrews,"Andrews\,Archie",AAndrews,
AAndrews,NY\Aandrews,EXCHLA01,,MS:GERCOM/LA/AANDREWS%
SMTP:AAndrews@LA.GerCom.com%X400:c=US;a= ;p=GerCom;o=LA;
s=Andrews;g=Archie;,,Recipients,

Remote,Marsha,Franklin,"Franklin\,Marsha",MFranklin,
MFranklin,,,SMTP:mfranklin@keytop.com,
MS:GERCOM/LA/MFRANKLIN%
X400:c=US;a= ;p=GerCom;o=LA;s=Franklin;g=Marsha;
%SMTP:mfranklin@keytop.com,,Recipients,0
```

Exporting a Directory

To export a directory, select Directory Export from the Exchange Administrator's File menu. This brings up the Directory Export dialog box shown in Figure 17.34.

Fill in the box, selecting the Exchange servers and recipients container(s) to be exported from. Specify an export file and indicate which of the three available types of directory objects you want to export: mailboxes, custom recipients, and/or distribution lists. Select a logging level and change the separators if necessary. In the Character Set section of the Directory Export dialog box, select Unicode if your directory entries contain special characters such as accents; otherwise ANSI is fine. If you want to include hidden directory objects, select that option.

When you're done filling in the information, click on Export to create your export file.

FIGURE 17.34

Setting up an Exchange
Server directory export

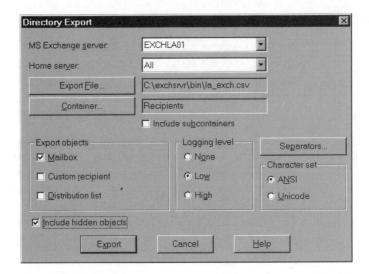

Going Beyond the Basic Export

You can specify which directory fields Exchange Administrator should export.
Just put the field names in the export file, before requesting the export. For
example, to export all of the standard mailbox fields listed in the previous section, plus company, department, title, address, city, state or province, and
phone number, enter the following header on a single line in the export file,
then request a directory export to the file:

```
Obj-Class,First Name,Last Name,Display Name,Alias Name,
Directory Name,Primary Windows NT Account,Home-Server,
E-mail address,E-mail Addresses,Members,Obj-Container,
Hide from AB,Company,Department,Title,Address,City,
State-Or-Province, Phone number
```

Moving Mailboxes between Exchange Sites

Back at the beginning of this chapter I showed you what a no-brainer it is to move mailboxes between Exchange servers in a site. Moving mailboxes between containers in a site, sites, or organizations is a bit more of a challenge. Here's how you do it.

Basically, you want to store a copy of your mailbox outside of the Exchange information store. From the client's Tools menu, pick Services. Using the resultant Services dialog box, click on Add and add a personal folder. Click OK your way out of the Services dialog box. You'll now see a new store in your Exchange client. Just drag and drop the folders and messages you want into the new store. You can't drag and drop either your Inbox or special folders. Just create new folders to hold the contents of these and drag and drop into them. Remember that you can mark and move or copy multiple messages and folders just by using the standard Windows item selection procedures; for example, Ctrl+click to select noncontiguous items.

When you're through filling up your personal folder, disconnect from your original mailbox and connect to the new one. Make sure that your newly created personal folder file is available. Use the Services dialog box to add your personal folder to your client. Drag whatever you want from the personal folder to your mailbox. Voilà! You've moved your mailbox to a new Exchange site or organization.

TIP You can also use Exchange Server's directory export function to ship out mailbox information for import at a new Exchange site or organization.

Working with Address Book Views

Address book views are one of the best new features of Exchange 5.0. They're containers that hold specially grouped images of your Exchange global address book. Address book views can be organized by such directory fields as the geographical locations or the departments in which Exchange recipients in your organization are located.

Address book views add hierarchical structure to what are usually flat views of recipients in the Exchange global address book and in Exchange Administrator. They make it easier for users to find addresses and for you to organize and manage Exchange recipients in Exchange Administrator. Address book views are especially useful in large organizations.

> **NOTE** Before Exchange 5.0, there was only one way to add structure to a global address book. You had to create a bunch of recipients containers and then create each recipient in the appropriate container. If you wanted to organize your global address book by department, you had to create a container for each department in your organization and then create each recipient in the container representing their department. Because it's difficult to move recipients to new containers after creating them—you have to export them to a file, modify the export file, and import the file—this method worked just fine, until someone was transferred to a new department.

Adding an Address Book View

To add an address book view, click on the Address Book Views container (see Figure 17.35). Next, open Exchange Administrator's File menu and click on New Other. Finally, select Address Book View from the menu that pops open. This brings up a dialog box for a new address book view as shown in Figure 17.36.

On the General property page, give the view display and directory names. Next, tab over to the Group By property page. As you can see in Figure 17.37, you use this page to set the directory fields that will be used to group recipient addresses. You can group to a depth of four levels. For example, if your organization is large, you might want to group by state, city, office building, and department. In Figure 17.37, I've set department as the only grouping field.

On the Advanced property page (see Figure 17.38), you can set two options and perform one action.

FIGURE 17.35

Preparing to create a
new address book view

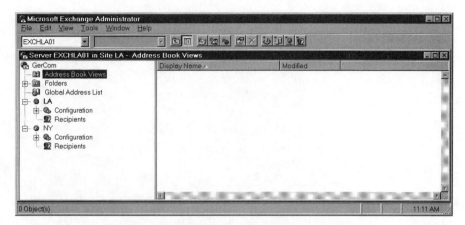

FIGURE 17.36

The dialog box used to
create new address
book views

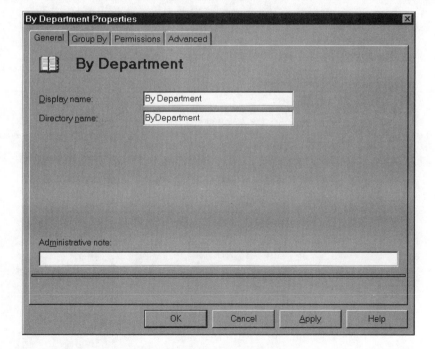

FIGURE 17.37

Setting address book
view grouping criteria

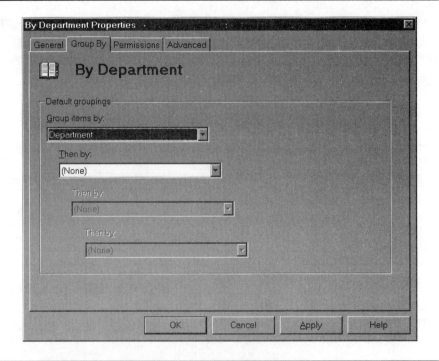

FIGURE 17.38

The Advanced
properties page for an
address book view

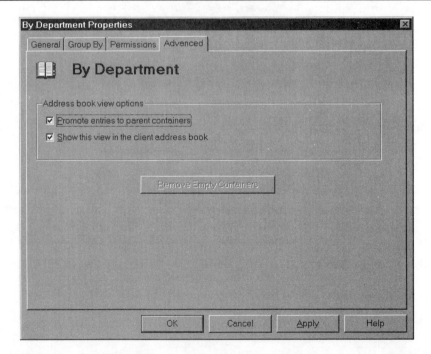

If you check 'Promote entries to parent containers' and your address book view is at least two levels deep, appropriate recipients will appear in all levels of the view, but the top level. For example, if you create a view named "Location" grouped by state, then by city and finally by department, recipients will show up in the appropriate state, city, and department container. No recipients will show up in the top-level container, "Location". If you don't check 'Promote entries to parent containers', recipients will show up only in the lowest level container, which is department in our example.

Check 'Show this view in the client address book' to make the address book view visible to Exchange client users. Click on 'Remove Empty Containers' to delete any subcontainers in the view that are empty, because all of the recipients that belong in the container have been deleted.

When you're finished with the address book view dialog box, click OK to start a process that will create the view. How fast the view is created depends on how many objects there are in your global address book and on how busy your Exchange server is. When all is done, you'll see a new address book view in your Exchange server's directory. This view will, of course, be replicated to other Exchange servers in your organization.

Figure 17.39 shows how an address book view organized by department looks in Exchange Administrator. Figures 17.40 and 17.41 show how a user sees the same address book view within an Exchange client.

FIGURE 17.39

An address book view as displayed in Exchange Administrator

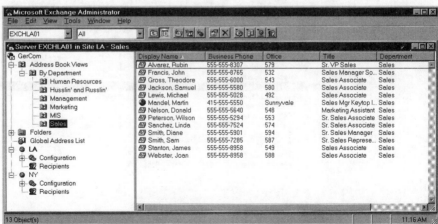

FIGURE 17.40

Selecting a container from an address book view within an Exchange client

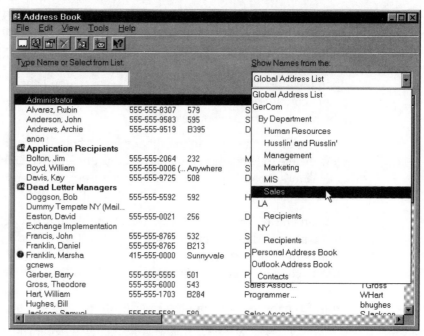

FIGURE 17.41

Selecting a recipient from an address book view container within an Exchange client

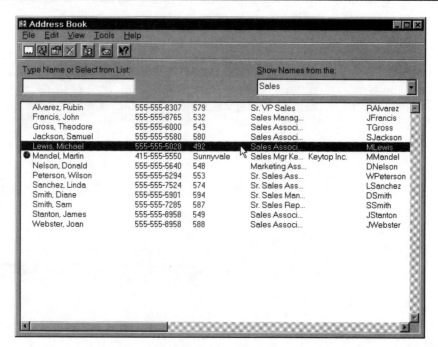

That Address Book Views Container

Perhaps you noticed that the master Address Book Views container shown in Figures 17.35 and 17.39 doesn't show up in any of the other figures in this book. That's because the address book views function was completed late in the Exchange Server 5.0 development cycle. Just days before this book went to press, I was able to get a copy of Exchange Server 5.0 with a complete implementation of address book views. There was just enough time for me to complete this section and no time to redo all of the figures in the book.

Adding an Address Book View Container

As you've just seen, address book view hierarchies are normally built automatically. You can also manually add an address book view subcontainer to an existing address book view container. These specially added containers are useful where the standard groupings you've selected for a view don't work. For example, the grouping set country-city-state for a view called "Location" works fine for the United States, which has states. It doesn't work for countries such as Greece that don't have states, but do have cities. For Greece, you need only country and city containers.

To create a new address book view subcontainer, click on an appropriate address book view container or subcontainer. Then, select 'Address Book View Container' from the New Other menu on the Exchange Administrator's File menu. When the dialog box for adding the container pops up, use the General property page to give the container display and directory names. Using our example, I'd use "Greece" for both names.

Next, tab over to the Group By property page. Here, you select the subcontainer that you want to group by and a grouping value for the field represented by the container that will hold your new address book view subcontainer. This sounds a lot more complex than it is, so let's turn back to our example. In Figure 17.42, I'm adding the new subcontainer to the container which represents the field *country*. I've requested that recipients be shown in the new subcontainer, if the value for the field *country* is "Greece." I've asked that subcontainers be created within the container Greece based on the value of the field *city*. In Figure 17.43, you can see the fruits of my labor.

FIGURE 17.42

Adding a new address
book view container

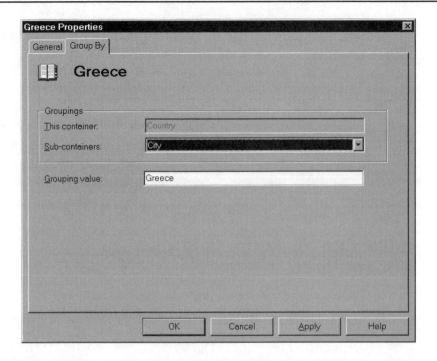

FIGURE 17.43

A newly added address
book view container

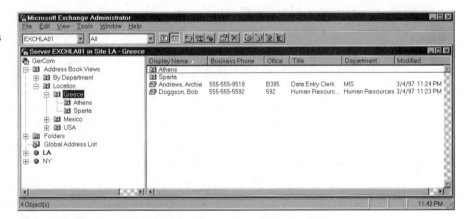

Adding to an Address Book View

Let's say Alicia Jones, who used to work in the Los Angeles Sales department of
GerCom, is transferred to the Marketing department in LA. I can change her

department by opening a dialog box for her mailbox and editing the department field. I can also simply move Ms. Jones from the Sales to the Marketing department address book view container.

It's not quite as easy as dragging and dropping the object. Instead, I click on Alicia Jones in the Sales container and select 'Add to Address Book View' from the Exchange Administrator's Tools menu. Then I select the appropriate container from the little address book view tree that pops up.

> **NOTE**
>
> *Add to Address Book View*, isn't exactly the right term for what you're doing here. You're really moving a recipient from one view to another by changing some of its attributes. The recipient inherits the attributes of the address book view hierarchy it's moved to and can no longer be found in the old hierarchy. Check it out. Double-click on the recipient after you've moved it to see its new attributes. Of course, you can quickly return to the old attributes by "adding" the recipient back to its old address book view hierarchy.

Other Advanced Exchange Administrator Options

The Exchange Administrator program provides a number of options that I haven't covered yet. I don't have the time or space to go into great detail about each of them, but I do want to make you aware of what they are and, in general, what you can do with them. You'll find these options in the Configuration container for a site.

Add-Ins

The Add-Ins container holds objects representing Windows dynamic link libraries (DLLs) that support one or another Exchange Server component. Add-ins include administrative components for the Internet Mail Service, the Microsoft Mail Connector, and the Free-Busy Connector that supports Schedule+. There is little you either can or need to do with these objects other than add an administrative note to them and change their permissions.

Addressing

The Addressing subcontainer holds three subcontainers: E-Mail Address Generators, Details Templates, and One-Off Address Templates. *E-mail address generators* are objects representing the DLLs that actually generate addresses. As with objects in the Add-Ins container, there's little you can or have to do with these objects.

Exchange clients use *details templates* to display the properties of a recipient or for other Exchange client functions, such as a search for a specific recipient. *One-off address templates* are used when an Exchange client user generates an address for a foreign e-messaging system. You can modify the graphical user interface or the DOS version of either template type by opening the template, tabbing over to the Template property page, and moving or editing old fields or adding new ones. When you choose to add new fields, a drop-down list shows you which ones are available. You can test changes you've made at any time without leaving Modify mode, and if you make a mistake, you can always revert to the original template.

In Figure 17.44, I'm modifying the details template for a mailbox by adding a new property page; in Figure 17.45, I'm testing my modifications. See the Exchange Server docs for more information on template modification.

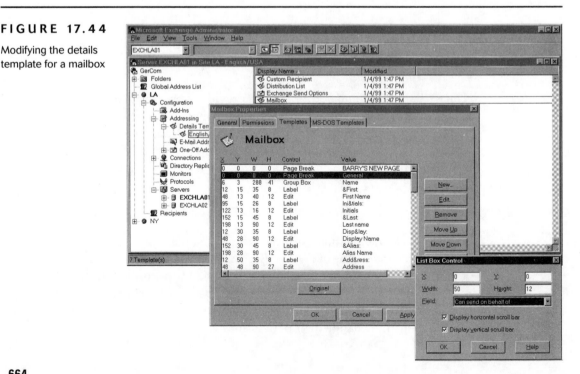

FIGURE 17.44

Modifying the details template for a mailbox

FIGURE 17.45

Testing a modified details template for a mailbox

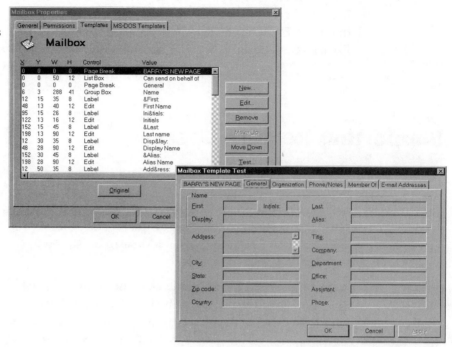

Remotely Administering Exchange and NT Servers

Using a Remote Access Service connection, you can administer your Exchange organization from any place with a telephone. As I get deeper and deeper into Exchange administration, I am finding remote connects invaluable. In fact, if you've got the Exchange Administrator along with the full suite of NT Server administrative tools on your remote Window NT Workstation or Server machine, you can pretty much kick back and manage your NT network without leaving the comfort of your easy chair.

Remote administration is no special trick. With a RAS connection in place and assuming that your remote NT workstation or server has been properly admitted to an appropriate NT domain, all you have to do is fire up Exchange Administrator and point it at the right Exchange server. Things may be a bit slow for certain functions, but you can do anything remotely that you can do when connected to the network.

If you're running NT Workstation, you can copy the server administration tools, User Manager for Domains, Server Manager, etc., from an NT Server CD ROM. With those tools in place, you'll add users and computers to your domains, start and stop Exchange and other NT services, and more, all without having to "go to the office."

Trust me: This is neat stuff. Try it. You'll like it. I promise.

Supporting Remote Users

Aside from ensuring that remote users install and set up their Exchange clients properly—as well as providing NT Remote Access Service (RAS) dial-in services and the modems and phone lines to support them—you don't have to do much else to support remote users on the server side. For more on the RAS, see *Mastering Windows NT Server 4*, by Mark Minasi, Christa Anderson, and Elizabeth Creegan (Sybex, 1996).

On the client side, the client installation software specifically asks if the client will be used for remote access. If you answer yes, then, each time you start up your Exchange client, you'll be asked if you want to connect to your Exchange server or work offline. Aside from a proper installation, the user needs to understand how to dial in to the network and use the Exchange client's folder synchronization capability. These topics are covered in *Microsoft Exchange Plain & Simple*, by Elizabeth Olson (Sybex, 1996).

Linking Exchange Client to Exchange Server over the Internet

You can connect your Exchange client to your Exchange Server without the benefit of RAS services. You can connect directly over the Internet through an Internet Service Provider (ISP). All you have to do is log into your ISP as usual. If your Exchange server is externally registered in the Domain Name Service so that you can ping it by name, you're pretty much ready. If the server isn't registered, you'll have to create an entry for the server in the HOSTS file on the computer where you're running the client. For more on the HOSTS file, see Minasi, et al.

Linking Exchange Client to Exchange Server over the Internet (Continued)

The Remote Procedure Calls that support Exchange client-server communications must be able to pass over the ISP-based link between your client and server. Technically, this requires that TCP/IP port 135 be enabled on all firewalls and routers between the client and server. You can test to see if this is the case by using a program developed by Microsoft, called "RCPPING.EXE". Check with the company for availability and source.

To connect your client to the server, get to the MS Exchange Settings Properties dialog box. In Windows 95 and NT 4.0, right-click on the Inbox icon on your desktop and select Properties. Double-click on Microsoft Exchange Server on the dialog box. Type in the name of your Exchange server as registered in the DNS or named in your HOSTS file. Then type in your mailbox's display name or alias and click on Check Name. You'll know that all is well if the display name for your mailbox shows up underlined. OK your way out of the various dialog boxes and open your mailbox. It takes a while the first time, but once your client is able to talk to the server directly over the Internet you will be able to do virtually anything you can do locally or with a RAS connection.

Supporting Roving Users

Some users sit at the same desk all day, every day. Others are moving around all of the time, often not even having a computer of their own. These users are often referred to as *roving users*. Basically, you want each roving user to have a directory on a server where they can pick up their Exchange and other settings every time they log in to the network, whatever workstation they use to log in.

The Exchange settings you're interested in are those for home server and mailbox name. You want a roving user to get the same server and mailbox name no matter what workstation they choose to log in on.

Supporting a roving Exchange user is no different from supporting a roving user who is working with any other software—Microsoft Word, for example. With Exchange you want to present the same server and mailbox name. With Word, your goal is for the user to get the same default template, window-size settings, etc. The specific procedures you must follow to support roving users depends on the workstation (and sometimes network) operating system you're using.

Fortunately, Microsoft has a tool for simplifying the job of setting up correct profiles for roving Exchange users. This tool (PROFGEN.EXE) can be found in the update to the Exchange Resource Kit. The update can be downloaded free from Microsoft's Exchange web site.

A Quick Look at Schedule+

Users of Microsoft's Schedule+ have available (free) and unavailable (busy) times in their schedules. This *free/busy* information, which is used by Schedule+ to automatically set up meetings and appointments, is stored in special hidden public folders. When they need to access recipient schedules to set up meetings, Schedule+ clients go to these hidden folders. To support cross-site Schedule+ activity, the Schedule+ free/busy hidden public folder for each site is represented in the Exchange hierarchy (see Figure 17.46). At a minimum, these free/busy folders include information for connecting to the site they represent. If one site's free/busy folder is replicated to other sites, then the replicas include free/busy information for the site they represent.

When a user tries to include a recipient located in another site in a scheduling effort and the site's free/busy folder hasn't been replicated, the Schedule+ client uses the contact information to connect to the other site. It then gets the schedule information it needs directly from the hidden public folder in the other site.

If public folder replication delays between sites can be tolerated when scheduling meetings and appointments, you can replicate free/busy folders among the sites in your Exchange organization. (See Chapter 14 for more information on public folder replication.) With replication, Schedule+ clients can access free/busy information for other sites by looking in the free/busy replicas at their own sites. There's no need for these clients to contact the other sites directly.

NOTE   To connect to free/busy folders in other sites, the Schedule+ client must be able to establish an RPC-based session with the Exchange server in the other site. This requires a hard-wired or dial-up RAS link. If such a link isn't possible, then cross-site folder replication is your only alternative, since it can be implemented on indirect links.

If you need to exchange free/busy information with older Schedule+ versions that are compatible with Microsoft Mail for PC Networks, you'll need to run the Schedule+ Free/Busy Connector, which is an extension of the Microsoft Mail Connector. See the Exchange docs for further information.

FIGURE 17.46

The Exchange hierarchy includes a Schedule+ free/busy public folder for each site.

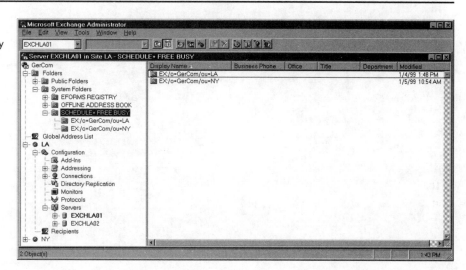

Conclusion

Wow! What a trip. You've learned a lot in this chapter, including how to create new information stores, move mailboxes, track messages, set up advanced security, import information into the Exchange directory, extract information for the Exchange directory from other sources, and export directory information from Exchange Server.

By now you should also have a basic grounding in migrating users from other e-messaging systems, using Exchange add-ins and e-mail address generators, editing Exchange's details templates and one-off address templates, moving mailboxes between sites, using address book views, remotely administering your Exchange and NT servers, supporting remote and roving Exchange users, and working with Schedule+.

I'd say that you're now almost an Exchange Server expert. All we have left are a set of exciting Internet protocols new to Exchange 5.0 and a tutorial on the use of electronic forms in the Exchange environment. Turn the page and we're off.

CHAPTER
EIGHTEEN

18

Advanced Exchange Server Internet Protocols

- Setting up and using Exchange Server support for Post Office Protocol client-server messaging

- Setting up and using Web browser (Hypertext Markup Language) access to Exchange Server

- Setting up and using Exchange Server support for the Lightweight Directory Access Protocol

- Setting up and using Exchange Server support for the Network News Transfer Protocol

- Setting general parameters for more than one protocol

This is one of the most exciting chapters in this book. Exchange Server 5 and higher come with a set of Internet-based client-server protocols that, taken together, raise it from a fairly tightly controlled, proprietary client-server product to a very open and flexible E-messaging system. Let's not waste any time. Onward into that rabbit hole again.

NOTE We're going to be looking at a ton of objects (tools) for managing and administering the Exchange advanced Internet protocols. As in earlier chapters, I'll skip over property pages on objects that have already been covered.

The Post Office Protocol

Exchange Server includes full support for Post Office Protocol version 3 (POP3). POP3 is a simple, but effective way for a client to pull mail from an e-mail server. There's no fancy support for folders or all of the fine bells and whistles you'll find in the Exchange and Outlook clients. For example, you can't access your Exchange server–based folders with a POP3 client. But, if you're looking for a lightweight client that can function readily over the Internet, POP3 isn't a bad choice.

IMAP4 Is Coming

The Internet Message Access Protocol version 4 (IMAP4) improves on POP3 in a number of ways. Unlike POP3 clients, IMAP4 clients *can* access folders on an e-mail server. IMAP4 also supports saving some settings, such as the appearance of client windows on the server. This lets you run IMAP4 clients on different computers and still see a similarly configured user interface when you log into your IMAP4 server account. Microsoft promised support for IMAP4 some time in 1997. Watch the web site www.microsoft.com/exchange for more information.

POP3 Set Up: The Exchange Server Side

The server side of POP3 protocol support is installed when you install Exchange Server. Once POP3 is installed on the server, your job is to set a few key parameters to customize your POP3 environment to the needs of your organization and users.

You can customize all POP3 parameters at both the Exchange site and server levels. This lets you set site-specific parameters and still have the flexibility to deal with special needs on one or more servers in the site. If that's not enough customization for you, you can even set some POP3 parameters at the individual mailbox level.

Let's get right to site level POP3 parameters.

Setting Up POP3 at the Site Level

The first step is to find the Protocols container for your site. See Figure 18.1 if you're having trouble finding the container.

The Protocols container holds configuration objects for all four of the advanced Internet services supported by Exchange Server. Double-click on the POP3 site defaults object to bring up the POP3 (Mail) Site Defaults Properties dialog box shown in Figure 18.2.

FIGURE 18.1

The site Protocols container and its four advanced Internet configuration objects

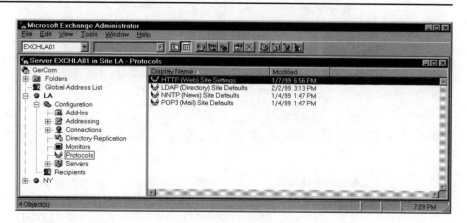

General Properties   You can enable or disable the POP3 protocol for the entire site on the General property page. The protocol is enabled by default. Deselect Enable protocol to turn off POP3 services for the site.

FIGURE 18.2

The General property page of the POP3 site configuration dialog box

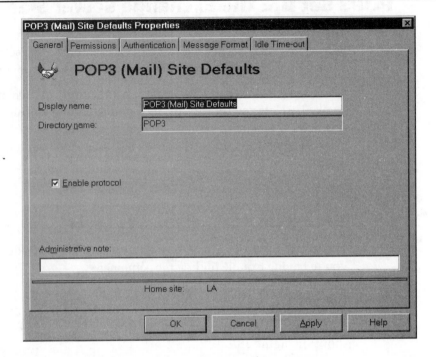

Throughout our discussions of the POP3 protocol, I'll be talking about what might be called "the big three POP3 clients:" Eudora Pro, Microsoft's Internet mail client, and Netscape's mail client. Coincidentally, all three of these products began to deliver a rich set of features when they reached the 3.0 version level. To save time and space, I'll use the "brilliant" term I coined just above when referring to these POP3 clients.

Authentication   Use the Authentication property page (Figure 18.3) to select the security levels that your Exchange Server POP3 service will support. All three of the authentication methods listed below are used to verify a POP3 user's NT account name and password. They are listed in order of increasing security.

- Basic (Clear Text) authentication is the least secure, but also the most ubiquitous security method used. All authentication is done in unencrypted text.

- Windows NT Challenge/Response uses standard NT account–based security and an encrypted password to authenticate users.

- Secure Sockets Layer (SSL) allows for encryption of the authentication process and all other communications between client and server. If you decide to use SSL authentication, be sure to read the Exchange Server documentation regarding setting up your Microsoft Internet Information and Exchange servers to support it.

All POP3 clients support clear text authentication. Windows NT Challenge/Response authentication is included in Microsoft Internet Mail and News versions 3.0 and greater. Microsoft, Netscape, and other vendors have promised Secure Sockets Layer support in future versions of their POP3 clients. Check with the vendor of your favorite POP3 client for the latest news on SSL support.

FIGURE 18.3

Setting the levels of authentication to be used by Exchange Server's POP3 service

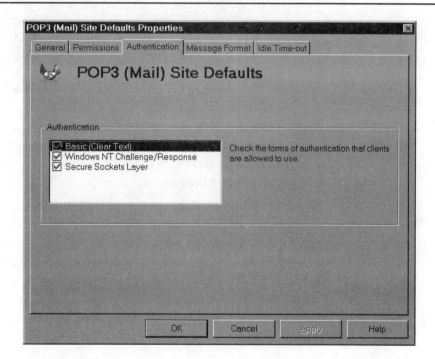

Message Format   You use the Message Format property page to set message-encoding parameters, the type of character set to be used in messages, and to tell Exchange Server whether to send documents in Exchange's rich-text format. See Figure 18.4.

FIGURE 18.4

Setting parameters for
message formatting

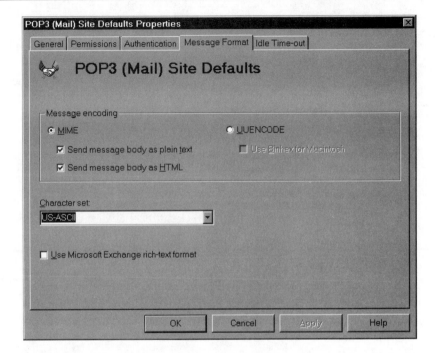

Message Encoding   The Internet supports the transmission of messages and attachments in 7-bit characters. Formatted text (fonts, bold, italic, underlined, etc.) or binary attachments, both of which require 8 bits, must be coded into a 7-bit format to traverse the Internet.

Like any single instance of the Internet Mail Service, an Exchange POP3 server can support either, but not both, of the two major encoding standards: MIME and UUENCODE. MIME is the newer and more popular encoding option. MIME can handle both formatted text and binary attachments. The big three POP3 clients all support MIME encoding.

If your POP3 client doesn't support MIME, you'll have to use UUENCODE. UUENCODE does not support formatted text. It just handles binary message attachments.

The Message Body   MIME-encoded messages can support plain text and/or HTML message bodies. Plain text is just what you'd expect: simple 7-bit characters, nothing more. It will work with any MIME-compatible POP3 client. HTML

(Hypertext Markup Language) is an Internet standard used in World Wide Web client-server systems. HTML supports fancy text formatting like different fonts, bold, italic, and color. The big three POP3 clients support HTML formatting.

If you choose both the plain text and HTML message body options, as I have in Figure 18.4, the MIME message will include versions of the message body in each format. The MIME-aware client will use the highest level format it can support.

If you pick the UUENCODE option, you can tell the POP3 server to use the Binhex encoding scheme for Macintosh POP3 clients. If you select Binhex, all messages will be sent in Binhex format. So you'd only want to use this option for an Exchange site dedicated to Macintosh POP3 clients.

The Character Set   Use the Character set drop-down list to select the character set to be used in outgoing POP3 messages. The list includes the basic ASCII option as well as a wide range of character sets for other languages. The options available on your Exchange server will vary with the language or languages supported on the server.

Microsoft Exchange Rich Text Format   Microsoft rich text format is another way to get fancy text formatting to a POP3 client. Microsoft's Internet Explorer 3.0 and greater can display rich text right in a message. Other POP3 clients will include rich text messages as attachments.

Idle Time-out   Folks like to stay connected to their mail and web servers. Each POP3 connection requires a little server overhead, especially if POP3 clients are periodically checking the server for new messages. Using the Idle Time-out property page, you can set a time after which a POP3 connection will closed. See Figure 18.5, which is all you'll need to figure out how to do this less-than-monumental task.

Setting Up POP3 at the Server Level

POP3 is very server-centric. Users must specifically log into the server where their Exchange mailbox resides. You can modify the POP3 parameters you set for your Exchange site on a server-by-server basis. In this way, for example, you could set up an Exchange POP3 server to support users of Macintosh POP3 clients and Binhex encoding or users whose clients require binary attachments encoded in UUENCODE as opposed to MIME format.

FIGURE 18.5

Selecting a time-out
period for POP3
connections

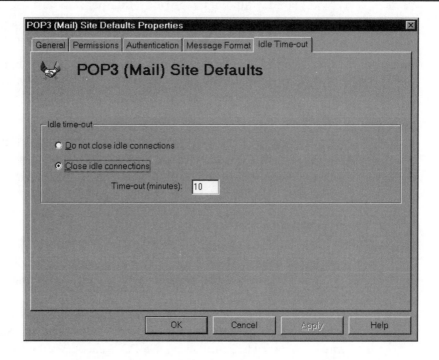

FIGURE 18.5

Selecting a time-out
period for POP3
connections

To modify POP3 parameters on a specific server, use the server-specific POP3 setup object, which is located in the Protocols container for each server. As you can see in Figure 18.6, the server-based POP3 configuration object lets you set all of the parameters you can set at the site level, as well as the logging levels to be used for server-based diagnostics.

Since we've already talked about all of the configuration options here, I'll leave it to you to make any server-based modification you need. Have fun.

WARNING   If POP3 services are turned off for a Site, you can't turn them on for a server. You can, however, turn POP3 services off for a server, if they are enabled at the site level.

FIGURE 18.6

The server-level POP3 settings dialog box

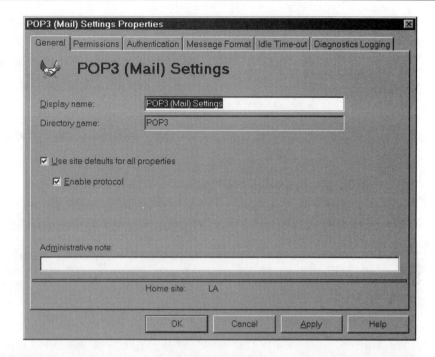

Sending Messages for POP3 Clients

POP3 clients pull their messages from POP3 servers. Simply put, POP3 servers are the source of incoming mail for POP3 clients. POP3 servers do not provide outgoing messaging services for POP3 clients. This service is provided by an Internet sendmail host.

Back in Chapter 15, I showed you how to use the rerouting capabilities of the Internet Mail Service to provide outgoing sendmail host services to POP3 clients as well as other servers. Check Chapter 15 for details on IMS routing.

Customizing POP3 Support for a Mailbox

To customize POP3 support for a specific mailbox, find the mailbox in the appropriate recipients container in Exchange Administrator and double-click on it. Tab over to the Protocols property page on the mailbox's properties dialog box (see Figure 18.7). Then double-click on the POP3 (Mail) object.

FIGURE 18.7

The Protocols property page of a mailbox Properties dialog box

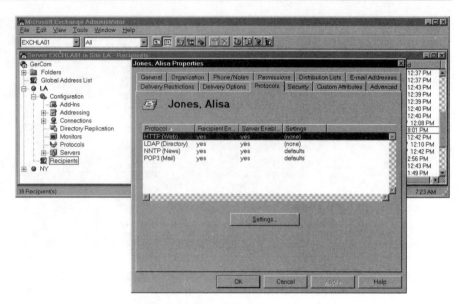

This brings up the Protocol Details properties dialog box shown in Figure 18.8. For a variety of reasons, security being a big one, you may not want all your Exchange mailbox users to access their mail using a POP3 client. To disable POP3 services for a mailbox, deselect Enable POP3 for this recipient.

FIGURE 18.8

Customizing POP3 support for a mailbox

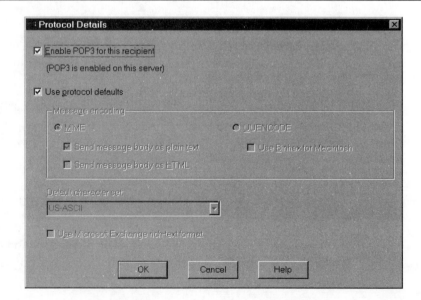

> **WARNING** If POP3 services are turned off for a server (or its site), you can't turn them on for a mailbox on that server.

Finally, as you can see in Figure 18.8, you can set message formatting options on a mail-by-mailbox basis. You can use these options to support clients that aren't standard for your site or server. For example, say you've set up a server that supports Macintosh users who require Binhex encoding. You also can support users of the Eudora client version 3 or greater on that server by enabling MIME message encoding and body text options for the mailboxes of Eudora users.

POP3 Set Up: The Client Side

I've always thought of POP3 clients as one of life's little miracles. You set some basic parameters, tell the client to check for mail on your POP3 server and your mail shows up. I'm sure that building sophisticated POP3 servers and clients is quite a task, but using them is really a snap. Let's get some clients configured so you can experience the miracle.

Start with Microsoft's POP3 Client

Though you can use any POP3-compliant Internet mail client to access your Exchange Server's POP3 server, you'll find that Microsoft's client is not only one of the best, but it's also enabled to support all four of the advanced Internet protocols I cover in this chapter. So I strongly suggest that you use the Microsoft client for the exercises in this book, even if you plan to use another one later on.

The Internet mail client and an Internet news browser client are packaged together in a single self-executing installation file. You can download the file from Microsoft's web site, www.microsoft.com.

Once they're installed, there are two ways to run the Internet mail and news clients. You can run them from the Windows 95 or NT 4 Programs menu, which you access through the Start button on the taskbar. You can also run either of the two programs from Microsoft's Internet Explorer. Click Explorer's Mail button and select Read Mail or Read News or select the program you want from Explorer's Go menu.

Getting Connected to an Exchange Server–based POP3 Server

First you need to set up your POP3 client to connect to an Exchange Server–based POP3 server. Before you start, you'll need to gather the following information:

- your Exchange mailbox alias name
- your NT account name, if it's different from your Exchange mailbox alias name
- the password for your Windows NT account
- your Windows NT domain name (optional)
- your POP3 e-mail address
- the name of your POP3 server (for incoming messages)
- the name of your SMTP server (for outgoing messages)

Let's take a look at how each of these is used to set up a POP3 client.

The POP3 Account Name   You'll use one or more of the first four items in the list above to set up your POP3 account name. When you're using Exchange Server's POP3 server, at the most basic level, the POP3 account name is the alias name of the Exchange mailbox you want to access with your POP3 client. My Exchange mailbox alias is bgerber, so, my POP3 account name is bgerber.

In Figure 18.9 I'm setting up the Microsoft POP3 client version 3 using the Options dialog box, which you'll find on the client's Mail menu. I've entered my account name in the Account Name field. Why, you may be asking, is "la\" included in that account name and what's my Password? As it turns out, a lot happens on your Exchange and NT servers when you're authenticated to access your Exchange mailbox through a POP3 client. Let's take a look at the authentication process.

You're authenticated to access your Exchange mailbox with a POP3 client in a number of ways. First, Exchange Server attempts to authenticate your use of your mailbox just as it would if you were using the Exchange client. That is, it attempts to authenticate you through the Windows NT security system. It needs to find your NT domain and account name and finally to validate that you've entered the correct password for that account. Then Exchange Server needs to check to be sure that your NT account is authorized to access the mailbox. Finally, it has to verify that your mailbox is enabled for POP3 services.

FIGURE 18.9

Setting client-side parameters required for connection to an Exchange Server's POP3 server (using version 3.0 of Microsoft's Internet mail client)

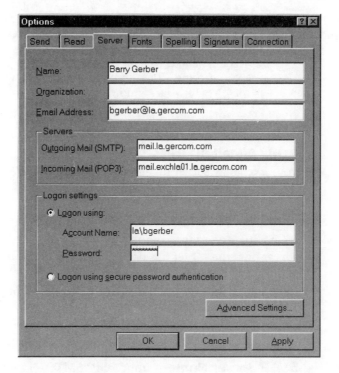

Because my Exchange mailbox alias and my NT account name are the same, I only need to enter my mailbox alias in the Account Name field and my NT account password in the Password field. Exchange Server then uses the mailbox alias and password both to authenticate me in the NT security system and to locate my Exchange mailbox. If my mailbox alias were different from my NT account name, I'd have to enter both of these in the following format: NT_user_account_name\mailbox_alias_name.

Now back to why "la\." "la" is the name of the NT domain where my Exchange Server LA site is located. As I mentioned earlier, NT security authentication starts at the domain level. Until your NT domain is known, it's not possible to begin authenticating your NT account name or password.

If I don't enter the name of my LA domain, Exchange Server will search through all known NT domains attempting to find the one I'm in. If my NT environment includes lots of domains, that could take a long time. By entering the name of my domain, I shorten the time it takes to gain POP3 access to my Exchange mailbox.

NOTE

If you're a non-Exchange Server–based POP3 client user, all of this may seem pretty complicated. After all, other POP3 servers don't require all this stuff. All you need enter in the POP3 Account field is your UNIX account name. If your Exchange mailbox alias and your NT account name are the same and you're willing to wait while Exchange Server searches for your NT domain, you can do exactly the same thing.

POP3 E-Mail Address   Your POP3 e-mail address is the Internet address for your Exchange server mailbox. In Figure 18.9, I've entered bgerber@la.gercom .com in the E-mail Address field.

POP3 Server Name   Your POP3 server name is the Internet address of the Exchange server where your mailbox resides. You can use the IP address of the server or, if the server has been entered into a Domain Name Server (DNS), you can use its Internet domain name. In Figure 18.9, I've entered the domain name for my Exchange server EXCHLA01 into the Incoming Mail (POP3) field.

The general convention with POP3 mail servers is to prefix the server's standard Internet name with the word "mail." Hence, mail.exchla01.la.gercom.com.

SMTP Server Name   Your POP3 SMTP server sends mail from your POP3 client out to the Internet. If you've chosen to use the Exchange Server Internet Mail Service to do this task, put in an Internet name or IP address that the POP3 client can use to contact the IMS server. If you're using another SMTP host for this purpose, enter the Internet name or IP address of that host. In Figure 18.9, I've entered mail.la.gercom.com in the Outgoing Mail (SMTP) field.

Other POP3 Client Settings

Various POP3 clients allow you to set a range of other parameters. One of the most important involves whether you leave copies of your messages on the POP3 server. To better understand this option, you need to understand that POP3 clients download each message that is on the server. If you don't leave copies of messages on the POP3 server, they aren't available when you access them with a different client on the same or a different computer.

Your POP3 server is also your Exchange server. If you don't choose to leave a copy of all messages downloaded by your POP3 client on the server, you won't be able to access them with another POP3 client or with the Exchange or Outlook client. Whether you leave copies or not depends on how you work. If you're going to work from one place with the POP3 client, you can suck all your messages down into that client and deal with them there. If you're going to use a POP3 client when you're away from the office and an Exchange or Outlook client when in the office, you'll want to be sure to leave a copy on the server.

In Figure 18.10, I'm using the Microsoft Internet mail client's Advanced Settings dialog box to make sure that a copy of all my messages will be left in my Exchange server mailbox. You get to this dialog box by clicking on the Advanced Settings button on the Options dialog box (see Figure 18.9).

FIGURE 18.10

Making sure that a copy of each message downloaded by the POP3 client remains on the Exchange server

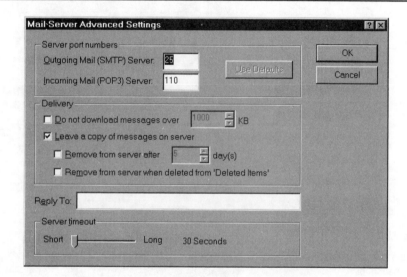

All POP3 clients offer a range of options for connecting to your POP3 server. In Figure 18.11, I've chosen a LAN-based connection using the Microsoft Internet mail client's Connection property page.

I'll leave it to you to explore the above and other client settings offered by your favorite POP3 client.

Eudora Pro 3.0 and Greater: Basic Configuration

Here's a quick basic configuration lesson for another POP3 client, Eudora 3. As you can see in Figure 18.12, a Eudora POP3 account includes both the POP3 account name and the POP3 server name. In Figure 18.13, I've set the name of my SMTP server, *mail.la.gercom.com*.

FIGURE 18.11

Selecting POP3 client-
server connectivity
options

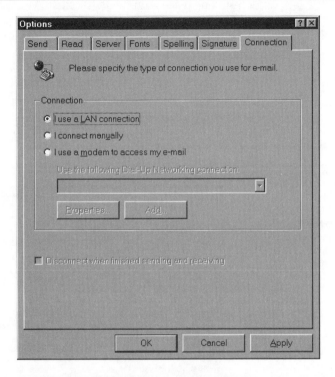

FIGURE 18.12

Setting POP3 account
information for
Qualcomm's Eudora
Pro 3.0 POP3 client

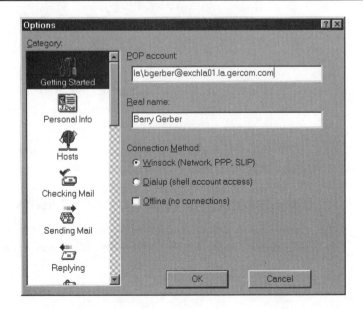

FIGURE 18.13

Setting POP3 server information for the Eudora Pro 3.0 POP3 client

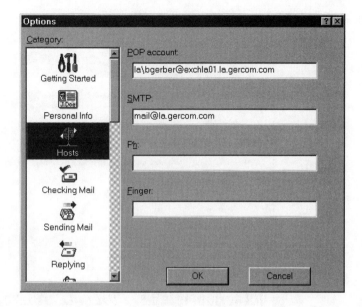

Did It Work?

Figure 18.14 shows the rewards of all the server- and client-side configuring we've been through. As you can see, we're looking at a message sent to me by GerCom's class clown, Rubin Alvarez. It was sent from his Exchange client and includes a couple of fonts that I can see in my Microsoft Internet mail client, because, in this case, my Exchange server's POP3 server is configured to send me messages in HTML format. In Figure 18.15, I'm enjoying the fruits of my labor with Eudora Pro 3. Very nice.

I'm going to leave it to you to figure out how to send and retrieve messages with your POP3 client. It's easy and, hey, what's life without new things to learn?

Troubleshooting POP3 Problems

Generally, I've found POP3 to be one of the easiest and least vexing protocols of all to use. If you do have trouble, there are three major troubleshooting tools for POP3 connects: protocol logging, POP3 event logging, and POP3 counters for NT's Performance Monitor. See the Exchange Server documentation for help using these.

FIGURE 18.14

Viewing an HTML formatted message with Microsoft's Internet mail client 3.0

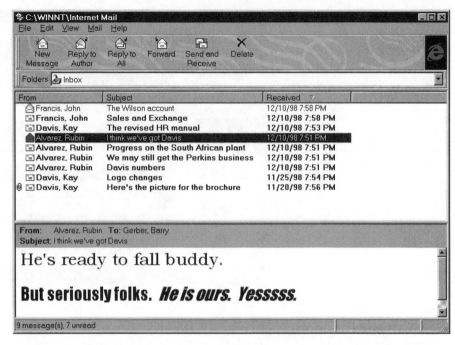

FIGURE 18.15

Viewing an HTML formatted message with Qualcomm's Eudora Pro 3.0

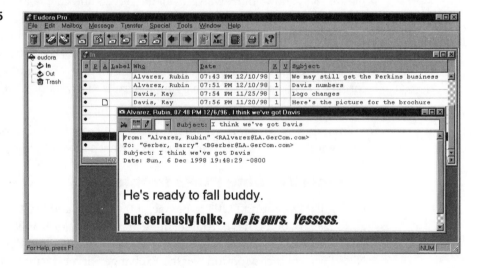

Web Browser Access to Exchange Server

Microsoft has put together several components that let you access mailboxes and public folders on Exchange servers. The whole thing works pretty simply, although, as with POP3, there's a lot of complexity behind the scenes.

Microsoft has created a new NT service called "ActiveX Server" or just "Active Server" (AS). AS is the link between NT applications and Internet-based users of those applications. AS interacts on one side with special programs (called "Active Server Components" or ASCs) that talk directly to an application like Exchange Server. On the other side, AS communicates with Microsoft Internet Information Server.

Users access ASCs through Internet Information Server using an Internet browser that is Java and frames capable. Both Microsoft Internet Explorer 3.0 and greater and Netscape 3.0 and greater meet this specification. The ASCs take data from applications, wrap it up in a nice user interface and translate the whole thing into Hypertext Markup Language (HTML), which is then sent to the browser through Internet Information Server.

In the case of Exchange Server, Exchange-specific ASCs take Exchange Server MAPI and Remote Procedure Call data and put it into an Exchange client–like user interface. The ASCs then translate all of this into HTML and ship the HTML code off to the browser through Internet Information Server.

WARNING Microsoft has issued warnings that the ASCs that come with Exchange Server 5 are just samples and not full-blown applications that you should expect to use with a massive number of users. The company has promised to release more sophisticated and robust Exchange ASCs. So, depending on when you read this book, some of the Exchange ASCs might be quite different from what I'll show you here. Keep an eye on www.microsoft.com/exchange for Exchange ASCs progress reports.

You can install support for AS either when you install Exchange Server itself or after that by running the Exchange Server setup program. If you need more information on AS installation, check out Chapter 7. For more on Internet Information Server, see Chapter 6 of this book and Microsoft's docs for IIS.

Active Server Component (HTTP) Set Up: The Server Side

Active Server or HTTP (Hypertext Transport Protocol) set up is pretty simple. You can configure HTTP at the site and mailbox levels. Unlike POP3, no server-level configuration is available.

Setting Up HTTP at the Site Level

Go to the site Protocols container and double-click on HTTP to open the HTTP Site Settings dialog box (see Figure 18.16). If you need a reorientation to the site Protocols container, take a look at Figure 18.1.

FIGURE 18.16

The HTTP Site Settings dialog box

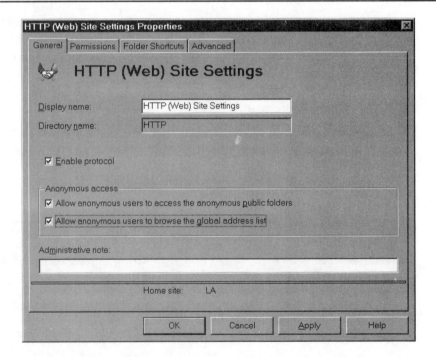

General Properties   As you can see in Figure 18.16, there's very little you need to do on the General property page. You can disable and enable the HTTP protocol and control anonymous user access to specific public folders and the global address list.

When you access your Exchange mailbox using the Exchange Server ASCs, Secure Sockets Layer (SSL) authentication is used. I discussed SSL in the section above on POP3. SSL authentication support for AS applications is provided by the Internet Information Server.

WARNING To access your Exchange mailbox with a web browser, your browser must support SSL as do the Microsoft and Netscape version 3.0 and greater browsers. If you have trouble getting to your Exchange mailbox with your browser, be sure it provides this level of support.

Anonymous or unauthenticated users cannot access Exchange mailboxes. They can, however, access specific public folders and the global address list. As you can see in Figure 18.16, you can enable or disable public folder and global address list access separately. This makes good sense, since you might be more than willing to have others accessing marketing or other information you might want to publish through public folders, but not getting into personnel information stored in your Exchange organization's global address list.

Folder Shortcuts You use the Folder Shortcuts property page to specify which public folders are displayed to anonymous users. See Figure 18.17. Click on the New button to bring up a dialog box to browse through your public folders and select the ones you want. See Figure 18.18. Select a folder and click on OK on the dialog box. The folder now shows up in the folder shortcuts list. See Figure 18.19.

Click on the Remove button on the Folder Shortcuts property page to delete public folders from the list.

WARNING The Folder Shortcuts page only specifies which public folders will be visible to anonymous users. By default, anonymous users have no rights to a public folder on the Folder Shortcuts list. To give them a level of access to a specific public folder, the folder's owner needs to open the Properties dialog box for the folder using an Exchange or Outlook client. Specific rights are granted on the Permissions property page of the dialog box. See Figure 18.20.

FIGURE 18.17

The Folder Shortcuts property page

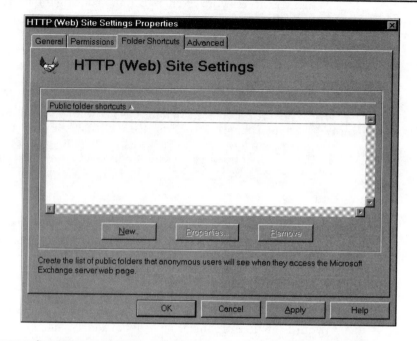

FIGURE 18.18

Selecting public folders to be displayed to anonymous Exchange Server users

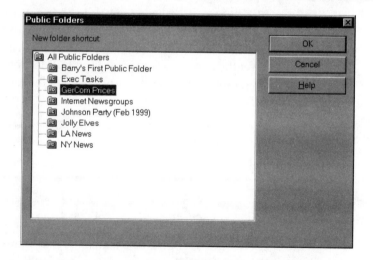

FIGURE 18.19

A public folder has been selected for display to anonymous Exchange Server users

FIGURE 18.20

Setting anonymous user access rights for a specific Exchange public folder

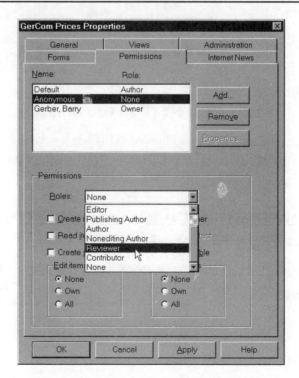

Advanced Properties   You can set a limit on the number of address book entries returned to an authorized user. See Figure 18.21. This helps limit server and network traffic.

FIGURE 18.21

Setting limits on the number of address book entries returned to an authorized user

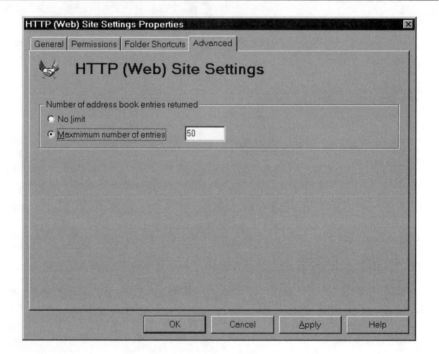

Setting Up HTTP at the Mailbox Level

If HTTP access is enabled at the site level, you can disable it for an individual mailbox. That's it. For specifics on finding the mailbox level Protocols container, check out the section of this chapter on customizing POP3 support for a mailbox.

Active Server Component (HTTP) Set Up: The Client Side

Client side setup is a breeze. Just specify that you want to connect to the Internet Information Server that supports your Exchange client plus "/exchange." In my case I connect using the URL http://la.gercom.com/exchange.

In Figure 18.22, I've entered my NT domain name and account name and password. The rules for logging into your Exchange mailbox through the Exchange ASCs are pretty much the same as the rules for logging in using a POP3 client. The one very nice exception is that you don't have to specify the server where your mailbox is stored. Since Microsoft controls this application, they've set it up so that the app finds your mailbox wherever it is in your site. That's why there's no server name in the URL I use to access the Exchange ASCs.

FIGURE 18.22

Entering authentication information for HTTP access to an Exchange Server mailbox

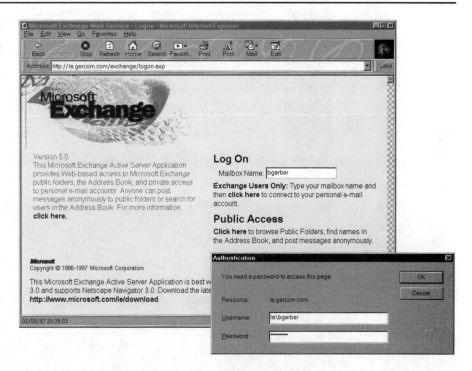

In Figure 18.23 I'm using Microsoft Internet Explorer web browser to review the list of messages in my Exchange mailbox. In Figure 18.24 I'm looking at my favorite message from Rubin Alvarez complete with HTML text formatting. Figure 18.25 shows an anonymous view of a GerCom public folder showing various Enter key options. It is internet publishing without our having written a bit of HTML code. Finally, Figure 18.26 shows an anonymous access to GerCom's global address list. Extremely nice.

FIGURE 18.23

Viewing a list of messages in an Exchange mailbox with Microsoft's Internet Explorer web browser

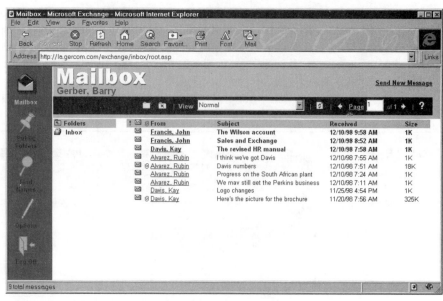

FIGURE 18.24

Viewing an Exchange message with a web browser

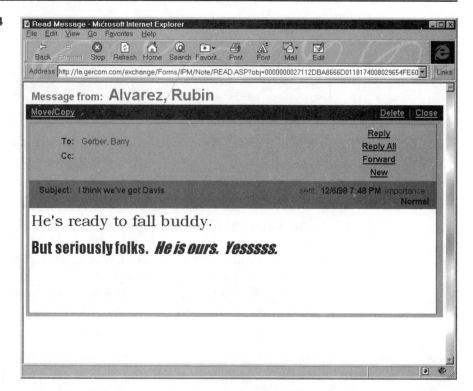

FIGURE 18.25

An anonymous user
views the contents of an
Exchange Server public
folder with a web
browser

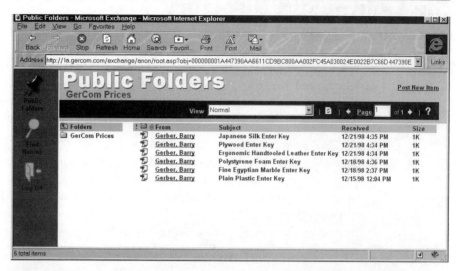

FIGURE 18.26

An anonymous user
views an entry in the
Exchange Server global
address list with a web
browser

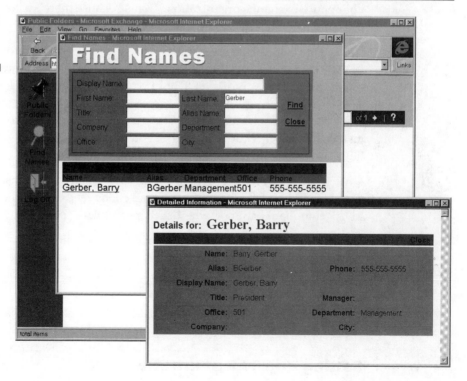

The Lightweight Directory Access Protocol

The Lightweight Directory Access Protocol (LDAP) is a client-server application that lets you browse, read, and search for information stored in an electronic directory. It was developed at the University of Michigan to allow access to an X.500 directory without all of the overhead required by the original X.500 Directory Access Protocol.

LDAP server support is installed when you install Exchange Server. Exchange Server's LDAP server accesses the Exchange directory database which, as I'm sure you're aware by now, contains data attributes such as recipient display names, phone numbers, and e-mail addresses. Upon request, the LDAP server returns directory data to LDAP-compatible clients. Server-to-client data transmissions are limited by the user authentication rules and directory attribute permissions that are in place on Exchange Server for the LDAP server.

What I'm about to say is really neat, so listen up! One LDAP server can serve your entire Exchange organization. That's because there's a copy of the Exchange directory for your entire organization on each server in the organization.

There are basic LDAP clients that you can use to directly browse through an LDAP-compatible directory. But the real power of LDAP comes with its integration into e-mail clients, like POP3 or IMAP4 clients. A POP3 client with integrated LDAP support provides not only access to a user's Exchange mailbox, it also provides access to Exchange Server–based address books. And you're not limited to just Exchange Server address books. You can also search any LDAP server you have access to.

Microsoft's POP3 Internet mail client version 3.01 and later supports LDAP. Check with your favorite Internet e-mail client vendor to find out if its product is LDAP compliant or, if not, whether there are plans to make it compliant.

Let's get our LDAP service up and running right now.

LDAP Set Up: The Server Side

You can configure LDAP parameters at the site, server, and mailbox level. We'll start with site-level configuration.

Setting Up LDAP at the Site Level

Find the LDAP configuration object in the Protocols container. Then double-click on it to open the LDAP (Directory) Site Defaults dialog box shown in Figure 18.27.

FIGURE 18.27

The LDAP Site Defaults
dialog box

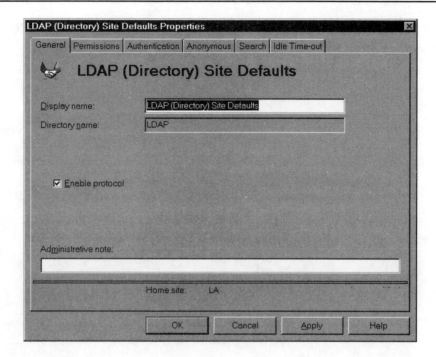

General Properties   As you can see in Figure 18.27, you know this page pretty well. Aside from the standard naming and note functions, you use the General property page to enable or disable LDAP for the site.

Authentication   Use the Authentication property page shown in Figure 18.28 to select the methods to be used for NT account name and password authentication. You have two options: Basic (Clear Text) or Secure Sockets Layer. I discussed these authentication methods in the POP3 section of this chapter.

You can choose either, both, or neither of these authentication methods. If you choose neither method, then only anonymous users will be able to access your Exchange Server directory with an LDAP client. Let's move on to anonymous access right now.

Anonymous   The Anonymous property page is used to enable or disable anonymous LDAP client access. See Figure 18.29.

FIGURE 18.28

Setting authentication
methods for LDAP con-
nections to Exchange
Server

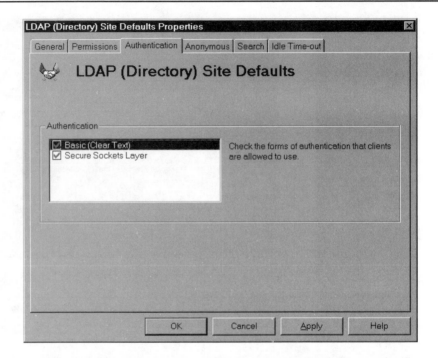

FIGURE 18.29

Enabling anonymous
access to an LDAP
server

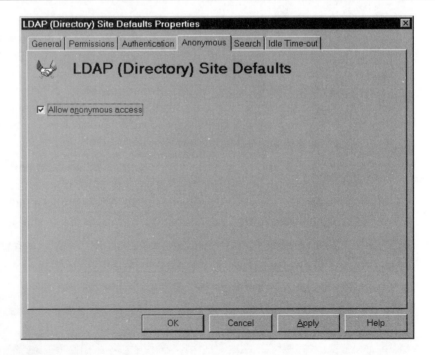

> **NOTE**
> You can limit what Exchange directory attributes are available to an anonymous or even authenticated LDAP user. To do this, use the Exchange Administrator's Directory Service Site configuration dialog box (Attributes property page). See the last chapter for more information.

Search   You use your LDAP client to ask an LDAP server to search for a string of characters in each entry in a specific directory field. For example, you might request a search for all instances of "Smith" in the Exchange last name field. The LDAP protocol allows a client to request that each search start at the beginning or end of an entry or anywhere within an entry. For example, a search for the string "jo" starting at the beginning of each last name entry in the directory will return all of the *Jo*neses, *Jo*hnsons and any other last name beginning with "Jo." A last name search for "sky" starting at the end of each entry will return names such as "Per*sky*," "Olin*sky*" and "*Sky*" itself. A search for "ro", starting anywhere within each last name entry, will return names such as "*Ro*wan," "C*ro*w," and "Domb*ro*."

When a search starts at the beginning of a directory entry, its called an "initial substring search" in LDAP parlance. A search that starts at the end of an entry is called a "final substring search" and a search that starts anywhere within an entry is called an "any substring search." Throughout the rest of this section, these terms will be italicized to avoid confusion.

Initial substring searches are fast. *Final substring searches* are slower than initial substring searches and *any substring searches* are the slowest of all. Slower searches can eat up resources on an Exchange server, so don't think of them only as inconveniences for LDAP client users. Any user of an Exchange server that is also an LDAP server could feel the impact of slower LDAP searches.

You use the Search property page shown in Figure 18.30 to tell your LDAP server how to deal with string searches. If you choose the first option, 'Treat "any" substring searches as "initial" substring searches', *final substring searches* aren't done at all and *any substring searches* are converted to *initial substring searches*. This assures fast searches, but may result in incomplete information, if the user submitted a final or any substring search.

With the second option, 'Allow only "initial" substring searches', *any substring searches* aren't even converted into *initial substring searches*. Only *initial substring searches* are honored. Running under this option, an LDAP server can easily match or exceed the search speed of the first option. If the final option, 'Allow all substring searches,' is selected, the LDAP server is allowed to perform any of the three types of searches. This option will almost always result in slower searches.

Before we leave searches, note in Figure 18.30 that you can also specify how many search results your LDAP server returns to an LDAP client. The higher this number, the lower your LDAP server's performance is likely to be. A setting of around one hundred should be about right for light LDAP client access. Twenty-five to fifty is best if you expect your LDAP server to get heavy duty use.

FIGURE 18.30

Selecting the method to be used for LDAP searches and the maximum number of search results to be returned

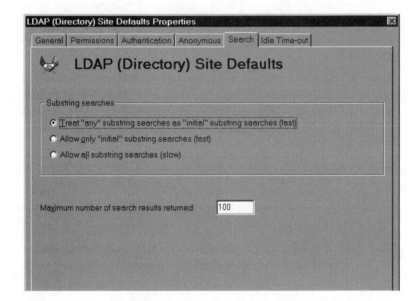

Setting Up LDAP at the Server Level

Server-level LDAP configuration options are the same as for the site. I'll leave it to you to go ahead and make any custom server settings that you need.

LDAP Set Up: The Client Side

In this section, I'll show you how to set up and test LDAP functionality in Microsoft's POP3-based Internet mail client. Be sure that you've installed version 3.01 or later of the client.

Setting Up the Windows Address Book

Before we jump into the client itself, we have to do a bit of LDAP configuration. This isn't done in the client itself, but in an application called Windows Address

Book. When you install the Microsoft Internet mail and news clients, Windows Address Book is also installed. Find it on the Windows 95 or NT 4 Programs menu and click on it to open it up.

Figure 18.31 shows the Windows Address Book window. To set up access to your LDAP server, select Directory Services from Windows Address Book's File menu. This brings up the Directory Services dialog box shown in Figure 18.32.

FIGURE 18.31

The Windows Address Book application

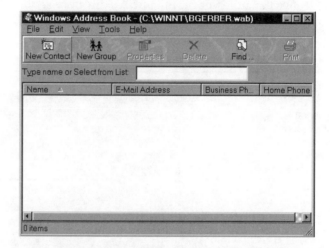

FIGURE 18.32

The Directory Services dialog box

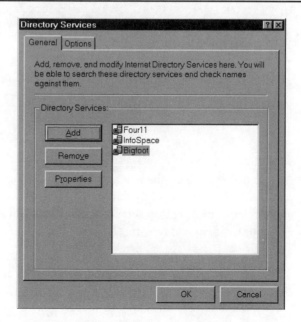

General Properties   Microsoft includes setups for some public directory services. The public services that are already set up for my LDAP client are Four11, InfoSpace, and Bigfoot. You need to add your Exchange organization's LDAP server or servers to this list of directory services. Click on the Add button to open a dialog box for adding a new LDAP directory service.

General Properties for a New Directory Service   In Figure 18.33, I've already filled in the friendly name for this service and the Internet domain name of the Exchange server running LDAP directory services for my Exchange organization. The Windows address book displays the friendly name whenever it refers to this particular directory service.

FIGURE 18.33

Configuring general properties for a new directory service

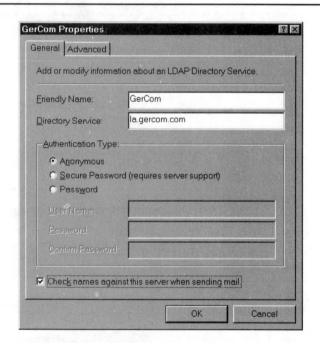

I've also checked the box at the bottom of the dialog box for my new directory service. The Microsoft Internet mail program will now request an LDAP-based search of this directory service when it attempts to resolve names I type into the To: or Cc: fields on new messages.

Use the Authentication Type area on your new directory service dialog box to set up your LDAP client to use any authentication options you selected when configuring LDAP on the server side. Select Anonymous if you enabled anonymous access on the LDAP server. Use Secure Password to encrypt any passwords sent to the LDAP server. Choose Password to enable Windows NT authentication. You can only select one of these options.

Advanced Properties for a New Directory Service   Next, tab over to the Advanced property page on your new directory service's dialog box. See Figure 18.34. If your searches time out, increase the search time-out value. If you want this directory service to send you more or fewer directory items, enter the number in the 'Maximum number of entries to return' field. You might request fewer items to lighten the network traffic load. Of course, whatever number of entries you request from the LDAP server you connect to, you'll never get any more than it has been configured to return.

FIGURE 18.34

Setting advanced properties for a new directory service

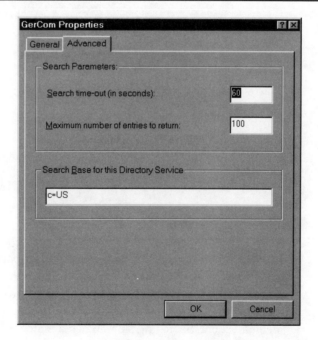

Use the search base option to broaden or narrow the scope of searches that you do. You use X.400 addressing parameters to change the scope of searches done using this directory service. The default is c=US, which means that only directory entries with a country value of US (United States) will be returned from searches of this directory service. You can use virtually any item available in a directory here or you can leave it blank to impose no limits at all on a search.

When you're done working with the Advanced property page for your new directory service, click on OK to register your new settings. This returns you to the General property page on the Directory Services dialog box. You should see your new directory service in the list on this page. See Figure 18.35.

FIGURE 18.35

A new directory service listed on the Directory Services General property page

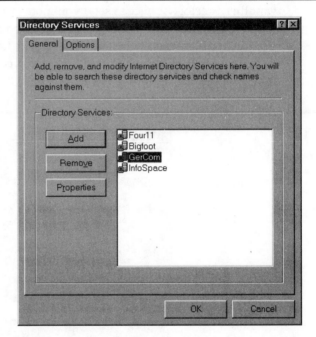

Options   Now tab over to the Options property page on the Directory Services dialog box. If you've chosen to search more than one directory service, as I have in Figure 18.36, this is where you set the search order that is used when your LDAP client attempts to resolve names you've typed into the To or Cc field of your Internet mail client. Searching stops when a match is found in any directory service on the list.

Do what you need to on the Options property page. Click on OK on the Directory Services dialog box when you're done, and you're finished configuring your LDAP client.

FIGURE 18.36

Setting the search order to be used when more than one directory service is specified for use by the Internet mail client

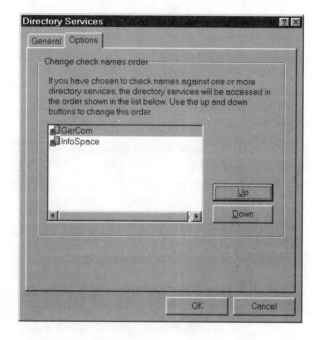

Did It Work?

Testing with the Windows Address Book   You can check your work right inside of Windows Address Book. Click on the Find button in the Windows Address Book window. This brings up the Find People dialog box shown in Figure 18.37. Select the friendly name of your Exchange LDAP service, type in a name or e-mail address to search for, and click on the Find Now button.

FIGURE 18.37

Setting search criteria for the Windows Address Book LDAP client

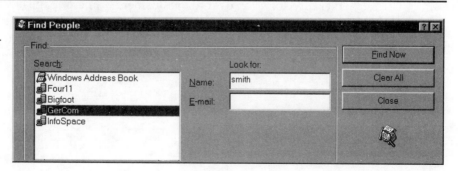

If all goes well, your LDAP client will connect to your LDAP server, request information on all people meeting the search criteria you set, and return the names to Windows Address Book. Figure 18.38 shows the results of my search for all of the Smiths in GerCom. Notice that the list includes Smiths at both my LA and NY site, proving that Exchange Server LDAP support is indeed organization-wide.

FIGURE 18.38

A list of Exchange user mailboxes and some of their directory attributes found using the search criteria set in Figure 18.37

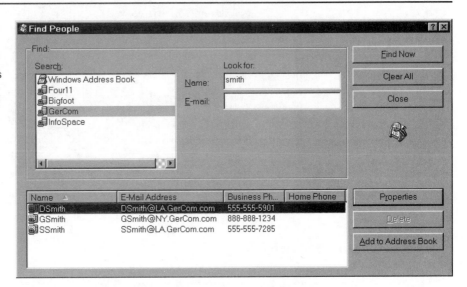

Pretty fantastic, huh? Well, folks, the show's only begun. Click on one of the names that's returned to bring up a properties dialog box for the person. See Figure 18.39. As you can see, I can add Gina Smith's address to my Microsoft Internet mail address book and I can look at a range of items from the Exchange Server directory. Tab over to the Business property page (see Figure 18.40) to see a ton of business-oriented info about the person. Why, if there was an entry in the Exchange Directory, you could even click the Go button down at the bottom of the page and be magically transported to Gina Smith's business web page.

FIGURE 18.39

Personal information found in an LDAP search of an Exchange Server directory

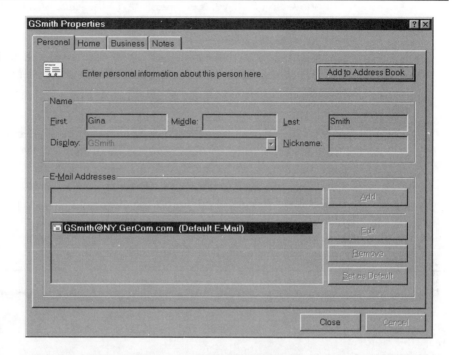

FIGURE 18.40

Business information found in an LDAP search of an Exchange Server directory

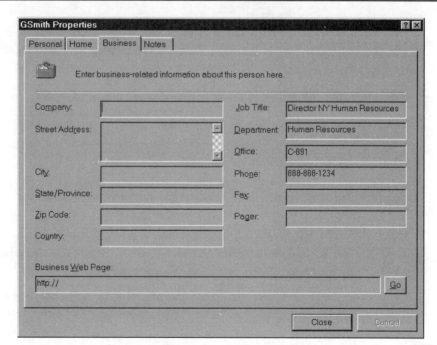

The show isn't over yet. Let's move on to the Microsoft Internet mail client.

Testing with an LDAP-aware POP3 Client   Open Internet mail client, which you'll find on the Windows 95 or Windows NT 4.0 Start button's Programs menu. For information on obtaining and installing the client, check out the sidebar *Start With Microsoft's POP3 Client*, which appears earlier in this chapter.

As you track through this section, follow along on Figure 18.41. Click on the client's New Message button. Type the last or full names of some Exchange users into the To or Cc fields of the message. Separate multiple names with semicolons. Next, click on the toolbar button with the little check mark and Rolodex card icon. Your client will initiate an LDAP search of any directory services you set up in Windows Address Book. If matches are found, the mail client replaces the names you typed in with the aliases of the appropriate Exchange mailboxes. If more than one match is found for a name you typed in, you'll be offered a list of names to choose from.

FIGURE 18.41

To and Cc field names have been resolved by an LDAP search of an Exchange Server directory

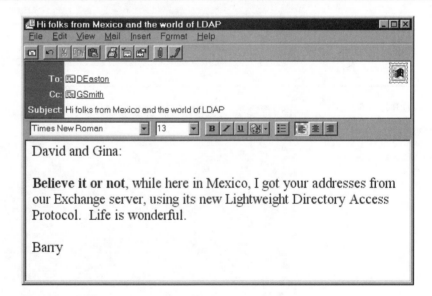

Finally, double-click on one of the resolved names in the To or Cc field. This brings up the same dialog box we saw back when we were working with Windows Address Book. See Figure 18.42.

Microsoft has worked several miracles here, but the overall effect is to give a POP3 client much of the addressing look and feel of the Exchange and Outlook clients. That's pretty nice, especially for a client that's absolutely free.

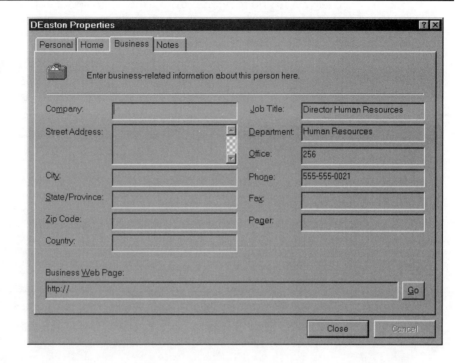

FIGURE 18.42

Viewing business information from an Exchange Server directory by double-clicking on a resolved name in the To or Cc field

The Network News Transport Protocol

Aren't these advanced Internet protocols fantastic? Well, we're not finished with these wonders yet. We've got one more to go, the Network News Transport Protocol (NNTP). NNTP supports those wild, woolly, and sometimes useful Internet newsgroups that are home to everything from the infamous and sometimes offensive *alt* to the fairly staid German language *zer* groupings. In-between, you'll find lots of computer- and business-relevant groups, as well as enough other stuff to keep you (or people who work at your place of business) delightfully distracted from work for hours.

All of the above is to warn you that you should very carefully consider the consequences of giving your users access to the newsgroups. One argument in their favor, aside from the truly useful groups that are out there on the net, is that you can use newsgroups for internal communications, too.

I'll leave it to you to ponder the business and social implications of NNTP. The good news is that, if you want newsgroups, Exchange Server 5 makes it about as easy as possible to set them up and make them available.

Once setup is done, your Exchange server acts just like any other NNTP server. Newsgroups from all over the world show up as public folders. Anyone who can get to those public folders by any of the means I've discussed in this and other chapters can get to the newsgroups on your Exchange server. In addition, your Exchange Server–based NNTP server fully supports standard news reader clients like Microsoft's Internet news client, FreeAgent or WINVN.

By whatever means someone gets to your Exchange NNTP server, if they have the rights to do so, they can post new or reply messages to any newsgroup or they can respond directly to the original sender of a news message by e-mail. Your server will see to it that those messages and postings are available not only locally, but, if you want, to users of the newsgroup outside of your Exchange site or organization.

If all of this isn't enough, your Exchange NNTP server can also feed its newsgroups to other NNTP servers. Couple all of this good stuff with the kind of user-friendly interface you've come to expect from Exchange Server and you've got it all NNTP-wise.

What's a USENET Newsfeed?

You'll often read or hear the term "USENET" used in very close conjunction with "newsfeed." A newsfeed is the regular transmission of a specific set of newsgroups from one computer to another. USENET is the network of computers that supports client and server Internet newsfeeds. One of your main tasks, should you choose to take your Exchange Server into the NNTP world, will be to find a USENET newsfeed provider and subscribe to that provider's service.

As a protocol, NNTP isn't the most obvious thing you'll ever encounter. There are lots of terms and concepts to master. The best way to get a handle on all of this is to jump in and get your hands dirty. So let's get to configuring and using NNTP on an Exchange server.

NNTP Set Up: The Server Side

Your NNTP server can perform a range of tasks. It can get newsfeeds from other NNTP servers, send its newsfeeds—including new postings from its users—to other servers, and send newsgroup information and messages to NNTP clients. I'll cover the first two of these below. The third happens without any intervention on your part, although, as you'll see, you can limit the folders that differently authenticated NNTP clients can access in your newsgroups.

The Newsfeed Configuration Wizard

Before you can actually set up a newsfeed, you'll need to make some arrangements with an Internet newsfeed provider. Many Internet Service Providers (ISPs) can supply you with a newsfeed. You should have the following in hand before you start the setup process:

- your provider's USENET site name (which is an Internet domain name)

- the Internet domain names or IP addresses of your provider's host servers (which might be the same as the USENET site name)

- the user name and password your Exchange NNTP server will use to log on to your provider's host computer (not all providers require these)

If all of this is new and strange to you, fret not. Your USENET provider will understand just what you need.

You can create as many newsfeeds as you like. To set up your first newsfeed, start from the Exchange Administrator's File menu and select New Other, then select Newsfeed. This brings up the startup page of the Newsfeed Configuration Wizard shown in Figure 18.43.

Click on Next to move on to the Wizard's next page, which is shown in Figure 18.44. On this page you specify the Exchange server where the newsfeed will be installed and a *USENET site name*. The installation server must support public folders. The USENET site name is the domain name or, more specifically, the *fully qualified domain name* of the server the newsfeed will be installed on.

I'm sure you've gotten the hang of Wizards by now. So, I'm going to stop prompting you to click the Next button when you're ready to move on.

On the next Wizard page (see Figure 18.45), you set the type of newsfeed this is to be. Inbound newsfeeds are those where you get news from your USENET provider. Inbound feeds fill up those public folders on your Exchange server. Outbound newsfeeds send new newsgroup messages to other NNTP servers.

FIGURE 18.43

The Newsfeed Configuration Wizard's startup page

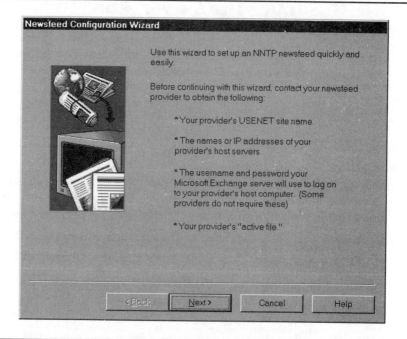

FIGURE 18.44

Setting information about the Exchange server where a newsfeed will be installed

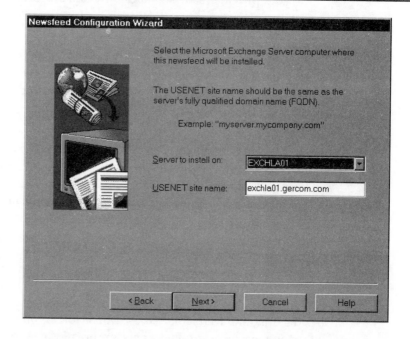

FIGURE 18.45

Setting the type of news-
feed to be supported by
an Exchange NNTP
server

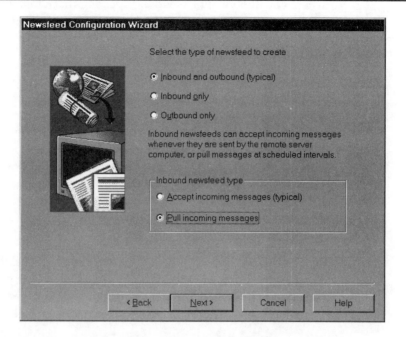

Outbound messages to your USENET provider reflect user postings in your
server's copy of each newsgroup. The USENET provider's NNTP server adds
these postings to its copy of each newsgroup. As one NNTP server passes its
updates on to another, each server's copies of the newsgroups grows to include
more and more of the messages posted by users in the wider USENET
newsgroup community.

Outbound newsfeeds also let you become a USENET newsfeed provider in
your own right. When your NNTP server sends newsgroup messages to non-
USENET providers, you become their provider.

NOTE In this section, I'm going to focus on getting a newsfeed from a USENET
provider. I'll discuss the technical aspects of becoming a USENET newsfeed provider in a later section.

Generally, you'll want to configure an Inbound and Outbound newsfeed for
feeds you get from a USENET newsfeed provider. Inbound-only feeds are fine

where you don't want to send user postings back to your USENET provider. We'll talk about outbound feeds later. Outbound-only feeds are best when you don't want to get news messages from a provider, but do want to send user postings to the provider.

Inbound newsfeeds can be of two types: push ('Accept incoming messages' in Figure 18.45) or pull ('Pull incoming messages' in Figure 18.45). In a push feed your USENET provider sends news messages to your NNTP server on its schedule. In a pull feed you go and get news messages from your provider on your schedule. Push feeds are best where you're after a large number of news messages and where a higher speed network is in place between your server and your USENET provider. Pull feeds work best when you need to access smaller numbers of news messages over slower networks, especially those of the dial-up persuasion. Pull feeds are also useful when you want to control traffic on your network, because you can specifically schedule when pull feeds happen on your Exchange server.

Though push feeds are the most widely used, I, rebel that I am, like pull feeds. So, in Figure 18.45, I've chosen a pull feed. Depending on which kind of feed you choose, you'll be shown somewhat different options from this point on. I'll let you know when selecting a push feed would have yielded other options.

If you've selected any combination of push/pull and inbound/outbound newsfeed, with the exception of a push type inbound-only feed, the Wizard next asks how you want to connect to your newsfeed provider. See Figure 18.46. Push type, inbound-only newsfeeds rely on another NNTP server to initiate the link and assume a LAN-based connection between your server and the remote server. So, if you're configuring a push type, inbound-only connection, you won't see this Wizard page.

As you can see in Figure 18.46, I've chosen a LAN-based connection. You can also use a dial-up link.

Before presenting the page in Figure 18.46, the Wizard checks to see if you've set up the Remote Access Service (RAS) and if you have a RAS phone book that might supply information for a dial-up. If you don't have a phone book, you'll see a rather scary message to that effect. Don't worry, unless you want to use RAS, you can ignore the warning. If you need RAS, you'll have to set it up and enter at least one number in the phone book. See Mark Minasi, et al., *Mastering Windows NT Server 4* (Sybex, 1996) for more on configuring RAS.

As with the previous Wizard page, you'll see the page shown in Figure 18.47 if you're configuring an inbound and outbound, pull type inbound-only, or outbound-only newsfeed. Use the drop-down list to tell your Exchange server how frequently it should connect to your newsfeed provider.

FIGURE 18.46

Setting the connectivity
method for a newsfeed

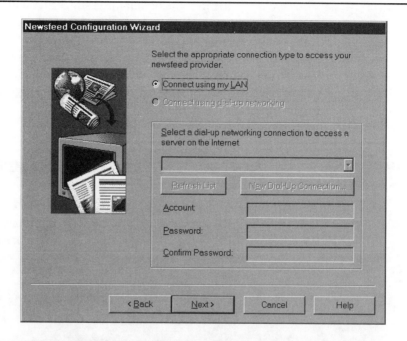

FIGURE 18.47

Setting connection
frequency for a
newsfeed

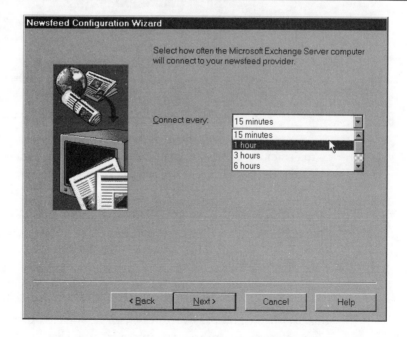

Now we're getting to some of that info I suggested you have close at hand when setting up your newsfeed. The next Wizard page is used to enter the USENET site name your newsfeed provider gave you. In Figure 18.48, I've entered the name of a USENET site Microsoft operated for the use of Exchange 5 pre-release users. My thanks to the good folks on the Exchange development team for giving me access to the site. By the way, this site ran on an Exchange 5 server and it worked very well throughout the period of my tests.

FIGURE 18.48

Entering the name of the USENET newsfeed site

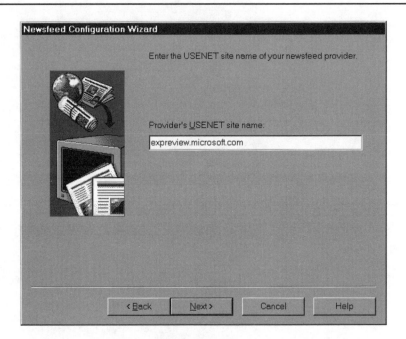

You enter the Internet domain name or IP address of host computers on the next Wizard page. See Figure 18.49. You can enter one or more hosts for a newsfeed. Some providers operate more than one host for redundancy and better performance.

Next you need to enter some security information. See Figure 18.50. Enter any user name and password information your USENET newsfeed provider gave you in the top two fields. The user name in the *Remote servers log in as* field is actually the name of an Exchange mailbox or custom recipient. If it's a mailbox, the password is the password of the NT account linked to the mailbox. NNTP servers connecting to your server to push messages to it or pull messages from it will use this user name and password. Click on Change to open the Exchange address list. Then select the appropriate recipient from the list.

FIGURE 18.49

Entering identifying information for news-feed hosts

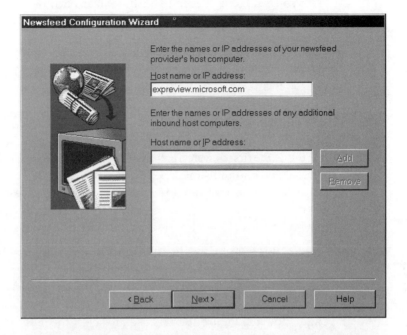

FIGURE 18.50

Setting security information for a newsfeed

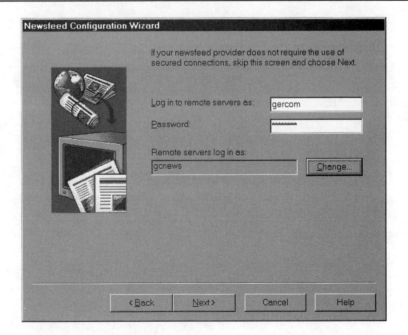

As you can see in Figure 18.51, the Wizard is now ready to install the Exchange Internet News Service. This is a standard NT service that supports newsfeeds. It's installed only once on an Exchange server. Since this is the first time I've installed a newsfeed on this server, the Wizard installs the Internet News Service. Click on Next to start installation of the service and your newsfeed. (Woops! I promised I wouldn't tell you to click on Next anymore. I just couldn't resist.)

At this point, you will be asked to enter the password for your site services account. That's the one you created before you installed your first Exchange server.

If this is the first newsfeed on this server, you're next asked to set the mailbox of the Internet news administrator. See Figure 18.52. This mailbox owns all of the Internet public folders. Its user can do such things as modify access rights to newsgroup folders, move folders around, and delete them. To set the Internet news administrator's mailbox, click on Change and select the mailbox from the address list that pops up.

Your NNTP server needs a list of the newsgroups available from your USENET provider. This is called the "active list." You can get a copy of the file from your provider by e-mail or you can download it using the FTP protocol. Alternatively, your Exchange server can download the file for you right now. The next Wizard page, shown in Figure 18.53, is used to select the method you'll use to make the file available to the Exchange NNTP server. As you can see, you can even tell the Wizard you don't have the file right now and go on configuring your newsfeed.

FIGURE 18.51

Exchange is ready to install the Internet News Service and a newsfeed.

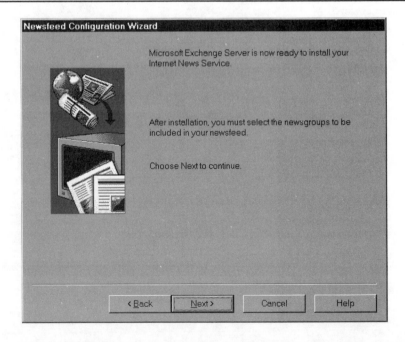

FIGURE 18.52

Setting the Exchange mailbox of the Internet news administrator

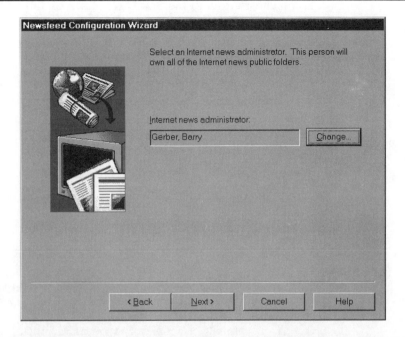

FIGURE 18.53

Specifying how and when an Exchange server can access the active newsgroups file for the USENET newsfeed provider

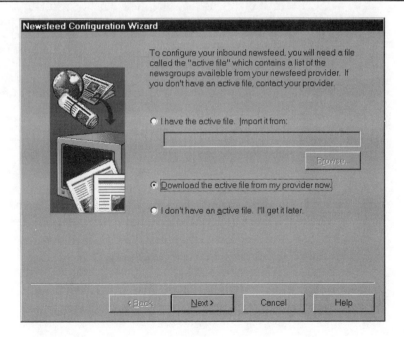

If you chose either of the first two options on the Wizard page shown in Figure 18.53, the next Wizard page you'll see will look something like the one in Figure 18.54. You're shown a tree with the newsgroups that are available to you.

Click on a folder and then click on Include to add the folder and its folders and/or newsgroups to the list of newsgroups you want to receive. In Figure 18.54, I clicked on the newsfeed itself (expreview.microsoft.com) and then on the Include button. As you can see in Figure 18.55, my server will get all of the newsgroups in the feed.

In Figure 18.56, I clicked on the newsgroup *migration* and then on the Exclude button to remove the migration newsgroup from the newsgroups my server will get.

WARNING Before we go much further, I've got to talk to you about what I call *newsoverfeeding*. With millions of users hitting USENET newsgroups every day, it shouldn't surprise you that your collection of news messages is going to grow very quickly. There are two keys to sanity here. First, carefully select and limit the newsgroups you'll support. Second, use the message aging functionality built into public folders to assure that messages are deleted from your newsgroup folders frequently. You now know how to select newsgroups from a newsfeed. I talked about public folder message aging back in Chapter 14. Set the public folder aging parameters based on how quickly a folder tends to grow in size. Some USENET news providers delete messages that are a day or two old from fast-filling newsgroups. So, don't feel bad if you have to wield a sharp, close-cutting razor.

When you click on Next this time, your Exchange server starts creating the new public folders that will hold your newsgroups. To entertain you while it does its thing, the server shows you the little progress dialog box shown in Figure 18.57. Actually, if you're installing a lot of newsgroups, folder creation can take quite a while. You'll welcome that little dialog box, if nothing else, as an indicator that your Exchange server hasn't crashed.

FIGURE 18.54

Preparing to select from a list of newsgroups available from a USENET newsfeed provider

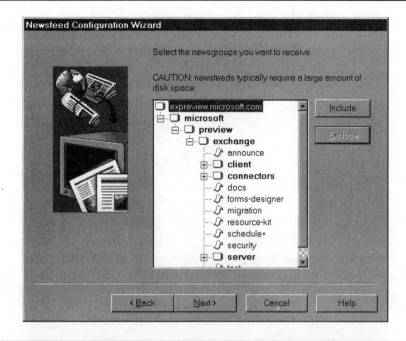

FIGURE 18.55

Selected newsgroups are displayed.

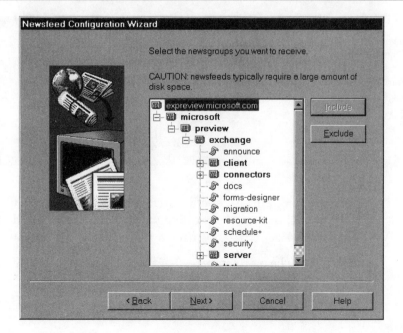

FIGURE 18.56

Deselecting a
newsgroup

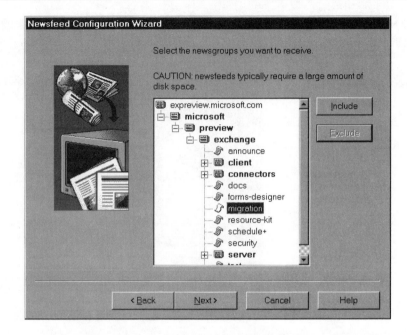

FIGURE 18.57

A dialog box showing an
Exchange server's
progress in creating new
folders to hold
newsgroups

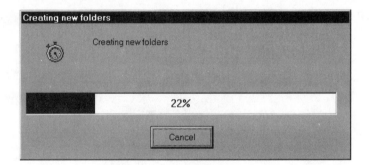

The Wizard page shown in Figure 18.58 tells you that you're finished at last. I won't bore you by repeating the important messages that are displayed on this final Wizard page. I'll just warn you to pay close attention to all of the messages.

I can be pretty impatient at times. So, immediately after I clicked Finish on the Wizard, I fired up my Exchange client to see what my public folders looked like. Sure enough, there were all of those newsgroup folders sitting in the Internet Newsgroups folder. See Figure 18.59.

FIGURE 18.58

A new newsfeed has been installed.

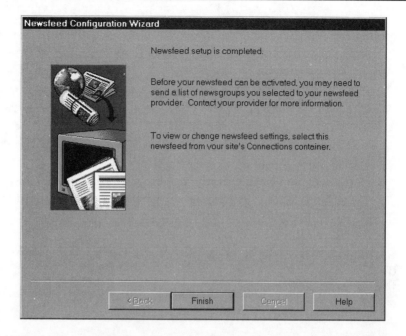

FIGURE 18.59

Viewing newsgroup folders with an Exchange client

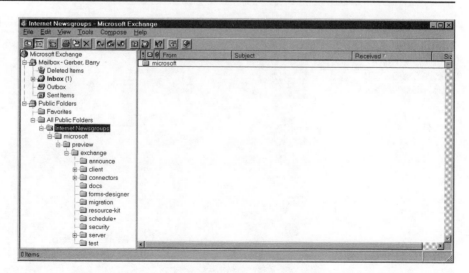

Imagine my disappointment when I found the folders themselves empty. They were empty, of course, because the time hadn't yet come for my first pull of newsgroup messages from my USENET provider. As you'll see later in this chapter, after an appropriate interval, my newsgroup folders did, indeed, fill with all the goodies from Microsoft's Exchange 5.0 preview newsfeed.

NOTE
While you're thinking about those newsgroup public folders, don't forget about public folder replication. Because they're nothing more than public folders, you can wholly or selectively replicate newsgroups across your Exchange organization. Just keep in mind the traffic that can be generated during such replication. If network bandwidth is limited between those of your Exchange servers that need to support newsfeeds, it might make more sense to subscribe to separate newsfeeds for each server.

Before we move on, take a look in the Connections container for the site where you installed the newsfeed. There's now an object for the feed in that container. I'll talk about that object in just a bit.

Administering and Managing the Exchange NNTP Service at the Site Level

Find the NNTP object in the site Protocols container and double-click on it. This brings up the NNTP (News) Site Defaults Properties dialog box shown in Figure 18.60.

FIGURE 18.60

The General property page of the NNTP (News) Site Defaults Properties dialog box

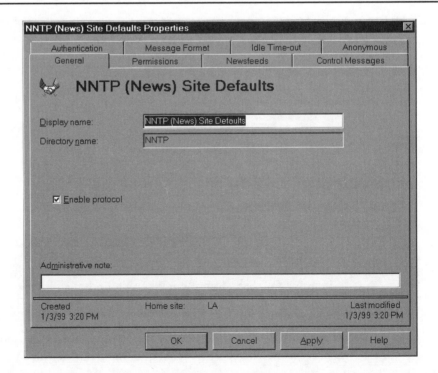

General Properties   You should be quite familiar with the General property page. It looks pretty much like the General pages for the three other advanced Internet protocols we've discussed in this chapter. You can disable and enable the NNTP protocol for the site on this page.

Newsfeeds   Tab over to the Newsfeeds property page. There's a lot behind that little newsfeed object in the list in Figure 18.61. Double-click on it to bring up a whole new dialog box for administering and managing each specific newsfeed. See Figure 18.62. This is the same dialog box you'd get if you double-clicked on the object for the newsfeed in the Connections container for the site where you installed the newsfeed.

Until I tell you otherwise, we'll be looking at the property pages on the Newsfeed Properties dialog box shown in Figure 18.63. When we've finished with these, we'll return to the NNTP (News) Site Defaults dialog box in Figure 18.61.

FIGURE 18.61

Preparing to open a newsfeed for administration and management

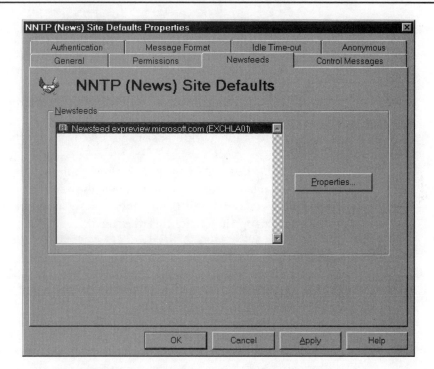

FIGURE 18.62

The General property page of the Newsfeed Properties dialog box

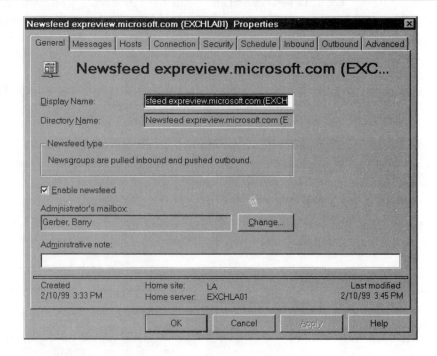

The Newsfeed Properties dialog box is chock-full of property pages. Many of them are carbon copies of pages you saw on the Newsfeed Configuration Wizard. Because you're familiar with those pages I'll cover only the ones that are new.

General Properties   As Figure 18.62 shows, among other things, you can disable or enable the newsfeed and change the administrator's mailbox for the newsfeed. By default, this is the mailbox you set as the Internet news administrator. You can change it here for this newsfeed.

Message Size Limits   You use the Messages property page to set size limits on incoming and outgoing messages. Figure 18.63 shows the defaults. The one MB max on outgoing messages is considered a fair limit on what users should be able to send to other newsgroups.

You can leave these settings as they are, unless you have a good reason for changing them. If you're worried about the disk space taken up by messages, it's better to limit the number of newsgroups you support, and/or use short public folder message aging settings, than it is to too narrowly limit message size. Small size limits could exclude messages that are key to understanding the conversational thread of a specific newsgroup.

FIGURE 18.63

Setting incoming and
outgoing newsfeed mes-
sage size limits

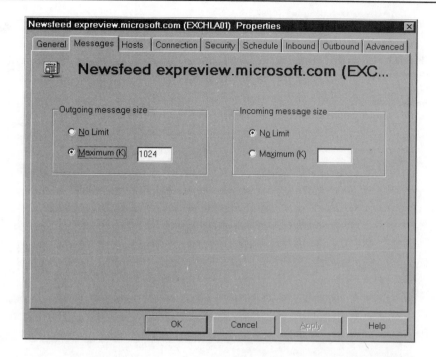

Hosts, Connection, and Security   The Hosts, Connection, and Security property pages on the Newsfeed Properties dialog box contain pages you saw back on
the Newsfeed Configuration Wizard. Check out the following figures and related
text for details on these pages:

- Hosts: Figures 18.48 and 18.49

- Connection: Figure 18.46

- Security: Figure 18.50

The Connection Schedule   You use the Schedule property page on the
Newsfeed Properties dialog box shown in Figure 18.64 to set how frequently
your NNTP server will connect to your USENET provider in order to send and
receive new messages. This schedule applies to outbound and inbound, pull type
inbound-only, and outbound-only newsfeeds. Pick the schedule that works for
your site's network traffic and your users' needs.

FIGURE 18.64

Setting a connection
schedule for inbound
and outbound, pull type
inbound-only, and out-
bound-only newsfeeds

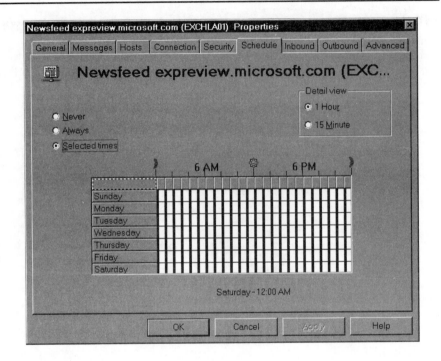

Inbound Settings Here's another property page with contents you've seen
before. Take a look at Figures 18.53 through 18.56 and accompanying text for
more information.

Outbound Settings If your newsfeed is of the inbound and outbound or
outbound-only variety, you can use the Outbound property page to specify the
newsgroups for which you'll send postings by your users back to your USENET
provider. See Figure 18.65. You'll remember that this is the way your users' postings get integrated into the image of the newsgroup beyond your Exchange
environment.

Advanced Properties Your Exchange server can fall behind in processing messages from your USENET provider, whether your newsfeed is push or pull. This
usually happens when a newsfeed includes a large number of messages. The
server puts messages into a queue and then processes them in the order received.
As the messages in a queue pile up, it takes longer and longer for the most current
messages to find their way into the appropriate newsgroup.

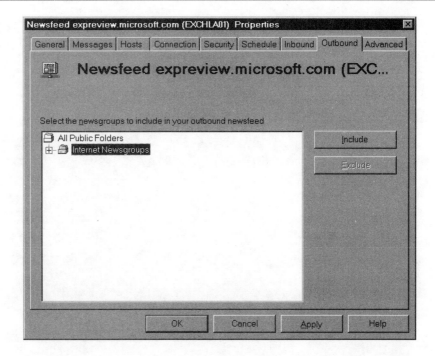

FIGURE 18.65

Selecting the news-
groups to be included
in outbound communi-
cations with a USENET
provider

To help speed things up, you can delete all unprocessed messages from their queue. The messages are lost, but, newsgroups being what they are, this is generally not considered a big deal. After all, you don't carefully preserve each daily edition of your newspaper as though it were a fine Moroccan leather-bound first edition of a literary classic.

You use the Advanced property page on the Newsfeed Properties dialog box to flush unprocessed newsgroup messages from their queues. To do this, click on Mark All As Delivered (see Figure 18.66). This deletes all of the messages in the queue and allows your server to catch up on its newsgroup message processing functions.

If you're getting a push newsfeed, all will be just fine after the flush. Each time your USENET provider connects to you, it sends only messages your server hasn't yet received. So, you'll get only messages that weren't sent to you before, not new messages plus a bunch of messages that you already deleted from the queue. If you're using a pull feed, when you flush the queue, the server resets the time base that is used to determine which messages your server needs from the USENET provider. The time base is set to the time when the queue was flushed. This assures that messages retrieved from your provider are no older than the time when the queue was flushed.

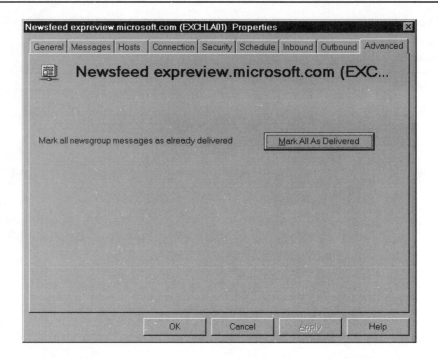

FIGURE 18.66

Clicking 'Mark All As Delivered' deletes all unprocessed news-group messages in this newsfeed.

Control Messages   OK, we're done with the Newsfeed Properties dialog box and ready to return to the NNTP (News) Site Defaults Properties dialog box. Figure 18.67 shows the Control Messages property page.

NNTP control messages are generated for new and deleted newsgroups and when someone makes a request to delete a single message from a newsgroup. You have to process control messages for new and deleted newsgroups. If you trust the newsfeed providing the new newsgroup, accept the group by highlighting its control message and clicking on the Accept button. If not, highlight the message and click on Delete.

Your Exchange server processes requests to delete an individual message automatically, if the person requesting the deletion is in your Exchange organization's global address list and the message originated from the organization. For other single item deletion requests, you get to accept or delete the control message.

FIGURE 18.67

Use the Control Message property page of the NNTP (News) Site Defaults dialog box to accept or reject messages about certain changes in a newsfeed.

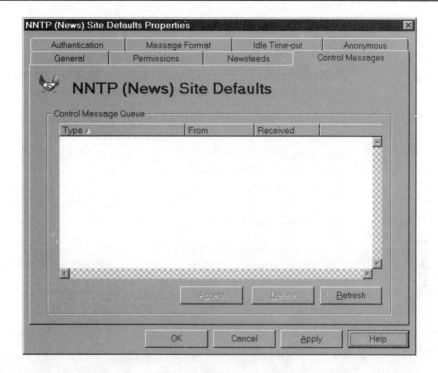

Authentication, Message Format, Idle Time-out, and Anonymous

You shouldn't have any trouble using the last four property pages on the NNTP (News) Site Defaults dialog box.

The Authentication page offers the usual three options for verifying NT account name and password: Basic (Clear Text), Windows NT Challenge/Response, and Secure Sockets Layer.

Use the Message Format page to choose between the MIME or UUENCODE message encoding standards and to send message bodies in plain text and/or HTML format. As you'll remember, the HTML format preserves text formatting such as type of font, bold, italic, and color.

You can set a time after which idle NNTP client connections are closed on the Idle Time-out page.

If you wish, you can enable anonymous access to your NNTP server on the Anonymous page. If anonymous access is enabled, anyone who knows the Internet domain name or IP address of your NNTP server can connect to it and participate in newsgroups that are available to anonymous users. By default, anonymous users are given Nonediting Author access to newsgroup folders. In just a bit, I'll tell you how to change that.

Administering and Managing the Exchange NNTP Service at the Server Level

To open the server-level object for administering and managing newsfeeds, double-click on the NNTP object in the Protocols container on the server of your choice. As you can see in Figure 18.68, your NNTP server-level options are pretty much what they are at the site level, except for the absence of the Control Messages property page and the presence of the Diagnostics Logging page. Control messages are dealt with at the site level only and diagnostic logging only makes sense at the server level.

Aside from the fact that you'll only be able to work with newsfeeds on the specific server, you should have no problem using any of the property pages on the server-level NNTP (News) Settings Properties dialog box. Check the last section if you need a refresher on any of the property pages.

FIGURE 18.68

Use the server-level NNTP (News) Settings Properties dialog box to administer and manage newsfeeds on a server.

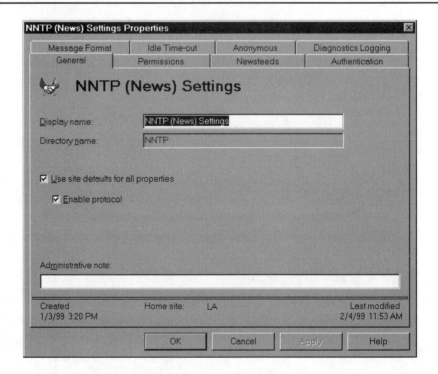

Administering and Managing the Exchange NNTP Service at the Mailbox Level

As with other advanced Internet protocols I've discussed here, at the individual mailbox level, you can disable or enable the NNTP protocol and set alternate message encoding options. See Figure 18.69.

FIGURE 18.69

Setting NNTP protocol options for an individual mailbox

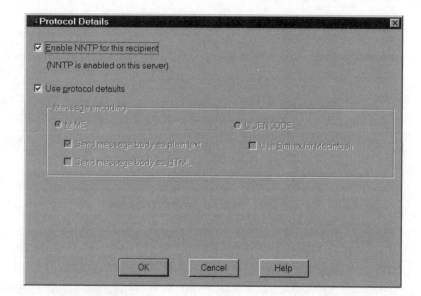

Managing Newsgroups

You will need to manage newsgroups in your Exchange client. You must be an owner of the newsgroup folder or folders you wish to manage. Here's a quick list of key newsgroup management how-tos:

- Create new newsgroups by adding a new folder wherever you wish in the Internet Newsgroups hierarchy.

- Turn an existing private or public folder into a newsgroup by dragging it into the Internet Newsgroups hierarchy.

- Remove an existing newsgroup by deleting it from the Internet Newsgroups hierarchy.

- Change anonymous user access to a newsgroup by opening the properties dialog box for the newsgroup folder, tabbing over to the Permissions property page, and setting the role assigned to Anonymous users. This role can range from Owner (not a good idea) to None, which locks anonymous users out of a newsgroup.

- Change newsgroup access for users authenticated through the NT security system in the same way as you change anonymous user access—which, for the record, is the same way you change public folder access for any Exchange recipient.

> **WARNING** Be sure that settings for anonymous web browser (HTTP) public folder access and anonymous newsgroup (NNTP) public folder access are harmonious. For example, you don't want to include a public folder in the list of folders available to anonymous web browser users and then disable anonymous access to it, because, for some reason, you want to limit NNTP client access.

NNTP Set Up: The Client Side

If you use your Exchange client or a web browser to access newsgroup folders, you don't have to do a thing. You access newsgroup folders just as you'd access any other public folder.

If you use a standard NNTP client like Microsoft's Internet news client, FreeAgent, or WinVN, you'll have to do a bit of configuring. You'll need to enter the Internet domain name or IP address of the Exchange server that supports your NNTP server. You'll also have to enter a user name and password, if you've disabled anonymous access or if non-anonymous users have access to newsgroups not available to anonymous users.

Each NNTP client has its own unique configuration and user interface. All of these are pretty straightforward. So I'll leave it to you to figure out how to set up and use your favorite client.

Did It Work?

You can test your newsfeed in lots of ways. First, check it out through your Exchange client. After allowing sufficient time for newsgroup messages to populate your newsgroup folders, take a look at a couple of newsgroups. In Figure 18.70, I'm using my Exchange client to look at messages in the Microsoft Exchange preview newsgroup *nntp*. Next, try reading one of the messages in the newsgroup, as I am doing in Figure 18.71. Then, just for fun, select a different personal view from your Exchange client's View menu. In Figure 18.72, I'm using a Group by Subject view on the nntp newsgroup.

FIGURE 18.70

Viewing an Exchange server–based newsgroup with an Exchange client

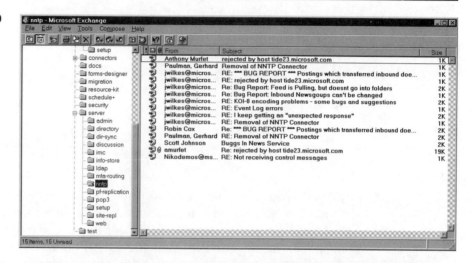

FIGURE 18.71

Reading a message in an Exchange server–based newsgroup with an Exchange client

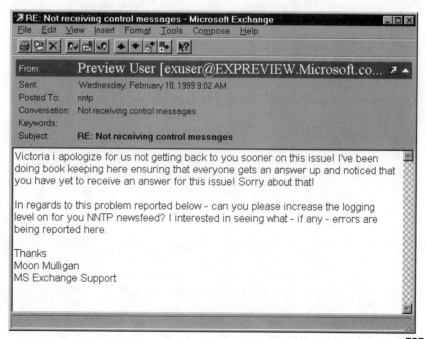

FIGURE 18.72

Looking at an Exchange server–based newsgroup with an Exchange client using a Group by Subject view

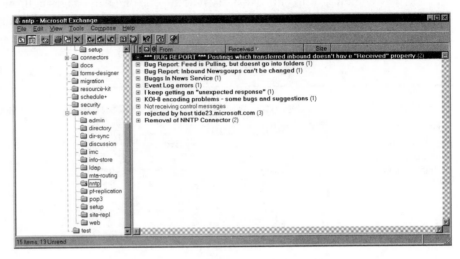

If all of this works and your newsfeed supports outbound communications with your USENET provider, try posting a new message to a newsgroup. Be sure to label the message as a test message. After a reasonable waiting period, you should be able to see your message in the newsgroup when you connect to another NNTP server outside of your Exchange organization, for example, to your Internet Service Provider's NNTP server.

Next, try accessing your newsgroups with a web browser. In Figures 18.73 and 18.74, I'm using my web browser to look at the same newsgroup and message as in Figures 18.71 and 18.72. If you need a refresher on web browser access to your Exchange server, take a look at my discussion of the client-side active server component setup earlier in this chapter.

Finally, connect to your NNTP server with a standard NNTP client. In Figure 18.75, I'm using the WinVN NNTP client to access the nntp newsgroup on my Exchange server. As above, I'm reading what by now should be a quite familiar newsgroup message.

I've been working with NNTP Exchange style for some time now and I haven't experienced any difficulties. If you have any problems getting NNTP services to work, make sure everything is properly configured, including your TCP/IP setup, the information you've entered about your USENET newsfeed provider, and the permissions you've set on your newsgroup public folders. If none of this helps, check the Exchange documentation for troubleshooting tips.

FIGURE 18.73

Viewing an Exchange
server–based newsgroup
with a web browser

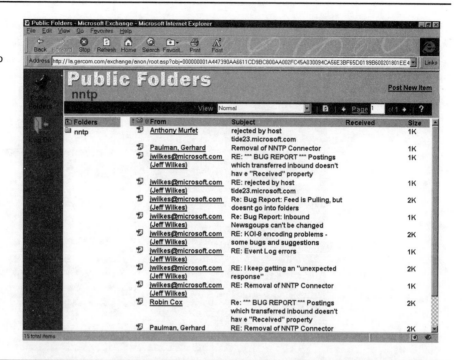

FIGURE 18.74

Reading a message in an
Exchange server–based
newsgroup with a web
browser

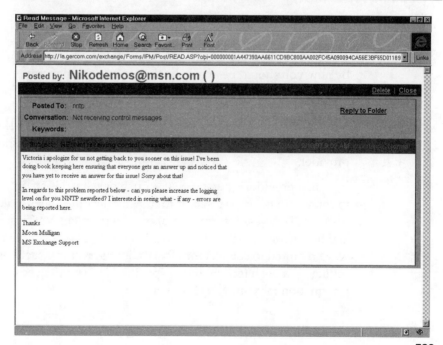

FIGURE 18.75

Viewing an Exchange
server–based news-
group and a message
in the newsgroup using
a standard NNTP client
(WinVN)

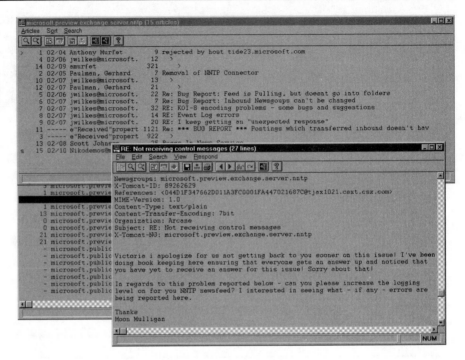

Becoming a USENET Newsfeed Provider

By now you should be an expert at configuring, managing, and administering a newsfeed to receive newsgroup messages from a USENET provider. With the knowledge you already have, you'll find it very easy to set up a newsfeed that provides newsgroup messages to other NNTP servers. Basically, you have to think of everything you've just been through from the perspective of a USENET provider.

From a provider's perspective, a push newsfeed is an outbound feed. You need to connect to the NNTP server to transfer new messages to it. To do this you need basic NNTP access information about the recipient NNTP server: its USENET site and host names or IP addresses and, if one has been set, the user name and password required to connect for NNTP client-server transactions. The person who is setting up a push feed on the recipient NNTP server needs the basic NNTP access information for your NNTP server.

To set up a pull newsfeed, the person at the recipient NNTP server needs the basic NNTP access information for your server. In a pull feed, the recipient NNTP server uses NNTP client technology to get newsgroup messages. So you don't have to do anything other than provide that basic NNTP access information.

> **WARNING**
>
> If you get into the newsfeed provider "business," be sure you protect the folders that shouldn't be seen outside of your organization. Use the Outbound property page on the Newsfeed Properties dialog box (see Figure 18.65) to exclude those sensitive folders from your feed to the recipient NNTP server.

That's all I need to say about the technical aspect of becoming a USENET newsfeed provider. Do remember to consider the kinds of loads that too many heavy-duty outbound feeds can put on your Exchange server. If you expect to get into this stuff big time, you should consider dedicating a pretty hefty chunk of computer to newsfeed provision.

Configuring Protocols Containers

To wrap up this chapter, I talk briefly about site- and server-level Protocols containers configuration. The parameters you set for these containers apply to all of the protocols in the container: HTTP, LDAP, NNTP, and POP3.

As you can see in Figure 18.76, which shows the site level Protocols Property dialog box, there are two configuration options we haven't discussed before: Connections and MIME Types. Use the Connections property page to set the IP addresses that your server should accept or reject connections from. See Figure 18.76. Use the MIME Types page (see Figure 18.77) to define new MIME content types that your Exchange server will use when it decodes MIME attachments. MIME-type definition isn't for us amateurs. So be sure you know what you're doing before you start cooking up new MIME types.

The server level Protocol configuration dialog box is exactly the same as the site level box, except that it lets you choose to use or not use site level settings. Nothing more need be said.

FIGURE 18.76

Setting the IP address of a server from which connections will not be accepted

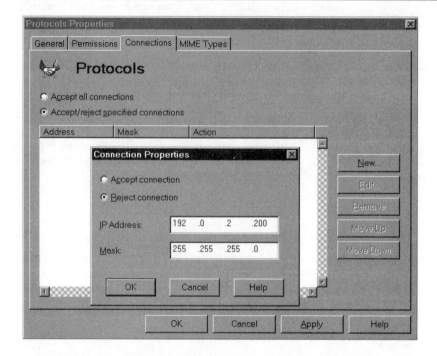

FIGURE 18.77

Use the MIME Types property page to configure new MIME content types.

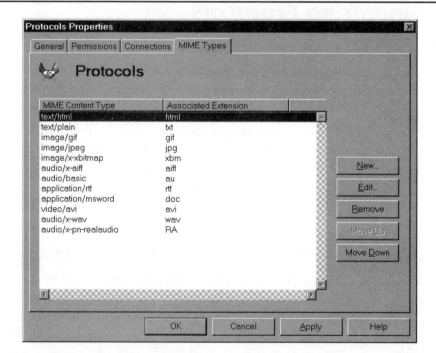

Protocol Policies

All of the protocols I've discussed here can leave your organization's e-messaging system open to malicious intrusions. These intrusions can come from inside or outside of your organization. For example, if you don't limit the data that an anonymous LDAP client user can access in your Exchange directory, competitors or headhunters could use the LDAP protocol to build a list of names and contact information to be used in recruiting away some of your organization's most valuable employees.

Protect your organization and yourself by encouraging the development of policies regarding these protocols. The source of this policy might be your organization's Human Resources department, a special committee, or executive management. Some issues that need attention include:

- Which of the protocols will we support?
- What kind of security do we want for authenticated users of the supported protocols?
- If we support them, will we allow anonymous access through the LDAP, HTTP and NNTP protocols?
- If we support the protocol, what kinds of POP3, LDAP, HTTP, and NNTP clients will we support? (Different clients might provide different levels of security.)
- What kinds of users will be allowed to use the different client options we support?

Conclusion

In this chapter you learned how to configure Exchange Server support for four advanced Internet protocols: the Post Office Protocol version3 (POP3), the Hypertext Transport Protocol (HTTP), the Lightweight Directory Access Protocol (LDAP), and the Network News Transport Protocol (HTTP). You also learned a bit about supporting clients for each of these protocols.

Now, for something completely different. In the next and final chapter of this book, we'll take a look at the Exchange Forms Designer and how you can use it to develop forms for use in customized applications.

CHAPTER
NINETEEN

19

Application Development with Exchange Forms Designer

- The Exchange application design environment

- Building an Exchange electronic form

- Installing an Exchange electronic form

Nobody likes filling in forms, right? Well, the answer probably seems obvious—until you consider the alternative: a blank piece of paper. Imagine doing your taxes without all those wonderful IRS and state forms. Imagine trying to process tax reports formatted every which way but clearly. Done right, forms—especially electronic forms—make it easier for users to get through complex or repetitive data-entry tasks with minimal pain. In addition, these forms help their creators collect data in a uniform manner and process it easily.

Microsoft Exchange Forms Designer (EFD) is a user-friendly front end, based on Microsoft's Visual Basic programming language, that lets you create slick electronic forms for use in the e-messaging world of Exchange. In some cases, you'll build forms to replace paper documents and automate the flow of work between groups in your organization. In other cases, you'll put together forms that totally change the way people do work in your organization.

Once you start working with EFD, you'll find yourself waking up at night with fantastic ideas for forms. Here are some examples:

- *Request forms*—used to ask for something:
    - Purchase orders
    - Computer program modifications
    - Computer hardware maintenance
    - Travel requests
    - Vacation or sick-day requests
- *Survey forms*—used to gather information:
    - Employee feedback on health insurance plans
    - User feedback on products or services
    - Employee participation in company picnics
- *Report forms*—used to provide required information:
    - Employee status reports to supervisors
    - Employee travel and mileage reports
    - Department head reports on success in staying within budget allocations
- *Other forms*—used for a variety of purposes:
    - standardized communications forms (for example, telephone notes, while-you-were-out memos)
    - forms for playing multiuser tic-tac-toe, chess, and other games

Your form-making should be informed by a clear understanding of the process you're automating and the people involved in that process. If this is the case, you'll be a winner, reducing paper shuffling and increasing the productivity and satisfaction of everyone involved. On the other hand, if you don't study processes and people carefully, you'll frustrate your bosses and users alike to the point that your forms will hinder rather than help the workflow you're trying to automate.

The Exchange Application Design Environment

As I indicated way back in the first chapter of this book, EFD isn't the only way to design applications. The Exchange application design environment includes the following:

- *Forms design tools:*

  - The Forms Designer—used to make your own forms

  - Form templates—predesigned forms for specific purposes

  - The Form Template Wizard—used to set up a new form based on form templates

- *Folder design tools:*

  - The Exchange client—used to create folders

  - Folder design cue cards—to guide you through folder design

- *OLE-2–based applications:* A word-processing document, a spreadsheet, or another element from an OLE-2–capable application such as Microsoft Word or Excel is pasted or inserted as an object into an Exchange message; the message *becomes* the application.

- *Exchange Application Programming Interfaces (APIs):* APIs are used to develop custom-coded applications using Visual Basic or C++.

Creating OLE-2 apps is just a matter of pasting or inserting the appropriate application object into an Exchange message. You don't need my help with that. To do justice to API-based application design, I'd need to write another book at least the size of this one. That's why I'm focusing this chapter on forms design—and even then, as you'll see, we'll only be able to touch the surface of this fascinating topic.

WARNING

Though EFD is easy to use, it's a full-featured program, and I can't possibly teach you everything you need to know about using it. My goal here is to show you how easy forms design can be and get you started doing a simple form with EFD. For more details, you'll need to look at the EFD documentation and, if you want to get into serious programming, a good book on Visual Basic.

Installation

EFD runs only in a 16-bit Windows environment. You can use a Windows 3.1x machine or Windows 95 or NT. When you run EFD in 95 or NT, the 16-bit code runs in the 16-bit mode of those operating systems. The Exchange client must be installed on the machine as well.

You'll find the EFD setup directory on the Exchange Clients CD-ROM. Just run SETUP.EXE in the directory, and in a few minutes you'll be on your way to forms designer heaven. If you need to install EFD on an Exchange server, be sure to stop the Exchange Server services before installation.

NOTE

There are or will be forms development options for Exchange that break the 16-bit barrier. For example, JetForm Corporation (Falls Church, VA) makes some nice products.

Building an Exchange Electronic Form

Find the EFD icon and double-click on it to start Exchange Forms Designer. If you accepted the default installation options, the icon will be in the same Windows program group as your Exchange client icon.

In Figure 19.1, EFD has just been opened. There are three objects on the screen. The dialog box opens at start-up to guide you through the forms development process. You can run the Forms Template Wizard, pick an existing template to use in building a new form, or open an existing form project.

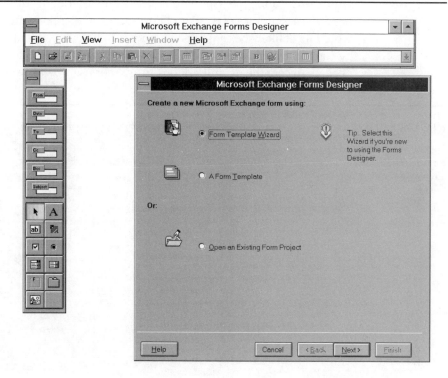

The long, thin horizontal rectangle at the top of the screen is EFD's basic menu and toolbar. The long vertical rectangle running along the left-hand side is a really useful toolbar that you can use to build your application.

Let's use the Form Template Wizard to start building a new form. The Wizard not only makes it very easy to get a new forms development project up and running, but it also gives you a good grounding in some key EFD concepts. Since the Form Template Wizard option is selected by default, just click on Next to move to the next page of the Wizard.

Getting Started with the Form Template Wizard

As Figure 19.2 indicates, you can do two things with an EFD form. You can *send* it to others, or you can *post* it in a public folder for others to use. Remember those words—*send* and *post*—and you'll have a far easier time with EFD. The Wizard page gives examples of Send and Post forms. A telephone message, for example, would most likely be sent to one or more Exchange recipients. A help-desk request, by contrast, would most likely be posted in a public folder for users to fill in as needed. Accept the default option 'To another user (Send)' and click on Next.

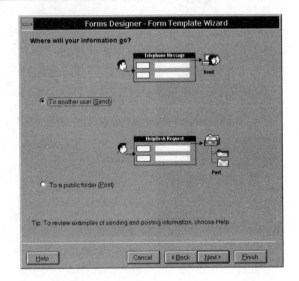

Because we told the Wizard that our form will be sent to others and not posted in a public folder, the Wizard now asks us questions about the form we will send. The next Wizard page asks if the form is for sending a new message or for responding to a message sent with another form (see Figure 19.3). You can create a Send form and a Response form and link them together; this lets you control both sides of the e-messaging process. Be sure 'To Send information' is selected and click on Next.

Next you're asked if you want your Send form to have a single window for both entering and reading information, or one window for entering information and another for reading it (see Figure 19.4). If it's okay for a recipient to edit information, choose the single-window option; otherwise, select two windows. For our example, be sure that the 'One window' option is selected and then click on Next.

FIGURE 19.3

Specifying whether the form is to send information or respond to an already-created form

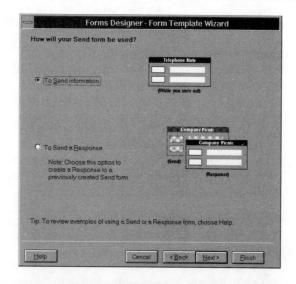

FIGURE 19.4

Specifying whether the form will allow editing of sent text

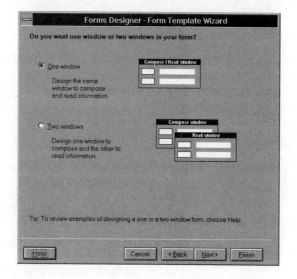

Now you can start building your form. In Figure 19.5, you can see that I've added a name and description for the form using the next Wizard page. The name and description show up in various places—for example, when you open the form for editing in EFD—so it's worth including them. As you can probably tell from my description, I'm going to make a form that people can use to tell me how they want to participate in GerCom's annual company picnic.

FIGURE 19.5

Adding a name and description for the form

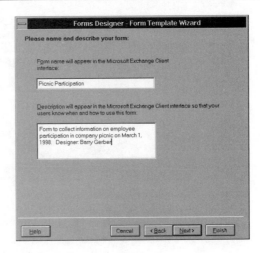

As you can see in Figure 19.6, the Wizard has done all it can for us. Now we're ready to get into some serious forms building with EFD. Click on Next, and we're off to forms development land.

FIGURE 19.6

The Wizard tells us that we are ready to build our form.

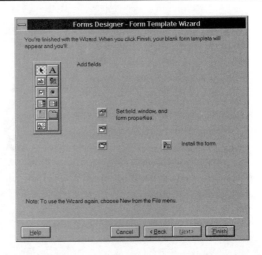

NOTE   Anytime you want to use the Form Template Wizard to set up another form, just select New from EFD's File menu. This brings up a dialog box similar to the one shown in Figure 19.1. Keep in mind that you can open only one form at a time in EFD, so you'll have to save and close your current form before you can start work on a new one.

Using EFD to Continue Building a Form

After a bit of churning, the Wizard opens a new EFD form that is all ready for you to work on (see Figure 19.7). Before you do anything else, it's a good idea to save your form at this point. To do so, select Save As from EFD's File menu. The default extension for forms is .EFP, so I saved my form as PICNIC.EFP.

FIGURE 19.7

A new form ready to be developed

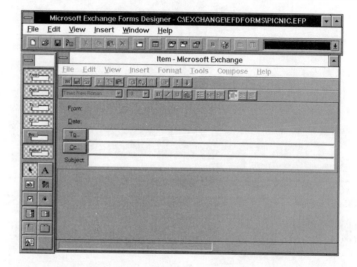

Notice in Figure 19.7 that the standard Exchange client formatting and other toolbars, as well as some standard Exchange e-messaging fields and buttons (From, Date, To, Cc, and Subject), are already in place. These fields are the appropriate ones for the Send message we originally asked the Form Template Wizard to set up.

EFD is object-oriented. Every field in a form is an object with editable properties. If I highlight a field—say, the To field—by clicking on it, its name (MAPI_To, in this case) is displayed on the horizontal toolbar (see Figure 19.8).

So that all forms adhere to Exchange standards, you can't move or resize standard Exchange e-messaging fields such as To or Subject. Therefore, even though a standard e-messaging field is displayed with all of its moving and resizing boxes and handles, you won't actually be able to move or resize it. You can, however, double-click on the field to open a dialog box that lets you view and edit the field's properties (see Figure 19.9).

Before we add any fields, let's take a quick look at some of the tools you have at your disposal with EFD. The vertical toolbar, shown in Figure 19.10, lets you do a number of forms development tasks with ease.

FIGURE 19.8

An Exchange electronic form with its To field selected

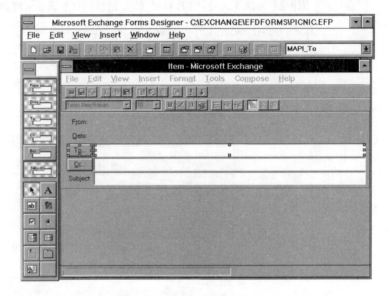

FIGURE 19.9

Viewing the properties of the To field

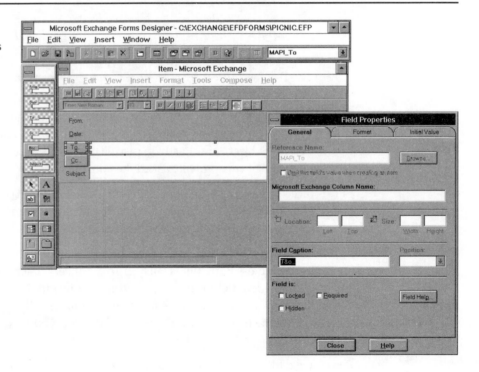

FIGURE 19.10

Exchange Forms
Designer's vertical
toolbar

The top six buttons let you add standard Exchange e-messaging fields. Except for the pointer button, which works like its equivalent in most applications, the vertical toolbar's buttons are used to add new fields to your form. Figure 19.10 shows the kind of field you can add with each button. Here's a quick rundown on each of those fields. Figure 19.11 shows a form I created with all of the fields in it.

- Entry field—a place to enter text

- Check box field—for options that can be toggled on or off

- Combo box field—lets you create a drop-down or other list box into which users can type

- Frame field—to group other fields

- Picture box field—for displaying a graphic image

- Label field—to provide text labels where needed

- Rich entry field—lets you enter formatted text, attachments, and the like; equivalent to the field in an Exchange message into which users enter messages

- Option button field—for multiple-choice options; users cannot select multiple option buttons on the same frame field

- List box field—lets you create a drop-down or standard list box from which users can select options but into which users can't type

- Tab field—provides tabbed pages to which you can add other fields

FIGURE 19.11

All of the fields that can be created on an EFD form

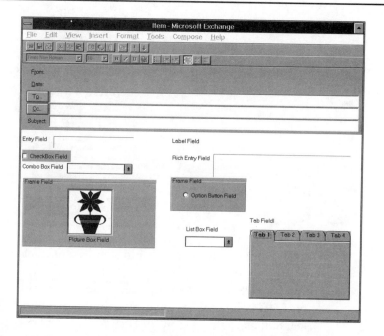

> **NOTE**
>
> If you'd like a copy of the form we're developing here, send me e-mail at gerber@deltanet.com. Include the words "EFD Form Picnic EFP" in the subject of the message and my auto-response Exchange Inbox rule will send a copy to you.

We're just about ready to add some fields to our form. First we need to do a couple of things to the form itself. To begin with, let's resize the form to make it a little bigger. Resizing is done just as it is with any Windows window: Just grab the bottom right-hand corner of the form with your mouse and drag away until the form window looks something like the one in Figure 19.12.

Now let's change the form's background color. Put your pointer anywhere on the background of the form and double-click. This opens the Properties dialog box for the window (see Figure 19.13). You can use this dialog box to set all kinds of attributes for the window itself; I'll leave it to you to explore all of its great features. To change the background color, click on the Format tab and then click on the Change button to the right of the little picture of an Exchange message (the one with the word *Background* above it). You will get a Color dialog box, which you can use to select a new background color. I've chosen white for my window.

FIGURE 19.12

Ready to begin developing a form with Exchange Forms Designer

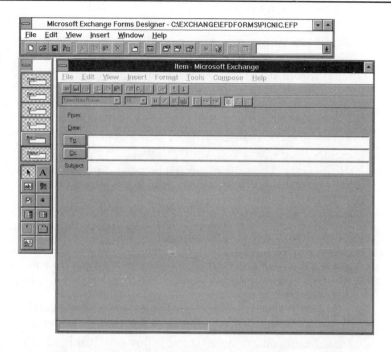

FIGURE 19.13

Changing a window's background color

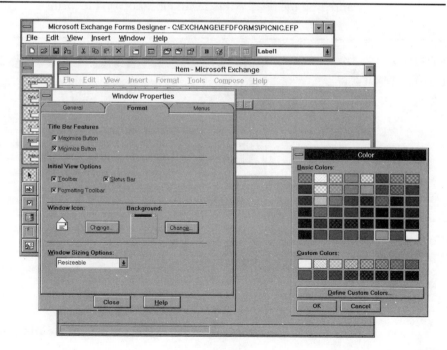

Now we're ready to add fields. As we move along, I'll show you how to do lots of neat stuff. Virtually everything you learn when adding one type of field can be used when you create other types. I'll tell you how to do a particular task as we set up a particular field; after that, I'll assume that you know how and when to use what you've already learned in creating other fields. As we go along, refer back to Figure 19.10 if you need to for the location of buttons on EFD's vertical toolbar.

First, let's add a label that will serve as the title of our form. Click on the label button (the one with the large capital letter *A* on it). Move your mouse to the general location where you want the label to appear—I'm putting mine at the top of the message. Then click your left mouse button once to place the label and bring up a little rectangular box with the word *label* inside.

Click inside the box until it's surrounded by a dark rectangle with seven small, solid boxes and one large box around it. You use the small boxes to change the size of the label field. Just put the pointer on one of the solid boxes, hold down the left mouse button, and drag to make the field larger or smaller. Resize your label field until it's about the size of the one in Figure 19.14.

Notice the larger solid box in the upper left-hand corner of the label rectangle? You use it to move the label field around the form. When you put the pointer on that box, the pointer turns into a little hand. Just hold down the left mouse button and drag the field to the desired location on the form.

FIGURE 19.14

Creating a title label for a form

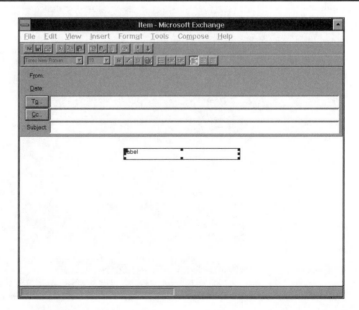

Next, click once on the label field and replace the word *label* with an appropriate form title (mine is 'The GerCom Picnic Is Coming Soon'). If the field is too small for the text you've added, resize it and drag the label field around the form until it's attractively placed (see Figure 19.15). To make the rectangular box with the little resizing boxes disappear, simply click on the form anywhere outside the field.

FIGURE 19.15

A label field resized to become the title of a form

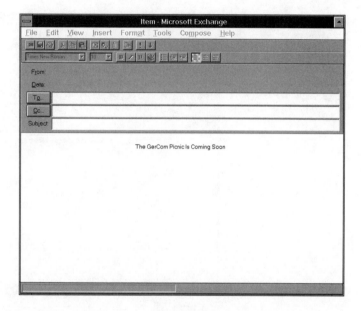

We took a lot of time fiddling around with sizing and placement on that first field. From here on, I'll leave it to you to do that kind of stuff on your own. Let's add another field.

For planning purposes, we need to find out what people will want to drink at the picnic. So let's create a set of multiple-choice options and a field for people to enter other preferences.

Because people should be able to select more than one drink option, we'll use checkbox fields grouped in a frame field to represent the options. (If we used options-button fields grouped on a frame, people would be able to select only one option in the group.) First, click on the frame field button on EFD's vertical toolbar; check out Figure 19.10 if you need a refresher on the toolbar buttons. Then click on the right-hand side of the form to create the frame.

We'll be offering four picnic drink options—coffee, tea, milk, and beer—so we'll need four checkbox fields. To create each field, click on the checkbox-field button on the vertical toolbar and then click on the frame you just created in roughly the spot where you want the checkbox to appear. Then place the four checkbox fields in a vertical line (see Figure 19.16).

FIGURE 19.16

Creating a set of drink options for a company picnic

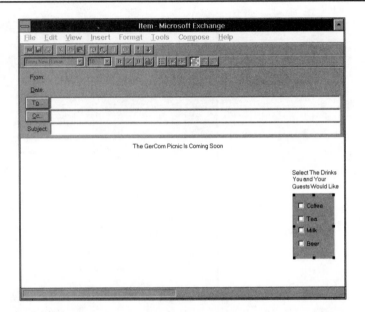

NOTE Once you place fields on a frame field, then drag the frame, its associated fields stay in place and move with it. This makes it easy to properly locate a frame field and its associated fields.

By the way, I didn't like the rather three-dimensional look of the standard frame field, so I double-clicked on the frame to bring up its Properties dialog box (see Figure 19.17). Then, on the Format property page, I changed the type of frame from Standard to the flatter-looking Panel design you see in Figure 19.16.

While the frame's Properties dialog box was open, I clicked on the Field Help button on the General property page to bring up the Field Help for Users dialog box shown in Figure 19.18. This lets me add something called *QuickHelp*, which a user can access by clicking on the field and then pressing the F1 key (or by selecting Current Field from the form's Help menu). I was also able to specify the text to be displayed on the form's status bar (the area at the bottom of the form) when the user's pointer enters the frame.

FIGURE 19.17

Changing a frame's format from Standard to Panel

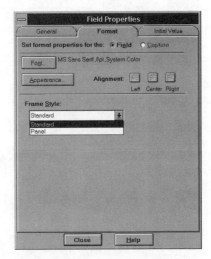

FIGURE 19.18

Adding help for a frame field

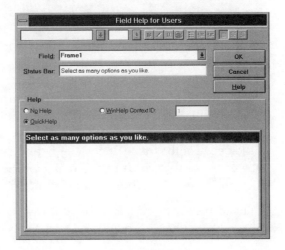

TIP

It's not easy to get a bunch of fields in line just by using your mouse. To vertically line up the four checkbox fields, use your mouse to move one of the fields so that its distance from the left edge of the frame is just as you want it to be. Then open the Properties dialog box for the field and, from the General property page, note the value of the field's Left Location (see Figure 19.19). Close that field's dialog box and then, in turn, open the Properties dialog box for each of the other fields, type in the correct Left Location value, and close the dialog box. When you're done, all of the checkbox fields will be equidistant from the left edge of the frame. In the alternative, you can position the topmost field where you want all fields to be left-aligned. Then, select all of the fields you want to align and choose Edit ➤ Align ➤ Left from the EFD menu bar.

FIGURE 19.19

Aligning a set of fields using the Properties dialog box for each field

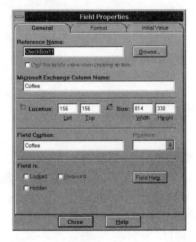

Close that field's dialog box and then, in turn, open the Properties dialog box for each of the other fields, type in the correct Left Location value, and close the dialog box. When you're done, all of the checkbox fields will be equidistant from the left edge of the frame. In the alternative, you can position the topmost field where you want all fields to be left-aligned. Select all of the fields you want to align and choose Edit from the EFD menu bar, then choose Align and Left.

Put a label above the frame for your Drinks checkbox fields. 'Select The Drinks You and Your Guests Would Like' seems to be a good choice for my form.

Now we need to add an entry field so people can type in other drink choices. Click on the entry field button on the vertical toolbar and place your text field below the Drinks frame with its four checkbox fields. Change the caption to Other Drinks, pretty up the formatting of the different fields, and you're done (see Figure 19.20).

FIGURE 19.20

A text entry field lets users indicate other drinks they would like.

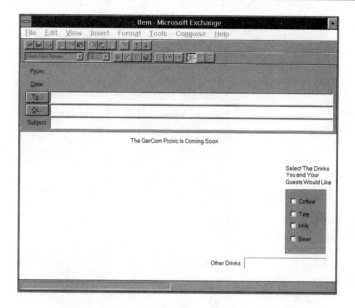

Now we need to create a set of checkbox fields so people can pick the main dish they want. We'll also provide an entry field to indicate a preference for other main-dish options.

Well, we're certainly not about to go through all the steps we just went through to create this new set of fields—we'll just copy and paste. Make sure your Drinks frame is selected; the rectangle with the resizing squares should be showing as in Figure 19.16. Select Copy from EFD's Edit menu (or use the keyboard shortcut, Ctrl+C). Then choose Paste from the Edit menu (or press Ctrl+V).

EFD will tell you that there are already fields with the same names as the ones you're trying to paste and will give you the option of either canceling the fields or renaming them to something unique. Choose the latter option. If you don't see the new frame and its associated checkbox fields, they've probably been pasted right on top of the old frame. In that case, just move the top frame with your mouse and you'll see the original frame underneath. You now have two identical frames and checkbox buttons. Move the copy to the left of the original.

Now edit the leftmost Drinks frame and its associated checkbox fields. Re-label the Coffee, Tea, Milk, and Beer fields to Hamburger, Turkey Burger, Veggi Burger, and Hot Dogs. Then copy, paste, and edit the Drinks label and the Other Drinks entry field so that they are appropriate for a main dish. When you're done, your form should look something like the one in Figure 19.21.

We'll need to know how many guests each person plans to bring and what kinds of games people will want to play. Add an entry box for the number of guests, plus a label and two list boxes for favorite games (see Figure 19.22).

FIGURE 19.21

The picnic form with main dish fields in place

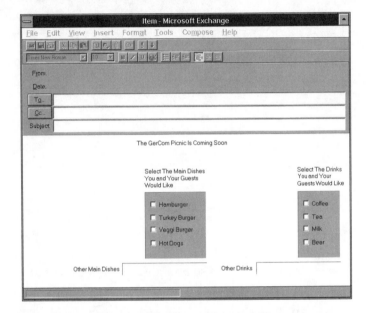

FIGURE 19.22

The picnic form now collects information on the number of guests and favorite games.

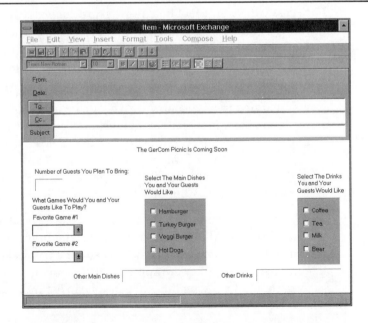

Right now those two list boxes for favorite games are blank; if form users opened the drop-down list, they'd find nothing to select from. To add some options, double-click on the first list box to bring up the Properties dialog box for the field. Under 'Specify values in the list' on the Initial Value property page, enter the names of a few games (see Figure 19.23).

FIGURE 19.23

Adding values to a list box

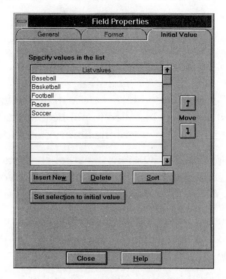

You can move any of your entries up or down in the list, using the two Move buttons on the right. If you want a particular value to show in the list box when a user opens the form, select it by clicking on it with your mouse and then click on 'Set selection to initial value'. When you're done, click on Close. Next, open the Properties dialog box for the second favorite-games list box and repeat the steps outlined above.

There's just one more thing to do before we finish. Double-click on the form's Subject field (it's right below the To and Cc fields in Figure 19.22). When the Properties dialog box for the field opens, tab over to the Initial Value property page and type in a default subject. That way you won't have to enter a new subject for each Exchange recipient you send the form to. My default subject is 'Survey For GerCom Picnic'.

That's it. We've finished creating our form. Be sure to save it. Now we need to install it in Exchange so that we can send it off to GerCom employees.

Installing a New Exchange Form

You can install a form in one of four locations:

- A public folder
- A personal forms library
- An organization forms library
- An Exchange client's private folder

Generally, Send forms are installed in forms libraries and private folders, while Post forms are installed in public folders. You use the same installation process to put a form into any of the libraries or folders.

From our discussions in earlier chapters, you should have a pretty good grasp of private and public folders, so I won't devote much time to them here. However, since forms libraries are a new subject, we need to spend a little time on them.

Each Exchange Server mailbox owner can store forms in a *personal forms library*. This library, which can be on the user's home server or a local hard disk, is available only to the user.

In addition, you can store forms in an *organization forms library* on an Exchange server. Like public folders, this type of forms library can be replicated between sites. With the appropriate security settings in place, users throughout your Exchange organization can access and use the forms in organization-wide forms libraries.

If you're planning to install a form in your own personal forms library or private folder, you don't have to do anything else prior to the installation. Before you attempt to install a form in a public folder, however, be sure the folder exists and that you have Owner-level permissions for it. Also, don't forget to give access permissions to the public folder to mailbox owners who need to use the form.

If you want to install a form in an organization library, you first have to create at least one organization forms library and give at least one Exchange mailbox owner the rights to administer the library.

Creating an Organization Forms Library

To create an organization forms library, select Forms Administrator from the Exchange Administrator's Tools menu. The Organization Forms Library Administrator dialog box pops up (see Figure 19.24). Click on New to bring up the Create New Forms Library dialog box, which is also shown in Figure 19.24. If this is your first organization forms library folder, just accept the default, Organization Forms, and click on OK to return to the Organization Forms Library Administrator dialog box.

FIGURE 19.24

Creating a new library for the organization-wide management of Exchange forms

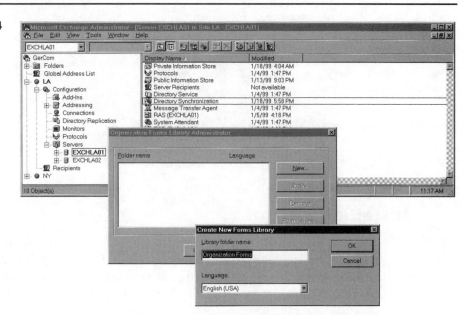

Now you need to give permission to one or more Exchange mailboxes or distribution lists to administer the forms library. Be sure the library name is selected, then click on Permissions. Use the resulting Forms Library Permissions dialog box to give the Owner role to anyone who will be creating and installing forms in the library (see Figure 19.25).

By default, the group 'Default' has Reviewer permissions for the library. Reviewers have full read rights to the library and the forms stored in it. All Exchange mailboxes belong to this group.

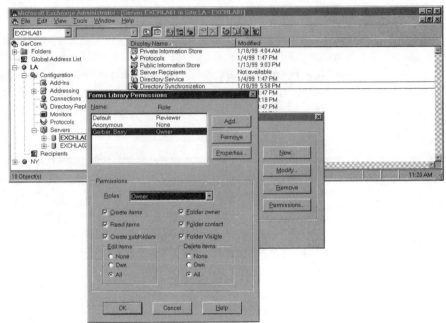

FIGURE 19.25

Giving an Exchange mailbox Owner permissions for an organization library

Installing a Form

Installing a new form is a piece of cake. With the form open in EFD, click on the install icon on EFD's horizontal toolbar (it's the fourth icon from the left) or select Install from EFD's File menu. The program will generate Visual Basic source code for the form and then compile it using the Visual Basic compiler.

> **NOTE**
>
> You can use the generated Visual Basic source code to modify your form in a variety of ways. For example, you can write Visual Basic code to total the numbers entered into a set of fields by a user and then place the total in another field.

When EFD is finished compiling your form, it asks you for the name of an Exchange client profile to use when it connects you to an Exchange server. Next, EFD uses the profile to link to the server. Then it presents you with a choice of forms libraries in which to store your form (see Figure 19.26). The list includes your personal folders, private (mailbox) folders, public folders, and any existing organization libraries. Generally, you'd store your own Send forms in personal folders, multiuser Send forms in organization forms libraries, and Post forms in public folders.

FIGURE 19.26

Selecting the forms library in which to store the form

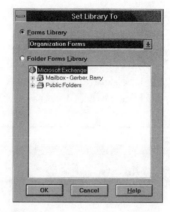

Select the option you want—I stored my form in the organization library I created above—and click on OK in the Set Library To dialog box. The Form Properties dialog box then pops up (see Figure 19.27). Enter a category and subcategory—they help immensely when you've got lots of forms—and fill in the Contact field. Then click on OK, and EFD executes the final form installation steps.

FIGURE 19.27

Entering category, subcategory, and contact information for a form

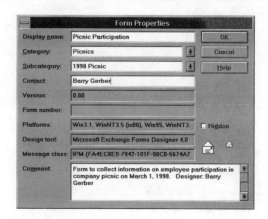

> **WARNING**
>
> Form installation takes time, and during most of that time you'll hear the hard drive on your EFD workstation whirring away. Have patience. The last thing you want to do is stop an already-long process and have to start it all over again.

Using a Form

To use the form we just created, select New Form from the Compose menu of your Exchange client. Exchange will show you which forms are available (see Figure 19.28). Select the form you created, and Exchange will install it on your machine and then present you with a copy of the form ready for sending.

FIGURE 19.28

Selecting a form to be used by an Exchange client

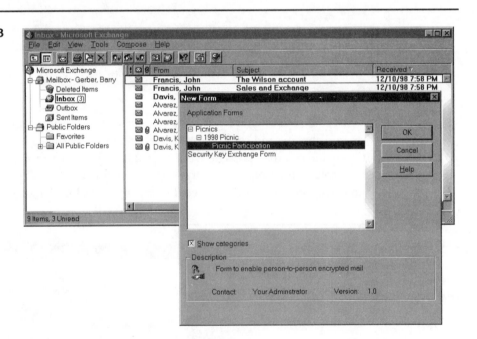

In Figure 19.29, I'm sending the GerCom picnic form off to Michael Lewis. In Figure 19.30, Michael Lewis has just finished completing the form.

When Michael Lewis clicks on the reply icon after filling in the form, a text-based reply message is generated that contains all the data entered into the form (see Figure 19.31). I receive Mr. Lewis's reply in a text message (see Figure 19.32). I can then manually process the replies I receive or—because the data is in a predictable format—write a program to process it. Pretty neat, huh?

FIGURE 19.29

Sending a form to an
Exchange recipient

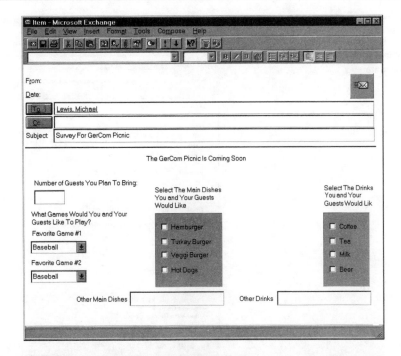

FIGURE 19.30

The data in a completed
form ready to be
returned to the form's
sender

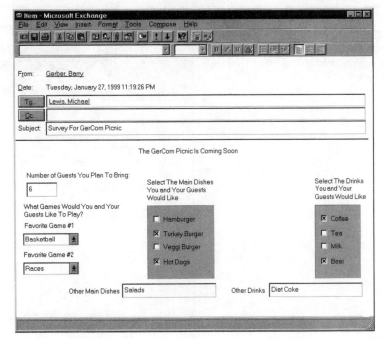

FIGURE 19.31

A text-based reply that contains all of the form's data

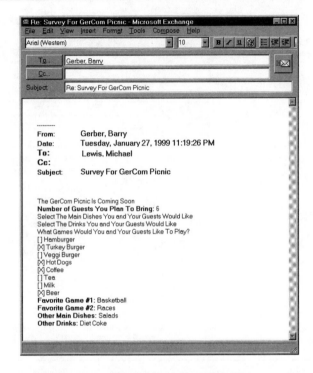

FIGURE 19.32

The reply as viewed by the original sender of the form

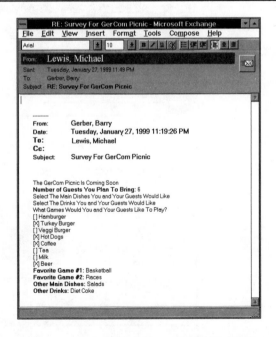

Don't Stop Here!

Unfortunately, we have to stop our exploration of EFD here, but don't let that stop you from exploring EFD further on your own. There are so many great things you can do with the program, such as creating Send and Response forms and linking them, and creating forms for posting in public folders.

EFD has a very good user interface. Combine that with its fine online help, and you can usually have a project based on newly discovered EFD features up and running in minutes. As with any piece of technology—Exchange Server included—your EFD watchwords should be *plan*, *do*, *test*, and *have fun*.

For example, while you have a form open, click on the Form Properties button on EFD's horizontal toolbar (see Figure 19.33). This is one of the most interesting of EFD's buttons. It lets you set up links between the current form and other forms, add various help features to the form itself, and even change the icons displayed when the form sits in an Exchange client's Inbox or folder.

FIGURE 19.33

Exchange Forms Designer's horizontal toolbar

Exchange Server comes with a number of sample forms–based applications. These apps support such functions as customer tracking and help desks. They're worth looking at both because they may help you understand how to build multiform applications and because they use Exchange's public folders to organize an app as well as deliver it to users throughout an Exchange organization.

Conclusion

In this chapter you learned about Exchange Forms Designer and how to use it to build, install, and deploy simple electronic forms. You also found out where to go to learn more about EFD and its supporting programming language, Visual Basic.

Well, folks, this is the last chapter of *Mastering Microsoft Exchange Server*. For me, researching and writing the book has been a lot of fun and relatively painless. I hope that your experiences with Exchange Server are as positive and rewarding.

INDEX

Note to the Reader: Throughout this index page numbers in **boldface** indicate primary discussions of a topic. Page numbers in *italics* indicate illustrations.

SYMBOLS

– (minus sign) in Exchange Administrator windows, 230
+ (plus sign) in Exchange Administrator windows, 230

A

Accept or Reject by Host options, Internet Mail Service Properties dialog box, 564
accessing
  Exchange Server program group, 211–212, *211, 212*
  messages remotely, 415
  NT accounts for the first time, 3853
  shared mailboxes, 403–405, *403, 404, 405*
accounts in NT Server
  accessing for the first time, 385
  creating, **241–242**, *241, 242*
  deleting when deleting mailboxes, 235
  extracting NT account lists for Exchange directory, 649–650, *650*
  granting accounts or groups rights to mailboxes, 241–242, *241, 242*, 248–249
  with inherited permissions, 247–248, *247*
Actions property page, server monitor Properties dialog box, 274–275, *275*
Active Server (AS), 57, 203, 689–697
  Active Server Components (ASCs), 57, 203
  client-side setup, **694–695**, *695, 696, 697*
  HTML (Hypertext Markup Language) and, 689
  HTTP Site Settings Properties dialog box, **690–694**
    Advanced property page, 694, *694*
    Folder Shortcuts property page, 691, *692, 693*
    General property page, 690–691, *690*
  overview of, 689
  server-side setup, **690–694**
    mailbox-level HTTP setup, 694
    site-level HTTP setup, 690–694
Add E-Mail Domain dialog box, 556, *557*
Add to Address Book View option, Administrator Tools menu, 286
Add to Favorites option, Exchange client File menu, 408
Add User or Group dialog box for mailboxes, 241–242, *241*
Add Users and Groups dialog box, 466, *466, 467*
adding
  address book view containers, 661, *662*
  address book views, 656–660, *657*
  Exchange systems to Dirsync systems, **592–601**
    Dirsync server settings, 598–599, *599*
    eliminating MS Mail SMTP gateways, 595
    setting up Dirsync requestors on Exchange servers, 592–598, *593*
    testing the setup, 600–601, *600*
  to Favorites folder, 408
  mailboxes to distribution lists, 250, *250, 251*
  servers to link monitors, 508, *509*
  servers to server monitors, 434, *435*, 508, *509*
Add-Ins container in Exchange Administrator, 663
Address Book dialog box. *See also* Global Address Lists; Microsoft Exchange Administrator; Windows Address Book
  creating views of, 286
  display name of public folders in, 310
  entering information about recipients managed by mailbox users, 244–246, *245*

entering mailbox user's manager information, 243, *243*

finding addresses in, 244

hiding shared mailboxes from, 406, *407*

importing folders, 410

Personal Address Books (PABs), 387, *388*

setting up Personal Address Books (PABs), 387, *388*

Address Book option, Exchange client Tools menu, 416

address book views, 655–663. *See also* views

adding, 656–660, *657*

adding address book view containers, 661, *662*

editing, 62–63

overview of, 655–656

Address Space property page

Dynamic RAS Connector Properties dialog box, 506

Internet Mail Service Properties dialog box, 557–559, *558*

Microsoft Mail Connector Properties dialog box, 575, *576*

Site Connector Properties dialog box, 474, *475*

X.400 Connector Properties dialog box, 498, *498*, *499*, 538

Address Type option, Internet Mail Service Properties dialog box, 554

addresses

creating or changing mailbox addresses, 251, *252*

e-mail addresses for distribution lists, 263

entering e-messaging address for custom recipients, 266, *266*

finding in Address Book dialog box, 244

POP3 e-mail addresses, 684

setting type of e-mail address for custom recipients, 265, *266*

Addressing subcontainer in Exchange Administrator, 664, *664*, *665*

administration group

creating, 195, 198–199, *199*

setting permissions for, 217–222, *218*

administration versus management, 228

Administrative Note field, mailbox Properties dialog box, 260

Administrator. *See* Microsoft Exchange Administrator

Administrator's Mailbox option, Internet Mail Service Properties dialog box, 554

Advanced property page

address book view Properties dialog box, 656–659, *658*

Directory Services dialog box, 705–706, *705*

Distribution List Properties dialog box, 264–265, *264*

HTTP Site Settings Properties dialog box, 694, *694*

Internet Mail Service Properties dialog box, 559–560, *559*

mailbox Properties dialog box, 257–260, *257*

public folder Properties dialog box, 526–527, *527*

Public Information Store Properties dialog box, 518, *519*

server Properties dialog boxes, 303–304, *303*

X.400 Connector Properties dialog box, 538–539, *538*

advanced search mode for finding user messages, 621–625, *621*

advanced security, 630–631, 635–643. *See also* security

advanced security tokens, **636**

enabling advanced security for mailboxes, **635–641**

on Exchange clients, 638–641, *638*

on Exchange servers, 635–638, *635*, *636*, *637*

Key Management (KM) Server and, 630–631

recovering security keys, 642–643

revoking, 643

sending and receiving digitally signed and encrypted messages, 642

Age Limits for All Replicas option, public folder Properties dialog box, 310

Age Limits property page, Public Information Store Properties dialog box, 518, *520*

alias names. *See also* naming conventions

for distribution lists, 261

for mailboxes, 114–115, *114*, 232

for public folders, 310

for shared mailboxes, 402

All option, Administrator View menu, 280

Anonymous property page

LDAP (Directory) Site Defaults Properties dialog box, 699–701, *700*

NNTP (News) Site Defaults Properties dialog box, 733–734

Anonymous users, 312

Append option, Backup Information dialog box, 340

Application Design option, Exchange client Tools menu, 417

Application Program Interface (API). *See also* Mail Application Program Interface

Common Mail Call (CMC) APIs, 14

overview of, 14, 747

applications. *See also* Forms Designer

client applications, 66

e-messaging–enable applications, 10, *11*

Exchange application design environment, 747–748

OLE 2.0 applications, 747

shared-file applications, 17–18, *18*

applying changes in Exchange Administrator, 246

architecture, **48–67**. *See also* hierarchy; main entries for specific components

client components, **64–66**

client applications, 66

Exchange clients, 64–65, *64*

forms, 66

Forms Designer, 66

Outlook client, 5, *8*, 65, 360

Schedule+, 5, *6*, 63, 65, 668–669, *669*

connectors, **58–63**

connections within sites versus connections between sites, 60

Dynamic RAS Connector (DRASC), 62

indirect site links and, 59–60, *59*, *61*, 121–122

Internet Mail Service (IMS), 62, 125

Message Transfer Agents and, 52

Microsoft Mail Connector (MMC), 62–63, 125

overview of, 58–60, *59*, *61*

Schedule+ Free/Busy Connector, 63

Site Connector, 61, 123

X.400 Connector, 61, 123–124

core components, **49–55**

directory service (DS), 49–50, *51*, *52*

information stores (ISs), 50–51, *52*, *53*

Message Transfer Agents (MTAs), 50, 52–53, *53*

system attendants (SAs), 54–55, *54*

optional components, **55–63**

Active Server Components (ASCs), 57, 203

Administrator program, 56

Directory Synchronization Agent (DXA), 57, 604–606, *605*

Exchange connectors, **58–63**

gateways, 63

Internet protocol servers, 57–58

Key Management Server, 57

Lightweight Directory Access Protocol (LDAP) servers, 58

Network News Transport Protocol (NNTP) servers, 58

Post Office Protocol (POP3) servers, 58

overview of, 48–49, *48*

archive bits, 334

AS. *See* Active Server

Association Parameters options in MTA Site Configuration Properties dialog box, 450

attachments, 9–10

Attributes property page, DS Site Configuration Properties dialog box, 320, *321*

Authentication property page

LDAP (Directory) Site Defaults Properties dialog box, 699–701, *700*

NNTP (News) Site Defaults Properties dialog box, 733–734

POP3 (Mail) Site Defaults Properties dialog box, 674–675, *675*

Auto Naming property page, Administrator Options dialog box, 232, *233*

automating backups, **349–353**. *See also* Backup utility

creating batch files, 350–351

using NT's Command Scheduler (WINAT), 351–353, *352*, *353*

AutoSignature feature, 416

Available Connections options, Internet Mail Service Properties dialog box, 560–561

B

backup domain controllers in NT Server, 79, 195, 424

Backup utility, **129–130**, **172–177**, **334–355**. *See also* Microsoft Windows NT Server

archive bits and, 334

automating backups, **349–353**

creating batch files, 350–351

using NT's Command Scheduler (WINAT), 351–353, *352*, *353*

Backup Information dialog box, **340–343**

Append option, 340

Backup Set Information options, 341–343, *342*, *343*

Hardware Compression option, 341

Replace option, 340, 343

Restrict Access to Owner or Administrator option, 340–341

Backup Status dialog box, 343–344, *344*, *345*

differential versus incremental backups, **335–337**

Exchange Server backups, **129–130**, **336–345**

backing up Exchange directory, 342, *342*

backing up Exchange servers and components, 129–130, 338–339, *339*

backing up information stores, 342–343, *343*

backing up NT Server drives, 339–340

Exchange Server component backup strategies, 336

Exchange Server transaction logs and, 337

monitoring backup progress, 343–344, *344, 345*

selecting Backup options, 340–343, *341, 342, 343*

installing tape device drivers, 172, *173*

restoring from Exchange Server backups, **345–349**

restoring Exchange directory, 347–348, *347*

restoring information stores, 347–349, *348*

selecting what to restore, 346–347, *346*

setting up, **174–177**, *174, 175, 176*

setting up tape drives, 172

testing backup routines, 340, **354**

types of backups, 335–336

bandwidth of networks, 108–109

basic search mode for finding user messages, 616–620, *617*

batch files for automating backups, 350–351

batch mode Exchange Server installation, 201

Binding Order property page, Setup Program Options dialog box, 372–375, *373*

BIOS chips and detecting RAM beyond 64MB, 150–151

buying hardware, 152, 154

By Message ID option for finding user messages, 622–625, *623, 624*

(

CAST-40 and CAST-64 encryption algorithms, 628

cc:Mail

cc:Mail Connector, **586**

changing cc:Mail site addresses, 236, *237*

Exchange Server and, 28

CD-ROM drives. *See also* hardware

detecting in NT Server installation, 156–157

IDE drives, 127, 156–157

setting up for NT Server installation, 151, 155

testing, 155

changing

applying changes in Exchange Administrator, 246

mailbox addresses, 251, *252*

organization display names, 293–294, *294*

recipient attributes, 280–282, *281, 282*

site addresses, 236, *237*

Character Set Translation options, Internet Mail Service Properties dialog box, 556

Clean Mailbox option, Administrator Tools menu, 286–287, *287*

Client Permissions option, public folder Properties dialog box, 311–312, *311*

client/server system, Exchange Server as a, 17–20, *19*

clients. *See also* Microsoft Exchange clients

NetWare clients, **379–380**

Exchange Server and, 380

routers and, 380

using Service Advertisement Protocol (SAP) Agents, 379–380

setting up NT Server clients, **189–190**

NetWare and other clients, 190

NT Workstation clients, 189, *189*

Windows for Workgroups clients, 190, *190*

setting up Windows 95 clients for NT Server, **181–189**

entering computer and login domain information, 186, *187, 188*

installing network adapter drivers, 183, *183*

installing network protocols, 184, *185*

installing network services, 185–186, *185*

installing Windows client software, 183–184, *184*

overview of, 181–182, *182*

rebooting Windows 95, 189

setting resource-sharing security options, 186, *188*

Clock property page, server monitor Properties dialog box, 276, 434–437, *436, 437*

closing Exchange Administrator windows, 238

CMC (Common Mail Call) APIs, 14

Collapse All option, Exchange client View menu, 412

Columns option

Administrator View menu, 280–282, *281*

Exchange client View menu, 411

Command Scheduler (WINAT) in NT Server, 351–353, *352, 353*

Common Mail Call (CMC) APIs, 14

complete-trust domain model, 85–86, *86*

Components property page, Setup Program Options dialog box, 372, *372*

Compose menu, 417–419. *See also* Microsoft Exchange clients

Forward option, 419

New Form option, 418

New Message option, 418

New Post in This Folder option, 418

overview of, 417, *417*

Post Reply in This Folder option, 419

Reply to Sender and Reply to All options, 418

WordMail Options option, 418

configuring

Eudora Pro 3.0, 685, *686, 687*

protocols containers, 741, *742*

UPS support in NT Server, 170–171, *170*

Confirm Exchange Site and Organization dialog box, 425, *426*

Connect to Server option, Exchange Administrator File menu, 238

Connected Sites property page, X.400 Connector Properties dialog box, 501–503, *501, 502,* 539

connecting

clients to Exchange Server via the Internet, 666–667

to Exchange Server-based POP3 servers, 682–684

legacy systems to Exchange, 134

to multiple Exchange servers in multiserver sites, 429–432, *430, 431*

Connection Parameters options, New MS Mail Connector (PC) MTA Service property page, 577

Connection Retry Values options in MTA Site Configuration Properties dialog box, 449

connections

defined, **122**

determining what is connected to what and how on networks, 108

versus links, **122**

planning connections to other systems, **133–136**

connecting or migrating legacy systems to Exchange, 134

connection options, 133–135

example, 135–136, *136*

Connections property page

Internet Mail Service Properties dialog box, 562–565

Microsoft Mail Connector Properties dialog box, 571–575, *572, 573*

Connector MTAs property page, Microsoft Mail Connector Properties dialog box, **576,** *576,* **579,** *579, 580*

connectors, 58–63. *See also* architecture; Dynamic RAS Connector; Internet Mail Service; Microsoft Mail Connector; Site Connector; X.400 Connector

cc:Mail Connector, **586**

connections within sites versus connections between sites, 60

gateways and, 63, **586–587**

indirect site links and, 59–60, *59, 61,* 121–122

Message Transfer Agents and, 52

overview of, **58–60,** *59, 61*

Schedule+ Free/Busy Connector, 63

Container Name option, mailbox Properties dialog box, 259

containers

Add-Ins container, 663

Addressing subcontainer, 664, *664, 665*

configuring protocols containers, 741, *742*

recipients and, 37–38

recipients containers

creating, **277–278,** *278, 279*

defined, **37–38**

types of, 306

recipients containers Properties dialog box, **277–278,** **306–308**

General property page, 277, *278,* 307, *307*

overview of, 277–278, *279,* 306–307

Permissions property page, 277, 307–308

Control Messages property page, NNTP (News) Site Defaults Properties dialog box, 732, *733*

copying files from CD-ROM disk in NT Server installation, 158–159

Create Connection dialog box, 574–575, *575*

Create Shortcut option, Exchange client File menu, 409

Create Windows NT Account dialog box, 242, *242*

creating

batch files for automating backups, 350–351

custom information fields for mailboxes, 257

custom recipients, **265–267**

entering e-messaging address for, 266, *266*

Properties dialog box, 267, *267*

setting type of e-mail address, 265, *266*

Dirsync systems with Exchange organizations, **601–604**

setting up Dirsync servers on Exchange servers, 601–602, *602*

setting up remote Dirsync requestors, 603, *604*

distribution lists, 260–261, *260*

domain accounts and groups in NT Server, 177–180, *178, 179*

Domain Name Service records for Internet Mail Service, 543–544

emergency repair diskette in NT Server, 160

Exchange Server administration group, 195, 198–199, *199*

folders, 408

forms, **418**, 418, **748–765**

    adding fields, 755–765

    editing fields, 763

    formatting and customizing with Forms Designer, 753–765, *753*

    starting with Form Template Wizard, 750–752, *750*

    starting Forms Designer, 748–749, *749*

information stores, 612–613, *614*

mailbox addresses, 251, *252*

mailboxes, 238, *239*

messages, 390–394, *391, 392, 393*, 413, 418

NT accounts, 241–242, *241, 242*

organization forms libraries, 766–767, *767, 768*

private folders, 408

public folders, 309, 313, 395–400, 408

recipients containers, 277–278, *278, 279*

shared mailboxes, 400–403, *401, 402*

shortcuts, 409

Site Services account, 196, 197–198, *198*

views of Address Book dialog box, 286

cross-domain trust relationships in NT Server, 80–81, *81*, 87, 456–459

Custom Attributes property page

    Distribution List Properties dialog box, 264

    DS Site Configuration Properties dialog box, 318, *319*

    mailbox Properties dialog box, 257

custom recipients. *See also* recipients

    creating, **265–267**

        entering e-messaging address for, 266, *266*

        Properties dialog box, 267, *267*

        setting type of e-mail address, 265, *266*

    defined, **42**

customizing

    Administrator toolbar, 288

    client toolbars, 394, 417

    POP3 server support for mailboxes, 679–681

D

Data Encryption Standard (DES) algorithm, 628

Database Paths property page, server Properties dialog boxes, 300–302, *301*

databases. *See* directory service; information stores

default server in multiserver Exchange sites, 428–429, *429*

Define Views option, Exchange client View menu, 412

Delete option, Exchange client File menu, 409

deleting

    folders, 409

    information stores, 613–614

    mailbox contents, 286–287, *287*

    messages, 409

    NT accounts with mailboxes, 235

Deliver Now option, Exchange client Tools menu, 413

Delivery Options property page, mailbox Properties dialog box, 254–255, *254*

Delivery Restrictions property page

    Distribution List Properties dialog box, 263

    Dynamic RAS Connector Properties dialog box, 506

    mailbox Properties dialog box, 252, *253*

DES (Data Encryption Standard) algorithm, 628

designing. *See also* planning

    Exchange application design environment, 747–748

    Exchange hierarchy, 43–44

    public and private folders, 417

designing Exchange systems, 96–143

    defining site boundaries, **118–121**

        example, 120–121, *120*

        networking domains and, 118, *118*

        and required networking capabilities, 119–120

    evaluating organization networks, **108–110**

        determining network bandwidth, 108–109

        determining what is connected to what and how, 108

        evaluating network's reliability, 109

        example, 109–110, *110*

    evaluating user needs, **97–105**

        example, 100–105

        overview of, 97–98

        questions to ask, 99–100

        upgrading workstations, 103–105

    naming conventions, **111–116**

alias names for mailboxes, 114–115, *114*, 232

display names for mailboxes, 113–114, *113*, 232

example, 115–116

for organizations, sites, and servers, 111–112

for recipient mailboxes, 112, *112*

organization's geographical profile, **105–107**, *105*, *107*

overview of, 96–97

planning connections to other systems, **133–136**

connecting or migrating legacy systems to Exchange, 134

connection options, 133–135

example, 135–136, *136*

planning intersite links, **121–125**

direct versus indirect connections, 59–60, *59*, *61*, 121–122

Dynamic RAS Connector, 62, 124–125

example, 125, *126*

Internet Mail Service, 62, 125

Microsoft Mail Connector, 62–63, 125

Site Connector, 61, 123

site link options, 121–123, *122*

X.400 Connector, 61, 123–124

planning servers and user links, **125–133**

backing up Exchange servers, 129–130

designing Exchange servers, 126–129

example, 131–133

fault tolerance and, 128

IDE versus SCSI-2 disk drives, 127

networking users, 130–131

rolling out the plan, **139–143**

defined, **139**

example, 140–143

overview of, 139–140

selecting a networking domain model, **116–117**, *117*

validating and optimizing design, **136–139**

defined, **136**

example, 138–139

guaranteeing message delivery, 137

message integrity, 137

message security, 137–138

optimization, 136, 138

system versatility, 138

detecting. *See also* finding

DHCP servers in NT Server installation, 162

existing software and hardware in NT Server installation, 157–158

hard disk and CD-ROM drives in NT Server installation, 156–157

RAM beyond 64MB, 150–151

determining

network bandwidth, 108–109

what is connected to what and how in organization networks, 108

device drivers, installing network adapter drivers for Windows 95 NT clients, 183, *183*

DHCP (Dynamic Host Configuration Protocol) servers in NT Server, 162

Diagnostics Logging property page, server Properties dialog boxes, 304–305, *305*

Dial Using option, Internet Mail Service Properties dialog box, 564

Dial-Up Connections property page, Internet Mail Service Properties dialog box, **560–562**

differential backups, 335–337

digital signatures, 57, 626–628

directories. *See also* Microsoft Exchange directory

system attendants and, 54

Directory Export dialog box, 653, *654*

Directory Import dialog box, 646–649, *647*

Directory Name field, mailbox Properties dialog box, 258

directory replication, 50, 295, 336, 370

multiserver sites and, 428

server-level directory service administration and, 446

setting up between sites, **479–486**, 507

cross-site public folder access and, 509

guidelines, **507**

setting up in the first site, 479–481

setting up in the second site, 481

testing the setup, 482–486, *482*

Directory Replication Connector dialog box, 479–486

General property page, 480, *480*

Schedule property page, 481, *481*

Sites property page, 484, *485*

directory service (DS). *See also* Microsoft Exchange directory

administration and management, **313–321**

overview of, 313–314, *315*

server-level administration and management, 320

server-level administration and management in multiserver sites, 445–446, *446*

site-level administration and management, 315–320

Directory Service Properties dialog box, 445–446, *446*

Directory Services dialog box, **703–707**

    Advanced property page, 705–706, *705*

    General property page, 704–705, *704*

    Options property page, 706, *706, 707*

DS Site Configuration Properties dialog box, **315–320**

    Attributes property page, 320, *321*

    Custom Attributes property page, 318, *319*

    General property page, 316, *316*

    Offline Address Book property page, 317, *318*

    Offline Address Book Schedule property page, 316–317

    overview of, 315–316

directory synchronization

    defined, **50**

    Directory Synchronization Agents (DXAs), 57, 604–606, *605*

    for Microsoft Mail for AppleTalk Networks, 590

directory synchronization with MS Mail PC systems, 590–606

    adding Exchange systems to Dirsync systems, **592–601**

        Dirsync server settings, 598–599, *599*

        eliminating MS Mail SMTP gateways, 595

        setting up Dirsync requestors on Exchange servers, 592–598, *593*

        testing the setup, 600–601, *600*

    creating Dirsync systems with Exchange organizations, **601–604**

        setting up Dirsync servers on Exchange servers, 601–602, *602*

        setting up remote Dirsync requestors, 603, *604*

    Directory Synchronization Agents (DXAs) and, 604–606, *605*

    Dirsync program

        defined, **590**

        Dirsync requestors versus servers, 590–591

        server settings, 598–599, *599*

    Dirsync requestor Properties dialog box, **592–598**

        Export Containers property page, 596–597, *596*

        General property page, 592–593, *593*

        Import Container property page, 594–595, *594, 595*

        overview of, 592

        Schedule property page, 598, *599*

        Settings property page, 597–598, *597*

    Dirsync Server Properties dialog box, 601–602, *602*

Disk Administrator applet in NT Server, 166–168, *166, 167, 168*

disk drives. *See* hard disk drives

disk duplexing, 72

disk mirroring, 72

disk striping with parity, 72

display adapters, setting up for NT Server installation, 151

display names. *See also* naming conventions

    for distribution lists, 261

    for mailboxes, 113–114, *113*, 232

    for organizations, 293–294, *294*

    for public folders in Address Book, 310

    for shared mailboxes, 402

displaying

    folders in Exchange clients, 411

    groups of messages, 412

    public folders, 309, 313, 400

    status bar in Exchange clients, 411

    toolbars in Exchange clients, 411

Distribution List Properties dialog box, 260–265. *See also* Microsoft Exchange Administrator

    Advanced property page, 264–265, *264*

    Custom Attributes property page, 264

    Delivery Restrictions property page, 263

    Display name and Alias name options, 261

    Distribution Lists property page, 262, *263*

    E-Mail Addresses property page, 263

    Expansion Server option, 261

    General property page, *260*, **261–262**

    including distribution lists in other distribution lists, 262, *263*

    Message Size Limit option, 265

    Notes field, 261

    overview of, 260–261

    Owner field, 261

    Permissions property page, 262

    restricting who can send messages to distribution lists, 263

    selecting members of distribution lists, 262

distribution lists. *See also* recipients

    adding mailboxes to, 250, *250, 251*

    creating, **260–261**, *260*

    display names and alias names for, 261

    including other distribution lists in, 262, *263*

recipients and, 42

restricting who can send messages to, 263

Distribution Lists property page, mailbox Properties dialog
box, 250, *250, 251*

DMA channels for network adapters, 153

Domain Name Service (DNS), 542–544, 548, *548*

domains in NT Server, 77–87

and defining site boundaries, 118, *118*

domain controllers, **79**, 163, 195, 424

domain models, **82–86, 116–117**

complete-trust domain model, 85–86, *86*

Exchange Server installation and, 194

master-domain model, 83–84, *83*

multiple-master-domain model, 84, *85*

selecting, 116–117, *117*

single-domain model, 82–83, *82*

granting domain access, **163, 177–181**

creating domain accounts and groups, 177–180, *178,
179*

granting access to servers and workstations, 163,
180–181, *180, 181*

installing NT servers in domains, **456–463**

installing the NT server, 456

setting cross-domain permissions, 460–463, *460, 462,
463*

setting up trust relationships, 456–459

overview of, **77–80**, *80*

setting up during NT Server installation, 163

trust relationships, **80–81**, *81*, 87, 456–459

DRASC. *See* Dynamic RAS Connector

drivers, installing network adapter drivers for Windows 95
NT clients, 183, *183*

drives. *See* hard disk drives

DS. *See* directory service

duplexing disks, 72

Duplicate option, Exchange Administrator File menu, 279

DXAs (Directory Synchronization Agents), 57, 604–606, *605*

Dynamic Host Configuration Protocol (DHCP) servers in NT
Server, 162

Dynamic RAS Connector (DRASC), 62, 124–125

Dynamic RAS Connector Properties dialog box, 503–507

Address Space property page, 506

Delivery Restrictions property page, 506

General property page, 503–505, *504*

RAS Override property page, 505–506

Schedule property page, 505, *505*

E

Edit menu

in Exchange Administrator, 279

in Exchange clients, 410, *410*

editing address book views, 62–63

EFD. *See* Forms Designer

.EFP files, 753

electronic forms. *See* forms

e-mail. *See also* mailboxes; messages

attachments, **9–10**

e-mail address generators, 664

e-mail addresses for distribution lists, 263

moving to public or private folders in Exchange clients,
22–23

POP3 e-mail addresses, 684

E-mail Addresses property page, mailbox Properties dialog
box, 251, *252*

E-mail Domain option, Internet Mail Service Properties
dialog box, 556, *557*, 564, *564*

emergency repair diskette in NT Server, 160

e-messaging. *See also* mailboxes; messages

defined, **4**

e-messaging-enable applications, 10, *11*

Exchange hierarchy and e-messaging addresses, 43–44,
44

Exchange Server and, 4–5

system attendants and e-messaging addresses, 55

Enable Message Tracking option, Internet Mail Service
Properties dialog box, 557

enabling advanced security for mailboxes, 635–643. *See also*
advanced security

on Exchange clients, 638–641, *638*

on Exchange servers, 635–638, *635, 636, 637*

recovering security keys, 642–643

revoking advanced security, 643

sending and receiving digitally signed and encrypted
messages, 642

encryption. *See* advanced security; Key Management (KM)
Server

entering

e-messaging address for custom recipients, 266, *266*

information about recipients managed by mailbox users,
244–246, *245*

mailbox user's manager information, 243, *243*

Escalation Editor dialog box, 271–273, *272*, 440, *440*

Eudora Pro 3.0

    configuring, 685, *686, 687*

    overview of, 5, *7*

evaluating

    organization networks, **108–110**

        determining network bandwidth, 108–109

        determining what is connected to what and how, 108

        evaluating network's reliability, 109

        example, 109–110, *110*

    user needs, **97–105**

        example, 100–105

        overview of, 97–98

        questions to ask, 99–100

        upgrading workstations, 103–105

Event Viewer in NT Server, 91–92, *92*

Exchange. *See* Microsoft Exchange

Exchange Forms Designer. *See* Forms Designer

Exit and Exit and Log Off options, in Exchange client File menu, 410

exiting NT Server, 169

Expand All option, Exchange client View menu, 412

Expansion Server option, Distribution List Properties dialog box, 261

Export Containers property page, Dirsync requestor Properties dialog box, 596–597, *596*

exporting directory information, 651–654. *See also* migrating

    directory export file structure, 652–653

    exporting directories, 653–654, *654*

    selecting fields, 654

    uses for, 652

Extended Mail Application Program Interface (MAPI), 14

extracting information for Exchange directory, 649–651. *See also* migrating

    extracting NetWare account lists, 650–651, *650*

    extracting Windows NT account lists, 649–650, *650*

F

FAT (File Allocation Table) file system, 158, 166–168, *166, 167, 168*

fault tolerance, and planning servers, 128

Favorites folder, adding to, 408

File menu

    in Exchange Administrator, **237–289**

        Close option, 238

        Connect to Server option, 238

        Duplicate option, 279

        New Custom Recipient option, 265

        New Distribution List option, 260–261, *260*

        New Mailbox option, 238

        New Other submenu, 267–268, *268*, 470, 494

        overview of, 237, *237*

        Properties option, 278

        Raw Properties option, 288–289

    in Exchange clients, **408–410**

        Add to Favorites option, 408

        Create Shortcut option, 409

        Delete option, 409

        Exit and Exit and Log Off options, 410

        Import option, 410

        New Discussion Folder option, 408

        New Folder option, 408

        overview of, 408, *408*

        Properties option, 409

        Rename option, 409

file name extensions, .EFP, 753

Filter option, Exchange client View menu, 411

filtering messages in folders, 411

Find Items option, Exchange client Tools menu, 416

Find Public Folders option, Exchange client Tools menu, 416

Find Recipients option, Administrator Tools menu, 285, *285*

Finder utility, 23

finding. *See also* detecting

    addresses in Address Book dialog box, 244

    matching NT accounts when creating mailboxes, 235–236, 242

    messages, 416

    public folders, 416

    recipients, 285, *285*

    system messages, 625, *626*

    user messages, **616–625**

        advanced search mode, 621–625, *621*

        basic search mode, 616–620, *617*

        By Message ID option, 622–625, *623, 624*

        Transfer Into This Site option, 621–622, *622*

Fixed-width Font option, Internet Mail Service Properties dialog box, 556

Folder and Address Book Display Name options, public folder Properties dialog box, 310

Folder Path option, public folder Properties dialog box, 313

Folder Replication Status property page
    public folder Properties dialog box, 526, *526*
    Public Information Store Properties dialog box, 520, *521*

Folder Shortcuts property page, HTTP Site Settings Properties dialog box, 691, *692, 693*

folders. *See also* public folders
    adding to Favorites folder, 408
    creating, 408
    deleting, 409
    displaying in Exchange clients, 411
    filtering messages in, 411
    folder views in Exchange clients, 412
    folder-level administration and management of cross-site public folder replication, 526–527, *526, 527*
    importing, 410
    offline folders, **413–415,** *414*
    personal folders
        overview of, 21–22
        versus private information stores, 41
    private folders, **15–16, 41**
        creating, 408
        defined, **15, 41**
        designing, 417
        in Exchange clients, rules for moving mail to, 22–23
        sorting, 15
        sorting and organizing messages in, 411
    renaming, 409
    synchronizing online and offline folders in Exchange clients, **413–415,** *414*

Font option, Administrator View menu, 283

Forms Designer (EFD), 66, 746–773
    creating forms, **418, 748–765**
        adding fields, 755–765
        editing fields, 763
        formatting and customizing with Forms Designer, 753–765, *753*
        starting with Form Template Wizard, 750–752, *750*
        starting Forms Designer, 748–749, *749*
    defined, **66**

Exchange application design environment and, 747–748

forms
    creating organization forms libraries, 766–767, *767, 768*
    installing, **766, 768–770,** *769*
    overview of, 13, *14,* 66
    personal forms libraries, 766
    saving, 753
    Send versus Post forms, 750, *750,* 766
    using, 770, *770, 771, 772*
    installing, 748
    toolbar, 753–755, *753, 755*
    uses for, 746–747, 773

forwarding messages, 419

Free/Busy Connector in Schedule+, 63

G

GALs. *See* Global Address Lists

gateways, 63, **586–587.** *See also* connectors
    eliminating MS Mail SMTP gateways, 595

General property page
    address book view Properties dialog box, 656, 661
    Directory Replication Connector dialog box, 480, *480*
    Directory Services dialog box, 704–705, *704*
    Dirsync requestor Properties dialog box, 592–593, *593*
    Distribution List Properties dialog box, 260, **261–262**
    DS Site Configuration Properties dialog box, 316, *316*
    Dynamic RAS Connector Properties dialog box, 503–505, *504*
    HTTP Site Settings Properties dialog box, 690–691, *690*
    Information Store Site Configuration Properties dialog box, 322, *323*
    Internet Mail Service Properties dialog box, 557, *558*
    LDAP (Directory) Site Defaults Properties dialog box, 699, *699*
    mailbox Properties dialog box, 239–242, *240*
    Message Transfer Agent Properties dialog box, 451–452
    Microsoft Mail Connector Properties dialog box, 571, *572*
    MTA Site Configuration Properties dialog box, 446
    NNTP (News) Site Defaults Properties dialog box, *726,* 727

organization Properties dialog box, 293–294, *294*

POP3 (Mail) Site Defaults Properties dialog box, 673, *674*

Private Information Store Properties dialog box, *326*, 327

public folder Properties dialog box, *309*, 310–313, 522, *523*

Public Information Store Properties dialog box, 514, *514*

recipients container Properties dialog box, 277

recipients containers Properties dialog box, 277, *278*, 307, *307*

server monitor Properties dialog box, 269–270, *269*

server Properties dialog boxes, 297, 298, *299*

Setup Program Options dialog box, 371, *371*

Site Addressing Properties dialog box, 528–529, *529*

Site Connector Properties dialog box, 472–473, *472*, 476–477, *477*

site Properties dialog box, 296, *296*

User Options dialog box, 365–366, *365*

X.400 Connector Properties dialog box, 495–496, *495*, 536, *537*, 537, 539, *540*

geographical profiles of organizations, 105–107, *105*, *107*

Global Address Lists (GALs)

addressing messages, 392, *392*

defined, **38**, **306**

displaying public folders in, 400

hiding shared mailboxes from, 406

granting

domain access in NT Server, **163**, **177–181**

creating domain accounts and groups, 177–180, *178*, *179*

granting access to servers and workstations, 163, 180–181, *180*, *181*

NT accounts or groups rights to mailboxes, 241–242, *241*, *242*, 248–249

other recipients access to a mailbox, 254–255, *254*

Group By option, Exchange client View menu, 411

Group By property page, address book view Properties dialog box, 656, *658*, 661, *662*

groups in NT Server, 177–180, *178*, *179*

H

hard disk drives

backing up NT Server drives, 339–340

detecting in NT Server installation, 156–157

IDE disk drives, 127, 156–157

partitions, setting up FAT or NTFS partitions in NT Server installation, 158, 166–168, *166*, *167*, *168*

SCSI-2 disk drives, 127, 156

setting up for NT Server installation, 154–155

testing, 154–155

hardware. *See also* CD-ROM drives; network adapters

NT Server Hardware Compatibility List (HCL), 152

purchasing, 152, 154

setting up server hardware for NT Server installation, **149–155**

CD-ROM drives, 151, 155

hard disk drives, 154–155

Hardware Compatibility List (HCL) and, 152

hardware requirements, 150–151

monitors and display adapters, 151

mouse, 152

network adapters, 152–153, 155

peripheral controllers, 151

purchasing hardware, 152, 154

RAM, 150–151, 154

SCSI-2 controllers, 151, 153, 155

serial ports, 152

testing for NT Server installation, **153–155**

CD-ROM drives, 155

hard disk drives, 154–155

memory, 154

network adapters, 155

Hardware Compression option, Backup Information dialog box, 341

hidden public folders, 309, 313

Hidden Recipients option, Administrator View menu, 280

Hide from Address Book option, mailbox Properties dialog box, 259

hiding

groups of messages, 412

recipients, 42

shared mailboxes from Address Book, 406, *407*

hierarchy, 32–45. *See also* architecture

conceptual view of, 32–33, *33*

designing, **43–44**

e-messaging addresses and, 43–44, *44*

Exchange management and, 43

Exchange Server object-orientation and, 32–33, *33*

organizations, **32**, **34**

recipients, **32**, **36–42**

    containers and, 37–38

    custom recipients, 42

    defined, **32**

    distribution lists, 42

    Global Address Lists and, 38

    hiding, 42

    mailbox agents, 37

    mailboxes, 38, 39–40, *40*, *41*

    overview of, 36–39, *37*, *39*

    public folders and, 38, 42

    site-level recipients containers, 37–38

servers, **32**, **35–36**, *36*

sites, **32**, **34**, *35*

Home Server field, mailbox Properties dialog box, 258

Home Server property page, User Options dialog box, 368–370, *369*

HTML (Hypertext Markup Language), 689

HTTP (HyperText Transport Protocol), 689–697

    client-side setup, **694–695**, *695*, *696*, *697*

    defined, **255**

    HTTP Site Settings Properties dialog box, **690–694**

        Advanced property page, 694, *694*

        Folder Shortcuts property page, 691, *692*, *693*

        General property page, 690–691, *690*

    server-side setup, **690–694**

        mailbox-level HTTP setup, 694

        site-level HTTP setup, 690–694

I

I/O addresses for network adapters, 153

IDE disk drives, 127, 156–157

Idle Time-out property page

    NNTP (News) Site Defaults Properties dialog box, 733–734

    POP3 (Mail) Site Defaults Properties dialog box, 677

IIS (Internet Information Server), 161, 164, 165, 195

IMAP4 (Internet Message Access Protocol version 4), 672

IMC. *See* Internet Mail Service (IMS)

Import Container property page, Dirsync requestor Properties dialog box, 594–595, *594*, *595*

Import option, Exchange client File menu, 410

importing. *See also* migrating

    information into Exchange directory, **645–649**

        import file structure, 645–646

        importing directory information, 646–649, *647*, *648*

    messages, folders, and address lists, 410

IMS. *See* Internet Mail Service

Inbox Assistant in Exchange clients, 415

incremental backups, 335–337

indirect site links

    connectors and, **59–60**, *59*, *61*, **121–122**

    setting up with X.400 Connector, 539–541, *540*

information stores (ISs)

    administration and management, **313–314**, **321–330**

        overview of, 313–314, *315*, 321–322

        server-level administration and management for private information stores, 325–329, *326*

        server-level administration and management for public information stores, 329–330, *330*

        site-level administration and management, 322–325, *323*

    backing up, **342–343**, *343*

    creating, **612–613**, *614*

    defined, **50–51**, *52*, *53*

    deleting, **613–614**

    Information Store Site Configuration Properties dialog box, **322–325**

        General property page, 322, *323*

        Public Folder Affinity property page, 325

        Storage Warnings property page, 325

        Top-Level Folder Creation property page, 323–324, *324*

    Information Store Storage Limits options in mailbox Properties dialog box, 259

    IS Maintenance property page in server Properties dialog boxes, 302, *302*

    New Information Store dialog box, 613, *614*

    Private Information Store Properties dialog box, **325–329**

        General property page, *326*, 327

        Logons property page, 327–328, *328*

        Mailbox Resources property page, 329, *329*

        overview of, 325–327, *326*

    private information stores

        defined, **21–22**

        mailboxes and, 39, 41

        versus personal folders, 41

server-level administration and management, 325–329, *326*

Public Information Store Properties dialog box, **329–330**, **514–522**

   Advanced property page, 518, *519*

   Age Limits property page, 518, *520*

   Folder Replication Status property page, 520, *521*

   General property page, 514, *514*

   Instances property page, 514–516, *515*, *517*

   Logons property page, 522

   overview of, 329–330, *330*

   Replication Schedule property page, 518, *519*

   Server Replication Status property page, 520, *521*

public information store server-level administration and management, 329–330, *330*

restoring, **347–349**, *348*

inherited permissions in NT accounts, 247–248, *247*

installing

   Active Server Components, 203

   Exchange Administrator, 217

   forms, 766, 768–770, *769*

   Forms Designer, 748

   Internet Mail Service, 204, 544–552, *545*

   Key Management (KM) Server, 628–630, *629*

   Microsoft Mail Connector, 570

   NT servers in domains, **456–463**

      installing the NT server, 456

      setting cross-domain permissions, 460–463, *460*, *462*, *463*

      setting up trust relationships, 456–459

   servers in sites, 424–428, *425*, *426*, *427*, 463–464, *464*

installing Exchange clients, **360–381**. *See also* Microsoft Exchange clients

installing Outlook clients, 360

installing Windows client software in network share mode, **374**

installing Windows client software on servers, **360–375**

   overview of, 360–361, *361*, *362*

   preparing client software for installation, 362–363, *363*

   selecting client installation point, 360, 364, *364*

   Setup program options, 370–375

   user options, 364–370

installing Windows client software on workstations, **375–378**, *376*, *377*, *378*

NetWare clients, **379–380**

   Exchange Server and, 380

   routers and, 380

   using Service Advertisement Protocol (SAP) Agents, 379–380

Setup Program Options dialog box, **370–375**

   Binding Order property page, 372–375, *373*

   Components property page, 372, *372*

   General property page, 371, *371*

   overview of, 370–371

   Services property page, 372, *373*

User Options dialog box, **364–370**

   General property page, 365–366, *365*

   Home Server property page, 368–370, *369*

   overview of, 364–365, *365*

   Read property page, 366–367, *367*

   Send property page, 367–368, *368*

   Spelling property page, 368, *369*

installing Exchange Server, 194–222

   postinstallation activities, **210–222**

      accessing Exchange Server program group, 211–212, *211*, *212*

      setting permissions for Exchange Server administrator group, 217–222, *218*

      starting Exchange Administrator, 214–217, *215*, *216*

      testing Exchange Server installation, 213–214, *213*

      troubleshooting Exchange Server problems, 214

   preparing for, **194–199**

      creating Exchange Server Administration group, 195, 198–199, *199*

      creating Site Services account, 196, 197–198, *198*

      gathering account information, 195–196

      gathering Exchange Server information, 196–197

      gathering NT Server information, 194–195

      installation path name, 196

      NT server computer name, 195

      NT Server domain model and, 194

      NT server roles and, 195

      security setup, 197–199

      selecting Exchange Server components for installation, 197

      testing server hardware setup, 194

   running Setup program, **199–210**

      batch mode installation, 201

entering organization and site names, 196, 205, *205*

entering Site Services account name and password, 196, 205–206, *206*

Exchange Server Performance Optimizer Wizard, 206–210, *207*, 212

file installation and system setup, 206–210, *207*

installing Active Server Components, 203

overview of, 199–200, *200*

selecting installation options, 200–204, *201, 202, 203*

selecting licensing mode, 204, *204*

installing NT Server, 73, 148–191

granting domain access, **163, 177–181**

creating domain accounts and groups, 177–180, *178, 179*

granting access to servers and workstations, 163, 180–181, *180, 181*

installing NT Server software, **155–164**

completing the installation, **164–169**

copying files from CD-ROM disk, 158–159

creating emergency repair diskette, 160

detecting DHCP servers, 162

detecting existing software and hardware, 157–158

detecting hard disk and CD-ROM drives, 156–157

domain setup, 163

the installation process, 162–163

installing Internet Information Server, 161, 164, 165

installing network adapters, 161

installing NT Server networking, 160–161

installing Service Packs, 149, 164–165

naming NT server, 160

ownership and licensing, 157, 159

selecting components for installation, 160

selecting networking protocols, 161–162

setting up FAT or NTFS disk partitions, 158, 166–168, *166, 167, 168*

Setup program's Installation Wizard, **159–163**

starting the installation, 156

installing uninterruptible power supplies, **169–171**

configuring UPS support, 170–171, *170*

selecting UPSs, 169–170, 171

serial ports and, 152

testing the UPS, 171

UPS defined, **169**

overview of, 73, 148–149

setting up clients, **189–190**. *See also* Windows 95 clients

NetWare and other clients, 190

NT Workstation clients, 189, *189*

Windows for Workgroups clients, 190, *190*

setting up NT Backup, **172–177**

Backup setup, 174–177, *174, 175, 176*

installing tape device drivers, 172, *173*

tape drive setup, 172

setting up server hardware, **149–155**

CD-ROM drives, 151, 155

hard disk drives, 154–155

Hardware Compatibility List (HCL) and, 152

hardware requirements, 150–151

monitors and display adapters, 151

mouse, 152

network adapters, 152–153, 155

peripheral controllers, 151

purchasing hardware, 152, 154

RAM, 150–151, 154

SCSI-2 controllers, 151, 153, 155

serial ports, 152

testing components, 153–155

setting up Windows 95 clients, **181–189**

entering computer and login domain information, 186, *187, 188*

installing network adapter drivers, 183, *183*

installing network protocols, 184, *185*

installing network services, 185–186, *185*

installing Windows client software, 183–184, *184*

overview of, 181–182, *182*

rebooting Windows 95, 189

setting resource-sharing security options, 186, *188*

Instances property page, Public Information Store Properties dialog box, 514–516, *515, 517*

Interchange property page, Microsoft Mail Connector Properties dialog box, **570–571**, *571*

Internet, connecting clients to Exchange Server via, **666–667**

Internet Information Server (IIS), 161, 164, 165, 195

Internet Mail Service (IMS), 541–569

installing, 204, 544–552, *545*

overview of, 62, 125, 541

setting up site links with, 568–569

TCP/IP protocol and, **542–544**

creating key DNS records for Exchange, 543–544

setting up TCP/IP protocol, 542–543

testing, 568, 569

Internet Mail Service Properties dialog box, 34, 553–568
   Address Space property page, **557–559**, *558*
   Advanced property page, **559–560**, *559*
   Connections property page, **562–565**
      Accept or Reject by Host options, 564
      Dial Using option, 564
      E-mail Domain option, 564, *564*
      Message Delivery options, 563
      overview of, 562, *562*
      Retry Interval option, 564–565, *565*
      Transfer Mode options, 562–563, *563*
   Dial-Up Connections property page, **560–562**
      Available Connections options, 560–561
      Logon Information option, 561
      overview of, 560, *560*
      Retrieving Mail option, 561
      Schedule option, 561–562
   General property page, **557**, *558*
   Internet Mail property page, **553–557**
      Address Type option, 554
      Administrator's Mailbox option, 554
      Character Set Translation options, 556
      E-mail Domain option, 556, *557*
      Enable Message Tracking option, 557
      Fixed-width Font option, 556
      Interoperability options, 555–556
      Notifications option, 554, *554*
      overview of, 553, *553*
      rich text formatting option, 556
      Send Attachments Using options, 554–555
      word-wrap option, 556
   overview of, 34, *35*
   Queues property page, **565**
   Routing property page, **566**, *567*
   Security property page, **566**, *567*
Internet Message Access Protocol version 4 (IMAP4), 672
Internet protocol servers, 57–58
Internet-enabled public folders, 15, *16*
Interoperability options, Internet Mail Service Properties
   dialog box, 555–556
interrupt requests (IRQs) for network adapters, 153
IPX/SPX protocol, installing, 161, 184
IRQs (interrupt requests) for network adapters, 153

IS Maintenance property page, server Properties dialog
   boxes, 302, *302*
ISA network adapters, 152

K

Key Management (KM) Server, 57, 626–636. *See also*
   advanced security
   advanced security and, 630–631
   defined, **57**
   installing, **628–630**, *629*
   overview of, 626–628
   passwords for, 633–636, *634*
   security settings for, 633–634, *634*
   setting encryption algorithms, 632–633, *632*

L

LDAP (Lightweight Directory Access Protocol), 58, 255,
   698–711. *See also* protocols
   client-side setup, **702–707**
   Directory Services dialog box, **703–707**
      Advanced property page, 705–706, *705*
      General property page, 704–705, *704*
      Options property page, 706, *706, 707*
   LDAP (Directory) Site Defaults Properties dialog box,
      698–702
      Anonymous property page, 699–701, *700*
      Authentication property page, 699–701, *700*
      General property page, 699, *699*
      Search property page, 701–702, *702*
   LDAP servers, 58
   overview of, 255, 698
   server-side setup, **698–702**
      server-level setup, 702
      site-level setup, 698–702
   testing, **707–711**
      with LDAP-aware POP3 clients, 710, *710, 711*
      Windows Address Book, 707–710, *707, 708, 709*
      Windows Address Book setup, 702–707
legacy systems, connecting or migrating to Exchange, 134

licensing

in NT Server installation, 157, 159

selecting Exchange Server licensing mode, 204, *204*

link monitors. *See also* server monitors

adding servers to, 508, *509*

defined, **438**

Properties dialog box, **438–444**

Bounce property page, 442–443, *443*

General property page, 438–439, *438*

Notification property page, 439–440, *439*, *441*

Recipients property page, 440, *441*

Servers property page, 440, *441*

links. *See also* multisite Exchange organizations

attachment links, **10**

versus connections, **122**

defined, **122**

planning intersite links, **121–125**

direct versus indirect connections, 59–60, *59*, *61*, 121–122

Dynamic RAS Connector, 62, 124–125

example, 125, *126*

Internet Mail Service, 62, 125

Microsoft Mail Connector, 62–63, 125

Site Connector, 61, 123

site link options, 121–123, *122*

X.400 Connector, 61, 123–124

setting up site links with Internet Mail Service, 568–569

setting up site-to-site links, **470–479**

setting up the first site, 470–476

setting up the second site, 476–478

testing connections, 478, *479*

setting up site-to-site links with Dynamic RAS Connector, **503–507**

Address Space property page, 506

Delivery Restrictions property page, 506

General property page, 503–505, *504*

RAS Override property page, 505–506

Schedule property page, 505, *505*

setting up site-to-site links with X.400 Connector, **494–503**

Address Space property page, 498, *498*, *499*

Connected Sites property page, 501–503, *501*, *502*

General property page, 495–496, *495*

Override property page, 500, *500*

Schedule property page, 496–497, *496*

Stack property page, 497, *497*

LoadSim utility, 99, 101, 105, 126–127

Local Postoffice property page, Microsoft Mail Connector Properties dialog box, **581**, *581*

Locales property page, server Properties dialog boxes, 299, *300*

Logon Information option, Internet Mail Service Properties dialog box, 561

Logons property page

Private Information Store Properties dialog box, 327–328, *328*

Public Information Store Properties dialog box, 522

logs

Log Messages option in New MS Mail Connector (PC) MTA Service property page, 576, *577*

transaction logs, 337

M

Mail Application Program Interface (MAPI). *See also* Application Program Interface; e-mail; e-messaging; Microsoft Mail

overview of, 14

Simple and Extended versions, 14

mailbox agents, 37

Mailbox Resources property page, Private Information Store Properties dialog box, 329, *329*

mailboxes. *See also* e-mail; e-messaging; messages; Microsoft Exchange clients

adding phone numbers and notes for mailbox users, 246, *246*

adding to distribution lists, 250, *250*, *251*

alias names for, 114–115, *114*, 232

cleaning, 286–287, *287*

creating, **238**, *239*

finding matching NT accounts when creating mailboxes, 235–236, 242

creating or changing mailbox addresses, 251, *252*

customizing POP3 server support for, 679–681

defined, **38**, **39–40**, *40*, *41*

deleting contents of, 286–287, *287*

deleting NT accounts when deleting, 235

display names for, 113–114, *113*, 232

enabling advanced security for mailboxes, **635–641**

on Exchange clients, 638–641, *638*

on Exchange servers, 635–638, *635, 636, 637*

entering information about recipients managed by mailbox users, 244–246, *245*

entering mailbox user's manager information, 243, *243*

granting NT accounts or groups rights to mailboxes, 241–242, *241, 242*, 248–249

granting other recipients access to a mailbox, 254–255, *254*

HTTP (HyperText Transport Protocol) mailbox-level setup, 694

Mailbox Owner permission, 249

Modify Admin Attributes permission, 249

Modify Permissions permission, 249

Modify User Attributes permission, 249

moving, 286, 615, *615*

moving between sites, 655

naming recipient mailboxes, 112, *112*

NNTP (Network News Transport Protocol) mailbox-level administration and management, 735, *735*

overview of, 21–22

Properties dialog box, **238–260, 635–638**

Add User or Group dialog box, 241–242, *241*

Advanced property page, **257–260**, *257*

Create Windows NT Account dialog box, 242, *242*

creating custom information fields, 257

Custom Attributes property page, **257**

Delivery Options property page, **254–255**, *254*

Delivery Restrictions property page, **252**, *253*

Distribution Lists property page, **250**, *250, 251*

E-mail Addresses property page, **251**, *252*

entering general information, 239, *240*

entering information about recipients managed by mailbox users, 244–246, *245*

entering mailbox user's manager information, 243–244, *243*

General property page, **239–242**, *240*

NT accounts with inherited permissions, 247–248, *247*

Organization property page, **243–246**

overview of, 238, *239*

Permissions property page, **247–249**, *247*

Phone/Notes property page, **246**, *246*

Primary Windows NT Account dialog box, 241, *241*

Protocols property page, **255–256**, *256*, 679, *680*

restricting who can send messages to mailboxes, 252, 253

Security property page, 635–638, *635, 636, 637,* 640–643, *641*

Send On Behalf Of permissions, 254–255, *254*

reconfiguring existing mailboxes, 259

roles for accounts with permissions on, **248–249**

Send As permission, 249, 255

shared mailboxes, **400–407**

accessing, 403–405, *403, 404, 405*

creating, 400–403, *401, 402*

display names and aliases, 402

hiding from Address Book, 406, *407*

permissions for, 405

sending messages to, 406

management versus administration, 228

MAPI. *See* Mail Application Program Interface

marking messages as read or unread, 410

master-domain model, 83–84, *83*

members, selecting for distribution lists, 262

memory

detecting more than 64MB, 150–151

setting up for NT Server installation, 150–151, 154

testing, 154

menus, pop-up menus, 409

Message Delivery options, Internet Mail Service Properties dialog box, 563

Message Format property page

NNTP (News) Site Defaults Properties dialog box, 733–734

POP3 (Mail) Site Defaults Properties dialog box, 675–677, *676*

Message Size Limit option, Distribution List Properties dialog box, 265

Message Sizes field, mailbox Properties dialog box, 258

Message Transfer Agents (MTAs)

administration and management, **313–314**, *315*

Connector MTAs property page in Microsoft Mail Connector Properties dialog box, **576**, *576,* **579**, *579, 580*

connectors and, 52

defined, **50, 52–53**, *53*

Message Transfer Agent Properties dialog box, **450–452**

General property page, 451–452

overview of, 450, *451*

Queues property page, 452, *453*

MTA Site Configuration Properties dialog box, **447–450**

    General property page, 446

    Messaging Defaults property page, 447–450, *448*

New MS Mail Connector (PC) MTA Service property page, **576–579**

    Connection Parameters options, 577

    Log Messages option, 576, *577*

    Options option, 578–579, *578*

    Polling Frequency options, 577

server-level administration and management in multi-server Exchange sites, 450–453, *451*

setting up MTA transport stacks, **489–494**

    overview of, 489–490

    setting up RAS MTA transport stacks, 492–494, *493*

    setting up TCP/IP transport stacks, 490–491, *490*, *491*, *492*

setting up RAS MTA transport stacks, 492–494, *493*

site-level administration and management in multiserver Exchange sites, 447–450, *448*

starting Microsoft Mail Connector MTA service, 581–582, *582*

TCP/IP MTA transport stacks, 490–491, *490*, *491*, *492*

X.400 Connector and MTA stacks, 536

messages, 390–395. *See also* e-mail; e-messaging; mailboxes

accessing remotely, 415

AutoSignature feature, 416

composing and sending, **390–394**, *391*, *392*, *393*, 413, 418

deleting, **409**

filtering in folders, 411

finding, **416**

forwarding, **419**

guaranteeing message delivery, 137

hiding or displaying groups of, 412

importing, 410

integrity of, 137

marking as read or unread, **410**

message security, **137–138**

reading received messages, **394**, *395*

replying to, **418–419**

restricting who can send

    to distribution lists, 263

    to mailboxes, 252, *253*

sending and receiving digitally signed and encrypted messages, 642

sending to shared mailboxes, 406

sorting and organizing, 411

system attendants and, 54–55

tracking system messages, **625**, *626*

tracking user messages, **616–625**

    advanced search mode, 621–625, *621*

    basic search mode, 616–620, *617*

    By Message ID option, 622–625, *623*, *624*

    Transfer Into This Site option, 621–622, *622*

Word as an Exchange client editor, 418

Messaging Defaults property page, MTA Site Configuration Properties dialog box, 447–450, *448*

microprocessors, multiprocessor support in NT Server, 90–91

Microsoft Exchange Administrator, 228–289, 292–331, 663–665

Add-Ins container, 663

Address Book dialog box

    creating views of, 286

    display name of public folders in, 310

    entering information about recipients managed by mailbox users, 244–246, *245*

    entering mailbox user's manager information, 243, *243*

    finding addresses in, 244

    hiding shared mailboxes from, 406, *407*

    importing folders, 410

    Personal Address Books (PABs), 387, *388*

    setting up Personal Address Books (PABs), 387, *388*

Addressing subcontainer, 664, *664*, *665*

administration versus management and, **228**

applying changes in, 246

creating custom recipients, **265–267**

    entering e-messaging address for, 266, *266*

    Properties dialog box, 267, *267*

    setting type of e-mail address, 265, *266*

creating distribution lists, 260–261, *260*

creating mailboxes, 238, *239*

creating NT accounts, 241–242, *241*, *242*

creating recipients containers, 277–278, *278*, *279*

directory service administration and management, **313–321**

    overview of, 313–314, *315*

    server-level administration and management, 320

    site-level administration and management, 315–320

Distribution List Properties dialog box, **260–265**

Advanced property page, 264–265, *264*

Custom Attributes property page, 264

Delivery Restrictions property page, 263

Display name and Alias name options, 261

Distribution Lists property page, 262, *263*

E-Mail Addresses property page, 263

Expansion Server option, 261

General property page, *260*, **261–262**

including distribution lists in other distribution lists, 262, *263*

Message Size Limit option, 265

Notes field, 261

overview of, 260–261

Owner field, 261

Permissions property page, 262

restricting who can send messages to distribution lists, 263

selecting members of distribution lists, 262

DS Site Configuration Properties dialog box, **315–320**

Attributes property page, 320, *321*

Custom Attributes property page, 318, *319*

General property page, 316, *316*

Offline Address Book property page, 317, *318*

Offline Address Book Schedule property page, 316–317

overview of, 315–316

Edit menu, **279**

File menu, **237–289**

Close option, 238

Connect to Server option, 238

Duplicate option, 279

New Custom Recipient option, 265

New Distribution List option, 260–261, *260*

New Mailbox option, 238

New Other submenu, 267–268, *268*, 470, 494

overview of, 237, *237*

Properties option, 278

Raw Properties option, 288–289

information store administration and management, **313–314, 321–330**. *See also* information stores

overview of, 313–314, *315*, 321–322

server-level administration and management for private information stores, 325–329, *326*

server-level administration and management for public information stores, 329–330, *330*

site-level administration and management, 322–325, *323*

Information Store Site Configuration Properties dialog box, **322–325**

General property page, 322, *323*

Public Folder Affinity property page, 325

Storage Warnings property page, 325

Top-Level Folder Creation property page, 323–324, *324*

installing, **217**

mailbox Properties dialog box, **238–260**

Add User or Group dialog box, 241–242, *241*

adding mailboxes to distribution lists, 250, *250*, *251*

Advanced property page, **257–260**, *257*

Create Windows NT Account dialog box, 242, *242*

creating or changing mailbox addresses, 251, *252*

creating custom information fields, 257

Custom Attributes property page, **257**

Delivery Options property page, **254–255**, *254*

Delivery Restrictions property page, **252**, *253*

Distribution Lists property page, **250**, *250*, *251*

E-mail Addresses property page, 251, *252*

entering general information, 239, *240*

entering information about recipients managed by mailbox users, 244–246, *245*

entering mailbox user's manager information, 243–244, *243*

General property page, **239–242**, *240*

granting NT accounts or groups rights to mailboxes, 241–242, *241*, *242*, 248–249

granting other recipients access to mailboxes, 254–255, *254*

NT accounts with inherited permissions, 247–248, *247*

Organization property page, **243–246**

overview of, 238, *239*

Permissions property page, **247–249**, *247*

Phone/Notes property page, **246**, *246*

Primary Windows NT Account dialog box, 241, *241*

Protocols property page, **255–256**, *256*

restricting who can send messages to mailboxes, 252, *253*

Send On Behalf Of permissions, 254–255, *254*

Message Transfer Agent administration and management, **313–314**, *315*

in multiserver sites, **428–433**

    connecting to multiple Exchange servers, 429–432, *430, 431*

    the default server, 428–429, *429*

    navigating site configuration hierarchy, 432–433, *432, 433*

in multisite organizations, **486–488**, *487*

Options dialog box, **232–236**

    Auto Naming property page, 232, *233*

    Delete Primary Windows NT Account When Deleting Mailbox option, 235

    Permissions property page, 233–235, *234*, 247

    Try to Find Matching Windows NT Account When Creating Mailbox option, 235–236, 242

organization Properties dialog box, **293–295**

    General property page, 293–294, *294*

    Permissions property page, 295, *295*

overview of, 20, *21*, 56, 212

preliminary settings, **232–237**

    changing site addresses, 236, *237*

    deleting NT accounts when deleting mailboxes, 235

    display name and alias options, 232, *233*

    finding matching NT accounts when creating mailboxes, 235–236, 242

    permissions options, 233–234, *234*, 247

Private Information Store Properties dialog box, **325–329**. *See also* information stores

    General property page, *326*, 327

    Logons property page, 327–328, *328*

    Mailbox Resources property page, 329, *329*

    overview of, 325–327, *326*

public folder Properties dialog box, **308–313**

    Age Limits for All Replicas option, 310

    Alias Name option, 310

    Client Permissions option, 311–312, *311*

    Folder and Address Book Display Name options, 310

    Folder Path option, 313

    General property page, *309*, 310–313

    Notes option, 312

    overview of, 308–310, *309*, 313

Public Information Store Properties dialog box, 329–330, *330*

recipients containers Properties dialog box, **277–278, 306–308**

    General property page, 277, *278*, 307, *307*

overview of, 277–278, *279*, 306–307

    Permissions property page, 277, 307–308

running remotely, 217

saving connections to Exchange servers, 288

server monitor Properties dialog box, **268–277**

    Actions property page, 274–275, *275*

    Clock property page, 276, 434–437, *436, 437*

    Escalation Editor dialog box, 271–273, *272*

    General property page, 269–270, *269*

    Notification property page, 270–273, *271, 272*

    Permissions property page, 270

    server monitors defined, **268–269**

    Servers property page, 273–274, *273, 274*, 434

    starting server monitors, 276–277, *276*

server Properties dialog boxes, **297–305**

    Advanced property page, 303–304, *303*

    Database Paths property page, 300–302, *301*

    Diagnostics Logging property page, 304–305, *305*

    General property page, 297, 298, *299*

    IS Maintenance property page, 302, *302*

    Locales property page, 299, *300*

    Services property page, 298

Site Addressing dialog box, 236, *237*

site Properties dialog box, **296–297**, *296, 297*

starting, 214–217, *215, 216*

System Attendant Properties dialog box, **313–314, 330–334**, *334*

Tools menu, **284–288**. *See also* Options dialog box

    Add to Address Book View option, 286

    Clean Mailbox option, 286–287, *287*

    Customize Toolbar option, 288

    Find Recipients option, 285, *285*

    Move Mailbox option, 286

    Options option, 232

    overview of, 284, *284*

    Save Connections options, 288

    Start Monitor option, 287

View menu, **279–284**

    All option, 280

    Columns option, 280–282, *281*

    Font option, 283

    Hidden Recipients option, 280

    Move Splitbar option, 283

overview of, 279–280, *280*

selecting what to view, 280

Sort By option, 282

Status Bar option, 284

Toolbar option, 283–284

viewing and changing recipient attributes, 280–282, *281, 282*

windows, **228–232**

closing, 238

moving splitbars, 232

multiple windows, 229–232, *229, 231*, 429–432, *430, 431*

Microsoft Exchange client installation, 360–381

installing Outlook clients, 360

installing Windows client software in network share mode, **374**

installing Windows client software on servers, **360–375**

overview of, 360–361, *361, 362*

preparing client software for installation, 362–363, *363*

selecting client installation point, 360, 364, *364*

Setup program options, 370–375

user options, 364–370

installing Windows client software on workstations, **375–378**, *376, 377, 378*

NetWare clients, **379–380**

Exchange Server and, 380

routers and, 380

using Service Advertisement Protocol (SAP) Agents, 379–380

Setup Program Options dialog box, **370–375**

Binding Order property page, 372–375, *373*

Components property page, 372, *372*

General property page, 371, *371*

overview of, 370–371

Services property page, 372, *373*

User Options dialog box, **364–370**

General property page, 365–366, *365*

Home Server property page, 368–370, *369*

overview of, 364–365, *365*

Read property page, 366–367, *367*

Send property page, 367–368, *368*

Spelling property page, 368, *369*

Microsoft Exchange clients, 20–23, 360–381, 384–419. *See also* mailboxes; messages; users

Active Server (AS) client-side setup, **694–695**, *695, 696, 697*

client components, **64–66**

client applications, 66

Exchange clients, 64–65, *64*

forms, 66

Forms Designer, 66

Outlook client, 5, *8*, 65, 360

Schedule+, 5, *6*, 63, 65, 668–669, *669*

Compose menu, **417–419**

Forward option, 419

New Form option, 418

New Message option, 418

New Post in This Folder option, 418

overview of, 417, *417*

Post Reply in This Folder option, 419

Reply to Sender and Reply to All options, 418

WordMail Options option, 418

connecting to Exchange Server via the Internet, **666–667**

creating public folders, 309, 313, **395–400**, 408

defined, **5**

Edit menu, **410**, *410*

enabling advanced security for mailboxes on, 638–641, *638*

Exchange Finder utility, 23

Exchange server outages and, 275

File menu, **408–410**

Add to Favorites option, 408

Create Shortcut option, 409

Delete option, 409

Exit and Exit and Log Off options, 410

Import option, 410

New Discussion Folder option, 408

New Folder option, 408

overview of, 408, *408*

Properties option, 409

Rename option, 409

HTTP (HyperText Transport Protocol) client-side setup, **694–695**, *695, 696, 697*

LDAP (Lightweight Directory Access Protocol) client-side setup, **702–707**

Microsoft Exchange Setup Wizard, 384–389, *385*

NNTP (Network News Transport Protocol) client-side setup, **735**

POP3 (Post Office Protocol) client-side setup, **681–686**

  configuring Eudora Pro 3.0, 685, *686*, *687*

  connecting to Exchange Server-based POP3 servers, 682–684

  other client settings, 684–685, *685*

  POP3 account names, 682–683, *683*

  POP3 e-mail addresses, 684

  POP3 server names, 684

  SMTP server names, 684

setting up newly installed clients, **384–389**, *385*

supporting remote users, 666

supporting roving users, 667–668

synchronizing online and offline folders, **413–415**, *414*

Tools menu, **412–417**

  Address Book option, 416

  Application Design option, 417

  AutoSignature option, 416

  Customize Toolbar option, 394, 417

  Deliver Now option, 413

  Find Items option, 416

  Find Public Folders option, 416

  Inbox Assistant option, 415

  Options option, 417

  Out of Office Assistant option, 416

  overview of, 412, *413*

  Remote Mail option, 415

  Services option, 403–404, 417

  Synchronize option, 413–415, *414*

View menu, **410–412**

  Collapse All and Expand All options, 412

  Columns, Group By, Sort, and Filter options, 411

  Folders, Toolbar, and Status Bar options, 411

  New Window option, 411

  overview of, 410, *411*

  Personal Views, Folder Views, and Define Views options, 412

views, 23

  defining, 412

  overview of, 23

  personal views and folder views, 412

windows

  client window, 389, *390*

  New Message window, 390–391, *391*

  opening, 411

working offline, **413–415**, *414*

Microsoft Exchange directory, 49–50, 232, 342, 645–654. *See also* directories

  backing up, 342, *342*

  defined, **49–50**, *51*, *52*, **232**

  exporting directory information, **651–654**

    directory export file structure, 652–653

    exporting directories, 653–654, *654*

    selecting fields, 654

    uses for, 652

  extracting information for, **649–651**

    extracting NetWare account lists, 650–651, *650*

    extracting Windows NT account lists, 649–650, *650*

  importing information into Exchange directory, **645–649**

    import file structure, 645–646

    importing directory information, 646–649, *647*, *648*

  restoring, **347–348**, *347*

Microsoft Exchange Forms Designer (EFD), 66, 746–773

  creating forms, **418**, **748–765**

    adding fields, 755–765

    editing fields, 763

    formatting and customizing with Forms Designer, 753–765, *753*

    starting with Form Template Wizard, 750–752, *750*

    starting Forms Designer, 748–749, *749*

  defined, **66**

  Exchange application design environment and, 747–748

  forms

    creating organization forms libraries, 766–767, *767*, *768*

    installing, **766**, **768–770**, *769*

    overview of, 13, *14*, 66

    personal forms libraries, 766

    saving, 753

    Send versus Post forms, 750, *750*, 766

    using, 770, *770*, *771*, *772*

  installing, 748

  toolbar, 753–755, *753*, *755*

  uses for, 746–747, 773

Microsoft Exchange Migration Wizard, 212, 644

Microsoft Exchange Server. *See also* designing Exchange systems

  administration group

    creating, 195, 198–199, *199*

    setting permissions for, 217–222, *218*

  cc:Mail and, 28

  as a client/server system, **17–20**, *19*

defined, **5**

e-messaging and, 4–5

future of, 9

Microsoft Mail for AppleTalk Networks and, 28

Microsoft Mail for PC Networks and, 27–28

NetWare clients and, 380

as an object-oriented system, 25, 32–33, *33*

Performance Optimizer Wizard, 206–210, *207*, 212

remote procedure calls and, 77, 78

scalability of, 26

SMTP (Simple Mail Transport Protocol) connector, 27

troubleshooting, 214

X.400 messaging systems and, 27

Microsoft Exchange Server installation, 194–222

  postinstallation activities, **210–222**

    accessing Exchange Server program group, 211–212, *211, 212*

    setting permissions for Exchange Server administration group, 217–222, *218*

    starting Exchange Administrator, 214–217, *215, 216*

    testing Exchange Server installation, 213–214, *213*

    troubleshooting Exchange Server problems, 214

  preparing for, **194–199**

    creating Exchange Server administration group, 195, 198–199, *199*

    creating Site Services account, 196, 197–198, *198*

    gathering account information, 195–196

    gathering Exchange Server information, 196–197

    gathering NT Server information, 194–195

    installation path name, 196

    NT server computer name, 195

    NT Server domain model and, 194

    NT server roles and, 195

    security setup, 197–199

    selecting Exchange Server components for installation, 197

    testing server hardware setup, 194

  running Setup program, **199–210**

    batch mode installation, 201

    entering organization and site names, 196, 205, *205*

    entering Site Services account name and password, 196, 205–206, *206*

    Exchange Server Performance Optimizer Wizard, 206–210, *207*, 212

    file installation and system setup, 206–210, *207*

    installing Active Server Components, 203

    overview of, 199–200, *200*

    selecting installation options, 200–204, *201, 202, 203*

    selecting licensing mode, 204, *204*

Microsoft Exchange Setup Wizard, 384–389, *385*

Microsoft Internet Explorer, 5, *7*

Microsoft Mail

  for AppleTalk Networks

    directory synchronization for, 590

    Exchange Server and, 28

  changing Microsoft Mail site addresses, 236

  migrating MS Mail users to Exchange, 569

  for PC Networks

    Exchange Server and, 27–28

    as a shared-file application, 17–18, *18*

Microsoft Mail Connector (MMC), 62–63, 125, 569–585. *See also* connectors

  installing, 570

  overview of, 62–63, 125, 569–570

  setting up PC post offices, 582–583, *583*

  starting MMC MTA service, 581–582, *582*

  testing MMC links, 584–585, *585*

Microsoft Mail Connector Properties dialog box, 570–581

  Address Space property page, **575**, *576*

  Connections property page, **571–575**, *572, 573*

  Connector MTAs property page, **576**, *576*, **579**, *579, 580*

  General property page, **571**, *572*

  Interchange property page, **570–571**, *571*

  Local Postoffice property page, **581**, *581*

  New MS Mail Connector (PC) MTA Service property page, **576–579**

    Connection Parameters options, 577

    Log Messages option, 576, *577*

    Options option, 578–579, *578*

    Polling Frequency options, 577

Microsoft Mail directory synchronization for AppleTalk networks, 590

Microsoft Mail directory synchronization for PC systems, 590–606

  adding Exchange systems to Dirsync systems, **592–601**

    Dirsync server settings, 598–599, *599*

    eliminating MS Mail SMTP gateways, 595

    setting up Dirsync requestors on Exchange servers, 592–598, *593*

    testing the setup, 600–601, *600*

  creating Dirsync systems with Exchange organizations, **601–604** setting up Dirsync servers on Exchange servers, 601–602, *602*

setting up remote Dirsync requestors, 603, *604*

Directory Synchronization Agents (DXAs) and, 604–606, *605*

Dirsync program

defined, **590**

Dirsync requestors versus servers, 590–591

server settings, 598–599, *599*

Dirsync requestor Properties dialog box, **592–598**

Export Containers property page, 596–597, *596*

General property page, 592–593, *593*

Import Container property page, 594–595, *594, 595*

overview of, 592

Schedule property page, 598, *599*

Settings property page, 597–598, *597*

Dirsync Server Properties dialog box, 601–602, *602*

Microsoft Outlook, 5, *8*, 65, 360

Microsoft Schedule+

Free/Busy Connector, 63

overview of, 5, *6*, 65, **668–669**, *669*

Microsoft Windows 95 client setup for NT Server, 181–189

entering computer and login domain information, 186, *187, 188*

installing network adapter drivers, 183, *183*

installing network protocols, 184, *185*

installing network services, 185–186, *185*

installing Windows client software, 183–184, *184*

overview of, 181–182, *182*

rebooting Windows 95, 189

setting resource-sharing security options, 186, *188*

Microsoft Windows NT Server, 23–24, 70–93, 172–177. *See also* Backup utility

accounts

accessing for the first time, 385

creating, **241–242**, *241, 242*

deleting when deleting mailboxes, 235

extracting NT account lists for Exchange directory, 649–650, *650*

granting accounts or groups rights to mailboxes, 241–242, *241, 242*, 248–249

with inherited permissions, 247–248, *247*

advantages of, 70–73

archive bits, 334

Command Scheduler (WINAT), 351–353, *352, 353*

Disk Administrator applet, 166–168, *166, 167, 168*

disk duplexing, 72

disk mirroring, 72

disk striping with parity, 72

domain controllers, **79**, 163, 195, 424

domain models, **82–86, 116–117**

complete-trust domain model, 85–86, *86*

master-domain model, 83–84, *83*

multiple-master-domain model, 84, *85*

selecting, 116–117, *117*

single-domain model, 82–83, *82*

domains

creating domain accounts and groups, 177–180, *178, 179*

and defining site boundaries, 118, *118*

granting access to servers and workstations, 163, 180–181, *180, 181*

overview of, **77–80**, *80*

setting up during NT Server installation, 163

trust relationships, **80–81**, *81*, 87, 456–459

Event Viewer, **91–92**, *92*

Exchange Server and, **23–24**, *24*

installing NT servers in domains, **456–463**

installing the NT server, 456

setting cross-domain permissions, 460–463, *460, 462, 463*

setting up trust relationships, 456–459

multiprocessor support, 90–91

networking protocols and features, 76–77, *76*

overview of, 73–74

Performance Monitor, **92–93**, *93*

RAID support, 71–73

Remote Access Server, 77

remote procedure calls (RPCs), 76, *76*

Server Manager, **89–90**, *89, 90*, 163, 180–181, *180*

services, 75–76, *75*

shutting down, 169

trust relationships, **80–81**, *81*, 87, 456–459

User Manager for Domains

creating domain accounts and groups, 178–180, *178, 179*

creating Exchange Server administration group, 198–199, *199*

creating Site Services account, 197–198, *198*

deleting accounts, 235

overview of, **87–89**, *88*

Windows Internet Naming Service (WINS), 162

Microsoft Windows NT Server installation, 73, 148–191

   granting domain access, **163**, **177–181**

      creating domain accounts and groups, 177–180, *178*, *179*

      granting access to servers and workstations, 163, 180–181, *180*, *181*

   installing NT Server software, **155–164**

      completing the installation, **164–169**

      copying files from CD-ROM disk, 158–159

      creating emergency repair diskette, 160

      detecting DHCP servers, 162

      detecting existing software and hardware, 157–158

      detecting hard disk and CD-ROM drives, 156–157

      domain setup, 163

      the installation process, 162–163

      installing Internet Information Server, 161, 164, 165

      installing network adapters, 161

      installing NT Server networking, 160–161

      installing Service Packs, 149, 164–165

      naming NT servers, 160

      ownership and licensing, 157, 159

      selecting components for installation, 160

      selecting networking protocols, 161–162

      setting up FAT or NTFS disk partitions, 158, 166–168, *166*, *167*, *168*

      Setup program's Installation Wizard, **159–163**

      starting the installation, 156

   installing uninterruptible power supplies, **169–171**

      configuring UPS support, 170–171, *170*

      selecting UPSs, 169–170, 171

      serial ports and, 152

      testing the UPS, 171

      UPS defined, **169**

   overview of, 73, 148–149

   setting up clients, **189–190**. *See also* Windows 95 clients

      NetWare and other clients, 190

      Windows NT Workstation clients, 189, *189*

      Windows for Workgroups clients, 190, *190*

   setting up NT Backup, **172–177**

      Backup setup, 174–177, *174*, *175*, *176*

      installing tape device drivers, 172, *173*

      tape drive setup, 172

   setting up server hardware, **149–155**

      CD-ROM drives, 151, 155

      hard disk drives, 154–155

      Hardware Compatibility List (HCL) and, 152

      hardware requirements, 150–151

      monitors and display adapters, 151

      mouse, 152

      network adapters, 152–153, 155

      peripheral controllers, 151

      purchasing hardware, 152, 154

      RAM, 150–151, 154

      SCSI-2 controllers, 151, 153, 155

      serial ports, 152

      testing components, 153–155

   setting up Windows 95 clients, **181–189**

      entering computer and login domain information, 186, *187*, *188*

      installing network adapter drivers, 183, *183*

      installing network protocols, 184, *185*

      installing network services, 185–186, *185*

      installing Windows client software, 183–184, *184*

      overview of, 181–182, *182*

      rebooting Windows 95, 189

      setting resource-sharing security options, 186, *188*

Microsoft Windows NT Workstation client setup for NT Server, 189, *189*

Microsoft Windows for Workgroups client setup for NT Server, 190, *190*

Microsoft Word as an Exchange client editor, 418

migrating, 134, 569, 643–654

   Exchange migration tools, 643–644

   exporting directory information, **651–654**

      directory export file structure, 652–653

      exporting directories, 653–654, *654*

      selecting fields, 654

      uses for, 652

   extracting information for Exchange directory, **649–651**

      extracting NetWare account lists, 650–651, *650*

      extracting Windows NT account lists, 649–650, *650*

   importing information into Exchange directory, **645–649**

      import file structure, 645–646

      importing directory information, 646–649, *647*, *648*

   legacy systems to Exchange, 134

migration source extractors, **644**

Migration Wizard, 212, 644

MS Mail users to Exchange, 569

minus sign (~-) in Exchange Administrator windows, 230

mirroring disks, 72

MMC. *See* Microsoft Mail Connector

Modify Admin Attributes mailbox permission, 249

Modify Permissions mailbox permission, 249

Modify User Attributes mailbox permission, 249

monitoring backup progress, 343–344, *344, 345*

monitors, setting up for NT Server installation, 151

mouse

    right-click menus, 409

    setting up for NT Server installation, 152

Move Mailbox option, Administrator Tools menu, 286

Move Splitbar option, Administrator View menu, 283

moving

    mail to public or private folders in Exchange clients, 22–23

    mailboxes, 286, 615, *615*

    mailboxes between sites, 655

    splitbars in Exchange Administrator windows, 232

MS Mail. *See* Microsoft Mail

MTAs. *See* Message Transfer Agents

multiple windows in Exchange Administrator, 229–232, *229, 231,* 429–432, *430, 431*

multiple-master-domain model, 84, *85*

multiprocessor support in NT Server, 90–91

multiserver Exchange sites, 424–453. *See also* sites

    Exchange Administrator in multiserver sites, **428–433**

        connecting to multiple Exchange servers, 429–432, *430, 431*

        the default server, 428–429, *429*

        navigating site configuration hierarchy, 432–433, *432, 433*

    installing additional servers in sites, **424–428**, *425, 426, 427*

    Message Transfer Agent Properties dialog box, **450–452**

        General property page, 451–452

        overview of, 450, *451*

        Queues property page, 452, *453*

    MTA Site Configuration Properties dialog box, **447–450**

        General property page, 446

        Messaging Defaults property page, 447–450, *448*

server monitors, **434–437**

    adding servers to, 434, *435*

    Clock property page, 434–437, *436, 437*

server-level directory service administration and management, 445–446, *446*

server-level Message Transfer Agent administration and management, 450–453, *451*

setting up link monitors, **438–444**, *439*

site-level Message Transfer Agent administration and management, 447–450, *448*

multisite Exchange organizations, 456–531. *See also* organizations

    adding servers to server and link monitors, 508, *509*

    Directory Replication Connector dialog box, **479–486**

        General property page, 480, *480*

        Schedule property page, 481, *481*

        Sites property page, 484, *485*

    Exchange Administrator in multisite organizations, **486–488**, *487*

    installing Exchange servers in sites, 424–428, *425, 426, 427,* **463–464**, *464*

    installing NT servers in domains, **456–463**

        installing the NT server, 456

        setting cross-domain permissions, 460–463, *460, 462, 463*

        setting up trust relationships, 456–459

    public folder Properties dialog box, **522–527**

        Advanced property page, 526–527, *527*

        Folder Replication Status property page, 526, *526*

        General property page, 522, *523*

        Replicas property page, 522–524, *524, 525*

    Public Information Store Properties dialog box, **514–522**

        Advanced property page, 518, *519*

        Age Limits property page, 518, *520*

        Folder Replication Status property page, 520, *521*

        General property page, 514, *514*

        Instances property page, 514–516, *515, 517*

        Logons property page, 522

        Replication Schedule property page, 518, *519*

        Server Replication Status property page, 520, *521*

    setting up cross-site permissions, **464–469**, *465*

    setting up cross-site public folder access, **508–513**

        advantages and disadvantages, 512–513

        overview of, 508–510

        setting up public folder affinity, 510–513, *511*

        testing, 511–512

setting up cross-site public folder replication, **508–510,** **513–528**

  advantages and disadvantages, 527–528

  at the folder level, 522–524, *523, 524, 525*

  folder-level administration and management, 526–527, *526, 527*

  overview of, 508–510

  at the server level, 513–518, *514, 515, 517*

  server-level administration and management, 518–522, *519, 520, 521*

setting up directory replication between sites, **479–486,** **507**

  cross-site public folder access and, 509

  guidelines, **507**

  setting up in the first site, 479–481

  setting up in the second site, 481

  testing the setup, 482–486, *482*

setting up MTA transport stacks, **489–494**

  overview of, 489–490

  setting up RAS MTA transport stacks, 492–494, *493*

  setting up TCP/IP transport stacks, 490–491, *490, 491, 492*

setting up site-to-site links, **470–479**

  setting up the first site, 470–476

  setting up the second site, 476–478

  testing connections, 478, *479*

setting up site-to-site links with Dynamic RAS Connector, **503–507**

  Address Space property page, 506

  Delivery Restrictions property page, 506

  General property page, 503–505, *504*

  RAS Override property page, 505–506

  Schedule property page, 505, *505*

setting up site-to-site links with X.400 Connector, **494–503**

  Address Space property page, 498, *498, 499*

  Connected Sites property page, 501–503, *501, 502*

  General property page, 495–496, *495*

  Override property page, 500, *500*

  Schedule property page, 496–497, *496*

  Stack property page, 497, *497*

Site Addressing Properties dialog box, **236, 528–530**

  General property page, 528–529, *529*

  overview of, 236, *237*

  Routing Calculation Schedule property page, 529

  Routing property page, 530, *530*

site Configuration Properties dialog box, 469, *469*

Site Connector Properties dialog box, **470–478**

  Address Space property page, 474, *475*

  General property page, 472–473, *472,* 476–477, *477*

  Override property page, 474–476, *475*

  overview of, 470–472

  Target Servers property page, 473, *474,* 477, *478*

site Properties dialog box, 464–466, *465, 468*

Multivalued Properties area, Directory Import dialog box, 649

N

naming

  Exchange servers, 111–112

  NT servers, 160

  public folders, 310

  renaming folders, 409

naming conventions, 111–116. *See also* designing Exchange systems

  alias names

    for distribution lists, 261

    for mailboxes, 114–115, *114,* 232

    for public folders, 310

    for shared mailboxes, 402

  display names

    for distribution lists, 261

    for mailboxes, 113–114, *113,* 232

    for organizations, 293–294, *294*

    for public folders in Address Book, 310

    for shared mailboxes, 402

  example, 115–116

  for organizations, sites, and servers, 111–112

  for recipient mailboxes, 112, *112*

navigating site configuration hierarchy in multiserver Exchange sites, 432–433, *432, 433*

NetBEUI protocol, installing, 161, 184

NetWare

  extracting account lists for Exchange directory, 650–651, *650*

  NetWare clients, **379–380**

    Exchange Server and, 380

    routers and, 380

    setting up for NT Server, 190

using Service Advertisement Protocol (SAP) Agents, 379–380

network adapters. *See also* hardware

installing, 161

installing drivers for Windows 95 clients in NT Server, 183, *183*

ISA bus cards, 152

setting up for NT Server installation, 152–153, 155

testing, 155

Network News Transport Protocol. *See* NNTP

networks

defining site boundaries and required networking capabilities, 119–120

evaluating organization networks, **108–110**

determining network bandwidth, 108–109

determining what is connected to what and how, 108

evaluating network's reliability, 109

example, 109–110, *110*

installing NT Server networking, 160–161

networking protocols and features in NT Server, 76–77, *76*, 184, *185*

system attendants and network connections, 54

New Custom Recipient option, Exchange Administrator File menu, 265

New Discussion Folder option, Exchange client File menu, 408

New Distribution List option, Exchange Administrator File menu, 260–261, *260*

New Folder option, Exchange client File menu, 408

New Form option, Compose menu, 418

New Information Store dialog box, 613, *614*

New Mailbox option, Exchange Administrator File menu, 238

New Message option, Compose menu, 418

New Message window in Exchange clients, 390–391, *391*

New MS Mail Connector (PC) MTA Service property page, 576–579. *See also* Microsoft Mail Connector Properties dialog box

Connection Parameters options, 577

Log Messages option, 576, *577*

Options option, 578–579, *578*

Polling Frequency options, 577

New Other submenu, Exchange Administrator File menu, 267–268, *268*, 470, 494

New Post in This Folder option, Compose menu, 418

New Requestor dialog box, 592, *593*

New Site Connector dialog box, 470, *471*

New Window option, Exchange client View menu, 411

New X.400 Connector dialog box, 494, *494*

newsgroups

managing, **735–736**

public folders and, 16, 396

NNTP (Network News Transport Protocol), 58, 256, 711–741. *See also* protocols

becoming a Usenet newsfeed provider, **740–741**

client-side setup, **735**

managing newsgroups, **735–736**

Newsfeed Properties dialog box, **727–732**

Advanced property page, 730–731, *732*

General property page, 728, *728*

Hosts, Connections, and Security property pages, 729

Inbound property page, 730

Messages property page, 728, *729*

Outbound property page, 730, *731*

Schedule property page, 729, *730*

newsfeeds defined, **712**

NNTP (News) Settings Properties dialog box, **734**, *734*

NNTP (News) Site Defaults Properties dialog box, **726–727, 732–734**

Authentication, Message Format, Idle Time-out, and Anonymous property pages, 733–734

Control Messages property page, 732, *733*

General property page, 726, *727*

Newsfeeds property page, 727, *727*

NNTP servers, 58

overview of, 256, 711–712

server-side setup, **713–735**

mailbox-level administration and management, 735, *735*

Newsfeed Configuration Wizard, 713–725, *714*

server-level administration and management, 734, *734*

site-level administration and management, 726–734, *726*

testing newsfeeds, 736–738, *737*

Notes field, Distribution List Properties dialog box, 261

Notes option, public folder Properties dialog box, 312

Notification property page, server monitor Properties dialog box, 270–273, *271, 272*

Notifications option, Internet Mail Service Properties dialog box, 554, *554*

NT. *See* Microsoft Windows NT

NTFS file system setup in NT Server installation, 158, 166–168, *166, 167, 168*

O

object-oriented system, Exchange Server as an, 25, 32–33, *33*

Offline Address Book property page, DS Site Configuration Properties dialog box, 317, *318*

Offline Address Book Schedule property page, DS Site Configuration Properties dialog box, 316–317

offline folders, synchronizing in Exchange clients, **413–415**, *414*

OLE 2.0
    attachment links, **10**
    OLE 2.0 applications, 747
    overview of, 12, *12, 13*

opening
    Exchange Server program group, 211–212, *211, 212*
    multiple windows for multiserver sites, 429–432, *430, 431*
    windows in Exchange clients, 411

Optimizer Wizard, 206–210, *207,* 212

optimizing Exchange systems
    example, 138–139
    overview of, **136, 138**

Options dialog box, 232–236
    Auto Naming property page, 232, *233*
    Delete Primary Windows NT Account When Deleting Mailbox option, 235
    Permissions property page, 233–235, *234,* 247
    Security property page, 638–640, *638*
    Try to Find Matching Windows NT Account When Creating Mailbox option, 235–236, 242

organization forms libraries, 766–767, *767, 768*

Organization property page, mailbox Properties dialog box, 243–246

Organization and Site dialog box, 425, *425*

organizations. *See also* multisite Exchange organizations
    creating Dirsync systems with Exchange organizations, **601–604**
        setting up Dirsync servers on Exchange servers, 601–602, *602*
        setting up remote Dirsync requestors, 603, *604*
    defined, **32, 34**
    display names for, 293–294, *294*

entering names for during Exchange Server installation, 196, 205, *205*

evaluating organization networks, **108–110**
    determining network bandwidth, 108–109
    determining what is connected to what and how, 108
    evaluating network's reliability, 109
    example, 109–110, *110*

geographical profiles, **105–107,** *105, 107*

naming, 111–112

Properties dialog box, **293–295**
    General property page, 293–294, *294*
    Permissions property page, 295, *295*

Out of Office Assistant, 416

Outlook, 5, *8,* 65, 360

Override property page
    Site Connector Properties dialog box, 474–476, *475*
    X.400 Connector Properties dialog box, 500, *500,* 537–538

Owner field, Distribution List Properties dialog box, 261

ownership in NT Server, 159

P

PABs (Personal Address Books), 387, *388*

partition setup in NT Server installation, 158, 166–168, *166, 167, 168*

passwords for Key Management Server, 633–636, *634*

paths
    Database Paths property page in server Properties dialog boxes, 300–302, *301*
    Folder Path option in public folder Properties dialog box, 313
    installation path name for Exchange Server, 196

PCI (Peripheral Component Interconnect) SCSI-2 controllers, 151, 153, 155

per server versus per seat licensing, 204

Performance Monitor in NT Server, 92–93, *93*

Performance Optimizer Wizard, 206–210, *207,* 212

Peripheral Component Interconnect (PCI) SCSI-2 controllers, 151, 153, 155

peripheral controllers, setting up for NT Server installation, 151

permissions. *See also* security
    Client Permissions option in public folder Properties dialog box, 311–312, *311*

granting NT accounts or groups rights to mailboxes, 241–242, *241, 242,* 248–249

NT accounts with inherited permissions, 247–248, *247*

roles for NT accounts with permissions on mailboxes, 248–249

Send On Behalf Of permissions, 254–255, *254*

setting cross-domain permissions in NT Server, 460–463, *460, 462, 463*

setting for Exchange Server administrator group, 217–222, *218*

setting up cross-site permissions in multisite organizations, 464–469, *465*

for shared mailboxes, 405

Permissions property page

Administrator Options dialog box, 233–235, *234,* 247

Distribution List Properties dialog box, 262

in Exchange Administrator Options dialog box, 233–234, *234,* 247

mailbox Properties dialog box, 247–249, *247*

organization Properties dialog box, 295, *295*

recipients container Properties dialog box, 277, *278*

recipients containers Properties dialog box, 277, 307–308

server monitor Properties dialog box, 270

server Properties dialog box, 297

site Properties dialog box, 296–297, *297*

Personal Address Books (PABs), 387, *388*

personal folders. *See also* folders; Microsoft Exchange clients

overview of, 21–22

versus private information stores, 41

personal forms libraries, 766

personal views in Exchange clients, 412

Phone/Notes property page, mailbox Properties dialog box, 246, *246*

ping utility, 424

planning. *See also* designing

connections to other systems, **133–136**

connecting or migrating legacy systems to Exchange, 134

connection options, 133–135

example, 135–136, *136*

intersite links, **121–125**

direct versus indirect connections, 59–60, *59, 61,* 121–122

Dynamic RAS Connector, 62, 124–125

example, 125, *126*

Internet Mail Service, 62, 125

Microsoft Mail Connector, 62–63, 125

Site Connector, 61, 123

site link options, 121–123, *122*

X.400 Connector, 61, 123–124

servers and user links, **125–133**

backing up Exchange servers, 129–130

designing Exchange servers, 126–129

example, 131–133

fault tolerance and, 128

IDE versus SCSI-2 disk drives, 127

networking users, 130–131

user links, **130–131**

plus sign (+) in Exchange Administrator windows, 230

Polling Frequency options, New MS Mail Connector (PC) MTA Service property page, 577

POP3 (Post Office Protocol), 58, 256, 672–688. *See also* protocols

client-side setup, **681–686**

configuring Eudora Pro 3.0, 685, *686, 687*

connecting to Exchange Server-based POP3 servers, 682–684

other client settings, 684–685, *685*

POP3 account names, 682–683, *683*

POP3 e-mail addresses, 684

POP3 server names, 684

SMTP server names, 684

versus Internet Message Access Protocol version 4 (IMAP4), 672

overview of, 256, 672

POP3 (Mail) Site Defaults Properties dialog box, **673–679**

Authentication property page, 674–675, *675*

General property page, 673, *674*

Idle Time-out property page, 677

Message Format property page, 675–677, *676*

POP3 servers, 58

Protocol Details properties dialog box, 680–681, *680*

server-side setup, **673–681**

customizing POP3 support for mailboxes, 679–681

server-level setup, 677–679

site-level setup, 673–677

testing LDAP (Lightweight Directory Access Protocol) with LDAP-aware POP3 clients, 710, *710, 711*

testing POP3 setup, 687, *688*

troubleshooting POP3 problems, 687

pop-up menus, 409

ports. *See* serial ports

Post forms, 750, *750*

Post Office Protocol. *See* POP3

Post Reply in This Folder option, Compose menu, 419

preparing for Exchange Server installation, 194–199

    creating Exchange Server Administration group, 195, 198–199, *199*

    creating Site Services account, 196, 197–198, *198*

    gathering account information, 195–196

    gathering Exchange Server information, 196–197

    gathering NT Server information, 194–195

    installation path name, 196

    NT server computer name, 195

    NT Server domain model and, 194

    NT server roles and, 195

    security setup, 197–199

    selecting Exchange Server components for installation, 197

    testing server hardware setup, 194

primary domain controllers in NT Server, 79, 163, 195

Primary Windows NT Account dialog box, 241, *241*

private folders, 15–16, 41. *See also* folders

    creating, 408

    defined, **15**, **41**

    designing, 417

    in Exchange clients, rules for moving mail to, 22–23

    sorting, 15

    sorting and organizing messages in, 411

private information stores. *See also* information stores

    defined, **21–22**

    mailboxes and, 39, 41

    versus personal folders, 41

    Properties dialog box, **325–329**

        General property page, *326*, 327

        Logons property page, 327–328, *328*

        Mailbox Resources property page, 329, *329*

        overview of, 325–327, *326*

    server-level administration and management, 325–329, *326*

processors, multiprocessor support in NT Server, 90–91

properties, Raw Properties option in Administrator File menu, 288–289

property pages, 34. See also specific Properties dialog boxes

Protocol Details properties dialog box, 680–681, *680*

protocols. *See also* HTTP; LDAP; NNTP; POP3

    configuring protocols containers, **741**, *742*

    DHCP (Dynamic Host Configuration Protocol), 162

    IMAP4 (Internet Message Access Protocol version 4), 672

    in NT Server

        overview of, 76–77, *76*, 161–162

        for Windows 95 clients, 184, *185*

    Protocols property page in mailbox Properties dialog box, 255–256, *256*

    SAP (Service Advertisement Protocol) Agents, 379–380

    security and, **743**

    SMTP (Simple Mail Transport Protocol)

        changing SMTP site addresses, 236, *237*

        eliminating MS Mail SMTP gateways, 595

        Internet Mail Service and, 542, 548, *548*

        SMTP gateway, 27

        SMTP server names, 684

    TCP/IP

        installing, 161, 162–163, 184

        Internet Mail Service and, 542–544

        TCP/IP MTA transport stacks, 490–491, *490, 491, 492*

Protocols property page, mailbox Properties dialog box, **255–256**, *256*, 679, *680*

public folders, 15–16. *See also* folders; recipients

    alias names for, 310

    creating, 309, 313, 395–400, 408

    defined, **15**

    designing, 417

    display name of in Address Book, 310

    displaying, **309**, **313**, **400**

    in Exchange clients

        overview of, 22

        rules for moving mail to, 22–23

    finding, 416

    hidden public folders, 309, 313, 400

    Internet-enabled public folders, 15, *16*

    naming, 310

    Properties dialog box, **308–313**, **397–398**, **522–527**

        Advanced property page, 526–527, *527*

        Age Limits for All Replicas option, 310

        Alias Name option, 310

        Client Permissions option, 311–312, *311*

        Folder and Address Book Display Name options, 310

        Folder Path option, 313

Folder Replication Status property page, 526, *526*

General property page, *309*, 310–313, 522, *523*

Notes option, 312

overview of, 308–310, *309*, 313, 397–398, *398*, *399*

Replicas property page, 522–524, *524*, *525*

Public Folder Affinity property page in Information Store Site Configuration Properties dialog box, 325

as recipients, 268

recipients and, 38, 42

replicating, 51

setting up cross-site public folder access, **508–513**

advantages and disadvantages, 512–513

overview of, 508–510

setting up public folder affinity, 510–513, *511*

testing, 511–512

setting up cross-site public folder replication, **508–510, 513–528**

advantages and disadvantages, 527–528

at the folder level, 522–524, *523*, *524*, *525*

folder-level administration and management, 526–527, *526*, *527*

overview of, 508–510

at the server level, 513–518, *514*, *515*, *517*

server-level administration and management, 518–522, *519*, *520*, *521*

sorting, 15

sorting and organizing messages in, 411

Usenet newsgroups and, 16, 396

Public Information Store Properties dialog box, 329–330, 514–522. *See also* information stores

Advanced property page, 518, *519*

Age Limits property page, 518, *520*

Folder Replication Status property page, 520, *521*

General property page, 514, *514*

Instances property page, 514–516, *515*, *517*

Logons property page, 522

overview of, 329–330, *330*

Replication Schedule property page, 518, *519*

Server Replication Status property page, 520, *521*

public information stores. *See also* information stores

server-level administration and management, 329–330, *330*

public key encryption, 57

purchasing hardware, 152, 154

Q

questions for evaluating user needs, 99–100

Queues property page

Internet Mail Service Properties dialog box, 565

Message Transfer Agent Properties dialog box, 452, *453*

R

RAID (redundant array of inexpensive disks)

NT Server support for, 71–73

stand-alone RAID systems, 72

RAM

detecting more than 64MB, 150–151

setting up for NT Server installation, 150–151, 154

testing, 154

RAS. *See* Remote Access Server

Raw Properties option, Exchange Administrator File menu, 288–289

Read property page, User Options dialog box, 366–367, *367*

reading received messages, 394, *395*

receiving digitally signed and encrypted messages, 642

Recipient Template option, Directory Import dialog box, 647–648

recipients, 32, 36–42. *See also* distribution lists; hierarchy; public folders

creating custom recipients, **265–267**

entering e-messaging address for, 266, *266*

Properties dialog box, 267, *267*

setting type of e-mail address, 265, *266*

custom recipients, 42

defined, **32**

distribution lists, 42

entering information about recipients managed by mailbox users, 244–246, *245*

finding, 285, *285*

Global Address Lists and, 38

granting other recipients access to a mailbox, 254–255, *254*

hiding, 42

mailbox agents, 37

mailboxes, 38, 39–40, *40*, *41*

overview of, 36–39, *37*, *39*

public folders and, 38, 42

public folders as, 268

site-level recipients containers, 37–38

viewing and changing recipient attributes, 280–282, *281*, *282*

viewing hidden recipients, 280

recipients containers. *See also* containers

creating, **277–278**, *278*, *279*

defined, **37–38**

Properties dialog box, **277–278**, **306–308**

General property page, 277, *278*, 307, *307*

overview of, 277–278, *279*, 306–307

Permissions property page, 277, 307–308

types of, 306

reconfiguring mailboxes, 259

records, Domain Name Service records, 543–544

recovering security keys, 642–643

Remote Access Server (RAS)

Dynamic RAS Connector (DRASC), 62, 124–125

Dynamic RAS Connector Properties dialog box, **503–507**

Address Space property page, 506

Delivery Restrictions property page, 506

General property page, 503–505, *504*

RAS Override property page, 505–506

Schedule property page, 505, *505*

Key Management Server and RAS public key encryption, 57

in NT Server, 77

remotely administering Exchange and NT servers, 665–666

serial ports for, 152

setting up RAS MTA transport stacks, 492–494, *493*

Remote Mail option, Exchange client Tools menu, 415

remote procedure calls (RPCs)

Exchange Server and, 77, 78

in NT Server, 76, *76*

renaming folders, 409

Replace option, Backup Information dialog box, 340, 343

Replicas property page, public folder Properties dialog box, 522–524, *524*, *525*

replicating

directories, 50, 295, 336, 370

public folders, 51

Replication Schedule property page, Public Information Store Properties dialog box, 518, *519*

Reply to Sender and Reply to All options, Compose menu, 418

replying to messages, 418–419

Request to Send (RTS) Values options in MTA Site Configuration Properties dialog box, 449

requestors. *See* directory synchronization

restoring from Exchange Server backups, 345–349. *See also* Backup utility

restoring Exchange directory, 347–348, *347*

restoring information stores, 347–349, *348*

selecting what to restore, 346–347, *346*

Restrict Access to Owner or Administrator option, Backup Information dialog box, 340–341

restricting who can send messages

to distribution lists, 263

to mailboxes, 252, *253*

Retrieving Mail option, Internet Mail Service Properties dialog box, 561

Retry Interval option, Internet Mail Service Properties dialog box, 564–565, *565*

revoking advanced security, 643

rich text formatting option, Internet Mail Service Properties dialog box, 556

right-click menus, 409

rights. *See* permissions

roles for NT accounts with permissions on mailboxes, 248–249

rolling out Exchange systems, 139–143

defined, **139**

example, 140–143

overview of, 139–140

routers, NetWare clients and, 380

Routing Address property page, X.400 Connector Properties dialog box, 539–541, *540*

Routing Calculation Schedule property page, Site Addressing Properties dialog box, 529

Routing property page

Internet Mail Service Properties dialog box, 566, *567*

Site Addressing Properties dialog box, 530, *530*

RPCs. *See* remote procedure calls

RTS (Request to Send) Values options in MTA Site Configuration Properties dialog box, 449

rules for moving mail to public or private folders in Exchange clients, 22–23

running
Exchange Administrator remotely, 217
Exchange Server Setup program, **199–210**
batch mode installation, 201
entering organization and site names, 196, 205, *205*
entering Site Services account name and password, 196, 205–206, *206*
Exchange Server Performance Optimizer Wizard, 206–210, *207, 212*
file installation and system setup, 206–210, *207*
installing Active Server Components, 203
overview of, 199–200, *200*
selecting installation options, 200–204, *201, 202, 203*
selecting licensing mode, 204, *204*

S

SAP (Service Advertisement Protocol) Agents, 379–380
SAs. *See* system attendants
saving
Administrator's connections to Exchange servers, 288
forms, 753
scalability of Exchange Server, 26
Schedule+
Free/Busy Connector, 63
overview of, 5, *6*, 65, **668–669**, *669*
Schedule option, Internet Mail Service Properties dialog box, 561–562
Schedule property page
Directory Replication Connector dialog box, 481, *481*
Dirsync requestor Properties dialog box, 598, *599*
X.400 Connector Properties dialog box, 496–497, *496*, 537
SCSI-2 controllers
detecting in NT Server installation, 156
setting up for NT Server installation, 151, 153, 155
testing, 155
SCSI-2 disk drives, 127, 156
SCSI-2-compatible tape drives, 172
Search property page, LDAP (Directory) Site Defaults Properties dialog box, 701–702, *702*
searching. *See* finding
security. *See also* Key Management (KM) Server; permissions
advanced security, **630–631, 635–643**

advanced security tokens, **636**
enabling advanced security for mailboxes on Exchange clients, 638–641, *638*
enabling advanced security for mailboxes on Exchange servers, 635–638, *635, 636, 637*
Key Management (KM) Server and, 630–631
recovering security keys, 642–643
revoking, 643
sending and receiving digitally signed and encrypted messages, 642
Key Management Server security settings, 633–634, *634*
message security, **137–138**
overview of, 26, 626–628
protocols and, **743**
setting resource-sharing security options for Windows 95 clients in NT Server, 186, *188*
setting up during Exchange Server installation, 197–199
system attendants and, 55
Security property page
Internet Mail Service Properties dialog box, 566, *567*
mailbox Properties dialog box, 635–638, *635, 636, 637*, 640–643, *641*
Options dialog box, 638–640, *638*
Select Inbound Message to Track dialog box, 621, *622*
Select Message to Track dialog box, 624, *624*
Select System Message to Track dialog box, 625, *626*
selecting
Backup options, 340–343, *341, 342, 343*
Exchange Server components for installation, 197
Exchange Server installation options, 200–204, *201, 202, 203*
Exchange Server licensing mode, 204, *204*
Exchange servers and components for backing up, 338–339, *339*
fields for directory export files, 654
members of distribution lists, 262
a networking domain model, 116–117, *117*
networking protocols in NT Server installation, 161–162
NT Server components for installation, 160
NT Server domain models, 116–117, *117*
uninterruptible power supplies, 169–170, *171*
what to view in Administrator View menu, 280
Send As mailbox permission, 249, 255
Send Attachments Using options, Internet Mail Service Properties dialog box, 554–555

Send forms, 750, *750*, 766

Send On Behalf Of permissions, 254–255, *254*

Send property page, User Options dialog box, 367–368, *368*

sending messages, 390–394, *391*, *392*, *393*, 413, 418

    digitally signed and encrypted messages, 642

    to shared mailboxes, 406

serial ports

    for Remote Access Server, 152

    setting up for NT Server installation, 152

    uninterruptible power supplies and, 152

Server Manager in NT Server, 89–90, *89*, *90*, 163, 180–181, *180*

server monitors, 268–277, 434–437. *See also* link monitors

    adding servers to, 434, *435*, 508, *509*

    defined, **268–269**

    in multiserver Exchange sites, **434–437**

    Properties dialog box, **269–276**

        Actions property page, 274–275, *275*

        Clock property page, 276, 434–437, *436*, *437*

        Escalation Editor dialog box, 271–273, *272*

        General property page, 269–270, *269*

        Notification property page, 270–273, *271*, *272*

        Permissions property page, 270

        Servers property page, 273–274, *273*, *274*, 434, *435*

    starting, 276–277, *276*

    synchronizing clocks, 435, 437

Server Replication Status property page, Public Information Store Properties dialog box, 520, *521*

server-level administration and management

    of cross-site public folder replication, 518–522, *519*, *520*, *521*

    of directory service, 320

    of directory service in multiserver Exchange sites, 445–446, *446*

    of Message Transfer Agents in multiserver Exchange sites, 450–453, *451*

    of NNTP (Network News Transport Protocol), 734, *734*

    of private information stores, 325–329, *326*

    of public information stores, 329–330, *330*

server-level setup

    for LDAP (Lightweight Directory Access Protocol), 702

    for POP3 (Post Office Protocol), 677–679

servers. *See also* multiserver Exchange sites; workstations

    Active Server (AS) server-side setup, **690–694**

        mailbox-level HTTP setup, 694

        site-level HTTP setup, 690–694

    adding to link monitors, 508, *509*

    adding to server monitors, 434, *435*, 508, *509*

    backing up, 129–130, 338–339, *339*

    clients and Exchange server outages, **275**

    connecting clients to Exchange Server-based POP3 servers, 682–684

    defined, **32**, **35–36**, *36*

    Dirsync servers, 590–591

    enabling advanced security for mailboxes on, 635–638, *635*, *636*, *637*

    in Exchange hierarchy, **32**, **35–36**, *36*

    granting access to in NT Server, 163, 180–181, *180*, *181*

    HTTP (HyperText Transport Protocol) server-side setup, **690–694**

        mailbox-level HTTP setup, 694

        site-level HTTP setup, 690–694

    installing NT servers in domains, **456–463**

        installing the NT server, 456

        setting cross-domain permissions, 460–463, *460*, *462*, *463*

        setting up trust relationships, 456–459

    installing in sites, **424–428**, *425*, *426*, *427*, **463–464**, *464*

    Internet protocol servers, 57–58

    LDAP (Lightweight Directory Access Protocol) server-side setup, **698–702**

        server-level setup, 702

        site-level setup, 698–702

    Lightweight Directory Access Protocol (LDAP) servers, 58

    naming Exchange servers, 111–112

    naming NT servers, 160

    Network News Transport Protocol (NNTP) servers, 58

    NNTP (Network News Transport Protocol) server-level administration and management, 734, *734*

    NNTP (Network News Transport Protocol) server-side setup, **713–735**

        mailbox-level administration and management, 735, *735*

        Newsfeed Configuration Wizard, 713–725, *714*

        server-level administration and management, 734, *734*

        site-level administration and management, 726–734, *726*

    planning, **125–133**

        backing up Exchange servers, 129–130

designing Exchange servers, 126–129

example, 131–133

fault tolerance and, 128

IDE versus SCSI-2 disk drives, 127

networking users, 130–131

POP3 (Post Office Protocol) server-side setup, **673–681**

customizing POP3 support for mailboxes, 679–681

server-level setup, 677–679

site-level setup, 673–677

POP3 server names, 684

Post Office Protocol (POP3) servers, 58

Properties dialog boxes, **297–305**

Advanced property page, 303–304, *303*

Database Paths property page, 300–302, *301*

Diagnostics Logging property page, 304–305, *305*

General property page, 297, 298, *299*

IS Maintenance property page, 302, *302*

Locales property page, 299, *300*

Services property page, 298

system attendants and, 54

Servers property page, server monitor Properties dialog
box, 273–274, *273, 274, 434, 435*

Service Advertisement Protocol (SAP) Agents, 379–380

Service Packs for NT Server, installing, 149, 164–165

services in NT Server

installing network services for Windows 95 clients,
185–186, *185*

overview of, 75–76, *75*

Services option, Exchange client Tools menu, 403–404, 417

Services property page

server Properties dialog boxes, 298

Setup Program Options dialog box, 372, *373*

setting

cross-domain permissions in NT Server, 460–463, *460,
462, 463*

encryption algorithms for Key Management Server,
632–633, *632*

permissions for Exchange Server administrator group,
217–222, *218*

resource-sharing security options for Windows 95 clients
in NT Server, 186, *188*

type of e-mail address for custom recipients, 265, *266*

setting up

cross-site permissions in multisite organizations,
464–469, *465*

cross-site public folder access, **508–513**

advantages and disadvantages, 512–513

overview of, 508–510

setting up public folder affinity, 510–513, *511*

testing, 511–512

cross-site public folder replication, **508–510, 513–528**

advantages and disadvantages, 527–528

at the folder level, 522–524, *523, 524, 525*

folder-level administration and management,
526–527, *526, 527*

overview of, 508–510

at the server level, 513–518, *514, 515, 517*

server-level administration and management,
518–522, *519, 520, 521*

directory replication between sites, **479–486, 507**

cross-site public folder access and, 509

guidelines, **507**

setting up in the first site, 479–481

setting up in the second site, 481

testing the setup, 482–486, *482*

Dirsync requestors on Exchange servers, 592–598, *593*

Dirsync servers on Exchange servers, 601–602, *602*

domains during NT Server installation, 163

Exchange clients, **384–389,** *385*

FAT or NTFS disk partitions in NT Server installation,
158, 166–168, *166, 167, 168*

indirect site links with X.400 Connector, 539–541, *540*

link monitors, 438–444, *439*

MS Mail PC post offices, 582–583, *583*

MTA transport stacks, **489–494**

overview of, 489–490

setting up RAS MTA transport stacks, 492–494, *493*

setting up TCP/IP transport stacks, 490–491, *490,
491, 492*

NT Backup, **172–177**

Backup setup, 174–177, *174, 175, 176*

installing tape device drivers, 172, *173*

tape drive setup, 172

NT Server clients, **189–190.** *See also* Windows 95 clients

NetWare and other clients, 190

NT Workstation clients, 189, *189*

Windows for Workgroups clients, 190, *190*

Personal Address Books (PABs), 387, *388*

public folder affinity, 510–513, *511*

RAS MTA transport stacks, 492–494, *493*

remote Dirsync requestors, 603, *604*

security during Exchange Server installation, 197–199

server hardware for NT Server installation, **149–155**

    CD-ROM drives, 151, 155

    hard disk drives, 154–155

    Hardware Compatibility List (HCL) and, 152

    hardware requirements, 150–151

    monitors and display adapters, 151

    mouse, 152

    network adapters, 152–153, 155

    peripheral controllers, 151

    purchasing hardware, 152, 154

    RAM, 150–151, 154

    SCSI-2 controllers, 151, 153, 155

    serial ports, 152

    testing components, 153–155

site links with Internet Mail Service, 568–569

site-to-site links, **470–479**

    setting up the first site, 470–476

    setting up the second site, 476–478

    testing connections, 478, *479*

site-to-site links with Dynamic RAS Connector Properties dialog box, **503–507**

    Address Space property page, 506

    Delivery Restrictions property page, 506

    General property page, 503–505, *504*

    RAS Override property page, 505–506

    Schedule property page, 505, *505*

site-to-site links with X.400 Connector Properties dialog box, **494–503**

    Address Space property page, 498, *498*, *499*

    Connected Sites property page, 501–503, *501*, *502*

    General property page, 495–496, *495*

    Override property page, 500, *500*

    Schedule property page, 496–497, *496*

    Stack property page, 497, *497*

TCP/IP protocol for Internet Mail Service, 542–543

trust relationships in NT Server, 456–459

Windows 95 clients for NT Server, **181–189**

    entering computer and login domain information, 186, *187*, *188*

    installing network adapter drivers, 183, *183*

    installing network protocols, 184, *185*

    installing network services, 185–186, *185*

    installing Windows client software, 183–184, *184*

    overview of, 181–182, *182*

    rebooting Windows 95, 189

    setting resource-sharing security options, 186, *188*

    Windows Address Book, 702–707

Settings property page, Dirsync requestor Properties dialog box, 597–598, *597*

Setup Advanced Security dialog box, 639, *639*

Setup program, **199–210**, **370–375**. *See also* Microsoft Exchange client installation

    running, **199–210**

        batch mode installation, 201

        entering organization and site names, 196, 205, *205*

        entering Site Services account name and password, 196, 205–206, *206*

        Exchange Server Performance Optimizer Wizard, 206–210, *207*, *212*

        file installation and system setup, 206–210, *207*

        installing Active Server Components, 203

        overview of, 199–200, *200*

        selecting installation options, 200–204, *201*, *202*, *203*

        selecting licensing mode, 204, *204*

    Setup Program Options dialog box, **370–375**

        Binding Order property page, 372–375, *373*

        Components property page, 372, *372*

        General property page, 371, *371*

        overview of, 370–371

        Services property page, 372, *373*

shared mailboxes, 400–407. *See also* mailboxes

    accessing, 403–405, *403*, *404*, *405*

    creating, 400–403, *401*, *402*

    display names and aliases, 402

    hiding from Address Book, 406, *407*

    permissions for, 405

    sending messages to, 406

shared-file applications, 17–18, *18*

shortcut menus, 409

shortcuts, creating, 409

shutting down NT Server, 169

signatures

    AutoSignature feature, 416

    digital signatures, 57, 626–628

Simple Display Name field, mailbox Properties dialog box Advanced property page, 258

Simple Mail Application Program Interface (MAPI), 14

Simple Mail Transport Protocol. *See* SMTP

single-domain model, 82–83, *82*

Site Addressing Properties dialog box, 236, 528–530

    General property page, 528–529, *529*

    overview of, 236, *237*

    Routing Calculation Schedule property page, 529

    Routing property page, 530, *530*

Site Connector. *See also* connectors

    overview of, 61, 123

    Properties dialog box, **470–478**

        Address Space property page, 474, *475*

        General property page, 472–473, *472, 476–477, 477*

        Override property page, 474–476, *475*

        overview of, 470–472

        Target Servers property page, 473, *474, 477, 478*

Site Services account

    creating, 196, 197–198, *198*

    entering name and password during Exchange Server installation, 196, 205–206, *206*

    Site Services Account dialog box, 425, *426*

site-level administration and management

    of directory service, 315–320

    of information stores, 322–325, *323*

    of Message Transfer Agents in multiserver Exchange sites, 447–450, *448*

    of NNTP (Network News Transport Protocol), 726–734, *726*

site-level setup

    for HTTP (HyperText Transport Protocol), 690–694

    for LDAP (Lightweight Directory Access Protocol), 698–702

    for POP3 (Post Office Protocol), 673–677

sites. *See also* links

    changing site addresses, **236**, *237*

    Configuration Properties dialog box, 469, *469*

    connections within versus connections between, 60

    defined, **32**, **34**, *35*

    defining site boundaries, **118–121**

        example, 120–121, *120*

        networking domains and, 118, *118*

        and required networking capabilities, 119–120

    entering names for during Exchange Server installation, 196, 205, *205*

    in Exchange hierarchy, **32**, **34**, *35*

indirect site links, **59–60**, *59*, *61*, **121–122**

installing additional servers in, 424–428, *425, 426, 427*

installing servers in, 424–428, *425, 426, 427, 463–464, 464*

naming, 111–112

navigating site configuration hierarchy in multiserver sites, 432–433, *432, 433*

planning intersite links, **121–125**

    direct versus indirect connections, 59–60, *59, 61,* 121–122

    Dynamic RAS Connector, 62, 124–125

    example, 125, *126*

    Internet Mail Service, 62, 125

    Microsoft Mail Connector, 62–63, 125

    Site Connector, 61, 123

    site link options, 121–123, *122*

    X.400 Connector, 61, 123–124

    Properties dialog box, **296–297**, *296, 297, 464–466, 465, 468*

    site-level recipients containers, **37–38**

Sites property page, Directory Replication Connector dialog box, 484, *485*

SMTP (Simple Mail Transport Protocol). *See also* protocols

    changing SMTP site addresses, 236, *237*

    eliminating MS Mail SMTP gateways, 595

    Internet Mail Service and, 542, 548, *548*

    SMTP gateway, 27

    SMTP server names, 684

Sort By option, Administrator View menu, 282

Sort option, Exchange client View menu, 411

sorting

    Exchange Server lists, 282

    messages, 411

    public or private folders, 15

Spelling property page, User Options dialog box, 368, *369*

splitbars in Exchange Administrator windows, 232

Stack property page, X.400 Connector Properties dialog box, 497, *497*

stand-alone RAID systems, 72

starting

    Exchange Administrator, 214–217, *215, 216*

    Exchange Server programs, 211–212, *211, 212*

    Microsoft Mail Connector MTA service, 581–582, *582*

    NT Server installation, 156

    server monitors, 276–277, *276*

status bar

    displaying in Exchange Administrator, 284

    displaying in Exchange clients, 411

Storage Warnings property page, Information Store Site Configuration Properties dialog box, 325

stripe sets with parity, 72

synchronizing. *See also* directory synchronization

    online and offline folders, 413–415, *414*

    server monitor clocks, 435, 437

system attendants (SAs)

    defined, **54–55,** *54*

    Properties dialog box, **313–314, 330–334,** *334*

T

tape drives

    installing device drivers, 172, *173*

    SCSI-2-compatible tape drives, 172

    setting up for NT Backup, 172

Target Servers property page, Site Connector Properties dialog box, 473, *474*, 477, *478*

TCP/IP protocol. *See also* protocols

    installing, 161, 162–163, 184

    Internet Mail Service and, **542–544**

        creating key DNS records for Exchange, 543–544

        setting up TCP/IP protocol, 542–543

    TCP/IP MTA transport stacks, 490–491, *490, 491, 492*

testing

    adding Exchange systems to Dirsync systems, 600–601, *600*

    backup routines, 340, **354**

    cross-site public folder access setup, 511–512

    directory replication setup between sites, 482–486, *482*

    Exchange Server installation, 213–214, *213*

    Exchange systems, **136–139**

        defined, **136**

        example, 138–139

        guaranteed message delivery, 137

        message integrity, 137

        message security, 137–138

        optimization, 136, 138

        system versatility, 138

hardware for NT Server installation, **153–155**

    CD-ROM drives, 155

    hard disk drives, 154–155

    memory, 154

    network adapters, 155

    SCSI controllers, 155

Internet Mail Service, 568, 569

LDAP (Lightweight Directory Access Protocol) with LDAP-aware POP3 clients, 710, *710, 711*

Microsoft Mail Connector links, 584–585, *585*

network adapters, 155

newsfeeds, 736–738, *737*

POP3 setup, 687, *688*

RAM, 154

server hardware setup during Exchange Server installation, 194

site-to-site links, 478, *479*

uninterruptible power supplies, 171

Windows Address Book, 707–710, *707, 708, 709*

Toolbar option, Administrator View menu, 283–284

toolbars

    customizing, 417

    displaying in Exchange clients, 411

    Forms Designer toolbar, 753–755, *753, 755*

Tools menu

    in Exchange Administrator, **284–288**

        Add to Address Book View option, 286

        Clean Mailbox option, 286–287, *287*

        Customize Toolbar option, 288

        Find Recipients option, 285, *285*

        Move Mailbox option, 286

        overview of, 284, *284*

        Save Connections options, 288

        Start Monitor option, 287

    in Exchange clients, **412–417**

        Address Book option, 416

        Application Design option, 417

        AutoSignature option, 416

        Customize Toolbar option, 394, 417

        Deliver Now option, 413

        Find Items option, 416

        Find Public Folders option, 416

        Inbox Assistant option, 415

        Options option, 417

Out of Office Assistant option, 416

overview of, 412, *413*

Remote Mail option, 415

Services option, 403–404, 417

Synchronize option, 413–415, *414*

Top-Level Folder Creation property page, Information Store Site Configuration Properties dialog box, 323–324, *324*

tracking, 616–625. *See also* finding

system messages, **625**, *626*

user messages, **616–625**

advanced search mode, 621–625, *621*

basic search mode, 616–620, *617*

By Message ID option, 622–625, *623*, *624*

Transfer Into This Site option, 621–622, *622*

transaction logs, 337

Transfer Into This Site option for finding user messages, 621–622, *622*

Transfer Mode options, Internet Mail Service Properties dialog box, 562–563, *563*

Transfer Timeouts (sec/K) options in MTA Site Configuration Properties dialog box, 450

troubleshooting

Exchange Server, 214

POP3 problems, 687

Trust Level field, mailbox Properties dialog box, 258

trust relationships in NT Server, 80–81, *81*, 87, 456–459

Try to Find Matching Windows NT Account When Creating Mailbox option, Administrator Options dialog box, 235–236, 242

managing, **735–736**

public folders and, 16, 396

User Manager for Domains in NT Server

creating domain accounts and groups, 178–180, *178*, *179*

creating Exchange Server administration group, 198–199, *199*

creating Site Services account, 197–198, *198*

deleting accounts, 235

overview of, **87–89**, *88*

User Options dialog box, 364–370. *See also* installing Exchange clients

General property page, 365–366, *365*

Home Server property page, 368–370, *369*

overview of, 364–365, *365*

Read property page, 366–367, *367*

Send property page, 367–368, *368*

Spelling property page, 368, *369*

users. *See also* clients

Anonymous users, **312**

evaluating user needs, **97–105**

example, 100–105

overview of, 97–98

questions to ask, 99–100

upgrading workstations, 103–105

planning user links, 130–131

supporting remote users, 666

supporting roving users, 667–668

utilities. *See also* Backup utility

Finder, 23

LoadSim, 99, 101, 105, 126–127

ping, 424

WINAT in NT Server, 351–353, *352*, *353*

U

uninterruptible power supplies (UPSs), 169–171

configuring NT Server UPS support, 170–171, *170*

defined, **169**

selecting, 169–170, 171

serial ports and, 152

testing, 171

upgrading workstations, 103–105

Usenet newsgroups. *See also* NNTP (Network News Transport Protocol)

becoming a USENET newsfeed provider, 740–741

V

versatility of Exchange systems, 138

video adapters, setting up for NT Server installation, 151

View menu

in Exchange Administrator, **279–284**

All option, 280

Columns option, 280–282, *281*

Font option, 283
Hidden Recipients option, 280
Move Splitbar option, 283
overview of, 279–280, *280*
selecting what to view, 280
Sort By option, 282
Status Bar option, 284
Toolbar option, 283–284
viewing and changing recipient attributes, 280–282, *281*, *282*
in Exchange clients, **410–412**
Collapse All and Expand All options, 412
Columns, Group By, Sort, and Filter options, 411
Folders, Toolbar, and Status Bar options, 411
New Window option, 411
overview of, 410, *411*
Personal Views, Folder Views, and Define Views options, 412
viewing
hidden public folders, 309, 313
recipient attributes, 280–282, *281*, *282*
views
of Address Book dialog box, 286
address book views, **655–663**
adding, 656–660, *657*
adding address book view containers, 661, *662*
editing, 62–63
overview of, 655–656
defining, 412
in Exchange clients, 23
defining, 412
overview of, 23
personal views and folder views, 412
overview of, 23
personal views and folder views, 412

Web browsers. *See* Active Server
WINAT utility in NT Server, 351–353, *352*, *353*

Windows. *See* Microsoft Windows
windows
in Exchange Administrator, **228–232**
closing, 238
moving splitbars, 232
multiple windows, 229–232, *229*, *231*, 429–432, *430*, *431*
in Exchange clients
client window, 389, *390*
New Message window, 390–391, *391*
opening, 411
Windows Address Book, **702–710**. *See also* Address Book dialog box
setting up, 702–707
testing, 707–710, *707*, *708*, *709*
Windows Internet Naming Service (WINS), 162
Wizards
Exchange Server Performance Optimizer Wizard, 206–210, *207*, 212
Form Template Wizard, 750–752, *750*
Internet Mail Wizard, 544–552, *545*
Microsoft Exchange Setup Wizard, 384–389, *385*
Migration Wizard, 212, 644
Newsfeed Configuration Wizard, 713–725, *714*
NT Server Installation Wizard, 159–163
WordMail Options option, Compose menu, 418
word-wrap option, Internet Mail Service Properties dialog box, 556
working offline with Exchange clients, 413–415, *414*
workstations. *See also* servers
granting access to in NT Server, 163, 180–181, *180*, *181*
upgrading, 103–105
World Wide Web browsers. *See* Active Server

X.400 Connector, 61, 123–124, 536–541. *See also* connectors
Message Transfer Agent stacks and, 536
overview of, 61, 123–124
Properties dialog box, **494–503**, **536–541**

W

X

Address Space property page, 498, *498*, *499*, 538

Advanced property page, 538–539, *538*

Connected Sites property page, 501–503, *501*, *502*, 539

General property page, 495–496, *495*, 536, 537, *537*, 539, *540*

Override property page, 500, *500*, 537–538

Routing Address property page, 539–541, *540*

Schedule property page, 496–497, *496*, 537

Stack property page, 497, *497*

setting up indirect site links, 539–541, *540*

X.400 messaging systems

changing X.400 site addresses, 236, *237*

defined, **27**

Message Transfer Agents and, 53

How to:

Become familiar with the concepts and terminology of Exchange Server *(see Chapters 1, 2, and 3)*.

Get a handle on the relationship between Windows NT and Exchange Server *(see Chapter 4)*.

Plan for an Exchange Server implementation *(see Chapter 5)*.

Measure the messaging load that an Exchange server can handle *(see Chapter 5)*.

Install Windows NT *(see Chapter 6)*.

Install Exchange Server *(see Chapter 7)*.

Use the Exchange Administrator Program *(See Chapter 8)*.

Create a new mailbox *(see Chapter 8)*.

Create a new distribution list *(see Chapter 8)*.

Create a custom recipient *(see Chapter 8)*.

Create a new public folder *(see Chapter 8)*.

Create a new server monitor *(see Chapters 8, 13, and 14)*.

Create a new link monitor *(see Chapters 13 and 14)*.

View hidden objects in a recipients container *(see Chapter 8)*.

Administer and manage objects in the Exchange Server hierarchy *(see Chapter 9)*.

Back up an Exchange server *(see Chapter 10)*.

Install and set up Exchange clients for Microsoft Windows so that users can install them from a network server *(see Chapter 11)*.

Become familiar with the Exchange client from a user's perspective *(see Chapter 12)*.

Add an Exchange server to a site *(see Chapters 7 and 13)*.

Administer and manage multiple servers in a site *(see Chapter 13)*.

Add sites to an Exchange organization *(see Chapter 14)*.

Administer and manage multiple Exchange sites *(see Chapter 14)*.

Create a new MTA transport stack *(see Chapter 14)*.